TimeOut

Athens

timeout.com/athens

Penguin Books

PENGUIN BOOKS

Published by the Penguin Group
Penguin Books Ltd, 80 Strand, London WC2R ORL, England
Penguin Books USA Inc., 375 Hudson Street, New York, New York 10014, USA
Penguin Books Australia Ltd, 250 Camberwell Road, Camberwell, Victoria 3124, Australia
Penguin Books Canada Ltd, 10 Alcorn Avenue, Toronto, Ontario, Canada M4V 3B2
Penguin Books (NZ) Ltd, cnr Rosedale and Airborne Roads, Albany, Auckland, New Zealand

Penguin Books Ltd, Registered Offices: Harmondsworth, Middlesex, England

First edition 2004
10 9 8 7 6 5 4 3 2 1

Copyright © Time Out Group Ltd 2004
All rights reserved

Colour reprographics by Icon, Crowne House, 56-58 Southwark Street, London SE1 1UN
Printed and bound by Cayfosa-Quebecor, Ctra. de Caldes, Km 3 08 130 Sta, Perpètua de Mogoda, Barcelona, Spain

Edited and designed by
Time Out Guides Limited
Universal House
251 Tottenham Court Road
London W1T 7AB
Tel + 44 (0)20 7813 3000
Fax + 44 (0)20 7813 6001
Email guides@timeout.com
www.timeout.com

Editorial

Editor Ruth Jarvis
Deputy Editor Sylvia Tombesi-Walton
Consultants Coral Davenport, Denny Kallivoka,
 Alexia Loundras
Copy Editor Jessica Eveleigh
Listings Checkers Marigo Alexopoulou, Helen Babbs,
 Georgina Doutsi, Joyce-Ann Gatsoulis, Sophia Krasaki,
 Cordelia Madden
Proofreader Marion Moisy
Indexer Jackie Brind

Editorial/Managing Director Peter Fiennes
Series Editor Ruth Jarvis
Deputy Series Editor Lesley McCave
Guides Co-ordinator Anna Norman
Accountant Sarah Bostock

Design

Art Director Mandy Martin
Acting Art Director Scott Moore
Acting Art Editor Tracey Ridgewell
Senior Designer Averil Sinnott
Designers Astrid Kogler, Sam Lands
Digital Imaging Dan Conway
Ad Make-up Charlotte Blythe

Picture Desk

Picture Editor Kerri Littlefield
Deputy Picture Editor Kit Burnet
Picture Researcher Alex Ortiz

Advertising

Sales Director Mark Phillips
International Sales Manager Ross Canadé
International Sales Executive James Tuson
Advertising Sales (Athens) Pivotal Media
Advertising Assistant Sabrina Ancilleri

Marketing

Marketing Manager Mandy Martinez
US Publicity & Marketing Associate Rosella Albanese

Production

Guides Production Director Mark Lamond
Production Controller Samantha Furniss

Time Out Group

Chairman Tony Elliott
Managing Director Mike Hardwick
Group Financial Director Richard Waterlow
Group Commercial Director Lesley Gill
Group Marketing Director Christine Cort
Group General Manager Nichola Coulthard
Group Art Director John Oakey
Online Managing Director David Pepper

Contributors

Introduction Coral Davenport. **History** Nick Wyke. **Athens Today** Brian Church, Paris Ayiomamitis. **Architecture** Martin Olofsson. **Greek Myth & Legend** Amanda Castleman. **Athens 2004** John Hadoulis. **Where to Stay** Joyce-Ann Gatsoulis, with contributions from Coral Davenport. **Sightseeing** Coral Davenport (*Zappeion: a stately stroll* Androniki Kitsantonis). **Beaches** Joyce-Ann Gatsoulis. **Restaurants** Denny Kallivoka, with contributions from Coral Davenport (*In search of souvlaki* Joyce-Ann Gatsoulis; *My kind of town, Taverna tips* Brian Church; *Greek wines* Petros Parayios). **Cafés** Joyce-Ann Gatsoulis, Yiannis Poulis. **Shops & Services** Cordelia Madden, with contributions from Coral Davenport, Angie Kartsatou and Konstantinos Sarkas. **Festivals & Events** Paris Ayiomamitis. **Children** Areti Daradimou. **Film** Martin Olofsson, Konstantinos Sarkas. **Galleries** Stathis Panagoulis. **Gay & Lesbian** Panagiotis Hatjistefanou, Christopher Nicholas. **Music** Coral Davenport, George Kolyvas, Martin Olofsson. **Nightlife** Alexia Loundras, Othonas Orfanos. **Sport & Fitness** Yiannis Kifonides, Chris Salmon. **Theatre & Dance** Ioanna Blatsou. **Getting Started** Ruth Jarvis. **Attica & the Mainland** Alexia Loundras (*Byron in Greece* Gulya Isyanova; *Delphi* Antonis Dimas). **Northern Peloponnese** Jonathan Cox (*Mycenae* Antonis Dimas). **Island Escapes** Androniki Kitsantonis. **Directory** Debbie Ellis, with contributions from Konstantinos Sarkas (*Greek for cheats, You're breaking up, Get in line* Brian Church; *Who let the dogs out?* Cordelia Madden).

Maps JS Graphics (john@jsgraphics.co.uk). Maps are based on material supplied by Road Editions. Athens Metro map copyright Attiki Metro 2003

Photography Jon Perugia, except pages 6, 16, 18, 20, 44 Hulton Archive; page 9 Archive Photos; page 13, 29, 231, 245 Getty Images/The Image Bank; page 17 © British Museum; page 21 Hulton Archive/Keystone; pages 38, 39 Mary Evans; page 41 ©Archivo Iconongrafico, SA/Corbis; page 45 Michael Nicholson/Corbis; page 47 Associated Press/Frank Augstein; page 102 Goulandris Museum of Cycladic Art; page 128 Vagelis Massias; page 147 Charlie Makkos; page 187 Hellenic Festival SA/Haris Bilios; page 225 Associated Press/Stavrakis Thanassis; pages 236, 238, 240, 241, 242 Chris Salmon; pages 247, 248, 250, 251, 252, 255 Jonathan Cox; page 257 Travel-Ink. The following images were provided by the featured establishments/artist: pages 56, 57, 65, 67, 68, 69,196, 197, 205.

The Editor would like to thank Carla Burt, Johnny Cash, Eleni Delimpaltadaki, Andy Hadjicostis, Ilias Heliopoulos, Tamsin Hudson, the Travel Bookshop, Giorgos Vamvakidis, Nick Wyke and all at *Time Out Athens*.

Contents

Introduction

At first glance, Athens can seem daunting. Many visitors, fresh off the airport shuttle, are dismayed by their first sight of Syntagma at midday: blinding sun, honking traffic, dusty scaffolding and fast food joints. At that moment, they wonder why they shouldn't follow the backpacking hordes in a quick trip up the Acropolis before making an island exit.

The first reason is obvious: it may be vast, confusing and sprawling, but Athens is home to some of world civilisation's most magnificent glories: the eternal Parthenon, which French poet Lamartine called 'the world's most perfect poem in stone', is the Agora, where, in the fifth century BC, democracy was born, Socrates corrupted the city's youth and Demosthenes's golden tongue held its citizens in sway. It's also where, a few centuries later, St Paul converted Athens' first Christians, in his famous 'Men of Athens…' speech, recorded for your reading pleasure in the Bible. These are the sights you've read about and will remember forever.

Of course, you knew all that. But one of the most rewarding reasons to explore Athens is discovering that, with a little effort and the right guidance, you can scratch the surface of the modern city and find yourself in some of the most interesting and beautiful neighbourhoods in the world. Athens is an endlessly layered entity: ancient marbles rub shoulders with incense-scented Byzantine churches, pastel neo-classical mansions, swarming markets, and gritty modern flats – all on one city block. The contrasts are fascinating, as is the cocktail of European, Balkan and Middle Eastern influences. The key to appreciating Athens is finding these juxtapositions, whether it be in a medieval chapel set among Cycladic-island style houses at the foot of the Acropolis, listening to *rembetika* in the Central Meat Market at dawn or tripping over ruins of the 480 BC Themistoclean Wall on your way out.

In the years leading up to the 2004 Olympics, Athens seems to have gained an edgy new energy. It's not just the requisite pre-Olympic facelift, though that has done much to make the city more visitor-friendly. Sights and museums have been renovated and central squares given facelifts; historic buildings have received fresh coats of paint and many central streets been converted from pot-holed, traffic-clogged nightmares to attractive walkways. All this activity, along with a new urban awareness, has triggered a boom in development in the once-empty, decrepit neighbourhoods west of the Acropolis. For the first time, Athens is seeing a surge in its contemporary art world, with dozens of former factories and warehouses being converted to galleries, which it seems can't be filled fast enough with the work of a rising wave of young Greek artists. These have been followed by hip cafés, experimental theatres, progressive nightclubs and art-filled fusion restaurants – in the shadow of the Acropolis, modern Athens is finally coming alive on its own terms.

ABOUT THE TIME OUT CITY GUIDES

The *Time Out Athens Guide* is the latest addition to the city guide series produced by the people behind London and New York's successful listings magazines. We also have an office in Athens, where a weekly Greek-language *Time Out* magazine is published. Staff there have contributed to this guide to ensure that it is crammed with local expertise.

THE LOWDOWN ON THE LISTINGS

Above all, we've tried to make this book as useful as possible. Transport information, opening times, admission prices, websites and credit card details are all included in our listings. And, as far as possible, we've given details of facilities, services and events, all checked and correct at the time we went to press. However, since owners and managers can change their arrangements at any time, we always advise readers to telephone and check opening times and other particulars. This is particularly the case during the Athens Olympics in August 2004. While every effort has been made to ensure the accuracy of the information contained in this guide, the publishers cannot accept responsibility for any errors it may contain.

PRICES AND PAYMENT

We have noted whether venues such as shops, hotels and restaurants accept credit cards or not but have only listed the major cards – American Express (**AmEx**), Diners Club (**DC**), MasterCard (**MC**) and Visa (**V**). Many businesses will also accept other cards, including Cirrus, Maestro, JCB, Discover and Carte Blanche, along with euro travellers' cheques issued by a major financial institution (such as American Express).

The prices we've supplied should be treated as guidelines, not gospel. Fluctuating exchange rates and inflation can cause charges, in shops and restaurants particularly, to change rapidly. If prices vary wildly from those we've quoted, ask whether there's a good reason. If not, go elsewhere. Then please write and let us know. We aim to give the best and most up-to-date advice, so we always want to know if you've been badly treated or overcharged.

THE LIE OF THE LAND
Athens is a city of distinct neighbourhoods, and we have used these to structure our sightseeing chapters. The same area classifications are used to divide other chapters, such as restaurants; for a map showing the divisions, see p290. Every location included in the book has a map reference. These refer to the street maps on pages 294 to 299.

TELEPHONE NUMBERS
The country code for Greece is 30. All Athens numbers start with 210, which needs to be dialled both from outside and inside the city. Where no alternative exists, we have given (and stipulated) a mobile telephone number. These start with a '6'. For more details of phone codes and charges, see p273.

ESSENTIAL INFORMATION
For all the practical information you might need for visiting the city – including visa and customs information, disabled access, emergency telephone numbers, a list of useful websites and the lowdown on the local transport network – turn to the **Directory** chapter at the back of this guide. It starts on page 262.

TRANSLITERATIONS
There is no standard system for the transliteration of Greek characters. We have chosen a method that reflects pronunciation as closely as possible. However, we have frequently broken our own rules where there seemed good reason to do so: for proper names with a well-established spelling; or when people or businesses had their own preferred version,

for example. We have chosen, however, not to duplicate the spellings given on street signs, since these are inconsistent and unrecognisable in speech. It's better to follow a map.

We have sourced maps with a similar, but not identical, transliteration system to our own.

LET US KNOW WHAT YOU THINK
We hope you enjoy the *Time Out Athens Guide*, and we'd like to know what you think of it. We welcome tips for places that you consider we should include in future editions and take notice of your criticism of our choices. There's a reader's reply card at the back of this book – or you can email us on athensguide@timeout.com.

There is an online version of this book, along with guides to 45 other international cities, at **www.timeout.com**.

The best vintage year?
'79.*

*1879.

1879. The foundation of the Boutari company. Celebrating 125 years in wine making, the Boutari family carries on defining the course of the Greek wine history. Respect of tradition, devotion to quality, alert to innovation and commitment to excellence are the reasons for honouring Boutari with the "Wine and Spirits" award "International Winery of the Year" for the 8th time.

BOUTARI
FIFTH GENERATION
www.boutari.gr

In Context

Features

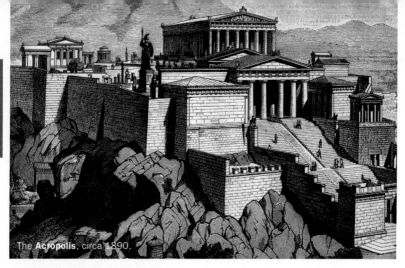

The **Acropolis**, circa 1890.

History

The rise and fall – and the rise again.

As with all great cities of the ancient world, any early history of Athens is an exercise in separating myth from (limited) reliable sources.

Graves and wells of neolithic settlers dating back three millennia before Christ have been found on the slopes of the Acropolis. Around 1500 BC the hill became known as Cecropia, after King Cecrops, the successor to King Actaeus, who had given Athens its primary name: Acte (from which the name of the region, Attica, also derives). Cecrops had been attracted by the hill's two copious springs.

But the city's founding myth rose out of a heroic showdown between the male god of the sea, Poseidon, and the female goddess of wisdom, Athena. Both were laying claim to Attica. According to legend, when Poseidon struck the rock of the Acropolis with his trident, a horse leaped out of rushing water. Athena replied by striking a nearby rock with her spear, and an olive tree appeared. The gods of Olympus declared Athena victor and she became protectress of the town, bequeathing the city both its name and, with the olive tree, an important symbol of peace and prosperity.

By 1400 BC the Acropolis had been fortified in the manner of a Mycenaean citadel. The Mycenaeans lived in independent communities clustered around palaces ruled by kings and dominated by a centralised religion and bureaucracy. Their warlike kingdoms were

a breeding ground for myths, and yielded the sources on the sack of Troy (which took place some time between 1230 BC and 1180 BC) and the destruction of Thebes that would inspire Homer when writing *The Iliad* four centuries later.

Under Dorian assault from the north and amid internal strife, most of the Mycenaean culture in Greece collapsed in 1200 BC. Somehow, though, the invasion bypassed Athens. This immunity later boosted claims of classical Athenians that they were autochthonous, that is, the true native inhabitants sprung from the soil of their land.

DARKNESS FALLS

Athens couldn't avoid, however, the shadow that veiled Greece during the period 1050 BC to 750 BC, known as the Greek Dark Age. The bitter infighting of the Mycenaeans had caused widespread poverty; the population plummeted and many people migrated to the Aegean Islands and the coast of Asia Minor.

Few, if any, written records survive from this period and our knowledge is limited to scant archaeological evidence. However, tombs from the age have revealed a proto-geometric style of pottery. This would later develop into the story-telling figurative urns, the archetypes of today's copies sold to tourists in Plaka. Other finds of ivory, gold and, particularly, iron indicate some notable advances in metallurgy, which helped Athens to emerge from its Dark Age.

CITY LIGHTS

The collapse of Mycenaean civilisation left a political vacuum in Greece. Around 800 BC Athens began incorporating the outlying villages into its city-state (*polis*) and within 50 years ruled the whole of Attica. By this time other Greek cities had also organised themselves into independent city-states, the most powerful being Chalcis, Corinth and Eretria. The main goal of the city-state was to avoid strong central political power and to share authority among its citizens. Power, however, was still largely concentrated in the hands of the wealthy and privileged. Centuries later, the Greek philosopher Aristotle (384 BC-322 BC; *see p11* **Three wise men**) insisted that it was the forces of nature that had created the city-state, and that anyone who existed outside the community of a city-state must be either a beast or a god.

A cultural and economic revival accompanied the emergence of the city-states across Greece and inspired new styles of warfare, art and politics. Greek colonies were established as far away as the Black Sea, present-day Syria, North Africa and the Western Mediterranean. Athens enjoyed a period of peace and remained the leading artistic centre in Greece until about 730 BC, when it was superseded by Corinth, both culturally and politically. The introduction of coinage and the spread of alphabetical writing came to Athens second-hand via Corinth. It would take until the late Archaic Age (700 BC-500 BC) for Athens to garner any real political clout.

> **'A harsh 'Draconian' code dealt with menial crimes, like the pilfering of cabbage, by capital punishment.'**

FROM TYRANNY TO DEMOCRACY

The Archaic Period is so called because of a plodding pace of change in comparison to the hyper-progressive Classical Age that succeeded it. It was, nevertheless, a seminal period that produced startling innovations in architecture and art, not to mention the poetry of Homer.

In Athens the city office merged into an annually appointed executive of nine archontes (chief magistrates). After serving his term, an archon became a life member of the council (called the Areopagus, because it met on the hill of Ares). An aristocratic group known as the Eupatridai ('sons of good fathers') had an exclusive right to these posts. The governing class was responsible for war, religion and law. Its hierarchy depended on wealth, gained either from commerce or agriculture.

Three wise men: Socrates

No Adonis, the short, stub-nosed Socrates (470 BC-399 BC) captivated young Athenians by teaching them to question everything. A man of action as well as of thought, he also fought for his native Athens in the First Peloponnesian War. In 399 BC a jury of democrats found him guilty of impiety and of corrupting the youth. He was condemned to death. Rather than take voluntary exile, he swallowed hemlock poison after explaining to his friends the immortality of the soul and his lack of fear of leaving this world.

Early works: A godly man, Socrates believed in a purely objective understanding of such concepts as justice, love and virtue as the basis of his teachings. His Socratic dialogues, responding to a pupil's question with another question, taught that answers to philosophical questions were hard to come by.

Major contribution: True moral wisdom lies in the self. A person's soul is directly responsible for their happiness. Socrates believed that all vice is the result of ignorance, and that no person is willingly bad; correspondingly, 'virtue is knowledge', and those who know what's right will act justly.

Apparently: Because Socrates claimed to know nothing, the Delphic Oracle called him 'the wisest man in Greece'.

Must read: He preferred the immediate impact of an argument in the agora to putting pen to papyrus. Our knowledge of Socrates is based on the writings of Plato and Xenophon, both his pupils. His brilliant defence at his trial is recorded in Plato's *Phaedo*.

His legacy: Plato attributed most of his personal works to the dialogues he had with Socrates.

If he were around today: He'd be a soft target for satire as he was in his own day. In Aristophanes's comedy *The Clouds*, he is ridiculed as the master of a 'thinking shop' where understudies distorted reason.

Easy quote: 'Know thyself.'

Three wise men: Plato

Born of a well-to-do Athenian family, Plato (427 BC-347 BC) was an instinctive authoritarian who admired the Spartans for their ruthless discipline and loathed the limp-wristed democrats who had condemned his mentor Socrates to death. After a spell as a tutor to the son of Dionysius I of Sicily, he returned to Athens to set up his Academy. He died at the ripe old age of 80.

Early works: His doctrine of Innatism stated that we all possess immortal souls so learning is just recollection from the soul's previous existence. Ergo, if you knew your Corinthian from your Doric columns in your past life, you will recognise them in this life.

Major contribution: Plato developed a dual vision of this ordinary world around us and another one of eternal divine perfection. So the tables that we see outside a taverna are just inferior copies of God's ideal template of 'tableness'. Apparently the mega-brained, guided by love and beauty, could see this pure form.

Apparently: There is more to life than the dim *Groundhog Day* existence that we are led to believe from birth. To escape that monotony we must train our minds to seek a better, 'more real' world. The individuals who persevere will discover 'goodness itself' and become the 'golden' leaders of a society comprising unquestioning silver, bronze and iron people. Plato's utopian visions were borderline dictatorial experiments. And what exactly were his forms, anyway?

Must read: *The Republic*, a model for a society blissfully in tune with itself where commoners and soldiers are governed by wise philosopher-chiefs.

Legacy: He kept later generations questing for ultimate mystical truths through the use of reason.

If he were around today: Plato's doctrine of equal rights for the sexes would go down well in a city that boasts its first woman mayor. But his cold-hearted notions of state-arranged marriages and having children removed from their parents at birth in order not to dilute public spirit with emotions, would offend most family-centric Greeks, not to mention Aphrodite.

Easy quote: 'The learning and knowledge that we have is, at the most, but little compared with that of which we are ignorant.'

Across Greece the replacement of monarchy by an aristocracy of nobles had left the common people with few rights. The resulting social tensions prompted a move towards tyranny, where despotically inclined individuals temporarily seized power in the city-states.

In 640 BC, bristling with victory in an event at the Olympic Games, an Athenian nobleman named Cylon attempted to overthrow the aristocracy and seize power in Athens. The coup failed. Undeterred and still upset with the political system, Cylon led an abortive attempt at tyranny in 632 BC. His army of mercenaries briefly occupied the Acropolis. When Cylon fled, his followers sought sanctuary at the sacred altar of Athena, from where they were lured down by promises of reprieve by the archon Megacles and then massacred by Athenian troops. Megacles and his family were banished in perpetuity for sanctioning the murders.

Continued unrest and the constant threat to the aristocracy's supremacy led to the archon Draco's strictly defined law code enacted in 621 BC. It was a harsh code (hence 'Draconian') that sidestepped pressing issues and dealt with menial crimes, such as the pilfering of cabbage, by capital punishment.

Relief came in the guise of Solon, a poet who became archon in 594 BC. His revised code alleviated the system of land tenure and debt for the peasants and implemented trial by jury. He reorganised the state by breaking the exclusive power of the aristocracy and established four classes of Athenian society based on agricultural wealth. A new council was set up, the Boule of 400 Representatives, a sort of popular assembly that sat alongside the Areopagus. Solon encouraged the development of lucrative olive and wine production in Attica, reformed the law courts and coinage, and invited foreign businessmen to the city.

Ideologically Solon paved the way to Athenian democracy, but in practice many of his reforms failed. As controversy heightened over the rule of the archontes, the opportunistic military leader Pisistratos seized power as a tyrant by occupying the Acropolis in 560 BC. Although he was expelled twice (the first time he had been reinstated as a result of a ludicrous plot whereby a woman rode into the city dressed up as Athena and proclaimed Pisistratos's virtues as leader), Athens flourished under his rule.

Arguably the most benign of Athens' tyrants, Pisistratos assembled a hefty navy and extended the city's boundaries on land. He improved the water supply and commissioned the Temple of Olympian Zeus and the rebuilding of the Old Temple of Athena on the Acropolis. A keen culture vulture, he sponsored historians, poets, sculptors and orators and revitalised the Festival of the Great Dionysia, which rivalled those at Olympia and Delphi.

Pisistratos died in 527 BC. He was succeeded by his son Hippias, who, though a patron to poets, became increasingly tyrannical after surviving an assassination attempt in 514 BC in which his brother Hipparchos was killed.

By 510 BC, following a consultation with the Delphic Oracle, Megacles's son Cleisthenes had rallied the support of the Spartans, the premier power of the time, and managed to drive Hippias out of Athens. The exiled tyrant tried to settle scores 20 years later with the help of a Persian army headed by Darius, only to be famously trounced at the Battle of Marathon.

Cleisthenes took over Athens, allied himself with the ordinary people (*demos*) and brought Solon's reforms back. He created ten new tribes based on place of residence to avoid the old political ties of kinship that had existed. Each tribe was composed of *demoi* (village units) with their own political apparatus. The Assembly (an attempt to make the different factions and regions of Athens into one people) now became the focus of political decision-making.

Cleisthenes also introduced the political safety valve of ostracism, whereby citizens could agree to remove a perceived troublemaker for ten years. This was democracy of sorts. All adult male citizens were enabled to speak and vote for, or against, motions put before the Assembly, but women, slaves and those not born of Athenian parents were excluded from the political process.

> **'For Athens and Sparta the spoils of war were short-lived, for they would soon be at each other's throats.'**

WAR STORIES

Athens had to get a series of Persian wars out the way before it could fully blossom as the cosmopolitan centre of its 'empire'. In 490 BC Darius followed up his threats for 'earth and water' from Athens by amassing an army at least 30,000 strong on the plains of Marathon. Famously a messenger ran the roughly 42 kilometres (26 miles) from the battle site to Athens to announce the news, and his efforts are immortalised in modern marathon races.

Darius expected an early surrender, but instead the vastly outnumbered Athenian hoplites made an impromptu charge and with their superior armour, astonishingly, drove the Persians away. The historian Herodotus, by no means a military expert, estimates the Persian dead at Marathon as 6,400 and the Athenians as only 192. A theory has recently evolved that the horsemen carved on the frieze around the wall of the Parthenon, part of the Elgin Marbles (*see p16* **Lost marbles**), might represent the 192 soldiers killed at Marathon.

In the war's sequel, ten years later, a fearsome army returned under the command of Darius's son, Xerxes I. By the time the invaders reached Athens, the vastly outnumbered citizens had been evacuated and the Persians burned an empty city. Traces of the 'non-event' have been recognised in bronze arrowheads found by archaeologists, their points twisted by striking against the rock of the Acropolis.

Athens was best placed to fight with its navy, built up from the proceeds of the discovery of a rich vein of silver a few years before. At the Battle of Salamis the Athenian general Themistocles ingeniously defeated the Persian navy by seducing its ships into

Pericles. *See p10.*

Perikles.

(Bd. I. S. 123.)

Nach der antiken Herme im Vatican.

Hadrian's Arch.
See p14.

a narrow channel, where the heavier Greek vessels proceeded to ram and sink them. The string of victories sent the Greeks' confidence sky-high.

But for Athens and Sparta the spoils of war were short-lived, for they would soon be at each other's throats. Both sides began collecting allies – Athens sided with the city-states in northern Greece, the Aegean Islands and the west coast of Asia Minor, while Sparta formed the Peloponnesian League with its neighbours, Olympia and Corinth. Athens' Delian League, so called because its treasury was originally located on the sacred island of Delos, moved to Athens in 454 BC. Gradually its members became more dependent on their head city and the Athenian Empire was formed.

Pericles (495 BC-429 BC), a politician from a distinguished local family, is the protagonist of Athens' Golden Age. He used tributes coaxed from members of the Delian League and materials brought back from expeditions to territories in Phoenicia and the Black Sea region to transform the city.

Eventually Pericles overstretched the empire by advising war on too many fronts at once, while at the same time stirring up resistance among allies by making harsh demands on them for protection against the Persians. In 446 BC Athens and Sparta agreed to a 30-year peace treaty. But the mutual mistrust continued.

GOLDEN YEARS

With the unflappable Pericles at the helm, peace – coupled with unprecedented power and income – heralded Athens' heyday as the intellectual and cultural centre of Greece and beyond. In just a handful of decades, from approximately 470 BC to 430 BC, many of the city's iconic buildings were built. The Acropolis, left ravaged by the Persians, took shape again. The fusion of Ionic and Doric order columns in the Parthenon and the sheer beauty of the Erechtheum proclaimed the city's imperial pre-eminence.

The rooftop pediments of other majestic buildings, including the Temple of Hephaestus (or Theseion), the Propylaia and the Temple of Poseidon on the hillside at Sounion (where Byron was to graffiti his name on a column; *see p243* **Byron in Greece**), strove towards azure skies. Such buildings, some of which still stand today, would prove to be the blueprint for the architecture of elegance and power down through the ages.

The progressive climate of the period allowed the arts full creative freedom. Drama entered its own golden age with the innovative political satire of Aristophanes and the classical tragedies of Aeschylus, Sophocles and Euripides; Pindar penned lyric poetry, while Socrates, and later Plato and Aristotle, laid the basis of Western philosophy. The glories of the

Golden Age were recorded by the historians Herodotus and Thucydides. The latter employed an advanced scientific approach that, for the first time, attempted to clear the historic landscape of dim myths and divine actions.

Sculptors abandoned the rigid formal styles of the Archaic Period for more naturalistic poses eased by the development of more malleable bronze casting techniques. Phidias's sculptures from the Parthenon are good examples of this powerful, new, liberating aesthetic. During the fifth century even the much-prized Attic red-figure pottery reached its artistic zenith, with detailed everyday scenes and mythological stories fired on black vases and wine vessels.

At the vanguard of this progress was Pericles. He never ranked higher than a general, but his sound intelligence and charisma as an orator allowed him to dominate the political scene and oversee the city's extraordinary boom. Thucydides believed that Pericles wielded a calming influence over the worst excesses of government. In an oft-quoted funerary speech, Pericles depicted an idealised state of democratic Athens: 'The city has succeeded in cultivating refinement without extravagance and knowledge without softness.'

Although Pericles also had praise for an individual's freedom, his ardent imperial streak still supported the subjugation of former allies. In terms of political and legal rights, Athenian citizenship was deemed superior to that of other cities within the empire. Out of a population of 200,000 at its peak, only 50,000 males were full citizens. In the mid century, at Pericles's request, citizenship was restricted to those born of both Athenian parents; this protectionism arguably backfired as it never allowed the conquered upper classes to become part of the Athens project.

Pericles's achievements were multifarious. He also proposed the building of the Long Walls around Athens' southern perimeter (linking the city to the port at Piraeus), commissioned the Parthenon, introduced the *theorica*, a state allowance to encourage poorer citizens to attend the theatre, and was a friend and sponsor to many of the leading philosophers and artists of the day, in particular Anaxagoras, Sophocles and Phidias. But with Pericles's demise and the onset of war, the Golden Age lost its sheen.

Three wise men: Aristotle

Born in Macedonia, at age 17 Aristotle (384 BC-322 BC) enrolled at Plato's Academy, where he studied for 20 years. On Plato's death he travelled in Asia Minor, then went back to Macedonia to tutor the young Alexander the Great before returning to Athens to found his own university, the Lyceum – known as the Peripatetic ('walking') school because discussions often took place around the grounds. When Alexander died, an anti-Macedonian backlash prompted Aristotle to leave Athens. He died in exile from a tummy bug.

Early works: The world is made up of forms, but these are only 'natural kinds' or species. By a process of induction a universal truth derives its meaning from proof of many individual instances of it. So observing several dogs bark we can make an informed guess that all dogs can bark.

Major contribution: A sculptor gives the marble (matter) of a statue shape (form). Form, a Hermes or Zeus perhaps, gives matter its essence and increases its actuality. Everything had a final cause or potential function, from simple objects to complex human beings. Therefore, he reasoned, there must be one divine first cause or 'prime mover'.

Apparently: Among living creatures there is a hierarchy of souls, from plants to animals to humans who alone have rational, reasoning souls.

Must read: Aristotle wrote over 400 works covering just about everything from crustaceans to the Athenian constitution. About 30 philosophical treatises, or lecture notes, survive.

His legacy: Aristotle's observations on the anatomy of marine life laid the blueprint for zoology. His study of logic using deductive arguments, or syllogisms (example: Every Greek is a person. Every person is mortal. Every Greek is mortal), was unsurpassed until the 20th century. The fields of astronomy, art, theology, politics, psychology and literary criticism all owe a debt to Aristotle.

If he were around today: He'd be the ultimate polymath, but Darwinists would give him a hard time.

Easy quote: 'Without friends no one would choose to live, though he had all other goods.'

BACK TO THE FRONT

The Peloponnesian War ran from 431 BC to 404 BC and was triggered when Athens placed Corfu, a colony of Corinth, under its power.

Thanks to Thucydides, detailed accounts of the war still exist. He attributed the 'real' cause of the conflict to Sparta's fear of Athens' expanding imperialism. On paper, Athens had the superior navy; Sparta, the sharper infantry. Pericles's strategy, therefore, was to make sudden navy raids and then retreat behind Athens' defensive walls when Spartan soldiers attacked. The plan might have worked had an epidemic in 430 BC not killed thousands of Athenians packed inside the city, including Pericles himself.

Athens held on for ten more years despite the devastation of its countryside and the loss of income from its silver mines and olive groves. After victories for both sides, including the prestigious capture of 120 Spartan soldiers by the Athenians, the fragile Peace of Nicias, named after the chief Athenian negotiator, was agreed in 421 BC.

But a succession of generals turned their backs on Sparta's offers for peace and took increasing risks. In 413 BC an overstretched invasion force led by Alcibiades, an ambitious student of Socrates, suffered a catastrophic defeat at Syracuse in Sicily. The damage was massive. Thucydides calculated that more than 40,000 Athenian troops and as many as 200 ships were lost in Sicily.

Before leaving for war, Alcibiades had allegedly taken part in a spree that desecrated the Herms, sculpted heads of the god Hermes that protected doorways throughout the city. Because he was thought to have once parodied the Eleusinian mysteries, the drug-fuelled initiation ceremonies for the cult of Demeter and Persephone, Alcibiades became a chief suspect and was recalled from Sicily for trial. Rather than face the Assembly, he fled to Sparta and was condemned to death in absentia.

After upsetting the Spartans by seducing the wife of one of its kings, Alcibiades sought refuge in Persia. He was itching to return to Athens, though, and, with the promise of Persian support, made contact with some Athenian oligarchs who were looking to take advantage of the ferment in the city. In 411 BC a moderate oligarchy failed and democracy was restored. Alcibiades switched sides to the democrats and led a four-year campaign regaining Athenian control in the Aegean. He rode back into Athens a hero and that year led the religious procession to Eleusis. Pursued by multiple enemies, Alcibiades was eventually blamed by the fair-weather Athenians for a naval defeat at Notium and he retreated to the safety of a castle.

The situation deteriorated in Athens when, in 406 BC, a 5,000-strong crew drowned and the people accused the generals of not having done enough to rescue the sailors. The generals were tried en masse at the Assembly, but Socrates, who happened to be chairman, refused to conduct the case as it contravened an Athenian citizen's right to an individual hearing. Such was the rancour among the people that they condemned the generals anyway. Six, including the son of Pericles, were summarily executed. As Aristotle later noted, ancient democracy was ever susceptible to mob rule.

By 404 BC the population of Athens had grown, but food lines were still cut off. The city had no choice but to surrender and its walls were supposedly dismantled to the sound of flute music while the freedom of Greece was proclaimed.

The war ended Athenian hegemony and shut down the Delian League. Sparta installed a brutal puppet regime in Athens called the Thirty Tyrants. This lasted just a year before Athenian rebels restored democracy.

> **'Apparently Alexander the Great loved Homer so much that he slept with a copy of *The Iliad* under his pillow.'**

MACEDONIA RISING

Although the fourth century BC began with the unjust death of Socrates, the baton in the quest for absolute truth was passed on to Plato and Aristotle, who became regular fixtures debating in the agora (market place). The Monument of Lysicrates was built and the polished speeches of Demosthenes, delivered at the people's Assembly, became another highlight of city life in this period. Fourth-century BC Greece was marked by complex power struggles between new alliances, yet more wars and a shift from city-states towards monarchy.

During the first third of the century Sparta and Thebes became embroiled in a feud that ultimately weakened both sides. Athens, fearful of the growing power of her north-western neighbour Thebes, switched allegiance and formed a coalition with Sparta. In 378 BC Athens revived her maritime ambitions and formed the Second Athenian Confederacy, composed of the cities and islands of the Aegean and Ionian seas. However, it lacked the backbone of the Delian League, having neither the resources nor the determination to impose its will, and soon overreached itself.

Crumbling under the weight of history: the **Parthenon**.

Ready to capitalise on the power vacuum among the squabbling Greek states was new player Macedonia. Its rise as a superpower was inspired by its king, Philip II, and his son Alexander the Great.

Athens, which had allies on the north-western border, had always been happy to see Macedonia weak. A step ahead of his fellow Athenians, Demosthenes realised that Philip's expansionist policies represented a real threat. In a series of well-varnished speeches known as the Philippics, he warned the Athenians how their indifference contrasted with Philip's energy and decisiveness. Speaking about a rumour that wanted Philip dead, Demosthenes said: 'Is Philippos dead? What does it matter to you? For if this Philippos dies, you will soon raise up a second Philippos by your apathy.' His powerful oratory, though, went unheeded.

The Macedonians made their move in 338 BC in a battle at Chaironeia, in central Greece. Fighting side by side in a phalanx formation and armed with 4.3-metre (14-foot) spears, Philip's light-footed army became a lethal porcupine that could skewer enemies before they got too close.

Post-victory, Philip sent Alexander to Athens on a diplomatic mission to placate the Greeks by returning the ashes of the Athenian dead who had fallen in the battle. He made no punitive demands and asked only that Athens should ally itself with Macedonia. Such had

been Alexander's brutal razing to the ground of Thebes when it rebelled in 336 BC, that Athens had the good sense to accept Macedonian rule.

Alexander didn't linger in Athens. Instead he marched east to create the Persian Empire by conquering most of the known world from present-day Turkey as far as Afghanistan, while still only in his 20s. Apparently he loved Homer so much that he slept with a copy of *The Iliad* under his pillow. On news that his brilliant life had been cut short by an illness in 323 BC, the people of Athens reputedly danced in the streets.

In the squabbles among generals that followed Alexander's death, Athens tried to seize back its independence, but was effortlessly defeated. Surrender meant the end of its proud tradition of naval power and the abolition of democracy. As if to symbolise the city's demise, Alexander's successor, Demetrios Falireas, installed a harem in the Parthenon. In 322 BC Athens' most eloquent advocate Demosthenes, who had been chased into exile by the Macedonians, chose suicide by poison rather than be captured.

HELLENISTIC 'GREEK-LIKE' ATHENS

In 307 BC Demetrios 'the Besieger' (so called because of his assault on the island of Rhodes) freed Athens and re-established democracy. This marked the beginning of the Hellenistic Age, which is characterised by a shift in perception from an insular city-state mentality to a view of the individual as part of an expansive empire. Adherents of Diogenes, the Cynics in particular, but also the Epicureans, and the Stoics, considered the achievement of self-sufficiency a means of protecting man from a random world at large. These new philosophical patterns were reflected in the arts. Portraits expressed not only the public role of the sitter, but also his or her inner thoughts and feelings. Sculpture was less serene than in the classical period, and began to embody the sensual and a sense of life's drama. Much impressive construction took place throughout the wider empire, but in Athens, notably, the Tower of the Winds and the Stoa of Attalos were built, the latter's neo-classical style echoing the glories of the past.

In 267 BC Athens and Sparta, with the support of the Egyptian king Ptolemy II, attempted one last time to undermine Macedonian hegemony. Demetrios's son Antigonos, however, proved too strong and when he counter-attacked not even the Spartans could save the day. Athens endured a Macedonian garrison until 229 BC but, although the city lost any further political claims to lead Greece, it remained an intellectual and cultural centre.

WHEN IN ROMAN ATHENS...
In the second century BC, Rome, the region's growing superpower, began to wrestle power from Macedonia in Greece. But it was not until 86 BC that the Roman general Sulla occupied Athens. One of his first acts, as a punishment for Athens having supported Mithridates's rebellion in Asia Minor, was to knock down its walls and siphon off art treasures to decorate Rome.

Under the Pax Romana (the imperial peace inaugurated by Augustus in AD 31), Athens benefited from Roman patronage as the intellectual capital of the Graeco-Roman world. In 66-67 Nero toured Greece and won everything he turned his hand to, from athletic to musical challenges – only a brave opponent would defeat a psychopathic emperor. In peacetime, tourists and the sons of Roman nobility, such as Cicero and Horace, flocked to the city to see its ancient sites and to study at its renowned university. As a token of the esteem with which Rome held all things Greek, emperors began to honour leading Greeks by electing them for the Roman senate and inaugurated a panhellenic festival.

Around this time modifications were made to the Acropolis with the construction of an elegant circular temple dedicated to Rome and Augustus, eastwards of the Parthenon. And the Emperor Claudius built a grandiose

stairway leading to the Propylaia, which provided a formal and symmetrical approach to the sacred hill.

But of all the Roman Emperors, it was the passionate philhellene Hadrian (117-38), who made the biggest impact on the city and its heritage. Not only did he introduce the Greeks to Roman laws and give them the rights of Roman citizenship, but he also repaired earlier fire damage to the Parthenon and built the Library to the east of the Ancient Agora. In addition, he solved the crucial problem of the city's water supply by building a great reservoir on the slopes of Lycabettus Hill, which collected water brought there by channels from Mount Parnes. His impressive architectural contribution included the continuation and completion in 131-2 of the Peisistratid Temple of Olympian Zeus and the erection of a huge gateway leading to the *peribolos* (precinct) of the temple, the Arch of Hadrian. The inscription over the monumental entrance reads: 'This is the Athens of Theseus, the old city' on one side, and on the other, 'This is the city of Hadrian, not of Theseus.' The words can still be discerned through the soot today.

Equally evident today is the Odeon of Herodes Atticus (Herodion), a Roman imperial theatre built into a natural slope of the Acropolis in the middle of the second century by the eponymous 'millionaire' and tutor to Marcus Aurelius. The auditorium could seat 50,000, and to this day hosts productions of the great Greek dramas.

During the reign of Valerian (253-60) the walls of Athens were rebuilt. But not well enough to repel the Germanic Heruli tribe, who stormed the city in 267 and left it in rubble. The remaining Athenians moved to a small area to the north of the Acropolis, where they fortified new walls built of marble salvaged from the ruined buildings.

GOODBYE TO THE GODS
According to the Roman writer Petronius, in the early first century AD one could find more gods than citizens in Athens. The well-travelled chronicler Pausanias agreed that the gods interested the Athenians more than anything else. In 52 AD St Paul had preached the gospels on the Areopagus. As the apostle shared his news with the Epicurean and Stoic philosophers on walks through the temples he was shocked to discover a city full of idols. Nonetheless, he was impressed by its beauty. The Athenians relished hearing about a religion whose God 'does not inhabit temples'. It appealed to them on a moral and intellectual plane, but they mocked the concept of resurrection. A handful, however, did

In Context

convert to Christianity, long before Constantine made it Greece's official faith in the early fourth century (323), when the Roman emperor moved his capital from Rome to the Greek city of Byzantium, renaming it Constantinople.

During the fourth and fifth centuries, Athens experienced a brief regeneration, with its neo-Platonic philosophical schools attracting important students (such as Julian the Apostate, Basil and Gregory) from all over the known world, only to fall into oblivion after Emperor Justinian closed them down in 529. By then, Athens, tormented by waves of Slavic barbarians, plague and earthquakes, had long since faded under the shadow of Constantinople.

> **'Athens, once worthily called the flower of the world, sunk to being the poorest and most miserable of cities.'**

BYZANTINE COMPLEXITIES

From about the sixth to the 13th centuries Athens entered another dark age. The former cradle of civilisation became a provincial satellite of the Byzantine empire and a minor centre of religious learning and devotion. Today, all that remains from this period are the foundations of some of the ancient temples that had been converted for early Christian worship and a handful of churches from the 11th and 12th centuries built on the Byzantine cross-in-square plan.

From the 13th century, a host of outsiders took advantage of Athens' run-down state. First came the French. After the creation of the Latin Empire of Constantinople in 1204, the city passed to Othon de la Roche, a French nobleman who became *megaskyr*, or great lord of Athens and Thebes. He was succeeded by his nephew, Guy I. Athens prospered under Frankish rule, and the magnificence of the Athenian court was recorded in mid century by a Catalan chronicler.

Then, in 1311 the duchy was captured by a band of Catalan explorers who a year later offered the ducal title to King Frederick II of Sicily, a member of the house of Aragón. The Aragón clan carried the title, but Athens was, in fact, governed by the Catalan Grand Company, an unreliable mercenary force that also acquired the neighbouring duchy of Neopatras in 1318.

As the French feudal culture faded, Athens sank into insignificance and poverty, particularly after 1377, when the succession was contested in civil war. Peter IV of Aragón assumed sovereignty in 1381, but ruled from Barcelona. On his initiative, the devastated duchy was settled by Albanians.

Eleftherios Venizelos.
See p19.

Lost marbles

Zealous plane-spotters and drunken holiday-makers are just blips in Anglo-Hellenic relations compared to the ongoing dispute over what the Greeks and PC press call the Parthenon Marbles and most Brits know as the Elgin Marbles.

In 1801, when Athens was still occupied by Ottoman forces, Lord Elgin, British ambassador to Turkey, had the 2,250-year-old sculptures by Pheidias removed from the frieze of the Parthenon and transported home. The aristocrat claimed he had an official licence for his deeds, but only an ambiguously worded Italian translation has survived. The Greeks counter-claimed that he had bribed and bullied his way with uncouth Turkish bureaucrats who were acting against the will of the Greek people.

With wars raging in Europe, it took Elgin more than ten years to get himself and the goods home. He wanted to keep the marbles, but debt forced him to sell them to the British Museum in 1816 for the princely sum of £35,000, though he complained to Parliament that they were worth twice that. Now housed in the rather austere Duveen Gallery, where up to six million people a year visit, to this day the museum claims that its possession of the marbles is legal. Despite a campaign by a handful of British MPs to return the marbles to Greece, the government takes its official line from the museum director, who won't budge. The museum says it is bound by Parliament to keep the sculptures.

Since the Greeks wrestled their independence from the Turks in the 1820s, they have been making noises for the sculptures to be returned. Then, as now, they argued that the works are integral to the artistic effect and context of the Parthenon, the highest symbol of Greece's ancient heritage.

Had Elgin acted as a cultural saviour or a vandal? The pros and cons are numerous. Actually, the Acropolis was twice besieged during the Greek War of Independence, so Elgin's actions might have inadvertently

---

Athens again shone briefly after its conquest in 1388 by Nerio Acciaioli, lord of Corinth and member of a family that was 'plebeian in Florence, potent in Naples and sovereign in Greece', according to the historian Edward Gibbon. Nerio helped to establish many of his compatriots as merchants in Athens. One of them, Cyriac of Ancona, kept illustrated diaries of his time in Greece; his scribbles offer a rare insight into lost monuments.

The next 50-odd years witnessed a tug-of-war for the city between the Republic of Venice and the Ottoman Turks. The Venetians had held Athens from 1394 to 1402, but in 1456 the fall of the Acropolis to the Turks marked the beginning of nearly four centuries of Ottoman rule.

Athens once again declined. The few remaining Greeks lived a semi-rural existence. They paid a tax to the Turks, but both Jesuit and Capuchin monasteries continued to thrive. The Erechtheum was used as a harem and the Parthenon, which had already been converted into a Christian church with a campanile, was refashioned into a Turkish mosque complete with minaret. A French naval officer visiting in 1537 wrote: 'Athens, once worthily called the flower of the world, has now, under heavy servitude, sunk to being the poorest and most miserable of cities.'

When Venetian troops besieged the Acropolis in 1687, the Parthenon, used by the Turks as a gunpowder store, was heavily bombarded – until that incident the sacred hill had been virtually intact. The Parthenon took a further hit in 1801, when the British ambassador to Constantinople Lord Elgin detached much of the frieze around the temple and shipped it to London (*see above* **Lost marbles**).

saved the marbles from more serious harm. And what damage the sculptures might have endured exposed to Athens' smog of recent years is anyone's guess. That said, apparently the British Museum caused irreparable damage to the marbles during cleaning in 1937-8.

The Greeks are no longer demanding ownership, but would like to see the marbles returned on loan in time for the 2004 Olympic Games, where they would be housed in a specially built museum in sight of the Acropolis.

To counter concerns about setting a legal precedent, Greek campaigners vow that the marbles are a one-off case and say their return would not threaten the status of other artefacts in the British Museum and beyond.

The debate continues. The only accord is based on the classical importance of the collection and their unique beauty. Something that Keats recognised, after hours of gazing at the marbles, when he wrote in his *Ode on a Grecian Urn*: 'Beauty is truth, truth beauty – that is all ye know on earth, and all ye need to know.'

Gibbon described the city's decline, writing about 18th-century Athenians 'walking with supine indifference among the glorious ruins of antiquity'. Foreign visitors, however, seemed more enthusiastic. The 1762 publication of *Antiquities of Athens* by the Society of Dilettanti prompted many travellers to visit the city as a sort of adjunct to the Grand Tour, and proved highly influential on Western neo-classical architecture.

GERMAN AND BRITISH ATHENS

In the late 18th century the Greek Nationalist movement gained momentum with the founding of a number of secret societies financed by exiled merchants. They were spurred on by philhellenic western European intellectuals such as Goethe and Byron, who did a first-rate PR job for the Greek cause. During the War of

Independence, Athens changed hands several times between the Turks and Greek liberators, with the Acropolis, as ever, the seat of power.

By 1827, when the Turks recaptured the hill (which they were to hold for the next six years), Athens had been all but evacuated. Even in 1833, when plans for the new nation had been drawn up by the 'Great Powers' of western Europe (Britain, France and Russia), Athens only held about 4,000 people housed below the north slope of the Acropolis.

Modern Athens began to take shape from 1834, when it took over from Nafplion as the capital of a newly independent Greece. If Ioannis Kapodistrias, the mastermind of the War of Independence, had not been assassinated in 1831, chances are that the capital would have remained in the Peloponnese. As it was, the reasoning of

Famine in Athens

In April 1941 the Greek prime minister Alexandros Koryzis shot himself in despair at the Germans' imminent occupation. A week later the Greek flag was lowered on the Acropolis and the Nazi swastika raised in its place. Across Europe, newsreels showed field marshal von Brauchitsch on the sacred hill that Hitler had dubbed the symbol of 'human culture'. So began a three-year period that Churchill called the 'long night of barbarism'.

Almost immediately Athenians started panic-buying and stripped the city's stores bare, partly in response to German scare-mongering that the departing British army had poisoned the water supply with typhoid bacilli. The ill-prepared German army had neglected to bring their own food supplies and arrived in Athens half-starving. Officers looted the city's warehouses and seized supplies. A combination of a debilitated Greek state infrastructure, ruthless plundering by the occupying force and a below-average harvest soon caused acute food shortages.

As a result, the country experienced rampant inflation, which created a black market in which olive oil became the chief commodity and the price of a loaf of bread reached two million drachmas.

As the Germans bickered with the Italians about who should feed Greece, official rations dwindled and soup kitchens, set up by charities, fed people just two or three times a week. Many resorted to eating weeds gathered from the outlying areas of the city. Desperate, people of all ages, particularly those from the slums created by an influx of refugees in 1923, took to the streets to beg.

Children waited patiently for soldiers to discard olive stones, fighting among themselves to suck the stone dry, while brave hawkers cried: 'Buy raisins. A handful will save you from Charon!' To make matters worse, snow fell in Athens that winter and the sub-zero temperatures fuelled disease. Physically and mentally exhausted individuals collapsed crying '*pinoue, pinoue*' ('I'm hungry') as they lay dying. The next morning their swollen bodies were slung in the back of a municipal truck bound for the cemetery.

Reports by German occupation officials that more food was needed in Athens were ignored by the Nazi high command in Berlin. In a memo to Reich leaders of the occupied territories, Goering wrote: 'I could not care less when you say that people under your administration are dying of hunger. Let them perish so long as no German dies.'

For the first time since mortality records began in the Athens/Piraeus zone, the death rate exceeded the birth rate. At the time the BBC's reported over 500,000 deaths during the winter of 1941-2, but more accurate studies put the figure at about 40,000 for the year ending October 1942. By this time grain supplies were arriving from the International Red Cross and the end was in sight.

In Context

the mediating powers was almost completely symbolic. They imposed a hereditary monarchy on Greece and at the tender age of 17 the Bavarian Otto I became the first king of the Hellenes (1832-62).

Installed in the only two-storey house in the city, the teenage monarch set about rebuilding much of Athens along neo-classical lines using German and French architects. The idea was to re-create the glories of the ancient city: broad streets were laid out in grid patterns, incorporating showpiece squares such as Syntagma, and lined with grand public buildings like the Royal Palace, the University, the Academy (built in marble from Mount Pentelicon) and the Observatory.

In keeping with the spirit of the new nation, German archaeologists, most notably Heinrich Schliemann, began stripping away the Frankish and Turkish embellishments on the Acropolis and Parthenon and at other key sites in the city. Clearly impressed by these treasures on a visit to the Acropolis in 1848, the English author Edward Lear wrote: 'Poor old scrubby Rome sinks into nothing by the side of such beautiful magnificence.'

By most accounts 19th-century Athens was a mild-mannered city of elegant tree-lined avenues. Its dwellings, built for the nascent professional classes, were similar in style to those of Victorian London. Most of these Ottonian-style houses have long since been replaced by concrete, though some of the best surviving examples are on Vassilissis Sofias.

In 1843, the explosive combination of Otto's autocratic rule and croneyism, the continued interference of foreign powers and declining economic conditions led to a bloodless revolution taking place in Athens. The people joined forces with political and military leaders to insist on the restoration of the constitution.

In the 1850s the population still numbered only 20,000 and economic progress was slow. There were no railway routes into the city, roads were poor and the export of currants provided the only source of national income. It was out of a climate of despondency that the governing creed of the century, the 'Great Idea' (Megali Idhea), developed. The thesis advocated a new Greek Empire by the gradual enlargement of Greece's territory at the expense of the declining Ottoman Empire. But for the rest of the century, it was to create tension between liberal and conservative forces. One expression of rebellion against tradition was an enthusiasm for use in literature of the demotic language (popular language) over *catharevousa* (a simplified form of ancient Greek), a debate that led to riots in Athens in 1901.

Between 1854 and 1857 the occupation of Piraeus harbour by the French and British armies increased the discontent among Athenians and eventually led to the expulsion of King Otto in 1862. This had been facilitated by a new generation of graduates from Athens University, which had been re-opened in 1837. However, much to the chagrin of the Greek intellectuals (and due to British influence in the Ionian Islands), George I was enthroned in 1863. He ruled until 1913 and proved a more capable leader than Otto (even if during the first 17 years of his reign there were nine elections and 31 governments). In 1870 George's rule was further marred by the kidnapping and murder of a group of wealthy British tourists on an excursion to Marathon; the crime became known as the Dilessi murders, and was one of more than 100 cases of the time.

Arguably Athens deserved its fin-de-siècle tag as the 'Paris of the eastern Mediterranean'. The opening of the Corinth Canal, begun in AD 62 and completed in 1893, made Piraeus one of the world's great ports. The merchant navy expanded and a shipping industry boom sparked a growth in manufacturing and banking.

Athens had a chance to show off its achievements to the world in 1896, when it hosted the first modern Olympic Games. The Panathenaic Stadium, which seated 70,000 people, was constructed on the site of the original fourth-century BC arena by an expatriate Greek tycoon. But such progress was precarious. A year later, when a dispute broke out over the control of Crete, the Turks were poised within a few days' march of Athens. Once more the city was saved from the Turkish army by the allied powers.

POPULATION BOOM

The man who had led the uprising to liberate Crete in 1905, Eleftherios Venizelos, was summoned to Athens following a coup d'état by an Athens garrison in 1909. Appointed Prime Minister in 1910, he was an advocate of liberal democracy, who doubled Greek territory during the Balkan Wars (1912-13) and sided with the Allies in World War I.

In March 1913, King George was assassinated by a madman and his son Constantine became king. Constantine, who was married to the sister of the German Kaiser, didn't want to get involved in the war and this caused much tension with Venizelos. For the first three years of the war Greece kept neutral and the city was occupied by British and French troops.

Greece's catastrophic post-war invasion of Smyrna resulted in the 1923 Treaty of Lausanne, which implemented a controlled form of ethnic cleansing and signalled the end of the Great Idea. In an exchange of religious minorities, 400,000 Turks left Greece, and almost one and a half million Christian refugees, mainly Greeks, arrived from Asia Minor. More than half of them came to Athens, where they founded shanty towns on the fringes of the city. The web of suburbs along the metro line to Piraeus bears testimony to the refugees' origins: Nea Smyrni, Nea Ionia, Nea Filadelfia.

At the same time as the slums were expanding, during the political bickering of the inter-war years, the American School began excavations in the Athenian Agora in 1931, culminating in the complete restoration of the Stoa of Attalos.

COMMUNIST FEARS

Although a republic was established between 1924 and 1935, its existence was threatened by repeated military coups. When Venizelos was exiled in 1935, King George II was restored to the throne by a rigged plebiscite. As prime minister he installed General Ioannis Metaxas, who ruled as a fascist-style dictator – his secret police dealt ruthlessly with leftist opponents and parts of Thucydides were banned from schools. Metaxas is best known for his curt reply of 'ohi' (no) to Mussolini's request to allow Italian soldiers to cross Greece. Apparently his actual response was 'C'est la guerre', but the proud Greeks prefer to remember the more emphatic riposte. The day of the rebuttal, 28 October 1940, is now celebrated as a national holiday.

In April 1941, Hitler's armies advanced suddenly into Greece. Athen's inhabitants suffered extreme hardships during the three-year German occupation in World War II, especially during the winter of 1941-2, when hundreds died daily from starvation (*see p18* **Famine in Athens**).

> **'Prime Minister Karamanlis noted: "We invented democracy. We were into it before it was cool."'**

During the war the Hotel Grande Bretagne in Syntagma Square housed successively Greek, British and German headquarters. Churchill, who was in Athens to show his support for the Greek government against the communists, escaped a bomb placed in the hotel's basement in December 1944 by staying aboard HMS *Ajax* in Piraeus harbour.

In December 1944 an open communist revolution broke out in the Thisio area after a demonstration had been fired on by police in Syntagma Square. Traces of action from the Battle of Athens that ensued can still be seen on some buildings in the city. For a brief time the government held only the Parliament building, neighbouring embassies and a part of Syntagma Square, while the palace garden was used as a common grave. British troops eventually restored order and at a conference called by Churchill on Christmas Day an armistice was arranged whereby Archbishop Damaskinos became regent.

The country's civil troubles of 1944-9 between pro- and anti-communist factions seriously retarded the city's recovery. Athens was virtually severed from the rest of Greece by roadblocks. Tragically, more Greeks were killed in the civil war than in World War II. In response to the distress and disorder, over a million Greeks set sail for a more prosperous existence in Canada, Australia and America. Many of those who stayed behind headed for Athens, where American aid was funding an industrialisation programme, in search of work.

After its wars Greece was isolated as the only non-communist state in the Balkans. Communism was declared illegal and the government introduced its infamous Certificate of Political Reliability (that gave proof that the holder was not a Red), which remained valid until 1962, and without which Greeks couldn't vote or easily find a job.

Eleftherios Venizelos. *See p19.*

Athenians strike against economic cuts in the 1990s. *See p22.*

In the 1950s and '60s the metropolis began to take on the sprawling shape that characterises it today. Land clearance for suburban building caused run-off and flooding, requiring the modernisation of the sewer system; at Piraeus in 1959 a burst sewer revealed four superb classical bronzes. The Mornos River was dammed and a pipeline over 160 kilometres (100 miles) long was built to Athens, supplementing the inadequate water supply.

Ideological conflict and political instability led to the seizure of power by a military Junta in 1967. Andreas Papandreou, who would later become prime minister, called it 'the first successful CIA military putsch on the European continent'. During this time persecution and censorship ruled. Greece's favourite actress Melina Mercouri was disenfranchised while out of the country, rembetika clubs were shut down and productions of the classical tragedies forbidden. Sadly during the Dictatorship of the Colonels (1967-74) many of the Turkish houses of Plaka and other neo-classical buildings were destroyed.

On 17 November 1973, student demonstrations against the Junta at Athens Polytechnic were brutally ended when tanks moved in, killing at least 34. The occasion provided the name for Greece's lethal November 17 urban guerrilla terrorist group, which has killed 23 targets, including British Brigadier Stephen Saunders, shot dead at point-blank range in Athens' traffic in June 2000. In 2002 Greek police had a breakthrough in rounding up its alleged members following a botched bombing in Piraeus; they were finally put on trial in 2003.

MODERN ATHENS

The Junta was finally felled in July 1974, after it had precipitated the Turkish invasion of northern Cyprus following a disastrous plan to assassinate President Makarios. Konstantine Karamanlis, a leading politician in voluntary exile, returned to streets full of jubilant crowds. As the new prime minister, Karamanlis noted: 'We invented democracy. We were into it before it was cool.' A ban on communist parties was lifted and later that year in a referendum the Greeks voted by two thirds for the abolition of the monarchy. When King Constantine finally revisited Greece in 1993 for a holiday, the government kept his yacht under constant surveillance by missile boats and planes. Not surprisingly, the tanned London-based king said he had no desire to overthrow the Greek constitution.

The new republic now looked to western Europe for orientation with the goal of joining the European Economic Community. On 1 January 1981, thanks to the manoeuverings of Karamanlis, Greece became the tenth member of the EEC. Later that year Andreas Papandreou's Panhellenic Socialist Movement (PASOK) party formed Greece's first socialist government, appealing to the electorate with the simple slogan '*Allaghi*' (change). Melina Mercouri was appointed Minister of Culture and wasted no time launching a campaign to return the Elgin Marbles to Greece. In 1985 Athens became Europe's first Capital of Culture.

Papandreou had his comeuppance when his amorous exploits with an air hostess were splashed across the newspapers and the party became tangled up in a financial scandal involving the Bank of Crete. But in January 1992 he was acquitted.

The 1990s were characterised by austere cuts by the government to attain some sort of economic stability and reactive strikes. Power passed from the New Democracy party (ND) back to Papandreou's PASOK. With a 52-strong cabinet on hand, Papandreou virtually ran the country from his private villa in Athens' exclusive Kifisia district, a suburb that had first become fashionable when Herodes Atticus built his villa there in the first century AD.

Since World War II Athens has drawn more than three million people from the countryside and now contains more than 40 per cent of the country's population. In such a megalopolis, the Greek saying that Athens is merely 'the largest village in Greece' is now seriously challenged.

A series of governments had neglected the city's expansion problems and by the early '90s Athens was saddled with a deserved reputation as one of the most traffic-polluted cities in Europe. In 1994, as a response to the worsening *nefos* (smog) that was adversely affecting ancient buildings and monuments, traffic restrictions were introduced in central Athens.

The failed bid for the 1996 Olympic Games inspired some improvements to the city – primarily a shiny new metro system and a gleaming modern international airport. But it was the awarding of the 2004 Games a year later that galvanised planners into action.

Plans were temporarily disturbed when a strong earthquake shook the city on 7 September 1999. It was the most powerful to hit the region in almost 200 years, killing 120 people and leaving 70,000 homeless. The quake measured 5.9 on the Richter scale and left minor cracks in one of the Parthenon's columns. It also damaged the pottery collection in the National Archaeological Museum.

Following the death of Papandreou in 1996, the Blairite Costas Simitis steered Greece to the European Monetary Union in January 2001 when the euro replaced the drachma, much to the relief of countless tourists. A year later, in 2002, the city elected its first female mayor, Dora Bakoyianni, who narrowly escaped an assassination attempt not long after her election.

Greece held the presidency of the European Union without incident for the first half of 2003. Athenians will be hoping that the Olympic Games will run just as smoothly and leave the city with a handsome infrastructure for future generations.

> ▶ For an architectural history of Athens, *see p30* **Architecture**, and for insights into early religion, *see p38* **Greek Myth & Legend**.

Key events

3200 BC Bronze Age in Cyclades and Crete.
Around 3000 BC Neolithic settlements
on the Acropolis hill.
1450 BC Myceans in Knossos.
Around 1400 BC The Acropolis is fortified.
1230 BC-1180 BC Destruction of Troy.
1200 BC Collapse of Mycenean culture.
800 BC Athens expands by incorporating
its surrounding villages into its city-state.
776 BC The first Olympic Games take place.
750 BC-700 BC Homer writes
The Iliad and *The Odyssey*.
750 BC-500 BC The Archaic Age.
594 BC Solon becomes archon of Athens.
496 BC Birth of dramatist Sophocles.
490 BC The Athenians defeat the Persians
(led by Darius) at the Battle of Marathon.
480 BC The Persians burn Athens.
470 BC-430 BC Pericles's programme of
civic improvement focuses on the Acropolis.
454 BC The Delian League moves to Athens,
signalling the start of the Athenian Empire.
431 BC-404 BC Peloponnesian War
between Athens and Sparta.
427 BC Birth of philosopher Plato.
399 BC Socrates is sentenced to death.
387 BC Plato sets up his Academy.
338 BC After winning the battle of
Chaironeia, the Persians led by Philip II
gain control over Athens.
336 BC Philip II's son Alexander
(the Great) inherits control of Athens.
323 BC Death of Alexander the Great.
322 BC Death of Aristotle and Demosthenes.
330 BC-215 BC Euclid and Archimedes
develop their mathematical theorems.
267 BC Athens fails to rise
against Macedonia.
148 BC Romans conquer Macedonia.
86 BC Roman general Sulla occupies Athens.
AD 31 The Pax Romana is inaugurated by
Emperor Augustus.
52 St Paul preaches the gospels to Athenians.
66-67 Emperor Nero tours Greece.
124-31 The Roman emperor Hadrian begins
architectural reconstruction in Athens.
232 Constantine moves the capital of the
Roman Empire to Constantinople.
380 Emperor Thedosius declares Christianity
the official religion of the Empire.
529 Emperor Justinian closes down
the philosophical schools in Athens.
600-1300 Athens goes into decline. Its
temples are converted to Christian churches.

1054 The Christian church is divided
into Roman and Greek orthodoxies.
1300-1456 A series of invaders (Franks,
Catalans, Venetians, Turks) occupy Athens.
1456 The Turks occupy the Acropolis.
They rule Athens for the next four centuries.
1687 In an attempt to recapture Athens,
the Venetians bombard the Parthenon.
1801 Lord Elgin removes part of the frieze
around the Parthenon and ships it to London.
1821 Start of the Greek War of Independence.
1828 Creation of the first free Greek state.
Its president is Ioannis Kapodistrias.
1831 Kapodistrias is assassinated.
1832 The Great Powers of western
Europe impose Bavarian King Otto as ruler.
1834 Athens becomes the capital of Greece.
1893 Opening of the Corinth Canal.
1896 The first modern-day Olympic Games
take place in Athens.
1910 Eleftherios Venizelos is appointed
Prime Minister.
1912-13 The Balkan Wars double the
territory belonging to Greece.
1913 King George is assassinated.
1917 Greece sides with the Allies in
World War I.
1923 Treaty of Lausanne authorises a
population exchange in Asia Minor. Greece
gains in excess of one million refugees.
1935 Venizelos is exiled; power is given
to general Ioannis Metaxas.
1941-42 German occupation.
1944 An assassination attempt against
Winston Churchill fails. The communist
revolution starts.
1944-49 Civil war tears Greece apart.
A mass exodus begins.
1967 The Junta seizes power.
1973 Student demonstrations against
the ruling colonels end in a blood bath.
1974 The Junta collapses.
1981 Greece's first socialist government
is elected into power. The country joins
the European Community.
1985 Athens is Europe's first Capital
of Culture.
1994 Traffic restrictions are introduced in
Athens in an attempt to reduce pollution.
1997 Athens is awarded the 2004 Olympics.
1999 An fatal earthquake hits Athens.
2001 The drachma is replaced by the euro.
2004 The Olympics come to Athens after
a 108-year hiatus.

Athens Today

Millions of visitors. Millions of complaints.

Or so it used to be. Disorganised, deafening and dirty, with stray dogs at the airport, Athens was shunned by visitors, except for romantic classicists, concrete salesmen, or backpackers and tourists heading to the islands.

No longer. Today Athens, home of the 2004 Olympic Games, is exerting its own pull. Most public clocks still show the wrong time, but the times are indeed changing. New airport, new metro, new determination. A cosmopolitan Mediterranean and European city is being born. And although much of this change would be only at discussion stage had it not been for the Olympics, there is a definite desire to move forwards in Greece. Athens has come of age.

NO SILENCE PLEASE, WE'RE GREEK

Not everything has changed, though. Greeks are still addicted to coffee and cigarettes. Some 44 per cent of Greeks over 15 smoke, the highest percentage in the European Union. Many of them are civil servants able to turn simple tasks into Herculean labours. Getting, completing and having the necessary forms processed (for anything – from driving licences to property permits) can take months. Athenians spend longer in queues than most other Europeans; waits up to 30 minutes are a weekly occurrence.

The capital, stuffed full of four million people, remains stunningly loud. Cars honk non stop, mobiles ring eternally and, anywhere you go, you will hear people shouting. The first time you think a murder is about to be committed, the tenth time you find it amusing, the 100th time you're the one shouting. On the night of a big soccer match, you can walk through Athens and follow every minute of the game as TVs blare out from private flats, coffeehouses, police stations and tavernas. Athenians love sport. There are almost as many basketball courts as there are churches.

'Surly shop assistants and snarling taxi drivers make Basil Fawlty look cuddly.'

Always look on the bright side of life in Athens, because it's nearly always there. You can't walk down a street without worrying about potholes. But you won't get mugged – Athens is the safest European capital hands down. Bag-snatching has gained in popularity in recent years, however, so hold on tight.

If Athens irritates you, the trick is to see the bigger picture. True, surly shop assistants and snarling taxi drivers make Basil Fawlty look polite and cuddly. People will invariably queue-jump or reverse over your foot. If you need directions or have a problem, though, nine in ten Athenians will stop to help, in English if they can. (Warning! Louts called touts will also stop to lure you to €100 drinks.) There's a refreshing accessibility to most public places, a hidden but healthy humanity and an all-round feeling of freedom. Bizarrely, in a country ruled by bureaucracy, even politicians can be gotten hold of quite easily. Greeks can have a private audience with a minister or MP simply by knowing a friend of a friend of a friend, or by approaching them in tavernas and restaurants, or on the beach during their holiday. It is a given that a politician will have time for a member of the public. This open-access system wasn't even marginally threatened by the attack on Mayor Bakoyianni in December 2002, when a deranged mechanic fired several shots at her car, injuring her driver and narrowly missing her.

BACK TO THE CENTRE

Something is clearly going right because by far the harshest judges of Athens – Athenians, who compare the place unfavourably with their native islands or other mainland escapes – are coming back to live in the centre of the capital.

While parts of Athens have a Third Worldish feel, with little or no infrastructure and regular (preventable) floods, quaint inner-city areas are being restored, highlighting the city's classical past and dragging it out of its Balkan shell. Old districts like night-loving Psyrri, bohemian/formerly anarchic Exarchia and tourist-saturated Plaka are now considered trendy, rather than dodgy, places to live in. A project to unify the city's archaeological zone into a pedestrian haven has made progress, backed by true culture-lovers and enthusiastic property buyers. The price of real estate, a common subject of discussion in cafés, has rocketed.

Incidentally, so has the cost of a cup of coffee (you'll get little change from a €5 note for some joe). September 2002 saw a nationwide shop and market boycott against the blatant overpricing in the advent of the euro. However, Greeks remain strongly pro-euro – a much more stable currency than the old drachma.

Athenians take a close interest in what's going on. There was genuine outrage when the central Platia Omonia facelift in 2003 revealed it to be almost totally concrete. *Candid Camera* couldn't have done a better job. A new facelift for the old facelift is in the works (*see p36* **Omonia moan**).

There's a long way to go, but Athens is heading in the right direction with more thought, care and follow-through being invested in the capital's appearance. New shopping avenues, such as the pedestrianised Ermou off central Syntagma Square, are mushrooming to compete with the traditionally filthy-rich area of Kolonaki.

TREE AT LAST

Greeks, devoted conspiracy theorists, have learned not to believe grand promises. The capital was going to be environmentally transformed by the 2004 Olympics, but this hasn't happened. Hemmed in by three mountain ranges, pollution levels in the city can soar on busy hot days, and the occasional *nefos* (smog) is still a problem. Environmental initiatives are often plagued by a complete lack of organisation or enforcement, one reason why Greeks are so massively pro-EU. Very few of Brussels' regulations will actually affect them.

Wild promises, like the planting of many millions of trees ahead of the Games, and even realistic promises, like solar heating for the athletes' village, were broken. To meet the deadline, the required tree-planting rate once allegedly reached an astronomical 80,000 a day or a mere 3,333 an hour (almost one a second). Annoyed Olympic organisers and environment ministry officials insist they were talking about saplings and plants and other little green things. Since nobody can be bothered to go round counting all these, the issue has withered away. The municipality says it will plant 10,000 trees but, outside of Panathenaic Stadium, don't expect a lot of green in Athens.

> **'So the family is all-important and the grubby sex sector sizzles. Contrasts are everywhere in Athens.'**

HAVE A LAUGH, COME TO ATHENS

This is a world-famous madhouse. Outside of the gigantic state-sector, most Athenians work seriously hard and quite a few have more than one job ('European prices, Third World salaries' is a much-heard complaint). Free time is precious. Why not enjoy it? Unfortunately, a major service provider is the sex industry, the capital's dirty and badly kept secret, which includes many Eastern European women working in appalling conditions.

So the family is all-important and the grubby sex sector sizzles. Don't be surprised, contrasts are everywhere in Athens. Taverna toilets can be filthy, private homes are invariably spotless. Armed guards on duty listen to the football on the radio. The capital is ostensibly left-wing and rebellious, yet many Greeks would take deep offence at someone going to a classical music concert in jeans and T-shirt. Athens can be more class-conscious and conservative than, say, London. Never admit your ignorance. Don't marry a postman.

ICARUS

No 1
airport
in the world

Greece takes pride in the No1 Airport in the world.
Athens International Airport has been acknowledged
as the best airport in the world in Overall Passenger
Satisfaction. We are proud of this success and we
will continue to offer you everything that makes
your travel a pleasant and unforgettable experience.
Thank you.

ATHENS
INTERNATIONAL AIRPORT
ELEFTHERIOS VENIZELOS

GREEN MAN, DEAD MAN

There's nothing like your first time when the car speeds through a clearly red traffic light, past the green man luring pedestrians to their death. Greek transport, with its dog-eat-dog/dog-run-over-dog attitude, used to be a microcosm of life in the capital. Transport is now getting its act together. Two modern-day miracles are the cheap, clean and efficient Athens Metro and the new airport, officially called Eleftherios Venizelos Airport, known locally as Spata Airport, or Athens International Airport on its website. Whatever its name, it's pretty darned good. Operating since 2001, Spata was voted the world's No.1 airport for its size in 2002. An overland train will link the Metro with the airport by the 2004 Games and a tram will connect the centre to the southern coast.

Getting around is becoming easier despite parts of Athens, in the run-up to the 2004 Olympics, being a 24-hour building site. The Olympics performed the vital role of getting big things finished and little things started. When the millions of arguments about the 'O' word have been forgotten, this will be its main legacy.

TEMPERS BOIL IN MELTING POT

A huge number of illegal migrants came in the 1990s – perhaps a million, or ten per cent of the country's population, equivalent to some 25 million going to the US. It's possible nowadays to get on a bus in Athens and not hear Greek. Albanians are often blamed, often rightly, for rising crime, the criticism dying down when Greek born-and-bred gang leaders are arrested.

In the long run, multiculturalism will be good for Greece, but the transition has been – and is – painfully hard, not least for the migrants themselves, whose treatment by employers and state alike has sometimes been atrocious. Many Greeks feel they're 'losing' their country, though a weekend journey through Greece shows the country is being fed and built by the same unwanted migrants. The powerful Orthodox Church – led by Christodoulos, a fiery ultra-nationalist who says he's just a patriot – objects to a planned mosque on the city's outskirts. Indefensibly, there is no official mosque in central Athens.

By mainstream European standards, most Greeks are robust nationalists. Greece has often been exploited in the past, and there's the wound of Cyprus, where Turkish troops to this day control the north. Deeply divided on domestic politics, Athens is a 99-per-cent society when it comes to foreign issues. TV stations will often promulgate one view (the second Gulf War was about oil, any criticism of the Athens Olympics was for US security firms to get contracts, etc), which is then willingly adopted by almost everyone. Some differing opinions are now heard on sensitive domestic subjects (such as the presence of a Muslim population in northern Greece), and Greek-Turkish relations are doing well, but the country desperately needs a politically incorrect, *Private Eye*-style taboo-buster. *Pontiki*, the main satirical magazine, never mocks Greece itself. It should.

LOOKING AHEAD

Athens ain't beautiful. It needs less smog, more trees. More pedestrians, fewer cars. Stop motorbikes racing along the pavement, bring on the street entertainers. Death to potholes, life to cycle lanes. Ban protests in the morning, make civil servants work in the afternoon. Public toilets yes (there are very, very few), cat poisoning no. More power to the amenable Dora Bakoyianni, the first female mayor, elected in October 2002, and less to unchecked property developers. And an end to earthquakes – the last big one, 5.9 Richter, killed 122 in September 1999 – would be nice.

Progress has come at a cost for the locals, including the blatant profiteering since the 2002 switch to the euro. Athenians complain that life here involves paying high European prices on low Greek salaries. Since costs have shot up all around the country, many Athenians now holiday in a place they know well. Athens.

We shall not be moved

You won't find this particular tradition on any postcard, but visitors are as likely to come across it face to face as they are the Parthenon – welcome to the city of protests.

Around once a week, angry demonstrators take over the centre of Athens, faithfully followed by cops and stray dogs. Star marchers include pensioners (who have got the time), taxi drivers, teachers and students. Drums beat and whistles blow as colourful banners and time-honoured chants denounce the frugal government or evil Americans, sometimes both. Adding to the fun, police routinely cordon off streets, old men with trolleys full of nuts do a roaring trade, protesters have a lovely day out and everyone's happy. Except, of course, ordinary Athenians stuck in the inevitable massive traffic jams.

Why so many protests? Since the typical Greek works for the cash-strapped state, demonstrations hit their employer directly.

Why so many in Athens? Marches in, say, up-north Kozani tend not to lead the evening's news. Why are protesters allowed to cripple the city centre at its busiest times? Ever since the 1967-74 military dictatorship, all governments have quivered at being called anti-democratic. The result is that as few as 200 people can paralyse the lives of hundreds of thousands. Truly big demos are organised two or three times a year by the major unions. Why do protests often take place on a Monday or Friday? Cynics would argue that many workers, instead of marching, can enjoy a long weekend and are therefore more likely to back the strike.

Ironically, the protests have demonstrated the future of Athens: car-free. The streets become beautifully empty and pollution drops dramatically. It's time to permanently 'greenify' the roads before the cars return.

But get ready for future marches staged by the gardeners of the city.

The **Propylaeum**. See p31.

Architecture

First there was the Acropolis – and then
it all went downhill from there.

Roughly speaking, Athens comprises
500 square metres of ancient marble and
many, many square kilometres of 1950s concrete.
Unlike Rome, which has developed more or less
harmoniously since its golden age, incorporating
and preserving successive waves of new
architecture, Athens reached its aesthetic peak
early on and, once the Romans departed, in
AD 395, trudged on to the present with
relatively little to show for it.

The reasons are historic: Athens effectively
became a backwater. But it's tempting to
hypothesise that so feted were the Acropolis
constructions, so technically miraculous and
rich in their aesthetics, ambition and materials,
that later Athenian builders felt unable to
compete. Certainly, rather than creating a fitting
environment, they have fashioned one that
flatters in relief. The Parthenon's hilltop location
guarantees that it is visible from around street
corners or between apartment blocks, dominating
the city's landscape. The temple is impressively
beautiful by any terms, but the contrast with the
concrete animal filling up the whole Athenian
basin and climbing up the surrounding mountains
makes it truly extraordinary.

Modern Athens is unique in its architecture,
or, rather, lack of it. The brutally uncontrolled
way the urban fabric has spread out around

the planned city centre has created a non-
monumental city with no or few connecting
open spaces, majestic boulevards or parks.
Despite the first impression of chaotic ugliness,
though, Athens is richer in small-scale meeting
places than most cities, which goes some way
towards explaining why it is sometimes called
'the largest village in Greece'. Look beyond its
concrete façades, alive with balcony greenery;
the David-and-Goliath meeting between a
microscopic 11th-century Byzantine church
and a 21st-century luxury hotel; or the calm,
glimmering city that you see beneath you from
Lycabettus at night; and you will find a city
that hasn't had the luxury to be picturesque.
Soon you might realise that the ugliness is
not that bad. You might even find it beautiful.

ANCIENT ATHENS

There is evidence of settlements on the
Acropolis as far back as the neolithic times,
around 5000 BC, and of the cult of Athena in
Mycenaean times (around 1500 BC). But the real
architectural fame for the Athenian hill started
in 510 BC. It was in the first century BC that the
last Peisistratid tyrant was overthrown and the
Delphic Oracle ordered that the Acropolis
should be the province of the gods, prohibiting
human occupancy of the sacred buildings
forever. Today the achievements of the ancient

architects stand as testament to one of the greatest legacies of Classical Greece – 2,500 years later they're still the most influential constructions in Western civilisation. (There's even a copy of the Parthenon in Nashville.)

> **'The Parthenon appears to be an ode to simplicity, but it is the most technically perfect Doric temple ever built.'**

The centrepiece of the Acropolis is the **Parthenon**, which French poet Lamartine called 'the world's most perfect poem in stone'. Standing on the location of earlier temples, the temple is dedicated to Athena's incarnation as virgin goddess (Parthenos). Its predecessor was the first Doric temple built entirely from marble – Athenian marble, to be precise, from the quarries of Mount Pentelicon. It was meant to be a monument to the Athenian victory over tyranny and to represent the triumph of democracy. However, the temple was destroyed when the Persians sacked Athens in 480 BC.

Thirty-three years later, in 447 BC, Pericles gathered the best architects available, Iktinos and Kallikrates, under the supervision of the sculptor Phidias, and briefed them to draw up a plan for a reconstruction of the Acropolis buildings worthy of the city's newly found cultural and political position. More or less all substantial remains visible today date from this extraordinarily short time, the golden age of Athens. The current Parthenon was completed in ten years, an astonishing achievement.

Though the Parthenon appears to be an ode to simplicity, it is the most technically perfect Doric temple ever built. The architects used their knowledge of mathematics to calculate the best way to create an impression of complete symmetry, even from a distance. The width and placement of columns, the distances between them, the volumes and angles – every measurement is a ratio derived from the golden mean system of proportion. Subtle modifications were applied to all straight surfaces: the columns, for example, bulge slightly around the middle and lean somewhat inwards; the corner columns are slightly larger in diameter than the other exterior columns, since they are seen towards the open sky; the stylobate has an upwards curvature towards its centre of six centimetres (2.3 inches) on the east and west ends, and of 11 centimetres (4.3 inches) on the sides. These adjustments counteract the illusion that straight lines, when seen from a distance, appear to bend. The effect of these behind-the-scenes calculations is a building that seems effortlessly natural and harmonious.

The temple stands on the conventional three steps, below which the foundation platform originally created for its predecessor remains visible. The cella consisted of two rooms end to end. Inside the colonnades, towards the end, stood Phidias's monumental gold-and-ivory statue of Athena Parthenos, representing the fully armed goddess with spear, helmet and aegis (shield), accompanied by a snake, and holding a statue of victory in her extended right arm. The ceiling was made of wood, with painted and gilded decoration. Light was let in, as was the norm in Greek temples, only through the doorway when the great doors were opened.

The Parthenon also showcased a hitherto unseen richness in both quality and quantity of sculptures. The Parthenon had countless more metopes than other temples, all of them brilliantly sculpted. Unusually for a Doric temple, which would normally only have friezes on the end façades or in the interior (if at all), the Ionic frieze continues around the full perimeter.

The other buildings in the Acropolis are equally important in their influence of later architecture; one famous example is the Brandenburger Gate in Berlin, inspired by the **Propylaeum**. This was the masterpiece of the architect Mnesicles. As a gateway it was intended to give a feeling of passing from the mundane world to the sacred; it also blocks the Parthenon from view, so that it appears all at once in its full glory. However, with work disrupted by the Peloponnesian Wars, the Propylaeum remains uncompleted.

Tower of the Winds. *See p33.*

Temple glossary

Architrave The main beam resting across columns.

Caryatid A column in the shape of a sculptured female figure, for example at the Erechtheum.

Cella In Greek *naos*, a plain room in the centre of the temple, not used in worship. It was the seat of the god and left empty except for an image.

Entasis The swelling in the middle of a column.

Hexastyle The most common temple style, with six columns on the short ends.

The Parthenon is an octastyle temple (eight columns).

Metopes Blank or sculptured panels above the columns.

Pediment The triangular upper part at the front of the temple, above the base of the roof.

Peristyle The colonnades surrounding the larger temples – which makes the Parthenon a peristyle octastyle temple.

Stylobate The base on which the columns and the walls of the cella are placed.

The **Erechtheum** is the most exceptional Ionic building on the Acropolis, built in 421 BC-406 BC. While the Parthenon exudes elegant simplicity, the grace of the Erechtheum, composed of two adjoining temples, is its unique complexity. An exception to all the rules, it looks like a different building from each of its four sides. The last of the great works of Pericles to be completed, the Erechtheum was regarded with great respect and its site considered particularly sacred. It included, among other relics: the tomb of Cecrops, the legendary founder of Athens, the rock that preserved the mark of Poseidon's trident, and the spring that arose from it. The south porch, known as the Caryatid porch, is the most famous of the four porches, elevated by the alluring Caryae maidens from which it possibly takes it name (the ones you see are concrete, the originals kept in the Acropolis museum). Just to the west of the temple is the spot where Athena's sacred olive tree stood.

The small, jewel-like **Temple of Athena Nike**, goddess of victory, is the earliest Ionic building on the Acropolis (424 BC), while on the slope of Acropolis stands the cradle of ancient drama, the sixth-century BC **Theatre of Dionysus**, rebuilt in the fourth century by Lycurgus and believed to have seated 17,000 spectators. This is where giants such as Aristophanes, Aeschylus, Sophocles and Euripides first presented their plays, and where the Festival of the Great Dionysia, a renowned drama competition, would take place. In 334 BC one of the winners, Lysicrates, built a monument to commemorate the victory. The **Lysicrates Monument** in Plaka is the only preserved choregic monument, and has been imitated by many neo-classical architects.

In the western outskirts of the **Ancient Agora**, the **Temple of Hephaestus**, also known as Theseion, is almost contemporary with the Parthenon. It may lack the Parthenon's extraordinary grace, but it is the best-preserved Greek temple. Externally, that is; the Byzantine Greeks converted it into a church, constructed an apse at the east end and gave the temple its present concrete vault. As in the Parthenon, over the porch the Doric frieze is replaced by a continuous Ionic frieze. The building is almost wholly of Pentelic marble, bar the lowest of the three steps, which is limestone.

> **'To show what a good man he was, Hadrian placed a statue of himself next to the one of Zeus in the Temple of Zeus.'**

The **Stoa of Attalos**, built in the second century BC by King Attalos of Pergamon as a centre of retail trade, is a two-storey colonnade. Completely renovated in the 1950s (but not as far as the original colours), the building currently serves as the Museum of the Agora. The white-marble temples that are so admired now are mere skeletons of what they used to look like. Originally they were heavily decorated, with gold and bright colours. The image of minimal classicism that they inspire today would not have impressed the architects of the old times.

Temples were only one, if important, part of the large sacred precincts with complexes of buildings, lined by sculptures and linked by processional roads, revealing imaginative and organic city planning. The situation outside these precincts was a totally different matter. Private houses from the era were mostly very simple and have left few remnants. The street plans were haphazard in Archaic and Ancient Greece, with narrow streets, except from the main Panathenaic Way.

ROMAN ATHENS

The Romans captured and sacked Athens in 86 BC, razing the fortification walls and destroying a substantial part of its Classical and Hellenistic monuments and artworks. Upon coming to power in 27 BC the Emperor Augustus embarked on a systematic reconstruction programme, showing respect and admiration for the local cultural heritage. In Rome public buildings and monuments were built imitating Athenian models, while in Athens new ideas of planning and architecture were introduced. The **Roman Forum** of Caesar and Augustus, with the impressive **Gate of Athena Archegetis** on its west side, was an open space intended as a market area. Just by the Roman Forum, the **Tower of the Winds**, also known as the Clock of Andronikos of Kyrrhos, was probably built in the mid first century BC. The tower was an early version of a meteorological station, for the nearby market merchants to know the time and wind conditions to calculate the approximate arrival time of their deliveries by sea.

The **Odeon of Agrippa**, in the Ancient Agora, was originally intended as a concert hall and showed clear evidence of the interaction of Eastern and Western architectural ideas and techniques. It was burned down by barbarians and later converted to a gymnasium. Now only three colossal statues remain to be seen.

During his reign, Hadrian implemented a large-scale building programme, and Athens expanded to present-day Zappeion, National Gardens and Syntagma. The grandest of all Hadrian's projects was the **Temple of Olympian Zeus** (AD 132), the foundation of which had been laid more than 600 years earlier. The Corinthian temple is the largest ancient temple on the Greek mainland.

To show what a good man he was, Hadrian placed a statue of himself next to the one of Zeus, in the sacred cella. **Hadrian's Library** was another of his grand works – its surviving walls, with their monumental Corinthian columns, stand just next to today's Monastiraki metro station. The **Arch of Hadrian** was erected by the Athenians on the border between the old city and the new to honour the imperial benefactor; the arch is now the starting point of Dionysiou Areopagitou, the newly pedestrianised street connecting the archaeological sites.

The **Odeon of Herodes Atticus** was built by the wealthy public benefactor as a memorial to his deceased wife. It is a fairly typical Roman theatre, with a semicircular auditorium hewn out of the rocky southern face of the Acropolis hill. The 4,500-seat theatre, with its 30-metre- (98-foot-) high arched façade, had a cedar roof when it was completed in AD 161. It is now the main venue of the annual Athens Festival.

BYZANTINE

In the fourth century, paganism was quashed by Emperor Theodosius, and Athens' temples, including the Parthenon, were converted into Christian churches. Justinian I's decision to close down the schools of philosophy (AD 529) was the final nail in Athens' coffin – the city started to decline. The so-called Dark Ages would last until around the ninth century, when the Byzantine Empire hailed a period of reconstruction and reorganisation that was to last until the 13th century.

Several small cruciform churches from this period still remain, scattered around the city, squeezed in by apartment blocks, gigantic office buildings and hotels. The interiors are

The **Athens Academy**.
See p35.

The effects of **polykatoikia**. *See p36.*

usually heavily decorated with mosaics portraying religious figures and the emperor, and marble sculptural ornamentation.

The 12th-century **Panaghia Gorgoepikoos** or Agios Eleftherios, which is sometimes also called the Little Cathedral, is built with material from ruins of older buildings. This is particularly evident in the upper part of the church's external walls, where fragments of classical marble friezes combine with contemporary reliefs to create a collage of Greek history. The **Church of the Saints Theodore** (on Evripidou) and **Panaghia Kapnikarea** (on Ermou) are two other examples of famous cross-churches dating from the 11th century. The **Kaisariani Monastery**, which was well outside the city when it was built, is now a short walk up on the mountainside from buzzy Kaisariani.

THE TURKS
After two centuries of Frank, Catalan, Florentine and briefly Venetian rule, Athens witnessed the arrival of the Turkish Sultan Mehmet II in 1456. The city would stay under Turkish rule until 1821. However, remarkably little remains from this long period. Athens was never much more than a garrison town and not much money was put into it. And much of what was built, was, understandably, destroyed after Greece was liberated.

The area of **Plaka** is built on the Turkish plan, but little is left to see. The oldest Ottoman mosque in Athens is the **Fethiye Tzami**, built in 1458 on the Roman Forum, now used as an archaeological warehouse. Across the street from the Tower of Winds stands one of the few Turkish remains, a gateway and a single dome from a *madrassa*, an Islamic school. The Museum of Traditional Greek Ceramics, just opposite Monastiraki metro station, is situated in the 18th-century **Mosque of Tzidarakis**, without the minaret.

THE SANITATION OF ATHENS
After Greece won its independence, many buildings that had been erected during occupation were unceremoniously demolished. This was partly out of rage against the former tyrants, but also, in the case of many Byzantine and Frankish buildings, because they had been built as extensions to classical monuments.

In the classical revival all these monuments were stripped of the details added over the centuries, the Acropolis being the most striking example. It is easy to imagine the sacred rock having looked the way it does now for last two millennia. But the Acropolis has hosted the fortress of every power since Pericles, and has been alitered accordingly. The Parthenon served as a Byzantine and Catholic church and as a medieval fortress (Kastro) under the Franks. Under Ottoman rule, it became a mosque, with minaret and all, and unfortunately a gunpowder arsenal, which led to the worst damage to date, when the Venetians found it a good idea to blow it up. The Erechtheum, the most sacred place on the rock, functioned as a harem. Not so long ago, in one of the darkest times in Athens' history, the Nazi flag was reluctantly floating in the wind from the Acropolis. Only at the last minute was the plan by German architect Schinkel to place the royal palace of the new Greek state on the Acropolis scrapped.

In the urge to clear the Acropolis from all the alterations since classical days, a vast cultural heritage has arguably also been erased, interrupting the flow of the city's historical continuity, not to mention the damage caused to the original buildings by the stripping craze.

NEO-CLASSICAL
When Athens was appointed royal seat and capital city of the independent Greece in 1834, there was already a detailed city plan by architects Stamatios Kleanthis and Eduard Schaubert, both students of Germany's main man in classical architecture, Friedrich von Schinkel. But after a series of dramatic

Putting the columns straight

Columns are, if anyone missed it, the most important feature of the three orders of Greek architecture, into which you can classify almost all classical and neo-classical buildings. The easiest way to differentiate them is their capitals (the decorative cap), although the entablature (the part of the building supported), the shaft and the base of the column are also relevant elements of the orders, which involved proportion as well as design.

The **Doric** order, expressing weight and strength, lacked a base and had a fluted column with a swelling in the middle, narrowing at the top with a capital like a cushion. The Temple of Hephaestus and the Parthenon are prime examples. The **Ionic** order had more slender proportions and was more ornamented. The column was taller and slimmer than its Doric counterpart, with a base, and the capitals are characterised by scrolls (or volutes). An example is the Temple of Athena Nike. The **Corinthian** was the most ornate of the three orders, with a high base and a capital decorated with acanthus foliage.

The orders are supposed to be linked to the ancient perception of the human figure: the Doric represents the male, the Ionic the female and the Corinthian the virginal. The Temple of Olympian Zeus is an excellent example of the Corinthian order. With all three orders, the pediments were made the occasion for figure sculpture.

alterations, the plan was suspended in favour of Leo von Klenze's programme. In his urge to promote a picturesque, human-scale city, Von Klenze narrowed the width of the streets, abolished the grand boulevards and minimised squares. A great plan, if Athens was never to grow bigger. Well, grow bigger it did, and Von Klenze can be held partly responsible for undermining the natural growth of the city, and for many of the problems Athens faces today.

Influential foreign architects poured into the city. They laid the ground for the Athenian school of classicism, maybe the most refined of all neo-classical styles. Their monumental buildings showed the way and set the building style of the city, creating a whole city centre of neo-classical buildings. The majority of these buildings have long since been replaced by modern apartment blocks. Some of the finest, though, such as the **neo-classical trilogy**

on Panepistimiou (comprising the National Library, the University of Athens and Athens Academy), the **Presidential Mansion** and the **Catholic Cathedral**, still stand as monuments of the first decades of modern Athens.

POST-WAR

The first wave of the mass expansion of Athens took place between the wars as a result of the Asia Minor catastrophe. Some of the capital's finest architecture derives from this time. The 1920s and '30s apartment blocks, for example, incorporated a Greek identity, which was inspired by Cycladic architecture (plain, white stone walls) and modernist ideas. Architects like Dimitris Pikionis and Aris Konstantinidis were trying to define the Greek identity through modern architecture.

To solve the housing problems in Athens caused by the massive wave of migration from the countryside in the early 1950s, government-commissioned entrepreneurs developed a system of part exchange, **antiparochi**, where land for building was acquired from its owner in exchange for an agreed number of apartments in the finished building. The construction companies didn't have to pay for land, the landowners didn't have to pay for their apartments, and everyone was happy.

Concrete was the obvious choice of material, being cheap, easily available and easily handled by unskilled labourers. The system encouraged the standardisation of apartment blocks, the so-called **polykatoikia**, and soon extended to office spaces and other commercial buildings. The role of the architects was taken over by engineers, owing to the contractors' obvious desire to achieve maximum profit. The result was a rapid

Omonia moan

In 1998, an initiative to undertake the most significant urban refurbishment of Athens in a century, the newly formed EAXA (Unification of the Archeological Works of Athens) held European competitions for the redevelopment of Athens' four major squares, Omonia, Syntagma, Monastiraki and Koumoundourou. All the winning designs were – much to many people's delight – by young Greek architects, and were praised by the press.

Five years and severe delays later, when Omonia, the first completed square, was unveiled, the dream of a new aesthetic era was stillborn. The architects' intentions had been largely ignored and the new square was generally received as a failure, by the public, the media and, not least, by the architects themselves. The city's politicians had been unable to resist interfering with the architects' vision. Flower planters scattered around the square and a sculpture by Giorgos Zongolopoulos had been added, the artist being an acquaintance of EAXA director Yannis Kalantidis. Kalantidis has said that the competitions were a mistake, claiming that the public spaces belong to the

citizens and not to the architects. The central idea of ground-lighting in the centre of the square was abandoned and various shelters for the entrances to the Metro omitted from the plan. The result is a sad joke to most Athenians and an unlovely, user-unfriendly square that most visitors find hard to access and hard to appreciate.

A committee has been set up by the Environment and Public Works Ministry and the Athens Municipality to evaluate the situation. Their final proposal – with less than a year to go to the Olympics – was a total redesign of the just-completed 5.9 million square.

As for the other squares: the conventional grey stone used in Monastiraki bears no relation to the square's original award-winning design, which featured multi-coloured mosaics, and three of the architects have sued EAXA over copyright issues. Syntagma, whose final conversion is delayed, will also see most of its original design abandoned (though it's looking good so far). Only Koumoundourou was completed both to schedule and to plans.

growth of new, practical housing, but with poor quality of design and construction. At the same time the brutally uncontrolled, often illegal and rapid way the city grew itself created a unique form of city (non) planning.

'The Olympic Games are going to change the face of Athens – exactly how much it is too early to say.'

Although the artistic quality of pre-war architecture was far ahead of that of the post-war polykatoikia, the concept was more or less the same, one not far from the modernistic Dom-Ino utopia of Le Corbusier: a standard box-like construction that could fit all possible activities. One of the results of this, and what makes Athens truly unique, is that it is, in a visual sense, an egalitarian city, with affluent areas sharing the same architecture and structure with poorer areas. Athens exemplifies the functional model of modernism, in taking density to the extreme, not allowing the luxury of space, striving for the simplest, non-decorative, non-monumental architecture possible. The architecture does not create or enhance in itself the character of an area; this falls to the people. As designated public spaces are rare, the streets had to become the public spaces, which has created an extremely lively street life.

MONUMENTS OF MODERNISM
Another result of the antiparochi is the almost total lack of monumentalism, except for the buildings on Leof Vas Sofias, whose construction was controlled by the government. A perfect example of monumentalism and a benchmark in the modern architectural history of Athens is the **American Embassy** (1959-61), designed by Bauhaus Walter Gropius. Unfortunately, nowadays, building works, tight security and police buses have eliminated the spacious surrounds and the free spirit of the initial design.

Also on a monumental scale is the **Athens Conservatory** (Rigillis & Leof Vas Konstantinou), finished in 1976, by Ioannis Despotopoulos, who studied under Walter Gropius in Weimar. The Conservatory was the only building to be completed in a planned Cultural Centre for Athens. Despite shortcomings in construction and implementation of design, it is still a fine example of the radical Bauhaus spirit. The **Athens Hilton** caused a huge controversy at the time of its construction (1958-63). Accused of being both foreign and offensive, it is now considered one of the finest examples of post-war modernism.

Although the prerequisites for creative activity were sometimes lacking, Athens never did want for gifted urban planners and architects, and there are many interesting talents around today – Dimitris and Suzanna Antonakakis, Zoe Samorkas, Pantelis Nicolacopoulos and Christos Papoulias, for example – who should stand to benefit from Athens' new international perspective and sense of self-esteem.

OLYMPICS LEADING THE WAY?
You can't make an omelette without breaking eggs. During pre-Olympic construction and traffic improvement projects, Athens has been at times more unbearable than ever. But the benefits are already having an effect. The two new metro lines in 2001, opened after almost 30 years of work, have improved public transport dramatically, although their coverage is limited. The new Eleftherios Venizelos International Airport is, of course, a fundamental improvement. Both the metro and the airport could be characterised as architecturally sterile, although the exhibits of the archaeological findings in some of the metro stations, such as Syntagma (see p105 **The city beneath the city**), give them character. A tram line to the southern coastal suburbs is included in a scheme to regenerate coastal Athens, turning its face to the sea again. New open places and parks are being planned, both in the central city and in the coastal areas, for example, at Faliro. Landmarks have been refurbished. The main streets and (the few) open places are being given dramatic facelifts. The refurbishment of Syntagma has given the place a real upswing, though the unveiling of the new Omonia square was a sad story, with architects' intentions ignored and the place looking as sad as ever (see p36 **Omonia moan**).

Two of the projects feature big-league international architects: the revamp of the Olympic Sports Complex is being done by the Spaniard Calatrava, and the much-debated (and delayed) New Acropolis Museum (see p77 **A glass house for the Marbles**) by Bernard Tschumi. When either will be ready is a question for the gods.

The Olympic Games are without a doubt going to change the face of Athens – exactly how much it is too early to say. But if more care had been taken in the planning of infrastructure; if the generous amounts of money had been better spent or, indeed, spent on their intended purposes; if architects' opinions had been taken into consideration, perhaps it could have been the true full-body treatment that this faded beauty so desperately needed and deserves.

Zeus, king of the gods. *See p40.*

Greek Myth & Legend

A religion of epic proportions.

The Hellenic deities weren't exactly role models. They lied, cheated, squabbled and toyed ruthlessly with humans. Zeus, king of the gods, assumed various shapes – white bull, swan, golden cloudburst – to seduce unwilling women. His enraged wife Hera persecuted his mistresses, even chasing one pregnant rival with a giant python and transforming another into a pet cow. The list of dirty divine deeds is longer – and messier – than a Greek gyro.

The gods' main spin doctors were Homer, whose epic poems *The Iliad* and *The Odyssey* kick-started Western literature in the eighth century BC, and Hesiod, who wrote *The Theogony* in the seventh century BC. Ancient critics sometimes found fault with these saucy tales. 'Homer and Hesiod have attributed to the gods everything that is a shame and disgrace among men, stealing and committing adultery and deceiving one another,' the philosopher Xenophanes later complained. Yet most Greeks didn't mind the bad behaviour, considering it just as instructive as a good example – and a far better yarn. Even firmly into the days of monotheism myths have been the backbone of education and entertainment. Scholars have memorised ripping tales, then recited them at dinner parties. Politicians have tweaked the stories for propaganda. Artists have depicted scenes on pottery, while poets and playwrights have plumbed this rich vein of melodrama.

The Ancient Greeks believed deities took a very active role in human affairs and destinies. They wooed them with lavish temples, prayers, rites, offerings and games, like the Olympics. The sacrifice of animals – usually bulls, sheep or goats – was especially popular. Priests would slit the creatures' throats, sprinkle the altars with fresh blood, burn the choice bits for the gods and foretell the future from the entrails.

People could worship any and all deities. Cities had patron gods, like Athena in Athens, as did the trades. New divinities were borrowed freely from other cultures and woven into local mythology. Oracles, like Delphi, transmitted the gods' cryptic advice and prophecies.

Cults were a major force in Greek society. The most famous took place just outside Athens, in Eleusis, the site of a sanctuary to the fertility goddess Demeter. The celebratory rituals known as Eleusian mysteries (*see also p237*) were shrouded in secrecy, but rumours of drunkenness and orgies continue to this day.

These pagan rites gave way to Christianity in 324 AD, but Greek myth lives on. The Romans, then the Renaissance, revived these tales, which have since become a cornerstone of Western civilisation.

THE GODS

One creation myth claims the deities and living creatures sprang from the stream Oceanus encircling the world. In the most common version, Mother Earth emerged from the chaos and bore her son, Uranus (sky), while she slept. He showered her with fertile rain and she gave birth to flowers, trees, beasts, birds, the hundred-handed giants, the early gods (Titans) and the one-eyed Cyclops.

Family strife led the Titans to attack Uranus. The youngest of the Titans, Cronus, cut off his father's genitals with a flint sickle and became sovereign. He married his sister Rhea, but insisted upon devouring their children, as prophecy declared that a son would dethrone him. He swallowed five babies, then Rhea wised up. She gave birth to Zeus in secret, then hid him with nymph nursemaids on Crete.

Zeus grew to manhood and poisoned his father's honeyed drink, causing Cronus to vomit up the elder siblings – Hades, Poseidon, Hera, Hestia and Demeter (*see p40* **A-Z of Greek gods**). With their help, Zeus vanquished the Titans and became king of the gods and heaven. A dozen major deities dwelled high on Mount Olympus, while Hades brooded in the underworld and Poseidon ruled the ocean. Earth remained a neutral zone.

> **'The capital's name honours Athena, goddess of wisdom. This bold, brilliant divinity governed all knowledge – from weaving to astronomy.'**

Supporting the 12 Olympians was a cast of thousands. The three Fates spun, measured and snipped the threads of mortal lives, the Furies punished evil-doers, while nine Muses inspired poets, artists and musicians. Trees contained beautiful female spirits (dryads), as did streams (naiads) and fields (nymphs). Lusty, goat-legged satyrs frolicked with wild women (maenads) in holy groves. Centaurs, skilled in sorcery and healing, raped and revelled. Other gods included Pan (shepherds), Asclepius (healing), Eros (love), Hypnos (sleep), Helios (sun), Selene (moon) and Nemesis (punishment).

THE GODDESS

The capital's name honours its patron Athena, goddess of wisdom. This bold and brilliant divinity governed all knowledge – from weaving to astronomy and battle strategy. She represented victory and noble defence, unlike Ares, the bloodthirsty god of war. Athena was also the goddess of wit, morality and clear air, and the protector of small children. The flute, yoke, trumpet and plough number among her inventions.

Her birth was extraordinary, even by Greek mythology's standards. In a fit of insecurity, worried that a son might surpass him, Zeus swallowed his pregnant first wife. Soon after a horrible migraine gripped the king of the gods. The pain grew so severe, he begged for his skull to be chopped open with an axe. Out sprang Athena, fully grown, armed and shouting.

Despite the splitting headache, Athena was her father's favourite. Zeus refused her nothing, even allowing her use of his mightiest weapon, the thunderbolt. She remained a virgin, lofty and pure, but still managed to have a son. The smith god Hephaestus tried to ravage her. She fought him off, but some of his semen brushed her thigh and fell to earth, growing into Erichthonius, an early king of Athens.

The **Trojan War**. *See p42.*

A-Z of Greek gods

Aphrodite
Goddess of: Love.
Strengths: Born naked from the sea foam; also has a magic love-inducing girdle.
Flaws: Addicted to adultery.
Roman name: Venus.
Symbols: Rose, apple, swan, Cupid (her son).

Apollo
God of: Light.
Strengths: Bestowed enlightenment, governed music, medicine, oracles and crops.
Flaws: Cheated in a musical contest, then flayed his rival Marsyas alive.
Roman name: Apollo.
Symbols: Lyre, bow, tripod, laurel wreath.

Ares
God of: War.
Strengths: This natural born killer fathered Eros (Cupid) and Harmonia (Harmony).
Flaws: Lost twice to Athena, the martial goddess of wisdom.
Roman name: Mars.
Symbols: Spear, torch, armour.

Artemis
Goddess of: The hunt.
Strengths: Despite her bloodthirstiness, she protected pregnant women and small children.
Flaws: This eternal virgin turned a peeping tom, Actaeon, into a stag and hunted him.
Roman name: Diana.
Symbols: Bow and quiver, new moon and hind.

Demeter
Goddess of: The earth and fertility.
Strengths: Taught people about agriculture, civic order and wedlock.
Flaws: Starved humans when Hades stole her daughter, then created winter.
Roman name: Ceres.
Symbols: Corn, basket, poppy, serpent.

Dionysus
God of: Wine.
Strengths: Roamed the globe with drunken nymphs, satyrs and wild women.
Flaws: The portable party often spun out of control. Limbs were torn. Lives were lost.
Roman name: Bacchus (aka Liber).
Symbols: Ivy crown, wand, fawn, panther.

Hades
God of: The underworld and the dead.
Strengths: In milder moods, he bestowed wealth or an invisibility helmet.
Flaws: Kidnapped his bride Persephone, whose enraged mother invented winter.
Roman name: Pluto.
Symbols: Three-headed dog Cerberus, pickaxe, cypress tree.

Hephaestus
God of: Fire and metalworking.
Strengths: His fabulous jewellery earned him Aphrodite, the love goddess, as his wife.
Flaws: She cheated on him constantly.
Roman name: Vulcan.
Symbols: Hammer, tongs, a lame leg.

Hera
Queen of heaven, and goddess of marriage.
Strengths: Routinely renewed her virginity bathing in a special spring.
Flaws: This jealous wife chased one rival with a python, kept another as a pet cow.
Roman name: Juno.
Symbols: Peacock, cuckoo, pomegranate.

Hermes
God of: Thieves, traders and messengers.
Strengths: Invented the lyre mere days after his birth (with gut from Apollo's stolen cows).
Flaws: Guided souls to the underworld.
Roman name: Mercury.
Symbols: Herald's staff, winged golden sandals, winged helmet.

Hestia
Goddess of: The hearth and civic harmony.
Strengths: Kept the home fires burning and avoided sexual intrigue on Olympus.
Flaws: Too dull to have one, really.
Roman name: Vesta.
Symbols: Sceptre, hearth.

Poseidon
God of: The ocean and flowing waters.
Strengths: Invented horses (or so he boasted).
Flaws: Caused storms and earthquakes.
Roman name: Neptune.
Symbols: Trident, chariot drawn by foam horses, dolphin.

Zeus
King of the gods, ruler of the sky.
Strengths: Saved his siblings by poisoning their cannibal father, the Titan Cronus.
Flaws: Raped his mother (who advised him not to marry his sister, Hera).
Roman name: Jupiter.
Symbols: Lightning bolt, clouds, eagle, oak.

Athena won the city in a contest against her uncle, the sea god Poseidon. He struck the cliff of the Acropolis with his trident and a salt-water spring gushed from the rock. Athena produced an olive tree. The gods voted her contribution more useful to humans – as it brought food, oil and shelter – and awarded her Athens.

The ancients celebrated her each year at the Panathenea festival. A grand procession wound up the Acropolis, dominated by Phidias's majestic statues of the goddess (one was so massive that sailors in the Saronic Gulf could see her lance and helmet). Her great temple, the mighty Parthenon (meaning 'virgin' in Ancient Greek) still stands today.

THE HEROES

Brave, handsome heroes obsessed with fame and glory star in many tales. More often than not, their ambition wreaked havoc.

Achilles is a prime example. Though he was a magnificent warrior, his 'destructive wrath brought countless sorrows' to his people during the Trojan War, as Homer recounted in *The Iliad*. His arrogance finally outraged the gods: mid battle, they directed an arrow to Achilles's only vulnerable spot – his heel. Hercules started poorly – with the murder of his wife and children in a bout of madness – but the strongman redeemed himself through the Twelve Labours.

Oedipus unwittingly murdered his father and married his mother (Sigmund Freud named his famous complex after this pitiful character). The great musician Orpheus played so sweetly, the gods allowed him to bring his bride back from death – on one condition: he couldn't look at her until they reached the surface. Riddled with doubt, he glanced back and lost her again. The heartbroken hero soon perished, torn apart by wild animals.

> **'Theseus was strong, but refined, smart and diplomatic, all qualities the ancient Athenians prized.'**

Jason, leader of the Argonauts, captured the coveted Golden Fleece, aided by the sorceress Medea. After ten years of happy marriage, he chucked her out. The vengeful woman murdered their children and his new wife, then fled in a chariot drawn by winged dragons. Medea reappeared briefly as Queen of Athens, stepmother to the hero Theseus. She attempted to poison him and was banished. Theseus went on to face the Cretan Minotaur, the half-man, half-bull, imprisoned in the Labyrinth, who devoured young Athenian boys and girls.

Athena, goddess of wisdom and patron of the city. See p39.

Present-day pagans

Superstitions live on in the land of the gods and occasionally mingle with religious and historical experiences. In Greece it's Tuesday 13 that is considered unlucky because Constantinople, the spiritual home of Orthodoxy and today's Istanbul, fell to the Ottomans on a Tuesday.

More recently, Elizabeth Taylor and Richard Burton drank a lot in Greece. According to the superstition, whoever gets the last drop of wine from the jug will be the first to marry.

Be a good visitor. During your stay, avoid giving anyone the evil eye (known in Greek as 'to mati') by doing a quick 'ftou-ftou' when necessary. Come again? Praise a man's work or envy a woman's looks and they could be given the evil eye, which makes them feel ill or run down. This superstition is taken seriously by a surprisingly high number of Greeks, young and old, including some priests. For ultra-hardcore believers, there are 'experts' who can remove the eye in a special ritual, but it'll cost ya. Much better to do a pre-emptive

ftou-ftou – the spitting sound with your lips – without unleashing anything. This magically protects the person in potential peril.

Some genuinely religious actions in Greece may seem a little forced to the outsider, but the belief is there. Even taxi drivers, not widely known for their purity, can cross themselves when racing past a church. Respect their religious rights, by all means, but make sure their hands go nowhere near the meter.

Like in any country, a few individual Greeks have their own little superstitions, such as never lighting a cigarette from a candle or automatically grabbing your privates when a priest goes by.

While Greeks are horoscope-crazy and not averse to delving through your coffee, it's rare for superstitions to form a major part of anyone's life. Rather, they add colour to an increasingly homogeneous world and will hopefully survive and thrive.

Touch wood.

He killed the monster with the help of Princess Ariadne, then callously abandoned her on the way home. His comeuppance was swift: nearing Athens, Theseus forgot to hoist the white sail, a sign of victory for his worried father Aegeus. The grieving king leaped to his death.

Theseus was strong, but refined, smart and diplomatic, all qualities the ancient Athenians prized. He united the Attica region and laid the foundations of democracy. Perseus, on the other hand, was more of an action hero. He decapitated Medusa, the snake-haired gorgon, whose gaze turned flesh to stone.

Odysseus was celebrated as the cleverest Greek. The wily king fought in the Trojan War to reclaim Helen, the most beautiful woman in the world. His return trip took years, rather than weeks. Homer's *Odyssey* traces this epic journey, plagued by shipwreck, witches, sirens and giant man-eating Cyclops. Finally Odysseus reached his homeland, the island of Ithaca, to discover his faithful wife Penelope besieged by greedy, pushy suitors. He slew them with a great bow and reclaimed his kingdom – an unusually happy ending for ancient mythology.

THE HUMANS

The first generation were the 'golden race', who lived without care. They never grew old, lived off the fat of the land, and died contented.

Next came the silver race, eaters of bread. They were so quarrelsome and ignorant that Zeus destroyed them. The insolent bronze race ate flesh and delighted in war.

A more noble age, known as the race of heroes, followed. Sired by gods on mortal mothers, the warriors at Troy and the Argonauts were part of this age. The fifth and final race, known as the race of iron, is beset by unworthy descendants: cruel, unjust, lustful and treacherous. Hesiod wrote: 'I wish I were not of this race, that I had died before, or had not yet been born.'

Prometheus stole fire from the heavens and gave it to humans. Enraged, Zeus created the first woman: intelligent, lovely Pandora (meaning 'the all-gifted'). The gods gave her a box, containing 10,000 curses. Curious, she opened it and released evil into the world. Pandora quickly slammed the lid, but hope alone remained inside.

The Greeks had a myth for every occasion, from the cradle to the grave. The countless stories tapped into a plethora of universal themes – jealousy, infatuation, ambition and loyalty, to name a few. Perhaps this resonance explains their continued popularity, nearly 2,800 years after Homer first captured them in song.

Athens 2004

Let the Games commence.

On 13 August 2004 Athens will open its gates to the Olympic Games for the second time in 108 years. It will be a historic moment for this venerable city, and one that will be measured against the 'best ever' Sydney 2000 Games and the promise of a colossal binge at Beijing 2008.

Some 10,500 athletes, over 21,000 media representatives and hundreds of thousands of spectators are expected to flock to the 17-day Olympic spectacle. Unaccustomed to such crowds, many local residents plan to flee for the duration of the event even as hoteliers and shopkeepers roll out the red carpet.

Greek organisers have promised to deliver a 'magical Games', but they must also impose foolproof security measures on the first Summer Olympics since 9/11. With 50,000 security personnel on duty around the city, it will be a delicate balance. All in all, it's a far cry from the carefree atmosphere of the first modern Games held in Athens in 1896.

A FRENCHMAN'S INSPIRATION

Originally, the Olympics were one of four sacred Pan-Hellenic Games, and Athens was just one of several participating city-states. Today, few remember the Pythian, Isthmian and Nemean Games. The continuation of the Games of Olympia is thanks to the efforts of a visionary Frenchman: Pierre Fredy, Baron of Coubertin. A sportsman and pedagogue, Coubertin lobbied incessantly in the late 1800s for co-operation between Europe's fledgling athletics clubs. He was convinced that only sport could combat the militarism taking hold of the continent.

The lofty Olympics, with their emphasis on athletic perfection and fair play, were ideal for the Baron's designs.

Coubertin's dream found a limited response among the Greeks, who had already tried (unsuccessfully) to revive the Olympics with sports and trade fairs 40 years earlier. Several Athens sportsmen immediately proposed their city as host of the first modern Games of 1896, but ran into trouble with their own government when the financial requirements of the task hit home. The Greek state, still recovering from bankruptcy a few years earlier, wanted no part in the matter. As the newly formed, Lausanne-based International Olympic Committee (IOC) debated whether to move the Games to Hungary instead, Greece's wealthy expatriate merchants stepped forward to save the day – and to pick up the tab for what turned out to be an enormously popular event.

JUBILATION AND NEAR-CATASTROPHE

A century later, Greece needed no urging to bid for the 2004 Games. Still bitter about losing the centenary Olympics to Atlanta, Athens went wild in September 1997 when its name came out of the host-city envelope. Promises to hold 'the best Games ever' poured freely along with the retsina, with the happy hosts noting that 70 per cent of the necessary infrastructure was already in place. Thanks to Greece's special connection to the Olympics, they promised, this would be an unforgettable homecoming.

How right they were. Confident they had plenty of time to handle the remaining work, the Greeks spent the first three years preening

That was then, this is now

Despite serving as Coubertin's model for today's Games, the ancient Olympics (known to have run between 776 BC and AD 385) had very little in common with the modern, inclusive version he envisaged. Originally associated with funerary and religious events, the early Olympics were designed to reinforce Greek consciousness and rejected other cultures. Some of the rules would cause outrage nowadays, like the outright exclusion of women from the Games (a view that the Baron himself could reportedly sympathise with). Other ideals, such as the sacred Olympic truce imposed to suspend any ongoing wars between competing teams, are unenforceable in our era. But the two competitions did have similarities. After all, athletes were only human, and human nature hasn't changed that much in the past two millennia.

Home ground

THEN Excepting the 175th Olympiad, which the dictator Sulla took to Rome, the ancient Games were held in the valley of Olympia in the western Peloponnese for over 1,000 years.
NOW The modern Olympics are supposedly on permanent rotation around the five continents. South America and Africa have yet to see an Olympiad, though. Most end up in Europe.

Number of sports

THEN The first known Olympiad in 776 BC had just one event, the *stadion* (a 192-metre race). By 200 BC, the list had grown to 18 competitions, including wrestling, boxing, the discus and the javelin, and now-obsolete events like running with armour and chariot-racing with foals.
NOW The Olympics currently have 28 sports and close to 300 events. In recent months, the IOC has been giving serious thought to trimming the roster to make room for 'new, spectacular' disciplines, like BMX bike racing.

Oddest sport

THEN The *apene*, a chariot race with mules, proved unpopular even in its own time. It was discontinued after 448 BC.
NOW The tug-of-war ran for six Olympiads before being scrapped in 1920. Tug-of-war enthusiasts are still lobbying to have the sport reinstated.

Duration

THEN Five days.
NOW Over two weeks.

Sports facilities

THEN One stadium seating 45,000, a hippodrome and a training gymnasium.
NOW Thirty sports venues with a combined capacity of over 500,000 seats are in use for Athens 2004.

Athletes' fashion

THEN Athletes performed naked, their bodies covered in oil. Trainers also went garment-free, a rule designed to root out disguised women lurking in the stands.
NOW Today's Olympic gear largely depends on personal taste and the exigencies of sports science. Sprinter Florence Griffith-Joyner was famous for her gaudy slacks and talon-long fingernails. Swimmer Ian Thorpe caused a sensation with his seal-slick wetsuit. And runner Cathy Freeman's hooded one-piece was one of the highlights of Sydney 2000.

Olympic medallists

THEN One in each event.
NOW Three in each event. In Athens 2004 'Olympic victor' status will be extended to all Greek athletes who finish in the top eight in any event. The title translates into a paid post in the armed services.

The **Panathenaic Stadium**, in 1896...

Awards, honours and perks

THEN The humble olive crown awarded at Olympia was no trifling matter. The Greeks believed that victory in the Olympics was a gift from the gods. City-states demolished a section of their fortifications to let their victorious sons through, and rewards often extended to cash prizes, free meals and tax exemptions. Victory odes and statues were popular honours.

NOW Modern Olympians can look forward to a fruitful future of sponsorship and product endorsement. In Greece, Olympic medallists also get posts in the armed forces, police and fire department.

Dirty tricks

THEN Bribery of opponents was the most frequent offence, particularly closer to Hellenistic times as the Games became increasingly professional. Nero is said to have bought most of his victories in the tragedy, lyre-playing and chariot-racing competitions of the 211th Olympiad. Athletes also used mushrooms, garlic, alcohol and opiates to enhance performance or relieve pain.

NOW Why bribe opponents when you can beat them, ahem, fair and square? A wide choice of performance stimulants of varying legality is available to today's athletes, including ephedrine, steroids, insulin, amphetamines and caffeine.

... and in the present day.

Penalties

THEN Rule-breaking at Olympia was rare, but the organisers still took their penalties seriously. Minor infringements like false starts were punishable by flogging. Athletes caught cheating were fined, the proceeds going to statues of Zeus bearing details of the crime. The stiffest sentence was reserved for married women caught taking part at or even just watching the Games – they were cast to their deaths from nearby Mount Typaeum. Women were expected to keep to their own Games at Olympia, the Heraia, though they could take part at the Olympics as chariot owners.

NOW Doping, the most common infraction these days, carries a hefty fine and the threat of sports suspension for a limited time; repeated offenders face higher fines and can be banned for life.

Undesirables

THEN Barbarians, murderers, slaves and married women.

NOW Terrorists, ticket scalpers and fake-goods peddlers.

Security requirements

THEN Two squads of officials with cudgels and scourges.

NOW Heavily armed police and troops, anti-aircraft rocket launchers and chemical warfare protection units.

Sport over politics?

THEN The Olympic Truce was sacred in the early Games. Special heralds travelled the length of the Greek world to announce a general armistice, allowing safe passage for athletes and pilgrims to Olympia. Even the Persian invasion failed to ruffle the Greeks, who carried on with the 75th Olympiad even as Leonidas and his Spartans stood their last at Thermopylae.

NOW Games and their truces are much less of a priority in the modern world. World Wars I and II swept aside the 1916, 1940 and 1944 Olympiads. The 1980 Olympics were organised by a Soviet state busy invading Afghanistan. The US, which was supporting the Afghans at the time, boycotted the Moscow Games. Two decades later, the Americans themselves hosted the Salt Lake City 2002 Winter Games while waging war on the Taliban.

their project plans and shuffling officials from post to post. It took them seven months just to get the Games' organising committee running, and another year to decide who would oversee the necessary construction. The IOC was alarmed, but held its peace until the excuses began to pile up – along with the delays.

In April 2000, after general elections in Greece changed the minister in charge of the Olympic preparations for the third time in three years, Lausanne finally warned the Greeks that their Games management was leading straight to disaster. Athens' reaction was to bring Gianna Angelopoulos-Daskalaki (the dynamic chief of the victorious 1997 bid) out of retirement to lead the 2004 Games organising committee (ATHOC).

BACK FROM THE BRINK

The members of the IOC now had someone to talk business with, but their troubles in Greece were far from over. They would soon discover the true challenge of turning Athens into a modern Olympic city, as construction works bogged down in archaeological finds, uncharted utility networks and citizens' lawsuits.

Like a stubborn mule, Greece's bureaucracy defied all efforts to speed up preparations. With Angelopoulos-Daskalaki clashing with ministers over slipping deadlines, the government and organising committee often spent more time at each other's throat than on the task at hand. The pace would pick up and then falter, leading IOC president Jacques Rogge to remark that Athens' preparations reminded him of a Greek sirtaki dance.

The word was out that the 2004 Olympics were going to be a first-class embarrassment. It took three years for the organisers to put Athens back on track, and by the time they did, the IOC was prepared to expect anything from the Greeks, even a last-minute miracle – which is what they apparently achieved.

As for the Greek public, it took some effort to convince them that seven years of hard work hadn't been spent on an outrageously expensive two-week blow-out. Had it not been for the Olympics, organisers argued, God knows when the new Eleftherios Venizelos Airport would have opened. The Olympics were also credited with speeding up construction of vital roads bypassing the choked city centre, a top-notch underground metro, a badly needed public transport upgrade, and enough new arenas to last Athens the next hundred years.

Neither as groundbreaking as Barcelona 1992 nor as environment-friendly as Sydney 2000, the Athens Games took a limited shot at urban redevelopment. The old airport and a coastal landfill site were turned into sports complexes, and an attempt to revitalise abandoned wetlands

east of the city was made through the creation of a rowing centre. But whether plans to turn these sites into park spaces after 2004 will be carried out in full remains to be seen.

Practicals

With many projects scheduled for completion only a month or so before the Olympics, plans will be in flux until the last minute. At time of press, Greek organisers had no definite details of hotel vacancies, ticket availability, transport arrangements or venue contact numbers. It is assumed that ATHOC will post this information on its website at **www.athens2004.com** (along with venue maps and daily updates). The City of Athens site (www.cityofathens.gr) is also worth a look.

August in Athens is usually stifling hot from 11am to late afternoon. Most stadia are roofed, but hats, light clothing and an adequate supply of water are still highly recommended. Bear in mind, however, that you will not be able to bring your own food and water into Olympic venues, which will have their own official vendors. Smoking will also be prohibited, even at outdoor events. It's almost worth buying a ticket just to watch organisers trying to enforce this restriction in a nation of nicotine addicts.

To accommodate the large numbers of visitors without tickets, Athens organisers also intend to set up locations offering live Games coverage, performances by Greek and international artists and other cultural goodies. Entrance will be free of charge. Details will be posted on the ATHOC and city websites.

Getting around

Public transport (hopefully air-conditioned) will be the best way to move around the city during the Games. The bus and trolley fleets were recently overhauled, and the metro is to be supplemented by a new tram line connecting Athens to the coast, where several Olympic events will be taking place. A separate rail link known as the 'suburban railway' is supposed to connect the city to the airport. Olympic ticket-holders will have free access to public transport on the day of their event. On routes connecting Olympic venues, public buses and trolleys will make use of special priority lanes.

According to the state-run Athens Urban Transport Organisation (OASA), over 20 bus and trolley lines will be serving sports venues from 5am to the end of the day's events. Lines linking up to the tram and metro will run on a 24-hour basis. Further information is supposed to be posted on OASA's website (www.oasa.gr), and included in leaflets distributed to the public.

Taxis will also operate during the Games, but for security reasons cabbies will be obliged to deposit passengers at least 500 metres (a third of a mile) from Olympic venues. Expect higher fares than usual, as well as a variety of excuses for the price hike – the cost of air-conditioning during the ride is a popular one.

Bringing your own car to events is unwise. Parking near Olympic venues will be prohibited, and only accredited vehicles will be allowed inside stadium parking lots. In addition, emergency measures like road closures will almost certainly be taken to facilitate athletes, judges and VIPs going to the Games.

Allow plenty of time to travel to events and remember that sessions can be rescheduled or cancelled. Ticket-holders can use the same ticket at rescheduled sessions, but there will be no refunds.

Accommodation

The modern-day Olympics may have taken 108 years to 'return home', but finding a temporary home for visitors to the Games may take as long. Virtually every medium-size to large hotel in Athens has been contracted by the Olympic organisers to house official visitors, exposing a hotel shortage in the city. As the international media warned of an accommodation shortage, thousands of Athenians decided to keep their

properties off the market believing they would get rich quickly by renting out their flats during the Olympics. Since then, amateurs have been setting up internet 'accommodations agencies' hocking flats at anything from highish to exorbitant prices (€500-€2,000 and up per day for average to luxury flats sleeping 4-10). While some appear to be getting the prices they demand (particularly at the high end), generally it is believed there will be more than enough supply to meet the demand, and prices will settle by the time you read this.

The issue appears not to be availability, but knowing who to trust. **Filoxenia 2004** is an ATHOC-organised consortium with some 5,000 homes (from basic furnished apartments to luxury villas) on its books. As the official route, this is probably the safest bet: a contract protects you and properties have been screened for suitability and location. Prices range from €280 to €440 a night per two-person flat for a minimum of six nights.

Independent agents will also have private homes for rent. Try the **Hellenic Association of Travel and Tourism Agencies** (HATTA) or the **Athens Realtors Association**.

Rooms in standard hotels will be almost impossible to find at short notice, other than through cancellations. Small hotels that don't attract block bookings are most likely to have availability. A list of all registered hotels,

The indomitable **Gianna Angelopoulos-Daskalaki**. *See p46.*

SPORT	VENUE	W 11	Th 12	Fr 13	Sa 14	Su 15	M 16	Tu 17	W 18	Th 19	Fr 20	Sa 21	Su 22	M 23	Tu 24	W 25	Th 26	Fr 27	Sa 28	Su 29
Opening	OCO			O																
Closing	OCO																			O
Archery	PS				O	O	O	O	O	O	O	O								
Athletics	OCO										O	O	O	O	O	O	O	O	O	
Athl. Marath.	PS																			O
Badminton	GOC				O	O	O	O	O	O	O	O								
Baseball	HCO					O	O	O	O		O	O	O		O	O				
Basketball	HCO				O	O	O	O	O		O	O	O	O	O	O				
Basketball	OCO															O	O	O	O	
Beach Volleyball	FCO				O	O	O	O	O	O	O	O	O	O						
Boxing	POBH				O	O	O	O	O	O	O	O	O	O				O	O	O
Canoe & Kayak	HCO						O	O	O	O										
Canoe & Kayak	SORCC													O	O	O	O	O	O	
Cycling	POMBV																		O	O
Cycling	ACC				O	O														
Cycling	VOC								O											
Cycling	OCO										O	O	O	O	O	O				
Diving	OCO				O		O				O	O	O	O	O	O	O	O	O	
Equestrian																				
Dressage	MOEC										O	O		O		O				
Eventing	MOEC					O	O	O	O											
Jumping	MOEC												O		O		O			
Fencing	HCO				O	O	O	O	O	O	O	O	O	O						
Football																				
Athens	ATH				O	O		O					O		O	O			O	O
Heraklio	Pank S	O	O		O	O		O			O	O		O			O			
Patras	Pamp S	O	O		O			O			O	O		O			O			
Thesslnk.	Kaft S	O	O		O	O		O			O	O		O	O			O		
Volos	Pant S	O	O		O			O			O									
Gymnastics																				
Artistic	OCO				O	O	O	O	O	O			O	O	gala					
Rhythmic	GOH																O	O	O	
Trampln.	OCO												O	O						
Handball	FCO				O	O	O	O	O	O	O	O	O	O						
Handball	HCO																O	O	O	O
Hockey	HCO				O	O	O	O	O	O	O	O	O	O	O	O	O			
Judo	ALOH				O	O	O	O	O	O										
Pentathlon	GOC																O	O		
Rowing	SORCC					O	O	O	O	O	O	O	O							
Sailing	AKOSC				O	O	O	O	O	O	O	O	O	O	O	O				
Shooting	MOSC				O	O	O	O	O	O	O	O								
Softball	HCO				O	O	O	O	O	O	O	O		O	O					
Swimming	OCO				O	O	O	O	O	O	O	O								
Sync. Swim.	OCO														O	O	O	O		
Table Tennis	GOH				O	O	O	O	O	O	O	O	O							
Tae-kwon-do	FCO																O	O	O	O
Tennis	OCO				O	O	O	O	O	O	O	O								
Triathlon	VOC																O	O		
Volleyball	FCO				O	O	O	O	O	O	O	O	O	O	O	O	O	O	O	O
Water Polo	OCO					O	O	O	O	O	O	O	O	O	O	O	O	O	O	O
Weightlifting	NOWH				O	O	O				O	O	O	O	O	O				
Wrestling																				
Freestyle	ALOH														O	O				O	O
Grec/Rom	ALOH														O	O	O			

VENUE LIST

ACC	Athens City Centre
AKOSC	Agios Kosmas Olympic Sailing Centre
ALOH	Ano Liossia Olympic Hall
ATH	Athens
FCO	Faliro Coastal Zone Olympics Complex
GOC	Goudi Olympic Complex
GOH	Galatsi Olympic Hall
HCO	Helliniko Olympic Complex
Kaft S	Kaftantzoglio Stadium
MOES	Markopoulo Olympic Equestrian Centre
MOSC	Markopoulo Olympic Shooting Centre
NOWH	Nikaia Olympic Weightlifting Hall
OCO	Athens Olympic Sports Complex
Pamp S	Pampeloponnisiako Stadium
Pank S	Pankritio Stadium
Pant S	Panthessaliko Stadium
POBH	Peristeri Olympic Boxing Hall
POMBV	Parnitha Olympic Mountain Bike Venue
PS	Panathenaic Stadium
SORCC	Schinias Olympic Rowing & Canoeing Centre
VOC	Vouliagmeni Olympic Centre

COLOUR KEY   O quarter final   O semi final   O final

private accommodation and camping grounds in Greece is available through the **Greek National Tourism Organization** (GNTO). You can also contact Athens hotels directly (*see chapter* **Where to Stay**) or the **Hellenic Chamber of Hotels**. Expect rates to be two or three times as high as in the usual high season.

Alternatively, choose a pleasant seaside resort outside Athens, with good transport links, and shuttle in and out of Olympics events. Tolo and Nafplio and are possibilities, as are the coastal areas near Corinth. Even nearby islands like Poros, Hydra and Aegina could be good options, as long as boat tickets are in place. (*For all, see* **Trips Out of Town**, *starting on p233*.)

You can also base yourself at a location close to your particular Olympic venue. For example, if you are mostly frequenting equestrian events, you might consider areas like Markopoulo or Kakia Thalassa. If sports events in Faliro and Ellinikon have booked up all the hotels there, try heading south, for example to Varkiza, where space might not be so cramped.

For the adventurous, creative alternatives include the cruise ships docked at Piraeus, Faliro and Glyfada marinas, which will provide accommodation for thousands of Olympics spectators. Some of Athens' campgrounds are also likely to have availability. And one of Athens' dirty little secrets is the dozens of 'day hotels' or 'couples hotels', which are generally – unlike in most other cities – thoroughly clean places in discreet, often residential neighbourhoods. These never make it into the guidebooks and are quite likely to be able to fit you in. English speakers may be hard to find at these places and services are somewhat minimal, but for the unfussy it might prove a cheap solution. Consult the back pages of local listings magazines, like *Athinorama* or *Exodus*, where day hotels are often advertised in the Sex section.

Athens Realtors Association

Information line 210 362 1930/rentals hotline 210 360 7060/www.athensrealtors.com.

Filoxenia 2004

49 Stadiou (4th floor), Omonia, 10559 (210 327 7408-9/fax 210 327 7444/www.filoxenia2004.com).

Greek National Tourism Organization

Tsoha 7, Ambelokipi, 11521 (210 870 7000/ www.gnto.gr). Metro Ambelokipi.
Karagiorgi Servias 2, Historic Centre (210 322 2545). Metro Syntagma.

Hellenic Association of Travel & Tourism Agencies

Iossif ton Rogon 11, Makrygianni, 11743 (210 923 4143/fax 210 923 3307/www.hatta.gr). Metro Akropoli.

Hellenic Chamber of Hotels

Stadiou 24, Omonia, 10564 (210 331 0022/ fax 210 322 5449/http://users.otenet.gr/~grhotels/ english.html). Metro Omonia or Syntagma.

Tickets

Tickets for all Olympic events can be bought online at **www.tickets.athens2004.com/en** or through the official agent of each national Olympic committee. Tickets not sold by April 2004 can be purchased at official ATHOC outlets (details can be found on the ATHOC website). Prices range between €10 and €300, depending on event round and seat location. Tickets to the opening or closing ceremony cost between €50 and €900. Touts will undoubtedly be turning out in force near every venue, but bear in mind that purchases from unauthorised dealers are illegal. For more details, check out the Athens 2004 website.

For a package deal including accommodation and tickets, the following agents are authorised by the relevant national Olympic committee to supply tickets (to residents only).

Australia

Sportsworld plc, Level 3, 73 Walker Street, North Sydney, NSW 2060 ([02] 9492 9100/fax +61 [02] 9518 5224/www.sportsworld-athens2004.com).

Canada

CoSport, PO Box 905, Far Hills, New Jersey 07931 USA (1 877 457 4647/http://cosport.net/can/eng/ Athens2004Packages.asp).

Great Britain

Sportsworld Group plc, New Abbey Court, Stert Street, Abingdon, OX14 3JZ (01235 541 173/fax 01235 537 768/http://www.sportsworld-athens2004.com).

South Africa

Fli Afrika Travel, 1st Floor Killarney Mall, Riviera Road, Killarney, PO Box 1650, Houghton 2041 ([0] 11 646 4862/4620/fax +27 (0)11 646 4883/ http://www.fli-afrika.com/olympics.htm).

United States

Cartan Tours – Sports Division, 1334 Parkview Avenue, Suite 210, Manhattan Beach, CA 90266 (1 800 360 2004/310 546 9662/fax 310 546 8433/www.cartan.com).

CoSport, PO Box 905, Far Hills, New Jersey 07931 (1 877 457 4647/fax 908 766 2033/http://cosport.net/us/Athens2004 Packages.asp).

Venue highlights

Two sports complexes, the **Athens Olympic Sports Complex** in the northern suburb of Marousi and the **Helliniko Olympic Complex** on the southern coastal strip,

In Context

will handle the bulk of the events during the 2004 Games. The other venues are spread far and wide, the farthest being the **Schinias Olympic Rowing Centre** and the **Markopoulo Equestrian and Shooting Centres**, 30 kilometres (18 miles) east of Athens.

The biggest highlight of them all is the **Panathenaic Stadium**, in the city centre. Built in less than a year on the remains of a stadium dating from 330 BC, the Panathenaic Stadium passed into legend in April 1896, when the first modern Games was held here. Apart from the seating, most of which was stone and wood at the time, little has changed. All marble today (hence its nickname of Kallimarmaro, 'beautiful marble'), this living part of Olympic history will host the archery tournament and the marathon finish.

The **Athens Olympic Sports Complex** (OAKA) will be the main hub of the Games. The entire complex was touched up after years of neglect, and all athletics, diving, swimming, tennis and water-polo events will be held here, as will the men's soccer final. The main stadium, with a seating capacity of 75,000, will also host the opening and closing ceremonies.

Near the coastal suburb of Glyfada, **Helliniko Olympic Complex** is the second key sports zone of the Games. The site of the old airport, Helliniko presented organisers with a 5.5-square-kilometre (2.12-square-mile) opportunity when the new airport became operational in early 2001. They seized on the situation by building every conceivable sports facility that wouldn't fit anywhere else, including baseball diamonds, hockey pitches and a fast-water canoe course. Helliniko will also host fencing and softball, the basketball preliminaries and the handball finals.

About five kilometres (three miles) to the north-west, the **Faliro Coastal Zone Olympic Complex** completes the trio of Athens's sports clusters. Regarded by the Greek government as a masterpiece of urban regeneration, the two-arena complex was carved out of a landfill and rubbish dump. It will host the beach volleyball and tae-kwon-do tournaments, and the handball preliminaries.

Two more Olympic venues are located within a kilometre of the Faliro Complex. **Karaiskaki Stadium**, home of local soccer powerhouse Olympiacos FC, is to host one of four preliminary rounds of the soccer tournament (the other three will be played in the cities of Thessaloniki, Patra, Volos and Iraklio, Crete). Across the road, the **Peace & Friendship Stadium** will host the volleyball tournament.

The Paralympics

From 17 to 28 September, Athens will also host the 2004 Paralympics. Some 4,000 athletes with a disability will be competing in 19 sports, some of them unique to the competition, like goalball, boccia and powerlifting. Sydney sold over a million tickets to the 2000 Paralympics. In Athens, where disabled people are hardly ever seen because it's impossible for them to get around, expectations are far lower. But the Games will leave a legacy of improved urban accessibility, as well as a glimmer of awareness for disabled rights that will hopefully catch on.

The local experience

Greeks firmly believe in the power of television. On an important sports night, they either hole up at home with a takeaway or go down the local coffee shop for repartee with fellow fans. There's not much chance they'll interrupt their holidays to watch men's trampoline or judo, but some events will be mobbed.

Weightlifting is Greece's biggest hope of Olympic glory. Triple-gold winners Pyrros Dimas and Kachi Kachiasvili are making a final appearance in Athens (their sessions are already sold out) and a young women's squad is ready to support them. The only problem is that the new Nikaia Olympic Weightlifting Hall can seat only 5,000 at a time.

Athletics will also be a hot event, all the more since Greece has other medal hopefuls on the field. After Costas Kenteris surprised the world with his 200-metre victory in Sydney 2000, Greek fans have been waiting for a repeat performance to silence persistent talk of a fluke. In the women's 100-metre dash, US Olympic champion Marion Jones returns to claim her fourth gold medal, but the home crowd is hoping that Sydney 2000 silver medallist Katerina Thanou will rise to the challenge.

Basketball always fires Greeks up, and since these Games are held on their turf, they think it's about time their national team won its first Olympic medal. As a result, the Greek team's matches will be packed solid. Sell-out crowds are also expected at the US Dream Team's matches, due to the presence of NBA stars such as Tim Duncan, Allen Iverson and Jason Kidd.

A showdown is expected in swimming, with Australian prodigy Ian Thorpe defending his laurels against US newcomer Michael Phelps. Thorpe cut his teeth in the Sydney Games, where he smashed two world records on his way to gold. But Phelps stole the show in the 2003 World Championships, where he broke five world records. Thorpe's response is eagerly anticipated in Athens.

50 Time Out Athens

Where to Stay

Where to Stay

The Greek propensity for haggling spills over into the hotel business.
Here's where to find executive-style rooms at bargain prices.

Athens' hotels went through a frenzy of restoration in preparation for the 2004 Olympics, and facilities were much improved, generally to international standards. There are good choices at all levels, though the boutique idea has yet to catch on – while a handful of hotels have that modern designer look, few could really be called charming, unique or personal. And the high-end international chains are not generally the best examples of their genre, with many clustered in concrete blocks along the not-very-nice Syngrou artery.

Service tends to be a bit more personal and less formal than in other European capitals, but also slightly lazier. Rooftop terraces, gardens, pools, cafés and lounges (and often great views) are particular pleasures of many an Athenian hotel; traffic noise one of their tragic flaws. The outdated rating system for hotels in Greece, which assesses hotels on an 'A-B-C-D' scale, is not a very meaningful guide to quality, and is set to be updated to the international 'star' rating system. Budget hotels are fairly plentiful,

but hotels offering shared facilities, and western European-style dormitory hostels, are rare. Private apartment rentals are also less common than in the rest of Europe.

RATES AND DATES

Asking how much a hotel room costs in Athens is a bit like asking the cost of a plane ticket: nobody really knows, and it changes every day. We list official summer-season (June-September) 'rack rates', merely as a price indicator and for comparison purposes. The reality is that rack rates are about as meaningful as published full-fare flight prices: they only apply to the traveller purchasing at the absolute last minute, or in periods of unusually high demand. Generally speaking, hotel rates in Athens are highly negotiable compared to other European capitals, and depend on the season, number of rooms required, length of stay and all too often the mood of the booking agent at the time of the enquiry. At expensive and deluxe hotels, travellers can expect discounts of at least 25

The best Hotels

For budget value
Amaryllis (see p67); King Jason (p67); Tempi (p63).

For mid-range value
Acropolis Select (see p55); Jason Inn (p67); Plaka (p57).

For four-star value
Metropolitan (see p71); Philippos (p57).

For views of the Acropolis
Adonis (see p59); Adrian (p55); Plaka (p57).

For rooftop pleasures
The Adrian's garden (see p55); the Exarcheion's bar (p65); the Jason Inn's restaurant (p67); St George Lycabettus's pool bar (p64).

For swimming pools
Athens Hilton (see p63); Oscar (p69); President (p65).

For business
Holiday Suites (see p63).

For history
Athens Hilton (see p63); Hotel Grande Bretagne (p59); Pentelikon (p71).

For style
Andromeda (see p63); Athenian Callirhoe (p53); Omonia Grand (p67); Plaka (p57).

For children
Athens Cypria (see p61); Divani Apollon Palace (p69).

For honeymooners
Grande Bretagne (see p59); Pentelikon (p71).

For feeling like a king
Kefalari Suites (see p72).

For being a king
Grande Bretagne (see p59); Pentelikon (p71).

Adrian Hotel. *See p55.*

per cent and even up to 50 per cent off rack rates merely by asking for 'special offers', 'corporate rates' or 'internet rates'. The same applies to mid-range hotels, which regularly rent rooms at 15 to 30 per cent below advertised prices. Discounts at budget hotels are less likely and, when granted, smaller. Off-season reductions are common, with rates falling by 25-40 per cent, but may apply only to June and September at budget hotels and the lower end of the mid-range scale in central Athens. In July and August, budget hotels rarely offer discounts, and finding a good budget room during this period can be a challenge.

Since upscale visitors tend to avoid central Athens in the summer and business travel slows, travellers can expect significant reductions during July and August at expensive and deluxe hotels downtown. Volume discounts can be requested for group stays, which could simply consist of a few friends travelling together. Athenian hoteliers know all too well that the average traveller spends just one night in Athens, and give discounts for longer stays.

Of course, visitors can relax and let someone else do the work: hotels offer travel agents generous discounts, which should be passed on to customers. Competition for international clients is so strong that foreign travel agents often offer lower hotel rates than are available within Greece.

Acropolis & Around

Deluxe

Athenaeum Intercontinental

Syngrou 89-93, Koukaki, 11745 (210 920 6000/ fax 210 920 6500/www.intercontinental.com). Metro Syngrou-Fix. **Rates** €352-€397 double; €606-€2,534 suite. **Credit** AmEx, DC, MC, V. **Map** p299 D9.

Athens' largest hotel specialises in efficient luxury. Identical but spacious rooms are furnished in cool white marble and blue and green fabrics, with finishing touches such as sunny sitting areas, double-headed showers, and two or more phones per room. The executive suite floors offer a private check-in, an Acropolis-view lounge with an all-day buffet and private meeting rooms on top of the vast conference facilities. But all business-like restraint melts away in the shamelessly decadent presidential suite, which has hosted prominent guests including Bill Clinton and the Rolling Stones. Café Zoe, the hotel's all-day restaurant, is a must.

Hotel services *Bars (2). Beauty salon. Business services. Concierge. Disabled: adapted rooms. Gym. No-smoking rooms. Parking (€12). Restaurants (2). Swimming pool (outdoor).* **Room services** *Air-conditioning. Bathrobe. Internet access: dataport/ ISDN. Hairdryer. Laundry/dry-cleaning. Mini-bar. Room service (24hrs). TV: pay movies/satellite.*

Athenian Callirhoe

Kallirois 32 & Petmeza, Makrygianni, 11753 (210 921 5353/fax 210 921 5342/www.tac.gr). Metro Syngrou-Fix. **Rates** €360-€400 single; €400-€470 double; €500-€540 suite. **Credit** AmEx, DC, MC, V. **Map** p299 E7.

When it opened in 2002, the Callirhoe was hailed as one of the most stylish hotels in Athens, promptly leading to the opening of copycats all over town. No matter: customers who appreciate design still have a few years to enjoy the sleek, sharp-edged metal-and-glass decor before it goes out of style; while the rooms, which feature fluffy duvets, leather sofas and, in the upper brackets, hot tubs, still hold a premium on comfort. Front rooms are larger and more shapely but suffer street noise.

Hotel services *Bar. Gym. No-smoking rooms/ floor. Restaurant. TV room.* **Room services** *Air-conditioning. Bathrobe (executive room & suites). Internet access: dataport/ISDN/web TV. Hairdryer. Laundry/dry-cleaning. Mini-bar. Room service (24hrs). TV: games/pay movies/satellite.*

H|P
HOTELS

Athens at its most relaxed

- **Peaceful Location:** at the foot of the Acropolis, in the museum neighborhood, within an easy stroll from Plaka, providing easy access to the main shopping, business areas and metro station.
- **Unique View of the Acropolis**
- **Comfort:** at the elegant and well equipped 90 guest rooms of Herodion hotel and 50 rooms of Philippos hotel, some ideally spacious for big families.
- **Taste:** Mediterranean cuisine at the atrium coffee shop viewing the green back garden and at the restaurant.
- **Cocktail Bar:** after an impressive performance at the Herodion Ancient theater you may continue your evening with a drink in a pleasant and friendly environment.
- **Roof Garden:** an impressive space, an enticing suggestion for private occasions, celebrations, dinners.
- **Conference and Banquet Facilities**

HERODION
HOTEL ★★★★
4 Rorbertou Galli str.,
Athens, t: +30 210 92 36 832
www.herodion.com

PHILIPPOS
HOTEL ★★★
3 Mitseon str., Athens,
t: +30 210 92 23 611
www.philipposhotel.com

Divani Palace Acropolis

Parthenonos 19-25, Makrygianni, 11742 (210 928 0100/fax 210 921 4993/www.divaniacropolis.gr). *Metro Akropoli.* **Rates** €350 single; €380 double; €480-€900 suite. **Credit** AmEx, DC, MC, V. **Map** p299 E7.

The closest luxury hotel to the Acropolis, the Divani Palace Acropolis is popular with wealthy Greeks and ideal for popping out to an evening performance at the nearby Herodeion. Think lots of pink, gilt, mirrors, and potted palms in the lobby and rooms. Two especially nice features are the roof garden, where visitors can enjoy drinks and a great Greek buffet, and the preserved glassed-in portion of the Themistoclean Wall in the foundations. **Hotel services** *Bar. Business services. Concierge. Garden. Laundry. No-smoking rooms. Payphone. Restaurants (2). Swimming pool (outdoor).* **Room services** *Air-conditioning. Bathrobe (suites only). Internet access: dataport/ISDN. Hairdryer. Hi-fi (suites only). Laundry/dry-cleaning. Mini-bar. Room service (24hrs). TV: pay movies/satellite.*

Ledra Marriott Hotel – Athens

Syngrou 115, Koukaki, 11745 (210 930 0000/ fax 210 935 8603/www.marriott.com). *Metro Syngrou-Fix.* **Rates** €335 double; €540-€1,540 suite. **Credit** AmEx, DC, MC, V. **Map** p298 C9.

The Marriott has all the amenities and mod cons of a high-end chain, but its main selling point is its staff, possibly the friendliest and most efficient in town. It's also got comfortable rooms, furnished in warm reds and oranges, with feather duvets, overstuffed armchairs and marble bathrooms. The business facilities are good and there is also a highly reputed Polynesian restaurant, the Kona Kai, and a rooftop pool with a gorgeous Acropolis view. **Hotel services** *Bar. Beauty salon. Business services. Concierge. Disabled: adapted rooms. Gym. No-smoking rooms/floors. Parking (€12). Restaurants (2). Swimming pool (outdoor).* **Room services** *Air-conditioning. Bathrobe (executive rooms & suites only). Internet access: dataport/ ISDN. Hairdryer. Hi-fi. Laundry/dry-cleaning. Mini-bar. Room service (24hrs). TV: pay movies/satellite.*

Expensive

Electra Palace

Nikodimou 18, Plaka, 10557 (210 337 0000/ fax 210 324 1875). *Metro Monastiraki.* **Rates** €180 single; €218 double; €273 triple; €280 suite. **Credit** AmEx, DC, MC, V. **Map** p295/p299 F5.

With a new neo-classical façade, renovation is turning this former eyesore into possibly the most attractive building in the area. Because of pre-Olympic renovations, many amenities like the pools, gym and business centre don't reopen until well into 2004, and construction noise in the next wing will be a nuisance. But when the dust settles, the Electra Palace is expected to be a welcome addition to Plaka, which otherwise lacks a smart, four-star, full-service hotel.

Hotel services *Bar. Business services. Concierge. Gym. No-smoking rooms/floors. Parking (€9). Restaurant. Roof garden. Swimming pool (indoor/outdoor).* **Room services** *Air-conditioning. Internet access: dataport/ISDN. Hairdryer. Laundry/dry-cleaning. Mini-bar. Room service (7am-11pm). TV: pay movies/satellite.*

Herodion Hotel

Rovertou Galli 4, Makrygianni, 11742 (210 923 6832/fax 210 921 1650/www.herodion.gr). *Metro Akropoli.* **Rates** €179 single; €229 double; €285 triple; €267 suites. **Credit** DC, MC, V. **Map** p299 E7.

Under the same excellent management as the Philippos (*see p57*), the Herodion shares its sibling's chief advantage: a location ideal for drooling at the Acropolis and excellent care and service for a moderately sized hotel. But where the Herodion differs from the Philippos is in the decor, which is much more subdued and traditional. Pink furniture with neo-classical touches dresses up the rooms, which have sumptuous adjoining marble bathrooms. The hotel amenities are good, with a green, atrium-like café, a cosy, yet quite elegant, bar/lounge, and a modest roof garden with as up-close-and-personal view of the Acropolis as you can get. **Hotel services** *Bar. Business services. Concierge. Disabled: adapted rooms. Garden. Laundry (self-service). Restaurants (2). Swimming pool.* **Room services** *Air-conditioning. Internet access: dataport/ISDN. Hairdryer. Laundry/dry-cleaning. Mini-bar. Room service (7am-1.30am). TV: satellite.*

Moderate

Acropolis Select Hotel

Falirou 37-39, Koukaki, 11742 (210 921 1610/ fax 210 921 6938/www.acropoliselect.gr). *Metro Syngrou-Fix.* **Rates** €123 single; €145 double; €168 triple. **Credit** AmEx, DC, MC, V. **Map** p299 E8.

An uninspired façade hides a wholly renovated interior and good value for money. While the neighbourhood is not quite as convenient as Plaka or Syntagma, the hotel is a short walk away from the centre, and close to the Acropolis and Syngrou-Fix metro station. The hotel is extremely well appointed and stylishly decorated throughout, with Italian furniture and original artworks. These are some of the most comfortable rooms in Athens for the price, although the en-suite facilities are a bit cramped. Knowledgeable and friendly staff complete the picture of a hotel setting good standards in Athens. **Hotel services** *Bar. Gym. Internet point. Laundry (self-service). No-smoking rooms/floors. Parking (free). Restaurant.* **Room services** *Air-conditioning. Internet access: dataport/ISDN. Hairdryer. Mini-bar. Room service (7am-11pm) TV: pay movies.*

Adrian Hotel

Adrianou 74, Plaka, 10556 (210 322 1553/ fax 210 523 4786/www.douros-hotels.com). *Metro Monastiraki.* **Rates** €90-€100 single; €110-€125 double; €135 triple. **Credit** MC, V. **Map** p295/p299 E5.

The Grande Bretagne

One of the brightest jewels to emerge from Athens' pre-2004 chrysalis of construction doesn't, at first, even appear to be Greek. The Hotel Grande Bretagne (*see p59*), which reopened this spring after a two-year, £70-million renovation, looks more like a lavish monument to Victorian England. But that's just the (sumptuous) surface. For over 150 years, events within the hotel have been inextricably bound to the turbulent history of modern Athens.

It was built as a mansion in 1842, the same year as the palace across the street, which housed Greece's first king and which today is home to the Greek Parliament. A few years later the culinary talents of one Stathis Lampsis, a teenage palace kitchen worker, caught the attention of King George, who paid for the young Greek to study in Paris. In 1874 the former scullery boy returned home a renowned epicure and bought the mansion, which he transformed into the new capital's first grand hotel. In the following decades the Grande Bretagne hosted visiting dignitaries such as Richard Strauss, Laurence Olivier and Mary Pickford and Douglas Fairbanks, along with generations of royalty.

The mid 20th century ushered in a dark period in the hotel's history. In World War II it served alternately as the military headquarters for the Greek, German and British armies; Winston Churchill was a guest. On Christmas Eve 1944, the night before Churchill was to participate in an important conference, a plot to blow up the hotel from the sewers was foiled. Many of this period's intrigues were whispered in the corners of the Grande Bretagne's salons, while its glittering ballroom hosted the resulting summits.

Those in charge of the recent renovations have made every effort to recapture the hotel's original grandeur, restoring antiques, oil paintings and hand-carved details exactly as they had been a century earlier. And within weeks of its reopening, the Grande Bretagne was again swept up in the tide of history. In April 2003, as Athens hosted the historic enlargement ceremony of the European Union, anti-globalisation protesters vented their ire by throwing stones into the lobby. But, as history has proven again and again, such events are all in a day's work for this legendary landmark, which shows every sign of presiding over the heated history of the modern Greeks for many years to come.

The Adrian is located on a street awash with tourists and souvenir shops. Hotel guests can watch the neighbourhood show from their balconies, but still close the door on it with double-glazed windows, or avoid it altogether with a back-facing room. The Adrian is appropriately priced in the mid-range category, with smartly fitted rooms in a strangely pleasant olive motif, Acropolis views from some rooms (for an extra fee), a friendly and professional management, a comfortable lounge area, and a beautiful shaded roof garden with an ideal Acropolis view. **Hotel services** *Internet point.* **Room services** *Air-conditioning. Hairdryer. Kitchenette. Mini-bar. TV: pay movies.*

Hotel Plaka

Kapnikareas 7 & Mitropoleos, Plaka, 10556 (210 322 2096/fax 210 322 2412/www. plakahotel.gr). Metro Monastiraki. **Rates** €99 single; €125 double; €145 triple. **Credit** AmEx, DC, MC, V. **Map** p295/p299 E5. On the smartness-per-euro quotient, the Hotel Plaka fares well. There may be more stylish hotels in Athens, but probably not in this price range. The decor is minimalist and sleek, but not cold. Rooms are all comfortably and smartly furnished, quiet and spacious. A roof garden offers great views of the Acropolis – as do some of the rooms. Unfortunately, the hotel is as well liked by tour operators as it is by guidebook writers, and is popular with groups. **Hotel services** *Bar (summer). Roof garden (summer).* **Room services** *Air-conditioning. Internet access: telephone line. Hairdryer. Laundry. Mini-fridge. Room service (7am-7pm, beverages only). TV: pay movies/satellite.*

Philippos Hotel

Mitseon 3, Makriyianni, 11742 (210 922 3611/ fax 210 922 3615/www.philipposhotel.gr). Metro Akropoli. **Rates** €132 single; €169 double; €210 triple. **Credit** AmEx, DC, MC, V. **Map** p299 E7. While virtually every downtown Athens hotelier claims to be 'under the shadow of the Acropolis', the Philippos really is. Its sleek ground-floor lobby, reception, lounge, and coffee bar are excellent examples of postmodern decor, mixing radically different design signatures with seamless elegance. The small rooms are much less extravagantly appointed. The service is generally good, catering to a mix of business and leisure travellers avoiding the 'copy-paste' mould of the giant international chains and seeking high style without exorbitant prices. **Hotel services** *Bar.* **Room services** *Air-conditioning. Internet access: dataport/ ISDN. Hairdryer. Laundry/dry-cleaning. Mini-bar. TV: satellite.*

Budget

Acropolis House

Kodrou 6 & Voulis, Plaka, 10558 (210 322 2344/fax 210 324 4143). Metro Syntagma. **Rates** €52-€80 double; €83-€96 triple. **Credit** MC, V. **Map** p295/p299 F5.

The Margi. *See p71.*

After 40 years in business, the verdict is still out on the Acropolis House – people either love it or hate it, as one traveller's faded elegance is another's old-fashioned shabbiness. The best and worst of Acropolis House is its long history: the hotel is housed in one of Plaka's oldest buildings and a protected landmark, retaining its original hand-painted frescoes, gilt-framed wall hangings, gloriously high ceilings and original fittings in the reception area. But the hotel has not been maintained well – the overall impression is dank, musty and a bit shabby. Rooms are outmoded, but practical, and management can be described in much the same way. **Hotel services** *Laundry (self-service). Non-smoking rooms.* **Room services** *Air-conditioning (some rooms). Fans (in non-a/c rooms). Internet access: telephone line. TV: satellite.*

Art Gallery Hotel

Erechthiou 5, Koukaki, 11742 (210 923 8376/ fax 210 923 3025). Metro Syngrou-Fix. **Rates** €65-€80 single; €80-€114 double; €100-€155 triple; €120-€165 quad. **No credit cards. Map** p299 E7. This small, family-run, homey hotel is located in a quiet residential area, within walking distance of the Acropolis. A mishmash of old family furniture and lovingly framed paintings from a locally celebrated impressionist artist who used the house as a studio decorate the interior. Rooms are very simple, all with wooden floors and flooded with light. At press time, the hotel was sprucing up, with badly needed bathroom renovations, floor refinishing and plans to add TVs and mini-bars to rooms. The earnest service and a good top-floor bar/lounge with views of Filopappou Hill and the Acropolis complete the picture. **Hotel services** *Bar. TV room.* **Room services** *Air-conditioning. Fan. Internet access: telephone line. Laundry service/dry-cleaning.*

St GEORGE
LYCABETTUS BOUTIQUE HOTEL
★ ★ ★ ★ ★

An emphasis on design and gastronomy

Le Grand Balcon

Room

Frame

St George Lycabettus hotel is a boutique style property located in the most exclusive quarter of Athens, Kolonaki. It is the preferred hotel of businessmen, show-biz and famous people in Athens. The Executive chef, Mark Enderborg from the renowed "Mirabelle" (1 Michelin star) and "Le Gavroche" (2 Michelin stars) of London has arrived in Athens ready to present his gastronomic creations.

The breakfast and the dining experience is trully unforgettable with aromas from the Greek seas in combination with the unique view of the Acropolis and Lycabettus hill. Frame lounge bar restaurant in the heart of Kolonaki cooking up a light modern cuisine in a casual yet elegant 60's-70's lounge atmosphere. Bubble chairs, sheepskin armchairs, miniature gardens hanging from the ceiling are just a few reasons worth visiting. In the summer months Frame's garden restaurant also hosts the stylish Bohemian bar where one can chill out listening to Smooth grooves and Conga beats. Trully an island vibe in the city center.

ST GEORGE LYCABETTUS BOUTIQUE HOTEL
2 Kleomenous St. 106 75 Athens, Greece
Tel.: (+3) 210 7290711-9. Fax: (+3) 210 7290439, (+3) 210 7247610
www.sglycabettus.gr, e-mail: info@sglycabettus.gr

Hotel Adonis

Kodrou 3, Plaka, 10558 (210 324 9737/ fax 210 323 1602). Metro Syntagma. **Rates** €44 single; €59-€70 double; €77-€88 triple. **No credit cards. Map** p299 F6.

Just next to the Acropolis House hotel – an excellent location – the Adonis offers very low room rates for a respectable hotel. The no-nonsense, experienced management serves breakfast up on the roof, where decor is still cheap 1960s bar/taverna, but the adjacent balcony with just a few tables has one of the best Acropolis views to be had at any budget. Rooms are quite sparsely decorated but are functionally and inoffensively furnished in new sets of modern furniture. Tiny en-suite bathrooms are balanced by large balconies in many rooms.

Hotel services *Bar. Roof garden.*
Room services *Air-conditioning (most rooms). Fan (non-a/c rooms). TV: satellite.*

Hotel Dioskouros

Pittakou 6, Plaka, 10558 (210 324 8165/ fax 210 321 9991/www.consolas.gr). Metro Akropoli or Syntagma. **Rates** €40 single; €60 double; €70 triple; €80-€100 quad. **Credit** AmEx, DC, MC, V. **Map** p299 F6.

Time Out Athens won't even list the few real hostels in downtown Athens, as they are miserably located and awfully managed. But, much like the Student & Traveller's Inn (*see below*), the Dioskouros retains the spirit of a hostel while offering better standards. Guests won't get en-suite bathrooms, spacious rooms or fancy furniture, but they will get a small, intimate hostel full of international independent travellers, a good clean bed, friendly staff, a dorm-bed option, a peaceful garden shaded with lemon trees to socialise in, and a quiet and excellent location on the edge of Plaka.

Hotel services *Bar. Cooking facilities (Oct-May). Garden. Internet point. Laundry. Payphone. Parking (free). TV area.* **Room services** *Air-conditioning (most rooms). Fan.*

Marble-House Pension

Anastasiou Zinni 35, Koukaki, 11741 (210 923 4058/fax 210 324 3551/www.marblehouse.gr). Metro Syngrou-Fix. **Rates** (breakfast not included) private bath €35 single, €43 double, €50 triple; shared bath €37 double, €44 triple. **Credit** MC, V. **Map** p299 D8.

The Marble-House Pension is in an off-centre location in an unexceptional but quiet area of the Koukaki neighbourhood. But for an off-centre location, it really couldn't be more convenient: just a three-minute walk away from Syngrou-Fix station, the pension is one metro stop or a brisk walk from the foot of the Acropolis, and two stops away from Syntagma. And for this minor inconvenience, travellers are rewarded with almost unbelievably low prices and a very hospitable atmosphere attracting young and young-at-heart budget travellers. With their wooden furniture, the rooms are thoroughly unobjectionable, and the courtyard is tranquil. Well worth the mini-trek.

Hotel services *Bar. Garden. No-smoking rooms/floors. Restaurant. TV room. VCR.* **Room services** *Air-conditioning (some rooms). Fan. Kitchenette (in two studios). Laundry. Mini-fridge. Room service (24hrs).*

Nefeli Hotel

Hatzimichali 2, Plaka, 10558 (210 322 8044/fax 210 322 5800). Metro Syntagma. **Rates** €60 single; €75 double; €96 triple. **Credit** MC, V. **Map** p299 E8.

Hidden away on an attractive residential street in Plaka, the Nefeli Hotel keeps a low profile, popularised solely by word of mouth over the years. Despite the discrete location, it's just around the corner from Plaka's lively main square, packed with outdoor cafés and tavernas. The hotel is well managed, with the type of excellent personal service rarely demonstrated in the budget category, which explains the high number of repeat clientele. The hotel was recently upgraded, but luckily the prices were not. Aside from occasional street noise, it's hard to find much wrong with the Nefeli – it just might be Plaka's best-kept secret.

Hotel services *Bar.*
Room services *Air-conditioning. Internet access: dataport/telephone line. TV.*

Student & Traveller's Inn

Kydathinaion 16, Plaka, 10558 (210 324 4808/fax 210 321 0065/http://users.forthnet.gr/ath/studentsinn). Metro Syntagma. **Rates** €50-€58 single; €60-€70 double; €75-€90 triple. **No credit cards. Map** p299 F6.

The owner of this practical budget hotel doesn't print brochures, offering one simple explanation: 'The location sells itself'. Indeed, the location is superb – on the outskirts of the more tasteful part of Plaka, within walking distance of Syntagma Square and metro station, on a quiet pedestrianised street. The inn has the clientele and casual, international camaraderie of a hostel, but the rooms and facilities of a simple hotel. Rooms are basic but cheery enough, and en-suite bathrooms are all newly renovated. Internet access and a green courtyard for socialising are more benefits.

Hotel services *Bar. Garden. Internet point. Payphone. Snack bar. TV room.* **Room services** *Air-conditioning.*

The Historic Centre

Deluxe

Hotel Grande Bretagne

Syntagma, 10563 (210 333 0000/fax 210 322 8034/www.HotelGrandeBretagne-ath.gr). Metro Syntagma. **Rates** €270-€350 double; €490-€3,000 suite. **Credit** AmEx, DC, MC, V. **Map** p295/p299 F5.

A manager at a competing five-star hotel recently admitted that there's no question about it: the Grande Bretagne stands head and shoulders above every other luxury establishment in town. Already a landmark steeped in history (*see p56*), the GB's latest

Where to Stay

Landmark glamour at the **Athens Hilton**. *See p63.*

claim to fame is its head-to-toe renovation, which recaptured its famed turn-of-the-19th-century opulence. Antique furnishings, handcarved architectural details, tapestried headboards and the like have all been painstakingly restored to their original glory. Extra touches like 24-hour personal butler service add the final decadent finesse. Standard rooms, however, are not spacious. If all this seems out of your price range, stop by for tea (served in hand-painted, gold-trimmed teacups), just to breathe in the history.
Hotel services *Bars (2). Beauty salon. Business services. Concierge. Disabled: adapted rooms. Gym. No-smoking rooms/floors. Restaurant. Swimming pool (indoor/outdoor).* **Room services** *Air-conditioning. Bathrobe. Internet access: dataport/ISDN. Hairdryer. Hi-fi. Laundry/dry-cleaning. Mini-bar. Newspaper. Room service (24hrs). Turndown. TV: pay movies/satellite.*

King George II

Syntagma, 10563 (210 728 0400/fax 210 725 8217/www.grecotel.gr). Metro Syntagma. **Rates** approx. €525 single; €525 double. **Credit** AmEx, DC, MC, V. **Map** p295/p299 F5.
Once one of Athens' most renowned hotels, the King George II has been closed for 14 years and renovated for the past three. Its opening in the spring of 2004 was highly anticipated and while architecturally it has been somewhat modernised from its 19th-century origins, it is still expected to recall some of its former glory days. With just over 100 rooms, the hotel is billing itself as a highly personalised, highly upscale ultra-deluxe residence with boutique-hotel qualities.

Hotel services *Bar. Beauty salon. Business services. Concierge. Disabled: adapted rooms. Gym. Limousine service. No-smoking rooms/floor. Restaurants. Swimming pool (indoor).* **Room services** *Air-conditioning. Bathrobe. Internet access: dataport/ISDN. Hairdryer. Hi-fi. Laundry/dry-cleaning. Mini-bar. Newspaper. Room service (24hrs). Turndown. TV: DVD (selected rooms)/games/pay movies/satellite.*

Expensive

Best Western Esperia Palace

Stadiou 22, 10564 (210 323 8001/fax 210 323 8100/www.esperiahotel.com.gr). Metro Panepistimio. **Rates** €190 single; €240 double; €285 triple. **Credit** AmEx, DC, MC, V. **Map** p295 F4.
The crown jewel of the Best Western chain in Athens, the Esperia Palace offers a superb location on what has always been one of the swisher stretches of the main thoroughfare connecting Syntagma and Omonia. The Esperia Palace walls seem to be oddly charged with history, even though the building is only 40 years old. Plush leather couches in the reception and good faux-antique furniture in the very cosy rooms lend the hotel an elegant air. The Athinaios bar-restaurant in the hotel has a more casual feel, with its exposed-brick-wall decor.
Hotel services *Bar. Concierge. No-smoking rooms/floor. Payphone. Restaurants (2).* **Room services** *Air-conditioning. Fan. Internet access: telephone line. Hairdryer. Laundry/dry-cleaning. Mini-bar. Room service (7am-11pm). TV: pay movies/satellite.*

Electra Hotel

Ermou 5, 10563 (210 337 8000/fax 210 322 0310).
Metro Syntagma. **Rates** €172 single; €209 double;
€258 triple. **Credit** AmEx, DC, MC, V.
Map p295/p299 F5.
The Electra is just a few metres away from
Syntagma Square on Ermou, the area's biggest
shopping street and the gateway to Plaka and
Monastiraki. The hotel offers spacious rooms dec-
orated in bright colours and quite comfortable, if
generic, furnishings, as well as soundproofing to
block out noise from outside. Service can be a bit
impersonal at this large hotel, but is adequate. A
large American-style buffet breakfast is included.
Hotel services *Bar. Business services. Concierge.*
Laundry (self-service). No-smoking rooms/floor.
Payphone. Restaurant. **Room services**
Air-conditioning. Bathrobe. Internet access:
telephone line. Hairdryer. Laundry/dry-cleaning.
Mini-bar. Room service (7am-12.30am).
TV: pay movies.

Moderate

Amalia Hotel

Leof Vas Amalias 10, 10557 (210 323 7301/
fax 210 607 2135/www.amalia.gr). Metro
Syntagma. **Rates** €90 single; €110 double; €132
triple. **Credit** AmEx, DC, MC, V. **Map** p295/p299 F5.
With fairly low rates, the Amalia offers good value
for money and has carved out a niche as a relatively
affordable four-star, full-service hotel in the
Syntagma area. While it cannot be called plush and
it has a fairly standard 'monohotel' quality about it,
rooms are spacious and clean and reception areas
are as you would expect of any typical international four-star hotel. The location – on a heavily trafficked main avenue to Syntagma Square – is the
hotel's obvious drawback, but the issue is addressed
well by double-glazed windows and balanced by the
beautiful National Gardens across the street.
Hotel services *Bar. Restaurant.* **Room services**
Air-conditioning. Internet access: telephone line.
Hairdryer. Laundry/dry-cleaning. Room service
(8am-10pm). TV: pay movies.

Athens Cypria Hotel

Diomias 5, 10563 (210 323 8034/fax 210 324
8792/www.athenscypria.com). Metro Syntagma.
Rates €85-€105 single; €115-€135 double;
€155-€175 triple; €183-€237 family room.
Credit AmEx, MC, V. **Map** p295/p299 F5.
A good option for families, this modest, friendly
oasis is set on a quiet street steps away from
Syntagma. Cool, simple blue-and-white rooms have
satellite TV and movies, hairdryers, and mini-bars.
There are several connecting family rooms, and the
hotel offers discounts for children up to 12 years old
as well as providing cribs free of charge.
Hotel services *Bar. Disabled: adapted rooms.*
Room services *Air-conditioning. Hairdryer.*
Laundry/dry-cleaning. Mini-bar. Room service
(7am-1am). TV: pay movies/satellite.

Hotel Carolina

Kolokotroni 55, 10560 (210 324 3551/
fax 210 324 3551/www.hotelcarolina.gr).
Metro Monastiraki. **Rates** (July-Sept) €70
single; €90 double; €115 triple; €140 quad.
Credit MC, V. **Map** p295 E4.
Originally a budget hotel; if a recent renovation
hasn't turned this frog into a prince, it has transformed it into a somewhat more exclusive affair –
with more exclusive prices to go with it. The pre-
war building lends the hotel a bit of character and
history lacking in many Athens hotels. Brightly
coloured matching furniture make the smallish
rooms more efficient and add a touch of warmth to
the rather sterile feel of the spick-and-span, tile-
floored rooms.
Hotel services *Bar. Garden. No-smoking rooms.*
Restaurant. **Room services** *Air-conditioning.*
Internet access: telephone line. Hairdryer. TV.

Budget

Cecil Hotel

Athinas 39, 10554 (210 321 8005/fax 210 321
8005/www.cecil.gr). Metro Monastiraki. **Rates**
€55 single; €80 double; €105 triple; €129 suite.
Credit AmEx, MC, V. **Map** p295 E4.
The Cecil's environs and the building housing it are
both a little ragged these days, but when it comes
to the things budget travellers really crave – clean,
crisp, pleasant rooms and breakfast areas; a convenient location for sightseeing; crucial amenities
like air-conditioning; and a resident cat that gives
the place a little personality – the Cecil delivers. The
hotel will soon be taking further steps to renovate,
including soundproofing to reduce noise pollution,
but until then visitors should request off-street
rooms to ensure a good night's sleep.
Hotel services *None.* **Room services**
Air-conditioning. Laundry/dry-cleaning.
TV: satellite.

Fivos

Athinas 23, Monastiraki, 10554 (210 322 6657/
fax 210 321 9921/www.consolas.gr). Metro
Monastiraki. **Rates** €35 single; €55 double;
€70 triple. **No credit cards. Map** p295 E4.
Under the same management as the Dioskouros
(*see p59*), the Fivos shares its strengths: dirt-cheap
clean rooms with few amenities and few preten-
sions. The location could hardly get more practical,
within spitting distance of the Monastiraki metro
and very close to all the major sites. At press time,
the street on which the Fivos stands was a bit gritty and noisy, but should be pedestrianised by mid
2004, which should considerably improve the feel
of the area. The hotel, much like the street, is evolv-
ing rapidly after being bought by a local travel
agency in mid-2003, so travellers should check for
new amenities.
Hotel services *Bar. Cooking facilities.*
Internet point. Snack bar. **Room services**
Air-conditioning (some rooms, from Apr 2004).

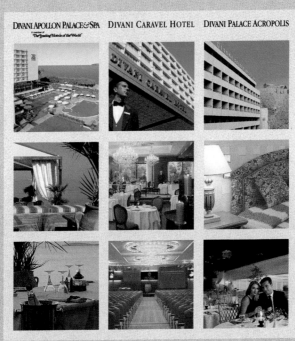

Tempi Hotel

Eolou 29, Monastiraki, 10551 (210 321 3175/fax 210 325 4179/www.travelling.gr/tempihotel). Metro Monastiraki. **Rates** €32 single; €40-€48 double; €60 triple. **Credit** AmEx, DC, MC, V. **Map** p295 E4.
For the traveller who has graduated from hostels but doesn't have a gold credit card, the Tempi is the perfect upgrade: the hotel has no curfews or dorm beds to contend with, but does offer some cost-saving features, like a simple but well-stocked kitchen for guest use and the option of shared bathrooms. The neighbourhood is convenient and safe, and the location on a pedestrianised street a relief from busy Athens.
Hotel services *Cooking facilities. Laundry (self-service). Payphone.* **Room services** *Air-conditioning. Fan. TV.*

Kolonaki & Around

Deluxe

Andromeda Hotel

Timoleontos Vassou 22, Ambelokipi, 11521 (210 641 5000/fax 210 646 6361/www.slh.com/andromeda). Metro Ambelokipi or Megaro Mousikis. **Rates** €435 single; €450 double; €500 junior suite; €550 executive suite. **Credit** AmEx, DC, MC, V.
Offering a more placid atmosphere than its competitors, the boutique-style Andromeda caters to business travellers averse to the faux-riche decor and impersonal feel of many large hotels in this category, but who still expect to be tended to in tasteful surroundings. Service is outstanding, the spacious rooms are all plushly decorated, and the hotel houses Etrusco, one of Athens' best-known Italian/Mediterranean restaurants. Garden rooms are preferable. The hotel also has new, very comfortable suites/apartments across the street to accommodate longer stays or families.
Hotel services *Bar. Beauty salon. Concierge. Restaurant.* **Room services** *Air-conditioning. Bathrobe. Fan. Internet access: ISDN. Iron (in apartments). Hairdryer. Hi-fi (in apartments). Kitchenette (in apartments). Laundry/dry-cleaning. Mini-bar. Room service (7am-11.30pm). TV: pay movies.*

Athens Hilton

Leof Vas Sofias 46, Kolonaki, 11528 (210 728 1000/fax 210 728 1111/ www.athens.hilton.com). Metro Evangelismos. **Rates** €375-€495 single; €405-€525 double; €435-€555 triple; €800 suite. **Credit** AmEx, DC, MC, V. **Map** p297 J5.
In Athens, the Hilton isn't just another standard multinational hotel – it's a veritable institution. It was for years the only hotel offering five-star accommodation and service in the city; its building design was a minor architectural milestone; scores of famous visitors have spent nights there; and its pricey eateries and lounges remain among the most talked about in town. The hotel is a city landmark, and Athenians have come to call the entire neighbourhood 'Heeltone'. A frenzied, thorough renovation is now complete and the results are lavish. Particularly fine are the bar and outdoor pool.
Hotel services *Bar. Beauty salon. Business services. Concierge. Disabled: adapted rooms. Garden. Gym. No-smoking rooms/floors. Parking (€35). Restaurants (3). Swimming pools (indoor & outdoor).* **Room services** *Air-conditioning. Bathrobe (in business/executive rooms). Internet access: ISDN/web TV. Iron (business rooms). Hairdryer. Laundry/dry-cleaning. Mini-bar. Newspaper (executive rooms only). Room service (24hrs). TV: pay movies/satellite/DVD (executive rooms).*

Divani Caravel

Leof Vas Alexandrou 2, Kolonaki, 16121 (210 720 7000/fax 210 723 6683/www.divanicaravel.gr). Metro Evangelismos. **Rates** €310-€460 single; €330-€490 double; €413 triple; €900 suite. **Credit** AmEx, DC, MC, V. **Map** p297 J5.
Boasting the most extensive facilities in Athens, the Divani's raison d'être is conferences. No doubt most conference-goers aren't paying list prices here, and that's a good thing, since better value can be found in Athens for the luxury traveller. The rooms, which have been completely renovated in the past two years, are certainly comfortable, and the rooftop pool offers great views of the city, but at these prices the rooms (not to mention the service, which can be so-so) should be a little more inspired.
Hotel services *Bar. Beauty salon. Business services. Concierge. Disabled: adapted rooms. Gym. No-smoking rooms/floors. Parking (€11). Restaurants (2). Swimming pool (indoor/outdoor).* **Room services** *Air-conditioning. Bathrobe (executive rooms). Internet access: dataport/ISDN (executive rooms). Iron (executive rooms). Hairdryer. Hi-fi (executive rooms). Laundry/dry-cleaning. Mini-bar. Newspaper (executive rooms). Room service (24hrs). TV: pay movies/satellite.*

Holiday Suites

Arnis 4, Kolonaki, 11528 (210 727 8690/ fax 210 727 8696/www.holidaysuites.gr). Metro Megaro Mousikis. **Rates** €460 junior suite. **Credit** AmEx, DC, MC, V.
Holiday Suites is trying hard to outshine the other contenders in the executive-travel category and is succeeding. While other hotels offer minimal executive comforts with maximum mark-ups on their standard rooms, Holiday Suites really delivers with large suites featuring fax machines and three telephones, plus a second line for data transfer and personal voicemail. There is a sauna, pool, free access to all the facilities at the nearby Holiday Inn, plus amenities like full stereos with wall-mounted speakers, DVD players, remote-controlled blinds, kitchenettes, refrigerators and sumptuous bathrooms.
Hotel services *Business services (at Holiday Inn). Gym (at Holiday Inn). Parking (€12). Swimming pool (outdoor – at Holiday Inn).* **Room services** *Air-conditioning. Bathrobe. Internet access: dataport/ ISDN. Iron. Hairdryer. Hi-fi. Kitchenette. Laundry/ dry-cleaning. Mini-bar. Newspaper. Room service (6.30am-midnight). TV: DVD/free movies/satellite.*

St George Lycabettus

Kleomenous 2, Kolonaki, 10675 (210 729 0711-9/ fax 210 729 0439/www.sglycabettus.gr). Metro Evangelismos. **Rates** €266-€313 single; €342-€399 double; €722-€1,669 suite. **Credit** AmEx, DC, MC, V. **Map** p297 H4.

Nestled among the pine trees on Lycabettus Hill, this intimate luxury hotel is steps away from Athens' top designer shops and museum row, though keep in mind that verdant surrounds in the centre do mean a steep hike or taxi ride up the hill. Your efforts are rewarded by designer rooms ranging from jewel-toned art nouveau to sleek black and white minimalism, and spectacular Acropolis panoramas from the rooftop pool bar and Le Grand Balcon restaurant. Downstairs, the '70s-themed lounge Frame is one of the trendiest nightspots in town.

Hotel services *Bars (3). Beauty salon. Business services. Concierge. Disabled: adapted rooms. Garden. Gym. No-smoking rooms. Parking (€14). Restaurant. Swimming pool (outdoor).* **Room services** *Air-conditioning. Bathrobe. Internet access: dataport/ ISDN. Hairdryer. Hi-fi. Laundry/dry-cleaning. Mini-bar. Newspaper. Room service (7am-midnight). TV: pay movies/satellite.*

Moderate

Airotel Alexandros

Timoleontos Vassou 8, Ambelokipi, 11521 (210 643 0464/fax 210 644 1084/www. airotel.gr). Metro Ambelokipi or Megaro Mousikis. **Rates** €132 single; €148 double; €170 triple. **Credit** AmEx, DC, MC, V.

This solid four-star hotel caters primarily to business travellers, who will certainly appreciate the executive-room amenities like dataports, room

safes, and tea and coffee facilities, as well as the car park and easy access to major Athens' business centres. But leisure travellers will equally appreciate the hotel rooms' homey interior design, whirlpool marble baths, nearby metro station, proximity to the concert hall, quiet neighbourhood location, and luxurious reception, lounge and restaurant. Something for all and sundry.

Hotel services *Bar. Parking (free). Restaurant.* **Room services** *Air-conditioning. Bathrobe. Internet access: dataport/ISDN. Hairdryer. Laundry/dry-cleaning. Mini-bar. Room service (7am-midnight). TV: pay movies/satellite.*

Golden Age Hotel

Michalakoupoulou 57, Kolonaki, 11528 (210 724 0861/fax 210 721 3965/ www.goldenage.gr). Metro Megaro Mousikis. **Rates** €102 single; €110 double; €132 triple. **Credit** AmEx, DC, MC, V.

A four-star quality hotel at mid-range prices, the Golden Age Hotel's only real drawback is its location on a heavily trafficked boulevard. But with a metro station and the Athens Concert Hall (Megaro Mousikis) a five-minute walk away and double-glazed windows soundproofing the large, bright rooms, the problem nevertheless loses some of its import. Another benefit is the small size of the Golden Age Hotel compared to other quality hotels in the neighbourhood, ensuring a more personal touch in the service.

Hotel services *Bar. Business services. Concierge. Disabled: adapted room. No-smoking rooms. Parking (€20). Restaurant.* **Room services** *Air-conditioning. Bathrobe. Internet access: dataport/ISDN. Hairdryer. Laundry/dry-cleaning. Mini-bar. Room service (24hrs). TV: pay movies/satellite.*

Omonia Grand Hotel.
See p67.

Xenos Lycabetus

Valaoritou 6, 10671 (210 360 0600/www.xenos lycabettus.gr). Metro Syntagma. **Rates** €130 single; €160 double; €380 junior suite; €470 suite. **Credit** AmEx, DC, MC, V.

This newcomer is a sleek, stylish boutique-style hotel. With just 25 rooms, the emphasis is on personal service. The location – on a pedestrianised street filled with cafés and upscale restaurants in a particularly fashionable part of Kolonaki yet extremely central – is perfect for the fashionatti. The hotel has its own popular café and restaurant in the area's upmarket vernacular. Rooms feature large, marble-swathed bathrooms, but they have a neutral, boxy modern style that's not quite as elegant as the area. But all in all, very good value for money.
Hotel services *Bar. Business services. Disabled: adapted rooms. Parking (€25/24hrs). Restaurant.* **Room services** *Air-conditioning. Internet access: ISDN. Hairdryer. Laundry/dry-cleaning. Mini-bar. Room service(24hrs). TV: pay movies/satellite.*

Budget

Exarcheion

Themistokleous 55, Exarchia, 10683 (210 380 0731/fax 210 380 3296). Metro Omonia. **Rates** €35 single; €45 double; €50 triple. **Credit** AmEx, DC, MC, V. **Map** p295 F2.

Like the Dryades (*see below*), the Exarcheion offers cheap rooms right in the middle of the student district, as well as the same uneven service. But unlike the Dryades, the Exarcheion is smack in the centre of the area's café/bar scene. If getting rest is a priority, ask for a high-floor room. The rooms are quite generously sized and clean, but, of course, at these prices they're rather simple. The rooftop bar is attractive for soaking up the feel of the buzzing neighbourhood below.
Hotel services *Bar. Cooking facilities. Garden. Internet point. No-smoking floors. Parking (free).* **Room services** *Air-conditioning. Internet access: telephone. Hairdryer. Laundry/dry-cleaning. Mini-fridge. Newspaper. Room service (7am-11pm). TV.*

Hotel Dryades/Hotel Orion

Emmanuil Benaki 105, Exarchia, 11473 (210 382 7362 /fax 210 380 5193). Metro Omonia. **Rates** €39-€45 single; €35-€60 double; €45-€72 triple. **Credit** AmEx, MC, V.

This quiet pair of hotels under the same management stands in a cul-de-sac on Strefi Hill. They have a kitchen available for guest use, which makes them a good option for independent travellers on tight budgets – although local tavernas do provide cheap dining options. The service can be unpredictable, but overall both hotels are good value. Owing to the low prices and the studenty Exarchia location the hotels – particularly the Orion – draw a young, international crowd.
Hotel services *Bar. Cooking facilities. Garden. Internet point. Parking (free).* **Room services** *Air-conditioning. Internet access: telephone line. Laundry/dry-cleaning. Mini-fridge. TV: satellite.*

President Hotel

Leof Kifisias 43, Ambelokipi, 11523 (210 698 9000/fax 210 692 4900/www.president.gr). Metro Ambelokipi or Panormou. **Rates** €73 single; €86 double; €103 triple. **Credit** MC, V.

This cubist giant offers several hundred standard rooms – convenient for the occasional hotel shortage, as they can usually be counted on for availability. The

Where to Stay

St George Lycabettus.
See p64.

PARK HOTEL
Athens

★ ★ ★ ★ ★

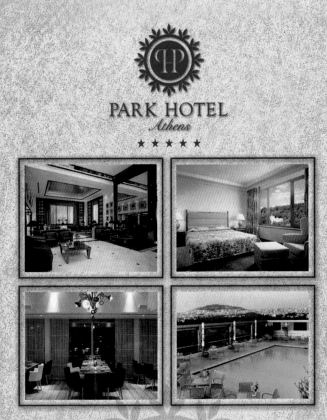

Centrally located overlooking Pedion Areos - one of Athens loveliest parks - and just steps away from the National Archaelogical Museum, the renewed **Park Hotel Athens** is the ideal choice for business travelers and those who seek a leisurely break. Throughout the hotel premises the discreet luxury and elegant style create a relaxing and intimate atmosphere.

The culinary creations combined with the elegant ambience and impeccable service, are the distinguishing marks of Alexandra's Restaurant, Park Café and the new trendy roof-top St' Astra restaurant-bar with a panoramic view of the Acropolis and Lycabettus hill. The hotel's Banqueting department and the "Park Catering Service" ensure that your social or business event, inside or outside the hotel, becomes an unforgettable experience.

10, Alexandras Avenue, 106 82 Athens - Tel: +30 210 8894500, Fax: +30 210 8238420
www.athensparkhotel.gr, e-mail: info@athensparkhotel.gr

place feels a bit dated. But, having said that, some rooms are quite charming and fine for the leisure or business traveller without any high-tech needs, and the rooftop pool is elegant.

Hotel services *Bar. Concierge. Disabled: adapted rooms. No-smoking rooms. Parking (€10). Restaurant. Swimming pool (outdoor).* **Room services** *Air-conditioning. Bathrobe. Internet access: dataport/ISDN. Hairdryer. Laundry/dry-cleaning. Room service (24hrs). TV: satellite.*

North of the Acropolis

Expensive

Grecotel Athens Acropol

Pireos 1, Omonia, 10552 (210 528 2100/ fax 210 523 1361/www.grecotel.gr). Metro Omonia. **Rates** €240 single; €300 double. **Credit** AmEx, DC, MC, V. **Map** p295 E3.

Although it is just across the street from the Omonia Grand Hotel (*see below*) and owned by the same chain (Grecotel), the Athens Acropol seems a world away and is less a jet-setters' dwelling than solid, standard, four-star conference-style hotel. Service is good, and both rooms and en-suite facilities are fairly spacious and simply furnished. Hotel facilities are somewhat dated, while the on-site fitness centre is small, but well equipped. The buzzing Platia Omonia is just outside the front door, with its metro station offering speedy access to all the city's major tourist sites.

Hotel services *Bar. Business services (across the street). Concierge. Disabled: adapted rooms. Gym. Non-smoking floor. Restaurant.* **Room services** *Air-conditioning. Dataport. Internet access: telephone line. Hairdryer. Hi-fi (in some rooms). Laundry/dry-cleaning. Mini-bar. Room service (7am-11pm). TV: DVD (on request)/pay movies/satellite.*

Omonia Grand Hotel

Pireos 2, Omonia, 10552 (210 523 5230/ fax 210 523 4955/www.grecotel.gr). Metro Omonia. **Rates** €250 single; €310 double; €500 junior suite. **Credit** AmEx, DC, MC, V. **Map** p295 E3.

The Grand is Omonia's only deluxe hotel, and sits upon a corner of the square. It calls itself a 'hip hotel', and clearly caters to a youngish, moneyed traveller wanting something stylish, ultra-contemporary and at the same time luxurious. And indeed the hotel does manage to carry off a modern, artful quirkiness alongside a touch of classic refinement. The front rooms, notably those on the corners, feature large windows, with views overlooking the busy Platia Omonia.

Hotel services *Bar. Business services. Gym (across the street). Internet point. Restaurant.* **Room services** *Air-conditioning. Dataport. Fan. Internet access: telephone line. Hairdryer. Hi-fi. Laundry/dry-cleaning. Mini-bar. Room service (7am-11pm). TV: DVD (suites)/pay movies.*

Budget

Amaryllis Hotel

Veranzerou 45, Omonia, 10432 (210 523 8738/fax 210 522 5954/www.greekhotel.com/athens/amaryllis). Metro Omonia. **Rates** €44 single; €55 double; €66 triple. **Credit** AmEx, MC, V. **Map** p295 E2.

One of the best deals in the Omonia area, the recently renovated Amaryllis has preserved its low rates and now offers even better value for money. In the midst of a busy commercial area, the hotel is on a comparatively quiet street but still close to the square. Ideal for those who are travelling on a budget but desire extensive facilities, the Amaryllis greets travellers with an airy marble-swathed lobby and reception and a café/lounge with plush seats. Rooms are cheery, bright and generally more agreeable than other budget hotels, though service can be sour.

Hotel services *Bar. Disabled: adapted rooms.* **Room services** *Air-conditioning. TV.*

Jason Inn

Agion Asomaton 12, Psyrri, 10553 (210 325 1106, 210 520 2491/fax 210 523 4786/www.douros-hotels.com). Metro Thisio. **Rates** €72 single; €88 double; €108 triple. **Credit** MC, V. **Map** p295 D4.

The hotel structure is unimpressive and the street it stands on nondescript, but the reward for taking just a walk to a more picturesque neighbourhood is worth it, with good access to sites and a somewhat more 'authentic' experience and lower prices than Plaka while just a short walk away. With standard-issue but pleasant rooms, an attractive rooftop garden restaurant and a staff that thoroughly understands the needs of its mid-range budget travellers, the Jason Inn is good value for money.

Hotel services *Bar. Disabled: adapted rooms. Garden. Restaurant.* **Room services** *Air-conditioning. Internet access: telephone line. Hairdryer. Mini-fridge. Room service (6am-2am). TV: satellite.*

King Jason Hotel

Kolonou 26, Metaxourgio, 10437 (210 523 4721/fax 210 523 4786/www.douros-hotels.com). Metro Metaxourgio. **Rates** €57 single; €72 double; €90 triple. **Credit** MC, V. **Map** p295 D3.

A recent renovation has lifted the profile of this hotel, and its customer comforts. Rooms are now a warm pine-wood style punctuated with bright colours. The attention to detail and progressive features like dataports and free internet access in all rooms (plus conveniences like room safes and hairdryers) are evidence of the King Jason's excellent reputation. The lounge, breakfast area and bar are all sleek and cool. Staff are friendly and seem to have a genuine interest in being of service to guests. The hotel's only shortcoming lies its decidedly unglamorous neighbourhood.

Hotel services *Bar. Parking (free). Restaurant.* **Room services** *Air-conditioning. Fan. Internet access: telephone line. Laundry/dry-cleaning. Mini-fridge. Room service (8am-midnight). TV: satellite.*

Beach luxury

While many visitors hurry to the Greek islands, travellers may not be aware that some of Greece's best spas and resorts are a quick drive from Athens. Several plush facilities along the strip of coastline known as the 'Athenian Riviera' (from Vouliagmeni to Cape Sounion) offer major pampering without the hassle of onward travel. Although the Athenian Riviera is still a world away from the laid-back islands, it also feels like a world away from Athens, and is ideal for those with just a couple of extra days to spare from the city.

The closest is the tranquil **Astir Palace Resort**, sprawling over a private pine-clad peninsula 25 kilometres (16 miles) from Athens. The resort's three hotels offer magnificent sea views, private beaches and dozens of activities ranging from windsurfing, tennis and jet-skiing to private pilates lessons.

Also in Vouliagmeni is the **Divani Apollon Palace & Spa**, which doesn't look at all like a palace but does pull off the deluxe hotel experience with taste and flair. Service is exceptionally good, as are hotel amenities: private beach, gardens, two outdoor swimming pools, a brand-new, full-service spa, Jacuzzi, a children's playground, tennis courts and, of course, plush rooms – many with panoramic sea views. The only unpleasantness here is a shameful double-pricing policy in which non-Greeks pay more than locals.

Western Athens

Budget

Hostel Aphrodite

Voda Michail 65, 10440 (210 881 0589/fax 210 881 6574/www.hostelaphrodite.com). Metro Larissa Station or Victoria. **Rates** €16-€18 dorm bed; €19-€20 quad bed; €45-€53 double; breakfast €1.50-€5. **No credit cards.** **Map** p295 E1.

Hostels in Greece usually offer the best of the genre – cheap beds and a young, convivial atmosphere – without maddening detractions like lockouts, over-stuffed rooms or bare-minimum service. Hostel Aphrodite is no exception. Beds are about as cheap as they come, extra services like travel and laundry are readily available, doubles and quads (some with private bath) are also available, and the multinational, young staff create a world-party atmosphere. The location is close to both rail and metro stations, but the gritty neighbourhood should be seriously taken into consideration.

Hotel services *Bar. Internet point. No-smoking rooms/floors. Payphone. TV room.*
Room services *Air-conditioning. Laundry.*

Grand Resort Lagonissi.

Travelling further down the coast, about an hour's drive from downtown Athens, is the **Grand Resort Lagonissi**, which lies on a peninsula between Athens and the ancient site of Sounion. As the name tells you, this is not merely a hotel but a resort complex constituting an entire village with numerous restaurants and even a chapel. And with 16 very well-kept and well-equipped beaches, guests are ensured their own place in the sun. The resort has a bit of something for everyone, including children's entertainment, extensive sports facilities, and beauty and spa services.

Astir Palace Resort

Apollonos 40, Vouliagmeni, 16671 (210 890 2000/fax 210 896 2582/www.astir.gr).

Rates 250- 400 single; 290- 440 double; 400- 3,000 bungalow; 750- 3,000 suite. **Credit** AmEx, DC, MC, V.

Divani Apollon Palace & Spa

Agiou Nikolaou 10 & Iliou, Vouliagmeni, 16671 (210 891 1100/fax 210 965 8010/www.divanis.gr/divaniapollon). **Rates** 260- 400 single; 280- 420 double; 1,200 suite. **Credit** AmEx, DC, MC, V.

Grand Resort Lagonissi

40th km Athens-Sounion highway, Lagonissi, 19010 (229 102 3911/fax 229 102 4534/www.lagonissiresort.gr). Closed Oct-Mar. **Rates** 388 single; 485 double; 685 triple. **Credit** AmEx, DC, MC, V.

Oscar Hotel

Filadelfias 25 & Samou, 10439 (210 883 4215/fax 210 821 6368/www.oscar.gr). Metro Larissa Station. **Rates** €60 single; €76 double; €91 triple. **Credit** AmEx, DC, MC, V. **Map** p295 D1.

Don't be put off by the ugly monolithic exterior and rather seedy neighbourhood of the Oscar; it's very close to Larissa Station, from where guests can be whisked to the foot of the Acropolis in ten minutes. 'A luxury you can afford' is how the Oscar describes itself, and while we can't quite muster the enthusiasm to call the Oscar luxurious, its airy, cool

marble and brass lobby with stained-glass ceilings and beautiful pool/rooftop bar with good city views are indeed impressive for a budget hotel. The somewhat uninspired rooms and the two-minute walk through the neighbourhood to the metro station are considerably less so, though.

Hotel services *Bar. Garden. Internet point. Parking (about €10). Restaurant. Swimming pool (outdoor).* **Room services** *Air-conditioning. Internet access: telephone line. Hairdryer. Laundry/dry-cleaning. Minifridge. Room service (6am-midnight). TV: pay movies/satellite.*

Syngrou & Southern suburbs

Deluxe

The Margi

*Litous 11, Vouliagmeni, 16671 (210 896 2061/
fax 210 967 3101/www.themargi.gr). Bus 116, 118.*
Rates €590-€800 single; €610-€800 double; €1,600-
€2,600 suite. **Credit** AmEx, DC, MC, V.
With its stone walls, distressed leather chairs,
antique trunks, randomly placed candles in silver
pots and gauzy linens draped over outdoor arches,
The Margi seems inspired by a Moorish castle. It's
all deliciously atmospheric, though rooms still offer
plenty of mod cons, including internet facilities and,
in upper price brackets, hot tubs. And castle-
dwellers never experienced such lavish American
buffet breakfasts or elegant lounge bars offering
sushi with their cocktails.
Hotel services *Bar. Concierge. Garden.
Internet point. No-smoking rooms. Parking
(free). Restaurant. Swimming pool (outdoor).*
Room services *Air-conditioning. Bathrobe.
Internet access: telephone line/dataport (selected
suites only). Hairdryer. Hi-fi (executive rooms only).
Laundry/dry-cleaning. Mini-bar. Room service
(24hrs). TV: DVD (executive rooms only)/satellite.*

Expensive

Metropolitan Hotel

*Syngrou 385, Faliro, 17564 (210 947 1000/fax
210 947 1110/www.chandris.gr). Bus B2, 126.*
Rates €175 single; €175 double; €225-€285 suite.
Credit AmEx, DC, MC, V.
Yet another hotel upgraded in the countdown to the
Olympics, the 360-room Metropolitan is now one of
the most luxurious in Athens; it is also one of the
more affordable luxury hotels in the city. Standard
double rooms come in pleasant earth tones and
seem slightly small only because they are crowded
with comforts. By contrast the executive rooms and
suites are positively palatial. The hotel has also
addressed its major drawback – accessibility to the
city centre; travellers can now take advantage of
the hotel's free shuttle bus to Syntagma, which
takes about 15 minutes.
Hotel services *Bar. Beauty salon. Business
services. Disabled: adapted room. Garden. Gym.
No-smoking rooms/floor. Parking (free). Restaurant.
Swimming pool (outdoor). TV.*
Room services *Air-conditioning. Dataport
(executive rooms & suites only). Internet access:
telephone line. Hairdryer. Hi-fi (executive rooms
& suites). Laundry/dry-cleaning. Mini-bar. Room
service (24hrs). TV: games/pay movies/satellite.*

Plaza Vouliagmeni Strand Hotel

*Litous 14, Vouliagmeni, 16671 (210 896
0066/fax 210 967 3628/http://agn.hol.gr/
hotels/plaza). Bus 114, 115, 116.* **Rates**
€165 single; €195 double; €225 triple.
Credit AmEx, DC, MC, V.

The Plaza Vouliagmeni describes itself as charming,
and that's truth in advertising as far as this publication is concerned. The hotel's regular clientele is testament to its personal, sincere service and makes it a
standout from other hotels in the area. The decor is
elegant but relaxed, in harmony with the surroundings. Its location on a quiet street bordering a residential area is a short walk from Vouliagmeni's
beaches, a yacht club, and seaside cafés and restaurants, but the hotel's own fine restaurant and casual
roof-garden café also offer great views.
Hotel services *Bar. Business services.
No-smoking rooms. Parking (free). Restaurant.*
Room services *Air-conditioning. Bathrobe.
Internet access: telephone line. Hairdryer.
Laundry/dry-cleaning. Mini-bar. Room service
(7am-midnight). TV: pay movies/satellite.*

Moderate

Palmyra Beach Hotel

*Leof Posidonos 70, Glyfada, 16675 (210 898 1183/
fax 210 898 1186/www.palmyra.gr). Bus A1, A2,
E96.* **Rates** €112 single; €125 double; €150 triple;
€250 suite. **Credit** AmEx, DC, MC, V.
These two value-for-money hotels in the seaside suburb of Glyfada, about 25 minutes away from downtown Athens, are under the same management and
have comparable rooms and identical prices. The
Palmyra is on the coastal side of Posidonos Avenue
and the larger Emmantina, across the road, slightly
closer to the golf course. The name is something of
a misnomer, but there is a large public beach a short
walk from the hotel. Both hotels are near to the main
square of Glyfada, southern Athens' shopping and
dining centre, a kilometre from the popular golf
course and within close proximity to the popular
south coast summer nightlife. Pools at each hotel are
another attraction, as are the free airport transfers.
Hotel services *Bar. Disabled: adapted rooms.
Garden. Internet point. No-smoking rooms. Parking
(free). Restaurant. Swimming pool (outdoor).*
Room services *Air-conditioning. Bathrobe.
Hairdryer. Laundry/dry-cleaning. Room service
(8am-midnight). TV: satellite.*

Northern suburbs

Deluxe

Hotel Pentelikon

*Deliyianni 66, Kifisia, 14562 (210 623 0650/
fax 210 801 0314/www.hotelpentelikon.gr). Bus
A7, B7, 550.* **Rates** €360 single; €440 double;
€560-€1,060 suite. **Credit** AmEx, DC, MC, V.
The height of grand old luxury, the Pentelikon, built
in 1929 and roused again with a 1980s renovation preserving its belle époque style, is less a hotel than a private estate. It is located in a residential neighbourhood
in Kifisia, just a short walk away from Kefalari
Square's cafés and eateries, and is Athens' only gold-
star Michelin-rated hotel. Grand staircases, ballrooms

and carefully kept gardens all preserve an age long gone. Many of Greece's famed politicians, artists and celebrities stayed here during the hotel's '30s heyday, and today a new generation of stars is spotted here. **Hotel services** *Bar. Business services. Concierge. Garden. Internet point. Parking (free). Restaurant. Swimming pool (outdoor).* **Room services** *Air-conditioning. Bathrobe. Internet access: telephone line. Hairdryer. Laundry/dry-cleaning. Mini-bar. Room service (6.30am-2am). TV: satellite.*

Kefalari Suites

Pentelis 1 & Kolokotroni, Kifisia, 14562 (210 623 3333/fax 210 623 3330/www.kefalarisuites.gr). Metro Kifisia. **Rates** €207-€448 single; €207-€448 double. **Credit** AmEx, DC, MC, V.
Until a few decades ago Kifisia was a genteel country escape for Athenians and consisted of aristocratic mansions such as this one. Nowadays Kefalari Suites is part of a square bursting with restaurants and cafés, but a sense of the past is still present in this unique hotel. A suburban haven, each room has a different theme like 'Jaipur', 'Camelot' and 'Africa'. **Hotel services** *Business services. Garden. Internet point. No-smoking rooms/floors. Parking (free). Restaurant. Jacuzzi (outdoor).* **Room services** *Air-conditioning. Bathrobe. Internet access: dataport. Hairdryer. Hi-fi. Kitchenette. Laundry/dry-cleaning. Mini-bar. TV: satellite/VCR (on request).*

Expensive

Hotel Caterina

Mikonou 3, Kefalari, 14562 (210 801 8495/fax 210 801 5218/www.hotelcaterina.com). Bus A7, B7, E92, 550. **Rates** €149 single; €220 double; €265 single suite; €295 double suite. **Credit** AmEx, MC, V.
A lot has changed since the Caterina began as a small, family-run holiday resort for Athenians, but the personal touches remain, though the hotel now attracts a largely business clientele. Returning guests enjoy the four-star service of this hotel, which retains the personality and care of a small country getaway. The attractive rooms are decorated with oriental rugs and dark-wood antique replica furniture, and the small lounge/lobby has the feel of a luxurious rustic inn. Kefalari Square's cafés and eateries are closeby. **Hotel services** *Bar. Business services. Internet point. No-smoking rooms. Parking (free). Restaurant.* **Room services** *Air-conditioning. Internet access: telephone line. Hairdryer. Laundry/dry-cleaning. Mini-bar. Room service (7am-11pm). TV: DVD (on request)/satellite.*

Piraeus

Moderate

Mistral Hotel

Alexandrou Papanastasiou 105, Piraeus, 18533 (210 411 7094/fax 210 412 2096/www.mistral.gr). Trolley 20 from Piraeus. **Rates** €90 single; €115 double; €138 triple. **Credit** AmEx, MC, V.

An oasis in the middle of one of Attica's most polluted and congested areas, the Mikrolimano neighbourhood, has a port lined with a good mix of both ordinary fish tavernas and gourmet restaurants. The Mistral, hovering above, is in the middle of a fashionable residential neighbourhood. Rooms are standard mid-range fare, with subdued blue motifs. A pleasant location for an overnight stay on the way to the islands, and a short distance (but a world away) from the noisy and polluted main port of Piraeus. **Hotel services** *Bar. Business services. Garden. Internet point. Parking (free). Restaurant. Swimming pool (outdoor).* **Room services** *Air-conditioning. Internet access: telephone line. Hairdryer. Laundry/ dry-cleaning. Room service (24hrs). TV: pay movies/satellite*

Attica region

Deluxe

Sofitel Athens Airport

Eleftherios Venizelos International Airport, Spata (210 354 4000/fax 210 354 4444/www.sofitel.com). Bus E92, E93, E94, E95, E96, E97. **Rates** €245 single; €270 double; €444 suite. **Credit** AmEx, DC, MC, V.
Since its opening along with Athens' new international airport, the Sofitel has been collecting compliments. One of the better airport hotels in Europe, the main draw is right next door and literally within easy walking distance. This five-star hotel has plenty of conference spaces in addition to its pleasant rooms. **Hotel services** *Bar. Beauty salon. Business services. Concierge. Disabled: adapted rooms. Gym. No-smoking floors. Parking (€25). Restaurant. Swimming pool (indoor).* **Room services** *Air-conditioning. Bathrobe. Internet access: dataport/ ISDN. Hairdryer. Hi-fi (executive rooms/suites). Laundry/dry-cleaning. Mini-bar. Room service (24hrs). TV: DVD (in suites only)/ games/pay movies/satellite.*

Camping

Athens Camping

Athinon 198, Haidari, 12136 (210 581 4114/ fax 210 582 0353). Bus A15, B15. **Rates** €5/person, €2.50/child under ten. Campers €5.50, caravans €3.50, cars €2.80, small tents €3, large tents €3.50, electricity €3. **Credit** MC, V.
Like most campgrounds, this one is in the middle of nowhere, although technically in Athens. An unattractive campsite, it is nevertheless fairly convenient, and offers a proper restaurant, mini-market for necessities, and laundry facilities on the grounds. It is within walking distance of a neighbourhood with plenty of dining options and provisions. A nearby bus takes campers to Omonia Square in 20-40 minutes. Reservations are recommended. **Hotel services** *Bar. Garden. Laundry (self-service). Parking (prices above). Payphone. Restaurant. TV room.*

Sightseeing

Features

Introduction

Do not be daunted by Athens' vast sprawl – rather enjoy the fact that most sights are within walking distance of the city centre.

THE ACROPOLIS AND AROUND

Most places of interest are in close proximity to the city's heart, soul, most prominent landmark and must-see sight: the **Acropolis**. Below the Acropolis, to the east, is the picturesque, if heavily touristed neighbourhood of **Plaka**, whose pedestrianised winding streets are chock full of ancient ruins, medieval churches, neo-classical museums and vine-covered tavernas.

South of the Acropolis is the green expanse of **Filopappou Hill**, the highest point in southern Athens and a cool, tree- and history-filled retreat from the bustling centre. Below Filopappou are the quiet, working-class districts of **Koukaki** and **Makrygianni**, which are starting to fill up with hip new nightspots and restaurants.

West of the Acropolis is the Agora, ancient Athens' marketplace for over 600 years. The site is flanked to the north by the colourfully grungy neighbourhood of **Monastiraki**, home to the modern city's best flea market, and to the west by once-decrepit, now hiply revitalised **Thisio**.

THE HISTORIC CENTRE

The modern city evolved east of the Acropolis. Within the area known as the **Historic Triangle**, bounded by Mitropoleos (Plaka's northern border), Athinas and Akadimias (the latter running north to join the unlovely Omonia traffic circle (*see below* **North of the Acropolis**) are the main sights of 19th-century, independent Athens. This is also the commercial heart of the city, containing both the colourfully chaotic Central Market and the Stock Exchange. Its most prominent sight is Platia Syntagma (Constitution Square), crowned by the giant yellow Greek Parliament building, guarded by kilted, pom-pom-shoed soldiers. To the south and east of Syntagma are the **National Gardens**.

KOLONAKI AND AROUND

East of the historic centre are two different faces of modern Athens. To the immediate west of Syntagma is **Kolonaki**, full of designer shops, models, embassies, MPs' homes and fabulous, expensive restaurants. And to the northwest is **Exarchia**, Athens' university district, home to student protests, leftist cafés, cheap bookstores and smoky *rembetika* clubs. The two are separated by the steep promontory of Lycabettus Hill.

NORTH OF THE ACROPOLIS

North of Monastiraki is the formerly run-down neighbourhood of **Psyrri**. For centuries, this was a dark, seedy place, populated mostly by craftsmen's workshops and hash dens. But in the late 1990s, galleries, followed rapidly by clubs and restaurants, moved in, and it's now the hottest nightlife neighbourhood in town. West of Psyrri are the neighbourhoods of **Keramikos** and **Gazi**, where new galleries and cafés are springing up among soulful 19th-century ruins.

North of Psyrri is **Omonia Square**, a major roundabout spouting several of Athens' main

Don't miss Athens

● As if we needed to tell you – if you do nothing else, be knocked off your feet at the sight of the most influential monuments in western civilisation at the **Acropolis** (*see p76*).
● Imagine Socrates corrupting the youth and get up close to the Temple of Hephaestus to see the adventures of Theseus and Heracles at the **Ancient Agora** (*see p76*).
● Ponder the sleek, minimalist take on prehistoric goddess cults at the **Goulandris Museum of Cycladic Art** (*see p102*).
● Admire the sumptuous re-creations of Ottoman-era rooms and Byzantine shrines, then splurge at Athens' best gift shop at the **Benaki Museum** (*see p102*).
● Walk in cool green glades and capture picture-perfect Acropolis views from the top of **Filopappou Hill** (*see p76*).
● Get lost among island-style houses and miniature churches in Athens' prettiest neighbourhood, **Anafiotika** (*see p85*).
● Have a sunset drink with a view all the way to Aegina from **Lycabettus Hill** (*see p101*).
● Watch the mini-skirted, pom-pom-shod *evzones* changing guard in front of the **Tomb of the Unknown Soldier** (*see p98*).
● Take in a moonlit performance of absolutely anything at the **Odeon of Herodes Atticus** (*see p76*).

boulevards. In the 19th century, Omonia was a genteel *platia*; today, it's still a central point through which most visitors will pass, but it's degenerated into a dodgy, traffic-clogged meeting point for drug addicts, prostitutes and down-and-out migrants. Most of the area around Omonia also fits that description, though the appearance of a few hip new art spaces and restaurants in nearby **Metaxourgio**, directly to the west of Omonia, hint that it may one day follow the gentrification path of Gazi and Psyrri.

ATHENS SUBURBS

Extending south along the Attic coast are affluent suburbs like **Glyfada** and **Vouliagmeni**, home to some half-decent beaches, glamorous seaside nightclubs and venues for Olympic events including sailing and beach volleyball.

North of central Athens, the suburbs of most interest to visitors include affluent, tree-lined **Kifisia**, filled with some of Athens' finest eateries, along with designer shops and a few small but well-run museums, and the upper-middle-class suburb of **Marousi**. This neighbourhood never drew tourists before the Olympics, but in summer 2004, Marousi will take centre stage: it is the home of the Athens Olympic Sports Complex, the main Olympic stadium, which will host the opening and closing ceremonies and most high-profile finals. After summer 2004, it's expected that it will remain a draw, for its multi-million-dollar architecture by renowned architect Santiago Calatrava, and the landscaped park around it.

PIRAEUS

Athens' sister city and main port has grown so large that it's now pretty much joined up with the capital, but still retains its own character, filled with waterfront tavernas and old *rembetika* dives.

SIGHTSEEING TIPS

Sightseeing in Athens, especially in summer, can be idyllic or hellish – much of which depends on timing. Central Athens at midday in the white-hot sun of midsummer should be avoided at all costs. Do most of your active sightseeing in the morning and evening. Some archaeological sites stay open later than official closing times on summer evenings, while some museums are initiating seasonal late-night hours – up to midnight – one day a week. And there's always the cinema to retreat to for a burst of air-con.

Spend early mornings wandering around and visiting museums. At noon, escape to the shady cafés and tavernas of Plaka for a leisurely outdoor lunch, followed by a visit to one of Athens' few well-air-conditioned museums. The Cycladic and Benaki Museums stay the coolest.

Guided tours

Private companies and travel agents can tailor walks to specific themes or interests, while guides provided by the **Union of Official Guides** can lead you around the archaeological sites of your choice.

Bus tours give a good overview of the best sites, so you can pick where you'd like to go back and spend more time.

Bus tours

The standard package bus tour of Athens lasts about four hours and includes a guided tour of the Acropolis and National Archaeological Museum; it also drives by most other major sites and finishes up with lunch in a Plaka taverna. Reservations can be made through most hotels or any travel agency. The tours run daily, year-round, and cost around €45. Reserve at least one day in advance. CHAT Tours and Key Tours are reputed to have good guides.

CHAT Tours

Stadiou 4, Syntagma (210 322 2886). Metro Syntagma. **Map** p295/p299 F5.
Tours depart from in front of Hotel Amalia (Leof Vas Amalias 10).

Key Tours

Kallirois 4, Southern Suburbs (210 923 3166/ www.keytours.gr). Metro Akropoli. **Map** p299 F7.
Tours depart from the head office, located on a major thoroughfare south of the Temple of Olympian Zeus.

Hop In Sightseeing

210 428 5500/www.hopin.com.
Tours departs at 9am daily from the Panathenaic Stadium (*see p110*) and take most of the major sights of Athens, allowing passengers to get on and off for stops of up to an hour. The ticket is good for 24 hours, so you can come back the next day. It's best to book both in advance. Hop In offers a courtesy pick-up service from or near your hotel.

Walking tours

Amphitrion Holidays

210 924 9701.
Educational and offbeat tours for individuals and small groups in Athens and the mainland.

Athenian Days

210 689 3828.
Custom walking tours of Athens for groups of up to four. Prices range from €50 to €70 per group.

Union of Official Guides

210 322 9705.
Licensed guides for individual or group tours, starting at about €120 for a four-hour tour of the Acropolis and its museum.

The Acropolis & Around

Rock of ages.

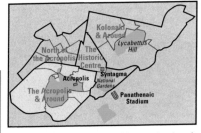

According to both myth and history, the city of Athens was born on the **Acropolis** (*see p77*). With its sweeping views of the landscape and sea, the high, jutting rock is a natural place for protection, administration and religious worship, and it has served these purposes for millennia. It's natural that the area around it, Plaka, is also the longest continually inhabited part of Athens, packed with seemingly endless layers of remains of the civilisations that have lived around the rock. The most impressive of these are from the fifth-century BC classical period, also known as the Golden Age of Athens, when Pericles built the complex of unforgettable temples, including the Parthenon, that now graces the top of the Acropolis. Around its southern base are complete classical structures like the **Theatre of Dionysus** (*see p83*) and the **Lysicrates Monument** (*see p87*), while many houses and restaurants in Plaka have remains of columns and ancient foundations in their basements.

Roman times saw the addition of structures like the **Roman Forum** (*see p87*) and the **Odeon of Herodes Atticus** (*see p83*). The Byzantines filled the area with dozens of frescoed, incense-scented churches. During the Ottoman occupation, Turkish overlords proclaimed their mastery by building mosques (like the one that remains in the Roman Forum) on ancient sites. Relics of Ottoman daily life also appear in the form of structures like Athens' only remaining Turkish bathhouse (*see p88*).

The best way to see all this is with a stroll on the stone-paved Unification of Archaeological Sites walkway, a beautiful, shaded route that runs through all of Athens' most important ancient sites. Its two major branches intersect below the **Areopagus** (*see p83*), where St Paul converted Dionysus, who later became the first bishop of Athens – the roads are named after these two, with Apostolou Pavlou (Apostle Paul) running north to south, and Dionysiou Areopagitou (Dionysus of the Areopagus) running east to west. Until very recently, these streets were congested with traffic. Their transformation to a pedestrian park is one of the few pre-Olympics works that's been universally hailed as a success.

To the north and east of those roads is the charming, if heavily touristed, area of **Plaka** (*see p84*) packed with ancient ruins, neo-classical houses, winding cobblestoned streets and tavernas overhung with bougainvillea.

To the south of the Acropolis is shady **Filopappou Hill** (*see p83*), the highest point in southern Athens and the best place to ramble through for outstanding views of the Acropolis.

On either side of Filopappou are the working-class residential districts of **Makrygianni** and **Koukaki** (*see p88*) to the east and **Petralona** to the west. A mix of cement-block flats and restored neo-classical buildings, these areas lack the instant charm and abundant sightseeing of Plaka, but because of their central location – and Athenians' new-found penchant for making the most of previously overlooked real estate – they are starting to come alive with chic restaurants, edgy modern tavernas and trendy new clubs appearing on their once-quiet old streets.

In the area just north of the Acropolis beats the true heart of classical Athens: the sprawling **Ancient Agora** (*see p90*), the marketplace where citizens and slaves haggled over the price of olive oil, where bureaucrats hammered out the tricky points of the first democracy, and where people like Socrates paced among the stalls asking mind-bending questions. The marble ruins of the Agora constitute the biggest, greenest and, some might say, most fascinating archaeological sites in Athens. On its north boundary is **Monastiraki** (*see p88*) the most colourful and attractive of the surrounding areas. Monastiraki has taken on the Agora's mantle of the marketplace: since Ottoman times, this small but vibrant quarter has been home to Athens' most famous flea market, filled with antiques and junk dealers, clothing and craft stalls, and hippies and migrants laying out their wares on rugs.

At the western boundary of the Agora is **Thisio** (*see p91*) a mix of cafés, galleries and buildings including a renovated 19th-century hat factory and the old royal stables. Thisio underwent a revival when the Unification of Archaeological Sites pedestrian way wound through its two main boundary roads, Apostolou Pavlou and the west end of Ermou. At the time of writing, the branch of Ermou that borders Thisio was being transformed into a walkway, a new aspect for Athens' main shopping thoroughfare. While its eastern end is stacked with high-end department stores, its Monastiraki stretch houses suppliers for the small workshops around the area – one shop sells only rivets, another only scales, another only metal wheels – and other specialist shops (designer coffee supplies, sexy mannequins), before segueing into the once-gritty, soon-to-be pretty and pedestrian western end.

Acropolis & Filopappou Hill

Maps p298, p299

Useful transport: Metro Akropoli, Monastiraki, Thisio.

Acropolis

Dionysiou Areopagitou (210 321 0219/www.culture. gr). Metro Akropoli. **Open** *Apr-Dec* 8am-sunset daily. *Jan-Mar* 8.30am-2.30pm daily. **Admission** €12; €6 concessions. Free to under-18s; free to all Sun Nov-Mar. **No credit cards. Map** p299 D6/E6.
Even jaded Athenians still catch their breath when they lift their eyes to the Acropolis. They're awed by more than sheer beauty: the Acropolis temples represent the greatest achievement of classical Greece, combining mathematical proportion with a glorious aesthetic to create an effect both human and sublime.

The Acropolis was a seat of royalty and religion as far back as the neolithic times. After the 11th century BC, however, everything grew up around Athena (*see p39*). Most of the Acropolis myths are associated with the goddess of wisdom: it was on this rock that she battled Poseidon for control of Attica's greatest city. The god of the sea struck the rock with his trident, and out gushed a spring, his offering to the people. Athena offered the more modest but wiser gift of the olive tree, and the citizens awarded her patronage of the city that still bears her name.

A glass house for the Marbles

Soon after Athens won the 2004 Olympics, Greeks began dreaming of another homecoming. For two decades, Greece has been trying to force Britain to return its most treasured antiquities – the statues of gods and warriors that once adorned the Parthenon, the pinnacle of classical Greek artistic achievement. The seventh Earl of Elgin cut the marbles off the temple in the early 1800s, then carted them back to England and sold them to the British Museum, which has since resolutely refused to return them (*see p16* **Lost marbles**).

The Olympics gave Athens the perfect opportunity to ratchet up the pressure on London: why not build a showcase for the missing marbles, and open it just in time for Greece's moment on the world stage? Ostensibly, the glittering $100-million new Acropolis Museum, now under construction at the foot of the Acropolis, was meant as a much-needed new home for the sculptures currently housed in the small, dusty, on-site museum. But the unveiled plans revealed that its centrepiece would be a top-storey room devoted to the Parthenon Marbles. The design, by Bernard Tschumi, is stunning: the room is to be all glass, with a direct view to the Parthenon, visually reuniting the sculptures and temple for the first time in 200 years. If the British refuse

a return in time for the Olympics, the Greeks will display the few marbles they still own, leaving the rest of the spaces significantly bare – in the hope that the thousands of 2004 visitors will join the wave of demand for the sculptures' return.

And the rest of the museum is nothing to sneeze at: the other Acropolis sculptures will be displayed better than they've ever been, and the space will allow for the display of treasures that have been languishing in storage for years.

Unfortunately, there's a hitch: the museum's construction was delayed by protesters who claim that the project threatens important finds on the new site – the remains of an early Christian village. Museum builders have countered by constructing the museum on stilts, with a glass view down to the site.

But the question looms: will it all be finished by summer 2004? At press time in late 2003, planners are saying there is no way the whole thing can open by then. But builders are working night and day to open at least the Parthenon room to the public, with heavy government pressure. Indeed, out of all the pre-2004 constructions in Athens, no other building bears such a weighty charge: the restoration of Greece's most glorious lost legacy.

The earliest Acropolis temples to Athena date from 650 BC, but it was during the late fifth century BC, known as the Golden Age of Athens, that the general Pericles launched an ambitious programme of works by Greece's greatest artists and architects, resulting in the timeless monuments we see today.

Though the temples' influence may be eternal, their physical state is not. The Acropolis (literally: 'top [of] city') has weathered invasions by the Spartans, Persians, Ottomans and Nazis, but its downfall may come from a more modern foe: the infamous Athenian smog is slowly eroding the marble. A team of international experts has been working for nearly 20 years to restore and protect the monuments, and there's hope that the project may be finished in time for the Olympics. In the meantime, you're bound to see a fair amount of metal swaddling the various structures during your visit, but don't despair: their architectural perfection survives the indignity of scaffolding.

The Acropolis is accessed through the imposing **Propylaeum**. The work of the architect Mnesicles, this gate obscures the view of the Parthenon and so stands alone on the horizon in all its grandeur, creating a theatrical passage from the profane to the sacred. The Propylaeum's north wing, known as the Pinakothiki (art gallery), was decorated with frescoes of scenes from Homer, and filled with recliners where visitors could rest. Construction on the Propylaeum began in 437 BC, but was suspended five years later with the onset of the Peloponnesian Wars, and never completed.

Acropotips

- Hold on to your ticket. It will give you free entry to all the other sites on the Unification of Archaeological Sites walkway for up to a week. The sites are: Acropolis site and museum, Ancient Agora (*see p90*), Theatre of Dionysus (*see p83*), Keramikos (*see p107*), Temple of Olympian Zeus (*see p100*) and Roman Forum (*see p87*).
- When you have your ticket checked, ask for a copy of the free guide to the site (in English). It's packed with info, but ticket-checkers usually don't bother to hand it out.
- Wear comfortable, rubber-soled shoes – the worn stone walkways are slippery and steep.
- Bring your own (large) bottle of water – the on-site vendors overcharge outrageously.
- Go first thing in the morning to avoid the heat and the crowds, or in the early evening to watch the sunset from the temples. After 5pm the colours are fabulous.

Usually, the first thing you'll see on the right after you've passed through the Propylaeum is the tiny, charming **Temple of Athena Nike**, built in 424 BC. There has been a temple to a goddess of victory at that spot since prehistoric times, as it protects the area most vulnerable to attack. At the time of writing, however, the temple had been completely dismantled for restoration; it should be returned in 2004. The originals of its small but exquisite friezes showing battle scenes with Greeks, Persians and gods are displayed in the Acropolis Museum.

The focus of the Acropolis is the **Parthenon**. The temple honours the incarnation of Athena as virgin goddess (Parthenos), and was designed and overseen by the sculptor Phidias in 447 BC-438 BC. Despite its apparent simplicity, the Parthenon is the result of countless advanced calculations. Every measurement used in the construction of the temple is based on the golden mean, a ratio-based geometrical system of proportion that still preoccupies mathematicians today. And to counteract the optical illusion that straight lines viewed from afar seem to bend, its columns bulge slightly, and lean a few degrees inward (if their lines were extended, they would eventually meet). The result of such intricate mathematical wizardry is to create a perfect structure, balanced in every way, that gives the impression of somehow being alive, radiating life.

The Parthenon's decorations were no less marvellous than its structure. The metopes were sculpted with scenes of gods and celebrated mortals, their dynamism and detail surpassing everything the Greeks had created up until then. The pediment sculptures were the most magnificent: the east pediment showed the birth of Athena, springing full-grown from the head of Zeus, and the west pediment showed Athena and Poseidon's battle for the city.

Though many of these sculptures survive, you won't see them in Greece. About two-thirds were removed from the Parthenon in the first decade of the 19th century by the Earl of Elgin, who carted them back to London and sold them to the British Museum, where they've stayed ever since (*see p16* **Lost marbles**). The Greek government has been campaigning passionately but unsuccessfully for their return since the 1980s; their latest gambit was a push for, if not a return, at least a loan of the marbles for the 2004 Olympics.

By the time Elgin came along, the Parthenon was no stranger to vandalism. Another of its original glories, a reportedly breathtaking 12-metre (40-foot) gold and ivory statue of Athena, disappeared after just a few centuries. The Byzantine emperors used the Parthenon as a Christian church, and the Ottomans later used it as a mosque. Under the Ottomans it also served as a gunpowder magazine, and when the Venetians shelled the building in 1687 the powder ignited and blew the roof off.

The simplicity of the Parthenon is contrasted by the fascinating complexity of the **Erechtheum** opposite. It was completed in 406 BC, on the spot where Athena and Poseidon battled for Athens. The

The **Parthenon**: graceful from every angle. *See p78.*

structure unites two separate temples: the east porch once sheltered an olive-wood statue of Athena, while the west porch was devoted to Poseidon. The most famous feature is the south porch, held up by six columns in the shape of voluptuous, drapery-clad maidens. These are known as Caryatids, possibly after the women of Caryae, who were famed for their beauty and served as Athenian slaves. This may have been what inspired Ottoman commanders to convert the temple to a harem during their occupation of the Acropolis; but like the Parthenon, the Erechtheum passed through such indignities unsullied and eternally lovely.

The Caryatids holding up the Erechtheum's porch today are copies; the originals are displayed in the on-site **Acropolis Museum** (free to Acropolis ticket holders). Though it's small and run-down, its holdings make this one of the most important museums in the world. Don't miss the sculptures that adorned the many shrines that rose and fell on the rock over the centuries, or the collection of votive statues and offerings to the gods. At the foot of the Acropolis, there's a glittering new €100-million museum under construction (*see p77* **A glass house for the Marbles**); the contents of the current museum will be moved to the new one upon completion.

Plaka: the old city

This walk wanders through a mix of colourful central streets and into tranquil, flower-filled corners that still seem astonishingly removed from the passage of time. It won't take you more than an hour and a half to do the following route. Sights range from 2,500-year-old ruins to incense-filled churches to modern-day museums. A word on the latter: this walk will take you past five of them, each a small, focused entity offering a slice of modern (read: of the past 500 years) Greek culture. While only the most fervent history buffs need feel obliged to see all five, keep in mind that the excellent displays therein are often overlooked by tourists blinded to all but fallen pillars and muscular *kouroi*, to their own detriment. Remember that most museums close around 2pm.

Start the walk at the Russian Orthodox **Church of the Holy Trinity**. It was built as a small chapel in the 11th century then, 800 years later, sold to the Russian government, which expanded it to its current size. Inside, look at the fine Russian embroideries on display. If you're lucky, you may hear the renowned female chanters practising. Cross the street and turn right on to Kydathinaion. This is a quintessential Athenian moment: the turn takes you suddenly from a modern, traffic-filled artery on to a stone-paved walkway lined with neo-classical mansions, leading straight to the heart of the old city. Head down Kydathinaion and on your right, you'll see the Byzantine **Church of the Transfiguration of the Saviour** (Kydathinaion 10, 210 322 4633), set in a shaded garden, around which neighbourhood men gather to play backgammon. Originally built in the 11th century, the church has been rebuilt and added to many times, and most of the current exterior dates from the 19th and 20th centuries. Opposite the church is the excellent **Museum of Greek Folk Art** (*see p87*), the biggest and most comprehensive of the museums on this walk. Continue down Kydathinaion to pleasant, leafy Platia Filomousou. At some point everyone visiting Greece passes through this shady *platia* lined with cafés, both old-world and modern-day.

At the bottom of the square, turn left on to Farmaki, which will take you to the **Church of St Catherine** (*see p86*). Turn right on to Lysikratous, which leads to the **Lysicrates Monument** (*see p87*). In the 17th century,

the monument was incorporated into a Capuchin monastery where Lord Byron stayed while writing the first canto of *Childe Harold*. The names of the branching streets reflect the celebrity guest: Vyronos (the Hellenised version of Byron) goes off to the south, while to the north Selley recalls Byron's Romantic buddy.

Have a gander round the souvenir shops on Adrianou and then continue on Thespidos, walking by the traditional taverna **Giouvetsakia** (*see p128*), with a history of over 50 years in Plaka. Walking straight along Thespidos will take you up to the base of the Acropolis. Turn right, following the rock to the whitewashed island-style **Church of St George of the Rock**. The church marks the entrance to **Anafiotika** (*see p85*; pictured top), a quirky hidden neighbourhood literally clinging to the side of the Acropolis. The steps carved into the rock at the left of the church will take you straight into Anafiotika's heart. Emerging, you'll likely find yourself on Pritaniou, near Mnisikleous, or Theorias, near Klepsydras. Head downhill on either Mnisikleous or Klepsydras, near the **Roman Forum** (*see p87*).

If you take Klepsydras, make a short detour at your second right on to Thrasvoulou, which will lead you to the **Church of the Holy Sepulchre** (*see p86*). Go back to Mnisikleous, continuing down the stairs. Turn left on to Kyrristou, which will lead you to the square of the Forum.

If you came via Klepsydras, you can head to the east side of the square and turn right on Kyrristou, to check out the recently restored **Turkish Baths** (*see p88*; pictured left). Now take a wander around the **Roman Forum** and the **Tower of the Winds** (*see p87*). On leaving, turn right on to Diogenous; on your left you'll see the **Museum of Greek Musical Instruments** (*see p87*), where you can listen to recordings of regional folk music. You could continue down Diogenous for lunch

under the enormous plane tree at **O Platanos** (*see p129*) before heading back to the Roman Forum on Diogenous.

Turn right at Eolou, then take your first left on Adrianou. On the right, you can look into the ruins of the once-luxurious **Hadrian's Library** (*see p90*). Follow the library to Areos, where you'll turn right, passing multinational street vendors on your way to Monastiraki. In an intriguing visual surprise the ancient library's next-door neighbour is a mosque, which you can go into to see the **Museum of Traditional Greek Ceramics** (*see p91*). From here you can now hop on the metro (at Monastiraki's brand-new station) to head anywhere in town.

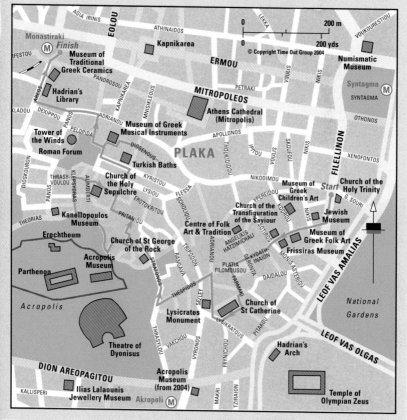

EVERYWHERE
Mythos
Excellent
Mythos
HELLENIC LAGER BEER
Mythos
BEER
ARROW/GRAFIS
MYTHOS LAGER BEER

Areopagus

Outside the entrance to the Acropolis. Metro Akropoli. **Map** p299 D6.

Named after Ares, the god of war, this high, slippery limestone rock began life in officialdom as Ancient Athens' highest court. According to myth, Orestes fled here after murdering his mother, Clytemnestra. Though the Furies had planned to kill him, Athena insisted on a jury trial (Orestes was acquitted), marking a transition from blood feuds to rule of law. Athens' judicial council convened on the same spot from the eighth to the fifth centuries BC. In AD 51, when Saint Paul visited Athens, it was here that he delivered his famous 'Men of Athens' sermon, converting Dionysus (a namesake, not the debauched god himself), who would later become the first bishop of Athens. The speech, immortalised in the Bible (Acts 17:22-34), is carved on a bronze plaque at the bottom of the rock, which is often visited by pilgrims who gather here to pray and sing hymns.

Odeon of Herodes Atticus

Dionysiou Areopagitou, near intersection with Propylaion (210 323 2771/www.culture.gr). Metro Akropoli. **Open** only during performances. **Tickets** vary with performance. **Map** p299 D6.

If the Theatre of Dionysus was the most important venue in classical Athens, this has been its equivalent since Roman times. Built in AD 174 by the wealthy Athenian Herodes Atticus, in memory of his wife, it has marvellous acoustics and a beautiful backdrop with tiers of Roman arches. The theatre is now the venue of the annual Athens Festival (*see p186*), hosting moonlit performances every summer. Many of the performances are of ancient Greek comedies

and tragedies, put on by the world's leading theatre troupes, but artists such as Pavarotti and the Bolshoi Ballet perform here as well. Though you can only enter the Odeon for performances, you can appreciate its architecture and setting from the outside and look down on it from the exit path from the Acropolis.

Theatre of Dionysus

Dionysiou Areopagitou (210 322 4625/www. culture.gr). Metro Akropoli. **Open** *May-Oct* 8.30am-7pm daily. *Nov-Apr* 8am-sunset daily. **Admission** €2; €1 concessions; free to holders of €12 Acropolis ticket. **No credit cards**. **Map** p299 E6.

This spot saw the birth of drama as we know it: it was the site of the sixth-century BC Festival of the Great Dionysia, honouring the god with performances that led to the renowned fifth-century BC drama competitions, with entries such as Sophocles's *Oedipus Rex* and Euripides's *Medea*. In its original state, the theatre sat 15,000. The best seats were reserved for the priests of Dionysus; you can still see the head priest's throne in the centre, carved with satyrs and adorned with lions' paws.

Filopappou Hill

Dionysiou Areopagitou & Apostolou Pavlou (no phone/www.culture.gr). Metro Akropoli or Thisio. **Map** p298 C7/p299 D7.

In antiquity, pine- and cypress-clad Filopappou was known as the Hill of the Muses, and poets thronged its slopes for inspiration. During wartime, generals garrisoned themselves atop it: as the highest point in southern Athens, it has sweeping views out to the sea, not to mention the best view to the Acropolis.

The **Tomb of Filopappus**. *See p84.*

Sightseeing

The 'fishing village' of **Anafiotika**, marooned in central Athens. See p85.

Today, the shady, path-lined hill is an ideal refuge from the parched, smoggy city – it's also covered with interesting, but rarely visited, monuments.

At the foot of the hill is the pretty, gingerbread-like **Church of St Dimitrios Loumbardiaris** (see below) built in 1460. Behind the church is the Tourist Pavilion (210 923 1665), a blissfully quiet, scenic little café offering sweeping views to the Acropolis.

As you start up the south side of the hill, which leads to its peak, you'll see a small cave said to be Socrates's prison, where the philosopher was held after being sentenced to death for corrupting the youth of Athens. One of those corrupted youths, Plato, wrote a version of his mentor's deathbed words in this prison in his *Phaedo*, a seminal work of Western philosophy.

At the peak of the hill is the AD 116 **Tomb of Filopappus**, a Roman senator who loved Athens so much he was made an honorary citizen of the city. This is the spot to whip out your camera and take that postcard-perfect shot of the Acropolis – and look all the way out over Athens to the sea. On the way down the hill, is Athens' **National Observatory**, Greece's oldest functioning research centre. It is housed in a beautiful neo-classical mansion. Further down the hill is a grassy, idyllic spot with some piles of stones and a few foundations. This is all that's left of the **Pnyx**, which could be considered the exact birthplace of democracy: when Athens converted from a rule of one governor to a rule by the people, in 594 BC, the Athenians built a 5,000-seat amphitheatre here, which was where the first voting by, of and for the people, for their own leadership, took place. This was also where great orators such as Demosthenes spoke to the assemblies before votes.

On the west side of the hill, cut into the green slopes, is the **Dora Stratou Dance Theatre** (see p232), which hosts performances of Greek folk dancing.

Church of St Dimitrios Loumbardiaris

Filopappou Hill, off Dionysiou Areopagitou (no phone). Metro Akropoli. **Open** during services. **Admission** free. **Map** p299 D6.

It's said that in 1656 an Ottoman commander garrisoned on the Acropolis planned to attack this church with cannon-fire on the feast-day of St Dimitrios. But the saint intervened: the garrison was struck by lightning, foiling the attack and earning the church its full name, which means 'Dimitrios the Bombardier'. Today, the church's decorations and scenic location make it a popular choice for weddings and baptisms.

Plaka

Maps p295 & p299

Useful transport: Metro Akropoli, Monastiraki, Syntagma.

Starting at the foot of the Acropolis, the old area of Plaka is a maze of narrow, cobblestoned, medieval streets that twist through ancient sites, tourist-packed *platias* and lovely Byzantine courtyards. The best way to explore it is simply to get lost among its enchanting passages. You'll almost certainly spend time on its main thoroughfare, the tourist-shop-packed Adrianou, which is named after the Roman emperor Hadrian and winds up to the library he built in AD 132; and in leafy, café-filled Platia Filomousou. The most beautiful section of Plaka is the tiny village of **Anafiotika** (*see below*), a cluster of Cycladic-island-style houses at the very base of the Acropolis.

In recent years, Plaka has been revitalised, becoming more than just a neighbourhood of old families with tourists walking through – the Greek Culture Ministry, along with several private arts and real-estate firms, has been buying up its old houses, restoring them to their former glory and transforming them into worthy new arts venues. Some of the best of these are the **Frissiras Museum** (*see p86*) and the **Museum of Greek Children's Art** (*see p87*).

Anafiotika

Bounded by Stratonos, Pritaniou & Alimberti. Metro Akropoli or Monastiraki. **Map** p299 E6.

This tiny district at the foot of the Acropolis is one of the most beautiful and quirky hidden spots in all of Athens. It was built in the 19th century by trades-men from the Cycladic island of Anafi, brought to Athens after the Greek War of Independence to build the king's palace. They missed home so much they re-created a pocket of it here, all dome-topped blue-and-white houses, covered with banks of bougain-villea, in a winding maze of passages. Walk quietly through the area: it's still very much occupied, in many cases by descendants of the original Anafiotes.

Athens Cathedral

Platia Mitropoleos (210 322 1308). Metro Monastiraki. **Open** 7.30am-7.45pm daily. *Mass* 6.30am Sun. **Admission** free. **Map** p299 E5/F5.
The enormous, lavishly appointed Athens Cathedral, known as Mitropolis, is one of Athens' best-known landmarks. It is the seat of the Greek Orthodox arch-bishop (often cited as the nation's most influential person) and is regularly packed when thousands of

You and me babe, how about it?

'England? Germany? France?' No, it's not roll call at the EU; it's the mating call of an indigenous species known as *kamaki*, the Greek male whose proud primary occupation is seducing foreign women. The term translates literally as 'spearfisher', a brilliantly illustrative metaphor requiring no further explanation. In Athens, the densest *kamaki* habitats are in tourist-filled Plaka and Syntagma, where the fishers can pick and choose among the choicest prey: the hundreds of blonde, long-legged northern Europeans getting lost on their way to the Acropolis, clearly in need of guidance around the city by its most charming and heavily hair-gelled residents.

Subtlety is not part of the game: once he's zeroed in on his choice, the ardent suitor will follow her for blocks, calling out guesses on her nationality, invitations to coffee and glowing assessments of her beauty.

But *kamaki* are more than just gigolos: in the 1980s, there was talk of the *kamaki* forming a union to be subsidised by the Tourist Board – after all, they argued, they were as much of a tourist draw as Greece's temples and beaches, and the sex-starved women whose vacations they brightened were pouring money into the economy with every overpriced cocktail they paid for.

The good news about *kamaki* is that while their street come-ons are aggressive, that's usually where it stays: Greece has a very low rate of rape or sex crimes. But crack a single

smile in response to his come-ons, and the *kamaki* will inevitably assume an invitation that may be very tough to wriggle out of.

One of the simplest ways to avoid the *kamaki*'s embrace is to wear a wedding ring. For added impact, tell your eager friend that your husband is Greek – he'll respectfully back away from a fellow countryman's property. You can also just shake your head and say (repeatedly), 'Sorry, not interested', or be culturally correct and attempt a brush-off in his own language: *Ase me, re!* (Leave me alone, buddy!). Of course, if you do fancy yourself a Shirley Valentine in search of some hot Mediterranean love, lord knows you've come to the right place.

A few things to keep in mind before running off with a handsome young Kostas or Stavros: expect that you'll probably pay for whatever meals or drinks precede your seduction; most *kamaki* lack gainful employment. Don't expect scintillating conversation. While most *kamaki* have mastered a few key phrases in the language of their conquests ('Such beautiful breasts!'), they'll expect to spend the majority of their time with you communicating in the international language of love. And most importantly, provide your own protection: surveys show that the preferred birth control method of Greek men is still withdrawal, and you might find that he's made it all the way to your hotel room, full of expectations, but without a single condom.

Traffic? What traffic? Newly pedestrianised **Apostolou Pavlou**. *See p76.*

Greek grandmothers turn out to kiss touring holy relics, or when Athens' high society comes for weddings and baptisms. Though the colourful frescoes and ecclesiastical objects are impressive, the building's architecture is fairly standard. Of far greater artistic importance is the tiny Panaghia Gorgoepikoos (also known as 'Mikri Mitropolis', or Little Cathedral) next door. It was built in the 12th century, on the ruins of an ancient temple devoted to the goddess of childbirth, Eileithyia. What makes it unique are its building materials: its walls are built entirely of Roman and Byzantine marble relics, sculpted with reliefs depicting the ancient calendar of feasts.

Centre of Folk Art & Tradition
Angelikis Hadzimichalis 6 (210 324 3972). Metro Akropoli. **Open** 9am-1pm, 5-9pm Tue-Fri; 9am-1pm Sat, Sun. **Admission** free. **Map** p299 F6.
The rooms in the family mansion of folklorist Angeliki Hadzimichali have been set up to depict the traditional Greek way of life, with house wares, ceramics and kitchen utensils from the 19th century. Museum exhibits include hand-woven costumes, embroideries and family portraits.

Church of the Holy Sepulchre
Thrasyvoulou (210 323 5810). Metro Syntagma or Monastiraki. **Open** by appointment. **Admission** free. **Map** p295 E5/p299 E5.
According to legend, this lovely church was built in the eighth century by the Byzantine empress Irene, an Athenian orphan. During the Turkish

occupation, the church's well was a hiding place for dissidents. The pretty, shady courtyard is filled with ancient bits of marble, and is a tranquil place to sit.

Church of the Holy Trinity
Filellinon 21 (210 323 1090). Metro Syntagma. **Open** Sun mornings and during choir rehearsals. **Admission** free. **Map** p295 F5.
Built in the 11th century, this church had some of its outer walls pulled down by the brutal Turk Ali Haseki in 1780, to help build fortifying walls around Athens. In later years, the church (also known as Agios Nikodimos) was sold to the Russian Orthodox Church, and in 1852 Tsar Alexander II had it restored with a new terracotta frieze and bell tower. Today it is still the stronghold of Russian Orthodoxy in Greece, and contains displays of ornate Russian embroidery. The church is famed for its chanters; stop by during Sunday services to hear them.

Church of St Catherine
Galanou & Goura (210 322 8974). Metro Akropoli. **Open** *May-Oct* 8am-noon, 5-7pm Mon-Fri; 7am-12.30pm, 5-10pm Sat, Sun. *Nov-Apr* 7.30am-12.30pm, 5-6.30pm Mon-Fri; 7am-12.30pm, 5-10pm Sat, Sun. **Admission** free. **Map** p299 F6.
This 12th-century church is built over the ruins of an ancient temple, possibly dedicated to Hestia, goddess of civic harmony, and some of those columns still stand at the base of the courtyard. Its many colourful frescoes have been restored well, and its choir is reputed to be one of the best in the city.

Frissiras Museum
Monis Asteriou 3 & 7 (210 323 4678/ www.frissirasmuseum.com). Metro Syntagma or Akropoli. **Open** 11am-7pm Wed, Thur; 11am-5pm Fri-Sun. *Guided tours* 12.30pm Sat, Sun. **Admission** €6; €3 concessions. **No credit cards. Map** p299 F6.
A stylish new addition to Athens' cluster of small museums, this collection of contemporary European paintings is fresh and eclectic, but all the pieces are linked by the same theme: the human form. The rotating display is housed in two beautifully restored neo-classical homes. In the three years since it opened, the Frissiras has already gained a name for spotting top new Greek and international talent.

Jewish Museum
Nikis 39 (210 322 5582/www.jewishmuseum.gr). Metro Syntagma. **Open** 9am-2.30pm Mon-Fri; 10am-2pm Sun. **Admission** €3; €1 concessions. **No credit cards. Map** p299 F6.
Archaeological digs have unearthed a synagogue in the Ancient Agora, which lends evidence to the existence of a Jewish community in Greece as far back as the fifth century BC. Some 87 per cent of the Jewish population of Greece was killed during the Holocaust, one of the highest percentages in Europe. This well-run museum has excellent displays documenting the history of the Jewish community in Greece, including engravings, religious and historical artefacts, intricate carvings and works of art, and written records dating back 2,300 years.

Kanellopoulos Museum

Panos & Theorias 12 (210 321 2313/
www.culture.gr). Metro Monastiraki.
Open 8.30am-3pm Tue-Sun. **Admission** €2;
€1 concessions. **No credit cards. Map** p299 E6.
Housed in a mansion in a pretty neighbourhood on
the slopes of the Acropolis, this small museum has
a fine collection of Greek art from the third century
BC to the 19th century. There's a beautiful display
of Byzantine jewellery with gorgeously worked
lapis, as well as a strong collection of icons, chalices
and other early Christian artefacts. Unfortunately,
despite the high quality of the items on show, the
layouts, displays and information about the works
leave much to be desired.

Lysicrates Monument

Platia Lysikratous (no phone/www.culture.gr).
Metro Akropoli. **Map** p299 F6.
Each year, winners of the Dionysian drama festival
(who included Aristophanes, Sophocles and
Euripides) were awarded a decorative tripod – the
ancient equivalent of an Oscar. In 335 BC, Lysicrates,
the producer of the winning play, built this marble
public display for his prize – ostentatious, perhaps,
but unbeatable PR. Six Corinthian columns are
arranged around a circular base, carved with
Dionysian emblems. In the 17th century, the monument was incorporated into a Capuchin monastery,
the foundations of which could be seen until recently
in a pleasantly overgrown green space around the
monument. However, in the summer of 2003, the
whole area was paved over with gravel, an aesthetically unfortunate move that has caused the area to
be dubbed 'a giant litterbox'.

Museum of Greek Children's Art

Kodrou 9 (210 331 2621/www.childrensart
museum.gr). Metro Syntagma. **Open** 10am-2pm Tue-
Sat; 11am-2pm Sun. Closed Aug. **Admission** €2;
free to under-18s. **No credit cards. Map** p299 F6.
Remember the scene in *Six Degrees of Separation*
when art dealer Donald Sutherland walks into a
classroom hung with children's paintings, and is
struck by how the five-year-olds paint like Matisse?
That's what it feels like when you enter this sunny
exhibition space, one of only two museums of this
kind in the world. Children's paintings are displayed
with the same dignity given the work of great
artists: the result is vivid, colourful, thought-
provoking and surprising. There are also daily
workshops and programmes for children.

Museum of Greek Folk Art

Kydathinaion 17 (210 322 9031/www.culture.gr).
Metro Syntagma. **Open** 10am-2pm Tue-Sun.
Admission €2. **No credit cards. Map** p299 F6.
The dimly lit, government-run building won't win
any prizes, but inside are five floors packed with
rich, beautiful folk art, including swoon-worthy
filigreed jewellery, fine embroideries worked with
gold and silver, and highly skilled stone and wood
carvings. Don't miss the room of wall paintings by
primitivist painter Theophilos Hadzimichali, transported intact from his home on the island of Lesbos.
Limited information in English, unfortunately.

Museum of Greek Musical Instruments

Diogenous 1-3 (210 325 0198/www.culture.gr). Metro
Monastiraki. **Open** 10am-2pm Tue, Thur-Sun; noon-
6pm Wed. **Admission** free. **Map** p295 E5/p299 E5.
There's a lot more to Greek music than the bouzouki
that plucked out the theme to *Zorba the Greek*. The
displays in this unassuming but fascinating little
museum trace how Asian, Middle Eastern and
European influences filtered through the Hellenic
sensibility to create instruments such as Byzantine
lutes, the sitar-like *santouri* and the *gaida* (a Balkan
take on the bagpipes). The instruments themselves
are beautiful, intricately carved with precious met-
als, ivory and tortoiseshell; the displays are accompanied by headphones playing recordings.

Roman Forum & Tower of the Winds

Eolou & Pelopida (210 324 5220/www.culture.gr).
Metro Monastiraki. **Open** 8am-7.15pm daily.
Admission €2; €1 concessions; free to holders
of €12 Acropolis ticket. **No credit cards.**
Map p295 E5/p299 E5.

One for the nosy: **Museum of Greek Folk Art.**

This is one of Athens' most interestingly layered sites. Its earliest and most striking feature is the marvellous eight-sided Tower of the Winds, built in 50 BC by Syrian astronomer Andronikos Kyrrhestas. The combination sundial, weathervane and water clock was unlike any other building in the ancient world.

A century later, the Romans shifted Athens' central marketplace from the sprawling Ancient Agora (*see p90*), building a smaller, more orderly one around the Tower. The Ottomans made their mark by building a mosque on the same site. In the 20th century, archaeologists used the Forum as a repository for unclassifiable small finds from all over Attica, which explains the presence of the odd Byzantine grave marker or garlanded sarcophagus.

Turkish Baths

Kyrristou 8 (210 324 4340). Metro Monastiraki.
Open 10am-2pm Wed, Sun. **Admission** free.
Map p295 E5/p299 E5.

Under Turkish rule, every Athenian neighbourhood had one of these public baths, used not only for steams and scrubs, but also as essential social meeting places. After Greece won independence, all Turkish baths in the city were destroyed except for this one, which has recently been renovated and reopened to the public. You can't actually bathe, but you can walk around the rooms and picture the languor of a lost era. Imagine being massaged on the marble slabs, dappled with light coming in through the pattern cut in the high domes, with scantily clad attendants fetching tea and scented oils.

Koukaki & Makrygianni

Maps p298 & p299

Useful transport: Metro Akropoli, Syngrou-Fix.

South of the Acropolis, opposite the Theatre of Dionysus, is Makrygianni, a residential district named after the Greek War of Independence hero General Yiannis Makrigiannis, whose name translates as 'John Long John'. There's a kilt-and-pointy-shoes-clad bronze statue of Makrigiannis just across from the neighbourhood's entrance, at the corner of Dionysiou Areopagitou and Vyronos. On the opposite corner is one of the most controversial spaces in Athens, the site for the New Acropolis Museum (*see p77* **A glass house for the Marbles**). It's also the site of the Acropolis Study Centre, originally built in 1834 as a barracks for the Greek royal police.

Further south, Makrygianni segues into Koukaki. There is little in the way of sightseeing in these neighbourhoods, which are modest but pleasant to wander in, but they do have several small, cosy tavernas and bars, and are starting to see a few trendier, chicer nightspots and well-run little hotels as well, as developers take advantage of the excellent location near the Acropolis.

Ilias Lalaounis Jewellery Museum

Karyatidon & Kallisperi 12, Makrygianni (210 922 1044/www.addgr.com/jewel/lalaouni). Metro Akropoli. **Open** 9am-4pm Mon, Thur-Sat; 9am-9pm Wed; 11am-4pm Sun. **Admission** €3; €2.30 concessions. Free to all 3-9pm Wed, 9-11am Sat. **No credit cards** (AmEx, MC, V accepted in shop). **Map** p299 E7.

Ilias Lalaounis is the only jeweller ever admitted to the French Academie des Beaux Arts. This claims to be a museum of the history of Greek jewellery, but really it's a fancy showcase for Lalaounis's interpretations of everything, from Hellenistic chokers to sexy Mycenaean body jewellery reconceived with modish 1960s influences. You can buy Lalaounis originals at the on-site boutique and take a look at the workshop, which claims to reproduce ancient designs using original techniques.

Monastiraki

Maps p295 & p299

Useful transport: Metro Monastiraki, Thisio.

Monastiraki takes its name from the tiny church that stands in its recently renovated main square, at the intersection of Ermou and Athinas. The church was originally built in the tenth century, and later destroyed. The one you see today was built in 1678, as part of a large, wealthy convent, whose buildings, over the next 200 years, spread all around the surrounding areas, up to what is now the Central Market (*see p97*). Most of the buildings were destroyed in the late 19th century during archaeological excavations and railway construction. All that remained was this tiny church, known as 'little Monastery' – in Greek, Monastiraki.

Platia Monastiraki provides one of the best vantage points to the layers of history that shaped Athens. Approaching the square from Ermou or Athinas, you see the Byzantine church in the foreground and, just beyond it, an 18th-century mosque, one of the most distinctive reminders of the Ottoman occupation (today the mosque is the **Museum of Traditional Greek Ceramics**; *see p91*). The classical temples of the Acropolis, rising above, give perspective to it all, even the modern traffic-clogged intersection in which you have to stand to get the best view.

Aside from the church, Monastiraki's main draw are its markets – both ancient and present-day. The beautiful (and recently pedestrianised and prettified) street of Adrianou runs along the edge of one of most important sights in the classical world: the **Ancient Agora** (*see p90*), for centuries the lively marketplace of Athens, where commerce, democracy and philosophy flourished all together. Though the Agora is a hallowed site

The **Hephaestum**. *See p91.*

rather than a lively marketplace today, its spirit lives on in the neighbourhood: on the north side of Adrianou is the Monastiraki Flea Market (*see below*), a bazaar that has flourished since Ottoman times. The market is centred on Platia Avyssinias and Ifestou, which, on Sunday mornings, are packed with barking peddlers from all over the Mediterranean.

Ancient Agora

Entrances on Adrianou and on the descent from the Acropolis, Monastiraki (210 321 0185/www. culture.gr). Metro Monastiraki or Thisio. **Open** *May-Oct* 8am-7pm daily. *Nov-Apr* 8am-5pm daily. Museum closes 30mins before site. **Admission** €4; €2 concessions; free to holders of €12 Acropolis ticket. **No credit cards. Map** p299 D5.

If you find the sprawling site confusing to navigate, that's partly because the market, founded in the sixth century BC, was the city centre for 1,200 years, witnessing the rise and fall of layers of overlapping *stoas* (colonnades fronting the market), temples and government buildings. But it's mainly because the market was far more than a place to shop: it was the centre of all public life, including arts, politics, commerce and religion. A typical Athenian, for whom participation in public life was as essential as breathing, would spend all day here: listening to the likes of Socrates, Demosthenes or Saint Paul hold forth among the oil and spice stalls, checking in at the circular *tholos*, where a council of 50 administrators were available 24 hours a day, and lighting a candle at the shrine to Hephaestus, which overlooked the whole scene. The latter is still the best-preserved classical-era temple in Greece – get up close and look at the friezes, which depict the adventures of Theseus and Heracles. The restored **Stoa of Attalos**, which functioned rather like an ancient shopping mall, today houses the excellent **Agora Museum**, focusing on artefacts connected to the incipient democracy.

Hadrian's Library

Dexippou & Areos, Monastiraki (www.culture.gr). Metro Monastiraki. **Map** p299 E5.

The Roman emperor Hadrian built this luxurious library in AD 132. Most of the space was a marble courtyard, with gardens and a pool. There were also lecture rooms, music rooms, a theatre and a small space for storing scrolls. Though the site is closed to the public, you can easily see the remaining Corinthian columns from the street.

Monastiraki Flea Market

Monastiraki (no phone). Metro Monastiraki. **Open** 8.30am-3pm Sun. **Map** 295 D5.

Platia Avyssinias comes alive Sunday mornings when Athens' best flea market fills the space and spills out on to the streets around it. Here's where you'll find everything you didn't know you needed: pink cut-glass Turkish liquor sets, 100-year-old telephones, antique carved-wood desks, gold-framed maps of the Balkans and Russian nesting dolls. Bring your haggling skills. For a guided walk around the area, *see p178* **Sunday morning in Monastiraki**.

Treasures of the **Ancient Agora Museum**.

Monastiraki: one big, pleasurable hussle. *See p89.*

Museum of Traditional Greek Ceramics

*Areos 1, Monastiraki (210 324 2066/www.
culture.gr). Metro Monastiraki.* **Open** *Sept-June*
9am-2.30pm Mon, Wed-Sun. *July-Aug hours vary.*
Admission €2. **No credit cards. Map** p299 E5.
Built in 1789 by the city's Turkish governor, this is
the only Ottoman-era mosque in Athens still open to
the public. After the fall of the Ottomans, the Greeks
stripped the mosque of its minaret and turned it into
a military barracks and then a jail. In 1918, it was
turned into a government-run museum of ceramic art,
against the wishes of many Greeks who would have
preferred to see all remnants of the hated occupants
destroyed. The collection here is small and limited
mostly to pieces from the second half of the 20th century – though many are beautiful, the main appeal
of the museum is just being in Athens' only mosque,
in the heart of what was the old Turkish bazaar.

Thisio

Maps p294 & p298

Useful transport: Metro Thisio, Monastiraki.

Thisio, the small but lively quarter west of the
Ancient Agora, takes its name from the best-
preserved classical-era temple in Greece. Though
the shrine was built to the god Hephaestus and
is formally known as the Hephaestum, among
its most notable features are the reliefs of
Athenian hero and king Theseus carved on
its metopes. It informally became known as
the Theseion (Temple of Theseus), lending
its name to the surrounding neighbourhood.

Until recently, Thisio was just a grubby, low-
rent neighbourhood at the far western end of
Ermou. But with the infusion of several new
art galleries, the renovation of old buildings
into cultural spaces, high-end restaurants and
trendy outdoor cafés, plus the addition of pretty,
paved walkways linking up the area with the
rest of Ancient Athens' major sites, suddenly
Thisio is hopping every night. The places to see
and be seen are around the newly landscaped
metro station, where all the pretty young things
hang out waiting for their dates; on Iraklidon
(named after Heracles, Theseus's companion
in those temple carvings); and quiet, tree-lined
Eptachalkou, home to cutting-edge galleries,
home-style *ouzeries* and a few small churches.

Melina Mercouri Cultural Centre

*Iraklidon 66 & Thessalonikis, Thisio (210 345
2150). Metro Thisio.* **Open** 9am-1pm, 5-9pm Tue-
Sat; 9am-1pm Sun. **Admission** free. **Map** p298 B5.
This former hat factory has undergone an industrial-
to-arts space transformation. The conversion kept
the original stone walls and airy spaces, but feels
like a fresh, modern venue for art exhibitions, which
pass through regularly. It does have one permanent
display: a well-executed re-creation of a 19th-century
Athenian street, with meticulously put-together shop
windows full of authentic paraphernalia like shoes,
food tins, rolling papers; a 'pharmacy' where the
chemist weighs out drugs on antique scales; and, of
course, a *kafenion*, with wrought-iron chairs, little
cups on marble tables and overflowing ashtrays.

Church of St Marina

*North-east edge of Filopappou Hill, Thisio (210 346
3783). Metro Thisio.* **Open** during services.
Admission free. **Map** p299 D7.
This cheerful church honours the protectress of
pregnant mothers and infants. St Marina's many
domes are higher and narrower than those of most
Orthodox churches, giving it a sprightly, buoyant
feel – definitely enhanced by the red-and-white-
peppermint striped façade. This is one of the most
popular churches in Athens, hosting a week-long
festival to the saint every July.

The Historic Centre

Grandiose neo-classical buildings, churches and the odd ancient ruin jostle for attention in the cradle of modern Athens.

The Historic Triangle

Maps p295 & p297

Useful transport: Metro Monastiraki, Omonia, Panepistimio and Syntagma.

The gritty, throbbing heart of modern Athens – the area between the triangle of boulevards formed by Akadimias, Mitropoleos and Athinas – was, until recently (by the standards of Athenian history, that is), little more than flowery meadowlands. Throughout ancient, Byzantine and Ottoman Athens, the commercial and cultural centre of the city remained based in the area around the Acropolis and Ancient Agora. The Themistoclean Wall, built in the fifth century BC, delineated the furthest edges of the city at the time – though today it runs through the part of town most packed with rushing Athenians. Yet a 19th-century letter about the **Hotel Grande Bretagne** (*see p56*), set smack in the middle of Syntagma, notes that guests were kept awake at night – not by traffic, but by the hooting of owls in the trees.

All that began to change after 1832, the year Greece wrestled its independence from the Ottoman Empire. The new country's first statesmen set out to build a neo-classical-style 19th-century capital, fusing their own neglected past with the ideals of contemporary Europe. They imported a Bavarian king, Otto, who brought along a host of northern European architects and planners. On the fresh, untouched ground outside the ancient capital, they laid out an orderly central triangle of boulevards: Ermou, Athinas and Panepistimiou. These are connected by three major squares: Omonia, Monastiraki and Syntagma. This area was filled with all the grand buildings

necessary for a new capital, buildings whose designs combined the sculptural lines of classical temples and the fanciful decorations of the architects' homelands.

Kick-start your neo-classical Athens experience in Akadimias, where the **Cultural Centre of Athens** (*see p93*) houses a fascinating and comprehensive collection of theatrical mementos, then head further west, to Panepistimiou, home to the **Neo-Classical University Complex** (*see p95*) and what is now the **Numismatic Museum** (*see p98*). The latter was originally Heinrich Schliemann's house, designed by fellow German philhellene Ernst Ziller (responsible for many of Athens' finest neo-classical buildings).

A couple of streets over, on Stadiou, is Greece's first modern Parliament building, today the **National Historical Museum** (*see p94*). At the intersection of Ermou and Stadiou, a grand new square (Syntagma) and a vast palace were built for the new king. The royal palace is now known as the **Parliament Building** (*see p98*). A short walk up Stadiou leads to **Platia Klafthmonos** (*see p98*), a famous gathering point for politicians, who would come here to commiserate on electoral defeats; on the square, the **City of Athens Museum** (*see p93*) was the first house built in Athens after the city was declared capital of the Hellenic Monarchy in 1834.

Commercial needs were also addressed. For centuries, Athenian merchants had plied their wares in the Ancient Agora; in 1870, the **Central Market** (*see p97*) was built on Athinas and since then has remained the capital's most vital and vibrant marketplace. Through the 19th and 20th centuries the historic triangle filled with shops and restaurants, old-time *rembetatika*, modern banks, shops and traffic of every kind.

But this area is no bastion of crisp modernity, by any stretch of the imagination. As with all of Athens, there are still many, many layers: dotted throughout the centre are some of Athens' oldest, smallest and most fascinating Byzantine churches, including **Church of the Saints Theodore** (*see p93*) and **Kapnikarea** (*see p94*). Almost all of them are still in use. And ancient Athens still makes an appearance, whether in the remains of the **Themistoclean**

Wall (sometimes surprisingly preserved, like the section in the foundations of the National Bank of Greece, on Eolou), or in the little sixth-century **Church of St John of the Column** (*see below*), which is actually built around an ancient Corinthian pillar.

In this part of town, monuments of exquisite beauty rub shoulders with soot-coated 1970s flats. Once-graceful neo-classical mansions now crumble into traffic-congested streets. But keep in mind that these contrasts may show you more of the true character of Athens than gazing at a thousand pillars.

Central Market
See p97.

Church of the Saints Theodore
Aristidou & Evripidou (no phone/www.culture.gr). Metro Panepistimio. **Open** generally mid morning-mid evening daily. **Admission** free. Map p295 E4. This tiny 11th-century church is one of Athens' oldest remaining Byzantine monuments. Many of the frescoes have been damaged by smoke and age, but towards the front and right there's a nice fresco of Saints Jacob, Thomas and Simon, with beautiful floral detailing beneath.

Church of St John of the Column
Evripidou 72 (no phone). Metro Omonia. **Open** generally mid morning-early evening daily. **Admission** free. Map p295 E4. Locally known as Agios Ioannis Kolonastis, this quirky little church is located at the intersection of Omonia's migrant community, Evripidou's spice market and Psyrri's gritty old workshops and edgy

new nightlife. This tiny chapel, dating from about the sixth century, was built around an ancient Corinthian column – possibly a remnant from an earlier temple to Apollo – which protrudes incongruously from the roof.

City of Athens Museum
Paparigopoulou 7, Platia Klafthmonos (210 324 6164). Metro Panepistimio. **Open** 10am-2pm Mon, Wed-Sat. **Admission** €5; €3 concessions. **No credit cards.** Map p295 F4. Otto, the first monarch – a teenager brought over from Bavaria – lived here while waiting for construction on the monarchy's first palace (now the Parliament) to finish. Most of the museum consists of re-creations of the rooms as Otto and his bride Amalia lived in them (much pink and gilt rococo – perhaps to remind them of home), including a throne room. There's also a collection of paintings of Athens when it was little more than a village and a fascinating model of the town as it was in 1842.

Cultural Centre of Athens
Akadimias 50 (210 362 1601/www.culture.gr). Metro Panepistimio. **Open** *Theatre Museum* 9am-2pm, 5-9pm Mon-Fri. **Admission** free. Map p295 F3. The pretty Cultural Centre is fronted by several statues of Greek notables, but everyone only looks at one sculpture: the woman whose robe seems to magically evaporate around her gravity-defying breasts is the famous Greek actress Kiveli, second wife of former Prime Minister George Papandreou. Inside the centre, there's a Theatre Museum with exhibits on the ancient Greek stage and lots of memorabilia from the likes of Melina Mercouri and Maria Callas,

Local hero Lord Byron is commemorated in marble. *See p100:* **Hadrian's Arch.**

Zappeion: a stately stroll

This three-hour route, taking you through lush greenery and past some handsome historical sites, makes for a pleasant and romantic afternoon walk.

It is impossible to rush a stroll through the **National Gardens** (see p100). Enter the grounds next to the Parliament Building on Leof Vas Amalias and lose yourself in a refreshing setting of towering palm trees, pines and cypresses, scattered with little bridges over brooks and shaded corners. At your exit, on the east side, a café with an ivy-covered terrace serves rather rough and ready fare but is a nice shady place to have a rest. Emerging from the park on to the immaculate Irodou Attikou – one of the most heavily policed streets in Athens thanks to its high-ranking residents – is an abrupt reality check.

Directly opposite the exit, on the right, are the **Maximou Mansion**, the prime minister's official residence, and the **Presidential Palace** – both neo-classical structures. The latter – home to Greece's kings until Constantine left the scene in 1967 – is guarded by Evzones who march solemnly towards each other at regular intervals.

At the end of Irodou Attikou, turn right on to Leof Vas Konstantinou, then continue on to Leof Vas Olgas and around 200 metres (220 yards) on you will see the elegant **Zappeion Exhibition Hall** on your right. Next door, the famed **Aigli Bistro Café** is a favourite haunt of politicians and artists, as well as of rich young things, as is reflected in its prices.

Strolling away from Zappeion and across the busy Ardittou will bring you to the marble **Panathenaic Stadium** (also known as Kallimarmaro; see p100) – a 19th-century reconstruction of the ancient Olympic Stadium and the site of the first modern-day Olympics

in 1896 and the Opening Ceremony for Athens 2004 – next to the pine-covered Ardittou Hill. Following Ardittou uphill will take you to the neighbourhood of **Mets**, one of the few central Athenian districts to have preserved some of its traditional flavour.

From Leof Vas Konstantinou, a left turn on to Nikiforou Theotokou will give you a taste of the neighbourhood – rows of pre-1940s houses with tiled roofs and flower-covered balconies on ascending levels of an uphill slope, connected by little staircases. Alternatively, turn right on to Markou Mousourou, and head towards **Pangrati** – another picturesque residential district.

The **Açai** bar (Markou Mousourou 1, 210 923 7109), on the corner of Markou Mousourou and Ardittou, has a roof garden with a sweeping view encompassing the Acropolis and Lycabettus Theatre. A short stroll along Markou Mousourou and a left turn takes you on to Archimidous – the mezedopolio **Xanthippe** (Archimidous 14, 210 756 0514) is great for dinner.

Going back down along Markou Mousourou you will come to Trivonianou on your left, which leads you to the striking Bauhaus-style entrance of Athens' **First National Cemetery** (see p110). This graveyard is a veritable museum, housing the works of Ianoulis Halepas, the famous belle époque sculptor from the Aegean island of Tinos, whose masterpiece I Koimomeni ('Sleeping Girl') is around 300 metres (330 yards) in on the right.

Leaving the cemetery, head down Anapafseos (directly opposite the cemetery gates) until you emerge on to a busy junction where you will see the **Temple of Olympian Zeus** (see p100) – the largest temple ever constructed in Greece, which now retains only

and a gallery that shows new works by Greek artists. At the back of the centre, you can join Athens' students and intellectuals for a spot of people-watching at its popular café.

Kapnikarea

Kapnikarea & Ermou (210 322 4462). Metro Monastiraki or Syntagma. **Open** 8am-2pm Mon, Wed, Sat; 8am-12.30pm, 5-7.30pm Tue, Thur, Fri; 8-11.30am Sun. **Admission** free. **Map** p295 E5.
The beautiful 11th-century church of Kapnikarea appears suddenly and felicitously, smack in the middle of the bustling shopping strip of Ermou. The church, dedicated to the Virgin Mary, was built over the ruins of an ancient temple dedicated to a

goddess, possibly Athena or Demeter. It is laid out in the typical Byzantine cross-in-square plan, with three apses on the east side and a narthex on the west. Inside, it is decorated with a mix of medieval mosaics and paintings by renowned 20th-century Greek artist Photis Contoglou.

National Historical Museum

Stadiou 13, Platia Kolokotroni (210 323 7617/ www.culture.gr). Metro Panepistimio or Syntagma. **Open** 9am-2pm Tue-Sun. **Admission** €3; €1.50 concessions; free under-18s. Free to all Sun. **No credit cards**. **Map** p295 F4.
The heroes of Greece's War of Independence were essentially bandits who lived in a network of

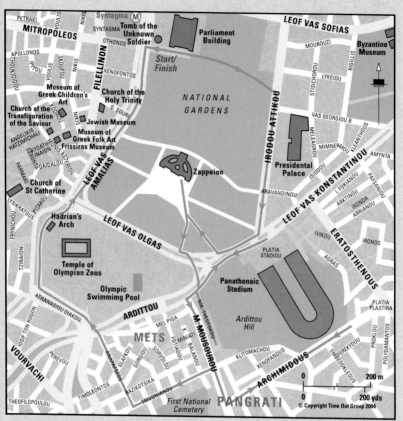

Sightseeing

some of its columns. On the same site, but in a somewhat better state of preservation, is **Hadrian's Arch** (*see p100*) – built in AD 131 in honour of the Roman Emperor Hadrian.

Continuing up Leof Vas Amalias will bring you back full circle to the National Gardens. Stop at the classic **Oasis** café (Irodou Attikou 4, open 8am-8pm) for a pick-me-up.

mountain hideouts during their rebellion. That doesn't seem to have precluded a taste for luxury, however: their paraphernalia, displayed here, includes lavishly engraved weapons and embroidered outfits galore. There are also paintings and engravings of key battles, personal items of war hero Lord Byron, and the embalmed heart of war hero and Greek president Konstantine Kanaris. The building itself was Greece's first Parliament, whose chamber is still preserved intact. The imposingly plumed bronze statue out front is Theodoros Kolokotronis, a lowly mountain bandit who became the war's greatest general. Even today, you may see floral wreaths left at the statue's base.

Neo-Classical University Complex

Panepistimiou, between Ippokratous & Sina (University 210 361 4301/Academy 210 360 0209/ Library 210 361 4413/www.culture.gr). Metro Panepistimio. **Open** *Library* Sept-July 9am-2pm Mon-Fri. *Academy & University* closed to the public. **Admission** free. **Map** p295 F4.

Though the formal name of this street is Eleftherios Venizelos, it's known to everyone – and even written on maps – as Panepistimiou ('University'), and that's all thanks to these buildings, among the most impressive structures in modern Athens. These models of neo-classical design were all built in the years after Greece gained independence, and exemplify what the new state hoped that it

Central Market

Athinas, between Sofokleous & Evripidou.
Metro Omonia. **Open** 7am-3pm Mon-Sat.
Map p295 E4.

For the truest flavours (and smells) of Athens, there's only one place to go: the sensory overload that is the city's Central Market. The enormous covered marketplace was built in 1870, and some of the establishments inside have remained pretty much unchanged since then. The blood-spattered, yellow-lit north side is the meat market, hung with carcasses of every description. Butchers expertly bark out prices while hacking with massive cleavers just centimetres from their fingers; definitely an awe-inspiring sight. The adjacent fish market is actually rather beautiful: sunlight streaming in from the high glass roof glitters off fish scales of every colour, while deep-purple squid glow against banks of crushed ice. Though this is one of the most old-school places in town, crass 21st-century commercialism has still managed to creep in. Hanging from the ceiling are rows of giant blue-and-white plastic fish, which Olympic organisers, in a promotional gambit, fitted out in Olympic sportswear, clipping football shoes and boxing gloves to some and stretching bikinis over others.

The streets surrounding the covered market are filled with spices, deli goods and livestock. On the fabulously fragrant **Evripidou** you can find spices from all over Greece; pick up some wild thyme or pungent Greek oregano to take home. **Armodiou** has shops full of live poultry and rabbits – meant for taking home to cook, not to frolic in the yard. Within the Central Market, **Papalexandris** (Sokratous 9) has wonderful olives, vine leaves and preserves.

Even when all the stores and stalls close up for the day, life still goes on in the market. It's also home to **Stoa Athanaton**, Athens' premier *rembetatiko* (*see p210*) where the music wails pretty much 24 hours a day. But for the true Central Market experience, stop by in the wee hours after a night of clubbing in nearby Psyrri. You'll find many fellow night owls at the three all-night restaurants inside the market, which all serve up market fare till dawn. Try **Taverna Papandreou** (Central Market, 210 321 4970) and order a bowl of *patsas*. It's a steamy, aromatic stew made primarily from pig intestines – though trotters sometimes make it into the brew as well. How can anyone want to eat this at any time of day? Greeks swear it's the best hangover preventive around – something about the tripe oil sealing in digestive juices. Look around and you'll see bleach-blonde babes in bite-sized skirts, suit-clad business folk and taxi drivers all digging in. Go ahead – what are you waiting for? It's the true taste of Athens.

Sightseeing

would become: a blend of its classical heritage and modern, Western-style statesmanship.

The central building housed Athens' first **National University**. It was designed by the Danish architect Hans Christian Hansen and built in 1842. The Ionian entryway columns are replicas of the columns of the Propylaeum, the entrance to the Acropolis. Inside the portico, there are colourful frescoes depicting Greece's first king, Otto, sitting on his throne surrounded by ancient Greek gods and heroes.

To the right of the University is the ornate, marble **Academy of Arts**, designed by Theophilus Hansen (brother of Hans Christian) and built in 1859. Its marble entry is based on the columns of the Acropolis temple Erechtheum, and its classical-style friezes are modelled after those on the Parthenon: one depicts the birth of Athena; another the battle between the gods and the giants. In front, the building is flanked by seated statues of Plato and Aristotle, while on either side rise high columns topped by statues of Apollo and Athena. On the far left is the **National Library**. It was built in 1902, and was also designed by Theophilus Hansen. Its entrance has Doric columns and is modelled after the Temple of Hephaestus in the Ancient Agora.

Though these three buildings were founded as the country's premier educational institutions, their stairs and huge courtyards are oddly empty – today's Athenian university students are rarely allowed within spitting distance of them. Most teaching takes place in gritty buildings around Patision, while the University is reserved for administrative offices and the Academy only opens for special events. The library is open to the public, but only students, public servants and others with special passes can enter the stacks. Even though you won't see students entering and leaving the buildings, you're unlikely to miss them altogether – along with anarchists and religious groups, they often hold demonstrations here, leafletting for the leftist cause *du jour* or assailing passers-by with hymns.

Numismatic Museum

Panepistimiou 12 (210 364 3774/www.culture.gr). Metro Panepistimio. **Open** 8.30am-3pm Tue-Sun. **Admission** €3; €2 concessions. **No credit cards.** **Map** p295 F5.

It's worth taking a look at this small museum, even if you're not interested in coins, just to walk around the beautiful mansion of Heinrich Schliemann, the famed German archaeologist who fulfilled his lifetime obsession when he discovered the rich Mycenaean kingdoms believed to be those described in *The Iliad*. The mansion is decorated with wonderful Pompeii-style frescoes and mosaics, carved marbles and moulded ceilings. It's a gorgeous showcase for the display of ancient gold, silver and bronze coins, many of them engraved with gods and mythical symbols. Featured displays include, among others, ancient Athenian coins bearing exquisite reliefs of Athena on one side and the owl, symbol of wisdom, on the other.

Parliament Building & Tomb of the Unknown Soldier

Syntagma (no phone/www.culture.gr). Metro Syntagma. **Open** *Parliament Library* 9am-1.30pm Mon-Fri. **Admission** free. **Map** p297 G5.

Once the domain of royalty, later a shelter for starving refugees, and today the seat of government, Greece's Parliament Building has many stories to tell. It was built in 1842 to house Otto, the Bavarian teenager imported to be Greece's first king. Over the next 70 years, the palace swung between opulence and neglect as various kings were exiled and returned. In 1923, after thousands of Greeks were forced to flee Asia Minor during the Greek-Turkish population exchange, the building acted as a shelter to the newly homeless. All this left it in a sorry state, and, after the return of a national parliamentary government in 1926, the building was gutted, renovated and reopened as a single-chamber council for the parliament.

Today it is the scene of parliamentary debates, broadcast on state television through a live in-house video camera. Most of the building is closed to the public, although its elegant library is open to researchers and often holds public exhibits.

In the square below the building is the Tomb of the Unknown Soldier, a monument to Greece's fallen. Carved on the tomb is a dying soldier, based on a fifth-century BC sculpture from Aegina, and an excerpt from Pericles's 430 BC funeral oration, given in honour of the Athenians who died in the Peloponnesian Wars. The tomb is guarded by the bizarrely costumed Evzones (*see p99* **Ministry of silly walks**), with a ceremonial changing of the guard every hour that is somehow both funny and moving to non-Greek eyes.

Platia Klafthmonos

Metro Panepistimio. **Map** p295 F4.

This square once played an important role in modern Greek politics. The name translates as the 'Square of Wailing', and it's where politicians who had lost office traditionally went to console each other after the elections. The sculpture in the centre is called 'National Reconciliation'.

Around the National Gardens

Map p297

Useful transport: Metro Akropoli, Evangelismos and Syntagma.

Once part of the royal palace and located southwest of the Historic Triangle, the National Gardens (*see p100*) are a godsend: thick, beautiful and shady, and dead in the centre of downtown Athens. Unsurprisingly, the real estate around them is among the city's most desirable. This is easy enough to see if you take a stroll down pretty Irodou Attikou, where you'll pass the lovely **Presidential Palace** (*see p94*), designed by Ernst Ziller (the

Sightseeing

Ministry of silly walks

Military folderol always looks a little ludicrous off the parade ground. But the Greek changing of the guard in front of the Tomb of the Unknown soldier outside the Parliament Building on the east side of Syntagma unquestionably takes the pom-pom. Tall, serious guards, called Evzones, clad in poufy miniskirts, white stockings, tasselled fez hats and red clogs adorned with giant pom-poms perform a slow, high-kicking dance that lifts those skirts up to eyebrow-raising heights. Though this is clearly a serious national ceremony, it's hard not to crack an incredulous smile when you see it (and, though they're supposed to stand stony-faced, the Evzones themselves aren't beyond a surreptitious wink in response).

The story behind the ritual is, however, a historic and rather moving one. No one in Greece wore such skirts (called *foustanellas*) before the 1820s, when the Greeks fought the War of Independence against their Turkish occupiers. The Greeks had no formal army – instead, the greatest fighters in the struggle were bands of outlaw brigands who waged rebellion from networks of caves in the mountains of northern Greece. These rebels, known as *kleftes* ('thieves'), adopted their own distinctive style of dress: knee-length white kilts, stockings and gorgeously embroidered vests (you can see many of these displayed at the National Historical Museum; *see p92*). They accessorized with fezes, fabulous moustaches, and shoes which, though they didn't have pom-poms, did have cords that pulled up the toes to give a jaunty look. It's not known why they chose this particular look, but one theory holds that the white skirts were the *kleftes'* version of the uniforms worn by Roman soldiers, re-interpreted centuries later, with an added Eastern flair.

Had the *kleftes* fought unsuccessfully, their flashy ensembles would probably have died with them, but in one of European history's most stirring underdog victories, these guerilla rebels wrested their country's independence from 400 years of occupation by the powerful Ottoman empire. Along with many other honours heaped upon them after independence, Otto, Greece's first king, had their *foustanella* declared the national military uniform; the teenage Bavarian king even took to wearing one himself.

Later, the *foustanella* was made the exclusive uniform of a new regiment, the Evzones – an elite fighting unit from which the royal guards were selected. Today, the Evzones are still an official branch of the Greek military, but there's no fighting involved – now they simply act as ceremonial guards. They are still selected from the ranks of Greek military conscripts, but the main qualifications are no longer fierceness and skill, but height and good looks.

As the role of the Evzones became more purely decorative, so too did their uniforms. The skirts inched up higher and higher, revealing plenty of muscular thigh. The cord that tied up the pointy-toed shoes slowly evolved into bits of fluff, which eventually turned into the luxuriant pom-poms of today. As for that high-kick march: in the words of an Evzone captain, 'It means nothing'. It was choreographed to be as formal and flourished as possible, a set of movements that did justice to the wearers' fabulous outfits.

You can watch the changing of the guard every hour on the hour; the most elaborate ceremony, with a band, is on Sundays at 10.45am. There's also an Evzone guard outside the Presidential mansion (*see p94*).

Sightseeing

Bavarian architect who created many of modern Athens' most important buildings), and, on the corner of of Leof Vas Georgiou, the stately **Maximou** building. The latter is the prime minister's official residence, though the current incumbent, Costas Simitis, prefers to live in his Kolonaki apartment. However, he still holds most official meetings here, and the entrance is regularly swamped with reporters and television vans. They have to get out of the way when the high-kicking Evzone guards march up the street – this whole scene, set against the verdant backdrop of the park, makes for a great modern Athenian moment.

Byzantine Museum

Leof Vas Sofias 22 (210 721 1027/www.culture.gr). Metro Evangelismos. **Open** 8.30am-3pm Tue-Sun. **Admission** free. **Map** p297 H5.

The Byzantine Museum has a world-renowned collection of icons, mosaics, sculptures and religious art. Renovation is more than doubling its permanent exhibition space, and never-before-seen parts of the collection – such as rare illuminated manuscripts – will be displayed for the first time. In addition, archaeologists recently discovered the site of Aristotle's Lyceum on the grounds; this ongoing dig will also be open to the public. Renovations will run through to 2006, during which time the museum will be open only intermittently – it's best to call ahead.

Hadrian's Arch

Leof Vas Amalias & Dionysiou Areopagitou (no phone/www.culture.gr). Metro Akropoli. **Open** 24hrs daily. **Admission** free. **Map** p299 F6.

To thank the Roman Emperor Hadrian for finally completing the Temple of Olympian Zeus (*see below*), Athenians built this arch in his honour in AD 131. Hadrian also saw to it that the arch clarified his own sovereignty. He had its west side inscribed: 'This is Athens, the ancient city of Theseus'. The east side was inscribed: 'This is the city of Hadrian and not of Theseus'. Sculptures of Theseus and Hadrian probably stood atop the arch. Nearby is some more honorific masonry: the statue of Byron at the corner of Amalias and Olga.

National Gardens

Leof Vas Amalias 1 (210 721 5019). Metro Syntagma. **Open** 7am-sunset daily. **Admission** free. **Map** p297 G5/G6.

The lush National Gardens were originally planted in 1839 as a private sanctuary adjoining the royal palace (now the Parliament). Amalia, Greece's first queen, brought in 15,000 domestic and exotic plants, many of which still remain. The garden was opened to the public in 1923, and is now a welcome deep-green – sometimes even jungly – oasis in the parched city centre. Winding paths lead past statues, fountains and a small bird sanctuary with such mock-natuaral abandon that it's actually possible to get lost. There is also a botanical museum, a duck pond, a playground and a handful of shaded cafés.

National War Museum

Leof Vas Sofias & Rizari 2 (210 725 2974/ www.culture.gr). Metro Evangelismos. **Open** 9am-2pm Tue-Sun. **Admission** free. **Map** p297 H5.

Admittedly, three sprawling floors on the history of Greek warfare, from Alexander the Great's battle plans through the sticky stew of the Balkan conflicts, might not be everyone's cup of tea. But a certain stripe of visitor will be in heaven. Meanwhile, anyone should enjoy a brief foray into the Saroglos Collection, which includes suits of armour, *Three Musketeers*-style foils and engraved Turkish scimitars. Outside there are real tanks and warplanes, which visitors can climb up into for a closer look. Interpretive panels are in Greek only.

Temple of Olympian Zeus

Leof Vas Olgas & Leof Vas Amalias (210 922 6330/www.culture.gr). Metro Syntagma. **Open** 8am-3pm daily. **Admission** €2; €1 concessions; free to holders of €12 Acropolis ticket. **No credit cards**. **Map** p299 F6.

In a city infamous for bureaucracy and construction delays, this colossal temple still holds the record for the longest tie-up – nearly 700 years. The tyrant Pisistratos commissioned the largest temple in Greece in 515 BC, ostensibly to honour Zeus, but mainly to keep his subjects occupied. After he was overthrown, the citizens of the new democracy refused to complete what they saw as a monument to tyranny. And so the Temple of Olympian Zeus languished for centuries, until the Roman emperor Hadrian recognised the opportunity it presented. He had the temple finished in seven years, fitted out with a gigantic gold-and-ivory sculpture of the god, and, for good measure, added a similar one of himself. Today only 16 of the original 104 columns remain, but their majesty still overwhelms.

Zappeion

Leof Vas Amalias (Exhibition Hall 210 323 7830). Metro Syntagma. **Open** *Garden* 24hrs daily. *Exhibition Hall* during exhibitions. **Admission** free. **Map** p297 G6.

On the south side of the lush and overgrown National Gardens are the orderly and well-cultivated Zappeion Gardens, centred on the stately Zappeion Exhibition Hall, built in 1888 by Theophilus Hansen, the Danish neoclassical architect who also designed parts of the University complex on Panepistimiou. As was typical of his designs, Hansen combined an entrance reminiscent of an ancient temple with a main body that referenced contemporary Mediterranean buildings, to pleasing effect. The building hosts conferences and exhibitions, the latter open to the public; it was also the first headquarters of the Olympic organising committee. The area in front of the building frequently hosts outdoor concerts and events, while the pretty complex of buildings just to the east of the Exhibition Hall includes the gourmet restaurant Aigli, a lovely restored mid-century outdoor cinema and Bedlam, a summer-only nightclub in the middle of the park.

Kolonaki & Around

Athens' most desirable address rubs padded shoulders with boho Exarchia.

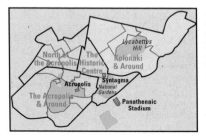

In ancient times, the high, green hill of **Lycabettus** (*see p103*), which rises between posh Kolonaki and bustling Ambelokipi, was considered an uninhabitable wilderness far from the centre of Athens. This is evident even in its name, which is believed to derive from the *lykaves*, or wolf-like creatures, that inhabited it. By the early 20th century, however, Athenians didn't seem so afraid of wolves there – the hill had become a popular place to graze sheep.

A mere century later, the foothills of Lycabettus Hill have been completely transformed: since the 1950s, Kolonaki has indisputably been the chicest address in

Athens, and today it's home to the city's top designer shops, trendiest restaurants, most see-and-be-seen cafés and impossible-to-get-into nightclubs, and block after block of pretty neo-classical mansions-cum-apartment-buildings housing diplomats and pop stars. At the time of writing, even Greece's prime minister, Costas Simitis, lived in Kolonaki, famously preferring his apartment to the official residence (*see p100*). This is the place to people-watch and spend money – though you can also enjoy Kolonaki without doing too much of the latter, just by strolling under its flowering trees and browsing its many art galleries.

On the north side of Kolonaki and Lycabettus is **Ambelokipi**, today a densely packed and busy district whose name, translated as 'little grapevines', also betrays its rural origins – it was once full of vineyards supplying Athenians with wine. Although Ambelokipi has no tourist sights or museums, it is a good area to keep on your radar – it's packed with good tavernas, restaurants, cinemas and, increasingly, small friendly nightclubs that lack both the chic cachet and the ludicrous prices of their Kolonaki brethren.

Athens' highest point: **Lycabettus Hill**. See p103.

Map p297

Useful transport: Metro Syntagma, Evangelismos.

The hotspot here is Platia Kolonaki, a smallish square that's a perpetual hive of activity, lined as it is with cafés, art galleries and designer shops. Radiating off the square are some of Athens' best streets for shopping and going out: start on Tsakalof or Patriarchou Ioakim for boutiques, or Milioni or Skoufa for a surfeit of chic places to imbibe caffeine or cocktails.

Heading uphill (and we really mean uphill) towards Lycabettus, you'll reach another good hub, this one a little quieter. Platia Dexamenis is home to the chic St George Lycabettus hotel (*see p64*) and its corresponding trendy café, Frame, plus one of Athens' nicest outdoor cinemas, the Dexameni (*see p193*). Heading west from here, you can see some of Athens' most exclusive real estate, mixed in with the elegant restaurants and shops that cater to its occupants. If you're here on a Friday morning, walk down Xenocratous, which hosts one of Athens' liveliest fruit-and-vegetable markets. You'll see housekeepers, old ladies and even high-heeled and pearl-clad matrons bargaining ferociously at the stalls below the mansions – a nice reminder that even in this most genteel of neighbourhoods, the old-fashioned village *laiki* (market) still thrives.

To the south, Kolonaki is bordered by the boulevard of Leof Vas Sofias, home to Athens' Museum Row: on the north side it's got the **Goulandris Museum of Cycladic Art** and the **Benaki Museum**, while on the south are the Byzantine (*see p100*) and National War museums (*see p100*).

Benaki Museum

Koumbari 1 & Leof Vas Sofias (210 367 1000/ www.benaki.gr). Metro Evangelismos or Syntagma. **Open** 9am-5pm Mon, Wed, Fri; 9am-midnight Thur; 9am-3pm Sun. **Admission** €6; €3 concessions. Free to all Thur. **No credit cards. Map** p297 G5.

This museum is housed in the gorgeously restored mansion of the wealthy 19th-century Benakis dynasty. It's also a pre-eminent collection: the works of Greek art, spanning the eras from antiquity to the 20th century, are top notch. Don't miss the sumptuous gold Hellenistic jewellery, the Byzantine shrines or the intricate re-creations of Ottoman-era sitting rooms. The gift shop is a destination in itself, offering exquisitely reproduced ceramics and jewellery.

Gennadius Library

Souidias 61 (210 721 0536/www.ascsa.edu.gr/ gennadius/genn.htm). Metro Evangelismos. **Open** 9am-5pm Mon-Wed, Fri; 9am-8pm Thur; 9am-2pm Sat. **Admission** free. **Map** p297 J4.

Turn-of-the-(19th)-century Greek diplomat John Gennadius scoured bookshops across Europe for rare and valuable publications on his country; the 27,000 gold-bound multilingual volumes he amassed represent the largest private collection on anything Greek. You can peruse whatever you desire within the luxurious reading room, as well as check out displays including Lord Byron memorabilia, the papers of Nobel laureate George Seferis and the first edition printed in Greek of Homer's works.

Goulandris Museum of Cycladic Art

Neofytou Douka 4 & Irodotou (210 722 8321/www. cycladic.gr). Metro Evangelismos. **Open** 10am-4pm Mon, Wed-Fri; 10am-3pm Sat. **Admission** €3.50; €1.75 concessions. **No credit cards. Map** p297 H5.

The world's largest collection of Cycladic art is one of Athens' must-sees. While Greek sculpture reached its pinnacle with the Parthenon Marbles, the first seeds in that tradition had been sown some 2,000 years earlier, in the Cycladic Islands of the Aegean. There, between 3,200 BC and 2,200 BC, a unique matriarchal culture flourished. Though contemporary with the Egyptians and Mesopotamians, it produced a totally different kind of art featuring elegant, angular, marble female figures with emphasised breasts and genitalia. The influence of the prehistoric figures can be seen in the work of Modigliani and Picasso, and they continue to inspire artists to this day. In addition to the fascinating Cycladic

Goulandris Museum of Cycladic Art.

The impressive entrance to the **Benaki Museum**. See p102.

pieces, the museum also owns a small but first-rate collection of ceramic items from the Classical period, as well as the adjoining Stathatos Mansion, a Bavarian-style neo-classical building designed by Ernst Ziller. There, among sparkling chandeliers, velvet drapes and antique furniture, the museum holds highly acclaimed temporary exhibits.

Greek Costume Museum

Dimokritou 7 (210 362 9513). Metro Syntagma.
Open 10am-1pm Mon-Fri. Closed Aug. **Admission** free. **Map** p297 G4.
This boutique-sized museum devoted to the history of clothing and fashion is appropriately located in the midst of Kolonaki's designer clothes stores. The 25,000 dresses and accessories include centuries-old folk costumes from every region of Greece, and copies of Minoan, Byzantine and Classical Greek fashions.

Lycabettus Hill

Funicular from Aristippou & Ploutarchou (210 722 7092). Metro Evangelismos. **Open** *Funicular* 9am-11.45pm daily (every 30mins). *Chapel of St George* Sun. **Admission** *Funicular* €4. *Chapel* free. **Map** p297 H4.
According to legend, Athens' highest hill was created when Athena took a piece off Mount Pentelicon, planning to augment the height of the Acropolis. En route to Athens, a messenger brought her bad news: in dismay, she dropped the rock, creating this promontory, which now projects proudly from the capital's poshest neighbourhood. On a clear day, there's a magnificent view of Athens and the Saronic Gulf from the peak, at the Chapel of St George.

Nearby, the outdoor amphitheatre (*see p208*) showcases music acts from Philip Glass to Calexico

all summer. At the summit, down a level from the chapel, the elegant restaurant Orizondes (*see p132*) offers highly praised cuisine with an unbeatable view. A handful of low-key cafés also dot the hill; a sunset drink at any is delightful. All this is accessible by road or paths through the pines, but beware: it's a steep walk. Many prefer to take the funicular up (€4 for the ride, from Hoida) and amble down.

Exarchia & Pedion Areos

Maps p295, p297

Useful transport: Metro Victoria.

Well-worn, bohemian Exarchia will never be known as a beautiful neighbourhood, but it holds a place in the heart of nearly every modern Greek, as evinced in the number of times it is referenced in Greek folk songs and novels from the 1970s onwards. It is home to the most important event in the nation's recent history, and still retains its legacy: it was here, in 1973, that the students of the **Athens Polytechnic** (*see p105*) rose up in protest against Greece's hated military dictatorship. Many of those students went on to become Greece's most prominent left-wing politicians; meanwhile, the neighbourhood has remained a gathering spot for students and intellectuals, its many cafés and tavernas alive with political debate.

While the front of the Polytechnic is often filled with students and demonstrators passing out leaflets against the Western imperialist disaster *du jour,* its next-door neighbour is often

Join the trendy and the beautiful in posh **Kolonaki**. See p102.

fronted by huge, shiny tour buses disgorging hundreds of people, all there to see one of the essential sights of Greece: the **National Archaeological Museum** (*see p105*), home to the mythical treasures of Mycenae, the sculptures of classical masters and much more.

On the east side of the Polytechnic, Stournari leads up to the heart of the neighbourhood, **Platia Exarchia**, *the* place to be for all your intellectual café-sitting needs. Its cafés and bars are always filled with students and old-time lefties, but you're just as likely to see middle-aged businessmen or taxi drivers having a drink – many Greeks like to come here when they feel the pull of their political consciousness. Don't be alarmed if you're approached by down-and-out figures asking for some change or a cigarette: they're harmless and won't protest if you say no. Of architectural interest in the square is the Bauhaus-style building that houses the Floral café: though faded and a bit tatty today, this was Athens' first apartment block, built in 1932-3. A down-at-heel feeling is endemic to the Platia Exarchia experience, and though there are plans to spruce the square up before the 2004 Olympic Games, they are unlikely to be sweeping.

Away from the square is a mix of scenically decrepit neo-classical houses, apartment blocks daubed with passionate graffiti and scores of used-book-and-record shops, hippie clothing stores, independent cinemas that show nothing but art flicks, simple tavernas serving up hearty, home-made food to accompany philosophical banter and some of Athens' best places to hear rembetika, the gritty Greek blues.

One of the best streets to see life in action in Exarchia is **Kallidromiou**, where you'll find a cluster of small old-time cafés much favoured by locals and intellectuals. Saturday mornings see this narrow thoroughfare transformed into one of Athens' largest outdoor markets as the bellowing vendors take over with their stalls of (mostly) fresh fruit and vegetables as well as flowers, herbs and fish.

If you follow Kallidromiou east, it eventually runs into **Neapoli**, a pretty but quiet residential district that acts as a buffer between the lefty grit of Exarchia on one side and the posh materialism of Kolonaki on the other. Appropriately, it is mostly populated by genteel but shabby writers and academics, who tend to frequent its many tavernas and *rembetatika*.

To the north of Exarchia and Neapoli is **Pedion Areos**, Athens' largest park. Despite this appealing qualification, some caveats must be noted: because of its location in a slightly down at heel area, the park is starting to see a fair number of homeless people, and a decreasing number of maintenance workers. That said, it is still spacious and green, decidedly welcome qualities anywhere in town.

Athens Polytechnic

Patision & Stournari. Metro Victoria.
Map p295 F2.
The date that resonates most deeply in the heart of many Greeks is 17 November 1973. On that day, thousands of students at the Athens Polytechnic rose up in protest against Greece's military Junta. The colonels countered with guns and tanks, killing 20 students. Though the day was one of the darkest in modern Greek history, it was also the turning point that led to the overthrow of the dictatorship the following year. Today the bravery of the students is commemorated with a moving monument to the slain in the Polytechnic's courtyard, which thousands of Greeks turn out to cover with flowers every year on the anniversary of their death.

Epigraphical Museum

Tositsa 1 (210 821 7637/www.culture.gr).
Metro Victoria. **Open** 8.30am-3pm Tue-Sun.
Admission free.
Located on the ground floor of the National Archaeological Museum (*see below*), with a separate entrance, this collection of inscriptions includes a 480 BC decree by the Assembly of Athens to flee the city before the Persian invasion; a sacred law concerning temple-worship on the Acropolis; and a stele with the Draconian laws on homicide.

National Archaeological Museum

Patision 44 (210 821 7717/www.culture.gr). Metro Victoria. **Open** *from May 2004* 8am-7pm daily. **Admission** €6-€10. *At the time of going to press, opening times and admission prices had yet to be finalised.* **No credit cards. Map** p295 F1/F2.

The city beneath the city

Living in one of the longest continually inhabited cities in the world (over 5,000 years and counting) is heaven for historians, but hell for builders: almost every major construction project in Athens' recent history has been held up by the accidental discovery of ancient remains. An Athenian digging a foundation for a backyard guesthouse might well stumble upon the tomb of Pericles – to the delight of archaeologists, but the dismay of the poor builder who just wants to get the job done. This explains why for years Athens was the only major European capital without a metro system: repeated attempts to dig subway lines were inevitably stalled by the discovery of tombs, foundations and temples – an archaeological treasure trove and a bureaucratic nightmare. But by the early 1990s, the government was determined to plough through and create a metro – an absolute requirement for hosting the Olympics. Thus began work on what has become simultaneously Athens' biggest construction project and archaeological dig ever. There were thousands of important archaeological discoveries, many of which were destroyed in the drive to get the metro done; but at least as many were preserved by the time the first stations opened up in 2000.

While subway digs are expected to continue well through to 2010, the first stations represent an admirable compromise between the need for modern transport and respect for ancient finds, plus a metro experience like none you'll have anywhere else: many stations have fascinating glassed-in stratigraphs revealing the layers of on-site

cultural remains, from 17th-century BC burial grounds, to fourth-century BC houses, to Roman baths, Byzantine aqueducts and Ottoman ossuaries – all on the same ground. Many stations are also mini-museums, with displays showing pottery, gravestones, and day-to-day artefacts like ancient children's toys or looms found on site. The excellent Syntagma station has the biggest display, with a vast stratigraph that includes a fourth-century BC burial ground, complete with a skeleton still in its tomb. Other stations worth checking out include Akropoli, which, in addition to displays of in situ aqueducts, has copies of the Parthenon Marbles, and Evangelismos, which opens into a cross-section of a first-century BC potters' kiln. Works are under way at the recently opened Monastiraki station, which will open on to an archaeological site along the banks of the ancient River Eridanos; while the still-under-construction Keramikos site, located underneath Ancient Athens' cemetery, has already produced a mother lode of first-rate finds.

The items displayed in the stations are a mix of originals and reproductions; a full display of the best metro dig finds is at the University of Athens Zografou campus (Iroon Polytehniou 9, 210 772 1000). Many of the stations display works by top contemporary Greek artists as well, making these stations must-see sights, even if you never actually take the train.

You can learn more about the subway displays at the Athens' metro website (www.ametro.gr).

This is more than just the top museum in Greece; packed full of a jaw-dropping array of classical treasures, it ranks as one of the most important museums in the world. In 2002, the museum closed for a full-scale renovation; it will reopen in spring 2004 with a facelift, reorganised collections and much more information accompanying exhibits. Post-2004 plans also call for a further expansion of the museum, allowing works that have long languished in its basement to be permanently displayed for the first time. During the expansion, some wings of the museum may be closed to the public – you may want to call ahead to find out the status of construction before your visit.

If everything is open, it's best to try to plan two visits – this museum is so densely packed with unmissable works that it's impossible to take it all in in one go. Classics buffs should by all means come here armed with their Homer and Pausanias, and feel the thrill of reading the words of the ancients describing magnificent works of art while gazing upon the actual objects.

Start in the ground-floor central hall (Gallery 4), home to some of the museum's most celebrated finds, the Mycenaean Antiquities. The Mycenaeans, renowned for their prowess as warriors, flourished during the 16th to 11th centuries BC, and fought the Trojans with the aid of Athena in *The Iliad*. Homer described their citadel, overseen by King Agamemnon, as 'well-built Mycenae, rich in gold'. All this was thought to be merely myth until German archaeologist Heinrich Schliemann unearthed their settlement in 1876. Drool over the stunning hoard he found, including a gold death mask, originally believed to be Agamemnon's but later dated to the 16th century BC, long before the king would have lived; a perfectly preserved 16th-century BC gold diadem; and the 15th-century BC golden Vaphio cups, embossed with scenes of capturing wild bulls and similar to cups described by Homer.

While Mycenae was training warriors and making gold swords, a highly advanced but more peaceful and matriarchal culture flourished on the island of Santorini, until it was buried under a volcanic eruption in the 16th century BC. Trapped under the ash and perfectly preserved were the exquisite Thira Frescoes (Gallery 48), colourful, graceful wall paintings showing scenes of prehistoric daily life: fishermen, flowers, birds, monkeys and boys boxing. These frescoes were damaged in the powerful earthquake that shook Athens in 1999 and have been closed to the public since then; they will be reopened for the first time, after careful restoration, in 2004.

The National Archaeological Museum is also the best place to trace the development of Greek sculpture. Galleries 7-13 are full of *koroi* from the seventh to fifth centuries BC. These statues of youths and maidens were the first monumental works in Greek art. The earliest are stiff and stylised, but by following the forms through the centuries, you can see artists learning to depict the body more naturalistically. Most impressive are the huge Anavyssos

Kouros and the lovely Phrasikleia Kore. Galleries 14-28 have some of the most marvellous achievements of sculpture in classical Greece. Most of the classical sculptures were made in bronze, which was later melted down and used for tools and weapons, but among those that survive is a famous 460 BC sculpture of a god, believed to be either Poseidon or Zeus poised to throw (depending on who it is) a trident or thunderbolt. There are also several later marble copies of the bronze originals, such as the one of an athlete binding his hair, a 100 BC copy of a bronze by the renowned sculptor Polycleitos, originally made in the fifth century BC.

These galleries also include many moving funerary sculptures: many were so large and luxurious, as families kept spending more and more money to create showier monuments, that they were actually banned in 317 BC. The scenes in these beautiful carvings typically show the deceased on the right and the survivors on the left, as well as an object characteristic of the dead.

The final sculpture galleries (29-33) show Hellenistic statuary dating from the second century BC to the first century AD. If you started your tour of Greek sculpture with the stiff, solid archaic monuments, now you can really see how far the artists have come. These sculptures are full of vigorous movement and sensuality, especially the 100 BC group of Aphrodite, Pan and Eros and the statue of a wounded Gaul.

Galleries 50-56 contain one of the world's richest collections of painted vases and pottery from the 11th to sixth centuries BC. Many of these depict fabulous scenes of mythical gods and warriors, such as the *krater* from 580 BC, showing the fight between Heracles and Nereus, and an early classical vase showing the rape of Helen by Theseus. Like the Thira Frescoes, these vases were damaged by the 1999 earthquake and have been kept away from the public since then; they are also due to be restored for the 2004 reopening.

A recent addition to the museum is a small but well-curated wing of Egyptian art. This should be viewed in conjunction with the earliest Greek archaic art, which borrowed heavily from Egyptian statuary before transforming it into something completely different. Feast your eyes on the sexy and well-preserved 715 BC bronze statue of the princess-priestess Takusit.

Pedion Areos

Leof Alexandras & Patision. Metro Victoria. **Open** 24hrs daily. **Admission** free. **Map** p295 F1.

Athens' largest park is a shady, welcome refuge from the surrounding smog and congestion, but not really a place to stroll if you are after scenic landscape. It has more of a working-class feel, with lots of old folks on benches, kids playing football and vagrants sleeping under trees. The park's proximity to the leftist district of Exarchia means it's frequently the site of political rallies, book fairs and free concerts by lesser-known Greek pop acts.

North of the Acropolis

A perennial favourite with artists and artisans (and the odd lowlife).

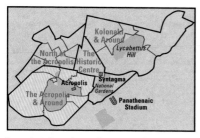

In ancient times the northernmost edge of Athens was the area of **Keramikos** (*see p108*). Named after its many ceramic workshops, it was separated by the Themistoclean Wall into two sections: the potters' quarters (within the city walls) and the cemetery (on the outside). Ancient Keramikos was full of edge-of-the-city activity: it was home to prostitutes who solicited soldiers returning through the city gates, money-lenders, wine-sellers and other shady dealers. Today those borders of Ancient Athens are in the centre of the modern city, but for years Keramikos and the neighbourhoods around it kept their ancient reputation intact, becoming home to a chaotic flea market, crumbling storefronts, humble workshops and hashish dens. But in recent years, bright, cool new restaurants, trendy cafés, hip artists' studios and clubs have been emerging.

To the south-east of Keramikos is **Psyrri**, which for centuries was a dark, scruffy quarter of workshops and craftsmen's studios. Today, these still run as they always have, but popping up among them are cutting-edge galleries, hipper-than-thou restaurants and nightspots and hole-in-the-wall music joints, making this the hottest place to go out in central Athens.

South of Keramikos, at the very end of Ermou, is **Rouf**, a truly revitalised former urban wasteland. On the northern fringe of this area is a huge former foundry, now transformed into a huge, multi-use arts complex (*see p108*) that, by proxy, has filled the surrounding streets with happening galleries, theatres and clubs galore.

Radiating out from Rouf and Keramikos are miles of decayed and decaying urban wilderness. To the south of Rouf are lonely abandoned factories, a few of which are gaining new life as dance clubs. To the north is **Metaxourgio**, a grey, congested cement-block-flat region where migrants pack into low-income housing. While this wouldn't seem the most promising spot for arts and nightlife, some venues have started to crop up, with planners taking advantage of low rent, proximity to the centre and the patina of authentic grunge wherever they can find it.

Psyrri

Map p295
Useful transport: Metro Monastiraki, Thisio.

Psyrri is one of the oldest neighbourhoods in Athens, filled with old-time workshops and decrepit buildings – though today craftsmen in old little shops are likely to have the hottest gallery of the moment as their next-door neighbour. By day the narrow streets may be full of a delivery of bricks or tools; but by night Psyrri comes alive with an ever-changing roster of entertainment, from traditional Greek *bouzoukia* to posh fashion-police-patrolled clubs to tiny, jazzy holes in the wall. Much of the action centres on the three squares of Iroon, Agion Anargyron and Agion Asomaton, where cheery tavernas, hipster-filled outdoor cafés and sleek DJ bars cluster irreverently around old churches. It's well worth getting lost in Psyrri's winding streets at night – there's always some new find cropping up on a once-forgotten corner.

Benaki Museum of Islamic Art
Agion Asomaton & Dipylou (210 367 1000/www. benaki.gr). Metro Monastiraki. **Opening hours & admission** to be confirmed. **Map** p295 D4.
Antonis Benakis, founder of the outstanding Benaki Museum (*see p102*), spent much of his life in Egypt, where he amassed a world-renowned collection of Islamic art. In spring 2004, two mansions in Psyrri will become home to the 8,000-piece collection – it will be one of the few museums in Europe devoted exclusively to Islamic art. Highlights of the planned exhibits include a celebrated collection of lustrous, elaborately painted ceramics; a filigreed tenth-century gold belt from Samarra, Iraq; a section of a carved early Islamic throne with stylised floral motifs and an inscription of blessings; and a 14th-century universal astrolabe, the only known surviving piece of medieval astronomical equipment of its kind. The museum will also display the entire marble-lined reception room of a 17th-century Egyptian mansion, transported piece by piece from Cairo. At the time of going to press, opening times and prices had not yet been determined; call or consult the website before you visit.

The industrial look of **Technopolis**.

Rouf & Tavros

Map p294
Useful transport: Metro Thisio.

Rouf's defining landmark is **Technopolis**, the foundry-turned-arts-centre at the crossing of Ermou and Pireos. A century ago, black exhaust from its smokestacks coated the surrounding area, giving it the name Gazi ('gaslands'). Today, the structure remains, with all the harsh beauty of its industrial architecture, but now the chimneys are illuminated with coloured lights that draw hipsters and art-world types to the complex's concerts and galleries. The revival of the once-sooty surrounding streets has been complete: Persefonis, the southern border street, is home to some of Athens' sleekest restaurants, and the smaller roads radiating off it are full of theatres, arts spaces and too-cool-for-school bars.

South of Rouf are the vast old factories of Tavros. Though these are not easy to get to, their sheer size seems to have inspired several transformations into clubs and party spaces.

Athinais
Kastorias 34-36, Rouf (210 348 0000/www. athinais.com.gr). Metro Metaxourgio or Thisio, then 20mins walk. **Open** 9am-10pm daily. **Admission** free. **Map** p294 B3.
Athinais exemplifies the best of the industrial-to-arts space conversions transforming Athens' downtown landscape: the former silk factory on the outskirts of Rouf, in the neighbourhood of Votanikos, is now

a sophisticated arts complex housing Greece's only Museum of Ancient Cypriot Art, containing treasures dating back to the ninth century BC, gallery spaces, a concert hall, a theatre and a cinema that screens classic or art films. It also has two excellent restaurants – lush Red (*see p139*) and the more affordable brasserie Votanikos (*see p140*) – and the sleek Boiler Bar. Be aware that the complex, still swathed in its original, 1920s stonework, has had no knock-on effect on the run-down, out-of-the-way surroundings, so if you come here, plan to spend the whole evening.

Foundation of the Hellenic World
Pireos 254, Tavros (210 483 5300/www.fhw.gr). Metro Kalithea. **Open** *Oct-May* 9am-2pm Mon, Tue, Thur; 9am-9pm Wed, Fri; 10am-3pm Sun. *June-Sept* 9am-4pm Mon, Tue, Thur; 9am-9pm Wed, Fri; 11am-3pm Sun. **Admission** free.
This vast, multi-purpose space is a fantastic use of a converted factory; it's a cultural centre devoted to multimedia and virtual-reality exhibits on Ancient Greece. These take you through sound-and-light tours of Ancient Miletus, the Temple of Olympian Zeus and the Ancient Olympics. There is also abundant theatre and gallery space, often used for educational programmes.

Technopolis
Pireos 100, Gazi (210 346 0981/www.culture.gr). Metro Thisio, then 10mins walk. **Open** 9am-9pm Mon-Fri during exhibitions. **Admission** free. **Map** p294 B5.
When the City of Athens bought this abandoned foundry and converted it into a huge, multi-purpose arts and performance space, it led to the transformation of the dingy surrounding neighbourhood, Gazi, into Athens' edgiest nightlife district, and kick-started a much-needed urban renewal trend: suddenly, Athenians cottoned on to the hipness of opening galleries and fusion restaurants in old lofts and factories all over town. The Technopolis buildings preserve their original industrial lines, and make an excellent host for everything from exhibitions of cartoon art to avant-garde theatre to rave concerts. The one permanent exhibit is the Maria Callas Museum, a small collection of the diva's personal items, including a handful of photos, mementos and costumes. If you visit the museum during the day, you'll need to find someone in the central office to let you in. Check local listings for exhibits and evening events.

Keramikos

Map p295
Useful transport: Metro Thisio.

The area around Keramikos, classical Athens' cemetery, looks pretty grim at first sight. It's centred on Iera Odos, a singularly ugly stretch of motorway lined by broken-down nightclubs and abandoned factories. This view becomes even more heartbreaking when you consider the history of this thoroughfare. For centuries Iera Odos ('Holy Road') was the road that priestesses and worshippers followed from the gate of Ancient Athens to Eleusis (*see p236*), site of the temples and rites of the mysteries of Demeter and Persephone, one of the most important religious cults of ancient times.

It might be surrounded by an ugly urban landscape, but there is hope for Keramikos. When you're walking among the sprawling ruins, especially in the rosy dusk, the surrounding crumbling industrial buildings add an element of harsh, poignant beauty so characteristic of Greece. The site itself was once home to potters' and artists' workshops, and centuries later that tradition seems to be starting up again, as contemporary studios are slowly appearing among the dark old buildings, followed, slowly but surely, by full-fledged hipster hangouts among the soulful modern ruins.

Keramikos

Ermou 148 (210 346 3552/www.culture.gr). Metro Thisio. **Open** 8am-7pm daily. **Admission** €2; free to holders of €12 Acropolis ticket. **No credit cards.** **Map** p294 C4.

During its life Keramikos has been many things – shrine, city gates, hangout of prostitutes and soldiers, artists' quarter, and the oldest and largest cemetery in Attica. What all these uses have in common is the site's location, at the edge of the (ancient) city. The site's name derives from the prevalence of potters' workshops on the grassy banks of the river Eridanos, which cuts through the site, and marked the north-west boundary of Ancient Athens. In 478 BC, that boundary was built in stone with the construction of the Themistoclean Wall around the entire city. The foundations of the wall still mark the outer edges of Keramikos.

Despite being built in haste, in fear of a sudden enemy attack, the walls were studded with grand gates. At the south-west edge of the site are the remains of the Dipylon Gate, the main entrance to Athens and the largest gate in Ancient Greece. The roads from Thebes, Corinth and the Peloponnese led to this gate, and many ceremonial events were staged here at important arrivals and departures.

To the south-east of the site is the Sacred Gate, reserved for priestesses to pass through on the road to Eleusis, to perform ancient Greece's most important religious rites, the mysteries of the goddess of agriculture, Demeter, and her daughter Persephone. Along the sides of the sacred road grew Athens' main cemetery, resting place for war heroes and wealthy statesmen – it was definitely prestigious to be buried here, as evinced by the many elaborate tombstones. The earliest tombs here are probably the seventh-century BC tumuli – high, round burial mounds built to honour great warriors. But 200 years later, the classical Athenians decided they wanted a lot more than just mounds of dirt, hence the showy monuments. The most distinctive of these is the fifth-century BC marble bull on the tomb of Dionysios of Kollytos, a man praised for his goodness, who died unmarried, mourned by his mother and sisters. The tomb of Dexileos, who died in 394 BC, shows a sculpture of the young man astride a rearing horse, while the lovely fifth-century BC stele of Hegeso shows the dead woman, seated on the right, taking a trinket from a box held by her maid.

As on the Acropolis, many of the sculptures exposed to the elements are copies, with the originals displayed in the small but fascinating on-site **Oberlander Museum**, which was closed through 2003 for renovations. The museum also contains fabulous cultural remains like pottery shards depicting erotic scenes, used in a brothel once on the site, and bits of marble carved with curses, which people would slip into the graves of their enemies.

Let them all hang: **Psyrri** (*see p107*).

Athens Suburbs

From beach towns to mansion living, Athens' suburban edges are anything but anodyne.

Sightseeing

Standing in Syntagma or negotiating the confusion of streets in the city villages that crowd the foot of the Acropolis, it's hard to imagine ever finding space, never mind peace, in this dynamic city. However, Athens' sprawling tentacles stretch way beyond its vibrant centre and cupped within the Athenian basin are myriad ways to escape the urban grind. From the breath of fresh, herb-scented air on Mount Hymettos and Lake Vouliagmeni's soothing medicinal waters to people-watching on Kifisia's posh shop-lined streets or strolling down glamorous Glyfada's be-and-be-seen promenade, the city's outskirts offer a whole new insight into Athenian life and leisure.

Eastern Suburbs

Maps p297 & p299

Useful transport: Evangelismos, Syngrou-Fix.

To the east of central Athens, just beyond the Zappeion Gardens and the Temple of Olympian Zeus, the ground starts to rise into the foothills of **Mount Hymettos**. The elevated eastern suburbs run along most of the 16-kilometre (ten-mile) length of the mountain. Most of these are fairly ordinary residential neighbourhoods, with **Pangrati**, the one closest to central Athens, the most interesting to visitors. Further up the mountain, you can take a break from smoggy central Athens with a walk on trails scented with fragrant wild herbs.

Pangrati

Pangrati's most dominant feature is the huge marble **Panathenaic Stadium** (*see below*), the site of the first modern Olympics in 1896. To the south of the stadium is the steep but lovely street of Markou Mousourou, shaded by flowering trees and filled with the scent of jasmine and bougainvillea from the balconies of neo-classical buildings. Markou Mousourou borders **Mets**, one of Athens' prettiest residential neighbourhoods. Heading up Markou Mousourou and then turning right on Trivonianou, you'll reach the entrance of the tranquil, shady and fascinating **First National Cemetery** (*see below*).

First National Cemetery

Anapafseos & Trivonianou (210 922 1621). Metro Akropoli or Syngrou-Fix, then 10mins walk. **Open** *May-Sept* 7.30am-8pm daily. *Oct-Apr* 8am-5pm daily. **Admission** free.

The wide, overgrown rows of century-old marble mausoleums in Athens' largest cemetery are good for a contemplative, off-the-beaten-path stroll. All of modern Athens' most famous are buried in lavish tombs here, including actress, Culture Minister and national heroine Melina Mercouri, War of Independence hero Theodoros Kolokotronis and Nobel laureate George Seferis. The cemetery is thickly planted with cypress trees, whose tall, pointed shape is believed to help guide souls up to heaven.

National Gallery

Leof Vas Konstantinou 50 (210 723 5857/ www.nationalgallery.gr/www.culture.gr). Metro Evangelismos. **Open** 9am-3pm, 6-9pm Mon, Wed; 9am-3pm Thur-Sat; 9am-2pm Sun. **Admission** €6.50. **No credit cards.** **Map** p297 J5.

The highlight of Greece's finest art gallery is a collection of El Greco's masterpieces. The museum is also a regular stop on the circuit of premier international exhibits, including recent showcases of Cézanne and Picasso.

Panathenaic Stadium

Leof Vas Konstantinou (210 325 1744/ www.culture.gr). Metro Evangelismos. **Open** 8.30am-2pm daily. **Admission** free. **Map** p297 G7/H7.

This enormous marble stadium, which boasts a seating capacity of around 50,000, was originally built in 330 BC to host the first Panathenaic Games. It later fell into ruins, and much of its marble was used for the construction of other buildings. In the 19th century, it was rebuilt to host the first modern Olympics (1896). The reconstruction used marble from nearby Mount Pentelicon, famed for its beauty – hence the stadium's nickname, Kallimarmaro, meaning 'beautiful marble'. That marble is now being meticulously cleaned and restored for the 2004 Olympics, when the stadium will host the archery competition and marathon finish; there is meanwhile limited access. The shady path atop the stadium is popular with local joggers.

Mount Hymettos

Behind Pangrati, the suburbs rise higher into the foothills of Mount Hymettos. One district that has taken good advantage of its situation is **Vyronas** (the Hellenised name of philhellene

Lord Byron), with its huge, attractive **Theatre of the Rocks**, aka Melina Mercouri Vrahon Theatre (*see p208*).

Behind Vyronas loom the higher slopes of Mount Hymettos, which the ancient Greeks believed was the original source of honey. It's not hard to see why. Honey from the mountain's abundant wild herbs – fragrant thyme, sage and lavender scent the air and make any walk up here a treat – is still considered among the finest in Greece.

The best way to experience Mount Hymettos is to visit the beautiful **Kaisariani Monastery** (*see below*), set in a pine and cypress copse on Ethnikis Antistaseos, the road to the top of the mountain. But everyone in Athens can enjoy one of Hymettos's most renowned qualities, even without ever setting foot on it: since ancient times, visitors and locals have been marvelling at the lovely rosy glow, and then deep-purple covering, that Hymettos takes on at sunset – even the forest of television aerials on top can't spoil the sublime effect.

Kaisariani Monastery

Kaisariani (210 723 6619). Bus 223 or 224, then 20mins walk. **Open** *Apr-Oct* noon-7pm Mon; 8am-7pm Tue-Sun. *Nov-Mar* 8.30am 3pm Tue-Sun. **Admission** €2; €1 concessions. Free to all first Sun June, Oct and second Sun July-Sept.

It's a mere 20-minute drive from Athens following the mountain road known as Ethnikis Antistaseos, but this Byzantine monastery on the pine-clad Mount Hymettos feels like a world away from the city. Look down over the splendid basin of Attica and breathe in the fragrance of the wild-thyme-covered hills. The cloistered monks still hold services in the two chapels, one built in the 11th century, the other 500 years later. Have a wander around the fresco-filled sanctuaries and feel free to taste the spring water gushing from the ram's-head fountain – it is said to boost fertility. The mountain trails outside the monastery are also worth exploring.

Northern Suburbs

Useful transport: Metro Irini, Kifisia, Marousi.

Heading north out of Athens, the boulevards of Leof Kifisias and Mesogeion run through increasingly expensive, spacious and leafy suburbs. Not that one could tell while driving on either road, though – they are filled with a huge, ugly build-up of randomly set shopping malls, business centres, supermarkets and billboards. But behind this façade are neighbourhoods like Paleo Psychiko, with its graceful neo-classical buildings, old flowering trees and diplomats' residences, and Neo Psychiko, home to cutting-edge gallery DESTE (*see p197*).

Athens' northern suburbs are framed by mountains on all sides – Tourkovounia to the west, Pentelicon to the north, Hymettos to the east. That means the wealthy residents who get to live on their foothills have space, clean air, greenery and a distinctively different climate from that enjoyed by the denizens of central Athens – in winter, these districts may see up to 30 centimetres (12 inches) of snow while downtown sees nary a flake. (The mountains

Goulandris Museum of Natural History. *See p112.*

Health springs eternal at **Lake Vouliagmeni**. *See p114.*

are also the reason that the city's infamous pollution ends up getting trapped in the lowland city basin.)

The two main suburbs of interest to tourists are **Kifisia**, 16 kilometres (ten miles) from central Athens, and **Marousi**, 12 kilometres (7.5 miles) from the city. The former is an attractive, wealthy and tree-lined district full of parks, cafés, posh shops, outstanding restaurants and two museums. It is a wonderful refuge from Athens in midsummer. During the Olympics, the main draw will be the suburb of Marousi. This once green-gladed area is home to the **Athens Olympic Sports Complex**, the main venue for the Olympic Games.

Because of their relative amount of space, other northern suburbs are also getting new, smaller Olympic venues, which means that all the roads and surroundings are being expanded and upgraded (as well as becoming more congested with works and buildings).

Kifisia

Kifisia started life as a cool, green and gracious summer resort for Athens' wealthiest citizens, who built airy neo-classical holiday homes along its neat, tree-lined streets. The urban sprawl of Athens didn't fully reach Kifisia until the 1970s; and though it's now a full-fledged suburb, it still retains the main qualities (shady, pretty and pricey) that made it so appealing to the early elite.

By far the easiest way to get to Kifisia is on the Line 1 metro, which terminates here. Walking out of the metro, you'll head up Adrianou, which flanks a pretty park filled with cafés. Continuing up the street, you'll pass Leof Kifisias to enter the commercial centre of

the area. This is focused around Kassaveti, Kolokotroni, Kyprou and Georganta streets, all lined with some of Athens' best restaurants and nightclubs, most expensive designer shops and chicest people-watching cafés.

Gaia Centre

Othonos 100 (210 801 5870). Metro Kifisia. **Open** 9am-2.30pm Mon-Thur, Sat, Sun. **Admission** €4.50; €1.50 concessions. **No credit cards**.

The Gaia Centre is part environmental research lab, part edutainment. The Centre, affiliated with the Museum of Natural History (*see below*) down the street, has three floors of well-made displays on ecosystems and the environment, including plenty of interactive video, computer and tactile displays. There's an exhibit on solar power, where you can cover and reveal the sun with varying degrees of cloud to see how fast it will run an engine; a touch-screen game where you can try to make your organic crop succeed on its own or by using pesticides; and a laser-light rotating-globe show every hour. The exhibits, designed in association with the London Museum of Natural History, are well made and a hit with kids. Unfortunately, almost all the information is in Greek.

Goulandris Museum of Natural History

Levidou 13 (210 801 5870/www.culture.gr). Metro Kifisia. **Open** 9am-2.30pm Mon-Thur, Sat, Sun. **Admission** €3; €1.20 concessions. **No credit cards**.

The extensive, excellently researched exhibit on Greece's rich natural wildlife makes the Museum of Natural History a fitting stop in leafy Kifisia. The displays include insects, mammals, birds, reptiles, shells, rocks, minerals and fossils. The botanical collections have over 200,000 species of Greek plants, 145 of which have been discovered only recently and recorded thanks to the museum's research.

Marousi

If you come to Athens for the Olympics, you'll come to Marousi. Up until the turn of the 21st century, this was little more than just a sprawling, upper-middle-class suburb, whose main attributes were a good hospital and a football stadium. Today Marousi is being completely transformed by the development of the **Athens Olympic Sports Complex**, along with some of the other biggest projects of the Games, including a gigantic broadcasting and press centre. At press time, Marousi was an area to steer clear of, a tangle of construction and perpetual traffic jams. It remains to be seen whether the new development will bring any permanent attractions after the Games.

Athens Olympic Sports Complex

Leof Kifisias 37 & Spiros Louis (210 683 4060/ www.sportsnet.gr/main_en.html). Metro Irini. **Open** *Summer 2004.*

The main, multistadium complex for the 2004 Olympics has long been Athens' biggest venue for sports and major concerts; but the stadium itself was shabby and its surrounds little more than a concrete wasteland. But after 2004, if all goes according to plan (a big 'if' in Athens), the stadium should be a major attraction. It's being expanded and redesigned by renowned Spanish architect Santiago Calatrava, whose airy, modern works for the Barcelona Games have become veritable landmarks. At press time, Calatrava's plans for the Olympic Complex included soaring, graceful glass-and-steel arches over the main stadium, a new velodrome and, most ambitious of all, the transformation of the surrounding area into a landscaped park filled with sculpture and lined with undulating glass-covered walkways.

If you travel to Athens after the Games and would like to see all this, a word to the wise would caution finding out how many of these plans did come to fruition before you go.

Museum of 20th-Century Design

Patmou 4-12, Technal Plaza (210 685 0611). Metro Irini. **Open** 9am-6pm Mon-Wed; 9am-8pm Thur, Fri; 10am-3pm Sat. **Admission** free.

This may once have been the most random museum in Athens: a stylish collection of furniture, lamps and interior design pieces by some of the top 20th-century architects (Salvador Dalí, Le Corbusier, Frank Lloyd Wright, Mies van der Rohe and Antoni Gaudí) located next to a football stadium in a far-flung suburb of the city. But now that the stadium is being converted to a landmark monument by Santiago Calatrava, whose name is starting to rank in importance with some of those displayed in the museum, it's all beginning to make some weird kind of sense. If you're at the stadium and inspired to see some more good design, it's a worthwhile place to visit.

Syngrou & Southern Suburbs

Map p298

Useful transport: Metro Syngrou-Fix; bus A2, E2.

Syngrou Avenue runs from the centre of Athens south to its coastal suburbs and beaches. Like the major arteries to the north, Syngrou is one of the ugliest roads around, lined with a haphazard smattering of big-box buildings, abandoned or run-down flat blocks (many built to house Greek refugees when they fled from Asia Minor in 1923), business centres and perpetual construction works.

But Syngrou does have its attractions. A lot of those big-box structures house Athens' largest nightclubs and *bouzoukia*. Their names, ownership and decor change almost every year, keeping them fresh, trendy and always exclusive, so international clubbing types should definitely put a night out here on their agendas. As with much in Athens, there's definitely a quirky appeal to making your way through a haphazardly gritty area, then suddenly finding yourself in one of the most wildly posh nightclubs in the Mediterranean; perhaps even more in driving by and seeing all the beautiful people lined up on the road's edge.

The northern part of Syngrou is also a hot-spot for Athens' sex industry, lined with strip clubs and, late at night, prostitutes and transvestites. Nothing wildly posh here: this is a particularly sleazy red-light district, staffed almost entirely by Eastern European women forced into the sex trade by their illegal status.

Once the road hits the coast, things get much better. From Syngrou, the busy Leof Posidonos, named after the god of the sea, runs along the coast through the wealthy seaside suburbs of Faliro, Glyfada, Voula and Vouliagmeni. The locals have taken to calling this area the 'Athenian Riviera', and there's something to be said for that: it's lined with clean, well-maintained public and pay-per-visit beaches (*see p117* **Beaches**), all invariably full of the requisite topless, thong-clad bathing beauties.

Between beaches are enormous, luxurious seaside nightclubs, which take over entertaining Athens' party people in summer, when the Syngrou clubs close down. Like their downtown equivalents, these spots are huge, seasonal, pricey and trendy, but they have the unbeatable added advantage of their wide, open-air beachfront locations. Some are open all day, drawing Athens' chicest and showiest to lounge and have coffee in their stunning settings. Many have decks that go right up to the water, swimming pools, gauzy draperies

Sightseeing

and model-perfect waiting staff. Some are also restaurants, importing brand-name chefs to serve up astronomically expensive and beautifully presented fusion food. All heat up after midnight, when long lines of designer-clad wannabes wait for admission from the fashion police at the doors.

At the time of writing, the area was undergoing huge changes, due mainly to the construction of major Olympic venues along the coast. Paleo Faliro is getting a double-stadium complex for tae kwon do and beach volleyball, while the beachfront suburb of Agios Kosmas is being transformed to host Olympic sailing events. The biggest transformation of all, however, is taking place at Hellenikon, where the vast space that used to be Athens International Airport is being turned into a multi-venue space for the Games. Its future use is as yet undecided: proposals range from the largest park in Europe to a racing-car track.

The two venues at Paleo Faliro are to be linked by an open-air seaside esplanade, which city planners say they'll line with greenery and cafés in the hope of making it a permanent attraction, but how attractive this project will be remains to be seen. It's also unclear how much these construction projects, or the prospect of Olympic visitors, will affect the adjacent beaches and nightclubs, many of which have operated illegally for years, but may be driven out during summer 2004.

Another transformation is taking place with the construction of a brand-new tram line running from central Athens to Vouliagmeni, meant to shorten and ease the trip from the city to the seaside and Olympic venues (and of permanent benefit to car-less visitors; the bus ride here isn't much fun). However, delays and protests against the project have led to the cutting of many planned stops, and to the shortening of the line. It will not be clear until after 2004 what shape this region will ultimately take.

Battleship Averoff

Trocadero Marina, Paleo Faliro (210 983 6539).
Metro Piraeus, then bus 909 to Oulen bus stop.
Open *Oct-Mar* 11am-1pm, 4-6pm Mon, Wed, Fri; 11am-3pm Sat, Sun. *Apr-Sept* 9am-1pm, 3-5pm Mon, Wed, Fri; 9am-1pm Tue, Thur; 11am-3pm Sat, Sun.
Admission €1. **No credit cards**.
Between 1910 and 1920, the Averoff was the fastest ship in the Greek fleet, and famously played a decisive role in the Balkan Wars, turning the tide between Greece and Turkey and forcing the return of Greece's major islands. Today the ship has been restored to its original state, and you can explore everything, from the bridge to the captain's luxurious quarters and the bowels of the engine room. On-board exhibits tell the stories of its wartime exploits.

Gracious **Kifisia**. *See p112.*

Lake Vouliagmeni

Leof Posidonos, Vouliagmeni (210 896 2239).
Bus A2 or E2 to Platia Glyfada; then bus 114.
Open *summer* 7am-8.30pm daily. *Winter* 8am-5.30pm daily. **Admission** €5. **No credit cards**.
This mixed fresh-and-saltwater lake is beautifully set inside a huge jutting rock on the inland side of the coast road. Its blue-green mineral-infused waters come partly from the nearby sea and partly from a deep, but still unknown freshwater source. What is known is that the water stays at an approximate 24°C (75°C) year round, making this a popular spot for winter bathing. The waters are said to be curative for conditions such as rheumatism, which explains the preponderance of genteel, elderly, bathing-capped crowds. They also appreciate the free parking, attractive landscaping of trees and flowered bushes, and pleasant, old-fashioned café on one bank. Behind the café, there is a small spa facility, where visitors can have hydrotherapy massages in the lake waters.

National Museum of Contemporary Art

Amvrosiou Frantzi 14 & Kallirois, Syngrou (210 924 2111).
The old FIX Beer brewery at this address is being converted into Athens' first comprehensive museum of modern art, which will display works by artists such as Ilya Kabakov, Gary Hill, Nan Goldin, George Hadjimichalis, Pavlos and Allan Sekula, as well as video art. However, the new space (which will include rooftop restaurant with sculpture garden) is still under construction and is not likely to be finished until 2006. In the meantime, the museum will display its collection at the Megaron Mousikis (*see p205*). At the time of going to press, museum staff were still unsure as to which works would be on display and what the opening times would be at the temporary location. Call the museum's administration offices on the above number for more details.

Piraeus

The place that launched a thousand ships.

Useful transport: Piraeus metro. For Mikrolimano, Piraeus metro then trolleybus 20.

Mikrolimano.

Thousands of years before it became Athens' main port, with ships departing daily for hundreds of islands, Piraeus itself was an island, separated from the mainland by a thin strip of water. Even after the waters fell away and it was joined to the land, it was almost another thousand years before the great Athenian general Themistocles, in the fifth century BC, recognised Piraeus' potential as Attica's best-situated natural harbour. Until then, Athenians had moored in the bay of Faliro, today a wealthy seaside suburb (*see p113*).

Themistocles had his new port built up to accommodate Athens' many ships, but his greatest accomplishment was the construction of the **Long Walls** in 478 BC. These fortifications, which surrounded the entire port and ran all the way back to the city of Athens, are still the most impressive remains in Piraeus today – walking through the modern city, you're likely to come upon fenced-off areas containing foundations of the walls and the settlements around them. In the mid fifth century AD, under Pericles, the city of Piraeus was laid out in blocks by Ippodamos of Miletus – it grew and thrived under the city plan, which is still the same one used today. In medieval times, the port became known as 'Porto Leone', after the colossal stone lion that guarded its entrance and that was taken to Italy by the Venetians in 1688.

By the 19th century, Piraeus was a busy, fast-growing city. In 1922, it grew even more: the Greek-Turkish population exchange brought thousands of refugees from Asia Minor to Greece; many of them settled in Piraeus. The port became known as a colourful but seedy place, full of hashish dens and dives where the Greeks from Turkey sang gritty rembetika. This image persisted into the mid century, immortalised in the movie *Never on Sunday*, where the whisky-voiced blonde film star Melina Mercouri (later Greece's Minister of Culture) played a singing prostitute who jumps in the port waters with visiting sailors.

Today Piraeus is a major commercial harbour, one of the main centres of transport and shipping in the Mediterranean. It's grown in size to the point where it's hard to say whether it's a sibling city to Athens, or just part of the city itself. There's no question that it retains its own character, though.

Most visitors to Piraeus arrive by train in the middle of the chaotic central harbour, surrounded by enormous ships, dozens of shipping company offices, street hawkers and people departing and arriving from all over the Med. Behind the station, around Alipedou and Skylitsi, is the **Piraeus Flea Market**. The market proper is held on Sundays from 7am to 3pm; a number of antique-cum-kitsch-cum-junk shops are also open during the week. A walk through this proletarian district will eventually lead you to Piraeus' must-see **Archaeological Museum**, housing the bronze sculptures of Athena and Artemis that graced the port in Themistocles's day.

South of the museum are Piraeus' two smaller and more scenic harbours, **Zea Marina** and **Mikrolimano**. The larger of the two is Zea Marina, also known as Pasalimani; this is the harbour for yachts plying the Saronic Gulf islands (and a good place to go millionaire-spotting). It's lined with buzzing cafés and bars, and is also home to the **Hellenic Maritime Museum**. Pretty **Mikrolimano**, filled with fishing boats and seafood restaurants overlooking the sea, is the main destination for tourists, and with good reason. Behind Mikrolimano rises the pretty neighbourhood of **Kastella**, Piraeus' most fashionable district. Lined with narrow streets, pastel-painted neo-classical mansions, it's possessed of the most lovely view of the entire harbour.

These days, the already-pretty Kastella is being given a makeover – fresh paint, new streetlights and the like – as are spots all over the port. That's because there are big plans for Piraeus during the 2004 Olympics. Due to a

Sightseeing

Piraeus

drastic shortage of hotel rooms for the event, Olympics organisers have booked 12 cruise ships to dock in the port during the Games, to act as 'floating hotels' for VIPs. At the time of writing, municipal officials still didn't seem quite certain how they were going to prepare for the visitors: it's expected that the area directly around the cruise ship berths will get a clean-up and beautification; and there are efforts being made at planting trees and flowers throughout the city. Culture Ministry officials say they'd like to transform the many archaeological sites, especially those with Long Wall foundations, into a linked archaeological park for the enjoyment of the visitors (and presumably their own residents), but it's unclear how much of this will come to pass.

Archaeological Museum of Piraeus

Harilaou Trikoupi 31, Pasalimani (210 452 1598/ www.culture.gr). Metro Piraeus. **Open** 8.30am-3pm Tue-Sun. **Admission** €3. Free to all Sun Nov-Mar. **No credit cards.**

That this smaller sister of the National Archaeological Museum (*see p106*) sees less than half the visitors of the downtown museum is perhaps understandable, but it's a shame nonetheless, for it is home to some of the most magnificent works of classical Greek art in existence. The greatest works of the Greek classical sculptors were generally done in bronze, but few survive, as most were melted down for weapons or tools in the intervening centuries. Some, however, were lost in the waters of Piraeus, where they stayed, perfectly preserved, for centuries, until they were found during an underwater excavation in 1959. Such is the fate that befell the marvellous bronze statues of Athena, Apollo and

Artemis, the undisputed stars of this museum. It's worth stopping by just to see Room 3, with the centrepiece of a brilliantly sculpted and perfectly intact bronze of Athena, believed to date either from the fourth century BC or from a first-century BC sculptor imitating the earlier classical style. Either way, it is a masterpiece, with a noble, helmeted head and a sash made of writhing snakes, and bearing the head of Medusa. In the same room is a well-sculpted bronze of Apollo, believed to date from around the sixth century BC, two lovely bronzes of Artemis and a perfectly intact fourth-century BC bronze tragic mask, with a wild, snaky beard, sunken cheeks and dramatically dismayed eyebrows.

Room 4 has another don't-miss: a large fourth-century BC shrine to the mother of the gods, with the goddess seated on a throne with a lion next to her.

Room 7 has what may have been the largest funerary monument in Ancient Greece. Built by a merchant from Istria for his son, the 'monument' is the size of a small temple, with larger-than-life sculptures of the merchant, his son and their servant surrounded by friezes of Greek heroes. It was the lavish ostentation of monuments like this that led to the banning of funerary monuments in Athens in 317 BC.

Hellenic Maritime Museum

Zea Marina (210 451 6264/www.culture.gr). Metro Piraeus. **Open** 9am-2pm Tue-Fri; 9am-1.30pm Sat, Sun. **Admission** €1.50; €1 concessions. **No credit cards.**

From Odysseus to Aristotle Onassis, the nautical world has always been fundamental to Greece's psyche. The 2,500 exhibits at this museum begin with models of prehistoric ships, and include sophisticated ancient navigating equipment, paintings, maps, flags, guns and models galore. Pieces of famous Greek battleships surround the exterior.

Beaches

Free-access strands of sand and luxury beach clubs are all in easy reach.

Lowest purchasing power; lowest per-capita salaries; highest per-capita auto fatalities… The advent of EU statistical reports, in which Greece consistently seems to be lagging at the bottom, may hurt the proud Greek psyche, but the country has managed at least one glowing statistical feat: it has by far the cleanest beaches in the EU. And while the Greek islands are famous for their pristine waters, what is less well-known is that the coastline around Athens, dotted with beaches, scores nearly as well.

In the past tourists and locals tended to shun urban resorts in favour of the islands; however, rising holiday costs in Greece, coupled with the improvement of local beaches, mean that more and more young Athenians and visitors are giving the coastline around the capital a go.

Beaches in the Athens area can be roughly divided into publicly maintained free beaches and semi-public, privately managed paying beaches. Heavy privatisation in the past few years means that very few of Athens' beaches are public and free, but they do exist and are reasonably maintained, if predictably crowded.

If you want more than just sea and sand from your ideal beach, then look to Athens' privately managed beaches. They are perfect for high-maintenance types and more closely resemble high-style clubs than merely convenient spots in the sand. And while they can be pricey, they do offer a number of services and conveniences. For the admission price you normally get an umbrella and chair, changing cabins, WCs and a cold rinse-off shower. Often there are also small children's playgrounds, a bit of greenery or small gardens, a snack bar or kiosk/mini-market, a first-aid station and sports facilities as well. Lifeguards are employed at all privately managed beaches, but should never be relied on, as they are often absent from their posts.

Athens' beaches are at their most crowded on summer weekends, between 11am and 2pm. The umbrella and chair you've paid for may not be available right away – a fact that you may or may not be informed of unless you ask. The roads too are busy at peak times and the buses full; a taxi is a sensible option.

Beaches usually close at sunset regardless of their stated 'official' hours. Sadly, midnight beach dips aren't an option except on public beaches; privately managed beaches are closed (and usually fenced off) at night.

The best Beaches

For avoiding the crowds
Agios Kosmas (see p118).

For joining the crowds
Kavouri-Vouliagmeni (see p119),
Astir Beach (see p120).

For proximity to the city centre
Edem Beach (see p117).

For spacious sands
Attica Vouliagmeni Beach (see p120).

For children
Agios Kosmas (see p118), Megalo
Kavouri (see p119).

For views
Attica Vouliagmeni Beach (see p120).

For social scene
Limanakia A & Limanakia B (see p120).

For watersports
Astir Beach (see p120).

For value for money
Voula A & Voula B (see p119).

Crime of any sort is still unheard of, although common-sense precautions like keeping an eye on your belongings apply. But your biggest trouble is likely to be getting socked by a tennis ball from 'rackets' players, which are ubiquitous on all beaches.

The best...

The following beaches are listed in geographical order, travelling from north (Faliro) to south (near Varzika). For more beach options, see p238 **Roadside beaches**.

Edem Beach ❶
Leof Posidonos coastal road, Paleo Faliro (in the Flisvos/Edem districts of Paleo Faliro). Tram from Syntagma area (from summer 2004)/bus A1, B1, B2, E1, E1 theta, E2, E2 theta, E19, 101, 217 or 010. **Open** 24hrs daily. **Admission** free.

Sightseeing

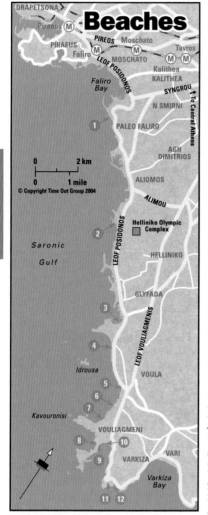

Beaches

Faliro Bay

Saronic Gulf

Helliniko Olympic Complex

Idrousa

Kavouronisi

Varkiza Bay

0   2 km
0   1 mile
© Copyright Time Out Group 2004

Athens' most urban beach may not be its best but is about to become its most convenient. Set in the seaside suburb of Faliro, as of June 2004 the beach connects directly with the centre via a brand-new tram line. Regular Athens buses also make the journey. A good way of approaching the beach is via Flisvos, one of Faliro's main centres, with plenty of eateries and cafés. A small boardwalk running between the coast and Leof Posidonos makes a good spot for lounging. The long beach, which is mostly sandy, with a few pebbles to contend with, comes to an end by the Hotel Poseidon. Since the beach is publicly

managed, it is free of charge, and although that means it's largely a self-service experience, the Hotel Poseidon offers private beach facilities (€4 buys a chaise longue, umbrella, beachside drink service, changing room, shower and lifeguard), while the nearby Edem taverna serves up meals at about €10-€15 per person. If driving, be aware that parking is notoriously difficult in the Paleo Faliro area.

Agios Kosmas ②

Off Leof Posidonos coastal road, Elliniko (next to the Ethniki Athlitiko Kentro [National Athletic Centre]). Bus A1, A2, B1, B2, E1, E1 theta, E2, E2 theta, E19 or 140. **Open** *mid May-mid Sept 9am-9pm daily.* **Admission** *Mon-Fri €5; €2 concessions. Weekends €8; €5 concessions.*

Agios Kosmas is a little tricky to find since it is a few steps from the main coastal road, but those making the extra effort will be rewarded with a perfect day out at one of Athens' smallest, most tasteful and peaceful beaches. Indeed, the size and overall calm help make Agios Kosmas feel a little more like a sleepy island resort rather than an Athens 'scene' beach. The water is clean and boosted by an extra filter/barrier in place for environmental pollution, while security guards are in place to throw out the human sort of pollution (guests behaving badly). Regulars as well as large groups can expect some discounts on request. Generally facilities, as well as the beach itself, are well-maintained. Bathrooms are especially modern and clean; outdoor showers less so. A small green garden is available for a little shade – and private parties on occasion; there is also a snack bar. The Olympic sailing events will take place almost directly in front of the beach, which may lead to its temporary closure in summer 2004.

Asteria ③

Entrance on Leof Vas Georgiou B, between Platia Katraki Vasos and Platia Kritis, Glyfada. Tram from Syntagma area (from summer 2004)/ bus A1, A2, E1, E1 theta, E2 theta, 114, 115, 116, 138 or 149. **Open** *Beach mid May-mid Sept 8am-9.30pm daily (last entry 8pm). Lifeguards on duty until 8pm. Pool area mid May-mid Sept 10am-7pm, 9pm-3am daily.* **Admission** *Mon-Fri €7; €3.50 concessions. Weekends €10; €5 concessions.* **Parking** *Cars €5; motorbikes €2.*

With entrance staff who act like bouncers, landscaped gardens and a nightclub, the Asteria feels like an exclusive beach club. And although Asteria isn't a private membership club, it is the priciest among Athens beaches and encompasses a giant complex and a huge beach on a bay in the seaside suburb of Glyfada, within easy access from the Athens' city centre. With immaculate WCs, extensive dressing rooms, huge gardens, a playground, a volleyball court, a pool complex, a few shops, watersports (water volleyball, inner tubes and blow-up teeter-totters) and several cafés, the Asteria is particularly popular with scenesters and upscale families. Which is not to say the beach has a really refined or restrained quality about it – it's as rowdy as any other beach and at high season can become a virtual sea of people. A unique feature is the elegant pool area, surrounded by cabanas, which transforms into a cocktail bar/café/lounge/disco at night (the €12 admission price also buys you a cabana and a cocktail).

Voula A & Voula B 4 5

Leof Alkyonidon, Voula.
Voula A: opposite the Asklipeo Voula Hospital complex; Voula B: close to the Voula Dimarhio (town hall). Bus A1, A2, E1, E1 theta, E2 theta, 114, 115, 116, 138 or 149 (Voula A); Bus A1, A2, or E1 (Voula B). **Open** *early May-mid Sept* 7am-9pm daily. **Admission** (each beach) €4; €1.50 concessions.
Under the same management and just one and a half kilometres (one mile) apart on the same street, these two private beaches are nearly identical. Both are on the less expensive side, and tend not to be as crowded as some of the other beaches. Both have generous grounds with gardens, generic snack bar, shops, as well as some sports facilities like beach volleyball. Voula A is directly next door to a large, pleasant beachside bistro/café, Palmie (meals around €15), while Voula B has tennis courts and has just finished building bungalows that may be rented out on a short-term basis beginning in 2004. The overall impression is not as marvellously stylish as some

other Athens' beaches and the facilities could be modernised a bit, but both are good value for money and, even at maximum capacity, neither feels cramped.

Kavouri-Vouliagmeni 6

Parallel to Iliou, near Agios Nikolaos church, in the Kavouri district of Vouliagmeni. Bus E1 theta, E2 theta, 114, 115, 116, 138 or 149. **Open** 24hrs daily. **Admission** free.
The incredibly popular Kavouri-Vouliagmeni is a long stretch of sand near the Divani hotel (*see p55*). This public beach is packed throughout the summer; if you can't find a patch of sand, join the others and play rackets by the sea. Though this is a strictly self-service resort, there is a string of fish tavernas (all rather upscale) alongside the beach, and some pleasant places for strolls amid them. The main problem here is definitely space, so if there isn't enough, head to the nearby Megalo Kavouri (*see below*).

Megalo Kavouri 7

Off Leof Kavouriou, in the Kavouri district of Vouliagmeni. Bus 114 (get off at Strofi Kavouriou, a small leafy square). **Open** 24hrs daily. **Admission** free.
Although set in the midst of one of the most expensive real-estate areas in all of Athens, Megalo Kavouri has a casual, distinctively downmarket feel.

Sightseeing

Astir Beach. *See p120.*

The large beach includes an up-close view of an ancient temple ruin on a tiny island right opposite. Shallow waters mean it's a good place for swimmers who are less than proficient, which is probably why swarms of families flock to it. Besides several nondescript, inexpensive cafés, no basic beach services are available (not even changing cabins or outdoor showers), but a shady, tree-dotted area just next to the beach makes for a great do-it-yourself picnic site. Parking is also readily available.

Astir Beach ⑧

Entrance via Plateia Aiglis, on Apollonos, Vouliagmeni Bay. Bus 114, 115 or 116 from Platia Glyfada. **Open** *mid May-mid Sept* 8am-8pm daily. **Admission** *Mon-Fri* €8; €4 concessions. *Weekends* €12; €6 concessions.

Directly across the street from Vouliagmeni public beach (*see below*), this private beach has a couple of real attractions that might be worth the hefty entrance fee: an ancient temple devoted to Apollo that cannot be seen unless you pay admission, and access to watersports otherwise unavailable on Athens beaches. The beach is adjacent to the Astir Palace (*see p69*), one of Athens' most beautiful resorts, but it's safe to say that the closely packed sun-seekers here are not having an Astir Palace experience. Still, the extensive range of watersports (hourly: waterskiing €25; parachuting €60; windsurfing €30; speedboat rental €200; sailing boat rental €45; all can be reserved in advance by calling 210 890 1775-54) is unique. Parking in July and August is extremely difficult. Easy access for the disabled is another positive distinguishing feature of Astir Beach.

Attica Vouliagmeni Beach ⑨

Opposite Platia Aiglis and next to Apollonos, Vouliagmeni Bay. Bus 114 from Glyfada. **Open** 24hrs daily. **Admission** free.

Just opposite the private Astir Beach (*see above*) is the free part of Athens' largest beach. Although lacking an ancient temple and extensive sports facilities, Attica Vouliagmeni is just as crowded as its neighbour, but somehow the huge, wide-open bay beach feels like it has enough space for everyone. The gorgeous view is free, the beach is self-service and definitely tends towards a younger crowd, so if that doesn't sound like your thing, continue on to the privately managed section of the beach (*see below*), which, although virtually the same beach, has a separate entrance.

Attica Vouliagmeni Beach ⑩

On Vouliagmeni Bay. Entrance at the point where Leof Athinas becomes Leof Posidonos, next to the Dimarhio (town hall) at Platia 24 Iouliou, Vouliagmeni Bay. Bus 114, 115, 116 or 340. **Open** *mid May-mid Sept* 8am-9.30 pm (last entry 8pm) daily. **Admission** €5. Animals not allowed.

Excellent value, and stylish to boot, the recently privatised Attica Vouliagmeni Beach (formerly known as Vouliagmeni A Beach) is perhaps the best

compromise between the high-frills Astir Beach (*see above*) and the service-less Attica Vouliagmeni free beach (*see above*). Set on an enormous stretch of sand on Vouliagmeni Bay, perhaps Athens' most beautiful coastline. A low-ish admission fee offers visitors an elegant chaise longue and umbrella, two snack bars, two small children's playgrounds, volleyball courts and a basketball court, and the other usual amenities like changing rooms, WC and open showers. Tennis courts can be booked for €10/hour. Part of the Olympic triathlon is scheduled to take place here, so most likely the beach will be closed for part of summer 2004.

... and the rest

While not exactly proper beaches, **Agnanti** and **Lambros**, two mini-beaches opposite Lake Vouliagmeni, deserve a mention. These makeshift beaches with stylish cafés and restaurants flanking them are very windy, so they are great for extra-hot summer days. However, they practically disappear in high tides. Both also boast shallow waters, making them good alternatives for those with little confidence in their own – or their children's – swimming abilities.

The two beachlets also have a nearby diving school (Vouliagmeni Diving Club, mobile 6934 603 707, accessible under a sign reading 'Akti Mezepoleio') offering various programmes ranging from one dive (€35) to a ten-day course with two dives daily for €350. The beaches have no closing hours, and can be reached via bus 114, 115 or 116 from Glyfada.

Limanakia A & Limanakia B ⑪ ⑫

Between Vouliagmeni and Varkiza. Bus 115, 116, 149, E1 theta, E2 theta. **Open** 24hrs daily. **Admission** free.

'Little Lake A' and 'Little Lake B' are total misnomers, as neither Limanakias is a lake. They are not really beaches either, but stunning, rocky coves set in from the ocean. Resting on an otherwise nondescript stretch of Athens coastline, they are easy to miss, but well worth a stop, if only to gape at the stunning rocks and cove, which are beautifully lit up at night. Descend down one of the small dirt paths leading steeply downhill towards the rocks. Limanakia B (just a short walk from A) leads down directly towards a quiet, rather private area of the rocks. A section of this beach is a well-known gay nudist haven (*see p201*). The steep rocky path at Limanakia A descends towards a café built into the rocks, which offers access to the water below. There's a bona fide scene at the rocks and the café/bar – which has island cantina-style music – is bursting with teenagers and 20-somethings, and is host to all-day parties throughout the summer.

Eat, Drink, Shop

Features

Restaurants

Meze forte.

In conference at **Symposio**. *See p127.*

Eating out is very much a part of Greek culture, and the balmy summer evenings are ideal for enjoying a meal outside in a leafy garden or overlooking the moonlit waves along the coast. If you want to dine with the locals, make your reservation for late evening – Greeks hardly ever go out for dinner before 10pm.

Recent years have seen a great improvement in all things gastronomic, with Athenians venturing away from trusted traditional taverna fare. The overall boom in the restaurant industry has brought a multitude of new trends with it, including classic foreign cuisines like French and Italian, as well as more exotic, multi-ethnic alternatives, Asian, Moroccan and fusion. The global craze for sushi has taken Greece by storm of late, with new restaurants springing up all the time. More and more chefs are now going abroad to train and then returning to Greece to put their newly found creative expertise to good use in the city's kitchens. Three Athens restaurants, **Spondi** (*see p145*), **Vardis** (*see p149*) and **Varoulko** (*see p151*), have all been awarded a Michelin star for their high standards.

In spite of an influx of modern trends, there's no real fear that the old-style taverna will go out of favour with the majority of the population. What has happened, though, is that these past couple of years have seen the birth of 'modern' tavernas aimed at the city's younger crowd, where traditional Greek food is served in a much fresher environment and with more attention to detail.

Making a table reservation is an absolute necessity in club-restaurants and in most quality eateries in general. Your tip should be around 10-15 per cent on top of the bill

Price guide

€ up to €20
€€ €21-€35
€€€ €36-€50
€€€€ €50 and over
For a meal for one including starter, main course and dessert.

(check whether service is included). Be warned that the combination of good food and a great eating environment doesn't come cheap in Athens – although the comparatively high restaurant prices in these places don't seem to deter people in the slightest. Seafood, in particular, is surprisingly expensive, and if it seems like it isn't, it's probably frozen.

GREEK EATS

Eating at traditional tavernas and *mezedopolia* is a must-do; unquestionably one of the best experiences to be had in Greece. Both serve the hearty, deeply flavourful dishes based on the precepts that have governed Greek cooking for centuries: fresh, seasonal ingredients, lots of extra virgin olive oil, local cheeses and a few fragrant herbs and spices. These are assembled sometimes with a wonderful simplicity that shows off the best of dishes, like *horta* (wild greens) with lemon, or sometimes with the inspired creativity that is a hallmark of much peasant food, and comes from taking the only ingredients available and combining them in the most interesting, flavourful way possible. An example of the latter is the winter classic, *stifado*, where rabbit is stewed with dark Mavrodaphne wine and hundreds of tiny onions.

Tavernas are friendly, cheap and informal, and usually have tables covered in butcher paper that is changed for each customer, cosy interiors lined with wine barrels (from which you may sometimes be asked to draw your own wine), outdoor gardens draped in bougainvillea, and cats winding their way around your chairs. Many tavernas have no written menus, and, even when they do, you'll often find that there's plenty of discrepancy between what's on the menu and what's in the kitchen. Usually, the waiter will just reel off what's cooking today, and you'll pick from his list. In many cases, customers are welcome – even expected – to go into the kitchen and just point to what looks most appealing. So don't be afraid to ask to do this. Though it may be intimidating, the taverna staff will consider it par for the course, and you can order exactly what you want, even without understanding a word of Greek.

There are three main types of dishes available. You'll start with a selection of *salates* (salads) and *orektika* (appetizers), a category that includes the dozens of aromatic dips like tzatziki, and small plates of cooked vegetables, like *kolokithokeftedes* (fried courgette-and-potato balls) or *mavromatakia* (marinated black-eyed peas). Main courses include simply grilled or roasted meat and fish, but vegetarians (or just those who don't want slabs of meat at every meal) should be sure to inquire about *mageirefta* (cooked stews, vegetable dishes, and casseroles, such as *briam* and moussaka). All this is accompanied with carafes of *hima* (local barrel wine), and often with the serenades of strolling musicians. For advice on choosing a good taverna, *see p144* **Taverna tips**.

If you're in the mood to sample dozens of dishes in one sitting – and to drink a lot – head to a **mezedopolion**. These serve mezes, lots of

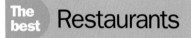

The best Restaurants

For gourmet food
Try **Spondi** (*see p145*), famous for its truffle-based dishes; **Vardis** (*see p149*), the first restaurant in Greece to be awarded a Michelin star; or seafood fusion at **Varoulko** (*see p151*).

For a meze feast
Pick and choose at **Athinaikon** (*see p129*).

For a traditional Greek taverna experience
Platanos (*see p129*) for a real 1940s feel, or **Mamacas** (*see p128*), a firm favourite with the young and trendy brigade.

For Greek contemporary cuisine
Apla Aristera-Dexia (*see p140*) offers modern, creative food in an enjoyable open-air setting.

For views
GB Roof Garden (*see p131*), **Orizondes Lykavitou** (*see p132*), **Pil Poul (O Kirios)** (*see p127*), **Moorings-Varoulko** (*see p145*) and **Le Grand Balcon** (*see p132*) all have lovely outlooks.

For the hippest scene
Join the fashionistas at **Balthazar** (*see p133*) or the beach lovers at **Island** (*see p145*) and **Septem** (*see p145*).

For the best seafood
If you're on a budget, try **Kollias** (*see p151*); for creative cuisine with a great view, head to **Varoulko** (*see p151*), its summer sister venue **Moorings-Varoulko** (*see p145*) and **Plous Podilatou** (*see p151*); and for an island feeling, **Jimmy & the Fish** (*see p151*).

For celebrity-spotting
Central and **48 The Restaurant** (for both *see p131*) attract showbiz VIPs.

Eat, Drink, Shop

Works of art hang on the wall,

but the palette is in the kitchen.

A unique restaurant that combines the opportunity
to buy or just enjoy Greek modern art
with creative Mediterranean cuisine.
Simply wonderful.

restaurant - gallery

small dishes, rather than large main courses, meant as much as an accompaniment to wine, ouzo and gossip, as sustenance. In some *mezedopolia*, the ordering couldn't be easier. The waiter will simply come out with a large tray of all the dishes available, and you'll choose from those. In others, you might pick from a menu or in the kitchen.

Though the focus is ostensibly on nibbles to accompany your meal, most *mezedopolia* serve dishes just as well-made and delicious as you'll find at a taverna. If it turns out this is your favourite way of eating – and it certainly has the advantage of allowing you to try everything – you can also turn your taverna experience into a meze feast. Tell your waiter you'll eschew the main courses, and simply order one of all the salads and appetizers.

Mezedopolia are also known as *ouzerie*, as ouzo, the aniseed-flavoured spirit distilled from the remains of grapes from the wine press, is the traditional liquid accompaniment. You'll also come across other members of the ouzo family: *raki* (the basic drink with or without the aniseed flavouring), *tsipouro* (with aniseed but slightly weaker than ouzo) or *tsikoudia* (Cretan *raki* without aniseed). All varieties are served with water and ice.

Acropolis & around

Creative cuisine

Edodi
Veikou 80, Koukaki (210 921 3013). Metro Akropoli or Syngrou-Fix. **Open** 8pm-12.30am Mon-Sat. **Average** €€€. **Credit** AmEx, DC, MC, V. **Map** p299 F7.
A beautiful neo-classical building in the central neighbourhood of Koukaki houses one of the humblest creative-cuisine restaurants in Athens. While the menu offers some interesting combinations, the flavours are not quite as delicate as we would like, but the prices are more affordable than other restaurants in the same category. The menu will initially pass before your eyes in the form of raw ingredients and later arrive ready to serve. Most of the desserts are fruit-based.

Event
Mnisikleous 7B, Plaka (210 331 5209). Metro Monastiraki. **Open** 11.30am-1am daily. **Average** €€€. **Credit** MC, V. **Map** p295/p299 E5.
Nikos Fanourakis is one of the few restaurateurs in the city who understands the similarities between a chef and an artist, and who knows how to bring out the best in both. His talents come together in this gallery-cum-bar-cum-restaurant (formerly the Athens

Eat, Drink, Shop

Cod and dips at **Bakaliarakia stou Damigou**. *See p128.*

Fashionable **48 The Restaurant**: for smart arses. *See p131.*

Gallery), where you can gaze at contemporary etchings and silk-screen prints by Greek artists while sampling successful fusion-Mediterranean cuisine. Seating is somewhat limited, but there are tables outside at which to enjoy a coffee in the morning, or food and drinks during the rest of the day.

Kouti

Adrianou 23, Monastiraki (210 321 3229).
Metro Monastiraki. **Open** 10.30am-1.30am Mon-Fri; 10.30am-2am Sat, Sun. **Average** €€. **Credit** AmEx, MC, V. **Map** p295/p299 E5.
With tables right next to the Ancient Agora in the hot months, this is the ideal location in which to relax and watch the world go by over a glass of ouzo, small delicacies and delicious salads. The menu is a bit limited and rather expensive, but the main dishes are well made.

Fish

Thalatta

Vitonos 5, Thisio (210 346 4204). Metro Thisio.
Open 8pm-12.30am daily. **Average** €€€.
Credit MC, V. **Map** p294/p298 B5.
The atmosphere at Thalatta, situated as it is in a beautifully restored house, with a tile-paved, flower-filled courtyard, tucked unexpectedly among Thisio's faded old factories, definitely has an edgy appeal of its own. Owner Yiannis Safos, originally from the island of Icaria, focuses on sourcing the freshest, most interesting fish that are pulled daily from the Aegean. Start with a selection from the top-quality raw bar, before moving on to dishes based

on regional recipes prepared with a touch of high-end flair: smoky grilled octopus with a brightly flavourful pumpkin purée and sundried tomatoes; sole from Messolongi with a sauce of porcini mushrooms and sweet wine; or a traditional fisherman's stew of monkfish with fennel and wild herbs. Finish with a tart lemon-peel sorbet.

French

Pil Poul (O Kirios)

Apostolou Pavlou 51, Thisio (210 342 3665). Metro
Thisio. **Open** 8pm-12.30am Mon-Sat. **Average** €€€.
Credit AmEx, DC, MC, V. **Map** p295/p299 D5.
The luxurious Pil Poul boasts an impressive and stylish tri-level balcony facing the Acropolis for the summer months and a slinky dining hall for the winter. The menu is generally – though not consistently – of a high standard and dishes such as the caprine rolled with prosciutto and the foie gras with caramelised endives are excellent.

Greek contemporary

Symposio

Erechthiou 46, Acropolis & Filopappou Hill (210 922
5321). Metro Akropoli. **Open** *May-Sept* noon-3am daily. *Oct-Apr* 8pm-3am Mon-Sat. **Average** €€€.
Credit AmEx, DC, MC, V. **Map** p299 E7.
Though its prices may be a little high, located as it is on the slopes of the Acropolis, Symposio is the perfect summer spot for dinner after a performance at the Herodeion. The quality of the ingredients here,

which in September might include wild mushrooms gathered in Epirus by the restaurant owner himself, carefully selected organic produce and delicious bread, is celebrated by local food fans. Due care goes into combining such fresh ingredients to create interesting, flavourful dishes. Be sure to ask for a table in the courtyard, with a view of the Acropolis.

Greek traditional

Bakaliarakia stou Damigou

Kydathinaion 41, Plaka (210 322 5084). Metro Syntagma. **Open** 6pm-1.30am Mon-Sat; noon-1.30am Sun. Closed June-Aug. **Average** €€. **No credit cards**. Map p299 F6.
This traditional, little basement tavern in Plaka is one of the best-known places in Athens to enjoy the traditional Greek fried cod with garlic dip. The space itself reveals the tavern's age. The interior is like something from a Greek 1950s film and the kitchen offers nothing more than the clean, clear taste of good old-fashioned Greek cuisine.

Café Avyssinia

Kinetou 7, Monastiraki (210 321 7047). Metro Monastiraki. **Average** €€. **Open** 10.30am-1am Tue-Sun. **Credit** MC, V. **Map** p295/p299 D5.
The Avyssinia, which from its upper level offers a view of the tin roofs of the flea market and beyond to the Parthenon, sees arty types gather here to feast on such titbits as mussel risotto, roast potatoes and

snails. Weekend lunchtimes are usually pleasantly hectic: to get here you must zigzag your way through the old books, weird serving dishes and rusty taps that are strewn about by the antiques sellers in the market.

Giouvetsakia

Adrianou 144 & Thespidos, Plaka (210 322 7033). Metro Akropoli. **Open** 10am-2am daily. **Average** €. **Credit** MC, V. **Map** p295 D5.
This family-run taverna is the place to head for a delectable roast lamb with pasta cooked in a clay dish – a traditional Greek *yiouvetsi*. People from all walks of life (including local characters, such as the old man with his hurdy-gurdy) can be seen walking past, while the area's tourist hot-spot character stops at the door. The wine list isn't impressive, but the decent house wine serves to make amends. The air-conditioned interior is welcome on hot summer days.

Mamacas

Persefonis 41, Thisio (210 346 4984). Metro Thisio. **Open** 1.30pm-1am daily. **Average** €. **No credit cards**. **Map** p294 B4.
Though modern in style and decor, Mamacas specialises in traditional Greek cuisine. The three pastel-coloured dining areas inside, and the tables down to street, fill up with a young and wealthy crowd – it's the hippest place in the area to go during the summer. The service can be nonchalant, but the central location makes up for it.

Balthazar. *See p133.*

Platanos

Diogenous 4, Plaka (210 322 0666). Metro
Monastiraki. **Open** noon-4.30pm, 7.30pm-midnight
Mon-Sat; noon-4.30pm Sun. **Average** €. **No credit**
cards. Map p295/p299 E5.

Platanos is one of the few tavernas left in Athens to
have preserved its 1940s feel so beautifully and
gracefully. Its heavily time-worn chairs have been
occupied by some of the greatest Greek personalities in politics and the arts, while the kitchen is still
run with an eye to treating both its local and foreign
clientele to good, well-cooked food. Try the white
wine and see if all the certificates it has received
from the Greek Wine Academy (since 1935) that are
hung on the wall are worth it. The lush, green environment of the open-air seating creates the impression of a village square, while the interior provides
a typical taverna feel.

Psarras

Erechthiou 16 & Erotokritou 12, Plaka
(210 321 8733). Metro Akropoli or Monastiraki.
Open 11am-1am daily. **Average** €€€.
Credit AmEx, DC, MC, V. **Map** p299 E6.

Psarras (meaning 'fisherman') is a recently refurbished and upgraded taverna. During the hot
summer days it's best to sit either at one of the tables
on the top floor, with a view of Lycabettus Hill, or
in the spacious courtyard across the street, where
tables have been placed on the different levels
of the yard. As far as the food is concerned, the
taverna offers delectable starters and a good selection of grilled meat and fish. Whatever you choose
for a main course, don't forget to place an order
for Psarras's all-time favourite: spicy greens with an
onion and tomato sauce.

Syn Athina

Iraklidon 2, Thisio (210 345 5550). Metro Thisio.
Open 9am-3am Mon-Thur; 9am-4am Fri, Sat.
Average €. **Credit** AmEx, DC, MC, V.
Map p294/p298 C5 .

Situated in a restored neo-classical building, Syn
Athina offers a splendid view of the Acropolis.
Outside, the tables on the pedestrianised street
are a great place to sit and people-watch. The menu
consists mostly of Greek classics.

Historic centre

Greek traditional

Athinaikon

Themistokleous 2 (210 383 8485). Metro Omonia.
Open 11.30am-12.30am Mon-Sat. Closed Aug.
Average €. **No credit cards. Map** p295 E3.

This central Athens institution has a four-page
list of mezes, and every one we have tried has
been consistently good. Among our favourites are
the *bekri* meze (drinkers' titbits such as pork marinated in wine and topped with hot salted cheese),
clams served in their shells, grilled octopus, shrimp

croquettes, *gigantes* in a rich tomato sauce and
ameletita (sautéed lamb testicles). The classic, comfy
surrounds feature dark, wooden beams, marble-
topped tables made from old-fashioned sewing
machines and framed mid 20th-century memorabilia
dating back to the restaurant's early years.

Diporto

Theatrou & Sofokleous (no phone). Metro Omonia.
Open noon-6pm Mon-Sat. Closed 2wks Aug.
Average €. **No credit cards. Map** p295 E4.

Ducking downstairs from the gritty streets and
packed Central Market, you'll enter a cheerful little
basement that has been the beating heart of this
Athenian neighbourhood for over 50 years.
Everyone comes here for lunch: blood-spattered
butchers from the market, suit-clad brokers from the
nearby stock exchange, artists, migrants, and even
ladies who lunch. If it's crowded, chef/owner/waiter
Barba Mitsos will sit you down at any table with
empty spaces, so be prepared to make friends. It's
not hard, over his simple, delicious and dirt-cheap
fare. Sometimes, he'll also decide what you're going
to have, and bring it to you without asking. Often
on offer are his buttery *gigantes*, warming chickpea
soup, fried *marides* and exceptional *horiatiki*. There
are only two things to drink: water, and wine drawn
directly from the barrels lining the walls.

Doris

Praxitelous 30 (210 323 2671/210 323 0177).
Metro Syntagma. **Open** 7.30am-6.30pm daily.
Average €. **No credit cards. Map** p295 F4.

Located at the same address since 1900, the
well-tended Doris restaurant is a leading advocate
of classic Greek cuisine. It serves rice pudding and
cream from early in the morning, while at lunchtime
it attracts all sorts of passers-by and employees
from neighbouring offices for its daily home-style
dishes. Most of the pots are empty by 3pm, so you
have to be quick.

Ideal

Panepistimiou 46 (210 330 3000). Metro
Panepistimio. **Open** *May-Sept* noon-midnight
Mon-Sat. *Oct-Apr* noon-1am Mon-Sat. **Average** €€.
Credit AmEx, DC, MC, V. **Map** p295 F3.

One of Athens' oldest restaurants, Ideal remains true
to the values of the family that has been running it
since 1922. Here you'll bump into old-time patrons
and loners enjoying one of the 20 daily specials.
The waiting staff provides quick and efficient
service, while the menu offers good home cooking
and classic Greek cuisine at very reasonable prices.

Kallimarmaro

Evforionios 13, National Gardens (210 701 9727).
Trolleybus 2, 4, 11. **Open** *May-Sept* 12.30pm-1am
daily. *Oct-Apr* 12.30pm-3pm, 7pm-1am Tue-Sat;
12.30-5pm Sun. **Average** €. **Credit** DC, MC, V.
Map p297 H6.

This establishment's comfortable interior furnishings, large windows framed with white curtains
and small tables dotted on the pavement make for

a welcoming environment. The menu is based on traditional Greek cuisine, one of the specialities being a rich cheese and leek pie. Popular main courses include chicken with Cypriot halloumi cheese, sultanas, pomegranate seeds and herbs cooked according to an ancient Greek recipe. The lamb en croute baked in a clay dish also draws the punters. Desserts include lovely, home-made (and filling) prunes, which are stuffed with walnuts and cooked in brandy and come with a chocolate sauce.

Mediterranean

GB Roof Garden
Grande Bretagne Hotel, Syntagma (210 333 0766). Metro Syntagma. **Open** *May-Oct* 7.30pm-2am daily. Closed Nov-Apr. **Average** €€€€. **Credit** AmEx, DC, MC, V. **Map** p295/p299 F5.
The rooftop restaurant of the Grande Bretagne Hotel offers luxurious dining with an unrivalled view of Syntagma Square, with the Parliament and the Acropolis serving as a backdrop. The space is modern and cultivated and the menu's fortes include excellent steak and fish on the grill. A few words of warning: a full meal can be quite pricey and booking a few days in advance is essential.

Olive Garden
Titania Hotel, Panepistimiou 52 (210 383 8511). Metro Panepistimio. **Open** 8pm-1am Mon-Fri; 8pm-1.30am Sat, Sun. **Average** €€. **Credit** AmEx, DC, MC, V. **Map** p295 F3.
A small piece of paradise in the centre of Athens, the Olive Garden is located on the top floor of the Titania Hotel. During summer evenings it provides an oasis of olive trees and beautiful flowers on its large veranda. In winter you can also enjoy a spectacular view of the Acropolis and the city lights at one of the tables by the glass-window in the pointedly hotel dining room. A classic meeting place for business-lunching stockbrokers, the Olive Garden's cuisine is Mediterranean, with an emphasis on Greek flavours.

Palea Vouli
Karytsi 7 (210 323 4803). Metro Syntagma. **Open** *mid Oct-Apr* noon-12.30am daily. Closed May-Sept. **Average** €€. **Credit** AmEx, MC, V. **Map** p295 F1.
Located next to Athens' Old Parliament – from which it derives its name – Palea Vouli serves coffee and food from lunchtime onwards. It's most enjoyable in summer, since the restaurant's outdoor tables, set up bang opposite the Old Parliament building, are shaded by the trees of Platia Kolokotroni and look across to the statue of General Theodoros Kolokotronis. The discreetly luxurious courtyard features cool marble surfaces, a palm tree and a stunning view of the Acropolis. The menu focuses mainly on Italian cuisine, although there are also a few interesting Greek selections to be had.

Oriental

Noodle Bar
Apollonos 11 (210 331 8585). Metro Syntagma. **Open** *May-Sept* 24hrs daily. *Oct-Apr* noon-midnight Mon-Sat; 5pm-midnight Sun. **Average** €. **Credit** MC, V. **Map** p295/p299 F5.
The simplicity and low prices at this pioneering (by Greek standards) noodle bar are the recipe of its success. Take a seat at one of the few outdoor tables and take in the surrounding neighbourhood. Aside from the noodles, the soups are worth a try too. And you'll be slurping in the company of a few Asian customers – always a good sign. You can order your dishes to go.

Kolonaki & around

Creative

Central
Platia Kolonaki 14, Kolonaki (210 724 5938/210 724 1059). Metro Syntagma. **Open** 11am-4am daily. Closed June-Sept, except 2004. **Average** €€€. **Credit** AmEx, MC, V. **Map** p297 H5.
Starting in the morning and running well into the early hours, this New York-style space is a favourite with stylish Athenians and local show-biz celebrities, who stop by for a cup of coffee, a sushi lunch, a relaxing drink at the bar, or a modern cuisine dinner to intense music. Its chocolate desserts are real winners.

Food Company
Anagnostopoulou 47, Kolonaki (210 363 0373). Metro Syntagma. **Open** 10am-midnight Mon-Fri; 10am-1am Sat, Sun. **Average** €. **No credit cards**. **Map** p297 G3.
At the bottom of Lycabettus Hill, this chic eatery is frequented by all sorts, from young couples rendez-vousing at one of the window tables to dog-walking old ladies picking up a takeaway to solitary types enjoying a peaceful read of the foreign newspapers at one of the pavement tables. Cold noodle dishes, lentil salad and carrot cake are recommended.
Other locations: Eleftheroudakis Bookshop, Panepistimiou 17, Historic Centre (210 325 8440).

48 The Restaurant
Armatolon & Klefton 48, Neapoli (210 641 1082). Metro Ambelokipi. **Open** *June-Sept* 1pm-midnight daily. *Oct-May* 1pm-midnight Mon-Sat. **Average** €€€. **Credit** AmEx, DC, MC, V.
This recent arrival on the Athens restaurant scene has set a new standard, combining a beautiful modern environment with exceptional cuisine and a wine list ranging from a perfectly respectable €20 table wine to fine labels in the €80 category. The space is modern but warm thanks to lighting by Arnold Chan – lighting designer for London's stylish Hakkasan. The creative cuisine menu, largely founded on immaculate preparation combined with

The menu

Avgolemono: a sauce made out of lemon, egg yolks and chicken stock. Also used for a soup made with rice, chicken stock, lemon and egg yolks.

Baklava: a pan-Middle Eastern sweet made from sheets of filo pastry layered with nuts.

Barbouni: red mullet, usually selected by the customer, grilled and served with olive oil.

Bekri meze: cooked pork marinated in wine, usually topped with melted cheese.

Briam: a vegetarian casserole of aubergines, courgettes, tomatoes, potatoes, bay and spices, similar to ratatouille.

Dolmades: young vine leaves stuffed with rice, spices and (usually) minced meat.

Fasolia plaki or pilaki: white beans in a tomato, oregano, bay, parsley and garlic sauce.

Fava: a dip made of puréed yellow split peas, usually topped with olive oil and chopped red onions.

Garides: large prawns, fried or grilled.

Gemista: tomatoes or peppers stuffed with a combination of rice, mince, herbs, pine nuts and raisins.

Gigantes or gigandes: white haricot beans baked in tomato sauce; pronounced 'yigandes'.

Halloumi or hallumi: a cheese traditionally made from sheep's or goat's milk, but increasingly from cow's milk. Best served fried or grilled. Primarily a Cypriot speciality.

Horiatiki: Greek 'peasant' salad of tomato, cucumber, onion, feta and sometimes green pepper, dressed with ladolemono (oil and lemon).

Horta: salad of wild greens.

Htipiti: tangy purée of matured cheeses, flavoured with red peppers.

Kalamari, kalamarakia or calamares: small squid, usually sliced into rings, battered and fried.

Kataifi or katayfi: syrup-soaked 'shredded-wheat' dessert rolls.

Keftedes or keftedakia: herbacious meatballs made with minced pork or lamb (rarely beef), egg, breadcrumbs and possibly grated potato.

Kleftiko: slow-roasted lamb on the bone (often shoulder), flavoured with oregano and other herbs.

Kokkinisto: chunks of meat – usually lamb or beef – baked with tomatoes and herbs in an earthenware pot, which seals in the juices and flavours.

Loukanika or lukanika: spicy coarse-ground sausages, usually made with pork and heavily herbed.

Loukoumades: tiny, spongy doughnuts dipped in honey.

top-quality ingredients (mostly delicate flavours) and a crisp, clear taste, has proved to be a great success with customers. The service is friendly, not stuffy, and sedate. Booking is essential.

Le Grand Balcon

St George Lycabettus Hotel, Kleomenous 2, Kolonaki (210 729 0712). Metro Evangelismos. **Open** 8.30pm-12.30am Tue-Sat. **Average** €€€. **Credit** AmEx, DC, MC, V. **Map** p297 J4.

Le Grand Balcon serves the creations of executive chef Marc Enderborg. Cleverly combined ingredients and colours, fresh fish and fine seafood compositions, such as the cappuccino shellfish soup flavoured with apple and curry, are real winners. These appetising offerings are complemented by an interesting list of wines and backed by music from resident DJs. Snow-white sofas and views of Athens and the Acropolis in the twilight make it an alluring setting for an unforgettable dinner.

Orizondes Lykavitou

Lycabettus Hill, Kolonaki (210 722 7065). Metro Evangelismos. **Open** noon-2am daily. **Average** €€€€. **Credit** AmEx, DC, MC, V. **Map** p297 J3.

Chef Yiannis Glendis injects new life into traditional Mediterranean dishes with some wacky experimentations, replacing the meat in the classic *giouvetsi* with ray and adding a retsina froth. On the meat front, Glendis's speciality is the Japanese Kobe beef, the price of which, unfortunately, you really don't want to know. The restaurant's location offers breathtaking views of the city. Check the funicular railway timetables to find your way up to the top of Lycabettus Hill.

Ethnic

Altamira

Tsakalof 36A, Kolonaki (210 361 4695). Metro Evangelismos or Syntagma. **Open** 1pm-2am Mon-Sat. **Average** €€. **Credit** MC, V. **Map** p297 G4.

Arabic, Chinese, Indian and Mexican cuisine successfully combined in a reasonably priced menu. In contrast to many other 'ethnic' food restaurants in Athens, here the dishes are originals and based on real know-how, while the colonial-style dining room is warm and inviting. When the waiters guide you through the endless menu – do try the

Loukoumi: 'Turkish' delight, made with syrup, rosewater and pectin, often studded with nuts.

Mageirefta: cooked vegetable dishes such as casseroles and stews. (This is a useful word to know in restaurants with no menus, where the waiter might say, 'We have such-and-such for salads, such-and-such for meats and such-and-such for mageirefta.' Also a useful word for vegetarians or people who don't want to eat hunks of grilled meat or fish at every meal.)

Marides: picarel, often mis-translated as 'whitebait' – small fish best coated in flour and flash-fried.

Melitzanosalata: purée of grilled aubergines.

Meze (plural mezedes): a selection of appetisers and main dishes that can be either hot or cold.

Moussaka(s): a baked dish of minced meat, aubergine and potato slices and herbs, topped with béchamel sauce.

Oktapothdi: octopus, usually grilled fresh and served with lemon and olive oil.

Papoutsaki: aubergine 'shoes', slices stuffed with mince, topped with sauce, usually béchamel or similar.

Pastourma(s): dense, dark-tinted garlic sausage, traditionally made from beef.

Saganaki: fried cheese, usually *kefalotyri*; also means anything (mussels, spinach) made in a cheese-based red sauce.

Skordalia: garlic and breadcrumb or potato-based dip, used as a side dish.

Soutzoukakia: baked meat rissoles, often topped with a tomato-based sauce.

Souvla: large cuts of lamb or pork slow-roasted on a rotary spit.

Souvlaki: chunks of meat quick-grilled on a skewer (known to London takeaways as kebab or shish kebab).

Spanakopitta: small turnovers, traditionally triangular, stuffed with spinach, dill and feta.

Spetsofai: a stew of sausages and peppers cooked with wine and bay leaf.

Stifado: a rich meat stew (often rabbit) with onions, red wine, tomatoes, cinnamon and bay.

Tarama, properly taramosalata: fish roe pâté, originally made of grey mullet roe (*avgotaraho* or *botargo*), but now more often cod roe, plus olive oil, lemon juice and breadcrumbs.

Tyropitta: like spanakopitta, but usually without spinach and with more feta.

Tzatziki: a dip of shredded cucumber, yoghurt, garlic, lemon juice and mint.

For a general eating-out vocabulary, *see p277*.

Eat, Drink, Shop

poppadoms with four dips from the Indian section – bear in mind that the portions are very big if you want to leave enough room for dessert.

Greek contemporary

Balthazar

Veranzerou 27 & Tsocha, Neapoli (210 644 1215). Metro Ambelokipi. **Open** *May-early Oct* 9pm-12.30am Mon-Sat. *Mid Oct-Apr* 9pm-12.30am daily. **Average** €€€€. **Credit** AmEx, MC, V.

The first Balthazar and its contemporary, Ratka, were the first 'in' places in Athens in the 1980s. Its owners have recovered something of its past glory with little thought for cost, a portion of which customers are called upon to share when the bill arrives. In winter, the *mise en scène* is a rather theatrical one inside the beautiful neo-classical building. In summertime the courtyard opens and Balthazar becomes the dining destination of choice for high society. The palm trees that adorn the well-proportioned and pleasantly lit dining area, create an out-of-Athens feel. This year the chef is Giorgos Tsaktsiras, who made a name for himself at Boschetto.

Cookou Food

Themistokleous 66, Exarchia (210 383 1955). Metro Omonia. **Open** 1pm-1am Mon-Sat. Closed 2wks Aug. **Average** €. **Credit** V.

This modern take on the classic Greek diner is primarily aimed at young local crowds. Imaginative decorative features include dried aubergines hanging from the ceiling, and tables hand-painted with little mottos. Such small details have endeared Cookou Food to many and make it a comfortable place to dine, even when going solo. Dishes marry tradition with just a little daring, such as chicken in an orange sauce.

Gantes

Valtetsiou 44, Exarchia (210 330 1369). Metro Omonia. **Open** 8pm-1am Mon; 1.30pm-1am Tue-Sun. **Average** €. **Credit** MC, V.

Traditional values meet contemporary trends in this chic restaurant. It's spacious and tranquil, with simple, modern decor. A variety of starters come from all around Greece, while for mains, the creative casseroles, such as the Byzantine chicken with honey, coriander and sultanas, are a delight. A stone-paved courtyard here overlooks Valtetsiou.

Prytanion

Milioni 7, Kolonaki (210 364 3353).
Metro Syntagma. **Open** noon-1am Mon-Fri;
noon-1.45am Sat, Sun. **Average** €€€.
Credit AmEx, DC, MC, V. **Map** p297 G4.
Located in one of the most cosmopolitan pedestrianised streets in Kolonaki, Prytanion is perfect for people-watching. The outside tables are shaded by trees and the wood-dominated interior is fully air-conditioned, with three different levels, where you can enjoy a meal or a drink to upbeat music. The food is generally great, though not always reliably so.
Other locations: Kolokotroni 37, Platia Kefalari, Kifisia (210 808 9160).

Greek traditional

Eleni

Anapiron Polemou 4-6, Kolonaki (210 721 8868).
Metro Evangelismos. **Open** *Sept-June* 8.30pm-1.30am Mon-Fri. Closed Sat, Sun and July-Aug. **Average** €€. **Credit** AmEx, MC, V. **Map** p297 J4.
This stylish restaurant combines modern design with traditional Greek cuisine, including light seafood mezes and home-style dishes. If you go with a group of friends book one of the two large sofas or one of the few outside tables. Sample the *cazan dipi*, an authentic Thessaloniki dessert, and try to save some room for the excellent yoghurt and sour cherry tart.

Maritsa's

Voukourestiou 47 & Fokilidou 15, Kolonaki
(210 363 0132). Metro Syntagma. **Open** 1.30pm-1.30am daily. **Average** €€. **Credit** AmEx, MC, V. **Map** p297 G4.
A chic and bohemian watering hole with tables outside on the stepped street of Fokilidou. The inside seating area is warm and inviting, reminiscent of a 1980s piano restaurant. The food is traditional, with such dishes as tasty fried courgette or chickpea patties and crispy fried mullet.
Other locations: Sofokleous 17, Historic Centre (210 325 1421).

Oikeio

Ploutarchou 15, Kolonaki (210 725 9216). Metro
Evangelismos. **Open** 1pm-12.30am Mon-Thur;
1pm-1am Fri, Sat. **Average** €. **Credit** MC, V.
Map p297 H4.
If you're looking for a cosy atmosphere and traditional Greek fare in Athens' most upmarket neighbourhood, this is the place to go to. The menu features a number of fresh salads and pies, while the oven-baked selections are tasty and well made. A few tables are placed on the pavement on sunny days, while indoors the small private balcony is the best spot to grab.

Ouzadiko

Lemos Shopping Centre, Karneadou 25-29,
Kolonaki (210 729 5484). Metro Evangelismos.
Open 12.30-6pm, 8pm-11.45pm Tue-Sat.
Closed Aug. **Average** €€. **Credit** DC, MC, V.
Map p297 H5.
Ouzadiko specialises in the small dishes that traditionally accompany a glass of ouzo – with a wide selection of ouzo and *tsipouro* to boot. But the cosy decor (dark wood, marble tables) and expanded menu set it apart from the regular run of ouzo joints. Everything, from the salads to the pies, is delicious and, if it's on the menu when you visit, make sure you try the roast pig, which is delectable if expensive. One of the most famous specialities here is the chocolate (as they call it) soufflé. It is, in fact, a *moelleux au chocolat* that even the French would envy. Avoid during a heatwave – it can get very hot and stuffy inside.

Rosalia

Valtetsiou 58, Exarchia (210 330 2933). Metro
Omonia. **Open** noon-2am daily. **Average** €. **Credit** AmEx, DC, MC, V.
The 'rose of Exarchia' offers a wide variety of traditional Greek dishes plus a few extras, such as chicken *à la crème* and a light *pannacotta* for dessert. Inside, wood panelling and photographs of Athens in the 1920s and '30s give the taverna a warm, homely feel, while a lush, vine-filled garden opens up to diners in the summer.

Vlasis

Pasteur 8, Ambelokipi (210 646 3060). Metro
Ambelokipi. **Open** 1-5pm, 9pm-1am Mon-Sat; 1-5pm Sun. **Average** €. **No credit cards**.
An all-time classic bourgeois restaurant serving traditional Greek food. When the starters tray comes round, be sure to try the aubergine with yoghurt, the leek pie and the *lachanodolmades* (stuffed cabbage leaves), which make an especially good choice during the winter. Signature main courses include pork with quince, rabbit in a tomato and shallot sauce, and lamb in an oregano sauce. When available, the grilled cuttlefish is strongly recommended. Warm cream pie and baked apples are just the thing for dessert. Booking is essential.

Italian

Boschetto

Athens Hilton, Leof Vas Sofias 46 & Evangelismos
Park, Kolonaki (210 721 0893). Metro Evangelismos.
Open 8pm-midnight Mon-Sat. **Average** €€€€.
Credit AmEx, DC, MC, V.
Boschetto serves modern Italian cuisine in a traditional-style venue, attracting mostly Greek and foreign business people. The main indoor seating area, though chic, could use a lick of paint. In summer ask for a table under the pine trees.

Il Parmigiano

Grivaion 3, off Delphou, Kolonaki (210 364
1414). Metro Panepistimio. **Open** noon-1.30am Mon-Sat. **Average** €€. **No credit cards**.
Map p297 G3.
This is a classic Italian trattoria – how much more classic can you get than to name yourself after a cheese? – the feel of which goes from serene at

La Pasteria
CUCINA ITALIANA

It takes two...to Pasta

Irresistible pasta dishes and all the delights of Italian cuisine in a uniquely Mediterranean atmosphere.

Restaurants:

Kolonaki: 18, Tsakalof st., Tel.: 210-3632032 • **Glyfada:** 6, V. Katraki st., Bizaniou Sq. Tel.: 210-8945085 • **N. Smyrni:** 15, K. Palaiologou st. Tel.: 210-9319146 • **Patision:** 58, Patision Ave. Tel.: 210-8250315 • **Alexandras:** 213, Alexandras Ave Tel.: 210-6455220 • **Bournazi:** Konstantinoupoleos st. & Har. Trikoupi st., 28th October Sq. Tel.: 210-5775133 • **El. Venizelos Airport:** Sky View/Olympus Plaza Tel.: 210-3538880 • **Kifisia:** 9, Kasaveti st., Tel.: 210-8085607 • **Palaio Faliro:** 7, Ag. Alexandrou st., Tel.: 210-9858880 • **Ag. Paraskevi:** 19, Ag. Ioannou st.

Open from 13:00 to 02:00   www.lapasteria.gr

My kind of town

Drunk or sober, stuffed or starving, few customers at **Varoulko** (*see p151*) would be able to explain the restaurant's name. Lefteris Lazarou, Varoulko's owner and Athens' celebrated chef, is one of the few. He'll even draw you a diagram. In ship-speak, the name means *derrick*, a cargo-carrying crane. Lazarou's father was a ship's cook.

Lazarou is likeable. Immediately. Rolling his own cigarettes, the words being served up from his smiling, saucepan-worn face are in easy, ordinary Greek out of noble consideration for the translator. For this alone he deserves a gold star (*see below*).

The man from Piraeus has mixed views on eating out in Athens: 'Many places have reasonable food... but really good food is only available in really good restaurants.' Such as his, but he's too modest to say so.

Indeed, Lazarou remains commendably down to earth for someone whose Piraeus restaurant (which decamps to Lake Vouliagmeni for the summer under the name of Moorings-Varoulko) is one of only three in Greece to have a coveted Michelin star.

How can normal-budget visitors to Athens know whether a taverna is any good before committing themselves? To the three 'classic' tests (Are there any Greeks there? Is anybody there? Does the owner carry a gun?), Lazarou adds this one: 'Whenever you see a big menu, the food is not good.' So where does he go? 'If I have a guest from abroad, the first place I go to eat something light around lunchtime is **Aigli Bistro Café** (Zappeion Gardens, Historic centre, 210 336 9363). Not cheap, but good.' Ouzo-ogler

Lazarou also recommends 'dropping by for mezes and an ouzo' at **Athinaikon** (*see p129*), close to Omonia.

In northern Athens, there's the bar/restaurant **Big Deals** (Harilaou Trikoupi 50, Kefalari, 210 623 0860). 'Not Deals... BIG Deals!' Boats many miles out at sea can hear his emphasis. In southern Athens, the **Lambros** restaurant (*see p149*) 'stands out from the rest' for this fresh-fish fancier. **Patroklos** (don't expect a phone number on an island where there is not even electricity) on the nearby small, non-inhabited island of Patroklos is great. 'But you need your own boat,' he adds, half-apologetically.

Lazarou likes to watch people, in a non-criminal sort of way. He recommends a Sunday beer at **Café Avyssinia** (*see p128*) if you've survived Saturday afternoons at **Artemis** (closed until sometime in 2004) inside the Piraeus meat market. 'I go to hear the traders shouting, to meet with people and' (surprise) 'drink an ouzo.' Elsewhere in Piraeus, the suggests the taverna **Panorama** (Irakliou 18-20, Kastella, 210 412 6713).

Away from food, Lazarou says visitors to Athens simply must walk around the Acropolis and adjacent areas of Plaka and Psyrri.

As for the 2004 Athens Olympic Games, no Greek wishing to live would publicly express doubts, but Lazarou seems genuinely confident: 'We Greeks do things at the last moment, but I think the Olympics will be fine and a big opportunity for the world to see Athens and taste Greek cuisine.' Including his, if they want a taste of gold-medal standards.

Eat, Drink, Shop

Padre Padrone

pasta e pizza

24 LEPENIOTOU STR. & OGYGOU - PSIRRI - TEL. 210 3318184

off-peak times to hectic during rush hour. You can eat at one of the tables outside on the tree-shaded pedestrianed street, or inside the stylishly simple restaurant. Succumb to the seafood *tagliolini* served straight from the pan, but save room for a traditional Italian *gelato fugato* for dessert. Service comes with a smile, while reasonable prices are a clincher. Booking is advised.

17
Lykavitou 2, Kolonaki (210 364 7049). Metro Syntagma. **Open** *May-Sept* 11am-2am daily. *Oct-Apr* 11am-2am Mon-Sat. **Average** €€€. **Credit** AmEx, DC, MC, V. **Map** p297 G4.
At lunchtime this unaffected restaurant is popular with Greek politicians, journalists and businessmen. The daytime menu offers mainly Greek selections; in the evenings a wider variety of Mediterranean-style dishes are available at higher prices. The careful, polite service and the light Greek songs every evening (the latter only in winter), all contribute to a thoroughly enjoyable night out.

Middle Eastern

Alexandria
Metsovou 13 & Rethymnou 7, Exarchia (210 821 0004). Metro Victoria. **Open** *June, July, Sept* 8.30pm-midnight Mon-Sat. *Oct-May* 8.30pm-2am Mon-Sat. Closed Aug. **Average** €€. **Credit** MC, V.
Alexandria offers a feast of Eastern flavours. Savour the summer specials – like octopus with chickpea purée or aubergine in a tomato sauce served with yoghurt – in the restaurant's courtyard, the entrance to which is at the rear, on Rethymnou. Indoors, earthenware vases and rows of small drawers displaying a bounty of herbs and spices create a distinctive atmosphere. Booking is essential at weekends and recommended at other times.

Oriental

Freud Oriental
Xenokratous 21, Kolonaki (210 729 9595). Metro Evangelismos. **Open** 9pm-1am daily. **Average** €€€. **Credit** MC, V. **Map** p297 H4.
The owner and host at Freud Oriental is the famous Manolis Koniotakis, formerly one of Athens' celebrity heart-throbs. The restaurant is elegant with elements of stone in the decor and the ambience of a Kolonaki residence. Beautiful but unpretentious painted ceilings, and low tables and chairs, contrast with its highbrow clientele: politicians, publishers, business people and movers and shakers. The menu offers excellent sushi as well as a choice of more complex and inspired dishes.

Golden Phoenix
Harilaou Trikoupi 96 & Gortinias (210 801 3588/ www.goldenphoenix.gr). Metro Omonia. **Open** Mon-Sat 7.30pm-1.30am; Sun 12.30pm-4pm. **Credit** AmEx, MC, V.

A very pretty and luxurious Chinese restaurant. Its wooden sculptures, scattered tables, lamps decorated with images of dancing geishias and traditional Chinese music all contribute to a warm, relaxing atmosphere in which to sample its Asian flavours. Recommended dishes include Peking duck (€15), lul lac beef (veal filet with mushrooms and baby corn in a sweet sauce) and pork dipper, and the Shanghai shrimp. The generous all-you-can-eat Sunday buffet (€25; €12.50 under-12s) is good value.

Kiku
Dimokritou 12, Kolonaki (210 364 7033). Metro Syntagma. **Open** *May-Sept* noon-1am daily. *Oct-Apr* 7.30pm-1am Mon-Sat. **Average** €€€€. **Credit** AmEx, DC, MC, V. **Map** p297 G4.
Kiku is favoured by the capital's sushi lovers and fans of Japanese cuisine in general. The clientele (high-powered Athenians and high-profile Japanese) doubtless eat at sushi bars abroad, and recognise the superb quality of the tempura, sukiyaki and the freshness of the fish used in the sushi and sashimi. The restaurant is air-conditioned.

Spanish

Agora
Hadziyanni Meksi 8 & Ventiri, Kolonaki (210 725 2252). Metro Evangelismos. **Open** noon-12.30am Mon-Thur; noon-1.30am Fri, Sat; 1-7pm Sun. **Average** €€. **Credit** AmEx, MC, V.
Despite Agora's central location, it's surrounded by so many trees that it provides a pleasant oasis, barely visible from the road. Sitting either inside the restaurant or in the garden, you'll find welcome respite from a busy day shopping. The never-ending menu includes a large variety of salads and pasta dishes, as well as meat and fish dishes in generous portions – all served under the watchful eye of the Austrian chef, while you are tended to by the young, smart waiting staff.

North of the Acropolis

Creative

Cousina Cine Psirri
Sarri 44, Psyrri (210 321 5534). Metro Thisio. **Open** 9pm-1.30am Tue-Thur, Sun; 9pm-2am Fri, Sat. **Average** . **Credit** DC, MC, V. **Map** p295 D4.
Conveniently located near theatres and cinemas, the jewel of Cousina is its roof garden on warm summer evenings, while the impeccable service and convivial atmosphere make it a welcoming restaurant for all seasons. Inside, the wood- and stone-panelled walls are complemented by a glass floor that looks down into the wine cellar. A new chef has injected fresh culinary ideas and imagination into the menu. The selection of mains may be limited, but a larger variety of starters includes such delights as orange salad, bruschetta with sweet onion, prosciutto and goat's cheese, and rabbit served in clay pots. For

dessert, try the raisin pudding with honey and glazed pears. Despite the pricey wine list (house wine from €15, other bottles from €40), Cousina packs the punters in late, remaining busy until well after midnight. A change of chef was in the works as this guide went to press.

Red

Athinais Complex, Kastorias 34-36, Rouf (210 348 0000). Bus A25, A26. **Open** 8.30pm-2am Mon-Sat. **Average** €€€. **Credit** AmEx, DC, MC, V. **Map** p294 B3.

Dark red dominates the colour palette, while the flavours can bring your blood to the boil. Summer diners can enjoy a variety of delicacies and pleasant music in the courtyard next to the old smokestack, which acts as a reminder of the venue's industrial history (*see p108*). Chef Yiannis Tselepis pumps up the flavour of the Mediterranean ingredients and creates inspired dishes such as the grilled smoked eel with champagne vinaigrette and lemon flower. Be sure to sample the appropriately silky-smooth desserts. The service, presided over by maître d'

Michalis Ladas, is exemplary. Michel Blanc, yes, he of Michelin three-star fame, has recently been appointed the consultant chef.

Greek contemporary

Apla Aristera-Dexia

Tzaferi 11, Rouf (210 342 2380). Trolleybus 21. **Open** *June-Oct* 9pm-1.30am Mon-Sat. Closed Nov-May. **Average** €€. **Credit** AmEx, MC, V.

This hospitable space is reminiscent of an open-air cinema, dressed in sky blue and white with a background mural of an upside-down Greek flag. Chef Karamolengos presents his innovative dishes, based on Greek cuisine, at the small wooden tables. The menu is indeed creative, featuring noteworthy fried treats and delectable desserts at friendly prices. Currently only open during the summer months, there is talk of winter opening hours. Look out for the branch in Kifisia (Charilaou Trikoupi 135 & Ekalis 39, 210 620 3102), with a character that transfers you back to an Athenian old-time classic café.

In search of souvlaki

For an empty stomach or wallet, it's a dream. Before a date, it can be a disaster. Souvlaki is Greece's original fast food: a pocket of hot, oily pita bread stuffed with greasy grilled meat, tomatoes, raw onion ringlets, garlicky tzatziki sauce and spices, wrapped tightly in a paper casing that diners slowly unwrap as they make their way through the sandwich – though never all at once lest the whole construction fall apart.

Souvlaki sounds straightforward, and like most Greek cuisine its simplicity is its virtue.

But behind this simplicity lies a labyrinth for the uninformed. To order correctly, you first have to learn the terminology: *gyro me pita* refers to the sandwich with shavings of rotisseried meat (*gyros* means 'circle'); *souvlaki me pita* is stuffed with chunks of skewered meat (*souvla* means 'skewer'); and *kebab me pita* is a skewered mix of ground beef, onions, garlic, and spices.

Next, it's essential to know that souvlaki is the all-encompassing term for all these varieties: 'let's get a souvlaki' could very well

Prosopa

Konstantinoupoleos 84, Rouf (210 341 3433). Metro Thisio. **Open** 8.30pm-2.30am daily. **Average** €€. **No credit cards. Map** p294 B4.

This bar-restaurant combines the fashionable with the alternative and attracts many of the city's artists and thespians. The decor indoors is modern and elegant, while during the summer months tables are moved outdoors to the pavement, where they acquire a bit more local colour with the passing train and street peddlers. The menu is much like any other bar-restaurant in town but the dishes are very well prepared and delicious. Make sure to order starters because the main course portions, such as the successful pork fillet with apricots, are rather small.

Votanikos

Athinais Complex, Kastorias 34-36, Rouf (210 348 0000). Bus A25, A26. **Open** 9am-2am daily. **Average** €€. **Credit** AmEx, DC, MC, V. **Map** p294 B3.

The pleasant, spacious courtyard of Votanikos is set in the modern, industrial Athinais cultural space. To the sounds of carefully selected Greek music, you'll have the chance to taste a range of traditional recipes from all around Greece. For dessert, the apple tart with calvados is a stand out.

Greek traditional

Archaion Gefsis

Kodratou 22, Metaxourgio (210 523 9661). Metro Metaxourgio. **Open** 1pm-1am Mon-Sat. **Average** €€€. **Credit** AmEx, DC, MC, V. **Map** p295 D2.

Greek cuisine doesn't get any more traditional than this – a meal prepared according to the recipes of the ancient Greeks, with all the ritualistic trimmings. Ancient Greek flavours abound at Archaion Gefsis, such as warm wine with honey or squid cooked in its own ink with pine nuts. The rather cheap-looking copies of ancient Greek vases and statues, in combination with the lyre music and flaming torches won't spoil your meal, though you may feel like you've stumbled on to the set of *Xena, Warrior Princess*. If you're in a large group, reserve the

mean 'let's grab a *gyros*'. With regard to the latter, it's definitely recommended you attempt pronouncing *gyros* with its throat-wrenching first letter gamma, as it's terribly uncouth to lazily utter 'jigh-rose'. And, whatever you do, don't ever call a souvlaki by its Turkish name: doner kebab.

As if that weren't enough to worry about, you also have to consider where you're ordering. Gyros and souvlaki sandwiches are either served as takeaway, or eaten quickly and ferociously on the premises at shoddy tables. It's a rare thing to order one of these sandwiches at a proper sit-down taverna, where, if you ask for a mere 'souvlaki' and not '*souvlaki me pita*', a huge plate of skewers garnished with tomatoes, tzatziki and pita bread will inexplicably arrive at your table. There's no logic to this, so there's no need to look for it.

Like everything else in Greece, even the timeless souvlaki is undergoing renovations. Nowadays, hunks of *gyros* are often shaved off with – horrors – electric knives, while the traditional and nicely complementary tzatziki is often replaced with a tasteless, vaguely mayonnaisey, generic *sos* (sauce). Lamb – which still flourishes in Greek-owned *gyros* joints abroad – is never available, with pork and often chicken the standard options. And as if answering the challenge of how one could possibly make the sandwich any

greasier, nowadays they often stuff a few chips inside your pita bread as well.

Asking where the best souvlaki in Athens is much like asking where to find the best curry in London or the best burger in New York, as everyone's got their favourite local. But the vast majority of Athenians agree that the new souvlaki franchises springing up should be avoided, whereas you can't go wrong with any of the three classic establishments that have taken over the entire block where Mitropoleos meets Platia Monastiraki in central Athens. At each one the service is as gruff as the grilled meats are tasty, greasy and cheap (around €1.50). All are good, but **O Thanasis** has a cult following among Athenians.

Bairaktaris

Platia Monastiraki 2, Plaka (210 321 3036). *Metro Monastiraki.* **Open** 10.30am-2am daily. **Credit** AmEx, MC, V. **Map** p295/p299 E5.

O Thanasis

Mitropoleos 69, Plaka (210 324 4705). Metro Monastiraki. **Open** 9am-2am daily. **No credit cards. Map** p295/p299 E5.

Savvas

Mitropoleos 86-88, Plaka (210 324 5048). Metro Monastiraki. **Open** 9am-3am daily. **Credit** DC, MC, V. **Map** p295/p299 E5.

Restaurant - Bar

Alexandras Av. & 31 Vurnazu str. Ampelokipi, Athens
Tel.:0030 210 6426238

8 Haj.Mexi & 9 Vediri (Hilton area) Ilisia, Athens
Tel.:0030 210 7252252 - 0030 210 7252242

e-mail: kouchris@otenet.gr

special dining area with seven settees. There are also tables set in the atrium, which is decorated with columns and a reproduction of the ancient *Fisherman of Santorini* fresco.

Oineas
Aisopou 9, Psyrri (210 321 5614). Metro Monastiraki. **Open** 6pm-2am Mon-Fri; noon-2am Sat, Sun. Closed 2 wks Aug. **Average** €. **Credit** V. **Map** p295 D4.

Everything about Oineas has a good vibe, from the colourfully kitschy Greek 1950s advertisements lining the walls inside to the lights, music and tables that spill out on to the streets of Psyrri on warm nights (that's half the year). Though some parts of this neighbourhood are all about being trendier-than-thou, Oineas manages to be both unaffectedly stylish and genuinely friendly. The same spirit carries over to the food, ideally suited to sharing with a group of friends. Take communal forkfuls from the huge salad of radicchio, chicken cooked with sesame seeds, shaved parmesan and a drizzle of reduced balsamic vinegar, then pass around the bite-sized *spanokopittas*, slices of roasted red pepper and feta terrine, and tender beef chunks cooked with capers and fresh herbs.

Stoa tou Vangeli
Evripidou 63, Psyrri (210 325 1513). Metro Omonia. **Open** 9am-7pm daily. **Average** €. **No credit cards**. **Map** p295 E4.

The interior decor at Stoa tou Vangeli is quirkily kitsch, dominated by yellowing posters of tropical beaches and the Swiss Alps. If you find the retsina-fortified clientele inside a bit too vocal, take a table in the little courtyard, where you'll be serenaded by the singing canaries. Try one of the casseroles, such as artichokes à la Polita, or cuttlefish with spinach. A good alternative is one of the catches-of-the-day – cod is recommended. Prices are very reasonable.

Taverna of Psyrri
Eschylou 12, Psyrri (210 321 4923). Metro Monastiraki. **Open** noon-1am daily. **Average** €. **No credit cards**. **Map** p295 E4.

The Taverna of Psyrri offers traditional Greek recipes, along with very fresh fish (not available every day), in warm surroundings. The inside walls are peppered with shadow puppets, while large, century-old wooden cartwheels act as chandeliers. The menu, which is deliberately mis-spelled, changes daily, in contrast to the generally tipsy clientele. The aroma of wine seeps through the floor-boards – the basement contains six barrels, from which you can refill your wine jug yourself. With its 120-year history, this is the place to enjoy something out of the ordinary in Psyrri. Non-smokers beware.

Zeidoron
Taki 10-12, Psyrri (210 321 5368). Metro Monastiraki. **Open** noon-1am daily. **Average** €€. **Credit** AmEx, MC, V. **Map** 295 D4.

Right on the main square of Psyrri, which on Friday and Saturday nights gets suffocatingly busy, the

Italian delights at **Padre Padrone**.

Zeidoron's main draw is its outdoor tables, offering a bird's-eye view of the action. The interior is really homely, though it can feel a little squeezed and too smoky. The menu offers everything from stuffed vine leaves to smoked salmon, but prices have more to do with the taverna's prime location than the food.

Italian

Padre Padrone
Lepeniotou 24, Psyrri (210 331 8184). Metro Thisio. **Open** 8.30pm-1.30am Tue-Sat; 1-7pm Sun. **Average** €€. **Credit** AmEx, MC, V. **Map** p295 D4.

Padre Padrone serves modern Italian cuisine in the heart of Psyrri. The best tables are upstairs, where there is a green and airy, conservatory-like feel. The pizzas are a particular draw on the menu; try the thin and crispy *caprese*. For dessert, opt for the yummy *cannoli*. This place doesn't fill up until late, so book a table for around 11pm.

Taverna tips

There are hundreds of tips for finding a good Greek taverna, but only one vital piece of advice upon which your life, or at least your stomach, depends: go where the Greeks go.

Walk past a taverna where you don't understand a word being spoken by the people eating outside and you've found your place. Local Greeks invariably choose the best tavernas – by taste, value for money and atmosphere. Don't worry, entering a taverna full of Greeks is nothing like going into a tightly knit English pub.

Ninety-nine percent of the battle for a good meal is won before entering the taverna. Once in, many tourists will be too polite to leave, however bad their meal. And there's little room for surprise. Tavernas tend to be uniformly bad, uniformly reasonable or uniformly excellent. Avoid places where someone outside is trying to drag you inside. Nearly always it's standard tourist fare – and possibly worse. Good tavernas let their cooking do the talking. Recommendations from hotels are sometimes not to be trusted as staff may have a particular place to plug.

If you're here for a few days, one option is to go for a small snack and see how you get on in a taverna before committing yourself to the full monty. The strong-willed can take up the invitation of many tavernas, good and bad, to look at food in their kitchens, and then leave without ordering.

Ignore set meals. They're not good value and, in some places, the food has already been served up on dozens of plates, waiting for people like you. Several outfits cater to the plate-breaking, bouzouki-dancing Greek stereotype. Have a good time by all means, but keep an eye on the bill.

To avoid being ripped off in tavernas you must have a menu to see the prices. Fresh fish can be extremely expensive, likewise bottles of wine. The taverna's own wine (ask for 'hee-ma'), served out of a barrel, is cheaper and usually perfectly acceptable. But when it's bad, it is bad.

Should you have a reasonable complaint, speak quietly with the waiter or, if not yet satisfied, with the owner. Greeks don't like being confronted in front of others. If you're getting nowhere, seek the help of fellow Greek diners. They will very likely back you up. There's nothing like a good argument to end a nice meal.

Oriental

Pak Indian

Menandrou 13, Psyrri (210 321 9412). Metro Monastiraki. **Open** 2pm-2am daily. **Average** €. **Credit** DC, MC, V. **Map** p295 D3.

As the name suggests, this is an Indian-Pakistani restaurant located on a street known for its spice stores and Asian supermarkets. Heavy wooden tables and chairs, a plethora of candles and upbeat Indian music make for a pleasant environment in which you'll run into more Greeks than Indians or Pakistanis. The menu has plenty of vegetarian selections, such as a delicious *dal chana* of white lentils with coriander and ginger.

Spanish

Tapas Bar

Triptolemou 44, Gazi (210 347 1844). Metro Thisio. **Open** 8pm-1.30am daily. **Average** €. **Credit** AmEx, V, MC. **Map** p294 B4.

Cheerful colours, an atmosphere that seems to have come straight out of a Pedro Almodóvar film and great easy-listening music combine to make the Tapas Bar the ideal place for a quick meal, taken either at the bar, one of the tables, or in the covered yard. The chicken or pork nuggets are great to go with a drink, particularly the inspired lemon cocktails, but if you're hungry one portion is unlikely to suffice. It's air-conditioned in summer and it gets so crowded at weekends that you'll find yourself elbow to elbow with your fellow diners.

Eastern suburbs

Creative

Spondi

Pyrronos 5, Pangrati (210 752 0658). Trolleybus 2, 4 or 11. **Open** 8.30pm-12.30am daily. Closed mid Aug. **Average** €€€€. **Credit** AmEx, DC, MC, V.

Spondi fully deserves its Michelin star, especially for its desserts – try the strawberries poached in red wine and spices, with vanilla and olive-oil ice-cream and you'll see what we mean. Don't even dare to leave without trying the red mullet over red lentil purée, truffle and tomato sauce or any of the truffle dishes. The atmosphere is pleasantly relaxed, with outside tables on three different levels in summer.

Fish

Trata (O Stelios)

Platia Anagenniseos 7-9, Kaisariani (210 729 1533). Bus 224. **Open** noon-1am daily. **Average** €€. **Credit** MC, V.

Excellently prepared Greek fish – from the northern Sporades, Lefkada, Aegina and Santorini – is the trademark at Trata. A speciality is the thick and tasty fish soup. The great food is complemented by rapid and polite service, which is essential for a restaurant where the open-air dining room and the tables outside on the square are always full. Sit in the interior hall of the taverna on cold, winter days. The tantalising and cosmopolitan wine list (perhaps the best in Athens) is another major plus.

Southern suburbs

Creative

Island

Limanakia Vouliagmeni, Vouliagmeni (210 965 3563). Bus A3, B3, then bus 114. **Open** *May-Oct* 9pm-2am daily. Closed Nov-Apr. **Average** €€€€. **Credit** AmEx, MC, V.

We reckon this is the most tasteful bar-restaurant in Athens. Ask for a table with a view of the bay of Varkiza. The newly opened area above the restaurant is pleasant to say the least, provided it's not too windy. The expensive and inclusive menu echoes that of the restaurant's sibling Central (*see p131*) in Kolonaki: from sushi to T-bone steak to plain old pasta to gourmet eccentricities where lobster meets foie gras. Parking is available.

Moorings-Varoulko

Vouliagmeni Marina, Vouliagmeni (210 411 2043). Bus A2, then bus 114. **Open** *May-Oct* 8pm-1.30am Mon-Sat; noon-5pm Sun. Closed Nov-Apr. **Average** €€€€. **Credit** AmEx, DC, MC, V.

The loved and lauded Varoulko restaurant (*see p151*) moves for the summer months to the beachfront here, with a magnificent view of Vouliagmeni Bay. The decor is in the same minimal ilk as its winter premises, with wooden floors reminiscent of a ship's deck. We'd recommend that you dine downstairs rather than in the Dock's café on the top floor, which adopts a clubby vibe in the evenings. Ask for a front table, ideally in a corner. To get to Moorings-Varoulko pass the Astir Resort Hotel and follow the road signs for the old Moorings restaurant at Vouliagmeni Marina.

Septem

Leof Vas Georgiou B58, Glyfada (210 894 1620). Bus A2. **Open** 9pm-2am Mon-Sat. **Average** €€€€. **Credit** AmEx, MC, V.

Septem is one of the loveliest restaurants on the coast, and among the few in the area where you will eat exceptionally well, especially mid week. The deck area, located right on the beach, is great for luxurious dining (both in quality and price) in a fun, light-hearted atmosphere. The chef does great things with seafood in line with Mediterranean culinary traditions. The wine list is in keeping with the quality of food and surrounds: it carries a selection ranging from some reasonably priced Greek varieties right up to seriously expensive foreign labels. You might want to avoid coming here on Saturday

Eat, Drink, Shop

nights as increased dining traffic might mean glitches in the kitchen – unless of course, you're planning to take advantage of the local nightlife at the Balux club next door.

Vive Mar
Karamanli 18, Voula (210 899 2453). Bus A3. **Open** noon-1am daily. **Average** €€€. **Credit** AmEx, DC, MC, V.

The decor is elegant on all three levels at Vive Mar, and all overlook the sea. This is a paradise of low lighting, palm trees and beat music. The cuisine is a creative blend based on Italian traditions, but the service appears to be in need of some improvement at times. A full meal will cost you a pretty penny, so try to get a table by the sea; it makes all the difference. Really, the view's the thing.

Greek wines

This may be the best time to drink wine in Greece since the bacchantes quaffed with Dionysus 6,000 years ago. Greece has always had ideal conditions for wine-making – dry, crumbly, sun-warmed soil, a wealth of old-growth vines and unique indigenous grape varieties. With these factors alone Greece has long produced good, drinkable, albeit simple wines. But it wasn't until the end of the 20th century that Greek wine-makers at long last began taking full advantage of what they had, bringing serious cultivation and ageing techniques to their vineyards.

Under this newly meticulous care, the Greek wine industry has undergone a complete transformation, producing complex, sophisticated wines with unusual varieties. Bottles bearing names like Aghiorghtiko, Xinomavro and Assyrtiko now make regular appearances atop lists in snooty wine mags, holding their own just fine with offerings of world-class vineyards.

You probably haven't seen many in your local wine shop, however, since distribution of some of the most interesting and unusual Greek wines outside the country is still low – and so are prices, at least within the country. All this means wine-drinking should be a top priority during your visit to Greece.

In restaurants, forsake the slim and pricey list of foreign wines, and order instead from the generally long lists of Greek wines. By all means ask your waiter or sommelier for recommendations. There's no shame in not knowing many of the vintages, some of which didn't even exist ten years ago. Most Greeks, justly proud of their top-quality new wines, will gladly guide to you towards the best Aghiorghtiko to accompany your *kokkinisto*, or a Malagousia to bring out the best in your grilled *barbouni*.

Don't make the mistake, however, of confining your wine-tasting to fancy restaurants. Every taverna serves its own *hima* (local barrel wine) – which, while not cultivated with the same care as its pedigreed, bottled siblings, is still made with grapes from the same good fine roots and soils, and is the best accompaniment to hearty taverna fare.

Another humble but much loved cousin of Greece's fine wines is retsina, a special favourite in summer. Retsina is wine with pine resin, which sounds bizarre, we know, and it's definitely an acquired taste – but once acquired, affection for retsina cuts across all boundaries of age and class.

To find out more about Greek winemaking, take a trip to the **Evharis Estate**. Spread over an area of 30 hectares, and just 50 kilometres (31 miles) from the city centre, on the road to the Peloponnese, this winery is equipped with a tasting room and a conference hall where the owners' large private collection of paintings are on display, as well as flower and herb gardens. Other drawing points include a traditional wine press, a private chapel and the estate's tranquil country setting.

Evharis Estate
Mourtiza, Megara (210 924 6940/ www.evharis.gr).

CHOOSING WINE
A handful of Greece's most well-known and frequently awarded labels are Lazaridis, Boutari, Hatzimichalis, Tsantali, Gaia, Skouras, Mercouri, Antonopoulos.

Best wine-growing regions
Attica: Produces uniformly good table wine and some outstanding vintages.
Cephalonia: An Ionian island especially renowned for Robola wines.
Macedonia: Northern Greek region home to well-established, award-winning wine producers Boutari, Tsantali and Lazaridis.
Nemea: Perhaps the finest wine-growing region in all of Greece, renowned for its deep, dark reds.

Fish

Akti
Leof Posidonos 6, Vouliagmeni (210 896 0448). Bus
A2, then bus 115. **Open** noon-1am daily. **Average**
€€. **Credit** MC, V.
A half-hour drive from the centre of Athens (as long
as there isn't too much traffic), this simple, classic

taverna is located right on the tideline and is a great
place to watch the sun go down. After taking a dip
in the sea, lounge about in your sarong and enjoy
lovely seafood titbits, including crab and cuttlefish.
If you want to secure a table close to the water, you'll
have to convince the powers that be that you're
intending to run up a steep tab. A tip is to get your
hotel receptionist to book a table for you.

Santorini: Almost nothing grows in its
volcanic soil but award-winning Assyrtiko
wine grapes.

Best grape varietals
Aghiorghitiko: Deep, red, velvety 'Saint
George' wines from Nemea are the rising
stars of Greek wine.
Assyrtiko: Greece's finest white wine,
redolent of honey and figs, comes from
the volcanic soil of Santorini.
Malagousia: A zesty, lime-y white grown
in western Greece.
Moschofilero: A fresh, summery white
grown in the central Peloponnese.
Robola: A robust red grape grown on the
Ionian islands.

Xinomavro: A dark, tannic, truffle-like red,
similar to Burgundy, grown in Macedonia.

Best reds
For any kind of game...
Domaine Katsaros 2000 (Cabernet
Sauvignon/Merlot, €22), Megas Oenos
by Skouras 2000 (Aghiorghtiko/Cabernet
Sauvignon, €15.50).
To complement char-grilled steaks...
Gaia Estate 2000 (Aghiorghtiko, €18.50).
... or Greek dishes...
Grand Reserve Naousa by Boutari 1997
(Xinomavro, €8.50).
... or poultry and mild cheeses...
Merlot, Domaine Hatzimichalis 2001
(Merlot, €22).
... or red meat and strong cheeses...
Ramnista by Kyr – Yianni Estate 1998
(Xinomavro, €9.20), Magiko Vouno 1997
by Nico Lazaridis (Cabernet Sauvignon/
Cabernet Franc/Merlot).

Best whites
To drink with seafood...
Moschofilero Boutari (€6), Trebbiano
Late Vintage 2000 by Nico Lazaridis
(€12.80), Chardonnay by Papaioannou
2001 (Chardonnay, €7), Sigalas Barrel
Santorini 2001 (Assyrtiko, €12), White
by Biblia Chora 2002 (Assyrtiko/Sauvignon
Blanc, €8.80).
... or white meat...
Mantinea Tselepos 2001 (Moschofilero,
€7), Domaine Gerovassiliou regional white
wine of epanomi Assyrtiko (Malagouzia, €10).
... or smoked salmon...
Malagouzia Porto Carras 2000
(Malagouzia, €11.50).

Best sweet wines
For chocolate and foie gras...
Vinsanto by Sigalas 1997 (Assyrtiko/
Aidani, €27).
... or traditional Greek desserts...
Samos Anthemis by Samos Cooperative
1995 (White Muscat, €13.50).

Eat, Drink, Shop

Dear Jane,

Hello from sunny Athens.
I'm having a wonderful
time. Acropolis is breath –
taking. I'm doing lots of
sightseeing, walking,
shopping and I can't stop
eating at Goody's!!! A
Great place with delicious
food... HIGHLY
RECOMMENDED!!!

22, Oak Road
London WD1 6HG
UK

Take care,
XXX Synthia

Goody's. Fast Casual dining in Athens

Goody's is the biggest chain of fast casual dining restaurants in Greece.
There are more than 70 restaurants located in several central areas,
almost everywhere in Athens and 170 in total all over Greece.
Visit Goody's and choose from a wide variety of value for money dishes,
made on the spot with fresh ingredients. Enjoy Premier Traditional
Sandwich, an authentic Mediterranean taste or Pita – Pita Goody's Pork,
a meal with a Greek touch. You can also have succulent burgers, fresh
salads, delicious pasta and many more, all magnificently cooked, all
offered at very reasonable prices. So make the right choice and taste
Greeks' favourite. Taste Goody's.

Ithaki

Apollonos 28, Vouliagmeni (210 896 3747). Bus A2, then bus 114. **Open** noon-2am daily. **Average** €€€€. **Credit** AmEx, DC, MC, V.

Glamorously located above Asteras beach. The food at this upmarket seafood restaurant is interesting, though not always as impressive as the magnificent setting. The menu features a wide selection of fish, prepared either simply or in exotic combinations.

Lambros

Leof Posidonos, Vouliagmeni (210 896 0144). Bus A2, then bus 115. **Open** 12.30pm-12.30am daily. Closed until Feb 2004. **Average** €€€. **Credit** AmEx, DC, MC, V.

This is a fish taverna with a romantic twist, aided by a fabulous view of the sea that's quite breathtaking by moonlight. The ethos here is quality food and fresh fish, which customers are invited to select from the restaurant display. The tables at the edge of the garden have a direct sea view.

Mythos tis Thalassas

Divani Apollon Palace & Spa Hotel, Agiou Nikolaou 10 & Iliou, Vouliagmeni (210 891 1100/www. divanis.gr/divaniapollon). Bus A2 then bus 114, 115, 116. **Open** 8pm-1am Mon-Sat. **Average** €€€€. **Credit** AmEx, DC, MC, V.

Dine on a jetty with refreshing sea breezes in summert or in the 1980s-style interior during the winter. The great seafood menu includes the likes of grilled octopus with yellow pies and paprika oil, and home-made *tortelloni* with peanuts and crabmeat. For chocolate lovers, the dark- and white-chocolate pyramid with strawberry sauce is a must.

Italian

San Marzano

Konstantinoupoleos 13, Glyfada (210 968 1124). Bus A3 or B3. **Open** 1pm-1am daily. **Average** €. **Credit** AmEx, MC, V.

San Marzano's modern yet friendly attitude is reflected in the well-thought-out decor, which includes paintings by artist Katerina Vagia. The food is innovative, with creative pasta sauces and pizzas. Try the Hellenica pizza (onion, Greek cheese, sausage and olives), the *farfalle* with fresh cream, or the *psaronefri* with mushrooms and baby tomatoes. San Marzano is owned by the Pizza Express chain, which means that you'll get the usual children's menu, and service with a smile too.

Northern suburbs

Creative

Beau Brummel

Agiou Dimitriou 9 & Agion Theodoron, Kifisia (210 623 6780). Metro Kifisia. **Open** 1-5pm, 8.30pm-12.30am Mon-Sat; 1-5pm Sun. **Average** €€€€. **Credit** AmEx, DC, MC, V.

In a kind gesture to less-affluent foodies, Beau Brummel has recently introduced a Sunday buffet with Greek specialities for €30 per person. The main menu offers contemporary and creative dishes, such as foie gras on red banana, and duck on a carrot mousse, as well as a selection of barbecue dishes – in most cases the animals are reared on the restaurant's own ecological farm outside Athens. The interior decor is based on stone and black wood; in the summer, there's a very modern outdoor area. The haute cuisine section of the restaurant is closed during summer, but the grill remains in operation.

French

Vardis

Hotel Pentelikon, Deliyianni 66, Kifisia (210 623 0650). Metro Kifisia. **Open** 9-11.30pm Mon-Sat. Closed Aug. **Average** €€€. **Credit** AmEx, DC, MC, V.

For years the only restaurant in Greece with a Michelin star, opulent Vardis remains the pull-out-all-the-stops standard for five-star classic French dining in Athens, and while you couldn't say it was modestly priced, it still represents good value for the experience. Expect tables glittering with gold and silver, pink marble, flawless service, showy but unforgettable cuisine and prices to match. Sublime starters might include pigeon cassoulet with foie gras in fig juice, or octopus boiled in milk with hazelnut sauce. Then try the superb veal with caramelised endive and orange; cockerel cooked with tarragon; or tender leg of lamb scented with fragrant citrus fruit and spring onions. In summer diners move outside to a lush poolside garden.

Greek contemporary

Gefseis me Onomasia Proelefsis

Leof Kifisias 317, Kifisia (210 800 1402). Metro Kifisia. **Open** 8.30pm-12.30am Mon-Sat. **Average** €€€. **Credit** AmEx, V.

This one's a must for serious foodies. Which is not to say anyone won't enjoy the stellar menus prepared by the talented Nena Ismirnoglou, who cut her teeth at New York's renowned Milos, or the beautiful setting in the garden of a restored Kifisia mansion. But the restaurant's very serious name, translated as 'Flavours of Designated Origin' is an irresistible siren song to a certain kind of food lover. Every ingredient is sourced from regional farmers throughout Greece; the kind who raise their lambs on herbs, grow every vegetable organically and personally hand-press their extra virgin olive oils. Not to be missed is the enormous array of Greek artisanal cheeses. Each month, Nena brings in cooks from a different part of the country to create speciality menus with a focus on the food and drink of Tinos one month, Thrace another, or the southern Peloponnese the next. Every dish on offer has a story, which the friendly staff will be happy to share.

Eat, Drink, Shop

Plenty more fish in the sea: **Diasimos**. *See p151.*

Middle Eastern

Pandeli

Pentelis 3, Kefalari (210 808 0787). Metro Kifisia, then bus 530. **Open** noon-midnight Tue-Sun. **Average** €€€. **Credit** DC, MC, V.

With culinary creations originating from Constantinople and Asia Minor and with decor to match, this restaurant is the latest word in Eastern luxury. The decor includes imported flooring from Istanbul and an open-air dining area (bathed in sunlight) that's just great for Sunday lunch; the copper serving pans are another especially nice touch. Don't, however, expect the same standard in food as Pandeli's mother restaurant in Istanbul.

Ya Hala

Kolokotroni 37, Platia Kefalari, Kifisia (210 801 5324). Metro Kifisia, then bus 530. **Open** 6pm-1.30am Mon-Thur; 1pm-2am Fri-Sun. **Average** €. **Credit** MC, V.

Ethnic cuisine in a pleasant environment and at relatively reasonable prices compared to those normally paid in the northern suburbs. Lebanese dishes, courteous service and Arabic music in what is otherwise a very European space. The fun here starts with the spicy aromatic food, peaks with the belly dancing and winds down with a few optional puffs on an aromatic hookah. Try the Château Ksara, an award-winning Lebanese wine.

Vegetarian

Vegge

Kolokotroni 9, Kifisia (210 808 0009). Metro Kifisia. **Open** 11am-midnight Mon-Fri; noon-6pm Sat, Sun. **Average** €€. **Credit** AmEx, DC, MC, V.

In a city of meat-eaters, Vegge is the only real choice for hardcore vegetarians, though don't expect too many surprises from the menu: lots of salads, pasta (better to choose the home-made varieties) and just a few meat alternatives with shellfish. Vegge attracts a broad age range and regulars are quick to grab a seat on the veranda – glassed in during the chillier months – to enjoy their meals to the accompaniment of smooth tracks along the lines of Frank Sinatra and Enya.

Piraeus

Fish

Diasimos

Akti Themistokleous 306 (210 451 4887). Metro Piraeus, then bus 904. **Open** 10am-1am daily. **Average** €. **Credit** AmEx, MC, V.

The main drag of the Freatida seaside area has a wonderful island feel to it. At Diasimos, this is especially distinct due to the 'live' decor: crates overflowing with cockles, shrimp and fish. Outside the restaurant you'll see octopuses hung up to dry. The service is quick, friendly and helpful.

Jimmy & the Fish

Akti Koumoundourou 46 (210 412 4417). Metro Piraeus, then trolley 20. **Open** 1pm-1am daily. **Average** €€€. **Credit** AmEx, DC, MC, V.

Eating at Mikrolimano is a must – for the lovely view of the sailboat-filled harbour and the cheerful, raucous calls of the fishermen. The problem is that most of Mikrolimano's seafood tavernas serve up little more than frozen-and-fried cookie-cutter platters. But Jimmy & the Fish stands far and away above the rest – you can tell right away just by looking at the stylish waiters in their body-hugging T-shirts and long, crisp aprons. The menu has plenty of well-made takes on fish and pasta (lobster spaghetti, squid ink risotto, and a signature dish of calamari stuffed with feta and prawns, coated with sesame seeds and cooked in ouzo). But serious fish lovers should ask for the catch of the day, which is grilled simply and served with a drizzle of olive oil and lemon – so good it doesn't need anything else.

Kollias

Stratigou Plastira 3 (210 462 9620). Metro Piraeus, then bus 832, 833. **Open** 7.30pm-1am Mon-Sat; noon-6pm Sun. **Average** €€. **Credit** AmEx, DC, MC, V.

The first wake-up call to the taste buds comes as soon as you sit down at the table: a coffee cup filled with the best fish soup (*kakavia*) in town, to be slurped down in one gulp. Following that, owner Tassos Kollias will take you on a tour of the kitchen so you can choose your own fish from his vast supply. Expect such delights as lightly fried gudgeon from Messolongi, or mytilene clams, a species now under the protection of the Ministry of Agriculture. There's a plant-filled terrace, and just across the road you'll find its cousin restaurant Ta 5 Piata (The Five Dishes), where you can order any five small dishes from the menu for €10.

Margaro

Hatzikyriakou 126 (210 451 4226). Metro Piraeus, then trolleybus 20 or bus 904. **Open** noon-midnight Mon-Sat; noon-5pm Sun. Closed 15 days Greek Easter. **Average** €. **No credit cards**.

Most of the seafood joints lining pretty Mikrolimano harbour are unreasonable priced and heavily touristed. So, those after the real flavour of Piraeus head to this cult favourite, located behind the harbour by the Greek naval officers' training base – which itself offers some surprisingly enjoyable views. You can hear the sizzle of the frying pans even before you step inside the charming courtyard of Margaro's. Opened in the 1930s and still run by the same family, Margaro is always packed, so get there early as it's not possible to book a table. Each night, colossal servings of shrimp, baby red mullet and whitebait come off the fires delectably crispy, to be enjoyed with a good house wine and a Greek salad.

Plous Podilatou

Akti Koumoundourou 42 (210 413 7910/210 413 7790). Metro Faliro. **Open** noon-12.30am daily. **Average** €€€. **Credit** AmEx, MC, V.

There's been an air of Santorini down in Mikrolimano ever since the Plous kitchen was taken over by chef Nikos Pouliasis. He has transferred all of his expertise from Koukoumavlos (the island's eminent eatery) and we just love the results. A must-try are the vegetable *dolmades* (stuffed vine leaves) with yoghurt, and the world-class Macedonian *halva* ice-cream with hazelnuts and strawberry coulis. The minimal decor inside gives the Mediterranean feeling, while the atmosphere outside in the sun is something of the French Riviera – though there's a bit too much of the Riviera in the prices.

Varoulko

Deligiorgi 14 (210 411 2043). Bus 049. **Open** *Nov-Apr* 8.30pm-1am Tue-Sat. **Average** €€€€. **Credit** AmEx, DC, MC, V.

Only three Athens restaurants have ever been awarded a Michelin star. Varoulko is one of them. Owner and chef Lefteris Lazarou (*see p137* **My kind of town**) still insists on calling himself a 'cook'. After his daily visit to the city's food markets he returns to his kitchen to create innovative seafood fusion dishes such as shrimp in vegetable sauce and squid with truffle oil and sweet garlic. The restaurant, with its minimalist interior, is located in a charming, busy Piraean neighbourhood. In summer the restaurant moves to the coast and becomes known as Moorings-Varoulko (*see p145*).

Greek traditional

Solon

Akti Themistokleous 284 (210 451 2340). Metro Piraeus, then bus 904. **Open** 10am-12.30am Thur, Sun; 10am-1am Fri, Sat. **Average** €. **No credit cards**.

There's more of a homely, comfortable feeling at Solon than in your average fish taverna. Soft colours on the walls, discreet decorative references to maritime life and two different dining rooms with interconnecting doors do the trick. The tables outside are just a few metres from the sea. The cuisine reflects the proprietor's good taste: the mussel-stuffed mushrooms – all of the mussel dishes are worth a try – and the filling shrimp and cheese frittata with tomatoes and herbs are both divine.

Eat, Drink, Shop

THE ESPRESSIONIST CAFÉS

Athens • 109, Veikou Ave., Galatsi • 78, Themistokleous & Valtetsiou Str., Exarchia • 95, Sapfous Str., Kallithea • 6, Eleftherias Square, Korydallos • 221, Alexandras Ave., Center • 118, Kifissias Ave. • 1, Perilkleous Str., Maroussi • 9, Dilaveri Str., Mikrolimano • Parsis Square, N. Ionia • 24, Ilission & Platanon Str., N. Kifissia • 2, Proussis & Fanariou Str., N. Philadelphia • 109, Imittou Str., Pangrati • 46, Kifissias Ave. & Granikou Str., Paradissos • 27, 28th Oktovriou Str., Patission • 15, El. Venizelou Str., Pefki • 87, 3rd Septemvriou Str., Victoria • 5, Sofokleous Str., Center • 5, Stadiou Str., Center • 14, F. Negri & I. Drosopoulou Str., Kypseli • 228, Thivon & Kanapitseri Str., Village Rendi • 57, G. Papandreou Str., Haidari • 65, A. Ioannou Str., A. Paraskevi • 3, Amfitritis Str., P. Phaliro • 29, A. Pavlou Str., Thisseio • 6, Gravias Str., Deree College, A. Paraskevi • 2, Aigaiou Str. & 141 Syngrou Ave., N. Smyrni • 146, Harilaou Trikoupi & Strofyliou Str., N. Erythrea • 112 - 114, Pendelis Ave., Vrilissia • 7, Milioni & Heraklitou Str., Kolonaki • 238 - 240, Kifissias Ave., Kifissia • 78 - 80, Konstantinoupoleos Str., Bournazi - Peristeri • 4, Pendelis Str., Halandri • 50, V. Konstantinou Str., National Gallery, Center • 23rd km National Road Athens - Lamia, Ag. Stefanos • 40.5 km National Road Athens - Korinthos, Megara

Thessaloniki • 15, Tobazi Str., Carrefour • 27, Aristotelous Str., Egnatia • 49, Nikis Ave., Paralia • 75, N. Plastira Str., Krini

Rest of Greece • 20, M. Alexandrou Str., Alexandroupolis • 11, Dodonis Str., Ioannina • Mavili Square, Ioannina • 50, M. Alexandrou Str., Katerini • 13 - 15, M. Alexandrou Str., Korinthos • 17, A. Nikolaou Str., Patra • 11, Radinou Str., Patra • 17, Akti Dymaion, Patra Veso, Patra • 202 km National Road Korinthos - Patra, Rio • 16, A. Diakou Str., Rhodes • 33, E. Antistassis Str., Serres • 12, Voudouri & Kallia Str., Halkida • Aigaiou Ave. & 66 Rodokanaki Str., Hios • 4 Akti Miaouli Str., Hania, Crete

Ferries • Blue Star Ithaki • Blue Star Paros • Blue Star Naxos • Superferry II • Sea Jet II • Kephalonia

Cyprus • 30 Stasikratous Str., Nicosia

Making good coffee is a form of art but it is only one part of the equation. The other part is the art of enjoying it. At Flocafé, the biggest coffeeshop chain in Greece, we specialise not only in making the best coffee but also in providing you with an excellent quality of products and services. Moreover, we offer you the atmosphere of socialisation, relaxation and entertainment that completes the equation.

THE ESPRESSIONIST CAFÉS

Cafés

Coffee is almost a religion in Athens. Join the congregation here.

To say that Greeks have a coffee culture is an understatement. Athenians' days often appear to be centred on their coffee rituals, and caffeine to be the fuel running the engine for the entire city. Coffee is to the Greeks what tea is to the Brits, except in Greece the process of partaking is very much a public display best enjoyed at a leisurely pace and out of doors. You may even wonder if anyone actually works in Athens – even at noon on a weekday you'll have to look hard to find yourself a free

table at one of the popular cafés in Thisio, Exarchia, Kolonaki or Plaka. Locals use the café as a library, a conference room and a living room: this is where newspapers are read, business deals agreed upon, marriage proposals made and hearts broken.

Coffee serves a ritual purpose, too: offering a cup to a visitor is the common denominator of Greek hospitality; it is always served at engagements and there is even a term – *kafes tis parigorios* (sympathy coffee) – for its

The clash of the coffees

Classic Greek coffee and upstart frappé compete as Athenians' caffeine of choice.

THE REAL THING

Legend has it that the Greeks opened the world's first coffee shop in Constantinople soon after the Ottoman occupation of the Byzantine Empire's former capital in 1475.

In this establishment the proprietors lovingly perfected the preparation and service of the beverage that today is a symbol of national pride: Greek coffee.

Coffee should be prepared in a *briki* – a long-handled small, wide-bottomed metal coffee pot narrowing at the lip. One small cup of water is put into the *briki*, which then goes on the stove to heat. When the water warms up, sugar (to taste) and one teaspoonful of coffee are stirred in. When the liquid starts to rise, the *briki* is whisked off the heat so as not to spoil the thick layer of froth (*kaimaki*) that forms as the coffee is about to boil. This froth is your god-given right. If you're ever in the pleasurable position of making Greek coffee, be sure to pour a bit into each cup before filling to the top, so that the precious *kaimaki* is evenly distributed among guests.

The *briki* cooks over an open flame, or more traditionally over hot sand, but under no circumstances should any self-respecting Greek – or *Time Out* reader – allow their coffee to be 'cooked' using the steam nozzle of an espresso machine, as is becoming alarmingly common at fast-food joints.

Finally, a Greek coffee is considered naked unless served with a glass of cold water. Another good accompaniment is a slice of *loukoumi*, a chewy candy dusted in powdered sugar that comes in many flavours, including cherry, lemon, almond and chocolate, as well as the traditional rose flavour.

Be warned: allow the coffee to stand for a few minutes before drinking it, so the grainy important role in soothing at Greek funerals and memorials. Don't be alarmed if you see someone at the next table doing strange things with an empty cup. They're probably just doing some fortune-telling from coffee grounds (*kafemandia*), which appeals to Greeks' superstitious nature. Professional *kafetsou* readers are bordering on trendy at the moment, with some commanding up to €30 a session.

COFFEE TALK

The local staples, the traditional Greek coffee (*cafe elliniko*) and the ubiquitous Nescafé-based frappé (*see p155* **The clash of the coffees**), are ordered unsweetened (*sketo*), moderately sweet (*metrio*) or extra sweet (*glyko*). You can also order all the usual Italian varieties,

French coffee (*cafe galliko*) and instant coffee (*nes*). 'With/without milk' is *me/horis gala*, and decaffeinated, though rarely available, is *horis cafe-eenee*. All coffee – particularly frappé – is served strong; ask for it *elafrees* (weak) if that's your preference. To order a cup of tea ask for *ena tsai*.

Classic Greek *kafeneio* are 'old men cafés', identifiable by their clientele of idle gents loitering over their coffees and arguing about politics, football or *tavli* (backgammon) in plain surroundings. Women or mixed groups, however, had best head to a *kafeteria* (modern café), where pretty much anyone under 60 gathers to socialise in less basic surroundings, often with quite loud music. Both also serve pastries and snack food to the appropriate degree of sophistication.

coffee can settle. Likewise, don't drain your cup or you'll get a nasty mouthful of *katakathi*, the undrinkable sludge-like sediment at the bottom of the cup. Not nice.

THE YOUNG PRETENDER

Greek frappé is a cold, heavily caffeinated frothy coffee drink that's become almost emblematic of Greece. Legend has it that in 1957 a Greek Nescafé salesman, on impulse, prepared the instant coffee in the same manner as Nestlé children's chocolate drink, producing a foamy creation that Nescafé then went on to promote with wild success.

Frappé owes its success to several factors. It satisfies the Greek need to while away the time over coffee (the tall glass it comes in lasts a lot longer than a wimpy demitasse); it supplies a hefty dose of caffeine to suit high local tolerance levels (some cafés instruct their servers to prepare the frappé with just two spoons of coffee for tourists, as opposed to the usual three for Greeks); and since it's cool and refreshing it goes down a treat in the hot Greek summer, when it becomes ubiquitous.

Though appearing elegant, the frappé is really rather humble: put a powerful dose of instant coffee, the desired amount of sugar, a few ice cubes and a splash of water in a cocktail shaker. Shake vigorously for 30 seconds or until foamy. Add one dash of evaporated milk and water; swirl to blend. Pour into a tall glass and serve with a straw.

Frappé lore is rampant. The foam – it should be of firm consistency – is critical, and the Greek press has suggested that some cafés add corn starch or egg whites to make it thicker. Apparently there's a black market for 'real' Greek Nescafé in the Greek neighbourhood of Astoria, New York City, since the manufacturing process required for instant coffee made to US tastes reportedly results in a different Nescafé that produces – horrors! – a different grade of foam.

'We have gastronomy and her definition:

the art of choosing, preparing, serving and... finally enjoying

Inside that concentrated and simple description belongs the cafè-Bar-Restaurant "**Athineon Politia**", where innumerable tries, innovations, secrets, knowledges and fantasy, can be found... With one and only receiver: **Your 5 senses...**

...i aristi polis ine i politia tis anthropinis psichis...
Platon

Αθηναίων Πολιτεία
———— CAFE • BAR • RESTAURANT ————

1, AKAMANTOS & APOSTOLOU PAULOU Str., THISSIO - ATHENS, TEL.: 210.3413.795, FAX: 210.3413.794
www.athinaion-politeia.com

Open your eyes, mister, the view's lovely at **Filistron**.

Cafés also offer alcohol, but they aren't somewhere you'd come to get drunk (insofar as Athenians ever do); for bars *see p213* **Nightlife**.

Acropolis & around

Amaltheia

Tripodon 16, Plaka (210 322 4635). Metro Akropoli. **Open** 10am-1am Mon-Thur, Sun; 10am-2am Fri, Sat. **No credit cards. Map** p299 E6.

This small, traditional pastry café specialises in dairy-based sweets that, while few in variety, are certainly good. Amaltheia is well known for its yoghurt (€4), which comes topped with honey and walnuts, chocolate sauce or diced fruit. But this is also a classic stop for Athens' younger crowds who want to enjoy delicious sweet (around €5.50 each) or savoury (€6.50) crêpes.

Athinaion Politeia

Akamantos 1 & Apostolou Pavlou, Thisio (210 341 3795). Metro Thisio. **Open** 9am-2am daily. **Credit** AmEx, DC, MC, V. **Map** p294 C5/p292 D5.

This is an old mansion transformed into a café with a great view of the crowds on Apostolou Pavlou. Coffee-drinkers who like classic flavours choose a Greek coffee from the traditional sand burner (€2.50), while the more adventurous may try an *espresso corretto* (€3.50), an explosive mix of espresso coffee and sambuca, after which you may be in need of a refreshing Terpsichori Crêpe (€6) with chocolate and fresh fruit.

Dioskouri

Dioskouron 13, Plaka (210 321 9607). Metro Monastiraki. **Open** *March-Oct* 8am-1.30am daily. *Nov-Feb* 8am-7pm daily. **No credit cards. Map** p299 E5.

While we wouldn't recommend the café for its frappé (€3), the tables offer a magnificent view of the Ancient Agora, with Gazi and Keramikos fading out into the urban Athenian background. We suggest you avoid this establishment on summer lunchtimes as there's little shelter from the sweltering sun; go at a cooler time of day.

Filistron

Apostolou Pavlou 23, Thisio (210 342 2897/ 346 7554). Metro Thisio. **Open** noon-1am daily. **Credit** DC, MC, V. **Map** p295/p299 D5.

In Ancient Greek *filistron* means 'manic passion' and the word was used to describe some of the gods of Olympus. Filistron is simply considered a pleasant hangout, known for its light meals, snacks and its coffee. Its beauty lies in its terrace, which is lush with climbers and flowers and offers a great view of the city. A delicious alternative frappé comes with a ball of vanilla ice-cream (€6) instead of milk.

Gallery Café

Adrianou 33, Monastiraki (210 324 9080). Metro Monastiraki. **Open** 10am-2am Mon-Fri; 9am-2am Sat, Sun. **No credit cards. Map** p295/p299 D5.

Located next to the Stoa of Attalos, the Gallery Café is recommended for its relaxed loungey atmosphere inside, good espresso (€2.60) and its chocolate roll

with a butterscotch sauce (€3.50). After 4pm, the bar starts offering cocktails (with or without alcohol) and cranks up the volume as an preface to a night out on the town.

Ionos

Geronta 7, Platia Filomousou, Plaka (210 322 3139). Metro Akropoli. **Open** 8am-2am daily. **No credit cards.** **Map** p299 F6.

Ionos is broadly considered one of the best places to get a decent frappé (€3.30) in Plaka. Alternatively, try the ice-cold 'special' chocolate milkshake (€5.60) or, if you are calorie-conscious, a fresh fruit salad (€4.40). Those who fancy a game can ask the waiter for a backgammon board.

Melina Café

Lysiou 22, Plaka (210 324 6501). Metro Akropoli. **Open** 9am-2am daily. **Credit** DC, MC, V. **Map** p295/p299 E5.

Located on a picturesque cobblestoned street, this café named after the legendary Melina Mercouri is a great place to enjoy a cappuccino (€3.20) with a slice of apple pie and vanilla ice-cream (€5.80).

Tristrato

Geronta & Dedalou 34, Plaka (210 324 4472). Metro Akropoli. **Open** 9am-1am daily. **No credit cards.** **Map** p299 F6.

A blast of cool air hits you as soon as you push open Tristrato's wooden door. Sweet-toothed folks should try the home-made baklava (€4), cream pie (*galaktoboureko*, €4) or cheesecake with cherries (€4.50). The menu is rich with tisanes, such as fresh mountain tea, as well as a broad selection of coffees.

Historic centre

Aiolis

Eolou 23 & Agias Irinis (210 331 2839). Metro Monastiraki. **Open** 10.30am-1am Mon-Wed, Sun; 10.30am-3am Thur-Sat. **No credit cards.** **Map** p295/p299 E5.

Though jam-packed and busy during the day, the pedestrianised shopping strip Eolou can become quite deserted at night, but the small tables of the Aiolis café, dotted outside the Church of St Irene, are hardly ever empty. This former local caff was given a facelift several years ago and transformed into a truly hip establishment that now attracts thirtysomethings for an espresso (€2.64), a chocolate soufflé (€6.18) or an exotic smoothie (€5.15), offered with or without alcohol.

Body Fuel

Stadiou 5 (210 325 7772). Metro Syntagma. **Open** 10am-7pm Mon-Fri; 10.30am-6pm Sat. **No credit cards.** **Map** p295 F4.

Primarily a snack stop with coffee also available, Body Fuel stands out for its nutrition-calculated salads with chicken, spinach and mushrooms (€4.20), low-cal smoothies, fresh fruit and veggie juices and vitamin-packed sandwiches. It's ideal for a light and tasty brunch and is handily central.

Flocafe

Stadiou 5 (210 324 3028). Metro Syntagma. **Open** *May-Sept* 7am-1am Mon-Fri; 8am-1am Sat; 10am-1am Sun. *Oct-Apr* 7am-midnight Mon-Fri; 8am-midnight Sat; 10am-midnight Sun. (Hours vary, depending on location.) **No credit cards.** **Map** p295 F4.

In Greece the popularity of this home-grown café chain has challenged the claim of newcomer Starbucks (on Skoufa in Kolonaki, popular and one of Athens' few no-smoking venues), but in a city that consumes this much coffee there's probably enough room for everyone. In addition to an enormous number of coffee options, Flocafe also serves up great snacks, small sandwiches, and dependably delicious desserts. Like many Greek cafés, the music and the conversations can get loud, especially in the evening. **Other locations:** throughout the city.

Grigoris

Krizotou 9 & Valaoritou 1 (210 364 4955). Metro Syntagma. **Open** 6am-8.30pm Mon-Fri; 7am-3.30pm Sat. **No credit cards.** **Map** p297 G4.

You'll find a Grigoris on almost every corner in Athens. It's a firm favourite with Athenians on the go who drop in for snacks ranging from cheese and spinach pies (€1) to mini pizzas (€1.50) and made-to-order hot and cold sandwiches. **Other locations:** throughout the city.

Yellow Café

Karagiorgi Servias 9 & Voulis (210 331 9029). Metro Syntagma. **Open** 7.30am-9pm Mon, Wed, Sat; 7.30am-10pm Tue, Thur, Fri. **No credit cards.** **Map** p295/p299 F5.

After a morning of sightseeing, pop in to the Yellow Café for a sandwich on home-made bread (from €3) followed by a chocolate brownie (€3) washed down with a strong espresso (€1.50).

Kolonaki & around

Blue Monkey

Voukourestiou 36, Kolonaki (210 364 1180). Metro Syntagma. **Open** 8am-8pm Mon-Fri. **No credit cards.** **Map** p297 G4.

A great place for a healthy snack, despite the occasionally sour service. The sandwiches cost around €4, and come with fillings of tomatoes, iceberg lettuce, salmon, prosciutto and rocket, and more.

Da Capo

Tsakalof 1, Kolonaki (210 360 2497). Metro Syntagma. **Open** 7am-midnight Mon-Sat; 8.30am-midnight Sun. **No credit cards.** **Map** p297 G4.

With an elite clientele and limited seating, Da Capo is renowned for its great cappuccino freddo (€3.50). Stand advised that it's all self-service. Check out the selections on display and order from a variety of (rather small and pricey) brioche sandwiches or fresh strawberry salad (€5) with or without Chantilly cream. In brief, it's expensive, but stylish.

Eat, Drink, Shop

Moschofilero Boutari

Great signatures cannot be imitated.

The privileged vineyards in the Mantinia region
at an altitude of 650 meters.
The most famous white Greek variety: Moschofilero.
The stringent criteria for the selection of grapes.
The winemaker's craft which reveals the uniqueness
of variety in Moschofilero Boutari.
The constant recognition in international
competitions.
The most popular Greek white wine.
Moschofilero Boutari. Your preference.
Simply because great signatures cannot be imitated.

BOUTARI

FIFTH GENERATION

www.boutari.gr

Everest

Tsakalof 14, Kolonaki (210 361 6791). Metro
Syntagma. **Open** 24hrs daily. **No credit cards.**
Map p297 G4.

The Everest chain is known for its custom-made hot
and cold sandwiches (from €2), as well as a range of
sweets and savoury pies. This branch is ideal for a
post-drinking late-night snack; there's also one on
the west side of Syntagma. Turnover is fast and so
is service; be ready to order (or point!).

Other locations: throughout the city.

Juice Up

Solonos 110 & Zoodochou Pigis, Exarchia (210 330
6755). Metro Panepistimio. **Open** 8am-9pm Mon-Fri.
No credit cards. Map p295 F3.

As you can guess from the name, this establishment
specialises in freshly squeezed juices (medium €2.50,
tall €3). There are also sandwiches, but it is the
juices we recommend.

L

Themistokleous 76, Exarchia (210 330 1215).
Metro Omonia. **Open** 9am-3.30am daily.
No credit cards.

This small and narrow café is one of the newest
additions to coffee-bar haven Exarchia. The yellow
tables outside are ideally positioned for both sun-
worshippers and people-watchers. This is a good
place to enjoy an espresso (€2.50) or a pannacotta
with a trickle of cocoa syrup (€5.50).

Salt & Sugar

Skoufa 37, Kolonaki (210 360 0603). Metro
Syntagma. **Open** 8am-1am daily. **No credit**
cards. Map p297 G4.

The air-conditioning indoors at this hip Kolonaki
hangout is a panacea for the sweltering summer
heat. It's popular with students from the nearby university, who drop in for coffee, as well as office workers on their lunch break. Try the *milopita*, a
French-style apple pie with caramel ice cream
(€5.90), and the quiche Lorraine (€ 5.10), delicious
and beautifully presented.

Ta Tria Gourounakia

Skoufa 73, Kolonaki (210 360 4400).
Metro Panepistimio. **Open** 8am-1am Mon-Fri;
10am-2am Sat; noon-2am Sun. **No credit**
cards. Map p297 G4.

This colourful and multifaceted café-restaurant-club
is named after the three little pigs of children's literature. The upbeat pop music puts a spring in your
step and it gets louder as the day wears on. The
small couches are invariably occupied by students
cramming over a cappuccino freddo (€3.50), books
and cellphones. Top favourites are the chocolate
soufflé (€7) and the cheesecake (€6.50). Another plus
is the especially friendly service.

Wunderbar

Themistokleous 80, Exarchia (210 381 8577).
Metro Omonia. **Open** 10am-3.30am daily. **No**
credit cards.

Table talk at **Ta Tria Gourounakia.**

Earthy colours reign here, and colourful sofas seat
a young, stylish crowd. Stop by for a very good
cappuccino (€3.50) in the daytime; in the evening a
clubby atmosphere pervades (*see p219*).

North of the Acropolis

Ta Serbetia tou Psyrri

Eschylou 3, Psyrri (210 324 5862). Metro
Monastiraki. **Open** 10.30am-3am daily.
No credit cards. Map p295 E4.

This café is dedicated to good home-made cakes.
There's a folk art feel to the hand-decorated furniture and more artistry in the kitchen, in the preparation of delicacies such as the *galaktoboureko* cream
pie (€3.50) and preserves (raspberry, cherry, grape,
bergamot, quince) served either with yoghurt or the
traditional northern Greek rice cream, *kazan dipi*.

Shops & Services

Chic and cheerful.

Whether you're searching for an elegant designer gown, a cheap and cheerful bikini, a traditional set of clinking worry beads or a box of handmade chocolates, Athens can provide everything you desire and more. You just need to know where to look.

The main central commercial areas of Greece's capital city nestle within easy walking distance of each other. Each sector has its own specialities and price brackets, as shops still tend to congregate like with like.

The traditionally moneyed district of **Kolonaki**, its northern sibling **Kifisia** and south suburban cousin **Glyfada** (the latter two originally the sites of holiday homes for rich Athenians before central Athens spread out its concrete tentacles and incorporated them into the urban sprawl) boast the most expensive designer boutiques selling the latest Greek and international fashions. Shoppers here are well turned out and dress to impress, whether they are flashing their gold cards at pricey emporia or just sipping a cappuccino at one of the chic pavement cafés.

The central street **Ermou**, although home to some of the most expensive real estate in Europe, tends to attract more affordable high-street clothing and footwear brands. Posses of teenagers gather along this pedestrian way to snap up the newest trends, while families flock here to buy bargain basics.

In the warren of roads between Ermou and Kolokotroni are excellent haberdashery shops and bargain clothing, while down towards **Athinas** the focus switches to hardware and food, culminating in the vast meat and fish markets and their surrounding satellite stalls selling cheeses, cold meats, herbs and spices and preserved vegetables (see p97 **Central Market**). Further into **Psyrri**, the Eastern immigrant influence manifests itself in the numerous shops selling Indian, Pakistani and Chinese foods and clothing.

Plaka and **Monastiraki** are the main tourist areas, with shops selling a variety of souvenir items, from leather bags and designer rip-off sunglasses to *flokati* rugs and traditional backgammon boards to antique furnishings and the ubiquitous priapic satyrs.

If you're after home furnishings, Athens has countless furniture and accessory shops. **Leof Vouliagmenis** and its parallel **Ilioupoleos**

are lined with an abundance of mainly locally made beds, lights, tables and sofas, while Kolonaki, Kifisia and the southern suburbs offer more expensive European imports.

Greek shops have rather complicated business hours, but in general they open from morning to mid afternoon on Mondays, Wednesdays and Saturdays, and morning to dusk on Tuesdays, Thursdays and Fridays. The traditional siesta has been all but done away with these days – while some of the smaller, family-run shops may close for a short break during the afternoon of late-opening days (Tuesday, Thursday, Friday), the large majority of stores stay open all day. Shops in designated tourist areas are allowed to open on Sundays, and department stores, supermarkets, florists and bakeries can open earlier and close later if they so choose.

Prices in Greece tend to be substantially lower than in other European countries and thus, depending on the exchange rate, good value for UK and US visitors. On top of this, sales are held in February and August.

Art & antiques

Astrolavos Artlife
Irodotou 11, Kolonaki (210 722 1200). Metro Evangelismos. **Open** 11am-3pm Mon, Wed, Sat; 11am-8.30pm Tue, Thur, Fri. **Credit** DC, MC, V. **Map** p297 H4/H5.
This modern art gallery and gift shop exhibits and sells artistic objects and paintings created by both up-and-coming and established Greek artists. Silk screens and originals are available from such local masters as Dimitris Mytaras and Alekos Fassianos.

Martinos
Pindarou 24, Kolonaki (210 360 9449/ www.martinosart.gr). Metro Syntagma. **Open** 10am-2pm Mon, Wed, Sat; 10am-8pm Tue, Thur, Fri. **Credit** MC, V. **Map** p297 G4.
The Kolonaki branch of Martinos has high-quality antique pieces from around the world, including eighth-century Chinese ceramics, African tribal masks and traditional Greek pottery. On the first floor there's a replica of a 19th-century Greek sitting room or *ontas*. The other branch specialises in Byzantine pieces and antiquities, but beware of buying one to take home – it is forbidden to take antiquities out of Greece without a special licence from the Archaeological Service (*see chapter* **Resources A-Z: Customs**). **Other locations**: Pandrosou 50, Monastiraki (210 321 3110).

Le Streghe son Tornate. *See p171.*

Zoumboulakis

Krizotou 7, Historic Centre (210 363 4454).
Metro Syntagma. **Open** 10am-8pm Tue, Thur,
Fri; 10am-3pm Mon, Wed, Sat. **Credit** AmEx, DC,
MC, V. **Map** p297 G4/G5.
The gallery has exhibitions by contemporary Greek
talents, while at the nearby shop you can buy num-
bered, signed silk screens or prints and objets d'art.

Books

Eleftheroudakis

Panepistimiou 17, Historic Centre (210 325
8440/www.books.gr). Metro Panepistimio.
Open *May-Sept* 9am-9pm Mon-Sat. *Oct-Apr*
9am-8pm Mon-Sat. **Credit** AmEx, DC, MC, V.
Map p295 F4.

International fashion

Outlets for the following international fashion and sportswear brands can all be found in central Athens:

Benetton Skoufa 20, Kolonaki (210 361 2451).
Bershka Ermou 50, Syntagma (210 331 4440).
Diesel Tsakalof 14, Kolonaki (210 360 0707).
DKNY Solonos 8, Kolonaki (210 360 3775).
Emporio Armani Solonos 4 & Milioni, Kolonaki (210 338 9101).
Ermenegildo Zegna Skoufa 18, Kolonaki (210 361 3700).
Escada Tsakalof 33, Kolonaki (210 361 3918).
Furla Patriarchou Ioakim 8, Kolonaki (210 721 6154).
Gant Kapsali 3, Kolonaki (210 722 2535).
Giorgio Armani Koumbari 8, Kolonaki (210 361 3603).
Gucci Tsakalof 27, Kolonaki (210 361 0870).
Guess Skoufa 14, Kolonaki (210 360 2511).
Karen Millen Anagnostopoulou 11, Kolonaki (210 362 3172).
La Perla Spefsippou 14, Kolonaki (210 729 9720).
Levi's Pindarou 19, Kolonaki (210 360 2066).
Louis Vuitton Voukourestiou 19, Kolonaki (210 361 3938).

Marina Rinaldi Skoufa 8 (Kolonaki, 210 363 8741).
MaxMara Akadimias 14 (Kolonaki, 210 360 2142).
Morgan Ermou 55 & Kapnikareas, Syntagma (210 324 1618). Ermou 30 (210 322 3202).
Naf Naf Ermou 45, Syntagma (210 321 6712).
Nautica Kanari 2, Kolonaki (210 361 7685).
Nike Tsakalof 34, Kolonaki (210 363 6188).
Paul & Shark Anagnostopoulou 6, Kolonaki (210 339 2334).
Polo Ralph Lauren Pindarou 22, Kolonaki (210 363 6342).
Puma Kanari 17 & Solonos, Kolonaki (210 361 0516).
Replay Ermou 53, Syntagma (210 324 5217).
Sisley Skoufa 17 & Irakleitou, Kolonaki (210 361 6200).
Tod's Voukourestiou 13, Kolonaki (210 335 6425).
Toi & Moi Panepistimiou & Em. Benaki 54, Historic Centre (210 384 0229). Ermou 75 (210 321 2611). Patision 127 (210 825 9556).
Tommy Hilfiger Milioni 3, Kolonaki (210 338 9420).
Wolford Skoufa 9, Kolonaki (210 363 2353).

Whether you're looking for the latest thriller, a copy of *The Odyssey* in Greek or a biography of Aristotle Onassis, this is the place to hunt. Eleftheroudakis's eight floors of English and Greek titles include literature, guidebooks and children's. For a break from browsing, pop up to the Food Company café.

Reymondos International Bookstore

Voukourestiou 18, Kolonaki (210 364 8189). Metro Syntagma. **Open** 8am-6pm Mon, Wed; 8am-8pm Tue, Thur, Fri; 8am-3pm Sat. **Credit** AmEx, DC, MC, V. **Map** p297 E4.
This tiny shop has the most comprehensive collection of foreign-language magazines in Athens, newspapers from most European countries, alongside fiction, classics, guidebooks and coffee-table tomes.

Department stores

Hondos Center

Omonia 4, Omonia (210 528 2800). Metro Omonia. **Open** *May-Sept* 9am-6pm Mon, Wed; 9am-9pm Tue, Thur, Fri; 9am-4pm Sat. *Oct-Apr* 9am-6pm Mon, Wed; 9am-8pm Tue, Thur, Fri; 9am-4pm Sat. **Credit** AmEx, DC, MC, V. **Map** p295 E3.

Use the shiny, hushed underground halls of the revamped and partly new metro station to get across the chaotic square to Hondos Center's gigantic ten-storey establishment. Whether it's a scale model of the Parthenon, a pair of socks or a three-piece suit you're after, this towering megastore will be sure to provide it. The swimwear selection is especially good, with a wide variety of labels including Dolce & Gabbana, Guess, Med, Moschino and Blue Point.
Other locations: throughout the city.

Lambropoulos

Eolou 99 & Lykourgou 2-6, Historic Centre (210 324 5811). Metro Omonia. **Open** *May-Sept* 9am-6pm Mon, Wed; 9am-9pm Tue, Thur, Fri; 9am-4pm Sat. *Oct-Apr* 9am-6pm Mon, Wed; 9am-9pm Tue, Thur, Fri; 9am-5pm Sat. **Credit** AmEx, DC, MC, V. **Map** p295 E3.
This department store offers seven floors of clothing, perfumes and cosmetics, bags, children's fashions and home accessories, along with an extensive collection of Athens 2004 Olympics merchandise – should you want to stock up on all the memorabilia. Plenty of Greek companies are represented, as well as fairly generic international labels.

Fashion

Budget

Authentic

Stadiou 56, Historic Centre (210 321 1728).
Metro Omonia. **Open** 9am-9pm Mon-Fri;
9am-4pm Sat. **Credit** MC, V. **Map** p295 E3.
Cotton/lycra tops, sporty trousers and factory
knits at rock-bottom prices. In winter all the clothes
are black or white, in summer hot pinks and
oranges sneak in. Don't forget that you generally
get what you pay for, and watch out for the returns
policy: there is no changing room here, yet if you
return a garment because it doesn't fit there is
no cash refund, only an exchange of the item for
something else.

Mango

Patision 122, Pedion Areos (210 823 3149).
Metro Victoria. **Open** *May-Sept* 9.30am-4pm
Mon, Wed, Sat; 9.30am-9pm Tue, Thur, Fri.
Oct-Apr 9.30am-4pm Mon, Wed, Sat; 9.30am-
8.30pm Tue, Thur, Fri. **Credit** AmEx, DC, MC, V.
This Spanish chain carries affordable versions of
catwalk looks on its rails while the designer origi-
nals are still being put together.

No Name

Athinas 8, Historic Centre (210 325 0291).
Metro Monastiraki. **Open** 9am-4pm Mon, Wed,
Sat; 9am-9pm Tue, Thur, Fri. **Credit** AmEx, DC,
MC, V. **Map** p295 E4.
A Greek company that creates affordable, fashionable clothing for both men and women. The
menswear line is simple and fairly basic, while the
womenswear is more overtly trendy. A good place
to pick up ephemeral fashion items as the fabrics
tend to be a bit on the perishable side.

Pull&Bear

Panepistimiou 56, Historic Centre (210 383 3538).
Metro Omonia. **Open** *May-Sept* 9am-6pm Mon,
Wed; 9am-9pm Tue, Thur, Fri; 9am-5pm Sat.
Oct-Apr 9am-6pm Mon, Wed; 9am-8pm Tue,
Thur, Fri; 9am-5pm Sat. **Credit** AmEx, DC,
MC, V. **Map** p295 F3.
Zara's little brother, Pull&Bear sells cheap, funky
streetwear. Drop in here for unisex khaki cargo
pants, slogan T-shirts, zip-up tops and chunky
Vans-type trainers.

2morrow

Kinetou 3, Monastiraki (210 324 7550).
Metro Monastiraki. **Open** hours vary; call ahead.
No credit cards. Map p295 D5.
This tiny, garment-packed shop sells a selection
of authentic '70s and retro vintage pieces collected
by designer Yota Caraba, as well as Caraba's own
unusual creations. Prices are as low as €5 for
second-hand tops, rising to €50 for one of Caraba's
hand-painted bikinis. The store keeps irregular
opening hours, so call before you head there.

Zara

*Stadiou 59, Historic Centre (210 324 3101). Metro
Omonia.* **Open** 9am-6pm Mon, Wed; 9am-9pm Tue,
Thur, Fri; 9am-5pm Sat. **Credit** AmEx, DC, MC, V.
Map p295 E3.
Everyone's favourite high-street chain, where you
can buy chic, classic quality clothing for men,
women and children at extremely reasonable prices.
Go early to avoid the crowds.
Other locations: Skoufa 22 & Pindarou, Kolonaki
(210 363 6340).

Mid-range

Anna Riska

*Ermou 26, Monastiraki (210 322 1661). Metro
Syntagma.* **Open** *May-Sept* 9am-4pm Mon, Wed, Sat;
9am-9pm Tue, Thur, Fri. *Oct-Apr* 9am-4pm Mon,
Wed, Sat; 9am-8.30pm Tue, Thur, Fri. **Credit** AmEx,
DC, MC, V. **Map** p295/p299 D5/E5.
Addressing a broad age range, this Greek chain sells
both trendy fashion items and a core line of basics,
including blazers, shift dresses and work suits. Take
a break from shopping at the attractive café upstairs,
where you can sip an ice-cold cappuccino freddo or
enjoy a freshly prepared salad or sandwich.

Artisti Italiani

*Ermou 22, Monastiraki (210 331 3857). Metro
Syntagma.* **Open** *May-Sept* 9am-4pm Mon, Wed,
Sat; 9am-9pm Tue, Thur, Fri. *Oct-Apr* 9am-6pm Mon,
Wed, Sat; 9am-8pm Tue, Thur, Fri. **Credit** AmEx,
DC, MC, V. **Map** p295/p299 D5/E5.
Milanese chic done the Greek way. Buy classic
items at prices that won't break the bank.

BSB

*Tsakalof 8, Kolonaki (210 339 2366). Metro
Syntagma.* **Open** 9am-4pm Mon, Wed, Sat;
9am-9pm Tue, Thur, Fri. **Credit** AmEx, DC,
MC, V. **Map** p297 G4.
All-the-rage clothes for teen and twentysomething
girls. Quality and lasting style are low on this Greek
brand's list of priorities, but if you're after bang-up-
to-the-minute fashions, BSB is well worth visiting.

DNA Stars

*Lekka 2 & Voulis, Historic Centre (210 331
0484). Metro Syntagma.* **Open** 9am-5pm Mon,
Wed, Sat; 9am-9pm Tue, Thur, Fri. **Credit** DC,
MC, V. **Map** p295/p299 F5.
An eclectic selection of clothes and accessories from
a variety of labels, including Jean Paul Gaultier, Miss
Sixty, Sandro, Peter Golding, Maje, Magilla, Miss
Selfridge and Homeless, as well as ethnic items from
Indonesia. While in the shop, pay your respects to
Carlos the tabby cat, who reclines languorously
behind the till, curling his paws and smiling.

Nine Below

Tsakalof 16, Kolonaki (210 362 5668).
Metro Syntagma. **Open** 10am-3.30pm Mon,
Wed; 10am-9pm Tue, Thur, Fri; 10am-4pm Sat.
Credit AmEx, MC, V. **Map** p297 G4.

Make the best out of your visit to Greece, by using the best maps of Greece available. Scenic routes in the countryside, remote beaches, picturesque villages and all sights worth visiting, clearly printed on the most accurate and updated maps of Greece. ROAD Editions maps are produced by experienced Greek cartographers. All ROAD Editions maps have a geophysical background from Greek military maps.

U.K. Distributor: PORTFOLIO, tel. 208 9979 000
12 Arachovis str. 106 80 Athens, Greece
tel. 0030 210 3640 723, fax 0030 210 3640 539
e-mail: road@enet.gr   www.road.gr

Cool urban European and US clothing labels, including Dico Copenhagen, Paul Frank, Soochi, 2Ckep and Punk Royal. There are customised vintage army pieces from London design company By and accessories from It's, Polder and Jerome Gruet.

Orfanidis
Kolokotroni 27, Historic Centre (210 323 5643).
Metro Syntagma. **Open** 9.30am-4pm Mon, Wed;
9.30am-8.30pm Tue, Thur, Fri; 9.30am-3.30pm Sat.
Credit AmEx, DC, MC, V. **Map** p295 F4.
Hand-picked garments for fashion-conscious girls and boys from Custo Barcelona, Energie, Guess and Dolce & Gabbana, and shoes by Adidas.

Sava
Akadimias 25, Historic Centre (210 364 1192).
Metro Syntagma. **Open** 9am-3pm Mon,
Sat; 9am-8.30pm Tue, Thur, Fri. **Credit** AmEx,
DC, MC, V. **Map** p297 G4.
Funky, fashionable clothes and accessories imported from lesser-known French, Italian and British brands. These trendsetting pieces are always distinctive.

Upmarket

Antonios Markos
Skoufa 21, Kolonaki (210 362 3036). Metro
Syntagma. **Open** 10am-4pm Mon, Wed, Sat;
10am-9pm Tue, Thur, Fri. **Credit** AmEx, DC,
MC, V. **Map** p297 G4.

Put a **Puma** in your tank. *See p164.*

As well as the eponymous Greek design duo's cool, classy garments for men and women, this minimalist gallery/shop stocks diverse pieces from a range of labels including Rokha, Anna Heylen, Bernard Willhelm, Xavier Delcour, Age and Dice Kayek. Also hats by Jacques le Corre, Irina Volkonskii bijoux and the complete range of Paul Frank, for which Antonios Markos has Greek distribution rights.

Carouzos
Patriarchou Ioakim 14, Kolonaki (210 724
5873). Metro Syntagma. **Open** 9.45am-3pm
Mon, Wed; 9.45am-8.30pm Tue, Thur, Fri;
9.45am-4pm Sat. **Credit** AmEx, DC, MC, V.
Map p297 H4.
Stock from all the biggest designers is sold at Carouzos. Calvin Klein, Miuccia Prada, Donna Karan, Salvatore Ferragamo, and Michael Kors for Celine are just a few of the class A international brands displayed in this Kolonaki institution's hallowed halls.

Ice Cube
Tsakalof 28, Kolonaki (210 362 5669). Metro
Evangelismos. **Open** 10am-4pm Mon, Wed;
10am-9pm Tue, Thur, Fri; 10am-3.30pm Sat.
Credit AmEx, DC, MC, V. **Map** p297 G4.
One of the most significant recent openings in Athens, this designer emporium boasts many of the hottest names in London fashion today – Lara Bohinc, J Maskrey, Liza Bruce, Frost French, Gharani Strok and Temperley to mention but a few – as well as a sprinkling of young Greek talents that add to the spice.

Prince Oliver Central
Anagnostopoulou 3, Kolonaki (210 364 5401).
Metro Syntagma. **Open** 9.30am-4pm Mon,
Wed, Sat; 9.30am-9pm Tue, Thur, Fri. **Credit**
AmEx, DC, MC, V. **Map** p297 H4.
Paul Smith, Etro, Paco Rabanne, Issey Miyake, Yohji Yamamoto and many other legends of the international fashion world are sold at this inspiring three-floor boutique located in the central Athens area of Kolonaki.

Rere Papa
Skoufa 62, Kolonaki (210 364 4300).
Metro Panepistimio. **Open** 11am-3pm Mon,
Wed, Sat; 11am-8.30pm Tue, Thur, Fri.
Credit AmEx, MC, V. **Map** p297 G4.
An idiosyncratic selection of garments and accessories, highlighted by the '50s-inspired retro creations of hot Greek girl design duo Rebecca Papastavrou and Renata Papazoglou (get the shop's name now?), plus imported labels, including Josep Font, For Design's Sake and Shelly's Shoes.

Sotris
Voukourestiou 41 & Tsakalof, Kolonaki (210 361
0662). Metro Syntagma. **Open** 9.30am-3.30pm
Mon, Wed, Sat; 10am-8.30pm Tue, Thur, Fri.
Credit AmEx, DC, MC, V. **Map** p297 G4.

Eat, Drink, Shop

Greek chic

Until recently, asking any non-Greek to name a fashion designer from this country would draw a complete blank. But lately, the success of Athens-born Sophia Kokosalaki in Milan, Paris and London has put the country that provides inspiration for so many of her popular creations on the fashion map.

Kokosalaki's mouthful of a name became, in 2002-03, the word most frequently pencilled into fashion editors' notebooks, whispered from stylist to celebrity client and emblazoned across catwalks at sell-out shows. The avant-garde 31-year-old artist may be one of the few Greek-born talents to make waves on the international fashion scene in recent years, but here in her country of birth there remains a goldmine of relatively untapped talent.

One of the best ways to introduce yourself to the work of the most noteworthy Greek fashion designers, struggling to make headlines in a country whose shopping populace is rigidly biased towards established Italian and French names, is with a visit to **Afternoon** (pictured, Deinokratous 1, Kolonaki, 210 722 5380). This stylish boutique is a proud testament to the best of Greek design today, gathering together a selection of garments and accessories made by some of the nation's brightest talents, including Deux Hommes, Vasso Consola, Smaragdi, Pavlos Kyriakides and Maro Zannia. Alternatively, pop into **Me Me Me** (Haritos 19, Kolonaki, 210 722 4890,

Take your pick from the latest creations dreamed up by Dolce & Gabbana, Prada, Marni, Miu Miu, Dior Homme, Comme des Garçons, Viktor & Rolf, Dries van Noten, Stella McCartney and many other catwalk favourites at this fashionistas' favourite.

Menswear

De Toute Facon
Voukourestiou 43, Kolonaki (210 361 4017).
Metro Syntagma. **Open** 10.30am-3.30pm Mon, Wed; 10.30am-8.30pm Tue, Thur, Fri; 10.30am-4pm Sat. **Credit** DC, MC, V. **Map** p297 G4.
Discerning gentlemen this way, please. This small, unobtrusive shop draws sartorially savvy customers who believe in paying for the best. Incomparably soft John Smedley tops, Duchamp cufflinks and ties, Cutler and Gros sunglasses, Alessandro Gherardeschi shirts and trousers and Trickers and Sabelt shoes.

Glou
Ermou 49, Historic Centre (210 331 3101-2).
Metro Syntagma. **Open** 9am-7pm Mon, Wed; 9am-9pm Tue, Thur, Fri; 9am-6pm Sat. **Credit** AmEx, DC, MC, V. **Map** p295/p299 E5.
Shirts, suits and casual clothing galore, and all at surprisingly affordable prices. This centrally located store also stocks the entire range of Puma sportswear as well as some Nike and Reebok items. But it gets even better: during the sales periods (February and August), Glou's prices are dropped to almost ridiculous depths. A suit for €50, anyone?

Incrocio
Kanari 8 & Merlin, Kolonaki (210 362 7768).
Metro Syntagma. **Open** *July-Aug* 9.30am-3.30pm Mon, Wed; 9.30am-9pm Tue, Thur, Fri; 9.30am-4pm Sat. *Sept-June* 9.30am-3.30pm Mon, Wed; 9.30am-8.30pm Tue, Thur, Fri; 9.30am-4pm Sat. **Credit** AmEx, DC, MC, V. **Map** p297 G5.

closed Sun), where you can browse through a pot-pourri of clothing by hot new names such as Apostolos Mitropoulos, Chara Lembessi, Angelos Bratis and Mia Oeser, as well as locally created bags, jewellery and objets d'art.

Eager for more? A wander around central Athens can incorporate the prêt-à-porter shops and haute-couture ateliers of many of Greece's most influential designers. **Yiorgos Eleftheriades YEShop** (Pindarou 38, Kolonaki, 210 361 5278, closed Sun), whose background is in costume design, produces edgy, unusual pieces – for both men and women – that unashamedly deconstruct and modernise classic elements for an unconventional silhouette. A favourite in Tokyo, Milan and Los Angeles, **Christoforos Kotentos** (4th Floor, Sachtouri 3, Psyrri, 210 325 5434, by appointment) dresses his devoted A-list clients in overtly sexy, luxurious garments in the softest nappa leather and barely-there lace. Meanwhile, up-and-coming talent **Lena Katsanidou** (Where to Wear, Alopekis 17 & Loukianou, Kolonaki, 210 722 3923, closed Sun) directs her capsule collection of unique leather bags and belts, sumptuous silk-and-satin tops and chunky, funky faux bijoux towards the flamboyant, trend-conscious twentysomethings of Athens' celebrity crowd.

More classic designs can be seen at the haughty boutique of **Michalis Aslanis** (Anagnostopoulou 16, Kolonaki, 210 360

4094, closed Sun), a diminutive genius who has been dressing the complete A-Z of Greek society since the 1970s, and at **Loukia**'s bustling atelier (Kanari 24, Kolonaki, 210 362 7334, closed Sun). Here, the flame-haired, softly spoken and self-effacing couturier dreams up incomparable creations for the confident, classy, elegant 21st-century woman. Well-to-do Athenian girls join a waiting list for one of Loukia's intricately detailed, beaded wedding gowns – if they are not being measured up for seductive, figure-hugging lace affairs at the quiet Plaka studio of celebrity designer **Celia Kritharioti** (Dedalou 8, Plaka, 210 323 0689, under construction. Temporarily: Leof Vas Sofias 4, Kolonaki, 210 725 5357, closed Sat-Sun).

Sadly there is little incentive for ambitious gifted designers to hone their skills for the Greek market. Home-grown fashion is not a lucrative industry in Greece – young talents are not encouraged by government support and other sponsorship or promotion as in many other countries, and even Greek buyers are reluctant to give up the secure status of Giorgio Armani, Donna Karan and the like for a relatively unknown local design brand. However, long-running talks of establishing a Greek Fashion Week may finally be coming to fruition, and in the meantime determined young talents such as Angelos Frentzos, Deux Hommes and Christoforos Kotentos follow in Sophia Kokosalaki's wake, flying the flag for Greek design overseas as well as at home.

Formal clothing for men who take pride in being well-dressed. Suits and ties by Hugo Boss and Giorgio Armani, shoes by Allen Edmonds and Bruno Magli, accessories by Trussardi and Burberry.

Oxford Company
Patriarchou Ioakim 12C, Kolonaki (210 721 1133). Metro Evangelismos. **Open** *May-Sept* 9am-3.30pm Mon, Wed, Sat; 9am-8.30pm Tue, Thur, Fri. *Oct-Apr* 9am-3.30pm Mon, Wed; 9am-9pm Tue, Thur, Fri; 9am-4pm Sat. **Credit** AmEx, DC, MC, V. **Map** p297 H4.
Take the inspiration of two Greek businessmen, the best of Italian fabrics and workmanship and a sensible pricing policy, and you get an extremely successful shirt-and-tie shop. The Oxford Company chain sells an impressive range of styles, shapes and patterns of shirts – for work or pleasure – to suit every age and taste. Also ties, cufflinks and a small selection of jumpers. Even if you are relatively bullish – or giraffish – of neck, you should still be able to find a shirt to fit.

Pagoni, Maison des Cravates
Voukourestiou 21A, Kolonaki (210 362 7649). Metro Syntagma. **Open** *May-Sept* 9am-4pm Mon, Wed, Sat; 9am-9pm Tue, Thur, Fri. *Oct-Apr* 4pm Mon, Wed, Sat; 9am-8.30pm Tue, Thur, Fri. **Credit** AmEx, DC, MC, V. **Map** p297 G4.
Looking for a designer tie? You name it, they got it at this tiny but comprehensively stocked neckwear emporium. Every label under the sun, from Cacharel, Fendi and Paul Smith to Walt Disney, is sold here. In summer, pick up an attractive (and laughably inexpensive) beach bag from the capsule collection made in India especially for Pagoni.

Sarafis
Patriarchou Ioakim 5, Kolonaki (210 722 5319/210 722 2802). Metro Syntagma. **Open** *May-Sept* 9am-3pm Mon, Wed; 9am-2pm, 5.30-8.30pm Tue, Thur, Fri; 9am-3.30pm Sat. *Oct-Apr* 9am-3pm Mon, Wed; 9am-8.30pm Tue, Thur, Fri; 9am-3.30pm Sat. **Credit** AmEx, DC, MC, V. **Map** p297 H4.

Eat, Drink, Shop

Casual clothing for active lads. Diesel, Levi's, Timberland, North Sails, O'Neill, Quiksilver, Murphy & Nye, Marlboro and other macho labels are stocked at this haven for (wannabe) sporty types. A limited range for outdoorsy girls is also available.

Children

Alouette

Pindarou 26-28, Kolonaki (210 362 8049). Metro Syntagma. **Open** *May-Sept* 9am-3.30pm Mon, Wed; 9am-8.30pm Tue, Thur, Fri; 9am-4pm Sat. *Oct-Apr* 9am-3.30pm Mon, Wed; 9am-9pm Tue, Thur, Fri; 9am-4pm Sat. **Credit** AmEx, DC, MC, V. **Map** p297 G4.

This spacious, well-laid-out store offers a range of reasonably priced Greek-made clothing alongside more pricey pieces by Lacoste, Gant and Miniman.

Lapin House

Anagnostopoulou 2, Kolonaki (210 724 6227). Metro Evangelismos. **Open** *May-Sept* 9am-3pm Mon, Wed; 9am-8.30pm Tue, Thur, Fri; 9am-4pm Sat. *Oct-Apr* 9am-3pm Mon, Wed; 9am-9pm Tue, Thur, Fri; 9am-4pm Sat. **Credit** AmEx, DC, MC, V. **Map** p297 H4.

Want to kit your kid out in mini creations by Prada, Moschino, Trussardi and Dolce & Gabbana? This is the place to browse, credit card at the ready.

Mothercare

Ermou 44, Historic Centre (210 323 8695). Metro Syntagma. **Open** 9am-4pm Mon, Wed; 9am-9pm Tue, Thur, Fri; 9am-5pm Sat. **Credit** AmEx, DC, MC, V. **Map** p295/p299 E5.

This international chain sells practical maternity clothing, garments for children from newborns to toddlers, pushchairs, cots and pretty much all an infant requires from the moment it comes into the world.

Mouyer

Kanari 8, Kolonaki (210 361 7714). Metro Syntagma. **Open** *May-Sept* 9am-3pm Mon, Wed, Sat; 9am-2.30pm, 5-9pm Tue, Thur, Fri. *Oct-Apr* 9am-3.30pm Mon, Wed, Sat; 9am-2.30pm, 5-8pm Tue, Thur, Fri. **Credit** AmEx, DC, MC, V. **Map** p297 G5.

Quality, well-fitted, durable footwear for children from four months old upwards. As well as Mouyer's own label, you'll find that imported brands from Italy and France are also stocked here. Adults who don't have overly large feet can shop here if they happen to have a penchant for children's styles – sizes go up to a European 40.

Neverland

Solonos 18, Kolonaki (210 360 0996). Metro Syntagma. **Open** 9am-3pm Mon, Wed; 9am-3pm, 5-8.30pm Tue; 9am-8.30pm Thur, Fri; 9am-3.30pm Sat. **Credit** DC, MC, V. **Map** p295 F3.

This delightful shop is a veritable Aladdin's cave of goodies for children, with its cuddly, realistic soft toys, its microscooters and board games, its lifelike dolls and its elaborately detailed sets of furniture and crockery for old-fashioned doll's houses. The kids may just never want to leave.

Second-hand

Dada

Emmanouil Benaki 82, Exarchia (210 381 5032). Metro Omonia. **Open** *May-Sept* 11am-6pm Mon, Wed, Sat; 11am-9pm Tue, Thur, Fri. *Oct-Apr* 11am-5pm Mon, Wed, Sat; 11am-9pm Tue, Thur, Fri. **No credit cards.**

Dada is bursting with imported second-hand clothing – dresses, shirts (€25-€30) and reasonably priced accessories for twenty to thirtysomethings. Don't worry too much about the state of the clothing – everything is sterilised and dry-cleaned.

Le Streghe son Tornate

Haritos 9, Kolonaki (210 721 2581). Metro Evangelismos. **Open** 10.30am-3.30pm Mon, Wed, Sat; 10.30am-8.30pm Tue, Thur, Fri. **Credit** AmEx, DC, MC, V. **Map** p297 H4.

This colourful second-hand store has a certain London feel about it and sells vintage designer clothes and accessories in the €40-€200 price range. If you're into geisha pendants, gold rings and clothing from the Far East, you're going to love this place.

Fashion accessories

Achilleas

Ermou 34, Historic Centre (210 324 9708). Metro Syntagma. **Open** 9am-4pm Mon, Wed, Sat; 9am-9pm Tue, Thur, Fri. **Credit** AmEx, DC, MC, V. **Map** p295/p299 E5.

This highly successful chain is Greece's home-grown equivalent of the UK-based accessory brand Accessorize. Not the best place if you're looking for lasting quality items, but it is great for cheap and up-to-the-minute bags, belts, sarongs, bijoux and hair baubles.

Arathymos

Kanari 10, Kolonaki (210 363 1673). Metro Syntagma. **Open** 9.30am-4pm Mon, Wed, Sat; 9.30am-8.30pm Tue, Thur, Fri. **Credit** AmEx, DC, MC, V. **Map** p297 G5.

Don't try to go anywhere in Greece without a pair of sunglasses – they are a necessity both for protection from the strong sun and as a fashion statement. This small but well-stocked shop has a wide selection of the coolest designer shades around. The staff are extremely helpful and have a knack of picking out the ideal sunglasses to suit each customer.

Folli Follie

Ermou 18, Historic Centre (210 323 0729). Metro Syntagma. **Open** 9am-3.30pm Mon, Wed, Sat; 9am-8.30pm Tue, Thur, Fri. **Credit** AmEx, DC, MC, V. **Map** p295/p299 F5.

There is nowhere better for reasonably priced, good-quality jewellery, watches, bags and scarves than this globally sold accessories chain, which started right here in Athens. The recently launched K Collection of one-off necklaces with precious stones is particularly impressive.

Eat, Drink, Shop

Cosmetics to fly for

In London they grace shelves in the hallowed halls of Harvey Nichols and Harrods, but here in their native land naturally based cosmetics lines Korres and Apivita can be found on sale for just a couple of euros at your local chemist.

The **Korres** range of products, made to homeopathic formulas incorporating a wide selection of indigenous Greek herbs and plants, includes shampoos, conditioners, face masks, creams and lotions, cleansers, body sprays, shower gels and a line of essential sunscreens. Before you head off to bake yourself on the idyllic island beaches, stock up on Aloe Vera-rich Sunscreen SPF 10-15 for the face and body and freshly scented Red Vine Hair Sun Protection Spray to keep your hair healthy and hydrated in the sun. Korres products are available from most chemists, but for the full range visit the birthplace of the brand (*see p175*). Britons meeting these innovative cosmetics for the first time will be pleased to hear that the first freestanding Korres store outside Greece opened on the King's Road in London in May 2003.

Like Korres, **Apivita**'s aromatherapy line harnesses the power of nature, using essential oils and plant extracts to address

Katerina Karoussos
Ploutarchou 7, Kolonaki (210 729 3690). Metro Evangelismos. **Open** *May-Sept* 10am-3pm Mon, Wed, Sat; 10am-2.30pm, 5.30-8.30pm Tue, Thur, Fri. *Oct-Apr* 10am-3pm Mon, Wed, Sat; 10am-2.30pm, 5-8pm Tue, Thur, Fri. **Credit** AmEx, DC, MC, V. **Map** p297 H4.

The inspired creations of Katerina Karoussos, Athens' most celebrated milliner, appear in theatrical productions, grace the heads of Athenian society ladies and are constantly photographed for top fashion magazines. Pop into Karoussos's Kolonaki store to see the wide selection of headgear: from elaborate, beribboned floral straw bonnets to simple, stylish fabric affairs. Alternatively, get measured up for a made-to-order hat of your choice. Be warned, though – bespoke hats take at least two weeks to create (longer in the busy summer season), so put your order in early.

Kem
Patriarchou Ioakim 26A, Kolonaki (210 721 9230). Metro Evangelismos. **Open** 8.30am-3pm Mon; 8.30am-3.30pm Wed, Sat; 8.30am-8.30pm Tue, Thur, Fri. **Credit** DC, MC, V. **Map** p297 H4.

This Greek bag-making chain sells seasonal selections of designer-influenced totes, evening bags, clutches, shoulder bags and luggage. Frequented both by professional women and trend-driven teenagers, Kem has established itself as a key player in the local accessories market.

Thiros
Skoufa 24, Kolonaki (210 362 8445). Metro Syntagma. **Open** 9.30am-3.30pm Mon, Wed, Sat; 9.30am-8.30pm Tue, Thur, Fri. **Credit** AmEx, DC, MC, V. **Map** p297 G4.

If you're heading for Thiros, the number-one Greek brand for handbags and capacious luggage

the needs of stressed city skin. The Express Masks – single-use packs offering effective solutions for problematic complexions – are particularly useful for travellers; pick up a packet or two (from the nearest pharmacy) of the Chamomile Cleansing Tissues and Deep Peeling with Olive Seeds to slip into your overnight bag.

The products of **Mastic Spa** (Iraklitou 1 & Solonos, Kolonaki, 210 360 3413, closed Sun) have yet to reach foreign shores except in the suitcases of visiting shoppers in the know. This comprehensive line, based on the healing oil of the mastic tree, which

flourishes only in the southern part of the eastern Aegean island of Chios, includes formulations for the hair, face and body. (Mastic products of all kinds, the more utilitarian included, are also available at **Mastiha Shop**, see p181.)

Another Greek cosmetics line takes its inspiration from ancient Greek beauty remedies. **Freshline** (Skoufa 10, Kolonaki, 210 364 4015, closed Sun) claims to use recipes used by the heroines of age-old Greek myths and legends for its frothy bath bombs, slabs of soap and preservative-free natural mud masks.

holdalls, be prepared to pay from around €80 upwards. As well as more conventional mono-chrome leather bags, there is a selection of Anya Hindmarch-inspired photo-emblazoned totes, some practical and stylish Tod's-style loafers, and ballet pumps in a range of joyful hues.

Underwear & swimwear

Aerakis

Skoufa 1, Platia Kolonaki, Kolonaki (210 362 4165). Metro Syntagma. **Open** 9am-3.30pm Mon, Wed, Sat; 9am-8.30pm Tue, Thur, Fri. **Credit** AmEx, DC, MC, V. **Map** p297 G4.

A treasure trove of extravagant underwear and swimwear from a selection of leading labels. Pretty, intricate lacy lingerie sets for ladies are provided by La Perla, Donna Karan, Chantelle and Cotton Club, while the menswear (sold

upstairs in a separate shop two doors down from the main entrance) includes boxers, vests, T-shirts, socks and even G-strings for more ostentatious beach-goers from renowned brands including Emporio Armani, Ferrè, Hom and Grigio Perla.

Filidono

Tsakalof 11, Kolonaki (210 361 6780). Metro Syntagma. **Open** 9.30am-3.30pm Mon, Wed, Sat; 9.30am-8.30pm Tue, Thur, Fri. **Credit** AmEx, DC, MC, V. **Map** p297 G4.

This abundantly stocked basement shop is where all the Athenian girls come to stock up on bikinis for the long hot summer. Brands include D&G, DKNY, Moschino, Replay, Calvin Klein and Blu Bay. There is also a range of sexy, vibrant-hued bikinis imported from Brazil that are cheap and cheerful but – due to the minimal cut of the bottom part – strictly for the toned of behind.

Baking hot in Athens

Atkins dieters will have a hard time sticking to their chosen low-carbohydrate menus here in Greece. Breakfast and snack staples are filo pastry pies with feta cheese (*tiropita*), spinach (*spanakopita*) or leek (*prasopita*). **Ariston** (Voulis 10, Historic Centre, 210 322 7626) is renowned throughout Athens for serving the tastiest, freshest cheese pies in town. Alternatively, Athenians munch on simple sesame seed-encrusted rings of baked bread (*koulouria*). Bought from the trays or baskets of the many street vendors who hawk both crusty and softer versions

of this traditional snack from dawn to mid morning, this is the ideal accompaniment to that first cup of coffee on arrival at the office.

Meals are always accompanied by chunks of bread, either rather lumpy village loaves (which even when freshly baked can often taste stale to foreign palates) or more innovative creations with olives, onions, walnuts or sun-dried tomatoes baked into them. Nestling in the shadow of the Acropolis, every morning the bakery **O Takis** (Misaraliotou 14, Makrygianni, 210 923 0052) gathers residents and passers-by

Intimissimi

Voukourestiou 27 & Solonos, Kolonaki (210 364 6996). Metro Syntagma. **Open** 9am-3pm Mon, Wed, Sat; 9am-9pm Tue, Thur, Fri. **Credit** DC, MC, V. **Map** p297 G4.
This high-street chain sells attractive underwear, nightgowns and a small selection of soft cotton jersey tops at extremely reasonable prices.

Vraki

Skoufa 50, Kolonaki (210 362 7420). Metro Panepistimio. **Open** 10am-3pm Mon, Wed, Sat; 9am-2pm, 5-9pm Tue, Thur, Fri. **Credit** MC, V. **Map** p297 G4.
A funky outlet selling Thessaloniki-made label Modus Vivendi underwear. Although the stock is

mainly for guys, there's some cotton briefs and vests for girls and unisex robes and tops too. Prices are very affordable.

Jewellery

Elena Votsi

Xanthou 7, Kolonaki (210 360 0936). Metro Evangelismos. **Open** 10am-3pm Mon, Wed, Sat; 10am-8.30pm Tue, Thur, Fri. **Credit** AmEx, DC, MC, V. **Map** p297 H4.
This talented Greek designer worked for Gucci's accessories division before launching her own line to the delight of A-list celebrities and jewellery aficionados. Votsi's impeccably finished creations are the epitome of classic Greek elegance.

drawn in by the delicious wafts of baking. Try the *koulouria*, baguettes and crusty olive loaves still warm from the oven – perfect for picnics.

From lunchtime onwards, Greece's famous pastries, cakes and sweetmeats come into their own. Baklava and *kataifi* are probably the best-known, although these rolls/triangles of honey-soaked pastry filled with nuts are actually of Middle Eastern origin. Forget your figure for half an hour, and enjoy a small punnet of gloriously sweet mini *baklavadakia* in different flavours selected for you by the staff at **Karavan** (Voukourestiou 11, Kolonaki, 210 364 1540). They're best consumed with a bitter cup of Greek coffee, tea with a slice of lemon, or just a glass of water (you'll need it).

Take a break from sightseeing in Athens' historical quarter, and stop for a slice of *karydopita* (walnut pie) with mastic-flavoured ice cream at **Tristrato** (Dedalou 34 & Geronta, 210 324 4472; *see also p157*). Situated in an old corner house on the edge of Plaka's main square, this old-fashioned coffee and tea shop is decorated like yiayia's (grandmother's) parlour, with upright settles and a display case full of dainty bone china. As well as sweets such as traditional *rizogala* (Greek rice pudding with cinnamon), *galaktoboureko* (pastry filled with confectioner's cream and sprinkled with icing sugar) and *milopita* (apple pie), To Tristrato is also known and loved for its savoury mushroom pies and teas with Greek mountain herbs.

Fanourakis
Patriarchou Ioakim 23, Kolonaki (210 721 1762). Metro Evangelismos. **Open** 9am-3pm Mon, Wed, Sat; 9am-2pm, 5.30-8.30pm Tue, Thur, Fri. **Credit** AmEx, DC, MC, V. **Map** p297 H4.
Incredibly intricate work in gold and white gold, often set with diamonds or other precious stones, represents the main part of this long-established jeweller's eclectic collection. The superbly detailed range of miniature silver beetle, butterfly and beetle brooches is one of Fanourakis's trademarks.

Lalaounis
Panepistimiou 6 & Voukourestiou, Historic Centre (210 361 1371). Metro Syntagma. **Open** 9am-3pm Mon, Wed; 9am-8pm Tue, Thur, Fri; 9am-2.30pm Sat. **Credit** AmEx, DC, MC, V. **Map** p297 G4/G5.

For decades the shops of Ilias Lalaounis, one of the earliest masters to make a name for Greek jewellery on the international stage, have been attracting discerning customers for its top-quality, Byzantine-inspired solid-gold necklaces, bracelets and earrings. The new DNA range incorporates more modern elements in an unusual series of molecular jewellery. There is also a Lalaounis Museum (*see p88*), which houses a several-thousand strong collection of Lalaounis designs past and present.

Petaie Petaie
Skoufa 30, Kolonaki (210 362 4315). Metro Syntagma. **Open** *July-Aug* 10am-2.30pm, 5-9pm daily. *Oct-June* 10am-3.30pm Mon, Wed, Sat; 10am-2.30pm, 5-8.30pm Tue; 10am-8.30pm Thur, Fri. Closed 2wks Aug. **Credit** AmEx, DC, MC, V. **Map** p297 G4.
This tiny, hole-in-the-wall shop sells a select range of works by talented young Greek jewellery designers, including Vangelis Polizo's amber inventions, Erato Boukogianni's coral-and-gold necklaces, Yiannis Tjovenis's collection of silver pieces and a range of ornate lucky-charm bracelets and casual turquoise-and-sea-glass bangles designed by the shop owner herself, Ioanna Kokolopoulou.

Shoes

Kalogirou
Patriarchou Ioakim 4, Kolonaki (210 335 6401). Metro Evangelismos. **Open** 9am-3.30pm Mon, Wed; 9am-8.30pm Tue, Thur, Fri; 9am-5pm Sat. **Credit** AmEx, DC, MC, V. **Map** p297 H4.
Shopaholics from all over Greece and Cyprus flock to jockey for viewing positions against the windows of this formidable Kolonaki shoe emporium, which sells a pricey selection of its own-brand footwear as well as the latest mouth-watering creations from Prada, D&G, Miu Miu, Tod's and Casadei. Well-off professional gentlemen buy their classic Church's brogues here.

Petridis
Platia Kolonaki 6, Kolonaki (210 723 8434). Metro Evangelismos. **Open** 9am-4pm Mon, Wed, Sat; 9am-9pm Tue, Thur, Fri. **Credit** AmEx, DC, MC, V. **Map** p297 H4
Fashionable, quality women's shoes from labels such as Pedro Garcia, Parallele, Vicini and Charles Jourdan, and traditional men's formal lace-ups from Petridis's own line, venerable Greek brand Mouriadis, Florsheim, Church's and Baldinini. It's also worth paying a visit, if you have time, to Petridis's stock shop (Mesogeion 253, Holargos, Northern Suburbs, 210 674 0592), where you can pick up many of the discontinued lines at greatly reduced prices.

Rollini
Ermou 16, Historic Centre (210 323 4838). Metro Syntagma. **Open** 9am-5pm Mon, Wed, Sat; 9am-9pm Tue, Thur, Fri. **Credit** AmEx, DC, MC, V. **Map** p295/p299 F5.

Eat, Drink, Shop

Mastiha, Loukoumia, Pasteli, Tsoureki, Ipovrihio, Sokolataki, Ouzo, Paksimadakia, Koulourakia, Glika tou Koutaliou, etc.

Sounds Greek to you?

Who says that you can't taste unknown... words? "Delicious" is our middle name and we come from Chios with love! Conquerors of the Mediterranean tradition and defenders of the indulging Greek aromas, we challenge you to taste, eat, smell, chew, swallow all mastihashop original goods and add a little something to your external beauty! **Is it clear now why mouzaka, bouzouki and sunset post cards are not the only things to take back home with you?**

It is!

karamella

Over-egging the pudding: **Amelie**. *See p177.*

A tempting selection of shoes for both men and women from Rollini's own brand are sold at this shop – as well as a selection of imported footwear by the likes of Pura Lopez, Dolce & Gabbana and sporty Puma.

Spiliopoulos
Ermou 63, Historic Centre (210 322 7590).
Metro Monastiraki. **Open** 9.30am-3.30pm Mon,
Wed, Sat; 9.30am-8.30pm Tue, Thur, Fri. **Credit**
AmEx, DC, MC, V. **Map** p295/p299 E5.
A bargain hunter's delight, this shop stocks seconds and last season's styles made by such sought-after names as Manolo Blahnik, Kate Spade, Narciso Rodriguez, Calvin Klein, Donna Karan and many others at a fraction of their original prices. We should really have kept this one a secret.

Food & drink

Chocolates

Aristokratikon
Karagiorgi Servias 9, Historic Centre (210 322 0546). Metro Syntagma. **Open** *May-Sept* 8am-4pm Mon, Wed, Sat; 8am-9pm Tue, Thur, Fri. *Oct-Apr* 8am-9pm Mon-Fri; 8am-4pm Sat.
No credit cards. Map p295/p299 F5.
Greece's original and best handmade chocolates. These nuggets of desire are made freshly every day in the kitchen of a Kolonaki mansion, from which the scent of cooking chocolate wafts temptingly each morning, then transported immediately to this classic Athenian shop. Don't miss the pistachio nut clusters and the unnervingly realistic rusty screws.

Greek specialities

Plain, simple, traditional Greek edibles are some of the most reasonably priced and best-appreciated souvenirs you can take back to your friends and relatives at home – and pretty nifty for a picnic, too. Keep away from the overpriced tourist-trap areas, and instead buy from the shops where Athenians themselves purchase their groceries. The busy area around the central meat market (on Athinas, near Omonia Square) – especially the spicy-scented Evripidou – is where you can find most Greek specialities, such as herbs, olives, cheeses, nuts and dried fruit, for sale.

Mesogeia
Nikis 52 & Kydathinaion, Plaka (210 322 9146). Metro Syntagma. **Open** 9am-5pm Mon, Wed; 9am-9pm Tue, Thur, Fri; 9am-4pm Sat; 10am-3pm Sun. **Credit** MC, V. **Map** p299 F6.
If you're in Plaka, do your food shopping at this small store packed to the gunnels with traditional (and often organic) goodies. The selection includes rusky *paximadia* (rusks), local olive oil, Greek wines and liqueurs, cheeses and other edible specialities gathered from all over Greece and its islands.

Tyria Outra
Sofokleous 17, Historic Centre (210 322 1135). Metro Omonia. **Open** 6am-9pm Mon-Sat.
No credit cards. Map p295 E4.
Cheeses, cold meats, fish marinated in oil, sweet, crumbling halva and stuffed veg pack the shelves and fridges of this unpretentious delicatessen.

Patisserie

Amelie
Pindarou 29 & Anagnostopoulou, Kolonaki (210 361 1573). Metro Syntagma. **Open** 10am-8pm Mon, Wed; 10am-10pm Tue, Thur-Sat. Closed August. **Credit** AmEx, DC, MC, V. **Map** p297 G4.
This French patissier sells designer desserts, pastel-hued macaroons and chocolates that are as scrumptious as they are elegant. The selection is minimal (only a few of each are created every day with ingredients imported from France), the packaging supremely chic and the prices high – this is boutique cake-shopping at its finest.

Supermarkets

Green Goat
Haritos 4, Kolonaki (210 722 6829). Metro Evangelismos. **Open** 9.30am-4pm Mon, Wed; 9.30am-8pm Tue, Thur, Fri; 10am-2pm Sat.
Credit MC, V. **Map** p297 H4.
This tiny shop is a haven of all that is organic: that's chicken, cereals, yoghurt, cleaning products, cosmetics, pasta, sausages, chocolate, beverages

Eat, Drink, Shop

Sunday morning in Monastiraki

A guided walk in shopping heaven.

The Monastiraki flea market, centred on Platia Avyssinias, should not be missed, no matter whether your idea of shopping is strictly designer or more like a couple of dirty postcards and a bottle of ouzo. Located next to Athens' Ancient Agora, where traders from throughout the Mediterranean once peddled their wares, crowded, colourful Monastiraki has become the meeting place for sellers of everything, from antique furniture and rare books to clothes, kitsch and junk from around the world. Sunday, when the rest of the city shuts down completely, is the liveliest market day, when dealers from all over crawl out of the woodwork to hawk their choicest and cheapest offerings.

and even sanitary items including babies' nappies. If they don't have what you want, helpful owner Rania is usually more than happy to order it for you – even if it is not otherwise produced in or imported into Greece.

Marinopoulos
Kanari 9, Kolonaki (210 362 4907). Metro Syntagma. **Open** *May-Sept* 8am-9pm Mon-Fri; 8am-6pm Sat. *Oct-Apr* 8am-8pm Mon-Fri; 8am-6pm Sat. **Credit** AmEx, DC, MC, V. **Map** p297 G5.

An average-sized city supermarket with a delicatessen section, dairy produce, fruit and vegetables, alcohol and beverages, cosmetics, tinned and frozen goods. The fresh bread tends to sell out by midday, so make sure you go early for your floury village loaf.

Vasilopoulos Delicatessen
Stadiou 19, Historic Centre (210 322 2405). Metro Panepistimio. **Open** *May-Sept* 8am-8.30pm Mon-Fri; 8am-3.30pm Sat. *Oct-Apr* 8am-8pm Mon-Fri; 8am-3.30pm Sat. **Credit** AmEx, DC, MC, V. **Map** p295 F4.

Pricier than other supermarkets, this deli is stocked with unusual brands like Green & Black's organic chocolate, gourmet eats, local specialities such as olive oil and feta cheese, and some generic household staples.

Wine & spirits

Cellier
Krizotou 1, Historic Centre (210 361 0040). Metro Syntagma. **Open** 9am-5pm Mon, Wed; 9am-8.30pm Tue, Thur, Fri; 9am-3pm Sat. **Credit** AmEx, DC, MC, V. **Map** p297 G4/G5.

A word to the wise: haggling is expected, indeed, de rigueur, no matter how low the initial price may seem.

When planning a day at the market, remember to start fairly early. Stalls and shops open at about 8.30am and close around 3pm.

Begin the walk at Thisio metro station, going down the newly pedestrianised Adrianou. Take note on your right of the sprawling ruins of the Ancient Agora, where fifth-century BC vendors once told riff-raff like

Socrates to shove off and stop scaring away customers. Continue down Adrianou, turning left on to Thisio, lined with twittering birdcages and traders selling fake furs, silver cutlery and Russian dolls on blankets. Have a poke around **Erato** (Thisio 9, 210 331 1991), a favourite bookstore of Athenian literati, full of foreign-language books, prints and leather-bound rare editions. Across the street, **Palaiopoleion O Alexandros** (Thisio 10, 210 321 5926, closed Mon) is a ▶

Cellier offers a great selection of fine wines, including many Greek vintages, champagnes and spirits. The goodie-packed Christmas and New Year's hampers are the original and best in Athens.

O Brettos

Kydathinaion 41, Plaka (210 323 2110).
Metro Monastiraki or Syntagma.
Open 10am-midnight daily. **No credit cards.**
Map p299 F6.
This dimly lit den, which is lined floor to ceiling with brightly coloured bottles and huge wooden barrels, sells home-distilled liqueurs as well as ouzo, either by the bottle (an ideal present for friends who like the odd shot of fiery liquor) or by the glass to eager patrons who gather around the hefty wood bar from around noon onwards.

Wine Garage

Xenokratous 25, Kolonaki (210 721 3175).
Metro Evangelismos. **Open** 11am-10pm Mon-Sat.
Credit AmEx, MC, V, DC. **Map** p297 H4.
This bright and modern shop stocks an excellent selection of local wines and imported vintages.

Health & beauty

Pharmacies

Korres

Ivikou 8, Pangrati (210 722 2774). Metro Syntagma.
Open *May-Sept* 8.30am-2.30pm Mon, Wed; 8.30am-2.30pm, 5.30-8.30pm Tue, Thur, Fri. *Oct-Apr* 8.30am-2.30pm Mon, Wed; 8.30am-2.30pm, 5-8pm Tue, Thur, Fri. **Credit** AmEx, MC, V. **Map** p297 H6.

fascinating jumble of oddities such as engraved art nouveau cigarette holders, tiny silver salt-and-pepper sets, erotic Arabic prints and antique medical supplies. The shop is co-owned by a Venetian and is often stocked with handmade Venetian carnival masks and colourful Venetian glass. Continue down Thisio, turning right on Astigos or Ermou, either of which will take you past a handful of intriguing junk shops while leading you to Platia Avyssinias, the heart of the market. In the centre of the square, dealers sell painted trunks, coloured cut-glass Turkish tea sets, frilly knickers, pastel-painted Jesus figurines and other such treasures from makeshift stalls. Those on the hunt for true antiques should explore the shops surrounding the square. Platia Avyssinias 3 can yield some good finds: at street level, **Costas Alexandros** (210 321 1580) has antique desk sets with ink bottles and working quills, battered marble-topped rococo writing tables, 1920s typewriters, Victrolas and old Greek toys. Downstairs,

Motakis (210 321 9005) is one of the few stores in Athens licensed to carry certified antique furniture. On the other side of the square, **Kouglanos** (Platia Avyssinias 6, 210 321 2473) has old Greek musical instruments, wooden signs from the early 1900s and funky upholstered furniture.

If you need a break, stop at **Café Avyssinia** (Kinetou 7, 210 321 7047; *see p128*), a family-run institution whose tables overflow into the market, and whose Arabic and French takes on Greek classics burst with flavour.

Leaving the square, turn left on to Ifestou. It's full of shops selling cheap clothes and trinkets, but keep your eyes open for the small entryways that lead downstairs into dusty storehouses of junk and treasure. Be sure not to miss Normanou, a sunny alley on the left of Ifestou. Here you'll find shops selling maps, prints, old photos, and everything else for your walls. Try **Darousos Theotokis** (Normanou 7, 210 331 1638) for prints of old Greek ads. Back on Ifestou, look for **Vavas** (*see p182*). Barely even a hole in

---

Converts to homeopathic medicine should head to this den of all that is natural and holistic. As well as cures for aches and pains, you will also find the complete range of Korres's own cosmetics here – this humble chemists is the home of the natural-based products that have taken London, New York and Paris by storm (*see p168* **Cosmetics to fly for**). The packaging is beautifully therapeutic too.

Litos

Stadiou 17, Historic Centre (210 322 2200). Metro Panepistimio. **Open** *May-Sept* 8am-2.30pm Mon, Wed; 8am-2pm, 5.30-8.30pm Tue, Thur, Fri. *Oct-Apr* 8am-2.30pm Mon, Wed; 8am-2pm, 5-8pm Tue, Fri. **Credit** MC, V. **Map** p295 F4.
One of the oldest surviving pharmacies in central Athens, this shop has everything you could need, and if by chance it doesn't, the friendly, English-speaking staff will order it for you.

Cosmetics

Beautyworks

Kapsali 10, Kolonaki (210 722 5511). Metro Evangelismos. **Open** 9am-4pm Mon, Wed, Sat; 10am-8.30pm Tue, Thur, Fri. **Credit** AmEx, DC, MC, V. **Map** p297 H5.
The full range of Shu Uemura products, as well as ranges from Kiehl's, Penhaligon's, Dr Hauschka and fragrances by Miller Harris, Floris and Acqua di

Parma. Don't miss the Rodial creams, made with antioxidant-rich pomegranate to combat cellulite and other toxin-related conditions.
Other locations: Kolokotroni 8, Kifisia (210 808 9070).

Body 'n' Soul

Fivis 17, Glyfada (210 894 5737). Bus A3 or B3. **Open** *May-Sept* 9.30am-3.30pm Mon, Wed, Sat; 9am-2.30pm, 5.30-9pm Tue, Thur, Fri. *Oct-Apr* 9.30am-3.30pm Mon, Wed, Sat; 9am-2.30pm, 5.30-8.30pm Tue, Thur, Fri. **Credit** AmEx, DC, MC, V.
Distinguished brands for beauty connoisseurs. These boudoir-like boutiques sell the most elusive products of the luxury cosmetics world, including make-up by Stephane Marais, T le Clerc and Nars, Creed perfumes, Caudalie grape-seed lotions and Hei Poa Tahitian oils. Also Kiehl's, Aesop's and OPI nail varnishes.
Other locations: Omirou 11, Neo Psychiko, Northern Suburbs (210 677 4554).

Heaven on Earth

Levidou 16, Kifisia (210 808 1151). Metro Kifisia. **Open** 9.30am-4pm Mon, Wed, Sat; 9.30am-8.30pm Tue, Thur, Fri. **Credit** AmEx, DC, MC, V.
As well as boasting sole representation of Annick Goutal perfumes in Greece, this suburban slice of paradise stocks the latest, trendiest international products. St Tropez cream, Bumble & Bumble hair-care, Bliss Spa treatments, Fresh cosmetics and Cellex-C cellulite lotions are some of the top sellers.

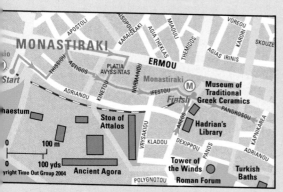

Ifestou ends at Monastiraki metro station. Just beyond the station, stamp and coin collectors should check out **Kiritisis** (Areos 1, 210 324 0544) – a tiny stall piled with coins, stamps, medals and wartime paraphernalia. Head up Pandrosou, stopping at **Stavros Melissinos** (*see p182*). As you'll see from the laminated magazine clippings peeling out front in the sun, the white-haired poet-shoemaker has morphed into

the wall, this tiny stand has been selling carved *tavli* (backgammon – the national pastime of Greece's café-sitters) sets for ages. At Ifestou 24, duck into the arcade of stores selling old Greek records. At the front of the arcade is **Nasiotis** (Ifestou 24, 210 321 2369), where bibliophiles can get lost in the stacks of rare and first editions, prints, old magazines and Greek movie posters.

a tourist-attraction parody of himself, more than happy to pose for pictures and push his books on guide-toting tourists. Be that as it may, this is probably still the best place in Athens to buy handmade leather Jesus sandals – there's a huge selection, which Melissinos (in keeping with his 'poet-as-man-of-the-people' image) custom-fits for each buyer.

Hondos Center

Omonia 4, Omonia (210 528 2800). Metro Omonia. **Open** 8.30am-8.30pm Mon, Wed; 8.30am-9pm Tue, Thur, Fri; 8.30am-5pm Sat. **Credit** AmEx, DC, MC, V. **Map** p295 E3.
This ubiquitous chain sells all the cosmetics you could need or want, from perfumes to shampoos and sun block. It also has a range of swimwear, underwear, bags and other accessories. This largest branch is a nine-floor emporium with clothing, books and a café with views across the capital. **Other locations**: Ermou 39, Historic Centre (210 322 068).

Make Up Spy

Anagnostopoulou 18, Kolonaki (210 360 9208). Metro Evangelismos or Syntagma. **Open** 9.30am-3.30pm Mon, Wed, Sat; 9.30am-8.30pm Tue, Thur, Fri. **Credit** AmEx, DC, MC, V. **Map** p297 G4.
Products from top-notch companies including Chantecaille, Laura Mercier, Nuxe, Urban Decay, haircare from Philippe B – this exclusive shop is the ultimate shopping ground for beauty buffs.

Sephora

Ermou 24, Historic Centre (210 331 3167/210 325 7744). Metro Syntagma. **Open** May-Sept 9am-6pm Mon, Wed; 9am-9pm Tue, Thur, Fri; 9am-5pm Sat. Oct-Apr 9am-6pm Mon, Wed; 9am-8.30pm Tue, Thur, Fri; 9am-5pm Sat. **Credit** AmEx, DC, MC, V. **Map** p295/p299 F5.

The Athens branch of the famous red-carpeted beauty supermarket is smaller than many of its international siblings, but it still manages to pack in a good many must-have brands. Check out Sephora's own line of affordable beauty accessories for simple beauty basics.

Hairdressers & barbers

Bitsikas Hairlines

Xanthippou 2, Kolonaki (210 721 3573). Metro Evangelismos. **Open** 12.30-6pm Tue, Thur, Fri; 12.30-4pm Wed, Sat. **No credit cards**. **Map** p297 H4.
Presided over by hair guru Stathis, this contemporary salon features a men's floor that resembles a futuristic airport lounge and a girlie pampering parlour for the ladies. Stathis is never domineering with his advice, and his opinion is always worth taking into consideration before you go under the knife.

Cut 'n' Go

Navarinou 6 & Ippokratous, Exarchia (210 363 1320). Metro Panepistimio. **Open** 10am-6pm Mon, Wed; 10am-8pm Tue, Thur, Fri; 10am-6pm Sat. **No credit cards**. **Map** p297 G3.
Good, simple hairdressing for men and women for less than €20 a cut. The Cut 'n' Go salon offers treatments with natural ingredients for damaged or stressed locks absolutely free of charge – which is definitely a bonus.

Ilias Zarbalis

Spefsippou 4 & Irodotou, Kolonaki (210 723 2939). Metro Evangelismos. **Open** 10am-5pm Mon; 8am-7pm Tue, Thur, Fri; 8am-5pm Wed, Sat. **Credit** MC, V. **Map** p297 H4.

Locks damaged by too much sun and sea can be chopped into a fashionable new look at this busy salon frequented by Athens' beautiful people. Check out the super-stylish new branch in Neo Psychiko, at Ethnikis Antistaseos 103 (210 675 4901), which more closely resembles an elegant furniture showroom than a hairdressing salon, and boasts luxurious massage armchairs at each of the styling stations.

Jacques Dessange

Spefsippou 13, Kolonaki (210 721 4395). Metro Evangelismos. **Open** 9am-6pm Mon, Wed; 9am-7pm Tue, Thur; 9am-8pm Fri; 8.30am-5pm Sat. **Credit** DC, MC, V. **Map** p297 H4.

Whether you want just a simple trim, your locks cut and styled into a funky new look, a tint to cover up those sneaky grey hairs or Dessange's world-renowned *balayage* do (freehand-painted Californian blonde highlights), this is the place to get it done properly.
Other locations: Lazaraki 10, Glyfada (210 898 1658-59).

Koureion ('Barber')

Apollonos 12, Plaka (no phone). Metro Syntagma or Monastiraki. **Open** 8am-3pm Mon, Wed, Sat; 8am-2pm, 5-8.30pm Tue, Thur, Fri. **No credit cards**. **Map** p295 E5/F5.

One of the few remaining truly traditional barber shops, complete with ancient shaving equipment, comfy leather chairs and a clientele that hasn't changed since the 1950s. You may not be able to get the trendiest haircut here, but visit for a glimpse of a fast-vanishing Athens.

Lia

Panepistimiou 18, in the arcade, Historic Centre (210 362 5260). Metro Syntagma. **Open** 9am-3pm Mon, Wed, Sat; 9am-6pm Tue, Thur, Fri. **No credit cards**. **Map** p295 F4.

This old-fashioned men's barber brings back images of '60s Athens, when men wore suits every day, sported well-polished brogues and took pride in keeping their hands handsome. Come here for a brisk, no-nonsense wash and cut, get your nails tidied up by the in-house manicurist at the same time, and you'll still have change from €30.

Opticians

Optika Stavrou

Akadimias 60, Exarchia (210 364 3012). Metro Syntagma. **Open** 8.30am-3.30pm Mon, Wed, Sat; 8.30am-8.30pm Tue, Thur, Fri. **Credit** AmEx, DC, MC, V. **Map** p295 F3.

If you've lost a lens or just want a trendy pair of shades, this optical shop has everything, from prescription lenses to the latest designer frames.

Spas

Indolent pleasure-hunters in search of a really luxurious spa experience should visit the newly opened spa at the **Hotel Grande Bretagne** (*see p59*).

Arome

Anagnostopoulou 36, Kolonaki (210 363 4014) Metro Evangelismos. **Open** 10am-7pm Mon-Fri; 10am-3pm Sat. **Credit** MC, V. **Map** p297 G4.

The polite and friendly staff at this small, select salon are expert at painless waxing, purifying peeling facials and pre-bikini slimming wraps, all using top-quality Anne Semonin aromatherapy products.

Cavalliert

1st Floor, Irodotou 18, Kolonaki (210 721 3546). Metro Evangelismos. **Open** 9am-1pm, 4-8pm Mon-Fri. **Credit** MC, V. **Map** p297 H5.

In their traditional Kolonaki apartment, Takis and Pambitsa Cavallieratos and their capable assistants cleanse, squeeze, knead, stroke and press away the troubles and imperfections that plague tired, unhealthy, badly nourished complexions. Pambitsa unblocks blackheads and purifies pores with her magic fingers that leave no redness or irritation, just clean, fresh skin; her husband Takis massages into thirsty, dehydrated cells creams handmade to the couple's own recipe from flowers and plants grown at their organic estate in southern Attica.

Cocoon Urban Spa

Souliou & Erifilis, Halandri, Northern Suburbs (210 656 1975). **Open** 10am-10pm Mon-Fri; 10am-6pm Sat. **Credit** AmEx, MC, V.

Face and body treatments from all corners of the globe to address common problems from stress to acne to cellulite. After your treatment, relax in the hammam and have a wallow in the jacuzzi, then join one of the innovative exercise classes, such as African dance with live drum music.

Home

I gata pou tin Iene Uccello

Al Soutsou 19, Kolonaki (210 364 2246). Metro Syntagma. **Open** *May-Sept* 9.30am-3pm Mon, Wed; 9.30am-2.30pm, 5.30-9pm Tue, Thur, Fri; 9.30am-4pm Sat. *Oct-Apr* 9.30am-3pm Mon, Wed, Sat; 9.30am-2.30pm, 5.30-8.30pm Tue, Thur, Fri. **Credit** AmEx, DC, MC, V. **Map** p297 G4.

Unconventional Italian and Greek-made furniture and household objects for tastefully quirky interiors.

Ionia

Patriarchou Ioakim 11, Kolonaki (210 722 4125). Metro Evangelismos. **Open** *May-Sept* 9am-3.30pm Mon, Wed, Sat; 9am-9pm Tue, Thur, Fri. *Oct-Apr* 9am-3.30pm Mon, Wed, Sat; 9am-8.30pm Tue, Thur, Fri. **Credit** AmEx, DC, MC, V. **Map** p297 H4.

This Greek institution offers a wide selection of reasonably priced, locally made china, crockery and cutlery. Whether you require a full dinner set for a wedding present or just a couple of cheap, comic mugs for the children, it's worth popping into Ionia.

Pallet Stores

Evangelistrias 17, Historic Centre (210 323 2344). Metro Syntagma or Monastiraki. **Open** 9am-6pm Mon, Wed; 9am-9pm Tue, Thur, Fri; 9am-5pm Sat. **Credit** AmEx, DC, MC, V. **Map** p295/p299 E5.

It's almost impossible to get in on a Saturday, and even midweek this cheap and cheerful shop is jam-packed with bargain hunters in search of odds and ends for the house. Candles, lamps, kitchen utensils, cups and saucers, even Christmas and Easter decorations – they're all here, if you can fight through the crowds to reach them.

Room Service

Irodotou 33, Kolonaki (210 723 0629). Metro Evangelismos. **Open** 9.30am-3pm Mon, Wed, Sat; 9.30am-2pm, 5.30-8.30pm Tue, Thur; 9.30am-9pm Fri. **Credit** AmEx, DC, MC, V. **Map** p297 A4.

A stylish range of sleek designs by sought-after contemporary European talents. The Kolonaki shop sells smaller objects – glasses, vases, lamps, accessories – while if you're after larger furnishings, such as a sofa or bed, the branch in southern Athens may better suit your needs.

Other locations: Fivis 16, Glyfada (210 894 6700).

Music

Metropolis

Panepistimiou 54, Historic Centre (210 380 8549). Metro Omonia. **Open** 9am-9pm Mon-Fri; 9am-6pm Sat. **Credit** AmEx, DC, MC, V. **Map** p295 F3.

Five floors of musical selections catering to most mainstream tastes. Prices average around €18 for an imported CD, but there are also plenty of sales racks with titles for €10 or less.

Music Emporioum

Ifestou 24, Monastiraki (210 331 0236). Metro Monastiraki. **Open** 9am-5pm Mon, Wed, Sat, Sun; 9am-8pm Tue, Thur, Fri. **No credit cards. Map** p295 E5.

It looks like a misprint, but this second-hand music shop really does add an extra 'O' into emporium. Come here for old LPs, EPs and singles of all types of music, costing from as little as €1 each.

Vinyl Microstore Didotou

34 Didotou, Exarchia (210 361 4544/www. popart.gr). Metro Panepistimio. **Open** 10am-5pm Mon-Fri; 10am-2pm Sat; occasional evenings. **Tickets** free. **No credit cards. Map** p297 G3.

This tiny independent record store is run by the owners of Pop Art Records, an independent label that stubbornly makes and sells beautifully packaged recordings of Greek bands. There are occasional performances: check in store for details – and at the same time, pick up the Greek indie-pop compilation *Try a Little Sunshine*, the ultimate non-mainstream Athens souvenir.

Souvenirs

Benaki Museum Shop

Koumbari 1 & Leof Vas Sofias, Kolonaki (210 367 1045). Metro Evangelismos or Syntagma. **Open** 9am-5pm Mon, Wed, Fri, Sat; 9am-midnight Thur; 9am-3pm Sun. **Credit** AmEx, DC, MC, V. **Map** p297 G5.

The perfect place to find a tasteful souvenir or gift, this shop sells replicas of ancient Greek artefacts, icons, jewellery and toys displayed in the museum, books on Hellenic and Byzantine history, modern Greek photography and art, plus postcards, silk scarves and local pottery.

Centre of Hellenic Tradition

Mitropoleos 59, Plaka (210 321 3023). Metro Monastiraki. **Open** *May-Sept* 9am-8pm daily. *Oct-Apr* 9am-6pm daily. **Credit** AmEx, DC, MC, V. **Map** p295 E5.

Although the entrance to this shop, tucked away in a small arcade, may seem somewhat unprepossessing, persevere and you will be rewarded with an extensive gallery filled with traditional pottery, ceramics, tapestry, embroidery, carvings, paintings and other handicrafts garnered from every corner of Greece.

Kori

Mitropoleos 13 & Voulis, Plaka (210 323 3534). Metro Syntagma. **Open** 9am-9pm Mon-Sat. **Credit** AmEx, DC, MC, V. **Map** p295/p299 E5.

A treasure trove for the discerning souvenir hunter, this small but well-stocked shop offers not only replicas and reproductions but also eye-catching, contemporary ornaments and jewellery made by talented young Greek artists.

Mastiha Shop

Panepistimiou 6 & Krizotou, Historic Centre (210 363 2750). Metro Syntagma. **Open** 9am-9pm Mon-Fri; 9am-5pm Sat. **Credit** MC, V. **Map** p295/p299 F5.

Just about everything you can imagine made with the famous mastic gum from southern Chios, which is said to be a panacea for all ills, from stomach ulcers to cancer. Whether you wish for mastic chewing gum, sweets, essential oils, candles, beauty products or just a book about Chios island, this is the place to find it. Don't miss the line of natural cosmetics made by Korres (*see p175*) especially for the Mastiha Shop.

R Touch

Athinas 17, Historic Centre (210 321 0285). Metro Monastiraki. **Open** 10am-5pm Mon-Sat. **No credit cards. Map** p295 E4.

Come to this store for elegant souvenirs, lucky charms, table accessories for the home, big rosaries and many other decorative objects made by Rodi Constandoglou, whose family has been in the trade since 1854. Her creations can also be found at the gift shops of the Benaki Museum (*see above*) and at the Folkloric Museum (*see p250*) in Nafplio.

Eat, Drink, Shop

Stavros Melissinos

Pandrosou 89, Plaka (210 321 9247).
Metro Monastiraki. **Open** 10am-6pm Mon-Sat;
10am-2.30pm Sun. **No credit cards.**
Map p295/p299 E5.

Plaka and Monastiraki are full of leather shops.
But generations of knowledgeable visitors from
all over the world instead duck into this rather less
flamboyant shop to stock up on Stavros Melissinos's
long-lasting, handmade leather sandals. The
smiling, Mad Professor figure began making shoes
in 1954, has expanded the original few styles to
around 32 classically inspired designs, and has
reputedly sold to John Lennon, Sophia Loren and
Jackie Kennedy Onassis.

Vavas

Ifestou 30, Monastiraki (210 321 9994).
Metro Monastiraki. **Open** 8.30am-8.30pm
Mon-Fri; 10am-2pm Sat, Sun. **No credit cards.**
Map pp295 E5.

So small you can barely step inside, this tiny
alcove can hardly be described as a shop, but it
still manages to stock a fine selection of traditional
wooden *tavli* (backgammon) boards. Prices start
from around €10. Look out for the unusual, hand-
painted sets.

Travellers' needs

Computer purchase & repairs

Apple Store

Akadimias 32, Historic Centre (210 364 1211).
Metro Panepistimio or Syntagma. **Open** 9.30am-
3.30pm Mon, Wed, Sat; 9.30am-8.30pm Tue,
Thur, Fri. **Credit** MC, V. **Map** p297 G4.

You can buy Macs and all the necessary (or not)
accessories here. If you have a problem with your
Apple computer, call the service line on 210 902 9212.

Germanos

Kanari 26, Kolonaki (210 361 5798). Metro
Evangelismos or Syntagma. **Open** 9am-4pm
Mon, Wed; 9am-8pm Tue, Thur, Fri; 9am-3pm Sat.
Credit AmEx, DC, MC, V. **Map** p297 G5.

The Germanos chain mainly sells and connects
mobile phones, but it also has a range of internet
services and can arrange PC repairs.
Other locations: throughout the city.

Laundry

Do It Yourself Laundry

Geronta 2, Platia Filomouso, Plaka. Metro Akropoli.
Open 8am-4pm Mon-Sat; 8am-1pm Sun. **No credit**
cards. **Map** p299 F6.

You don't really have to do it yourself. Just bring
along a sack of your dirty washing, leave it
with the ladies here and two hours later you will
be presented with neatly laundered and dried
garments. One machine load costs €8.

Katsaounis

Pindarou 27, Kolonaki (210 362 0960).
Metro Evangelismos. **Open** 7am-5pm Mon-Fri.
Closed Aug. **No credit cards. Map** p297 G4.

Dry-cleaning of all fabrics, including more delicate
ones such as suede.

Luggage

In the area around Monastiraki metro station
you can find plenty of shops selling all kinds
of suitcases, rucksacks and holdalls, often at
ridiculously low prices. For something more
upmarket, visit **Stefanidis** (Lekka 7, Historic
Centre, 210 322 3806), which sells hard cases
by Delsey and Samsonite, as well as bags
by Kipling, Diplomat, Roncato and Polo. The
larger branches of **Hondos Center** (*see p164*)
also sell a reasonable selection of luggage from
international brands.

Photographic

Aris Giagtzoglou & Sons

Lada Christou 5-7, Historic Centre (210 324
1780/323 3886). Metro Panepistimio. **Open**
8am-4pm Mon-Fri. **No credit cards. Map** p295 F4.

This small photo shop does quick, good-quality film
development, reprints, copies and enlargements, and
sells a range of camera accessories and albums.

N Pikopoulos Camera Service

Lekka 26, Historic Centre (210 322 5650/210 323
5409). Metro Syntagma. **Open** 9.30am-5.30pm
Mon-Fri. **No credit cards. Map** p295/p299 F5.

Repairs and service for all types of camera are
carried out here. Don't be put off by the unpromis-
ing entrance – take the lift to the third floor and you
will be greeted by walls of photographic equipment
and helpful staff.

Travel agents

Travel Plan

Lada Christou 3, Historic Centre (210 323 8801).
Metro Panepistimio. **Open** 8.30am-5pm Mon-Fri;
8.30am-2pm Sat. **Credit** AmEx, DC, MC, V.
Map p295 F4.

Probably Athens' largest travel agency, Travel
Plan can organise your flight home, book your
accommodation while in Greece, sort out your
transport to the islands, or arrange an idyllic cruise
around the Aegean.

> ▶ **Market forces** For a guide to Athens'
> unmissable Central Market, *see p97;*
> for a tour of the atmospheric Monastiraki
> flea market *see p178* **Sunday morning**
> **in Monastiraki;** and for Piraeus's flea
> market *see p115.*

Arts & Entertainment

Festivals & Events

Whether your bag is Greek tragedies, sporting events or political marches, Athens has got it in spades. And let's not forget those religious festivities...

Home to almost half of Greece's population, Athens is, not surprisingly, the focal point of most events and activities of significance. This is the case all year round, but never more so than in the summer months. While in the past many Athenians would escape the maddening summer heat, the capital's varied menu of cultural events is now forcing more people to postpone their holidays to breathe in something more than just pollution.

Notorious for setting up naff busts of ancient Greek heroes with his name scribbled all over them, former mayor Dimitrios Avramopoulos can at least be credited for tapping into the city's outdoor potential. The New Year celebrations at Syntagma, though nothing to write home about, are putting people back on the streets. Local municipalities organise summer festivals and newly pedestrianised avenues and long-neglected inner-city areas now serve as the stage for innovative modern-art exhibitions, book fairs and music festivals, and the city's splendid outdoor ampitheatres stage concerts, plays and festivals. Running an election campaign on an environmental and cultural platform, Avramopoulos's successor, conservative-backed Dora Bakoyianni, is widely expected to press on with the effort to 'humanise' the city.

Although it got off to a rocky start and was a victim of budget cuts, the Cultural Olympiad 2001-2004 – a programme developed by the Greek culture ministry to promote global cultural exchange through artistic events – has hosted many outstanding international performances under its banner.

For more information on events taking place in Athens during your stay, consult *Kathimerini* (a supplement of the *International Herald Tribune*), *Time Out Athens* or visit www.athensnews.gr (updated weekly).

Spring

Agia Evdomada (Easter Week)

Various churches around Athens, including Mitropolis. Metro Monastiraki. **Map** p295/p299 E5/F5. **Date** Mar/Apr.

Equivalent in importance to Christmas in Britain, Pascha (Easter) in Athens is a rewarding and colourful experience drawing deep on Greece's rich Orthodox heritage. With roots stretching back to ancient rites of spring, Greek Orthodox Holy Week is a splendid display of Byzantine ceremonial traditions. On the evening of Good Friday, every church decorates an *epitaphios* (bier) representing Christ's funeral, which is then lugged along in a hymn-chanting procession through the city streets. The most important procession begins at the Mitropolis cathedral and winds through the streets of central Athens. It's a great opportunity to get lost in Plaka, wandering from church to church taking in a hallowed atmosphere of incense, hymns and bell chimes. At midnight on Holy Saturday, candles are lit and firecrackers let off to celebrate the *anastasi* (resurrection) of Christ. People greet each other with the message 'Christos anesti' (Christ is risen). To celebrate the end of Lent, on Easter Sunday (Kiriaki tou Pascha) lambs are roasted on a spit.

Labour Day

Date 1 May.

Labour Day is usually celebrated with a mass exodus to the countryside for picnics. For those who stay in town there are marches organised by left-wing groups and workers' unions.

Summer

The Athens Festival

Information 210 322 1459/www.hellenicfestival.gr. Lycabettus Theatre, Lycabettus Hill, Kolonaki. Metro Evangelismos or Megaro Mousikis. **Map** p297 J3. *Odeon of Herodes Atticus, Acropolis. Metro Akropoli.* **Map** p299 D6. **Date** May/June-Sept/Oct.

The Athens Festival is the urban incarnation of the Hellenic Festival. Since its inception in 1945, it has been a major highlight of the Greek capital's summer cultural activities (especially since indoor venues tend to suspend activities). Music concerts ranging from jazz to classical along with drama and dance productions take place at the Odeon of Herodes Atticus and at the Lycabettus Theatre. One couldn't ask for better settings – the latter boasts the best views of the city from the top of the hill, while the former offers the classical splendour of the Parthenon as a backdrop for the performances. At the Herodeion heels are frowned upon (for fear of damage to the marble), even though Athenian socialites tend to ignore the rules. Stilettos are not an issue at the Lycabettus, and a small bus shuttling to the theatre from the foot of the hill means that you can give your Manolos a good outing without fearing that the heels might get lodged in a rocky crevice. Massive Attack, Moby, Madredeus and Alvin Ailey are some of the names to play at the Lycabettus in recent years, while the Herodeion has been graced by Maria Callas and just about every contemporary great from Monserrat Caballé to Luciano Pavarotti. For big-name events, book well in advance – tickets tend to sell out pretty quickly.

Acropolis Rally
Various locations throughout the city. Information www.acropolisrally.gr. **Date** mid June.
Launched 50 years ago, the rally has developed a huge following. The route starts at the foot of the Acropolis and takes drivers through rugged terrain on the Greek mainland for three days before leading them to the finish line at the Panathenaic Stadium. Join the rest of Athens by standing at the side of the road and watching the drivers whizz past.

Glyfada Festival
Exoni Theatre, Hydras 11, Glyfada (210 891 2200). Bus A1. **Date** June-July.
Situated in the eerie surroundings of an abandoned quarry, this festival has been hosting contemporary

Greek singers such as Nikos Papazoglou, Orpheas Peridis and Dionyssis Savvopoulos since 1992.

Rematia Festival
Rematia Theatre, Halandri, Northern Suburbs (210 680 0001). Metro Halandri. **Date** June-July.
The search for Greece's musical roots has really taken off in recent years and thousands gather at this open-air theatre to watch live shows with a focus on traditional Greek and ethnic music from the Balkans and Asia.

Vyronas Festival
Melina Mercouri Vrahon Theatre, Vyronas (210 765 5748). Bus 214/tram 11. **Date** 6wks June-Sept.
The municipality of Vyronas has done a pretty good job of attracting well-known Greek and foreign acts to an otherwise drab area. Fifteen years on, the festival (dubbed the People's Festival) offers jazz, rock, ethnic and contemporary Greek music at good prices under the shadow of a huge rocky outcrop. Although locked in a legal battle with the government over the illegal construction of the theatre, the Vyronas authorities are winning public support.

The **Odeon of Herodes Atticus**, venue for the Athens Festival.

Staging the classics

Between July and September, cultured and not-so-cultured Athenians usually get away on hot weekends to Epidaurus (*see p249*), an ancient site a couple of hours' drive (or ferry journey) from the city, for two major events in the Hellenic Festival.

In the Ancient Theatre, a respected programme of classical Greek drama is held throughout July and August. Even if you don't understand the language well enough to follow what's going on on stage, armed with a little knowledge (*see p229* **Understanding the ancients**) you should still be able to appreciate it, along with the fact that you're having exactly the same night out as the local Ancient Greeks, thousands of years ago. Renowned for its acoustics and beauty, the theatre, which dates back to the fourth century BC, has a capacity of 14,000.

Coach and ferry trips there and back are arranged by Hellenic Festival organisers, and at weekends extra buses are added to the usual schedule. You can also get a package including show tickets and a dinner cruise across the Saronic Gulf (approx 45; more information on 210 429 1501).

Set amid fragrant citrus groves, the nearby Little Theatre of Ancient Epidaurus, of the same vintage, offers a more intimate atmosphere than its big brother. The 2,000-seat venue has hosted the Musical July festival since 2002, providing an impressive stage for music concerts, from classical to Greek.

For more information on the area, which is worth a longer visit, *see p249*.

Hellenic Festival Box Office

Panepistimiou 39 (210 322 1459/www.greek festival.gr/). **Open** *Summer* 8.30am-4pm Mon-Fri; 9am-2.30pm Sat. **Credit** MC, V. **Map** p295/p299 F5.
Tickets for the both the Epidaurus Festival and Musical July are available here, at the Herodeion box office and at the two Epidaurus venues' box offices, which open two hours before the performance. Credit card bookings are accepted on the above number until 4pm on the day of the performance.

Rockwave Festival

Various venues around Athens. Information (210 882 0426/www.didimusic.gr). **Date** 3 days early July.
Since 1996, Rockwave has been taking its ear-splitting show to venues in and around Athens, to the delight of hairy head-bangers and pale Goth-rockers. The festival also includes juggling events and parties. It took a miss in 2003, but its organisers, Di Di Music, are preparing a harder comeback for 2004.

Anti-Racism Festival

Ilisia Park, Zografou, Western Athens (210 381 3928). Bus 222, 221 or 235. **Date** early July.
This three-day event is organised by the Network for Social Support for Refugees and Immigrants. Since its debut in 1996, the festival hasn't looked back, involving some 40 migrant communities and more than 100 human-rights and anti-racism groups. The event includes live music and dance by ethnic groups (recent festivals have showcased Syrian, Kurdish and Thai acts), exotic refreshment stalls and a chance to mingle with people from Athens' various foreign communities.

International Aegean Sailing Rally

Along the Saronic coast. Hellenic Offshore Racing Club, 4 Papadiamanti, Mikrolimano, Piraeus (210 412 3357/210 411 3201/www.aegeanrally.gr/ www.horc.gr). **Date** early July.
Sailing fans have been heading down to the coast for one of Greece's biggest sailing events since 1964.

Organised by the Hellenic Offshore Racing Club, the regatta gathers contestants from all over the world. Watch from any of the seaside suburbs.

WOMAD

Venue to be confirmed. Information: Cultural Olympiad (www.cultural-olympiad.gr). **Date** early July.
The ethnically diverse WOMAD festival first graced Athens' events calendar in 2001. It was cancelled in 2003, but the organisers promise that it will be back with a bang in the year of the Olympics.

Full Moon Day

Acropolis & Roman Forum, Acropolis & Plaka. Metro Akropoli or Monastiraki. **Map** p299 E6/E5. **Date** 9pm-1am, 2nd wk in Aug.
Since it began five years ago, Full Moon Day has been a major success, drawing thousands to experience the city's archaeological sites under the moonlight. Live outdoor cultural events are also held.

Athens International Film Festival

Various venues around Athens (210 606 1363/ www.aiff.gr). **Date** 10 days, 2nd wk in Sept.
Not to be confused with the better-known Thessaloniki Film Festival, the AIFF is becoming an important event in its own right. Local buffs get to feast on more than 100 features and short films from over two dozen countries.

Arts & Entertainment

International Month of Photography

Hellenic Centre of Photography, Chatzichristou 3, Makrygianni (210 921 0545/www.hcp.gr). Metro Akropoli. **Map** p299 E7. **Date** Mid Sept-mid Oct.
Always expanding its subject matter, this month-long event brings together different photographers, from young Greek artists to established international names, like the Mexican Juan Rulfo, whose work was highlighted in 2003.

Athens Book Fair

Dionysiou Areopagitou, Acropolis (210 330 3942). Metro Akropoli. **Map** p299 E6. **Date** Late Sept.
Now in its third decade, this highly popular 16-day book fair hosts books from a wide range of Greek publishers. Dozens of stands and over 300 publishers set up, while buskers and food stalls complete the picture. In 2004, the fair will take place under the Acropolis, as its regular venue, Pedion Areos park, is receiving a makeover.

Trash Art – Marathon of Creation & Recycling

Technopolis Gallery, Pireos 100, Rouf (210 346 0981/www.athens-technopolis.gr). Metro Thisio, then 10mins walk. **Map** p294 C4. **Date** Oct.
Founded in 1998, Trash Art (which is exactly what it sounds like) is as popular as ever. Fashion events inspired by recycling are also held in parallel. Some of the city's best DJs set the tone for the funky parties that follow.

Ochi Day

Date 28 Oct.
This national holiday commemorates Greece's resounding rejection '*ohi*' ('no') of an ultimatum from Italy's Benito Mussolini demanding that his troops be allowed to pass through Greece during World War II. School parades take place in the heart of the city (Leof Amalias, in front of the Greek Parliament).

Winter

Athens Marathon

(210 755 2888/www.athensmarathon.com). **Date** Sun early Nov.
Runners from Greece and abroad follow the original 42-kilometre (26-mile) route of Phidippides, the man who ran to Athens from Marathon in 490 BC to report that the invading Persian army had been defeated before dropping dead from exhaustion. The race begins at the modern village of Marathon and ends at the Panathenaic Stadium (site of the first modern Olympic Games in 1896).

17 November

Begins at the Athens 'Metsovio' Polytechnic (Triti Septemvriou) and ends at the US Embassy, Leof Vas Sofias. Metro Omonia. **Date** 17 Nov.
Although to outsiders 17 November is inextricably linked to the urban guerrilla group of that name, it's also the day that marks an important event in Greece's recent troubled history. Every year without fail, a march takes place to commemorate the night of 17 November 1973, when the military dictatorship brutally ended a student protest in the Athens Polytechnic, killing 34 demonstrators. The uprising's tragic end was a factor in the downfall of the Junta the following year. Organised by left-wing groups and workers' unions, the march has broad appeal and cuts through generations. The US embassy is pelted with eggs and other objects and graffiti are sprayed on neighbouring buildings – in protest at Washington's widely acknowledged support for the army generals. Depending on the political climate of the time, there is sometimes a stop at the British embassy. Although more sedate in recent years, in the past the march would routinely deteriorate into street clashes between gate-crashing self-styled anarchists and riot police.

Christmas & New Year

Date 24, 31 Dec & 5 Jan.
Not as important as in western Europe, but still a major event on the Greek calendar. Children sing carols door to door while charity group do their rounds. After midnight on New Year's Eve, a cake (*vassilopitta*) containing a coin is sliced. The person who gets the coins is blessed with good fortune for the year to come.

Epiphany

Along the Piraeus coast. **Date** 6 Jan.
The traditional Blessing of the Water is steeped in Orthodox tradition, with roots stretching perhaps as far back as pagan antiquity. The faithful congregate by the sea to watch the spectacle of young males dive into chilly waters to retrieve a cross hurled by the priest. The diver who gets the cross is blessed with good fortune.

Apokries (Carnival season)

Various locations. **Date** Last wk in Feb/beginning of Lent.
Municipal orchestras and choirs, jugglers, mime artists, singers and float parades take to the streets to whip up euphoria. Dress-up parties and lots of booze are the norm. A pervasive anything-goes atmosphere grips the city, particularly in Plaka, where groups of young males roam around bashing just about anybody with plastic clubs. Celebrations climax with the traditional party (*koulouma*) on Kathari Deftera (Ash Monday), with kite-flying spectacles and picnics at Filopappou Hill. Ash Monday also marks the beginning of Megali Sarakosti (40-day Lent fast) leading to Easter.

Independence Day Parade

Leof Vas Amalias, in front of Parliament. **Map** p297 G5. **Date** 25 Mar.
Military fighter jets whizz by as Athenians turn out in droves to watch the military and school parades celebrate the proclamation of the Greek revolution in 1821 against the Ottoman Empire. The feast of the annunciation is also celebrated.

Arts & Entertainment

Children

Cover your kids in sunscreen and let them play.

Okay, so it's true. Athens isn't exactly the most enthralling city for children and there is a dearth of organised facilities for young visitors. But this paradoxical society adores children. Even in the heart of Athens, away from the major arteries, local youngsters still play in the street without having to fear strangers or even cars, and, with the exception of bars, there are no public places where children aren't welcome. Your kids may even make some Greek friends without having to battle against the language barrier – locals learn English at a young age.

Animal encounters

Attica Zoological Park
Yalou, Spata, Attica (210 663 4724). Bus 319; when the bus terminates change to bus 304, 305; bus stop Zoological Park. **Open** *May-Sept* 9am-8.30pm daily. *Oct-Apr* 9am-5pm daily. **Admission** €10; €8 under-12s. **Credit** MC, V.
This is the only zoological park in Athens that treats the animals with any respect. Visitors can see lions, apes and many different kinds of birds.

Cinema

A trip to the cinema can make a good family break from slogging around the sights. There are the usual multiplexes dotting the city and its suburbs, but kids are more likely to appreciate a trip to an outdoor cinema, though screenings are evening-only. Most films are shown in their original language, but cartoons and other films aimed at a youngsters are commonly dubbed. Listings in the press should indicate this.
For cinema listings *see p192* **Film**.

Eating & drinking

Children are allowed in all restaurants, and genuinely welcomed in most. For fast-food junkies there are plenty of Pizza Hut and McDonald's outlets as well as Greece's own home-grown hamburger (and more) joint, Goody's. Dinner tends to be a late-evening meal.

Palai Pote
Grigoris Lambraki 75, Glyfada (210 963 2739). Bus A3 or B3 to bus terminal. **Open** *June-Sept* 1pm-2am daily. *Oct-May* 8.30pm-2am Tue-Sat; 1-7pm Sun. **Credit** V.
This classic Greek restaurant comes highly recommended for its indoor play area.

San Marzano
Leof Konstantinoupoleos 13, Glyfada (210 968 1124). Bus A3 or B3 to bus terminal. **Open** 1pm-1am daily. **Credit** AmEx, MC, V.
On Sundays (1.30-4.30pm) this Italian restaurant entertains kids with clowns, face-painters and magicians.

Museums

At the **Foundation for the Hellenic World** kids can follow in the footsteps of Thalis, the father of philosophy, with a virtual-reality tour around Ancient Militos, while a trip to the **Museum of Greek Children's Art** (*see p87*), with its focus on works by youngsters, might be inspiring for budding artists.
The **Greek Children's Museum** in Plaka has educational programmes about 'adult' professions that prepare kids for the future with tours of various workplaces like a bank and a factory. Greeks are proud of their traditional shadow-puppet theatre (*karaghiozis*), so a visit to the **Spathario Museum of Shadow Puppets** (*see below*) is also a good idea.
Future pilots can get the feel of being in the cockpit of a World War I plane at the **National War Museum** (*see p100*), while the displays at the **Museum of Greek Musical Instruments** (*see p87*) offer interactive fun for musical types.

Foundation for the Hellenic World
Pireos 254, Tavros (210 342 2292). Metro Kalithea. **Open** *Mid Sept-mid June* 9am-4pm Mon, Tue, Thur, Fri; 9am-8pm Wed; 11am-3pm Sun. *Mid Sept-mid June* 9am-2pm Mon, Tue, Thur; 9am-9pm Wed, Fri; 10am-3pm Sun. **Admission** €7.25; €4.75 under-12s. **No credit cards.**

Greek Children's Museum
Kydathinaion 14, Plaka (210 331 2995). Metro Akropoli. **Open** 10am-2pm Tue-Fri; 10am-3pm Sat, Sun. Closed July, Aug. **Admission** free. Programmes €5. **Map** p299 F6.

Spathario Museum of Shadow Puppets
Leof Vas Sofias & Ralli D, Platia Kastalias, Marousi (210 612 7245). Metro Marousi. **Open** 10am-1.30pm Mon-Fri. **Admission** free.

Parks

Neither the layout nor the climate of Athens lend themselves to parks in the traditional sense of the word (lawns and flowerbeds). However,

Arts & Entertainment

the **National Gardens** (*see p100*), near Syntagma, with their duckpond, mini-zoo, playground and narrow winding paths shaded by towering trees, make for a pleasant stroll with younger children.

Another park worth a mention is the **Municipal Park of Glyfada**, a couple of blocks inland from the marina, where kids can work on their rollerblading, cycling and skateboarding skills.

Municipal Park of Glyfada

Bus A3 or B3. **Open** 9am-9pm daily.

Playgrounds

Indoors

Indoor play-areas aim to cater for English-speaking kids, so your little ones will have no problem in communicating with the entertainers in the venues below. You can let your children run free all you like – they'll be safe and well looked after.

Balloons

Georgiou Papandreou 49, Zografou, Eastern Suburbs (210 777 7861). Bus 222 or 235 to IKA bus stop. **Open** 10am-1pm, 5.30-9.30pm Mon, Wed, Fri; 5.30-9.30pm Tue, Thur; 10am-2pm, 5-10pm Sat; 10am-10pm Sun. **Admission** €5.50 (unlimited juice included). **No credit cards**.
A well-organised playground with loads of games and toys for children up to the age of seven. **Other locations:** Leof Kifisias 243, Kifisia (210 808 1883).

Paramithi

Ifigenias 39, Nea Ionia, Northern Suburbs (210 271 1811). Bus A8. **Open** 10am-2pm, 5-10pm Mon-Fri; 10am-10pm Sat, Sun. **Admission** €7. **No credit cards**
Inside a fake medieval castle kids are given the opportunity to play, watch shows and have some serious fun. For children up to 12.

Outdoors

Almost every neighbourhood in Athens has its own small public playground. Those worth mentioning are in the National Gardens and Municipal Park of Glyfada (*see above*).

Sightseeing

Start your day early with a quick visit to the Parliament Building in Syntagma, where you can watch the slow-motion goose-stepping *evzones*, the personal guards of the Greek president (*see p99* **Ministry of silly walks**). Then head down to Plaka and enjoy a tour of the

capital's oldest neighbourhood on the open 'train' that departs from the corner of Eolou and Adrianou (duration 35mins, €5, €3 under-12s).

Older kids will get more out of a visit to the Acropolis (*see p77*) if you employ the services of a guide (book on 210 322 0090), and though Athens' most famous landmark may not inspire the same awe in young children that it does in adults, its slopes are fun to explore.

When temperatures soar up past 35°C (95°F), it's best to avoid the city centre. Take the metro and head north to Kifisia (*see p112*), where kids are big on the 'grand tour' by horse-drawn carriage (Platia Kefalari, €15/15mins). The neighbourhood also has many green spaces – ideal for picnics, but don't forget the sunblock.

Swimming

Most Greek children swim before they walk, and a visit to a beach is not only fun in its own right but a good way to integrate. For suggestions *see p117* **Beaches**. The water is clean and free of dangerous currents or drop-offs, but note that lifeguards can be unpredictably absent.

To visit a public pool you need a certificate from a paediatrician. It's not really worth the hassle, so use hotel pools (*see p228*) and beaches.

Theme parks

Agios Cosmas Go-Kart Centre

Leof Posidonos, Agios Kosmos, Southern Suburbs (210 985 1660). Bus A2 to 2nd Agios Cosmas bus stop. **Open** 9am-3am daily. **Admission** €10/10mins. **No credit cards**.
This place is situated next to the Agios Cosmas beach, opposite the Hellenikon Olympic Complex, which makes it convenient for a cool dip in the sea after a crazy Go-Kart race. For ages 10 and over.

Allou! Fun Park

Kifisou & Petrou Ralli, Rendi, Southern Suburbs (210 425 6999). Tram 21 to Kan Kan stop. **Open** 5pm-1am Mon-Fri; 10am-2am Sat, Sun. **Admission** free. Each ride €3-€5. **No credit cards**.
This is the closest you'll get to Disneyland in Greece. Attractions like the Carousel, Super Kangoo and Bongo are recommended for younger children. Adults will enjoy La Isla, where they can try their hand at rafting, and the adrenalin-inducing Shock Tower. There are lots of refreshments on site.

Oropos Water Park

Chalkoutsiou, Skala Oropou, Attica (22950 37570/1). Bus to Oropos from Mavromataion, bus stop Skala. **Open** *31 May-6 Sept* 11am-7pm Mon-Fri; 10.30am-7.30pm Sat, Sun. **Admission** €9; €7 5-11s; free to under-4s. **No credit cards**.
This well-organised, safe and highly recommended water park provides a kiddies' pool, waterslides, a restaurant and snack bar.

Arts & Entertainment

Film

Original English-language versions, low ticket prices and balmy outdoor screens make Athens a *Cinema Paradiso* for film fans.

Athens provides great hunting grounds for cinemaniacs, with a wide range of repertory screenings, small art-house theatres and massive multiplexes. The capital also hosts small, independent festivals, such as the Athens International Film Festival (*see p188*) and the Panorama Film Festival, which showcases European films with limited distribution deals.

But what makes Athens really special are the open-air summer cinemas, operating from May to September. While most cities write the summer off as a dead season for cinema, in Athens high on the list of summer-night entertainment options is lounging with a cold drink, a snack, even a cigarette, to recap on one of last year's films, watch a Hitchcock classic or attend a late-night cult screening of Lynch or the Coens. In backyards, gardens and on rooftops, these cinemas are uniquely atmospheric. There's often a small bar or traditional kiosk; decoration is floral; and the dark star-covered sky is your ceiling. The only indications of the real world out there are the sometimes very visible signs of the cinema's sponsor – on the chairs you sit on and often on a huge banner above the screen. But if that's the price we have to pay for the survival of these amazing cinemas, it's a small sacrifice.

Along with the outdoor screens, Athens offers a good range of cinemas, from art houses and small neighbourhood theatres to the usual sterile multiplexes. The latter apart, most indoor venues close in summer. In terms of repertoire, here as everywhere else, Hollywood product tends to dominate, but it is also possible to find European and independent films. Films are shown in their original language and subtitled in Greek.

GREEK CINEMA

Although Greece is not exactly known as the cradle of major film festivals or great celluloid production, things have been moving in the right direction in recent years – the biggest film festival in the Balkans, the Thessaloniki International Film Festival, has been going from strength to strength, and the domestic film industry has just started to recover after a long period in the doldrums.

The Greek film industry lived its golden age in the 1950s and '60s. During this time domestic film production won international renown through the likes of Michael Cacoyannis, the director of *Alexis Zorba* (*Zorba the Greek*, 1964), actresses Melina Mercouri and Irene Papas, and composers Manos Hadjidakis, who scored *Pote tin Kyriaki*, aka *Never on Sunday* (1960), and Mikis Theodorakis (*Zorba the Greek*). The number of films produced annually was over 60, compared to around 20 nowadays.

This fertile creative ground gave rise to the internationally acclaimed New Greek Cinema, an auteur school similar to the French New Wave that blossomed in the early 1970s. Directors had to work under the censoring eye of the Junta, but some profoundly personal and poetic films were made during this time, like Theo Angelopoulos's *Anaparastassi* (*Reconstruction*, 1970) and Alexis Damianos's *Evdokia* (1971).

After the Junta, the film industry made a brief artistic recovery, but the introduction of the video in the 1980s almost wiped it out. The '90s saw an increase in Greek output, with box-office hits like Olga Malea's debut film *O orgasmos tis ageladas* (*The Cow's Orgasm*, 1996) and Sotiris Goritsas' *Valkanisateur* (*Balkanisateur*, 1997). In 2000, *Safe Sex* topped the country's ticket sales chart, the first Greek film to do so in 30 years.

On the international stage, Greek cinema is synonymous with auteur Theo Angelopoulos, one of the great European filmmakers. The 1998 winner of Cannes' Palme d'Or with *Mia aioniotita kai mia mera* (*Eternity and a Day*), Angelopoulos is now celebrating 40 years in the industry. His slow, contemplative and intellectual works present rather a different picture to most other Greek films.

TICKETS AND INFORMATION

Adult ticket prices tend to hover around €6-€8. English-language listings can be found in *Athens News* and *Kathimerini*. Screening hours at outdoor cinemas are normally around 9pm and 11pm. During the lighter summer months, it is wise to catch the late screening (11pm), since Mother Nature doesn't switch the lights off until about half an hour into the earlier show. Don't forget that they have intermissions here, so don't leave if you find the ending a bit abrupt – it's just half time. And, this being Greece, you can smoke in the open-air cinemas.

You can't beat **Cine Paris** for sheer atmosphere.

Some Athenian cinemas carry the name of their sponsors. Since these may change, we have used the original name of the venue; be ready for variations in local listings.

Summer cinemas

The **Trianon** (see p195) and **Alfaville** (see p194) indoor cinemas convert to open-air venues in summer.

Aigli – Village Cool

Zappeion (in the National Gardens), Historic Centre (210 336 9369/6970). Metro Syntagma. **Tickets** €7. **No credit cards. Map** p297 G6.
This classic outdoor cinema, built in the early 20th century, is located in the National Gardens, in the centre of Athens. Run by the Village chain, it shows mainly American blockbusters.

Athinaia

Haritos 50, Kolonaki (210 721 5717). Metro Evangelismos. **Tickets** €7; €5 concessions. **No credit cards. Map** p 297 H4.
Tell anyone you went to the Athinaia last night, and the first question will be: 'How was the cheese pie?' And then maybe they'll ask what film you saw. Apart from the legendary home-made *tiropitas*, this is a good modern summer cinema with a half-decent sound system. However, that's an irrelevance on Friday and Saturday nights, when the loud buzz from the bars on Haritos, literally outside the cinema, will make it impossible to hear a single line of dialogue.

Cine Paris

Kydathinaion 22, Plaka (210 324 8057/210 322 2071). Metro Monastiraki. **Tickets** €7; €6.50 concessions. **No credit cards. Map** p 295 F6.
One of the largest open-air cinemas in the city and the only one in Plaka, Cine Paris is perched on a rooftop, right in the thick of things. If you sit up high

you can alternate your gaze between a 20th- or 21st-century blockbuster and that really famous fifth-century busted block of rocks, the Acropolis.

Ciné Psirri

Sarri 40, Psyrri (210 324 7234/210 321 2476). Metro Thisio. **Tickets** €7; €5 concessions. **No credit cards. Map** p295 D4.
Situated in the heart of urban Psyrri, this cinema has a good bar in the back of the yard, its own restaurant and a repertoire of modern (and not-so-modern) classics (think Coen Brothers, Bergman and Hitchcock) mixed with reruns of last year's blockbusters. Recently, even the decor has turned Hitchcockian, with the cinema's whisky-making sponsor managing to place its little grouse on just about every free space in the cinema…

Dexameni

Platia Dexamenis, Kolonaki (210 362 3942/210 360 2363). Metro Evangelismos. **Tickets** €7; €5 concessions. **No credit cards. Map** p297 H4.
Situated on a quiet little square in the heart of the neighbourhood of Kolonaki, this cinema next to an *ouzerie* is surrounded by green. On offer: late-night Friday and Saturday screenings of art/cult films. You might sometimes be surprised by the new soundtrack to your favourite film, though – the poor sound system has a hard time competing with the mainstream music from the adjacent outdoor Mykonos-style Frame bar. Britney Spears accompanying *Eraserhead*, anyone?

Ekran

Zoodochou Pigis & Agathiou, Exarchia (210 646 1895). Metro Panepistimio, then 10mins walk. **Tickets** €7; €5 concessions. **No credit cards**.
A good old cinema in Exarchia. Everything is just as it should be: a little kiosk with a little old woman selling pre-printed tickets, and a little old man next to her cutting it for you and selling photocopied programmes for the films.

Hero worship

Ancient Greece is hot property in Hollywood right now, as studios scramble to launch a new generation of sword-and-sandal epics. ('Toga saga', another genre description batted about, is of course technically inaccurate; Ancient Greeks dressed in chitons, which doesn't quite have the same ring to it.)

Ridley Scott's *Gladiator* was a runaway hit in 2000, and its success revived the genre, long neglected since the 1963 Elizabeth Taylor flick *Cleopatra* threatened to bankrupt Twentieth Century Fox.

Alexander the Great is receiving the royal treatment with two major biopics, directed by Oliver Stone and Baz Luhrmann. In the 4th century BC the charismatic king expanded his father's modest Balkan domain as far as the Himalayan foothills, rewriting western history en route. Stone's version, due out first in 2004, fizzes with conspiracy theories about Alexander's life and death. The script – co-written by the director and Oxford academic Robin Lane Fox – even tackles his controversial sex life. Colin Farrell (pictured) plays mainstream's 'first bisexual action hero'. Alexander dallies with the Queen of the Amazons, as well as his childhood friend,

lover and general, Hephaestion (Jared Leto). 'Back then there was no term for bisexuality,' Farrell told the BBC. 'It was just the way society was. People made love to men and women. It was only later on you had to pick one side of the fence.'

Luhrmann's film doesn't dwell on the lurid details in such depth. Instead, the *Moulin Rouge* director choses to explore the cultural impact of the conqueror's nine-year campaign. The 2005 release stars the high-powered duo of Leonardo di Caprio as Alexander and Nicole Kidman as his mother, Olympia.

Troy, meanwhile, caused an early flutter with publicity shots of Brad Pitt in his battle skirt as Achilles. This adaptation of Homer's *Iliad*, out in 2004, is directed by Wolfgang Petersen (*The Perfect Storm*). Other stars include Eric Bana, Orlando Bloom and Julie Christie. Pitt's Achilles will probably see more action than his literary counterpart, who spends most of the epic sulking in his tent. Purists may be dissatisfied on many points, however: Petersen has omitted the Greek gods, who meddle ferociously in the original poem.

Director Neil Jordan (*The Crying Game*) is also ransacking the classics library. He's chosen Homer's second masterpiece,

Arts & Entertainment (sidebar)

Riviera

Valtetsiou 46, Exarchia (210 383 7716/210 384 4827). Metro Panepistimio. **Tickets €7; €5 concessions. No credit cards.**

Your average desktop speakers are probably more efficient than Riviera's sound system. And then you have to contend with the insects and leaves falling on you from the big trees, and lush vegetation covering a good portion of the screen. But don't let that put you off – they show good films here and some of Athens' friendliest bars and restaurants are just around the corner for the post-movie post-mortem.

Thisseion

Apostolou Pavlou 7, Thisio (210 347 0980/ 210 342 0864). Metro Thisio. **Tickets €6.50; €5** concessions. **No credit cards. Map** p294/p298 C5.

The Thisseion is one of the beneficiaries of the newly completed pedestrianisation project connecting the ancient monuments. While it used to suffer heavily from the traffic outside, it is now one of the quietest cinemas in town. Add to that the view of the Acropolis and the countless cafés and bars in Thisio, and you have a serious contender for best open-air cinema in Athens.

Art-house & rep

Alfaville Bar Cinema

Mavromichali 168, Exarchia (210 646 0521). Metro Panepistimio, then 15mins walk. **Tickets** €6.50; €5 concessions. **No credit cards.**

In Exarchia, Athens' alternative 'hood, the Alfaville rules. This classic, slightly run-down cult cinema in a theatre-dense area is a true art house, offering retrospectives of '60s Japanese film, French New Wave and so on. In summer, the roof opens and the cinema becomes an open-air venue.

Apollon

Stadiou 19, Historic Centre (210 323 6811). Metro Panepistimio. Closed July-mid Sept. **Tickets €7. No credit cards. Map** p295 F4.

One of the home cinemas of the Athens Film Festival Opening Nights and the Panorama Festival (and one of the most popular downtown cinemas), the Apollon shows mostly European films.

Astron

Leof Kifisias 37, Ambelokipi (210 692 2614/210 692 4823). Metro Ambelokipi. Closed July-mid Sept. **Tickets €7; €6 matinées; €5.50 concessions. No credit cards.**

chronicling Odysseus's long, convoluted journey home after the Trojan War. Spanish actor Javier Bardem will play the lead role when production starts in 2004.

George Clooney may charge into battle as Leonidas, leader of the brave Spartans at the Battle of Thermopylae, where a mere few hundred warriors turned back the vast Persian hordes in 480 BC. Michael Mann's film, *Gates of Fire*, draws on Steven Pressfield's historical novel, as well as Herodotus, the 'father of history' (aka the 'father of lies').

The stirring tale also attracted the attention of Twentieth Century Fox, who asked screenwriter Erik Jendresen to update a 1962 film, *The 300 Spartans*, about the same battle.

Cameras are rolling elsewhere in the Ancient World. Vin Diesel is to play Carthaginian general Hannibal Barca in a film by the genre's past master, Ridley Scott. Oscar-winner Denzel Washington is lined up for the same role in another production. And Warner Bros is developing a new Cleopatra film, based on the two-part novel by Karen Essex.

A nice but not spectacular venue on the cinema high street of Athens, Leof Kifisias. What makes this cinema special is the live jazz in the bar in the intervals, an excellent customer-care measure.

Attikon

Stadiou 19, Historic Centre (210 322 8821). Metro Panepistimio. Closed July-mid Sept. **Tickets** €7.50; €7 concessions. **No credit cards. Map** p295 F4.
Built as a theatre in 1914 and converted to cinema four years later, the Attikon is arguably the flagship cinema of Athens. After its restoration, it boasts handsome plaster arches and an impressive chandelier. The programme includes European and American quality features. Along with the Danaos (*see below*), this is also one of the home cinemas of the Athens International Film Festival.

Danaos

Leof Kifisias 109, Ambelokipi (210 692 2655). Metro Panormou. Closed July-mid Sept. **Tickets** €7. **No credit cards.**
For Athenians the name Danaos is synonymous with seriously non-Hollywood, quality films and the Athens International Film Festival in September. However, this duplex cinema also entices with a nice bar and film books for sale in the foyer.

Trianon

Kodrigtonos 21 & Patision 101, Pedion Areos (210 821 5469/210 822 2702). Metro Victoria. **Tickets** €7; €5.50 concessions. **No credit cards.**
This art-house cinema, which converts to an open-air venue in the summer, offers retrospectives of the great directors, house festivals and screenings with live music.

Multiplexes

One of the main attraction of the mutiplexes is their air-conditioning, making them a natural escape from a fetid summer day. Most are in the outskirts, several strung out along Stadiou and Leof Kifisias.

Aello Cinemax

Patision 140, between Tinou & Kefallinias, Pedion Areos (210 825 9975/210 821 5327). **Tickets** €8. **Credit** AmEx, MC, V.
The closest multiplex to central Athens has six theatres showing a mix of mainstream hits and independent flicks. The theatres are all modern, with Dolby Digital sound systems, air-conditioning and a heavily stocked concession stand.

Galleries

Athens' raffish contemporary art scene is a phoenix rising
from the debris of the city's old industrial districts.

Over the past few years Athens has developed
a vibrant contemporary art scene, with new
galleries scheduling international programmes,
artist-run initiatives, a new National Museum
of Contemporary Art and such ventures as the
winter Outlook international contemporary
art exhibition. Finally, it looks as if the city
is finding its place as one of Europe's centres
of contemporary art.

In recent decades, Greek artists have been
mostly consumed with themes of local identity.
Those who had an international career –
Kounellis, Lucas Samaras, Takis and Cryssa
among others – lived, worked and built their
reputations outside of the Greek borders. Lately
this has begun to change, with a younger and
very active generation of artists who use an
international vocabulary in their work and
focus on international exposure. Two
characteristic examples are **Maria
Papadimitriou** and **Ilias Papailiakis**.
Papadimitriou was the 2003 winner of the
DESTE prize for Greece's best artist, and has
participated in major exhibitions including

Frankfurt's Manifesta 4 and represented Greece
in the 2002 Biennale of Sao Paolo. Most of her
work is based around social issues and is made
in a context of collaborations and collective
efforts that link art with society. Her most
prominent project is TAMA, a series of social
interventions with a community of Gypsies
living outside Athens, that aims to document
but also better their living conditions.
Papailiakis represented Greece in the 49th
Venice Biennale in 2001, and also took part
in Arco 04 (in Madrid), where Greece was the
invited country. His paintings are centered on
imagery of prey and hunted or dead animals
drawn from the history of art, and also contain
strong personal references.

Most galleries close for the summer between
July and September, and there's usually little
to see between scheduled shows during the
rest of the year. It's a good idea therefore
to phone ahead or to pick up a copy of the
free brochure *Art & the City* (available at
most galleries and online, in English, at
www.artandthecity.gr) to find out what's on.

DESTE Foundation. *See p197.*

AD gallery

Pallados 3, Psyrri (210 322 8785). Metro Monastiraki. **Open** noon-9pm Tue-Fri; noon-4pm Sat. **Map** p295 E4.

In operation for more than ten years, AD gallery focuses primarily on conceptual Greek art. Its repertoire has included such international artists as Angus Fairhurst and Jan Fabre; it also represents well-known mid-career artists such as Maria Loizidou and Cris Giannakos, while collaborating with legend of Greek modernism Nikos Kessanlis.

a.antonopoulou.art

Aristofanous 20, Psyrri (210 321 4994). Metro Monastiraki. **Open** 4-9pm Tue-Fri; noon-4pm Sat. **Map** p295 D4.

The work of renowned architect Aris Zampikos Angeliki Antonopoulou's gallery is one of the best-designed art spaces in Athens – and also boasts a great view of the Psyrri area. It concentrates on Greek contemporary work: artists who have exhibited here include Alexandros Psychoulis, Sia Kiriakakos and Maria Papadimitriou.

The Apartment

5th Floor, Voulis 21, Syntagma, Historic Centre (210 321 5469). Metro Syntagma. **Open** noon-8pm Wed-Fri; noon-3pm Sat. **Map** p295/299 F5.

Located on the fifth floor of an office building in Syntagma and owned by curator Vassilios Doupas, The Apartment has a mixed exhibition programme of Greek and foreign artists such as Jessica Graig-Martin, Caroline May and Kostas Avgoulis. The gallery's mission is to exhibit and promote the work of international emerging artists, and it encourages artists to work on a project basis.

Bernier/Eliades

Eptahalkou 11, Thisio (210 341 3935/www.bernier-eliades.gr). Metro Thisio. **Open** 10.30am-8pm Tue-Fri; noon-4pm Sat. **Map** p294/p298 C5.

One of the oldest and most important galleries in Athens, Bernier/Eliades was founded in 1977 by Jean Bernier and Marina Eliades and, over the years, has shown a wealth of big names (try Tony Cragg, Juan Munoz, Tony Oursler, Thomas Schutte and George Lappa for size). Perhaps the most significant contribution of the gallery is its efforts to introduce the Greek public to international contemporary art.

The Breeder Projects

Eumorfopoulou 6, Psyrri (210 331 7527/www.thebreedersystem.com). Metro Monastiraki or Thisio. **Open** 1-8pm Wed-Sat. **Map** p295 D4.

The Breeder showcases some of the most interesting and upcoming young contemporary artists – Jim Lambie, Henrik Haakansson, Mark Titchner, Brian Griffiths, Dionisis Kavalieratos and Ilias Papailiakis to name but a few. The gallery runs a very active international programme, featuring solo presentations, group shows and gallery swaps.

DESTE Foundation

Omirou 8, Neo Psychiko, Northern Suburbs (210 672 9460/www.deste.gr). Bus A5, A6, A7. **Open** 10am-6pm Mon-Fri; noon-4pm Sat.

This private exhibition space owned by über-collector Dakis Ioannou is now open to the public.

Industrial strength

Athens is a city that has learned to make the most of its ruins, whether by charging tourists (a deserved) €12 to see the temples of the Acropolis or by displaying 2,500-year-old drainpipes to ooing-and-aahing crowds in the gleaming new metro stations. Until recently ancient ruins alone were the city's main draw. And, while it's true that no trip to Athens would be complete without a visit to the Parthenon, it's also well worth taking a look at the exciting way in which Athenian artists and urban developers are starting to exploit some more modern ruins.

To the west of downtown Athens, outside the edge of the classical city, lie miles of crumbling industrial district dotted with the remains of what were once among eastern Europe's biggest factories, foundries and warehouses. Many are beautifully built, with clean, steel lines, stone walls and vast amounts of space – features that haven't gone unnoticed by a new breed of hip Greek entrepreneurs. Slowly but surely these abandoned factories are being transformed into galleries, performance venues and 'multi-use arts spaces', displaying cutting-edge contemporary art against the 19th-century backdrops of their former-factory shells.

The success of these spaces has led to a surge in the quality and quantity of Athens' contemporary arts scene, simultaneously prompting a flurry of hipper-than-thou bars and clubs to open up in their surrounds. In spite of all these new flowers budding in its midst, the area remains decidedly gritty, with a block of grey old factories for every shiny new transformation. This edgy contrast only enhances the street-cred cachet of attending an opening at any one of these fresh, young galleries, the best of which are listed below.

Athinais

Kastorias 34-36, Rouf (210 348 0000/www. athinais.com.gr). Metro Metaxourgio or Thisio, then 20mins walk. **Open** 9am-10pm daily. **Admission** free. **Map** p294 B3.
Located in the middle of one of the grungiest streets in town, this converted silk factory has acres of gallery space for posh art

Eleni Koroneou

Mitseon 5-7, Makrygianni (210 924 4271/www. koroneougallery.gr). Metro Akropoli. **Open** 11am-1pm, 5-8pm Tue-Fri; 11am-2pm Sat. **Map** p299 E7.
There are few galleries in town that are as well respected as Eleni Koroneou. First opened in 1988 with a programme centred on painting and photography, its recent shows have included Martin Kippenberger, John Bock and Lila Polenaki. The gallery has also contributed to Artforum Berlin, Art Athina and Art Brussels.

Els Hanappe Underground

Melanthiou 2, Psyrri (210 325 0364/ http://els.hanappe.com). Metro Monastiraki. **Open** noon-4pm Wed, Sat; noon-8pm Thur, Fri. *12-31 Aug* 8pm-midnight daily. **Map** p295 E4.
The emphasis at Els Hanappe Underground is on content rather than media. Committed to showing young artists from Glasgow, London and Los Angles, who work in diverse styles and media, its past exhibitions have made their mark with artists such as Dave Muller, Adam Chodzko and Katja Strunz. Vangelis Vlahos and Despina Isaia are among the young Greek artists also represented here.

Gazon Rouge

Kolokotroni 57, Historic Centre (210 331 9101/ www.gazonrouge.com). Metro Monastiraki or Syntagma. **Open** 10am-10pm Mon-Sat. **Map** p295 E4.

One of the young, trendy galleries that have recently opened in the historical centre of Athens, Gazon Rouge focuses mostly on the younger generation of Greek artists and artist-initiated shows – past exhibitions have featured performances by rising art star Georgia Sagri. The gallery space incorporates a coffee shop.

Ileana Tounta Contemporary Art Centre

Armatolon-Klefton 48, Lycabettus, Neapoli (210 643 9466/www.art-tounta.gr). Metro Ambelokipi. **Open** 11am-8pm Tue-Fri; 11am-3pm Sat.
Opened in October 1988 and recently refurbished, the Ileana Tounta gallery includes two exhibition halls, an art shop and the stylish 48 restaurant (*see p131*). The gallery holds shows by contemporary Greek and foreign artists such as Joao Onofre and Sophia Kosmaoglou.

Millefiori Art Space

Haritos 29, Kolonaki (210 723 9558). Metro Evangelismos. **Open** 10.30am-3pm Mon, Wed, Sat; 10.30am-8.30pm Tue, Thur, Fri. **Map** p297 H4.
Recently opened, this energetic, young gallery hosts interesting group shows mostly by British artists. Past collaborations have been with Phillip Allen and Christian Ward. Located on the first floor of a charming neo-classical building in the hip street of Haritos. the Millefiori also has a small shop, where you can find books on art as well as Philip Treacy millinery.

Arts & Entertainment

openings, a cinema, theatre, symphony hall, two gourmet restaurants and a sleek, high-end bar. *See also p108.*

Benaki Contemporary Arts Centre
Pireos 256 & Andronikou, Rouf (www.benaki.gr).
Set to open in mid 2004, this vast new arts centre, which has already scheduled some high-profile exhibitions, is a vote of confidence from the old-school, old-money Benakis family (of the Benaki Museum; *see p102*) that former factories are the future of art in Athens. The name is to be confirmed.

The Factory
Pireos 256, Rentis, Western Athens (210 480 1315). Bus 041 from Omonia. **Open** 10am-8pm daily.
The new home of the Athens School of Fine Arts attracts a mix of bohemians and high-art types to its shows, which include retrospectives by British photographers Gilbert and George, new work by top contemporary Greek artists and the final shows of the fine-art students.

National Museum of Contemporary Art
Amvrosiou Frantzi 14 & Kallirois, Syngrou (210 924 2111). Metro Syngrou-Fix. **Open** 10am-7pm Tue, Wed, Fri; noon-10pm Thur; 11am-7pm Sat, Sun. **Map** p299 E8.
Now under construction in the former FIX beer factory, this looks set to become one of the most important museums in Athens when it fully opens in 2006. Meanwhile, exhibits from its temporary collection are shown at the Megaron Mousikis concert hall.

Technopolis
Pireos 100, Gazi (210 346 0981/www. culture.gr). Metro Thisio, then 10mins walk. **Open** 9am-9pm Mon-Fri during exhibitions. **Admission** free. **Map** p294 B5.
The smokestacks of this former foundry are illuminated in neon-red as an aesthetic statement, and beneath them are held everything from exhibits of trash art to concerts by British indie groups. *See also p108.*

Nees Morfes Gallery
Valaoritou 9A, Kolonaki (210 361 6165). Metro Syntagma. **Open** 10am-noon, 6-9pm Tue-Fri; 10am-3pm Sat. **Map** p297 G4.
The oldest contemporary art gallery in Athens, Nees Morfes was established by Julia Dimakopoulou in 1959. The gallery's focus over the years has been painting, particularly abstraction, holding solo presentations of established Greek painters. Recently the gallery has introduced a programme that includes younger artists as well.

Rebecca Camhi
Themistokleous 80, Platia Exarchia, Omonia (210 383 7030/www.rebeccacamhi.com). Metro Omonia. **Open** by appointment only.
Formerly located in a 1930s hotel on Sofokleous, Camhi's gallery used to be the most beautiful art space in Athens. However, it has relocated to this new address until further notice. The gallery, inaugurated in 1995, showcases contemporary Greek and international artists and regularly holds parallel events such as talks by artists and curators. Past collaborations have included Nan Goldin, Rita Ackermann, Nobuyoshi Araki and Nikos Alexiou.

Unlimited Contemporary Art
Kriezi 1 & Sarri, Psyrri (210 331 4375/ www.unlimitedcontemporary.com). Metro Monastiraki. **Open** 2-8pm Tue, Wed, Fri; noon-4pm Sat. Closed July, Aug. **Map** p295 D4.

Artists Vassilis Balatsos and Ghislaine Dantan opened this gallery in 1996. International artists such as Erwin Wurm, Bernhard Martin and Uri Tzaig feature in this two-level, apartment-like space, as well as solo exhibitions of younger artists.

Xippas Gallery
Sofokleous 53D, Historic Centre (210 331 9333/210 331 9341/www.xippas.com). Metro Omonia. **Open** noon-8pm Tue-Fri; noon-4pm Sat. **Map** p295 D1.
The Athens outpost of the established Greek-owned Paris gallery, Xippas was designed by renowned architect Eleni Kostika. At 500 square metres, it's one of the largest and best-designed commercial spaces in Athens. Artists exhibited here have included Takis, Vic Muniz, Nikos Baikas and Peter Halley.

Zoumboulakis
Platia Kolonaki 20, Kolonaki (210 360 8278/www. zoumboulakis.gr). Metro Evangelismos or Syntagma. **Open** 11am-2pm, 6-9pm Tue-Fri; 11am-2pm Sat. **Map** p297 G5.
One of the best-known and commercially successful gallery-names in Athens, the two Zoumboulakis galleries are operated by second-generation dealer Daphne Zoumboulaki. With a focus on figurative Greek painting, the gallery collaborates with established artists such as Yiannis Moralis. An art shop at the Krizotou gallery (*see p163*), where you can buy silk-screens and editions by famous artists like Yiannis Tsarouhis, rounds things off.

Gay & Lesbian

Now you see it, now you don't: Athens' gay scene has one foot in the rave and the other still firmly in the closet.

Athens' gay and lesbian scene reflects the contradictory nature of the city itself. On the one hand there are westernised, Euro-style bars and clubs, whose vibe will be very familiar to any visitor coming over from Europe, the USA or Australia. On the other, there is a thriving underground scene that reflects the real, multi-ethnic Athens and its cross-cultural character. This part stands somewhat uneasily between the untamed Middle Eastern mentality and the sensual southern European way of life. Naughty, but nice. Its exotic feel will probably appeal to visitors who don't want an exact replica of what they already have at home.

The proliferation of fashionable gay bars has brought gay life out of the closet and into the limelight and laid the foundations for a young, hip and confident new scene. Despite these exciting developments, however, there is little sense of community among gay people in Athens. Plenty of 'gay' bars exist, and they're only too happy to welcome a hip and sexy crowd into their premises, but these same businesses are reluctant to put their hand on their heart (or, indeed, in their pocket) to offer moral or financial support to much-needed community and health projects. This lack of support and involvement may explain the general lack of solidarity among gays and lesbians in Athens. Gay Pride does not exist as such; over the years various individuals, whose main objective appears to be one of self-promotion, have attempted to organise marches and demonstrations. These events have had low turnouts, owing to poor organisation, internal squabbles and little support from society as a whole. Mr Gay Greece, an annual beauty pageant whose raison d'être remains unclear, is probably the only event that appears to take place with any degree of consistency (for the last couple of years at least…).

The lesbian community in Athens is small and discreet. Clubs specifically aimed at gay women are shockingly thin on the ground, which leads women to frequent lesbian-friendly places (of which there are a few), or to make do with meetings at women's centres (which double as social occasions).

Still, from a visitor's point of view, Athens' gay scene is diverse, vibrant and well worth checking out. The listings that follow divide the city's hangouts into two categories: mainstream

and alternative. Unless otherwise stated, venues welcome both gays and lesbians. The age of consent is 15.

INFORMATION

Deon (www.deon.gr), a glossy Greek freezine found at most gay bars and clubs, includes English-language listings for bars, clubs and cruising. *The Greek Gay Guide*, a pocket-size book with full listings and gay information for Greece and Cyprus, is on sale at kiosks, especially around Omonia.

Mainstream

Cafés

Kirki

Apostolou Pavlou 31, Thisio (210 346 6960). Metro Thisio. **Open** 10am-2am daily. **No credit cards.** **Map** p299 D5.
This outdoor café offers a stunning view of the Acropolis and a selection of tasty hot and cold mezes. Kirki is where gay Athens whiles away the lazy summer afternoons and evenings and, though it's mostly a gay crowd, it is one of the more lesbian-friendly places in Athens.

Sto 54

3rd Floor, Magna Graecia Hotel, Mitropoleos 54, Plaka (210 331 8781/www.sto54.com). Metro Monastiraki or Syntagma. **Open** 6pm-2am daily. **No credit cards.** **Map** p295 F5.
Beautiful, torch-lit terrace bar with great views of that old temple on the hill. Comfortable wicker chairs make this the ideal spot for sunset drinks or star-lit nightcaps. In winter the drinks and snacks move indoors, a somewhat cosier affair with wooden floors and tasteful homoerotic paintings on the wall. Mostly male crowd, but lesbian-friendly.

Bars

In August some of the following bars and clubs may be closed, so a phone call is advised before you step out. Not all clubs and bars charge an entrance fee. If they do, it should never be higher than €10, unless there's a guest DJ or a special show; your entrance fee often allows you to claim a free drink. Things rarely get going before 1am, so don't despair if you get there early and the place is empty.

Aleco's Island

Basement, Tsakalof 42, Kolonaki (no phone). Metro Syntagma. **Open** 11pm-3am daily. **No credit cards.** **Map** p297 G4.

The classic Athenian gay bar. Aleco is a warm and welcoming host, and the relaxed, homely atmosphere he generates is popular with bears and the over-25 crowd. One of the few places where you can go and have an early drink – that is, around 11pm.

Bee

Miaouli &Themidos, Psyrri (210 321 2624). Metro Monastiraki. **Open** noon-3am Mon-Thur, Sun; noon-5am Fri, Sat. **Credit** MC, V. **Map** p295 E4.

This café/bar with a fresh, modern pastel interior serves snacks, coffees and juices to a mainly straight trendy crowd during the day; at night, however, it becomes livelier and more gay. There are pavement tables and in the summer the action spills out on to the street, where a good-looking crowd hangs out, checks the talent and gets ready for a big night.

Blue Train

Konstantinoupoleos 84 & Iera Odos, Rouf (210 346 0677/www.bluetrain.gr). Metro Thisio, then 15mins walk. **Open** 7.30pm-3am Mon-Thur, Sun; 8.30pm-5am Fri, Sat. **No credit cards.** **Map** p294 B4.

The silent railtracks lying adjacent to this hip lounge bar introduce an edgy, industrial element, contrasting nicely with the stylish decor inside. Good music and outdoor seating complete the picture.

Dare

1st Floor, Tsakalof 5, Kolonaki (no phone). Metro Syntagma. **Open** noon-midnight daily. Closed Aug. **No credit cards.** **Map** p297 G4.

A welcome respite from the boutiques of Kolonaki, this relaxed lounge bar provides the perfect excuse to put your feet up with a vodka & tonic and chill out to some blissful tunes. Dare is one of the few daytime venues around and is ideal for an evening drink before the other bars heat up.

Fairy Tale

Koletti 25, Exarchia (210 330 1763/www.fairytale.gr). Metro Omonia. **Open** 6pm-3am Mon-Sat; 2pm-3am Sun. **No credit cards.** **Map** p295 F3.

This small, cosy bar in the student area of Athens serves light snacks and coffee on Sunday afternoons. It draws a mostly lesbian crowd. Be warned: the loud (Greek) music isn't exactly conducive to conversation.

Floga

2nd Floor, Persefonis 19, Rouf (210 341 3952). Metro Thisio, then 10mins walk. **Open** 10pm-4am daily. **No credit cards.** **Map** p294 B4.

A slightly old-fashioned venue offering thoroughly modern views of Gazi's converted gasworks. In this relaxed bar the owners are warm and friendly, and the barmen hot and sexy.

Granazi

Lempesi 20 & Kallirois, Makrygianni (210 924 4185/www.granazi.gr). Metro Akropoli. **Open** 11pm-3.30am daily. **No credit cards.** **Map** p299 E7.

Frappé & sympathy at **Kirki**. *See p200.*

One of the oldest gay bars in Athens, this joint plays mainly Greek music to a generally older crowd. Opened at a time when gay activities were confined to indoor spaces, Granazi had the insight to combine mock stone walls, Greek columns, plastic plants, mirrors and even street lamps to create a terrace, albeit a rather haphazard affair.

Clubs

Musically, Greek gay clubs are an acquired taste. If it's London- or New York-quality dance music you're after, your best bet is the super-trendy **U-Matic** (Leof Vouliagmenis 268, Neos Kosmos, 694 536 3700 mobile), a taxi ride from the centre, or the established **Plus Soda** in Thisio (Ermou 161, 210 345 6187/www.plussoda.com) – both are very gay-friendly.

Cone

Triptolemou 35, Rouf (210 345 8118). Metro Thisio, then 10mins walk. **Open** midnight-4.30am daily. **No credit cards.** **Map** p294 B4.

Small, and sometimes unsure of its sexuality, this venue gets busy at weekends and caters to fans of Greek music.

Flying In

Trikoupi Harilaou 34, Piraeus (no phone). Metro Piraeus. **Open** 11pm-late Fri, Sat. **No credit cards.** Friendly, fun and a little trashy in a good way, Flying In specialises in Greek music.

Get all dolled up for **Koukles**, Athens' most popular drag-show joint.

Kazarma

*1st Floor, Konstantinoupoleos 84 & Iera Odos,
Rouf (210 346 0677/www.ka3arma.gr). Metro
Thisio, then 15mins walk.* **Open** 11.30pm-5am
Thur-Sun. **No credit cards. Map** p294 B4.
At this stylish, intimate club from the team behind
Blue Train (*see p201*), a large red, pod-like central
bar dominates, giving the place a futuristic 1960s
feel. The coolness of the interior is compounded by
graffiti motifs on the wall and grey podium-style
tables. Kazarma attracts a stylish, young crowd with
its blend of pop and house from the TNT DJ team.

Koukles

*Zan Moreas 3, Koukaki (no phone). Metro Syngrou-
Fix.* **Open** 11.30pm-3am Mon, Wed-Sun. **No credit
cards. Map** p299 D8.
Koukles (meaning 'dolls') has the best drag show
in Athens on Friday and Saturday nights, when it
becomes the premier transvestite hangout.

Lamda

*Lempesi 15, Makrygianni (210 922 4202/
www.lamdaclub.gr). Metro Akropoli.* **Open** 11pm-
4am daily. **No credit cards. Map** p299 E7.
Although this is one of the oldest gay clubs in
Athens, a recent facelift has ensured it also remains
one of the busiest. Expect the usual mix of pop, dance
and Greek music on the main dancefloor; downstairs the low-ceilinged bar area can get intense and
cruisy, and there is a darkroom off to one side.

Lizard

*Apostolou Pavlou 31, Thisio (210 346 6960).
Metro Thisio.* **Open** midnight-4am Sat, Sun.
Closed summer. **No credit cards. Map** p299 D5.
Although in many ways outdone by the influx of
newer, trendier venues, Lizard remains a bit of an
institution for a mixed gay and lesbian crowd
and is still worth checking out. It's normally
open at weekends only, so it's advisable to give
its sister venue Kirki (*see p200*) a quick ring to
confirm opening times.

Mayo

*Persefonis 33, Rouf (210 342 3066). Metro Thisio,
then 10mins walk.* **Open** 10.30pm-6am daily. **No
credit cards. Map** p294 B4.
A simple fusion of white walls and glass creates
a hip, contemporary space. Glass doors open on
to a softly lit outdoor lounge area, and a spiral
staircase takes you up to the large terrace. This
breezy roof area gets packed at weekends with
a mixed gay/straight crowd and offers a welcome
respite from the balmy summer nights; you also
get the best views of Gazi and the cool industrial
landscape from here.

Play My Music

*Konstantinoupoleos 78, Rouf (210 341 1141).
Metro Thisio, then 15mins walk.* **Open** 10pm-4am
Tue-Thur; 10pm-6am Fri, Sat. **No credit cards.
Map** p294 B4.

Big, buzzing bar/club with sleek, contemporary interior, large video wall, great DJs and good lighting. The outside terrace area is ultra-modern and stylish, with white leatherette benches; the space is illuminated by dozens of candles set on the dark-wood tabletops.

Sodade

Triptolemou 10, Rouf (210 346 8657/www.
sodade.gr). Metro Thisio, then 10mins walk.
Open 11pm-3.30am daily. **No credit cards.**
Map p294 B4.
One of the first of a new breed of trendy bars to spring up in the newly revitalised Gazi area, Sodade continues to attract a young, fashion-conscious crowd. A glass corridor separates two bar areas: the first is heaving, playing a mix of dance music and Greek hits; the second has a more relaxed vibe. For complete relaxation, escape to the courtyard and lay back with your drink on the Bedouin-style sofas.

Alternative

Bars

Fantastiko

Aristotelous 37, Northern Suburbs (no phone).
Metro Victoria. **Open** 10.30pm-3am Mon-Fri, Sun;
10.30pm-5am Sat. **No credit cards. Map** p295 E1.
Groups of young guys hang out on the leatherette seats scoping out the clientele. Cute Romanian and Albanian go-go dancers take their turn jumping on to the makeshift stage, gyrating under a little disco ball every Saturday at around 2am. All this under the watchful gaze of an armless Adonis peering out over the mirrored bar.

Gallery

Smirnis 9 & Acharnon 52, Northern Suburbs
(210 825 1966). Metro Victoria. **Open** 11pm-
3.30am daily. **No credit cards. Map** p295 E2.
Greek music and a multi-ethnic male-only clientele.

Live Bait

Filis 34, Northern Suburbs (210 882 2134).
Metro Victoria. **Open** 11pm-4am Wed-Sun.
No credit cards. Map p295 E1.
At the busiest of the alternative bars, young men and their admirers congregate around a central oval bar. The DJ creates a party atmosphere at the weekend, ensuring this place is not solely about 'business'.

Strass

Odysseos Androutsou 32, Koukaki (210 922 1622).
Metro Syngrou-Fix. **Open** 10.30pm-4am daily.
No credit cards. Map p298 C8.
Popular with drag queens and their admirers.

Test Me

Pipinou 64, Northern Suburbs (210 822 6029).
Metro Victoria. **Open** 10.30pm-3am daily.
No credit cards.

A friendly meeting place popular with an older crowd wishing to make contact with their younger fans. Uninspired decor with simple wooden bar; music plucked at random from the barman's CD collection. Men only.

Saunas

Athens Relax

Xouthou 8 & Sokratous, Omonia (210 522 2866).
Metro Omonia. **Open** 1-8pm Mon-Sat. **No credit**
cards. Map p295 E2.
Fairly standard men's sauna featuring all the usual facilities, such as steam room, rest rooms, sauna, private cabins, lockers, bar, showers and masseurs. The large white-tiled steam room is worthy of note, resembling a sexually charged Turkish haman.

Ira Baths

Zinonos 4, Omonia (210 523 4964). Metro Omonia.
Open noon-8pm Mon-Sat. Closed bank holidays.
No credit cards. Map p295 D3.
Ideal for fans of *Midnight Express*, this traditional mens' baths incorporate sparse cells, complete with spring-sprung iron beds, used ashtray, metal dust-bin, complimentary plastic slippers and a very austere white-tiled ante-room furnished with mar-ble slab and shower. Each unit is locked with a key on a chain and there is even a small hatch at the top of the door allowing you to scour the corridors and complete your prison fantasy. You are shown to your cell by a little old lady in a pinafore who gives you a towel and bar of soap – highly surreal.

Cruising

Many Greek gay men live closeted lives. Not to be found in gay bars, they are more likely to be found frequenting the adult cinemas around Omonia (eg Star Cinema, 10 Agios Konstantinou, 210 522 5801, www.star-cinema.gr) or sex shops with video cabins (eg Silver Star, Klisthenous 7, 210 522 5311, www.silverstar.gr).

Despite massive renovation, Omonia retains its seedy image and is frequented by young hustlers who take their clients to one of many hotels in the area that rent rooms by the hour.

If you're planning a stroll in the park, it is wise to always carry your passport with you, as police raids are not unheard of.

Beaches/swimming

Don't miss out on the beautiful, rocky gay nudist beach Limanakia (*see p120*). It's on the coastal road to Sounion, at the end of a steep downhill climb. Take bus A1 or A2 (from Piraeus) or the B1 or B2 (from Athens) to Varkiza and get off at the Limanakia B stop, at the canteen. Or, better still, ask a Greek friend to take you there.

Music

Chaotic sound pollution and intimate musical moments.

Athens oozes with music. It's played in taxis, bars, tavernas, garages, butchers and street markets, on portable radios stretched to their limits. Volume always on eleven. It's Greek folk or pop music, or one of the billion combinations thereof. Lonely accordionists walk up and down quiet neighbourhoods playing the same sad tune over and over again, sometimes outplayed by bands with guitar, clarinet and drums, trying to catch the coins that people throw from the balconies.

Classical music came late to Greece, allowing other genres to flourish. The variety here is remarkable: monophonic Byzantine chants, electropop, Greek folk and *rembetika* (blues, loosely), symphony orchestras, 'art music' and an exuberant, bouzouki-accompanied version of pop. Silence is not an option.

TICKETS AND INFORMATION

Tickets can be bought from the relevant venues and from ticket agencies such as Tickethouse. On the net, www.cultureguide.gr lists most events. For smaller venues, see the listings in the weekly English-language *Athens News* or *Ekathimerini* (www.ekathimerini.gr).

Tickethouse

Panepistimiou 42 (210 360 8366/www.tickethouse. gr). Metro Panepistimio. **Open** 10.30am-6pm Mon-Fri; 10.30am-3pm Sat. **No credit cards.** **Map** p295 F4.

Ticket Hellas

1st Floor, Aithrio department store, Agiou Konstantinou 40, Marousi (210 618 9300/www. ticket-hellas.gr). Metro Marousi. **Open** 9.30am-6pm Mon-Fri; 10am-3.30pm Sat. **Credit** MC, V.

Classical & Opera

Few people travel to Athens for a night out at the opera; indeed, for a city of this size, the chances to hear classical music are few. But then, Athens is not like any other European city. Classical music is a relatively new phenomenon here. In 1828, when the Turks left the country and the first generation of Greek composers like Nikolaos Mantzaros and Manolis Kalomiris started out, Beethoven had been dead a year and the rest of the world was well into the Romantic era.

Although there are performances of classical music in the city every week, the scene is very centralised, most of the action taking place in the Athens Concert Hall, the **Megaron Mousikis**. Inaugurated in 1991 and part funded by the state, Megaron is the brainchild of publishing tycoon Christos Lambrakis, a very powerful man in Greek cultural and media life (too powerful, say some). Aesthetically, the building is reminiscent of the new Athens metro – it's functional and clean, but characterless and sterile, and not a place where you would want to linger. And while that's acceptable for a subway, for an arts venue it's a bit of a downer. But for Athens, the Megaron is more than just a music venue. The long-awaited building also embodies the modern cultural aspirations of the city, its desire to be on a par with any other EU capital.

The other main venue is the **Ethniki Lyriki Skini**, or Greek National Opera. One would expect the country that gave the world Maria Callas to honour her memory by celebrating the opera company where she started her career. But no. The Lyriki Skini, founded in 1939, has never had a permanent home and is still in temporary accommodation at the Olympia Theatre on Akadimias. But the audience has tripled over the past three years and is loyal and enthusiastic despite the inadequate premises.

Other venues worthy of a mention are the foreign institutes, such as the **Goethe Institut**, the **Italian Institute** and the **French Institute**, which regularly schedule classical music concerts. The Goethe Institut is quite an institution – in the 1960s, Günther Becker, one of the forgotten heroes of Athens' musical life, started to arrange concerts of German and Greek contemporary music there. During the Junta years the institute became a meeting point for composers, musicians and music lovers, playing a vital role as a centre of unofficial art.

In the summer, the action moves from indoor venues to various outdoor theatres. One of the main programmes is the **Athens Festival** (*see p186*), running from May to September, with the major events, including concerts and operas from the main Greek orchestras and big international names, taking place in the **Odeon of Herodes Atticus** (*see p76*) and at the **Lycabettus Theatre** (*see p208*).

Considering the limited number of venues, the amount of Athens-based classical groups is impressive, with two symphonic ensembles, two major chamber orchestras and the opera orchestra. Apart from the **Camerata Friends**

The pride of musical Athens: **Megaron Mousikis**. *See p205.*

of **Music**, none of them can compete with the top orchestras in Europe, but they are able to surprise under the leadership of an inspired conductor.

Venues

Principal venues

Ethniki Lyriki Skini (Greek National Opera)

Olympia Theatre, Akadimias 59-61, Historic Centre (210 361 2461/www.nationalopera.gr). *Metro Panepistimio.* **Open** *Box office 9am-9pm daily.* **Tickets** €20-€50. **Credit** MC, V. **Map** p295 F4, p295 F3.

The Greek National Opera is a competent company that hasn't had the means to develop fully owing to the limitations of its temporary home: the Olympia Theatre seats only 900. Artistic director Loukas Karytinos runs the activities in the problematic venue while fighting for a new purpose-built opera house. The indoor opera season runs from November to May. In the summer the company plays at the Odeon of Herodes Atticus and sometimes tours other parts of Greece and abroad. The Acropol Theatre at 9-11 Ippokratous, near Panepistimiou, stages operettas and children's operas.

Megaron Mousikis (Athens Concert Hall)

Leof Vas Sofias & Kokkali, Kolonaki (box office 210 728 2333/information 210 728 2000/www. megaron.gr). *Metro Megaro Mousikis.* **Open** *Box office 10am-6pm Mon-Fri; 10am-2pm Sat.* **Tickets** €15-€90. **Credit** AmEx, DC, MC, V.

The Megaron hosts mainly operas and symphonic and chamber music, from Greek and international names; it is also the home of the Camerata Friends of Music. The main Hall of the Friends of Music, renowned for its flawless acoustics, seats around 1,960; the smaller Dimitri Mitropoulos Hall around 450. The recent expansion, due for completion in 2004, includes the brand-new Alexandra Trianti Hall, which seats 1,750. The expansion will transform the Megaron into a major cultural centre housing conference halls, exhibition areas, a music library, shops and restaurants. The season runs from October to June.

Other venues

Athens French Institute

Sina 31, Kolonaki (210 339 8600/www.ifa.gr). *Metro Panepistimio.* **Open** 8am-9pm Mon-Fri. **Tickets** free. **Map** p297 H3.

Supergreeks

Nikolaos Mantzaros (1795-1862)
The composer of the Greek national anthem was a follower of the Italian school.
Manolis Kalomiris (1883-1962)
This Vienna-trained artist embarked on a musical war against the Italian influences. He was also the founder of the new Greek National School of Music, and the leader of three of its academies.
Nikos Skalkottas (1904-49)
A student of Schönberg, Skalkottas is widely known for his orchestral settings of Greek folk dances. His works are still played frequently.
Dimitri Mitropoulos (1896-1960)
One of the first Greek composers to use atonal and 12-tone techniques in his music. Became a conductor of major international renown, heading, among others, the Berlin State Opera, the New York Philharmonic and the Metropolitan Opera, also in New York.

Iannis Xenakis (1922-2001)
Worked as an architect with Le Corbusier before becoming a composer, and drew from his background in mathematics and engineering when creating his music. He is reputed to be one of the most pioneering and influential modernists of the 20th century.
Mikis Theodorakis (1925-)
& Manos Hadjidakis (1925-94)
After World War II Theodorakis and Hadjidakis worked within a popular neo-folklore/urban tradition, using simple instrumentation. Known as *entekno*, their music has become the quintessential Greek sound and is still played in both concert halls and tavernas. Theodorakis also played an important role in the resistance to the Junta.
Leonidas Kavakos
One of the leading violinists internationally, Kakavos is also the artistic director of the Salzburg Camerata.

Goethe Institut
Omirou 14-16, Historic Centre (210 366 1000/ www.goethe.de/om/ath/). Metro Syntagma. **Open** 8am-9pm Mon-Fri. **Tickets** free-€10. **No credit cards. Map** p295 F4.

Hellenic-American Union
Massalias 22, Kolonaki (210 368 0000/www.hau.gr). Metro Panepistimio. **Open** 9am-10pm Mon-Fri. **Tickets** free. **Map** p297 G3.

Ensembles

Athens State Orchestra
210 725 7601/www.megaron.gr or www.athensfestival.gr **Open** June-Sept.
'The main symphony orchestra in the history of Greek music' (as it calls itself) was formed over 100 years ago, though the current name goes back only to 1942, when the ensemble was assured the state funding it is still under. The current chief conductor, Vyron Fithedjis, is committed to performing new (and rediscovering old) Greek music.

Camerata Friends of Music
210 724 0098/www.megaron.gr.
Formed in 1991 as the Megaron house band, in just over a decade this chamber orchestra has, under the devoted leadership of Alexandros Myrat, achieved international renown. Respected Academy of St Martin-in-the-Fields maestro Sir Neville Marriner was recently appointed artistic director, adding lustre. The other leading figure is Myrat, who has been with the orchestra from the start.

ERT National Symphony Orchestra
Symphony office 210 606 6802/ Megaron Mousikis box office 210 728 2333/ Athens Festival box office 210 322 1459/ www.megaron.gr or www.athens festival.gr **Open** June-Sept.
The Radio Orchestra sticks mostly to recording for radio and TV, so the chances to see it in concert are few and far between. However, the ensemble does occasionally perform at the Megaron and more often at the Athens Festival in the summer.

Hellenic Group of Contemporary Music
Megaron Mousikis box office 210 728 2333.
This ensemble was formed by composer/conductor Theodore Antoniou, professor of composition at Boston University, and the president of the National Greek Composers Organisation.

Orchestra of the Colours
210 362 8589/check www.megaron.gr or www.orchestraofcolours.gr for performances.
The legendary composer/conductor Manos Hadjidakis formed this ensemble in 1989 with the intention of performing works not usually included in conventional repertoires. The maestro succeeded in this heroic task by investing in extensive rehearsing hours and financing his vision with his own money. Since Hadjidakis's death in 1994, the orchestra has been under a shaky state patronage. The current chief conductor of the Orchestra of Colours is Miltos Logiadis.

Byzantine Sacred Music

The fact that Greece 'missed' the first centuries of Western classical music is more than compensated by its alternative musical history.

In ancient Greece music was considered the highest form of art. It is believed to have accompanied everything, from religious rites to labour. Lately, there have been many efforts to re-create the music of ancient Greece, but since sound couldn't be recorded on marble, it's hard to say how close to the source the results are, and how much ancient music has influenced later Greek music. What is certain is that even in 21st-century Greece music remains omnipresent.

The greatest contribution to the Greek music world was made without doubt by the unique Byzantine chant, a musical system dating back to the first centuries of Christianity as the scholarly music of the vast Byzantine empire. Created long before the Western system, with its own principles and a sophisticated use of notation, the Byzantine chant is still alive, though maybe not kicking. After the fall of the empire in 1453, the Greek-Christian Orthodox church pursued its own course of artistic expression.

Byzantine music has remained essentially vocal. It is monophone and has inherited microtonal intervals, probably from the music of ancient Greece. Without the use of harmony or counterpoint, it has created a world of rich melodies and complex musical forms. The Byzantine chant forms a solid base from which, much later, Greek secular music has sprung.

Venues & ensembles

The best place to catch some Byzantine chants is Sunday mass. Chants start at 7am and go on until 11am. Agias Irini on Eolou is the home of the renowned Greek Byzantine Choir (210 862 4444/www.cs.duke.edu/~mgl/gbc/), performing the classic monophone chants on Saturdays (winter only) and Sundays. At Agios Dionysos on Skoufa it is possible to hear the rival (and less common) school of polyphonic chant.

Rock & Pop

If Athens set the world standard, bands like Calexico, Tindersticks and Godspeed You! Black Emperor would top international charts. In recent years major world tours have stayed away from Greece owing to the renovation of the stadia for the Olympics, and the quality bands that do visit are fanatically received.

Greece has never had a band with any real international success. Dig really deep and you come up with progressive rockers Aphrodite's Child, big in France in the 1960s, and Leuki Symphonia, who are said to have been on MTV in 1989. After that, you have to look at George Michael's Cypriot origins, Robert Plant's 1975 car accident in Greece and the Greek wife of that guy in Pink Floyd to get close to anything that would qualify Greece for the rock Hall of Fame.

This doesn't mean that there's no scene, though. The grandaddies of Greek rock, Trypes, which formed in 1983 and disbanded recently, were domestically influential and popular. Indie rockers Closer recently released a couple of good albums and now Pyx Lax and Raining Pleasure enjoy a fair amount of success. The latter supported the Dandy Warhols at their recent Athens gig and was the second English-speaking band in Greece ever to be signed to a multinational label. On an underground level, there are local bands, but not enough small clubs for them to play or fan and small-label support to generate a buzz.

More vital is the electropop scene. In the 1990s electro pioneers Stereo Nova could have easily competed on the international stage had there been any interest in promoting them. Now there's a handful of small labels, like Floor Filler Production, Bios Records, Antifrost and Pop Art Records, promoting some quality artists, some of them surprisingly experimental, such as Barcelona-based Ilios (Antifrost), Drog-A-Tek and Poptraume (Bios), who caught John Peel's attention and whose first single was voted Record of the Month in *Record Collector* in 2003. Other bands to look out for are Crooner, Hometaping and Spy F & the Zakulas (Pop Art Records). The commercial offspring of the genre are dadaist electro-poppers Mikro, who had a massive hit in 2003 with the track *MikroTronicPlasma*.

Two annual festivals take place in Athens with an impressive cast of international experimental electronica artists: the Electrograph Festival (www.electrograph.gr), featuring more experimental noise and electro-acoustic music, and the Bios Festival (www.biofighter.gr), with names like Mouse on Mars, PanSonic and Fennescz.

Venues

An Club
13-15 Solomou, Exarchia (210 330 5056).
Metro Omonia. **Open** from 9pm Fri, Sat. **Tickets** €10-€25. **No credit cards. Map** p295 E2.
One of Athens' smallest but most beloved rock clubs is set right in the heart of rocker- and anarchist-packed Exarchia. This is a great place to catch local

acts as they play their first riffs towards stardom. International bands like Electro Lane and Kid 606 also play here.

Ark No.6

Pireos 254, Rouf (210 338 8400). Metro Tavros. **Open** 10am-6pm daily. **Tickets** €15-€35. **Credit** DC, MC, V.

This massive warehouse hosts festivals and international acts. Recent performers include Public Enemy, Mogwai and Calexico.

Bios Pireos 84

Pireos 84, Metaxourgio (210 342 5335/www.bio fighter.gr). Metro Metaxourgio. **Open** 11am-4am daily. **Admission** free. **No credit cards. Map** p294 C2.

The brand new Bios Pireos 84 (*see also p221*) is the contemporary arts venue of graphic designers/festival/record label Bios. In September 2003 it opened its doors to all kinds of new technology arts (with the focus on music) with exhibitions, a café and a book and music shop. The annual Bios festivals will continue in the new space.

Free2go Club 22

Leof Vouliagmenis 22, Kinossargous, Southern Suburbs (210 924 9814/www.club22.gr). Metro Syngrou-Fix. **Open** from 11.30pm Wed-Sun. **Tickets** €12 incl drink Wed-Fri; €16 incl drink Sat, Sun. **No credit cards.**

Famous for its increasingly popular themed parties, Free2go also organises gigs with acts like Thievery Corporation. In the summer, the venue relocates along the coast, in Glyfada.

Gagarin 205 Live Music Space

Liosion Thymarakia, Vathi, Western Athens (210 854 7600). Metro Attiki. **Open** 10pm-3am Thur-Sun. **Tickets** €20-€30. **Credit** MC, V.

Smaller than Rodon (*see below*), though it looks identical. This converted garage has been turned into a mid-sized venue featuring artists like Beth Orton, Fun Lovin' Criminals and Godspeed You! Black Emperor. It also converts to a cinema from time to time, showing music films.

Half Note Jazz Club

17 Trivonianou, Kinossargous, Southern Suburbs (210 921 3310/www.halfnote.gr). Metro Syngrou-Fix. **Open** Box office 10am-6pm daily. **Tickets** €28 (incl one drink) ; €20 concessions. **Credit** AmEx, DC, MC, V. **Map** p299 F8.

The Athens jazz scene circles more or less entirely around this legendary venue. A great club with the right atmosphere, attracting international and Greek names in both jazz and world music.

Lycabettus Theatre

On top of Lycabettus Hill, Kolonaki (210 722 7209). Metro Evangelismos or Megaro Mousikis, then 10mins walk. Funicular every half hour 9am-11.45pm daily from corner of Aristippou & Ploutarchou. **Open** Theatre June-Sept. Box office from two hours before performances. **Tickets** €30. **Credit** AmEx, MC, V. **Map** p297 J3.

This modernistic amphitheatre, which hosts major acts, local and international, was created by one of the country's most important architects, Takis Zenetos. Its summer music festivals have hosted everyone from hip-hopper Guru to contemporary classicist Philip Glass. From up here, the chaotic city becomes a calm carpet of lights far below. Tickets can be pricey, but you can listen for free by climbing up the surrounding rocks (though agility is definitely required). You don't even need to bring your booze: freelance entrepreneurs climb around selling ice-cold drinks.

Melina Mercouri Vrahon Theatre

Vyronas (210 764 8675/210 766 2066). Bus 214/trolleybus 11. **Open** Theatre June-Sept. Box office from 6pm. **Tickets** €15-€25. **Credit** MC, V. **Map** p299 E5.

This outdoor theatre, impressively located in front of a cliff face, hosts concerts by top Greek musicians, with a liberal sprinkling of international acts – from an African drumming festival to Brit-poppers Suede.

Mikromousiko Theatro (Small Music Theatre)

33 Veikou, Koukaki (210 924 5644/www.anet.gr/smt). Metro Akropoli. **Open** 9pm-3am Thur-Sun. **Tickets** €5-€15. **No credit cards. Map** p299 E7.

As the name suggests, this is a tiny venue holding around 100 people – if they squeeze. It features local bands, and has begun to bring in visiting rock acts too, while maintaining its advanced experimental electronica and improvisation series, culminating in the annual 2:13 Festival. Nick Cave's violinist Warren Ellis's band Dirty Three played here last year to a packed and ecstatic house.

Rodon 24

Marni 24, Omonia (210 524 7427). Metro Omonia. **Open** 11am-5pm daily. **Tickets** €10-€25. **Credit** MC, V. **Map** p295 E2.

The oldest rock club in Athens (and for a long time the only one) was opened in a converted mid-century cinema in 1987 by The Triffids. The name alone brings tears to the eyes of the average Athenian concert goer. Around 1,800 capacity.

Rembetika & Folk

Arguably the only genuine Athenian music, **rembetika** can be described as songs from the urban underworld (or the Blues of the Balkans). The roots of the genre can be traced to the 1920s Piraeus hash dens, populated by the immigrants from the big population handover between Greeks and Turks. Drawing inspiration from Turkish café music, or *aman*, *rembetika* adopted a simple style and instrumentation, and became the voice of the dispossessed and miserable immigrant workers in Piraeus. Originally the main instruments were the

The truest of all *rembetes*

One of the most important Greek musicians is probably Markos Vamvakaris. Synonymous with the Greek soul and often mentioned as the father of *laiko*, Vamvakaris was born in 1905 in extreme poverty on the island of Syros. At the age of 15 he came to Piraeus, where he got a job at the slaughterhouse. He ended up in prison several times for being caught in *tekes* (hash dens). The myth goes that in the early 1920s he heard Old Nikos from Aivali playing bouzouki and swore that if he didn't learn to play the instrument he would cut his hand off with a meat clever... Six months later he played the instrument like a devil and by his first recording sessions, in 1932, he had composed a considerable number of songs.

Many of the early lyrics refer to the underworld and hashish smoking, but later became much more than that. He never achieved great financial success, but when he died, in 1967, he was one of Greece's best-loved musicians, and maybe the single most influential person on the Greek music scene. His life was that of a true *rembetis*, an outlaw clashing with the police, enjoying his narghile and moving around the *tekes* of underground Piraeus. Vamvakaris was part of the legendary Piraeus Quartet with Stratos Payoumdzis, Giorgos Batis and Anestos 'Artemis' Delias. The latter's fortune was short-lived: he died in the streets at the age of 29, after becoming addicted to hard drugs.

bouzouki and the smaller *baglamas*; the rhythm was tapped with feet, spoons on glasses or anything else to hand. The lyrics, often improvised, focused mainly on prostitutes, drugs and how to humiliate the police. *Rembetika* became popular during the 1930s, turning some of the poor *rembetes* into stars driving Rolls Royces, before falling into oblivion until a new generation, oppressed by the Junta, rediscovered the old songs and their rebellious lyrics, and turned them into their national songs of freedom.

The legendary names are the members of the Piraeus Quartet: Stratos, Markos, Batis and Artemis (*see above* **The truest of all *rembetes***), later joined by the bouzouki wizard Yiannis Tsitsanis, also connected with the westernisation of *rembetika*. Today, *rembetika* is synonymous with Greek music and seen as a fundament in much of the contemporary stuff. The real stuff doesn't exist anymore, except on a number of excellent recordings, but several live venues are keeping *rembetika* alive. The quality of the singers varies a lot, but there are still a couple of guys out there with that old *rembetes* feel in their veins. And *rembetika* certainly exists in the hearts of the Greek people. It's truly amazing listening to generations of Greeks at family gatherings, singing along to old *rembetes* praising hookers and dope.

Rembetika should not be confused with **folk music**, which in Greece differs widely from region to region and is a major chapter in itself, with influences from ancient Greece, Byzantine music and all the other occupying powers. A good place to hear the real stuff is at the **Dora Stratou Garden Theatre** (*see p232*), where it comes complete with authentic costumes and

everything. Don't be put off, though – this is not a touristic Real Greek Music show, but a serious institution based on extensive ethnographic research under the direction of professor Alkis Raftis. Another artist to look out for is Domna Samiou, who recorded thousands of folk songs in villages across Greece and is counted as one of the finest folk singers around. She co-operates with young musicians such as *lyra* player Sokratis Sinopoulos. Percussionist Andreas Pappas creates a tasteful blend of folk music and modern sounds with his group Krotala.

Venues

Rembetika

Mnisikleous

Mnisikleous 22 & Lysiou, Plaka (210 322 5558/210 322 5337). Metro Monastiraki. **Open** 10pm-6am Thur-Sun. **Admission** free. **Credit** V. **Map** p295/p299 E5.

One of the few year-round *rembetatika*, this has the requisite smoky inside and a beautiful outdoor terrace for summer nights. Gravel-voiced *rembetis* Bobbis Tsertes brings authentic grit to his performances, with occasional arty twists.

Perivoli t'Ouranou

Lisikratous 19 & Leof Vas Amalias, Plaka (210 322 2048). Metro Akropoli. **Open** Oct-May 10pm-3.30am Thur-Sat. **Admission** free. **Credit** AmEx, MC, V. **Map** p299 F6.

Located right by the Acropolis, this tasteful venue has remained in business for over three decades on a fine entertainment-and-food principle. Home to respectable old-school *laiko* and *rembetika* acts, it

Arts & Entertainment

has maintained a delightful traditional character suggesting Athenian nightlife 'for mature crowds' as it was in 1960s.

Stoa Athanaton

Sofokleous 19, Historic Centre (210 321 4362).
Metro Omonia. **Open** 3-7.30pm Mon-Sat.
Admission free. **No credit cards. Map** p295 E4.
Athens' premiere *rembetatiko*. Old-timers with suits and cigars shower musicians with flowers, and, when the mood strikes, dance passionately to songs of heartbreak and destitution. Reservations are a must on Friday and Saturday.

Taximi

Harilaou Trikoupi & Isavron 29, Exarchia
(210 363 9919). Metro Omonia, then 15mins walk.
Open *Sept-May* 10pm-2am Wed-Sun. **Admission** free. **No credit cards**.

Most of Greece's greatest *rembetika* musicians have played here, but the atmosphere remains deliciously old-timey, illuminated mostly by red candles and burning cigarettes. The smoke-stained walls are adorned with black and white pictures of the greats.

Folk

To Baraki tou Vasili

Didotou 3, Kolonaki (210 362 3625). Metro
Panepistimio or Syntagma. **Open** 10.30pm-3am daily. **Tickets** €13 (incl one drink). **No credit cards. Map** p297 G3.
A small, cosy venue in a quiet street, run by a music freak who unfailingly introduces performers to audiences. It stages up and coming local acts, both traditional and contemporary, and, less frequently, established artists, too.

The Posh & Becks of Athens

Skiladiko princess Despina Vandi and AEK striker Demis Nikolaidis

They are happy, beautiful and successful. The only thing that differentiates the Greek singer-footballer couple from their British equivalents is that Vandi is still successful in her own right and that Nikolaidis is maybe slightly less talented than Beckham, wears tighter jeans and, for sure, would never wear a headband. Their recent wedding was broadcast live on all TV channels, days before

and after, and when Nikolaidis did a Beckham and moved from his old club AEK Athens to Paris SG in June 2003, the cameras were there – at the airport, in the limousine, at the press conference. The Parisian team, however, was not overly impressed by Nikolaidis's physical condition, and Nikolaidis immediately left for... Atletico Madrid, where he bought a house just next to his role model.

Greek Popular Music

Greek popular music, or **laiko** (literally 'music of the people'), descends from the gritty, Eastern strains of *rembetika* (*see p208*) but morphed, via 1950s lounge singers, plate-smashing nightclubs and an affinity for love songs and glitter, into a one of a kind music (and entertainment) experience that blends the centuries-old bouzouki with the showmanship and big hair of Western pop.

There are different strains of *laiko*, but in the same way that most Western pop can trace its origins to gospel, jazz and blues, Greek popular music owes its beginning to the earthy, almost Middle Eastern sounds of *rembetika*. In the 1950s and '60s, as opulent nightclubs made their appearance in Athens, a few musicians who'd once made their names in *rembetatika* began emerging into this larger, showier world. They replaced the dark lyrics of *rembetika* songs with softer themes of love and longing, accompanied by dazzling, showy bouzouki musicianship. Bigger bands, bigger hair, sparkling costumes and floorshows soon followed. This music, and the clubs that play it, are called **bouzoukia**, after the primary instrument involved.

In the 1960s, *bouzoukia* became famous for over-the-top revelry, with customers breaking plates during songs, and dozens of stories, like the gentleman who paid $100 for a pair of scissors to cut his favourite singer's evening gown into a mini-dress. Much of this attitude prevails in today's *bouzoukia* – though breaking plates has been replaced by throwing flowers. Though all this revelry and consumption may seem like a Western influence, it actually comes from the same deep, dark roots as the music's *rembetika* ancestry: a fatalistic Balkan sensibility that destruction and death may well come tomorrow, so it's best to live it up to the dizzying heights tonight.

In modern Athens, *bouzoukia* fall into a couple of different categories. Though all favour fancy stage-shows, vast consumption of alcohol, liberal spending and thoroughly decked-out performers and clientele, some play a high quality of more traditional Greek music, with old-school singers like Costas Makedonas, Dimitris Bassis, Eleni Tsaligopoulou, Gerasimos Andreatos and Yiannis Kotsiras.

Another branch of *bouzoukia* is heavily mixed with Western, commercial pop – these performances tend to favour laser-light spectacles and catchy tunes that are often made into videos. The kings and queens of this scene

Bouzoukia's best side: **Yiannis Kotsiras**.

are just as likely to perform in tight leather pants and bustiers as in sparkling evening gowns. The ruling divas here are Anna Vissi, Kaiti Garbi and Despina Vandi (*see p210* **The Posh & Becks of Athens**).

The lowest form of *bouzoukia* is called **skiladiko**, literally, 'dog clubs'. These are places where the level of tackiness and ostentation is so high, and the quality of music (and level of décolletage) so low that they attract the lowest class of customer – fascinating if you're into cultural anthropology, but not recommended if you are interested in real *bouzoukia* music. If you want to see this scene, it's best to book a table at one of the clubs (for which you'll also pay for an obligatory meal). Expect the cost of ticket, meal and drinks for a couple to run around €200 – more if you buy flowers to throw at the singer.

But *laiko* isn't confined only to the kitschalicious world of *bouzoukia*. There's also a much less commercial and more sophisticated take on modern Greek music. In the 1960s, when nightclub singers were co-opting *rembetika* and marketing their pop version to the masses, Greece's most celebrated classical composers, Mikis Theodorakis and Manos Hadjidakis (*see p206* **Supergreeks**), combined traditional Greek music with Western-style symphonies, and

Laiko-pop and a fun attitude rule at **Romeo**.

accompanied them with lyrics by major poets, including Nobel Prize winners Odysseus Elytis and George Seferis. These innovative and beautiful pieces are usually performed at Greece's most prestigious venues, as part of high-profile festivals. But what's also important about them is that they laid the groundwork for a new type of *laiko* called **entekno**, meaning 'art music', a sophisticated and more difficult to define sound, found in small clubs and record stores, rather than in *bouzoukia*. *Entekno* still sounds very Greek but is definitely open to various influences, generally more folky and international rather than Western and commercial. *Entekno* artists like Socrates Malamas, Orpheas Peridis and Thanassis Papaconstantinou tend to be deep-digging songwriters rather than straight-out entertainers. But, even so, they can provide

a heady night on the strength of their material and rapport with fans. Shows are usually limited to short runs at clubs with 400-500 capacities, because the acts aim to 'keep it real'.

Venues

Bouzoukia

Apollon
Syngrou 259, Nea Smyrni, Southern Suburbs (210 942 7580). Metro Moschato, then 10mins walk. **Open** noon-9pm. **Tickets** *standing room* €15 (incl one drink); *table for four* €150 (incl alcohol). **Credit** AmEx, DC, V.
One of Athens' most popular venues, showcasing top acts like the Greek take on Britney Spears, Peggy Zina, as well as classic divas like Kaiti Garbi. Expect extravaganza shows with dozens of costume changes, laser light effects and wailing declarations of passion.

Fever
Syngrou & Lagoumitzi, Neos Kosmos, Southern Suburbs (210 921 7333). Metro Neos Kosmos. **Open** *Dec-May* from 10.30pm daily. Open season may vary. **Tickets** *Table for four* €100 (incl alcohol). **Credit** AmEx, DC, V.
Massive space with high-tech stage mechanisms that recently featured the Madonna of Greece, the queen of *skiladiko*, the greatest: Anna Vissi.

Gazi
Ierofanton 1 & Pireos, Rouf (210 347 4477). Metro Thisio, then 10mins walk. **Open** hours vary; call ahead. **Tickets** prices vary. **No credit cards**. **Map** p294 C4.
Quite an industrial-style place to host classical *laiko*, featuring artists such as the king of *laiko* Notis Sfakianakis and up-and-coming stars like Antonis Remos.

Romeo
Kallirois 4, Syngrou (210 922 4885). Metro Syngrou-Fix. **Open** *Box office* 4pm-6am. **Tickets** *Table for four* €120 (incl alcohol). **Credit** AmEx, MC, V.
One of the hottest places for *laiko*-pop. In the summer the club moves to the coastal area and becomes Romeo +, at Ellenikou 1, Glyfada (210 894 5345).

Entekno

Zygos
Kydathinaion 22, Plaka (210 324 1610). Metro Syntagma. **Open** from 11pm Fri, Sat; from 10pm Sun; days vary. **Tickets** €15 (incl one drink); *table for two* €60 (incl alcohol). **No credit cards**. **Map** p299 F6.
This historic venue, one of the few in the city centre, recently came back to the limelight of Athenian *entekno* with shows by one of the biggest names in Greek music, Giorgos Dalaras.

Nightlife

In the city that parties 24/7, style and stamina are prerequisites.

It's no wonder 'hedonism' is a Greek word. The pursuit of pleasure has always been integral to the Greek way of life, and for Athenians in particular nightlife is sacred. It's how city-dwellers keep sane. In the summer bars and clubs are a necessary distraction from the sweltering blanket of heat that descends over the city and offer an escape from the purgatory of sleepless nights. In the winter they fill up with those eager to find a warm refuge to while away the dark, damp nights.

But Athens' style-conscious barflies have got certain standards to uphold. And, with Athenians keen to keep up with their European neighbours, recent years have seen a deluge of unfeasibly swanky bars, trendy clubs and bohemian dens – all served by top home-grown and international DJs. You want it? They've got it. From Bond-era elegance and Manhattan cool to ethnic chill-out and space-age minimalism, the city glows with temptation and the promise of excess.

These nightspots are crammed into the city's crowded fabric, between shops, markets and restaurants. This fundamental lack of space, coupled with the Greek hereditary fondness for gossip, has inadvertently determined the city's nightlife culture. Although no self-respecting venue would ever be without its resident DJs, club (multi-storeyed and writhing with dancing bodies) are outnumbered by DJ bars-cum-clubs. That's not to say Athenians don't like to boogie – anyone who's seen *Zorba the Greek* will know the urge to shake that tush is engrained in the nation's bones – but that, bar the few space-graced places, these vibrant social folk have to content themselves with mere enthusiastic wiggling.

That said, the Greeks are proud of their stamina. They start late, around midnight, and go on all night, every night, with Saturdays being the busiest. And really, not much kicks off until the early hours. But it's worth noting that, in true laid-back Athenian fashion, opening hours are anything but rigid. Places are likely to shut early if they're not busy, or to stay open beyond advertised hours. The only certainty is the hedonistic pursuit of pleasure.

WHERE TO GO

Athens' social scene is largely clustered in areas. Twenty years ago, the winding streets of **Psyrri** were a pocket of iniquity littered with brothels and prowled by the underworld. Tidied and trendied up, these days the area retains only a hint of its illicit past. Still, it's just enough to add a decadent edge to its bar-lined, labyrinthine streets.

Above Psyrri glows the tower of Gazi, within the area of **Rouf**. Gazi was formerly the city's gasworks but has now been converted into an arts centre (*see p108*). Around this imposing structure are secret streets lined with eclectic bohemian gems and all-out boisterous hangouts, which are positively heaving at the weekend.

On the other side of Platia Omonia lies **Exarchia**. Home to anything alternative, this area was (and to some extent still is) the centre for left-wing and radical student-led politics. Although the anarchist bookshops have now made way for pulsating student-friendly nightlife, Naomi Klein's *No Logo* should still make for a great conversation starter. Not so in **Kolonaki**. Lined with more-money-than-sense boutiques, its sloping city-centre streets make up Athens' uptown and are filled with cool and ultra-glamourous, fashionable bars, interspersed with the odd buried, chilled-out den.

The summer months see Athenians decamp en masse to the islands. Those who can't flee head for the suburban beaches of **Glyfada** and **Vouliagmeni** and their sharp-dressing, palm tree-lined superclubs for a heavy dose of glitz to the tune of pounding house and Euro pop.

Acropolis & around

+ Soda

Ermou 161, Thisio (210 384 0205/www.plussoda.com). Metro Thisio. **Open** *Sept-May* midnight-3.30am Thur; midnight-6.30am Fri, Sat. Closed June-Aug. **Admission** Thur €10 (inc drink); Fri, Sat €15 (inc drink) before 1.30am, €20 (inc drink) after 1.30am. **No credit cards. Map** p294 C4.
This ultra-cool superclub, with its industrial vibe, plays host to a weekly roster of international guest DJs. The lithe, fetish-dressed podium dancers gyrate to the strains of hard, spiritual and progressive house, and the young mixed crowds follow suit until dawn. Between June and August, the club operates from its Glyfada base on the site of the old airport.

Inoteka

Platia Avyssinias 3, Monastiraki (210 324 6446). Metro Monastiraki. **Open** 8pm-6am daily. **Admission** free. **No credit cards. Map** p295 D5.

Set in the middle of Athens' antiques market, this shadowy, minimalist beacon offers electropop, scuzzy leftfield beats and dirty house to an inspiring crowd. The outdoor tables, set away from the frazzled basslines, offer a good alternative to the traditional quiet drink.

Interni

Ermou 152, Thisio (210 346 8900). Metro Thisio. **Open** 8.30pm-4am daily. Closed July-Aug, except 2004. **Admission** free Mon, Tue, Thur-Sun; €20 (inc 1 drink) Wed. **Credit** AmEx, DC, MC, V. **Map** p294 C4.

Stylishly minimalist, this designer bar-cum-club (with a summer sister club on Mykonos) is the epitome of 21st-century glamour. Perch on the leather bean bags and couches that fill the ground floor and enjoy fabulous cocktails in the lux, Bond-esque surroundings. As the night wears on and the spacious room fills, DJs crank up the house, R&B and ethnic lounge music. On Wednesdays, Interni hosts Bootycall, a popular R&B and soul club night.

Stavlos

Iraklidon 10, Thisio (210 346 7206). Metro Thisio. **Open** 9am-3am daily. **Admission** free. **Credit** AmEx, MC, V. **Map** p294 C5.

With its tree-lined courtyard and clientele of local artists, Stavlos oozes creative cool. Soft strains of funk, soul and jazz add to the smooth ambience, but as the sun sets the mood pricks up as DJs spin anything from house and electropop through to drum 'n' bass and retro classics. Particularly nice on a lazy Sunday.

Historic centre

Aiolis

Eolou 23 (210 331 2839). Metro Monastiraki. **Open** 10.30am-1am Mon-Wed, Sun; 10.30am-3am Thur-Sat. **Admission** free. **No credit cards. Map** p295 E5.

Open all day, this arty joint, offering a good selection of wines, welcomes sophisticated, trendy crowds of all ages to recharge their batteries in its warm, wooden atmosphere. Chilled-out freestyle electro, reggae and R&B sounds drift gently from the bar's speakers, while smart bamboo blinds keep the lighting soft and inviting.

Bar Guru Bar

10 Platia Theatrou (210 324 6530). Metro Omonia. **Open** 9.30pm-3.30am daily. Closed 14 June-30 Sept. **Admission** free, though special events may incur an entrance fee of up to €30 for the top-floor club. **Credit** AmEx, MC, V. **Map** p295 D4.

This lively and amiable bar-cum-club is run with a passion that is contagious. A mixed crowd of young, funky folk and VIPs flocks here to party in the fun, oriental-themed atmosphere, where the music – '70s soul to grizzled house and R&B – is as bright as the vibe. Scattered with cushions, the first floor is a great chill-out zone, offering the perfect retreat from the intimate dancefloor upstairs.

Kolonaki & around

Balia

Haritos 43, Kolonaki (210 723 3019). Metro Evangelismos. **Open** 9pm-3.30am daily. **Admission** free. **No credit cards. Map** p297 H4.

Sleek, stylish and red all over, this funky little bar with a disco vibe is like sitting in a tube of Chanel lipstick. Balia is busiest in the summer, when the preppy crowd spills out on to the pedestrianised street to mingle with those from neighbouring bars.

Balthazar

Tsocha 27, Ambelokipi (210 641 2300). Metro Ambelokipi. **Open** 9.30pm-4.30am daily. **Admission** free. **Credit** AmEx, V.

Now into its third decade, Balthazar is where the fashionable and well-heeled go to show off and enjoy cocktails in the smart, island-esque courtyard. New R&B nights add a much-needed zing to this Athenian old faithful.

Briki

Dorilaiou 6, Platia Mavili, Kolonaki (210 645 2380). Metro Megaro Mousikis. **Open** Sept-July 9am-3.30am daily. Closed Aug. **Admission** free. **No credit cards.**

There's an infectious laid-back vibe to this intimate dive, a cross between arty and kitsch. A mixture of eclectic tunes from funk and acid jazz to R&B and rock keeps the atmosphere warm, while Briki's killer air-con system ensures no-sweat chilling.

City

Haritos 43, Kolonaki (210 722 8910). Metro Evangelismos. **Open** 9pm-4am daily. **Admission** free. **No credit cards. Map** p297 H4.

With metallic columns propping up the ceiling and decadent red walls, there's more than a little *Bright Lights, Big City* vibe to this smart bar. The music – soft strains of disco, R&B and the poppier side of house – plays second fiddle to chattering voices, which is just how the label brigade who flocks to City to catch up and chat up likes it.

Decadence

Voulgaroktonou 69 & Poulxerias, Strefi Hill, Exarchia (210 882 3544). Metro Ambelokipi. **Open** 10.30pm-4am daily. **Admission** €6 (inc 1 drink) Mon-Thur, Sun; €8 (inc 1 drink) Fri, Sat. **No credit cards.**

A student crowd crams itself into Decadence's two levels (bar on the ground floor, pumping club above) for a fix of thrashing and moshing to the club's searing alternative-rock offerings.

En Delphis

Delphon 5, Kolonaki (210 360 8269). Metro Panepistimio. **Open** 8pm-4am daily. **Admission** free. **No credit cards. Map** p297 G3.

Seemingly inspired by the movie *Boogie Nights*, this spacious, stylish bar is heavy on '70s decor, all chrome, wood and bold patterns. A soundtrack of chart pop and house beats draws a sassy crowd to

Sophisticated **Soul**. *See p222*.

En Delphis. In the upstairs room you'll find plenty of quiet lounging space on the soft red seats and window-side benches.

Galaxy
Athens Hilton, Leof Vas Sofias 46, Kolonaki (210 728 1000). Metro Evangelismos. **Open** 8pm-3am Mon-Thur, Sun; 6pm-4am Fri, Sat. **Admission** free. **Credit** AmEx, DC, MC, V. **Map** p297 J5.
Situated on the top floor of the newly renovated Athens Hilton (*see p63*), this impossibly chic, classic lounge bar is one of the best places to catch the pink Athenian sunset. Decorated with one eye on the '60s and the other firmly on the 21st century, it's easy to feel underdressed in anything other than Gucci – though, thankfully, anything goes. However, the spectacular views, including a bird's-eye take on the Acropolis, come at a price as drinks are on the expensive side. But hey, you get what you pay for. And that includes cocktails.

Jackson Hall
Milioni 4, Kolonaki (210 361 6546). Metro Panepistimio. **Open** noon-3am daily. **Admission** free. **No credit cards. Map** p297G4.
With its walls covered in sports memorabilia and tacky trinkets, Jackson Hall has a whiff of the theme bar about it. But, despite the decor, situated as it is on this stylish Kolonaki pedestrian thoroughfare two doors down from Armani, it's popular with a smart, older set. This is the place to people-watch at the outdoor tables, serenaded by R&B and smooth pop.

Mo Better Club
Themistokleous & Koletti 32, Exarchia (210 381 2981/www.mobetter.gr). Metro Omonia. **Open** 10pm-4am Tue-Sun. **Admission** free. **No credit cards. Map** p295 F2.
For 14 years this cosy, space-age club (think *Barbarella* crossed with *Austin Powers*) has been seducing a young student crowd with its pumping

EVERYWHERE

MYTHOS LAGER BEER

For DJ talent

+ **Soda** (*see p213*) offers a weekly roster of international DJs, as well as featuring plenty of hot home-spun talent. Alternatively, visit the throbbing **Free Your Base** (*see p221*).

For feeling richer than you are

Air those Manolos at either the über-stylish **Privilege** (*see p222*) or **Destijl** (*see p223*), at the seaside.

For glamour

The sleek, glossy interior and million-dollar views at **Galaxy** (*see p215*) are hard to beat for that glamourous feel, though the stylish minimalism of **Interni** (*see p214*) runs a close second.

For going solo

Small and friendly, **Skoufaki** (*see below*) and **Tribeca** (*see p219*) across the road, are both very welcoming, as is **Aiolis** (*see p214*).

For a house-party feel

Fun and funky, both **Mommy** (*see below*) and **Tribeca** (*see p219*) ooze with that all-important home comfort.

For an intimate experience

The laid-back vibe of **Briki** (*see p214*) is perfect for breaking the ice, but if it's hushed sophistication you want, visit Psyrri's **Bar Aspro** (*see p219*).

For outdoor schmoozing

Visit the new swanky garden at **Soul** (*see p222*), or for a more chilled-out experience head for **Nipiagogio** (*see p221*).

For a quiet one

Sip wine at **Aiolis** (*see p214*) or visit **Stavlos** (*see p214*) for a laid-back Sunday at the foot of the Acropolis.

For rubbing shoulders with the in-crowd

Head out to **Mamacas** (*see p221*), heaving with Athens' wheelers and dealers, or check out **Balthazar** (*see p214*) for a dose of old-school chic.

For shiny happy people

Lounge about on cushions in the Thai-themed **Bar Guru Bar** (*see p214*), or sip a warming *rakomelo* in the inviting lo-fi atmosphere of **I Psyrra** (*see p221*).

---

mix of alternative rock, hip hop and electronica. Wednesday nights are marginally more mellow, with soulful funk sliding off the decks.

Mommy

Delphon 4, Kolonaki (210 361 9682). Metro Panepistimio. **Open** mid Sept-June noon-4am daily. Closed July-mid Sept. **Admission** free. **Credit** MC, V. **Map** p297 G3.

Step through Mommy's enormous doors and you step into a glorious, 1960s-inspired cartoon world. Coolly boisterous and very popular, this trendy club is set out like a house. Each room has its own theme, from the OTT kitchen decked out in kitsch accessories to the plush low sofas, Afghan rugs and oversized lamps in the lounge. Trendsetters mingle with sharp-dressing Polo and Hilfiger types as DJs spin a spectrum of tunes from frazzled electro to soulful R&B and joyous pumping house.

Palenque Club

Farandaton 41, Platia Agiou Thomas, Ambelokipi (210 775 2360). Metro Ambelokipi. **Open** 9.30pm-3.30am daily. **Admission** €10 (inc 1 drink). **No credit cards.**

Need to work on your tango? Then worry not, as Athens' premier Latin club offers early-evening dance lessons (9-11pm) for those who need to limber up and get their hips swaying. The hot, Latin rhythms (sambas and tangos through to bossa nova, Cuban jazz and funk) flow as freely as the luscious Mojitos here.

Rock 'n' Roll

Lioukianou 6, Kolonaki (210 721 7127). Metro Evangelismos. **Open** Oct-Apr 9pm-5am Tue-Sat; 9-11pm Sun. Closed May-Sept. **Admission** free. **No credit cards. Map** p297 H4.

Typical of Kolonaki's sleek environs, this DJ bar serves a style-conscious crowd nuggets of electro, house and pop in a comfortable setting. There's even a little dancefloor here, for those in the mood for wiggling their tush.

Skoufaki Café

Skoufa 47-9, Kolonaki (210 364 5888). Metro Panepistimio. **Open** 10am-4am Mon-Sat; noon-4am Sun. **Admission** free. **No credit cards. Map** p297 G4.

There's a bright Mexican-cantina look about this laid-back bar – from its orange walls peppered with Inca-inspired paint patterns to the funky Latino-spiked lounge, jazz and pop tunes that colour the place. Popular with a twentysomething, bohemian crowd, Skoufaki makes for a pleasant stopover all day (and night) long.

Arts & Entertainment

Island. See p223.

Tribeca

Skoufa 46, Kolonaki (210 362 3541). Metro
Panepistimio. **Open** 10am-3am Mon-Thur, Sun;
10pm-4am Fri, Sat. **Admission** free. **No credit**
cards. Map p297 G4.

There's a distinctly Manhattan feel to this, newish
incredibly hip bar, which is akin to a minimalist living room. Young and energetic go-for-it crowds, and
the odd VIP, pile into the small indoor space to jig-
gle (and on occasion sing) along to a rainbow of alternative pop tunes; expect White Stripes, Joy Division,
Red Hot Chili Peppers and Talking Heads. The side-
walk tables are quieter, but crackle with the same
swish atmosphere.

Wunderbar

Themistokleous 80, Exarchia (210 381 8577).
Metro Omonia. **Open** 10am-3.30am daily.
Admission free. **No credit cards.**

During the day, stylish young Athenians flock to the
Wunderbar to splay out on its loud, rainbow-bright
sofas (*see p159*). After dark they squeeze into this
café/mini club, for a dose of equally loud electro-
clash, techno and everything in between.

North of the Acropolis

Astron

Taki 3, Psyrri (no phone). Metro Monastiraki.
Open 9.30pm-4am daily. **Admission** free.
No credit cards. Map p295 D4.

House and pounding alternative pop blare away in
this small, dark rabbit warren of a club. A year-
round hotspot (quite literally so in the summer
months), it's often filled to bursting point, with its
young crowd spilling out on to the narrow street.
Ironic glowing photos of sunsets set in fluffy frames
lighten up the heady atmosphere.

Bar Aspro

Aristofanous 4, Platia Psyrri, Psyrri (210 331 3218).
Metro Monastiraki. **Open** 8.30pm-3.30am Mon-Thur,
Sun; 8.30pm-6am Fri, Sat. **Admission** free.
No credit cards. Map p295 D4.

Aspro (meaning 'white') by name and by nature, this
sleek wine bar showcases art on its virginal walls.
Its soothing (and very flattering) lights and sultry
strains of funky soul, jazz and Latin music at a con-
versation-friendly volume make this a relaxed setting for a long drink.

Bee

Miaouli 6, Psyrri (210 321 2624). Metro
Monastiraki. **Open** noon-3am Mon-Wed, Sun;
noon-5am Thur-Sat. **Admission** free.
No credit cards. Map p295 E4.

With a penchant for spoon chandeliers and cheesy
sunset backdrops, this whitewashed, gay-friendly
bar welcomes a smart, thirtysomething crowd to
mingle and schmooze to lounge and smooth R&B
music. Come the weekend, the vibe steps up a level
as DJs opt for house and upbeat R&B.

FREE2GO Club22
TELESTET

Meet the most successful club in town in one of Athens central avenues. At the beginning of Vouliagmenis Avenue (near the Panathenaic Stadium and Temple of Olympian Zeus), FREE2GO Club22 has created its own tradition by throwing the most successful parties in daily basis.

The best
club in Athens

A different theme party is happening every night at FREE2GO Club22. The club's resident djs along with the guest (Greek and foreigners) play the greatest music hits of all kinds and all times making us dance all night long.

Apart from clubbing in FREE2GO Club22 you can attend multi cultural events such as concerts, stand up comedy shows and theatre performances.

22 vouliagmenis ave.   tel: 210 9249814   www.club22.gr   info@club22.gr

Adulterated drinking

Sightseeing? Check. Shopping? Check. Siesta? Check? Right. Now all that's left to do is let your hair down. But don't let it down too far. There's particular reason to keep your wits about you here: some of Athens' drinking dens seem to have adopted a rather bad habit of late – adulterated alcohol.

Lined up behind the shiny bar, those familiar branded bottles of whisky, vodka – whatever – may not be exactly what they claim to be. In a bid to save a few pennies, some venues have taken to diluting their spirits with illegally imported rough – and potent – alcohol. Known by Athenians as *bombes*, these unpure shots can be potentially lethal in large enough doses. Down a few and your tastebuds will hardly notice. But your head (and liver) will most certainly know about it.

Although this underhand practice is not widespread, it is worth being aware of it. To avoid your drink being spiked, your best bet (as always) is to do as the locals. If everyone is drinking bottled beer – there's a reason.

Bios Pireos 84

Pireos 84, Metaxourgio (210 342 5335). Metro Metaxourgio. **Open** 11am-4am daily. **Admission** free. **No credit cards.** Map p294 C2.
Situated among artists' studios, the atmosphere in this massive warehouse space is one of cutting-edge creativity. Regularly hosting exhibitions, Bios is frequented by artists, their art is projected on to the spartan concrete walls and even the tables (functional art) are for sale. Strains of house, dance, electro, avant-garde noise and trippy chill-out, ooze or blare, depending on the DJs' mood, throughout the day and into the night.

Free Your Base

Ermou & Avliton 6-8, Psyrri (no phone). Metro Monastiraki. **Open** Oct-May 10.30pm-4am daily. Closed June-Sept. **Admission** free. **No credit cards.** Map p295 D4.
This throbbing, womb-like club rattles with progressive house and techno, warmed up with the odd bout of hip hop. While ferocious bongo-players prop up the DJs downstairs, seek refuge from the club's pulsing intensity in the upstairs harem-like booths, sumptuously scattered with pillows.

Gazaki

Triptolemou 31, Rouf (210 346 0901). Metro Thisio. **Open** 9pm-4am Mon-Thur, Sun; 9pm-5am Fri, Sat. **Admission** free. **No credit cards.** Map p294 B4.
Decorated in rustic reds and ethnic prints, Gazaki brims with bohemian charm. The tunes here are eclectic – just like the savvy crowds who flock to this gregarious, yet relaxed, club. Come the weekend, the place is as bustling as a Moroccan market.

I Psyrra

Miaouli 19, Psyrri (210 324 4046). Metro Monastiraki. **Open** 3pm-5am daily. **Admission** free. **No credit cards.** Map p295 E4.
Run by a lovely woman called Agape (or 'Love'), and haphazardly decorated with kitsch 1950s bric-a-brac and odd ends from the neighbouring market, I Psyrra (meaning 'the midge') is a tiny and wonderfully relaxed bar. A hip, studenty crowd spills out on to the pavement to sip *rakomelo* (a traditional island hot toddy spiced with cinnamon) and chill to the funky indie vibes.

Mamacas

Persefonis 41, Gazi, Rouf (210 346 4984/www. mamacas.gr). Metro Thisio. **Open** 2pm-4am daily. **Admission** free. **No credit cards.** Map p294 B4.
Mamacas (meaning 'mother's') is quiet and civilised throughout the afternoon and early evening. But as the night wears on, the atmospheric island-vibed nightspot teems with Athenians primed for a long night out. As the DJ spins a selection of techno, trance and Euro pop, the venue's roof pulls back to reveal the starry night sky – for that true summer sensation.

Micraasia Lounge

Konstantinoupoleos 70, Rouf (210 346 3851). Metro Thisio, then 10mins walk. **Open** 7pm-4am daily. **Admission** €12-€15. **No credit cards.** Map p294 B4.
Popular with a more mature clientele, this smart, bar-lounge is a carefully executed culture clash. Exotic sounds complement the lush East-meets-West surroundings.

Nipiagogio

Elasidon & Kleanthous 8, Gazi, Rouf (210 345 8534). Metro Thisio, then 10mins walk. **Open** 10pm-3.30am daily. **Admission** free. **No credit cards.** Map p294 B4.
Set in an old kindergarten, Nipiagogio (or 'kindergarten') retains the kind of fun, carefree vibe synonymous with finger painting. Silhouetted kiddie designs line the walls, stained-glass flowers spruce up the place and the chill-out lounge is decorated with animal prints. A small dancefloor at the top end of the room is packed with a friendly bunch of twenty- to thirtysomethings who relive their childhood – well, sort of – to lively house, '80s hits and retro classics. A dream-like walled garden, lit with fairy lights and floating, light-air balloons, acts as a second chillout room, where the specially selected soothing tunes just about colour the air.

Tribes

In daylight, as its bustling swarms scurry from A to B, Athens resembles an anthill at rush hour. But as the sun sets, the city is transformed and – refreshed after the siesta – far more exotic beasts crawl out of the ancient woodwork. These days, Athens is inhabited by three very distinctive tribes. Though difficult to spot in the city's frantic daily grind, they reveal themselves at night when they flock to the city's watering holes.

The first and most prevalent of these tribes is the **label brigade**. Like Africa's elegant gazelles, both male and female of the species are impeccably turned out. Styled by the likes of Klein, Hilfiger and other purveyors of preppy chic, they fill the stylish streets of Kolonaki and congregate around Haritos like sophisticated clones. On occasion, they are also known to venture out as far as **Mamacas** (*see p221*) in Gazi, while the truly exclusive don Manolos and Armani to roam the glossy realm of **Privilege** (*see p222*).

The second tribe – the smallest – includes the peacocks of Athens clubland. Intensely proud of their individuality, these trendsetters

would rather pluck out each hair on their gel-set mini-mohican than be spotted sporting the same asymmetrical '80s accessory. They are a creative mash of influences that change their fashion inspiration as often as they change their socks and can be found ruffling their feathers at the likes of **Mommy** (*see p217*), **+ Soda** (*see p213*) and in the arty circles of **Bios Pireos 84** (*see p221*).

The remaining night stalkers are remarkable for their sense of relaxed urban cool. These casual meerkats try much less hard than the other species, and tend to be the youngsters on the scene. Clad in mostly denim, less of their energy is spent posing (a defining characteristic of both other tribes) and is reserved instead for boisterous social bonding. This amicable lot is found scattered around **I Psyrra** (see *p221*), lining the pavements outside **Astron** (*see p219*) and wiggling away in **Nipiagogio** (*see p221*).

Yet, however definitive these Athenian groups may seem, inter-tribe mingling is widespread. Athens' nightlife is on the whole a welcoming place – open and accepting – whatever you wear.

Privilege

Agias Eleousis & Kakourgodikiou,, Psyrri (210 331 7801). Metro Monastiraki. **Open** *end Sept-May* midnight-3.30am Thur; midnight-6.30am Fri, Sat. Closed June-late Sept. **Admission** Thur €10 (inc drink); Fri, Sat €15 (inc drink) before 1.30am, €20 (inc drink) after 1.30am. **No credit cards**. **Map** p295 E4.

If you've got a beard, forget it. Rigidly face-policed, this is one of Athens' most exclusive watering holes. The chart-pop superclub is awash with shiny surfaces and boudoir-style VIP rooms, where a mixed crowd of beautiful and/or rich and/or famous Athenians dress up to watch each other make like models and sip cocktails.

So Bar

Persefonis 23, Rouf (210 341 7774). Metro Thisio, then 10mins walk. **Open** 10pm-4am Tue-Sun. **Admission** free. **No credit cards**. **Map** p294 B4.

Situated directly opposite the converted gasworks that give the area of Gazi its name, So Bar is a gloriously intense experience – only funky-coloured lights brighten up the utilitarian darkness of this industrial-themed bar. Pounding progressive house and electro are the order of the day and, come Saturday night, the long narrow room is

packed to bursting point. But, when it all gets too much, the assembled students and trendy twentysomethings retreat to the outside tables for a breather.

Soul

Evripidou 65, Psyrri (210 331 0907). Metro Monastiraki. **Open** 9pm-4am daily. **Admission** free. **No credit cards**. **Map** p295 E4.

This sophisticated and über-smart bar is incredibly popular with just about everyone, mainly owing to its new island-inspired garden. But, thankfully, there's plenty of space for all; either standing under the swaying banana trees or scattered on cushions beneath the bamboo shelter. Things at the stylish inside bar are more of a squeeze, but the breezy blend of chart pop, hip hop, R&B and house helps to keep the mood chipper.

Athens Suburbs

Bo

Karamanli 14, Voula, Southern Suburbs (210 895 9645). **Open** 10pm-5am daily. **Admission** €10 (inc 1 drink) Mon-Fri, Sun; €15 (inc 1 drink) Sat. **Credit** AmEx, DC, MC, V.

With tables that spill on to the beach and a distinctly tropical bar on the upper levels, this summer superclub overflows with a slinky island vibe and draws a very swish, mixed crowd. As tunes go, '80s hits and, as is quite common on the big seaside nightspots, a small dose of Greek pop rule.

Destijl

Karamanli 4, Voula, Southern Suburbs
(210 895 2403). **Open** *Apr-Sept* 10.30pm-5am daily. Closed Oct-Mar. **Admission** €7 Mon-Thur, Sun; €10 Fri-Sat. **Credit** V.
Although undeniably elegant, Destijl's pink and white colour scheme does lend the place a bit of a seashell feel. With a vigilant door policy – and with drinks erring on the expensive side – this is where the bold and beautiful twenty- to thirtysomethings flock for their fix of mainstream hits and Greek pop. Be sure to brush up if you want to get in.

Island

Limanakia Vouliagmeni, Vouliagmeni,
Southern Suburbs (210 965 3563). **Open** 9pm-4am daily May-Sept. **Admission** €3 Fri, Sat.
Credit AmEx, MC, V.
With its setting overlooking the Saronic Gulf, there's a distinctly Aegean feel to this slinky outdoor club. Its soft decor and enchanting sea view make Island a lush spot for a romantic night out, where ethnic beats, house and disco woo a fashionable, mixed crowd. Drink prices are a tad steep.

Moonshine

A Papandreou 15, Glyfada, Southern Suburbs
(210 968 0775). **Open** 9.30-3.30am Mon-Sat; 11-3am Sun. **Admission** free. **No credit cards**.
Surrounded by palm trees and cacti, and fuelled by funk, soul and indie rock, this relaxed and friendly, intimate crowd-puller is ideal for a warm-up drink – though the mighty fine Margaritas could well extend your stay.

Skipper's

Pier 1, Kalamaki Marina, Kalamaki,
Southern Suburbs (no phone). **Open** 9pm-4am daily. **Admission** free. **No credit cards**.
You can spot Skipper's a mile off. Built to resemble the deck of a large ocean liner, its tall protruding mast is strung with fairy lights and glows like a naked Christmas tree on the skyline. Get there early on Fridays and Saturdays to bag a seat on the impressive deck. The music, ranging from flamenco and salsa to trip hop, attracts a more mature pack.

Piraeus

L'Action Folie

Ath Dilaveri 9-11, Mikrolimano (210 417 4325).
Metro Piraeus. **Open** 9am-5am daily. **Admission** €3.
No credit cards.
Perched on the Piraeus seafront, this dimly lit, cosy café-bar is a perfect people-watching base from which to observe the port's raucous bar-hoppers trooping past. The music here (mainstream chart pop) isn't terribly inspired, but the warm, friendly atmosphere more than makes up for it.

L'Action Folie.

Sport & Fitness

Trekking up the Acropolis is not the only sporting activity in Athens.

When it comes to sport in Athens, the Olympics (*see chapter* **Athens 2004**) have, reasonably enough, received a lot attention. But there's more to the city's sporting landscape than those 17 days in August 2004. While perhaps not having the range of public sporting facilities of its northern European counterparts, Athens does offer plenty of ways to break a sweat, and that's quite aside from its watersports.

For those who prefer to experience sport from the comfort of a grandstand seat, this metropolis also boasts more participants in both basketball's Euroleague competition and football's Champions League than any other European city. So, Olympics or no, let the games commence.

Spectator sports

Visit any Athens newsagents and you'll find an array of daily sports newspapers providing colourful testament to the importance of basketball and, particularly, club football in Greek life. And with the big three clubs – **Olympiacos**, **AEK** and **Panathinaikos** – all competing at the highest European level in both sports, Athens fans have never had it so good.

But there is a blot on the spectating landscape: during the preparations for the 2004 Olympics, many teams will be forced to play in smaller temporary accommodation while their usual homes are upgraded for use in the Games. As a consequence, where previously tickets had been easy to come by on the day of all but the biggest games (the Greeks are a nation of armchair fans), the limited number of seats in the new venues will make buying in advance during this transitory time a good idea. At the time of writing there were no confirmed dates for teams to return to their done-up home grounds, but when they do, tickets purchases shouldn't present the same problem and spectators will benefit from new, loftier stands.

Football

Athens and neighbouring Piraeus are home to ten of the 16 teams in Greek football's top flight (A'Ethniki Katigoria) in 2003/4. But, although Nea Smyrni-based minnows Panionios finished an impressive fifth in 2002/3, it's Olympiacos, Panathinaikos and AEK that tend to grab both the attention and the top spots.

Of the big three, **Olympiacos** are the strongest – Greece's most popular side have won seven consecutive league titles between 1997 and 2003. But they were given a close run in 2002/3 by **Panathinaikos**, only overcoming the all-greens on the nail-biting final day of the season. Off the field, **AEK** have suffered from a precarious financial position and ground-sharing problems, but their success in getting through a tricky qualifying round to join Olympiacos and Panathinaikos in the 2003/4 Champions' League group stages proved that, on the pitch at least, the future looks healthy.

Meanwhile, the Greek national team pipped Spain to the top of the qualification group for Euro 2004 – their first appearance in the European Championships since 1980.

AEK
210 822 4666/www.aekfc.gr.
Following the demolition of their Nikos Goumas home (Kappadokias 2, Nea Filadelfia, Northern Suburbs), AEK have been ground-sharing with other local teams, including Panathinaikos. The arrangements have not gone too smoothly, however, and at one point in late 2003 AEK found themselves homeless.

Olympiacos
Zea Marina, Piraeus (210 414 3000/ www.olympiacos.org).
Olympiacos's usual home in Piraeus – Karaiskaki Stadium (nearest metro Faliro) – is being upgraded for use in the Olympic football tournament. Until then, the team will relocate and will play at the 21,000-capacity Georgios Kamaras Stadium (Leof Vas Iraklio 119, Rizoupoli, Northern Suburbs, nearest metro Perissos).

Panathinaikos
Irodou Attikou 12A, Historic Centre (210 8093630/ www.pao.gr).
After 16 years of self-imposed exile at the Olympic Stadium, Panathinaikos returned to the Apostolos Nikolaidis Stadium (Leof Vas Alexandras 160, Ambelokipi, nearest metro Ambelokipi) in 2000. However, since it's impossible to enlarge this historic downtown stadium from its 16,600 capacity, plans are afoot to move to a new ground within the next few years.

Foul play

'This is the last straw,' fumed Greek Sports Minister George Lianis in March 2003, 'things have gone far enough.' He was speaking after Olympiacos supporters attacked senior AEK officials in the VIP area during the half-time of an Athens derby between the two rivals.

Hooliganism has been a problem for almost as long as the Greek game has existed, and teams are frequently forced to play games in neutral stadia or behind closed doors as punishment for their fans' misdemeanours. Indeed, even after Lianis promised to implement measures to combat the violence, the 2003/4 season began with hundreds of AEK and Iraklis supporters throwing seats at each other during a September 2003 match.

But don't let that put you off. While passions, and tempers, do run high at Greek football matches – particularly at derby games between the big three teams (AEK, Panathinaikos and Olympiacos) – experiencing that intensity is a heady thing. We've seen people punching the wall until their hands bleed when their team concedes a goal, and the atmosphere is big, loud and tense, with fireworks and all.

Avoiding trouble isn't prohibitively difficult at any of Athens' ten top-flight clubs. If you speak Greek (or can find an English-speaking official), ask where the quiet part of the ground is. If not, your best bet is to look at the kind of people going through the turnstiles – families, naturally, tend to stick to the mellower sections, while the areas attracting tough young men armed with banners and attitudes are best avoided. Either way, expect the fierce policemen on the gate to confiscate anything remotely resembling a weapon – even an excess of coins is frowned upon.

Once inside, you'll see many people sitting on thin squares of polystyrene – bought from vendors outside and usually skimmed towards the pitch at the end. Some grounds sell alcohol, though most fans keep themselves charged up with coffee, pistachios and flailing outbursts at the referee. You might not understand much of what they're shouting (the word *malaka*, loosely meaning 'wanker', crops up a lot), but at least one word is universal – the Greek for offside is, handily, offside.

Basketball

Basketball has become increasingly popular in Greece since the men's national team won the European Championship title in 1987. Most of the teams in the top division of the national league are linked to football clubs and the trinity of **Olympiacos**, **Panathinaikos** and **AEK** dominates here too. But, where Olympiacos set the standard in football, Panathinaikos are the team to beat in basketball – they won the Greek league and cup double in 2003 to add to their European club championship success in 2002.

AEK

Meandrou 83 & Filadianon, Nea Filadelfia,
Northern Suburbs (210 252 3003/www.aekbc.gr).
AEK usually play in the 18,700-capacity Olympic Sports Hall (Leof Kifisias 37 & Spiros Louis, 210 683 4060, www.sportsnet.gr/main_en.html, nearest metro Irini), which is being upgraded for use as a basketball and gymnastics venue for the Olympics. Until then, they're playing in the 2,500-capacity Zofria Indoor Hall (Dionysou 17, Nea Liosia, Northern Suburbs, bus A12).

Olympiacos

Zea Marina, Piraeus (210 414 3000/
www.olympiacos.org).
Olympiacos's usual home in Piraeus, the impressive 15,000-capacity Peace & Friendship Stadium (Leof Posidonos, Faliro, nearest metro Faliro) is currently being upgraded for use as the Olympic volleyball venue. Until then, catch the team at the 2,200-capacity Korydallos Indoor Hall (Plataion 3, Korydallos, Western Athens, bus A17).

Panathinaikos

Leof Kifisias 38, Paradisos Amarousios,
Northern Suburbs (210 610 7160/www.paobc.gr).
Like AEK, the all-greens usually play in the Olympic Sports Hall (*see above*). While it gets upgraded, they'll be shooting hoops in the 1,800-capacity Sporting Indoor Hall in Patisia (Ilia Zervou 58, Patisia, Northern Suburbs, nearest metro Aghios Eleftherios).

Sporting activities

Bungee jumping

Liquid Bungee

Halkida Bridge, Evvia Island, 60km (37 miles)
north-east of Athens (210 970 4435/mobile 6937
615 191/www.bungee.gr). Trains from Larissa
station. In spring, Liquid Bungee organises its own
bus to the site. Call for more details. **Open** *Apr-Oct*
11am-5pm Sun. Closed Aug, Nov-Mar. **Rates**
€40 per jump. **No credit cards.**
The folks at Liquid Bungee were the first to offer organised bungee jumping in Greece – they've been

helping adrenaline-rush addicts jump off Halkida Bridge since 1993. Jumps cost €40 (that's €1 for every metre you fall), and that includes a certificate and 24 photos of the breathtaking event.

Gyms

Joe Weider Gym

Leof Vouliagmenis 366, Ilioupoli, Eastern Suburbs
(210 991 0731/www.joeweider.gr). Metro Dafni,
then bus A3, B3 or 171. **Open** 24 hours from 6am
Mon-10pm Sat; 10am-10pm Sun. **Membership**
€10 per day. **Credit** AmEx, DC, MC, V.
The Joe Weider Company has nine gyms dotted throughout Athens, the most central of which is in Ilioupoli (for other locations visit www.joeweider.gr, which, at the time of writing, was planning to put an English-language section up soon). The gyms are clean and airy, with a good range of up-to-date equipment, aerobics classes and a sauna. All welcome day guests and are open 24 hours a day (except on Sundays).

Mini soccer

Mini-soccer fields have been sprouting up all around Athens recently, attracting mostly

men and a few women, who proudly don the kit of their favourite teams and head on to the synthetic pitches in teams of between five and eight. Pitches can be booked at a cost of around €60-€80 per hour. So, should you and your friends fancy a kick-about, call one of the numbers listed below and book yourselves a game. Just so long as there's enough of you to form one team, the people in charge should be able to organise some opposition.

Paradise

Metamorfoseos 100, Agios Sotiras, Acharnes, Northern Suburbs (210 246 6466). Bus A9. **Rates** €60 for 1hr 15mins. **No credit cards**.

Protasof Club

Kapodistriou 2 & Marathonomachon, Cheroma, Vari, Southern Suburbs (210 9653 400). Metro Dafni, then bus 171. **Rates** €60 per hr. **No credit cards**.

Running

The old Panathenaic Stadium (*see p110*) is popular with joggers, who either use the track on the surrounding hill or run up and down the marble stadium's steps. The National Gardens are a reasonable central option, though they can often be people- and pushchair-choked. If you prefer a more sociable jogging experience, try going out with the Athens branch of the Hash House Harriers. Entirely non-competitive and requiring no level of fitness, the ad-hoc group meets weekly at 7pm on Mondays during summer and 11am on Sundays in winter. An hour's run or walk around town or into the surrounding hills is followed by a taverna meal and drinks – this is as much about socialising as exercising. Visitors are welcome; you can often cadge a lift from a metro station. Contact Brian Kirman on 69 4 696 9154 (mobile), visit the Harriers' website (www.athenshash.com) or look for listings in the *Athens News*.

Scuba diving

For more watersports, *see p117* **Beaches**.

Dive Adventures

Damareos 43, Pangrati, Eastern Suburbs (210 756 0552). Trolleybus 2. **Open** call for details. **Rates** €40-€70 per dive; €100 for two dives. **Credit** AmEx, DC, MC, V.
This specialist company organises diving excursions

Athens Hilton. *See p228.*

both in Attica and the nearby islands. Participants must hold a diving certificate. Equipment provided.

Vythos

Leof Eleftheriou Venizelou 56, Nea Smyrni, Southern Suburbs (210 933 3260/mobile 654 0254/ www.vithos.com). Bus 110. **Open** 8am-3pm Mon, Wed, Sat; 5-9pm Tue, Thur, Fri. Closed Sun. **Rates** from €25. **Credit** AmEx, DC, MC, V.

As well as organising classes for beginners, Vythos operates experienced divers' excursions around the coast of Attica. The cost ranges from €25 to €40 for short dives, depending on the equipment needed, while the two- to three-week courses start at €240.

Swimming

Summertime in central Athens can be sweltering, so it's nice to know that there are plenty of pools open to the public where you can cool off. Though hotel pools are rather pricey, you may find them preferable to their municipal counterparts owing to the excessive admission bureaucracy of the latter.

Athens Hilton

Leof Vas Sofias 46, Kolonaki (210 728 1000). Metro Evangelismos. **Open** *May-Sept Outdoor pool* 10am-6pm daily. Closed Oct-Apr. *Year-round Indoor pool* 10am-6pm daily. **Rates** €20 Mon-Fri; €35 Sat, Sun. **Credit** AmEx, DC, MC, V.

The Hilton's impressive outdoor swimming pool – the largest in central Athens – was an integral part of the hotel's €96 million refurbishment and re-opened in August 2003 with a swanky party. If you want to lounge around the pool with the in crowd, this is the place to go. And at 20 per day during the week, it isn't bad value for the luxury. A new fitness centre is due to open in 2004. Call ahead for details.

Athens Municipal Swimming Pool

Leandrou & Iphigenias, Kolokynthous, Northern Suburbs (210 515 3726). Metro Sepolia. **Open** 8.30am-6pm Mon-Fri; 9am-2pm Sat, Sun. Closed Aug. **Rates** €24 for 13 swims per mth. Members only. **No credit cards.**

To swim here you'll need a health certificate from a pathologist or a cardiologist, another one from a dermatologist, two passport-sized photos and a photocopy of your passport. So, if you're in Athens only for a short stay, you're better off heading to one of the hotel pools.

Holiday Inn

Michalakoupolou 50, Kolonaki (210 727 8000). Metro Megaro Mousikis. **Open** *May-Sept* 10am-7pm daily. Closed Oct-Apr. **Rates** €20 (towels incl). **Credit** AmEx, DC, MC, V.

The Holiday Inn's pool isn't exactly big, but, with superb views of Lycabettus Hill, its smart rooftop setting (complete with a bar and restaurant) is a great place to cool down and unwind while Athens life continues apace beneath you.

Tennis

Pete Sampras may be the son of Greek immigrants, but Eleni Daniilidou – who rose into the Women's WTA Top 20 rankings in 2003 – is the nearest Greek tennis has to its own star. There are plenty of courts in Athens for budding Serenas and Leytons to practise. As well as the tennis courts at the public beaches of **Voula A** (*see p119*) and **Attica Vouliagmeni** (*see p120*), the following courts are worth trying.

Athens Tennis Club

Leof Vas Olgas 2, Historic Centre (210 921 5630). Metro Syntagma. **Open** Non-members 7am-2pm Mon-Fri. **Rates** Non-members €15 per person. **No credit cards.** **Map** p299 F6.

This centrally located upmarket club has ten outdoor courts (six clay, four artificial grass), all of them floodlit. There are also three squash courts and a gym. All these facilities come at a price.

Ilioupolis Municipal Court

Angelou Evert 1 & Keffalinias, Ilioupoli, Southern Suburbs (210 993 0452). Bus 237. **Open** 5pm-9pm Sat; 9am-9pm Sun. **Rates** free.

These five clay and three hard courts are free to use and therefore very busy.

Ten-pin bowling

Athens Bowling Centre

Patision 177, Patisia, Northern Suburbs (210 865 6930/210 866 5573). Metro Ano Patissia. **Open** 10-2am daily. **Rates** €4.50 per game. **No credit cards.** Recently renovated eight-lane alley that, while perhaps not Athens' best, is certainly its most central.

Super Bowl

Kanapikeri 10, Rendi, Western Athens (210 561 3447/561 3678). Bus B18. **Open** 10am-2am daily. **Rates** €5 per game; €3 concessions; €3.50 Mon-Thur am. **Credit** MC, V.

This 30-lane, well-equipped modern bowling centre is worth the short trip out of town.

Trekking

Trekking Hellas

Filellinon 7, Plaka (210 331 0323/www.trekking.gr). Metro Syntagma. **Open** 9am-5pm Mon-Fri. **Rates** €15-€30. **Credit** AmEx, DC, MC, V. **Map** p295/p299 F5.

Attica's countryside will come as a pleasant surprise for those who thought Greece was nothing but sun, sea and sand. Trekking Hellas's simple yet interesting four-hour trek close to Athens is highly recommended. Starting in the foothills of Mount Parnitha at the Church of St Triada, it takes you through Skipiza spring and ends up at the Bafi lodge. It costs €20 and includes a picnic lunch.

Theatre & Dance

Take in a show in the birthplace of drama.

Theatre

With more than 350 productions each year and around 160 venues, Athens can claim to be one of the world's great theatre cities. The variety of shows on offer is astonishing: ancient and contemporary Greek drama, classics by Shakespeare, Chekhov and Ibsen, experimental multimedia performances, recent London and New York hits, comedies, musicals and European and US imports (Cirque Nouveau and the Black Theatre of Prague are regular visitors). The scene is flourishing: in the past five years or so several new theatres have been built, most of them in the formerly underdeveloped areas north of the Acropolis (Psyrri, Gazi, Metaxourgio and Votanikos). These venues' style and design are far from the usual notion of theatre luxury found in the central venues around Kolonaki (thick red carpets, velvet seats, elaborate sets): instead they combine the post-industrial design ethic of the surrounding buildings with the most up-to-date technological equipment and facilities.

Most productions, naturally, are in Greek. That shouldn't stop you enjoying the landmark experience of watching ancient drama in an amphitheatre contemporary to its conception, as at Epidaurus (*see p188*), or in the Roman Odeon of Herodes Atticus (*see p83*), where you can occasionally see the classics in English, too.

SEASONS AND FESTIVALS

The theatre season runs from mid October to the end of April, after which many companies leave town to tour the provinces. In summer, the focus shifts to the open-air theatres (Park, Alsos and Athineon) in the triangle made by Leof Alexandras, Patision and Prigiponison, which usually host light comedies or *epitheorises*, a theatrical descendant of Aristophanian comedy with sharp political and social commentary punctuated by musical numbers. You could also attend a performance by a renowned international guest company at the Odeon of Herodes Atticus (Herodeion) or Lycabettus Theatre during the acclaimed Athens Festival (*see p186*).

TICKETS AND TIMES

Many of the mainstream theatres are closed on Mondays and Tuesdays. Performances start late, at around 8.30-9.30pm, and at weekends there are additional matinées. Shows popular with young audiences usually have an after-midnight performance on Fridays or Saturdays.

Understanding the ancients

Seeing ancient drama in its birthplace, preferably in an amphitheatre where it would have been performed in classical times, is a quintessential Greek experience. It's best to make a summer trip to the Ancient Theatre of Epidaurus (*see p188*), but there are also frequent performances in Athens.

Theatre goers will know that classical theatre is far from dull. At times it gives Tarantino a run for his money with its violence and wry social commentary. It is, admittedly, in Greek, however, so it makes sense to take a translated text with you (*see p163* for English-language bookshops) or read the plot summary in the programme before the lights go down.

Most shows use modern theatrical conventions and technology, and they are all translated into modern Greek. They do not have an all-male cast, as they used to in the classical period, except for some Aristophanes productions. Accordingly, the actors very rarely wear masks as they used to. Costumes tend to be modern or stylised in keeping with the overall design; rarely, though, you will see the typical ancient Greek costumes (long pleated white dresses). Generally speaking, the productions are faithful to the originals. Which means that they do without an interval: bringing cushions and refreshments is a good idea.

The most commonly produced plays are Aristophanes's gender-reversal comedy *Lysistrata* and Sophocles's tragedy *Oedipus Rex*, with those writers' other works also common, along with those of Euripides.

Ticket prices are €15-€25, with the cheapest offered by theNational Theatre and for matinées at all venues. Students pay a little over half price. You can buy your tickets directly from theatre box offices, which are open 10am to 1pm and 5pm-9pm on performance days, or book in advance by credit card at an agency such as Ticket Hellas for an additional 16.5 per cent charge. For most of the shows at the Megaron Mousikis, Olympia Theatre and Herodeion, you should book as far as a month in advance.

Tickethouse

Panepistimiou 42 (210 360 8366/www.tickethouse. gr). Metro Panepistimio. **Open** 10.30am-6pm Mon-Fri; 10.30am-3pm Sat. **No credit cards.** **Map** p295 F4.
Useful central walk-in office, but cash only.

Ticket Hellas

1st floor, Aithrio department store, Agios Konstantinou 40, Marousi (210 618 9300/www. ticket-hellas.gr). Metro Marousi. **Open** 9.30am-6pm Mon-Fri; 10am-3.30pm Sat. **Credit** MC, V.

Major venues & theatres

The larger theatres in central Athens usually stage large-scale commercial productions, whereas the cosier ones are used for more experimental drama or dance shows.

Amore (Theatro tou Notou)

Prigiponison 10, Pedion Areos (210 646 8009/www. amorenotos.com). Metro Victoria. **Open** *Box office* 10am-10pm daily. Theatre closed July, Aug. **Tickets** €20; €14 concessions. **No credit cards.**
The Guardian has defined Amore as the equivalent of London's Royal Court, and rightly so. With up to eight productions annually and collaborations with

Theatre tips

● Greek productions rarely begin on time, except for those at the Herodeion and the Theatre of Epidaurus.
● Ushers/usherettes at smaller theatres expect to be tipped.
● Greek theatres are smoker-friendly during the intervals.
● In commercial shows, the audience applauds when their favourite actor enters the stage.
● Matinées are a unique experience even for Greek theatre goers. These shows are mostly favoured by older people who love to comment on what happens on stage – and not discreetly, either. It's literally a play within a play.

distinguished directors from the UK and Germany, Amore has broken through the formerly stagnant waters of the Athenian scene and offered shelter to some of the most promising young Greek talents. Its artistic directors, Yiannis Houvardas and Thomas Moshopoulos, have worked extensively throughout Europe, London included.

Coronet

Frynis 11, Pangrati (210 701 2123/ www.coronet.gr). Metro Evangelismos, then 20mins walk. Theatre closed May-Sept. **Tickets** prices vary. **Credit** MC, V. **Map** p297 J7.
This former cinema has been renovated into a cosy theatre with good facilities and some of the most advanced technological equipment in town. It plays host to a variety of companies, including the Black Theatre of Prague, whose unique dream-like technique is famous all over the world. The Czech performers use body language and mimicry so you can feel comfortable that your Greek will not be tested.

Ethniki Theatro (National Theatre)

Agios Konstantinou 22-24, Omonia (210 522 3242/ www.n-t.gr). Metro Omonia. **Open** *Box office* 10am-1pm, 5-10pm Tue-Sun. Theatre closed June-Oct. **Tickets** €12; €7 concessions. **No credit cards.** **Map** p295 E3.
Located in a beautiful neo-classical building, the National Theatre is a repertory theatre that hosts a variety of shows: classic, modern, musicals. The theatre also has several other locations scattered around Omonia, such as the Experimental Scene, which for the past two years has been performing to rave reviews under its new director, Stathis Livathinos.

Free2Go Club22

Leof Vouliagmenis 22, Eastern Suburbs (210 924 9814/www.club22.gr). Metro Syngrou-Fix. **Open** *Box office* 11.30am-8pm, days vary. Theatre closed May-Oct. **Tickets** prices vary. **No credit cards.** **Map** p299 F7.
Stand-up comedy, cabaret and drag shows all feature at this venue, one of the most alternative and innovative clubs in town. After the show, the dancefloor stays open till the early hours.

Ilisia Ntenisi

Leof Vas Sofias 54, Kolonaki (210 721 0045). Metro Megaro Mousikis. **Open** *Box office* 10am-1pm, 5-9pm Tue-Sun. Theatre closed May-Oct. **Tickets** €25-€29; €23 concessions. **Credit** V.
Located almost opposite the Megaron Mousikis, Ilisia Ntenisi is named after Greek star Mimi Denisi, who also produces the most extravagant and exuberant shows in town, with musicals her forte. One of her recent roles was the lead in *Victor/Victoria*. The venue is one of the largest in town, with thick red carpets, velvet seats and a huge stage. A short walk south, at Papadiamantopoulou 4, is an intimate studio-like venue, Ilisia Volanaki, which usually presents contemporary plays featuring the most promising young Greek actors.

Catch the classics at the scenically endowed **Herodeion**. *See p83.*

Kelsos Bar

*Leof Vouliagmenis & Kelsou 4, Eastern Suburbs
(210 921 7951/www.kelsos.gr). Metro Syngrou-Fix.*
Open *Box office* 9-10pm Wed-Sat; 7-8pm Sun.
Theatre closed May-Oct. **Tickets** €10; €8
concessions. **No credit cards. Map** p299 F8.
Five years ago the Plani Theatre Company opened
the Kelsos, the first bar theatre in town. Since then
other companies have followed its example and
nowadays bar theatres are an established presence.
They are especially pop-ular among young audiences because the (cheap) ticket for the show also
buys them a drink and the freedom to smoke.

Lambeti

*Leof Alexandras 106, Ambelokipi (210 646 3685).
Metro Ambelokipi.* **Open** *Box office* 10am-1pm,
5-9pm Tue-Sun. Theatre closed Apr-May. **Tickets**
€24; €16 concessions. **No credit cards.**
Named after Elli Lambeti, a distinguished 20th-
century Greek actress with an international career,
this theatre is one of the oldest and biggest venues
in Athens. An astonishing version of Edward
Albee's *Who's Afraid of Virginia Woolf?* was one of
the theatre's most recent hits.

Odou Kykladon

*Kikladon 11, Northern Suburbs (210 821 7877).
Metro Victoria.* **Open** *Box office* 10.30am-1.30pm,
5-9pm Tue-Sun. Theatre closed June-Nov. **Tickets**
€19; €13 concessions. **No credit cards.**
The artistic director of this venue, Lefteris Vogiatzis,
is one of the most acclaimed directors in Greece. The
venue hosts both modern and classic drama.

Theseion

*Tournavitou 7, Keramikos (210 325 5444). Metro
Thisio.* **Open** *Box office* 10am-1pm, 6-9pm Mon-Fri; 6-
9pm Sat, Sun. Theatre closed July-Aug. **Tickets** €20;
€14 concessions. **No credit cards. Map** p295 D4.

This loft-like venue hosts one of the most experimental and internationally renowned theatre
companies in Athens, the Theseum Ensemble, under
the innovative direction of Michail Marmarinos. One
of their productions, *The National Anthem*, which
ran for two consecutive years in Athens and abroad,
has won awards in many local and foreign theatre
festivals. The Theseum Ensemble has also inaugurated a new period of collaborations with companies
from Denmark and Germany.

To Treno sto Rouf

*Leof Konstantinoupoleos & Petrou Ralli, Rouf
(210 529 8922/mobile 6937 604 988). Metro T
hisio, then 15mins walk.* **Open** *Box office* 10am-2pm,
6-9pm Tue-Sun. **Tickets** €20; €14 concessions.
No credit cards. Map p294 A5/p298 A5.
This unique venue stages performances in the
carriage of a train. The shows are followed by a
candlelit dinner in an Orient Express atmosphere.

Dance

With Dimitris Papaioannou, the distinguished
choreographer and dancer of Omada Edafous,
taking creative responsibility for the opening
and closing ceremonies of the 2004 Olympics,
a wealth of opportunities have opened up for
younger artists, and contemporary dance is
thriving. However, classical ballet companies
barely exist in Athens, except for the graduates
of the Public School of Orchestral Art and the
foreign guest companies visiting during the
summer festivals or on tour at the Megaron
Mousikis during the winter. Bear in mind that
May is dance month, when almost all the local
companies show their most recent works in
diverse mini-festivals.

Arts & Entertainment

Dora Stratou Garden Theatre.

THE COMPANIES

Groups worth looking out for include established Papaioannou's Omada Edafous, alternative Konstantinou Rigou's Octana, ecstatic Ermi Malkotsi, Dimitri Sotiriou and Kiki Baka's Sinequanon and newcomers such as Katerina Papageorgiou's AdLib and Fotis Nikolaou's X-it.

Venues

Dora Stratou Garden Theatre

Filopappou Hill, Acropolis (central box office 210 324 4395/site box office 921 4650/www.grdance.org). Metro Akropoli, then 15 mins walk. **Open** Central box office (Skoliou 8, off Adrianou 122, Plaka) 10.30am-2.30pm Mon-Fri; site box office from 7.30pm performance days. Theatre closed Oct-May. **Performances** 9.30pm Tue-Sat, 8.15pm Sun. **Tickets** €13. **Credit** MC, V. **Map** p298 C7.

Formed by folk-music pioneer Dora Stratou, this venue is also known as 'the living museum of Greek dance'. The 900-seat garden theatre is located in the beautiful surroundings of Filopappou Hill. Dances, songs and music are presented in the form they were (or are still) performed in the villages where they originated, thanks to Stratou's meticulous research. Even the costumes are museum pieces, handmade in villages a century ago. Dora Stratou also offers workshops in Greek folk dance and culture, with English-speaking instructors. The daily programme includes dance classes, visits to the theatre's extensive wardrobe of over 2,500 village-made costumes and entrance to the evening's performance.

Kalamata International Dance Festival

Pan Kessari 6, Kalamata (27210 83086/ 90886/http://dikeho.conxion.gr). **Tickets** €20; €10 concessions. **Credit** MC, V.

Held in Kalamata, a Peloponnesian city less than three hours away from Athens, this is the most important dance event in Greece. It usually takes place in July, and the performances are held in a variety of venues. Audiences have the chance to see not only the best-known Greek groups, but also the *crème de la crème* of the international dance scene.

Leda Shantala 'Shantom'

Tripoleos 35A & Evoias, Halandri (210 671 7529/ www.shantala.gr). Metro Halandri. **Open** *Box office* 10am-8pm Mon-Fri. **Tickets** prices vary. **Credit** MC, V.

This brand-new venue is home to choreographer and dancer Leda Shantala, who has spent many years studying Indian culture and the way it is portrayed through the art of dance.

Megaron Mousikis

Leof Vas Sofias & Kokali, Kolonaki (210 728 2000/ www.megaron.gr). Metro Megaro Mousikis. **Open** *Box office* 10am-6pm Mon-Fri; 10am-2pm Sat. On performance days 10am-8.30pm Mon-Fri; 10am-2pm, 6-8pm Sat, Sun. Theatre closed July-mid Sept. **Tickets** prices vary. **Credit** AmEx, DC, MC, V.

Olympia Theatre

Akadimias 59-61, Historic Centre (210 361 1516/361 2461/364 3725/www.nationalopera.gr). Metro Panepistimio. **Open** *Box office* 9am-9pm daily. Theatre closed May-Sept. **Tickets** prices vary. **Credit** MC, V. **Map** p295 F3.

The Olympia Theatre, home of the Greek National Opera, Lyriki Skini, and Megaron Mousikis are the places to go to for classical ballet. The posh venues host lavish productions by some of the world's foremost dance companies. Book well in advance.

Roes

Iakhou 16, Rouf (210 347 4312). Metro Thisio, then 15mins walk. **Open** *Box office* hours vary. Theatre closed mid June-late Oct. **Tickets** €12-€22. **No credit cards. Map** p294 B4.

A minimalist venue that accommodates some of the city's most established companies.

Arts & Entertainment

Trips Out of Town

Features

Getting Started

Ancient sites, mountain heights, city living and seaside chilling.

Nafplio. See p249.

The image of Athens in tourist terms (ancient and busy; ugly, polluted) is so different from that of the rest of Greece (ancient and peaceful; beautiful, azure sea) that you could be excused for thinking that they were in two different countries. And, indeed, unless you're on a touring or dual-centre holiday, or happen to own a yacht, parts of the Greece of popular imagination – Crete and Corfu, for example – are out of your reach from Athens. But many of the country's quintessential attractions are very much accessible from the capital, from idyllic beaches a 80-kilometre (40-mile) drive down the Attica peninsula and islands a 40-minute hydrofoil trip away to heavy-hitting archaeological sites at Delphi and Olympia and characterful cities such as likeable Nafplio and the emerging Patra.

GETTING AROUND

Buses run from Athens to all the major destinations covered in this chapter, though it can be problematic to travel between them. You can get to parts of the Peloponnese by rail, but there fewer trains than there are buses, and there's little or no saving on journey time. Car-hire companies are given on page 265: driving is a far simpler business out of the Athens traffic, and most road signs are transliterated into English. You'll need a good map: Road Editions' Greece map is the best we've found available locally, but it's impractically large: we recommend you buy one in your home country. The AA/AAA's are good. If there are several of you, a taxi is a reasonable option for destinations in Attica. You can also arrange trips through travel agents (see p184) and tour operators (see p75).

TOURIST INFORMATION

Tourist information is only patchily available. Use the Greek National Tourist Organisation's internet database (see p275) ahead of your journey. Many destinations have a Tourist Police office (dial 171 country-wide), where you can ask for advice if you have any difficulties.

BASICS

Hotel rates are given as a range (from the cheapest double room in low season to the most expensive in high season) and should be taken as guidelines only: they are the official 'rack' rates and will rise and fall with the availability of rooms. During the Olympic period all bets are off: prices, especially for areas with convenient access to the venues, will put their prices up (and will likely be booked solid). On the plus side, restaurants and other venues, including ancient sites, may extend their opening times.

Phone numbers are given as dialled locally and from Athens; calling from outside Greece you need to preface them with the country code 30.

The best Destinations

Temples

Byron's favourite, the impressive and atmospheric **Sanctuary of Poseidon** (see p239); the remote and romantic **Sanctuary of Artemis Brauron** (see p243); majestic **Delphi** (see p245).

Ancient sites

The atmospherically abandoned theatre at **Thorikos** (see p240); sprawling, significant **Ancient Corinth** (see p246); the perfectly preserved theatre at the **Archaeological Site of Ancient Epidaurus** (see p249); **Olympia** (see p252), home of the first Olympics.

Urban escapes

Relaxed **Nafplio** (see p249), especially its lovely Old Town; buzzy, zestful **Patra** (see p254).

Island excursions

Lunch or dinner in **Aegina Town** (see p256); a day out on picturesque **Hydra** (see p258).

Trips Out of Town

© Copyright Time Out Group 2004

Attica & the Mainland

Dive into the crystal-clear waters of the Aegean or dip into Attica's rich archaeological history.

The holiday brochures seldom peddle the area immediately around Athens as a holiday paradise. And indeed there are more fabulous beaches, more picturesque towns and villages and more impressive ancient sites elsewhere in Greece. But the Attican peninsula has its charms. On its west coast, the scenic road to the lovely temple of **Sounion** takes you over headlands to tiny fingernail coves, sandy beaches and some great fish restaurants; on the east are some lesser known and therefore atmospherically deserted ancient sites, such as **Thorikos** and the **Sanctuary of Artemis Brauron**, along with the resort of **Porto Rafti** and the port of **Rafina**, neither of them devoid of interest. Further away, but still within striking distance, are two major sites: **Marathon**, interesting more for its history than the ruins that remain, and majestic **Delphi**.

Athens Environs

Mount Parnitha National Park

Snow-capped in winter and a tinderbox during the long, hot summer, Mount Parnitha – Attica's highest mountain at 1,413 metres (4,636 feet) – towers over the Athens basin. On a good day (that is, smog permitting), the views of the sprawling city beneath are quite breathtaking, but for Athenians, the pine-strewn rugged mountain is famous mainly for two things: as the epicentre of the devastating earthquake of 1999 and for its hotel/casino, the formerly illustrious **Mont Parnes**.

Served by a funicular, the casino boasts all the usual slot machines, as well as 54 gaming tables, including roulette, baccarat and blackjack. And, if you're feeling peckish, it even offers a reasonably priced buffet dinner (€9), complete with cracking views, in the glass-walled dining room.

Mont Parnes has recently been bought by the Hyatt hotel group and is set to undergo long-overdue renovations. All rooms are already out of action but, for the moment, the lobby and casino remain open and retain a sepia-tinted (if a little nicotine-stained) retro feel that harks back to its glamorous 1960s heyday, when even

Greek royalty would try their luck at the roulette tables – you half expect Dean Martin's Rat Pack to come strolling in chewing on fat Cubans. But take off the rose-tinted specs and it's hard to deny that the place is in dire need of a lick of paint (and then some). It is one of the best-situated hotels in the Athens area, but Hyatt will certainly have its work cut out to restore Mont Parnes to former glories.

Aside from spinning the wheels of fortune (and gawping at the view), Parnitha offers little other reason to make the trip out of town. There are a few hiking and mountain-biking routes, but these are poorly signposted. However, the area will play host to the Olympic mountain-bike event, so facilities are bound to improve.

Mont Parnes

Karageorgi 2, Parnes (210 246 9111/210 246 9115/ www.mont-parnes.gr). **Open** 4pm-4am Mon-Fri; 9am-4am Sat, Sun. **Admission** €6 (includes a complimentary drink). **Credit** DC, MC, V. **Dress code** Smart. No under-18s. Passport ID required.

Getting there

By bus
The casino runs a free bus service with pick-ups and drop-offs from outside the Athens Hilton Hotel (Leof Vas Sofias 46). The bus leaves at 4pm and 6pm and takes over an hour to reach its destination; return trips leave the casino at 10.30pm, 1.45am and 2.45am. Otherwise take bus 714 from Platia Vathis (also known as Platia Anexartisias), near Omonia. Tickets: ct45 regular; ct20 student.

By car
Take National Road 1 (Ethniki Odos) towards Mount Parnitha, which is clearly signposted. From the foot of Parnitha you can either drive up the winding mountain road or take the funicular (€1) to the summit. The funicular runs every 15 minutes from 7am until about 4am all year round (except when very windy).

Ancient Eleusis

Once a glorious sanctuary devoted to Demeter, goddess of harvest and fertility, these days Eleusis is not so much a lush, hallowed ground as a marble scrap heap strewn with ancient rubble. Perched on the edge of the dusty, modern-day refinery town of Elefsina, 16 kilometres (ten miles) from Athens, Eleusis is the rough diamond of Attica's archaeological sites. Granted, it's not pretty to look at, but its vast mass of discarded marble blocks, crumbling walls and column stumps tells of a rich history.

First built in 2000 BC, the site is entrenched in the worship of Demeter and became home to the Eleusian mysteries – the name given to the cult's secret initiation process and ceremonial rites. As their name implies, little is known of what form the rituals took, but the Romans certainly took to them, spreading the cult throughout the pre-Christian world.

Because of its proximity to Athens, Eleusis was an important strategic stronghold and fought hard to retain its independence. However, despite its fortified walls, it was conquered many times – by the Athenians on a number of occasions, and later by the Romans. But all embraced the cult and added their architectural signatures to the sanctuary.

Eventually, though, after being conquered by Alaric's Visigoths in AD 395, Eleusis was abandoned and largely left to fend for itself until 1821, when it served as a military camp in the Greek War of Independence. Those intervening centuries go some way to explaining the chaos of the site today. Fortunately, a good (and air-conditioned) on-site museum filled with well-preserved relics is there to help you appreciate the sprawling chaos.

Ancient Eleusis (site & museum)
Gioka 1, Platia Eleusis, Elefsina (210 554 6019).
Open 8.30am-3pm Tue-Sun. **Admission** €3; €2 concessions; free to under-18s. **No credit cards.**

Where to eat & drink

Unless refinery-spotting is a major passion, Eleusis is Elefsina's only draw. However, for a quick bite, **Café Tost** (Dimitrios 3, 210 556 1487, snacks from €1.20) is a well-priced café on the road directly opposite the site entrance. It serves soft drinks, coffee, beer, and some fairly basic snacks. Those hankering for a bit of a sea view with their food should head south of the site to Elefsina's small port, which is dotted with cafés.

Getting there

By bus
Take either the A16 or the B16 bus from Platia Koumoundourou near Omonia and get off at the Strofi bus stop. The site is a mere five-minute walk from there. Buses depart frequently and take an hour. Tickets: ct45 regular; ct20 student.

By car
Take the Athens-Patras motorway towards Elefsina. Leave the motorway at Elefsina and from there follow the road signs to the archaeological site.

West Coast

Leof Posidonos – which runs from south Athens to the headland of Sounion with its quietly awe-inspiring temple – is a dusty old road that isn't quite as grand as its name suggests. But, flanked to the north by lazy towns, rugged hills and (for some bizarre reason) a whole lot of fireplace sellers, and to the south by countless secluded beaches, it's crammed with worthwhile coastal stop-offs offering a taste of Greek seaside life.

The road to Sounion

VARKIZA
Sleepy Varkiza offers a peaceful alternative to its posher, more bustling neighbour, Vouliagmeni. This is a pretty little harbour town where many Athenian families make their summer homes, drawn by the narrow shingle beach, which is made up of a string of natural, shallow coves with calm waters and handy free canvas shelters offering shade from the fierce summer sun. The leafy seaside promenade, along the main stretch of beach, is littered with cafés and restaurants offering the usual ice-creams, frappés, soft drinks and meals. For an inexpensive lunch

The Sanctuary of Poseidon at **Sounion**.
See p239.

Roadside beaches

As well as the beaches (*paralias*) in the coastal towns, you can stop almost anywhere along Leof Posidonos and find yourself a spot for a swim and a sunbathe. From organised seafronts offering umbrellas and deckchairs to secluded coves that emerge suddenly from the jagged rocks, there's a beach at every turn (*see also chapter* **Beaches**). Just park on the hard shoulder or on the edge of the beach and cool off in the welcoming waters.

Five kilometres (three miles) out of Varkiza lies the secluded horseshoe bay of **Lombarda Beach** (pictured). With cheery chart pop drifting from the beach bars' speakers, this sandy strip, set away from the road, has a fun island feel. Even the sea is laid-back – shallow and calm, protected as it is by the rocky cliffs.

Further up the road is **Grand Resort Lagonissi** (Leof Posidonos, 22910 76000, www.lagonissiresort.gr, closed mid Oct-March; *see also p69*), a hotel whose plush pool and beach the public can use for a fee of €8 on weekdays and €12 at weekends. A deckchair and umbrella are included, though the fun things (watersports, massages, banana rides) are only available to hotel guests, so you might prefer to head a kilometre (half a mile) further east to a very inviting strip of beach where you can sample the same sparkling Mediterranean sea for free.

Located between the towns of Saronida and Anavyssos, **Eden Beach** represents the middle ground between Lagonissi's luxury and the no-frills options. This pretty, rounded bay with crystal-clear waters in front of the Eden Hotel is served by a café/bar offering drinks and light snacks. Deckchairs and umbrellas are available for hire.

The long, flat bay of **Legrena**, around eight kilometres (five miles) from Cape Sounion, is dotted with gorgeous secluded beaches. The Capet Cove, on the edge of Legrena Bay between Harakas and Legrena, is one of the most scenic, but can get a little busy at weekends.

If bathing in the shadow of ancient monuments is a particular ambition, head for the **Aegaio Hotel beach** on the western side of Cape Sounion or, for a more rugged (and private) dip, walk down the steep path that cuts down the left side of the Cape on the last stretch of road up towards the archaeological site.

option, visit **Artopolis** (Platia Varkiza & Leof Posidonos, no phone, snacks from €1.50). This bakery offers excellent-value freshly made *tyropitas*, *spanakopitas*, ice-creams, traditional biscuits and baklava, which you can eat perched on one of the many seafront benches.

Further round the bay, beyond the fishermen mending their nets, the eastern side of the harbour is flanked by a strip of sandy beach.

SARONIDA

As the most cosmopolitan (and largest) of the coastal road stop-offs, Saronida attracts a trendier crowd than the rest and, come the weekend, the town's sandy seafront swells with well-heeled Greek families escaping the Athens heat. The town is equipped to handle the onslaught and its main strip – leading up from the beach – is filled with fashionable eateries, bars and ice-cream parlours. Among them is the swanky **Il Vento Art Caffè** (Leof Saronidas 4, 22910 80080, main courses €10-€15), which, as its name suggests, takes pride in its smart decor (white armchairs at every table) and art-covered walls. Further up the road is the popular and industrial-themed **Reverso Café-Restaurant** (Leof Saronidas 20, 22910 61331, main courses €5-€9), serving a wide range of food as well as an impressive choice of ice-creams and cocktails.

PALEA FOKEA

Perched on the eastern end of Anavyssos Bay, Palea Fokea is more a village than a town. But with its lively café-lined main square, quaint marinas and sandy beaches, it's a good stop-off before the final assault on to Cape Sounion.

The bustling no-frills souvlaki joint **Ta Thythima** (Platia Eleftherias 9, 22910 38834, closed lunch daily, souvlaki sandwich €1.50) is well worth a visit for its succulent grilled chicken and lamb kebabs, as well as first-rate gyros. Of the fish restaurants that line the seafront at the top end of the town, **Remvi** (Leof Sounion 14, 22910 36236, mezes €2.50-€6) and **The Four Brothers** (Leof Sounion 6, 22910 40843, mezes €2.50-€6) are two of the best, offering excellent mezes, fresh calamari, grilled octopus and whitebait, as well as a wide range of fish by the kilo (€20-€40 per kilo) and meaty taverna staples. And if you want to avoid Sounion's sunset hordes, why not watch the sun slip behind Anavyssos Bay from the cool, grapevine-roofed **Cafe Fokea** (Leof Sounion 8, 22910 36468, main courses about €10) on the seafront.

Sounion

With its stunningly well-preserved columns and unrivalled position on a dramatic cliff above the blue Aegean, the **Sanctuary of Poseidon** at Cape Sounion is one of the most impressive ancient ruins this side of Delphi (hence the steady stream of tourist coaches). Dedicated to the god of the sea, the temple dates back to the fifth century BC. If its proud Doric columns seem impressive from miles away, then up close they are simply breathtaking – particularly in the evening, when large crowds gather to watch the sun set over this most evocative of sites. Indeed, Lord Byron (*see p243* **Byron in Greece**) was so taken by this cliff-top marvel that, when he visited in 1810, he etched his name into one of the temple's statuesque marble columns (a laurel wreath goes to anyone who can spot his legendary tag). Byron (who later referred to the temple in his *Don Juan*) wasn't the first or last to add his mark, but these days attendants are on hand to stop any wannabe graffiti artists.

Set back behind the road that leads to the Sanctuary of Poseidon, 500 metres (1,600 feet) below, is the blink-and-you'll-miss-it **Temple of Athena**. The scattered ancient rubble is not quite as impressive as the main attraction, but from this smaller sanctuary it is possible to get a great view of the towering big daddy of a ruin way up on the hill set back against the brilliant Attica sky. A well-stocked gift shop sells guidebooks and touristy knick-knacks.

Sanctuaries of Poseidon & Athena

Cape Sounion (22920 39363). **Open** 9am-sunset daily. **Admission** €4; €2 concessions; free under-18s. Free to all Sun in Nov-Mar. **No credit cards.**

Where to eat & drink

The site's cliffside café/restaurant (22920 39190, main courses €7-€8) is surprisingly good value, especially considering the excellent view it offers, and pleasantly shaded.

Getting there

By bus

From Mavromataion, near the Pedion Areos park, board either of the two buses (210 823 0179) heading towards Sounion; both terminate at the Sanctuary of Poseidon. Buses leave every hour, 6.30am-5.30pm, and take an hour and a half. Check the timetable for the return journey – the last bus to Athens leaves Sounion only a short while after sunset. Tickets: €4.30; €3.20 student.

By car

If you are in too much of a hurry to enjoy the calming sea views from the coastal Leof Posidonos, take the Attiki Odos motorway in the direction of Lavrion and from there follow the signs for Sounion and the archaeological site.

Trips Out of Town

The archaeological site of **Rhamnous**.

Thorikos

Perched on top of Velatouri Hill, by a small bay just north of the Sounion headland, the **ancient theatre** at Thorikos is an archaeological mole hill compared to neighbouring cliff-top Sounion. There are no attendants here – in fact there isn't even a proper car park or an entrance fee, and information about the site is only available at the Lavrion Museum, two and a half kilometres (one and a half miles) away. But while Thorikos' scattered ruins, overrun by weeds, might not be as instantly impressive as Poseidon's towering marble columns, they are no less fascinating.

Dating back to the Mycenaean period in the sixth century BC, Thorikos became a miners' town processing metal from the nearby mines at Lavrion. These days the settlement is best known for its impressive (and unusually oval-shaped) theatre. Built into the hillside overlooking olive groves, the amphitheatre is charmingly rough and ready, but despite its age (and obvious need for a gardener) the remains are incredibly well preserved.

Further back at the top of the hill there's also a sanctuary dedicated to Demeter and her daughter Kore, while scattered down the hill's west slope are the remains of a few houses.

Lavrion Museum
Platia Iroon Polytechniou, Lavrion (22920 22817). **Open** 10am-3pm Wed-Mon. **Admission** €2; €1 concessions. **No credit cards.**

Getting there

By car
Turn right out of Sounion towards Lavrion. Once in Lavrion, follow the signs to the archaeological site.

East Attica

Destinations are covered in north-to-south order.

Rhamnous

With its serene hilltop setting overlooking the Euboian gulf, the remote settlement of Rhamnous might look peaceful, but it's a site steeped in military history. Dating back to the sixth century BC, Rhamnous was home to the cult of Nemesis, goddess of retribution, and a grand temple dedicated to her once stood here. Appropriately, it's thought that the statue of the goddess within the temple was sculpted from the slab of marble that the Persians, confident of their victory at the Battle of Marathon in 490 BC, brought with them to build their triumphant memorial. Happily for the Greeks – though not for those cocky Persians – their assailants were vanquished and Nemesis received her well-won trophy.

Further down the hill is the fortress of Rhamnous – still under excavation and currently not open to the public. The fortress was permanently manned by an Athenian garrison and protected by a mighty 800-metre-long (half-mile) wall. Military buildings were enclosed on its upper level, with a gymnasium, a unique natural theatre, burial grounds and private homes beneath. Sadly, little remains of either the sanctuary or the fortress after they were systematically destroyed by Christians at the turn of the fifth century AD.

Temple of Nemesis
Rhamnous (22940 63477). **Open** *Summer* noon-5.30pm Mon; 8am-7pm Tue-Sun. *Winter* 8.30am-3pm daily. **Admission** €2; €1 concessions. Free to under-18s; free to all Sun in Nov-Mar. **No credit cards.**

Getting there

By car

Take the Athens-Lamia motorway in the direction of Agios Stephanos and Marathonas, then follow the signs to Grammatiko. When the road forks as you enter the village, follow it down the small hill to the right. After about a kilometre (half a mile) the road bends to the right up a winding mountain road. Stay on this road for just over seven kilometres (four and a half miles) until you reach a T-junction. Turn left and follow the signs to Rhamnous.

Marathon

The archaeological site of Marathon is, of course, 42 kilometres (26 miles) from Athens, across the Attican peninsula on the Rafina Coast, and about three kilometres (two miles) from nondescript Marathonas town. It's more fascinating for the story it tells than for what ruins remain. It's basically a large mound, but a mound that evokes a sense of the ancient past, along with the serenity of a cemetery.

It was here that in 490 BC the Battle of Marathon was fought, in which an army of 10,000 Athenians and Plataeans defeated 25,000 Persian invaders by ambushing the foreign army from the sides. The Greeks' victory was conclusive: compared to 6,000 Persian dead, they lost just 192 men in the battle. The Tomb of the Fallen, a huge dome rising out of the ground in which the Greeks who died in the battle were buried, commemorates them.

Most famously, however, the Battle of Marathon gave rise to the modern race that still bears its name. After the battle, the messenger Pheidippides ran the 42 kilometres (26 miles) to Athens to relay news of the Greeks' tremendous triumph. However, once there, having informed Athens of the victory, Pheidippides collapsed and died on the spot. The 2004 Olympic marathon will start from here and will retrace Pheidippides's steps.

The **Marathon Museum** lies two and a half kilometres (one and a half miles) to the west. Due to reopen in summer 2004, it houses battle relics that tell the tale of the Greeks' amazing victory. Note that there is no public transport between the site and the museum.

Archaeological site of Marathon

Spyrou Louis, Marathonas (22940 55462).
Open 8am-3pm Tue-Sun. **Admission** (includes entry to museum) €3; €2 concessions; free to under-18s and EU students. **No credit cards.**

Marathon Museum

Plataion 114, Vranas, Marathonas (22940 55155).
Open 8am-3pm Tue-Sun. **Admission** (includes entry to archaeological site) €3; €2 concessions; free to under-18s and EU students. **No credit cards.**

Where to eat & drink

There is nowhere worthy of recommendation to eat either at the ancient site or in Marathon town. Your best bet is to head for Fragma at Marathon Lake (*see p242*).

Getting there

By bus

From the bus terminal at Mavromataion (210 821 0872), near the Pedion Areos park, take any bus to Marathonas, Grammatiko or Souli, and alight at the Tymvos bus stop. From there it is a short walk to the site. Buses depart every hour 5.30am-10.30pm and take two hours. Tickets: €2.50; €1.90 student.

By car

Take Mesogeion in the direction of Marathonas. Prior to reaching the town, follow the brown archaeological-site signs for Tymvos.

After Marathon, relax at **Fragma**. *See p242.*

Worship Artemis at **Brauron**. *See p243.*

Marathon Lake

Situated on the site of the ancient Marathon lake, inland from Marathon, this massive reservoir was Athens' sole water supply right up until the 1950s. Although the dam (built in 1925) no longer shoulders such responsibility, it remains an impressive sight. Made out of marble, the structure, which measures 50 metres (160 feet) in height and 300 metres (a fifth of a mile) in length, rises imposingly out of the lake, surrounded by pine forests.

Although no one is allowed too close to the water, it is possible to walk on trails in the surrounding hills for beautiful views of the lake. Plus, the spanking new and very smart Fragma restaurant on the east side of the dam offers a particularly stunning view of the serene lake from it spectacular terrace. Alternatively there are observation platforms at either end of the dam and picnic areas on the west side from which to take in the sights.

Where to eat & drink

The fashionable and wonderfully situated café/restaurant **Fragma** (210 814 3415, main courses €20-€25) offers light snacks and traditional meze during the day and adventurous, well-presented modern European cuisine in the evenings (from lunchtimes at weekends). Dinner bookings are advisable.

Getting there

By car
Take Mesogeion in the direction of Marathonas. Once in the town, follow the well-marked signs to the lake ('*limni*').

Rafina

There's little reason to visit Athens' second port other than to catch a ferry, but there are certainly worse places to kill time in if you do. Rafina may be smaller and more out of the way than Piraeus, but ferry tickets from here to the Cyclades are generally cheaper, a taxi from the airport is just €20 and there are plenty of buses, making Rafina a convenient alternative starting point for any island-hopping adventure.

And as ferry ports go, this one's not so bad. The catamaran and ferry ticket offices line the harbour front, but round to the right, on the south side of the town, lies a small but pleasant strip of beach. Rising above the harbour is Rafina's main square and, far from fulfilling any sailor clichés, it's a clean, wide, tree-lined space flanked by modern cafés and bars. Among the best are the bright and airy **Café Estoril** (Platia Rafina, 22940 22490) – unmissable with its yellow chairs – and the more elegant, brushed-wood and chrome-decorated **The Square** (Platia Rafina, 22940 23400), both of which serve a selection of beers, cocktails, coffee and snacks. Head up the hill to the right of the square to find a very reasonably priced restaurant, **O Vraxos** (Platia Taxidromeiou, 22940 22307, fish €37-€47 per kilo), which serves tasty fish mezes.

Any further information can be obtained from the offices of the **Rafina Port Authority** (22940 22300), by the port.

Getting there

By bus
Buses (210 821 0872) for Rafina leave from Mavromataion, near Pedion Areos park, every half hour and take an hour and 15 minutes.

By car
Take Mesogeion and head north towards Christopoulo and Pinkermi; from there follow the signs to Rafina. For the coastal route, take Mesogeion and head north in the direction of Loutsa. Once there, follow the signs to Rafina.

From the airport
An Airport Express bus connects Eleftherios Venizelos with Rafina. This route is run by coach company KTEL (22940 23440). Single tickets cost €3; the journey takes about 20-30 minutes.

Byron in Greece

The admiration and love that Lord Byron felt for Greece, a 'beautiful country, with seasons all a-smile' and especially Athens ('Athens holds my heart and soul/Can I cease to love thee? No!') are well known. The feeling was reciprocated. When Byron died in 1824, weakened by an epileptic fit and thus unable to fight off a severe cold, the Greeks insisted on keeping his heart, and buried it beneath his statue in the Garden of Heroes in Mesolongi. Their affection for the English poet carries on to this day, with streets and children still being named after him.

Byron became fascinated by Greece at an early age. Born with a club-foot and becoming a sensitive and shy child, he spent most of his time reading. He was especially captivated by the glorious history and heroic myths of Ancient Greece, and it is no surprise that later in his life he was so appalled by Lord Elgin's pillaging of the Parthenon: 'Dull is the eye that will not weep to see/Thy walls defaced, thy mouldering shrines removed...'

He had a somewhat unstable childhood. His father, whom he scarcely knew, committed suicide and his mother treated him in an emotionally inconsistent manner. His nurse was rumoured to have made sexual advances to him, and he became infatuated with three of his cousins. The combination of this with his literary genius led him to become a self-willed young man, who vehemently resisted any attempts to control him. This is perhaps another reason why Byron admired Greece so much. Despite being under Turkish rule since the 14th century and despite attempts at oppressive assimilation, the Greeks managed to maintain their own cultural and national identity, traditions and religion virtually intact.

On coming of age and after leaving Cambridge University, Byron set off to travel around southern Europe with his friends. He first came to Greece in December 1809 (and visited it twice more over the next four months) and fell in love with not only the countryside, the sunshine, the architecture and the moral tolerance of the people, but also with a number of girls, about one of whom he wrote *Maid of Athens, Ere We Part*. He spent a lot of time on Platia Lysikratous, in central Athens, where he wrote some of *Childe Harold's Pilgrimage*. He also left his mark, quite literally, on the Sanctuary of Poseidon in Sounion, where he joined the vandalistic tradition of scrawling one's name into the columns. He even swam five kilometres (three miles) across Hellespont (the Dardanelles).

It was 12 years before Byron was to return to Greece. In 1823 the country was in upheaval and fighting for freedom from the Ottoman Empire. Byron had the honour of being appointed by the London Greek Committee as their agent in this cause. He threw himself into it with gusto, personally and financially, donating thousands of pounds to set up and arm the brig *Hercules*, although he himself never got to see any military action.

Lord Byron was an enigmatic and cynical man who effortlessly made women swoon, and perhaps there is more to his love of Greece than is known. Unfortunately his memoirs, which were deemed too scandalous even by his closest liberal-minded friends, were thrown in the fire after his death at the age of just 37.

Sanctuary of Artemis Brauron (Vravrona)

This impressive ancient site, 40 kilometres (25 miles) east of Athens, stands pretty much in the middle of nowhere. But its remoteness only adds to its romance. Surrounded by lush grasses and shady trees, this well-preserved temple is dedicated to Artemis, goddess of childbirth and hunting and protectress of animals. It dates back to the fifth century BC, when the worship of the goddess was the official cult of Attica. The site was particularly important during the Festival of Artemis, which took place every four years. For this occasion young girls aged between five and ten – priestesses in training – would wear bear skins and perform a ritual 'bear dance' where they'd imitate the movements of the goddess's favourite animal to celebrate her. You can still see the quarters where the young girls slept, as well as the impressively preserved temple – and, thanks to its remote location, chances are that you'll have the place to yourself.

The well-presented museum (which charges a separate entrance fee) is a kilometre (half a mile) further along the road and houses votive offerings found at the sanctuary.

Trips Out of Town

Bear in mind that the site is miles from any town, and bars and restaurants are hard to come by. However, there are several fruit and veg vendors on the road to the sanctuary who would probably welcome a little custom.

Sanctuary of Artemis Brauron & Museum

Vravrona (22990 27020). **Open** 8.30am-3pm Tue-Sun. **Admission** *Sanctuary* €3; €2 concessions. Free to under-18s; free to all Sun in Nov-Mar. *Museum* €3; €2 concessions; free under-18s. Free to all Sun in Nov-Mar. **No credit cards**.

Getting there

By bus

Take the 304 bus from the Ethniki Amyna metro station until it terminates, at Loutsa. The site is a 15-minute taxi journey from there. Buses depart frequently throughout the day. Tickets: ct45 regular; ct20 students.

By car

Take Mesogeion and head north in the direction of Loutsa. Once there, follow the signs for the Sanctuary of Artemis at Vravrona.

Porto Rafti

Once the exclusive summer playground of the wealthy, these days Porto Rafti welcomes a more varied crowd for the sunny season. Nowadays smart three-storey apartments stand tall over the grand old villas, while small boats mingle with flashy yachts in the peaceful bay.

Porto Rafti's family-friendly shingle beach is broken up into protected natural bays so it's perfect for paddling toddlers. Above, on the tree-lined promenade, young Greeks cool off in a string of fashionable shaded café-bars (open 10am-4am), whiling away the afternoons drinking frappés and playing *tavli* (backgammon) until the sun sets and beyond.

Where to eat & drink

The parasol-shaded **Café Status** (Leof Gregou 87, 22990 72603, closed Mon-Thur from Oct to May) is among the busiest daytime cafés and at night it grooves to R&B and chart hits. The luxuriously whitewashed **Café del Mar** (Leof Gregou 41, 22990 75698) on the southern tip of the town exudes an island-esque chilled-out vibe during the day, while at night DJs pump chart pop from the popular nightspot's speakers. Further along the strip, the trendy **Smart Café** (Leof Gregou 67, 22990 72270) has a funkier feel and less mainstream music.

Getting there

By bus

Buses depart about every hour 6am-9pm from the Pedion Areos bus terminal (Mavromataion 29, 210 821 0872), next to the corner of Patision and Leof Alexandras.

By car

Take Mesogeion and head towards Markopoulo. Once there, follow the signs for Porto Rafti.

Further Afield

Delphi

A majestic landscape at the foot of Mount Parnassus, the archaeological site of Delphi (22650 82312) is on a plateau overlooking the silver-leaved olive groves of Amphissa and the gulf of Galaxidi. According to ancient Greek legend, Zeus released two eagles at opposite ends of the world and Delphi is where they met.

At first a place where Mother Earth and Poseidon were worshipped, Delphi later became the Sanctuary of Pythian Apollo, before yet still more gods (including Dionysus and Athena Pronaia) became associated with the sacred location. Delphi was also the seat of the mystical oracle, the site of the first political allegiance among the city-states (the Amphictyonic League) and, along with Olympia and Delos, one of the most important sanctuaries in the ancient world.

Inside the **Temple of Apollo** was the sanctum of the oracle where the Pythia (the priestess who delivered the oracle) would pronounce the dubious, and sometimes incomprehensible, prophecies in a state of holy intoxication. Following the victorious Battle of Marathon against the Persians, the Athenians asked the Pythia for an oracle in view of the next great upcoming expedition. The priestess pronounced that wooden walls would save the city. Taking the risk, the Athenians navigated their ships against the Persians and annihilated the Persian fleet in Salamis, ruling the seas for many years to come and imposing conditions according to their interests.

Follow the Sacred Way and gaze upon the offerings of the Athenians (Treasury of the Athenians) and other various treasuries, the Ancient Theatre in which theatrical and lyrical competitions were held, and the excellently preserved Stadium, where sports events took place as part of the Pythian Games, the second most important festival in the ancient world after the Olympic Games at Olympia.

The Tholos at **Delphi**. See p244.

Next to the Sanctuary of Apollo is the **museum** (closed for refurbishment except for the Charioteer Hall until summer 2004). On the other side are the **Temple of Athena** and the Tholos, an impressive circular structure.

For hikers, the European path E4 offers a magical route (approximately seven hours) from the village of Agoriani (€20 taxi ride from Delphi) to the archaeological site of Delphi.

Museum
Delphi (22650 82312). **Open** *Oct-Mar* 8.30am-2.45pm daily. *Apr-Sept* 8.30am-6.45pm daily. **Admission** free. Closed until summer 2004.

Sanctuary of Apollo
Delphi (22650 82312). **Open** 8.30am-2.45pm Mon; 7.30am-6.45pm Tue-Sun. **Admission** €6. **No credit cards**.

Sanctuary of Athena
Delphi (22650 82312). **Open** *Late Mar-late Sept* 7.30am-8pm daily. *Late Sept-late Mar* 7.30am-sunset daily. **Admission** free.

Where to eat & stay

You'll find Greek specialities with a fabulous view at **Epicouros** (Vas Pavlou 33, 22650 83250, closed dinner Nov-Mar, main courses €10), while **Vakhos Taverna** (Apollonos 31) has a family atmosphere, with traditional Greek cuisine, reasonable prices and a view over the valley below.

Delphi's most luxurious hotel is the A-class **Amalia** (Apollonos 1, 22650 82101, rates €141-

€190 double; €230 during Aug/the Olympics), where facilities include a restaurant, bar, swimming pool and a majestic view over the olive groves towards the gulf of Galaxidi. The **Acropole** (Philellinon 13, 22650 82675, rates €45-€75 double) is ideal for those seeking peace and quiet, while the **Xenia Hotel** (Apollonos 69, 22650 82151, rates €90-€120 double) has nice views and serves breakfast on the veranda.

Getting there

By car
Delphi is 178 kilometres (111 miles) from Athens on the Athens-Thessaloniki national road. Take the turning to Arachova-Delphi at the 84th kilometre.

By bus
There are six buses daily from the Liosion bus station. Information is available from KTEL Fokidos (210 831 7096). The fare is €11.

EXCURSIONS
The picturesque town of **Arachova** is 12 kilometres (eight miles) from Delphi on the main Athens-Delphi road. There are numerous rooms and hotels as well as some excellent tavernas – ask to try the locally produced cheese (*formela*), honey and red wine – and a vast market of traditional products in the main street with wooden goods and rugs. A further 24 kilometres (16 miles) towards Athens, the 11th-century Byzantine monastery of **Osio Loukas** is beautiful both in its setting and its rich art and architecture, with notable mosaics.

Northern Peloponnese

Head to this peninsula for a little drama, a look at some of Ancient Greece's most spectacular treasures and a feat of engineering.

The massive Peloponnese peninsula defines the southernmost part of the Greek mainland. But for a narrow strip of land (now cut across by the Corinth Canal), this wild, mountainous expanse, rich in historical significance and scenic grandeur, would be an island (its name means 'island of Pelops'). The north-eastern Argolid and Corinthia regions contain some of the most celebrated remains of antiquity: **Mycenae**, centre of an influential early Greek culture and legendary home of Agamemnon; **Ancient Corinth**, destroyed and then rebuilt by the Romans, overseen by the eyrie-like fortress of Acrocorinth; the magnificent theatre of **Epidaurus**, the largest and most complete Greek theatre in existence. And these are just the highlights.

To make the best of these sites, it's wise to find a local base, and they don't come any prettier and more relaxed than the town of **Nafplio** on the Gulf of Argolis. For something completely different, head west along the Gulf of Corinth to the lively, youthful port of **Patra**, gateway to the Ionian islands and Italy. Often overlooked by visitors, it's a messy but vibrant centre with a lively nightlife and the best carnival in Greece. South of here is ancient Olympia, venue of the original Olympic Games.

Ancient Corinth & Acrocorinth

One look at a map is enough to tell you why the city of Corinth played such a pivotal role in classical times. Commanding the narrow Isthmus of Corinth, it controlled both the lucrative sea route between the Adriatic (via the Gulf of Corinth) and the Aegean (via the Saronic Gulf), and the land route between the Peloponnese and the rest of the Greek mainland.

The city rose to prominence during the eighth century BC on the back of commerce. It founded the colonies of Corcyra on Corfu and Syracuse on Sicily, and was a major player in the various city-state power struggles that characterised the succeeding centuries (siding with Sparta against Athens in the ruinous Peloponnesian War at the end of the fifth century BC).

In 146 BC, following the Roman defeat of the Greek cities of the Achaian League, the vengeful Romans razed the city, which was then abandoned for a century. In 44 BC, however, Julius Caesar decided to rebuild Corinth on a grand scale as the provincial capital. The city prospered anew, becoming famed for its wealth (and moral laxity, if St Paul is to be believed), until major earthquakes in the fourth and sixth centuries AD reduced it to rubble. It is the ruins of the Roman Corinth that can be seen today.

Modern Corinth is a hot, dusty, utilitarian sort of place, resited on the Gulf of Corinth in the mid 19th century. Give it a miss, and concentrate on the dual attractions, a few kilometres inland, of the remains of **Ancient Corinth**, and, looming above it, the spectacularly sited fortifications of Acrocorinth.

The excavated area of the ancient city, centred on a huge agora (market place), reveals only a fraction of what was once a vast settlement. The remains are fairly confusing, so it is wise to buy a guidebook. The one stand-out structure is a surprising survival from Greek Corinth, the seven remaining Doric columns of the fifth-century BC Temple of Apollo. Look out too for the Roman Fountain of Peirene, which stands beside a stretch of the marble-lined Lechaion Way. The site museum contains a fine selection of finds, all labelled in English, but, disappointingly, without any attempt to put them into their historical context.

While the excavations are certainly fascinating, most visitors will get more of a thrill out of ascending the rocky outcrop that supports the ruined citadel of **Acrocorinth**. Once home to Ancient Corinth's acropolis (and, on its highest peak, to a temple to Aphrodite tended by 1,000 sacred prostitutes), Acrocorinth became a formidable fortress in the Middle Ages, and was used until the end of Turkish rule in 1830.

The approach is via three gates that provide an architectural history lesson about the castle's various keepers. The first is Turkish, the second Frankish and Venetian, the third Byzantine. Beyond, a range of ruins is scattered over the huge expanse of the rock-strewn hilltop, still largely encircled by its walls. A Frankish keep perches on the second highest peak, and it's well worth

Trips Out of Town

The Corinth Canal

But for a mere six-kilometre (four-mile) strip of land, the Peloponnese peninsula would be an island. And if it were, how much quicker and safer navigation between the Adriatic and Aegean seas would be. Such was the problem that vexed minds as long ago as 602 BC, when Periander, tyrant of Corinth, considered, then rejected (following dire warnings from the Delphic Oracle), a plan to sink a canal across the isthmus.

The journey around the dangerous southern cape of the Peloponnese added 185 nautical miles to a ship's voyage between the two seas. Such was the risk and cost of the journey that, in the early sixth century BC, the Corinthians constructed a limestone-paved road called the *diolkos* between the Corinthian and Saronic Gulfs (traces of it are still visible today). Along this road ran the *olkos*, a wheeled cart that laboriously transported ships from one sea to the other. It proved a huge source of income and prestige for Corinth.

Yet the dreams of forging a nautical route across the isthmus persisted. In 307 BC another attempt was made. Demetrios Poliorcetes started a canal, before being scared off by Egyptian engineers, who persuaded him that differences in sea levels would result in the islands of the Saronic Gulf sinking under the waves.

The next serious attempt came in 67 AD, when Nero forced 6,000 Jewish slaves to start digging. They had created a trench 3,300 metres (10,830 feet) long and 40 metres (131 feet) wide before domestic troubles in Rome forced the Emperor back home and the project was abandoned.

The Byzantines tried, the Venetians tried. But time and again the enormity (and cost) of the task proved overwhelming.

It wasn't until the technological advances of the Industrial Revolution that the canal project finally seemed feasible. A plan was considered, then put aside, by the new Greek government soon after the country gained its independence from the Turks in 1830. It was the opening of the Suez Canal in 1869 that provided the spur – the Greeks assigned the mammoth task to a French company soon after. But yet again it stalled.

In 1881 Hungarian general Stefan Tyrr took over the project, and work commenced the following year. The canal took 11 years to complete, and followed almost exactly the route proposed by Nero 1,800 years earlier.

It measured 6,346 metres (20,820 feet) in length, was 24.6 metres (81 feet) wide at sea level and around eight metres (26 feet) deep, and caused 12 million cubic metres (423,792,000 cubic feet) of earth to be displaced. On 25 July 1893 the Corinth Canal opened to traffic.

The greatest irony of this stupendous engineering feat, which was two and a half thousand years in conception, is that within a century of its opening the development of super container ships, easily able to round the Peloponnese and too large for the canal, rendered it all but obsolete.

City of 1,000 sacred prostitutes: **Acrocorinth**.

the effort of climbing up to Acrocorinth's highest point (a tough half-hour hike from the car park) to gasp at the staggering 360-degree views from the summit.

Acrocorinth
No phone. **Open** 8am-7pm daily. **Admission** free.

Ancient Corinth Site & Museum
27410 31207. **Open** *Apr-Oct* 8am-7pm daily. *Nov-Mar* 8am-5pm daily. **Admission** €6. **No credit cards.**

Where to eat & drink

In terms of views, **Acrocorinthos**, a café/restaurant by the entrance to Acrocorinth, certainly has the edge over the many touristy tavernas in the village that has grown up around the ruins of Ancient Corinth. However, for the ultimate atmospheric experience, take a picnic up to the peak of Acrocorinth.

Mycenae

In the eighth century BC, in his epic poems *The Iliad* and *The Odyssey*, Homer spoke of the 'well-built Mycenae, rich in gold'. According to *The Iliad*, Agamemnon, king of Mycenae and the richest and most powerful king of Greece, headed the Greek expedition to Troy. Caused by the abduction of Helen, wife of Menelaus, king of Sparta and brother of Agamemnon, by Paris, the son of the king of Troy, the ten-year war (1193 BC-1184 BC) brought

with it the heroic deeds of Achilles, the cunning of Odysseus and even divided the gods of Olympus.

Until the 19th century these poems were regarded as little more than enthralling legends. Then, in the 1870s, the amateur archaeologist Heinrich Schliemann (1822-90), ignoring the jeers of his professional counterparts, struck gold: first by excavating Troy in present-day Turkey, and then Mycenae. He uncovered the graves of more than a dozen people, all bedecked in gold and jewels, and was convinced he'd found the tomb of Agamemnon. Although these were later dated to at least 300 years earlier than the Trojan War, Schliemann had found evidence of Mycenae's wealth at its peak.

Neolithic settlements first appeared in Mycenae in the sixth millennium BC. In the late Bronze Age, the kingdom was the most powerful in Greece, holding control over the Aegean, and building a legacy of grand palaces and fortified constructions before beginning to wane around 1200 BC.

The citadel of Mycenae is surrounded by a gigantic wall so impressive that the Ancient Greeks believed it to have been built by a Cyclops, one of the fierce one-eyed giants described in Homer's *Odyssey*. It can be entered through the impressive Lion Gate, with the main path leading up to the ruins of Agamemnon's Palace, the Throne Room and the Great Court.

The best-preserved Mycenaean structure by far, however, lies outside the bounds of the citadel. The immense royal *tholos* tomb (built

Trips Out of Town

with blocks of stone, tapering to the top, and then covered with earth) is misleadingly known as the Treasury of Atreus or the Tomb of Agamemnon, but it was built several hundred years before Agamemnon's era.

The remains of the magnificent gold treasures of the Mycenaean civilisation are housed at the National Archaeological Museum in Athens (*see p105*).

It is worth buying a guidebook and perusing the excellent site museum before attempting to make sense of the ruins, which, tombs aside, are relatively scant and confusing.

Archaeological Site of Mycenae & Museum

27510 76585. **Open** noon-7pm Mon; 8am-7pm Tue-Sun. **Admission** €6; concessions €3. **No credit cards.**

Where to eat & drink

The village of Mycenae offers plenty of touristy eating options. One of the best places lining the main road is **Mycinaiko** (27510 76724, main courses around €7). Go for whatever's been cooked fresh on the day.

Epidaurus

Henry Miller dedicated over ten pages of his book *The Colossus of Maroussi* to the magical landscape of Epidaurus ('open, exposed… devoted to the spirit') and the surrounding area.

At the top of the archaeological site is the Ancient Theatre, which dates back to the fourth century BC. Unearthed by Greek archaeologists at the beginning of the 19th century, it is today the largest and best preserved of its kind. The theatre seats up to 14,000 spectators and is renowned for its amazing acoustics – drop a coin in the centre of the amphitheatre and the sound will be heard as far as the highest seat.

Today, classical dramas are performed at this venerable venue during the annual Epidaurus Festival (*see p188* **Staging the classics**), an experience that will send a shiver down your spine when you consider that someone almost certainly sat in the same seat watching the same play more than 2,000 years before you.

At Epidaurus you'll also find the **Sanctuary of Asclepius** (dedicated to the Greek god of medicine), which includes the Katagogeion and the Temple of Asclepius, as well as the remains of a *tholos*, a gymnasium and a stadium.

Archaeological Site of Ancient Epidaurus

27530 22009. **Open** 8am-7pm daily. **Admission** €6. **No credit cards.**

Where to eat

Build up a healthy appetite exploring the sites, then head to the village of Lygourio, four kilometres (two miles) from Epidaurus, where you'll find the famous **Leonidas** taverna (Epidavrou 103, 27530 22115, closed Mon-Fri Oct-Mar, meal without drinks €10-€12). Decorated with photographs of performances at the Ancient Theatre and serving delicious traditional Greek cuisine, Leonidas has over the years catered for a multitude of cast members and was reputedly Melina Mercouri and her husband Jules Dassin's favourite.

Getting there

By bus

From Kifissos station in Athens (100 Kifissou, 210 513 4110) to Nafplio there are 15 buses daily (€9); from Nafplio to Mycenae four local buses daily at 10am, noon, 2pm and 6pm (€2); from Mycenae to Nafplio four local buses daily at 11am, 1pm, 3pm and 7pm (€2).

From Kifissos station to Lygourio two buses run daily (€8.60); from Nafplio to Epidaurus four local buses daily at 10.15am, noon, 2pm and 2.30pm, which return at noon, 1pm, 4pm and 6pm (€2). There is also a local bus service between Nafplio and Lygourio (KTEL Argolidos, 210 513 4588).

Organised tours to Mycenae and Epidaurus are available from Chat Tours (210 323 0827; €69 inc admission and guide, €79 with lunch) and Key Tours (210 923 3166; €69 inc admission and guide, €79 with lunch).

By car

Take the Athens-Corinth-Tripolis national road to reach Ancient Corinth. Follow the signs to Argos-Nafplio and, after 9km (5 miles), turn left for the archaeological site of Mycenae. For Epidaurus (27km/16.5 miles from Nafplio) follow the signs to Lygourio-Epidaurus.

Nafplio

Easily the most agreeable spot to base yourself in the north-eastern Peloponnese is Nafplio. The origins of this relaxed little town – named after Nafplius, son of Poseidon – are obscure, and it wasn't until the Byzantines fortified the settlement at the end of the 12th century that it emerged as an important commercial and strategic regional centre. The following centuries saw it pass through many hands – Franks, Venetians, Turks – before it enjoyed a brief five-year glow of national importance as the capital of the newly independent Greek state. (Athens took over this role in 1834.) In 1831, the country's first leader, Ioannis Kapodistrias, was shot dead in a vendetta outside the church of Agios Spyridon (the hole made by the fatal bullet is still visible behind a glass panel beside the door).

Trips Out of Town

Modern Nafplio is split between a workaday new town and a lovely Old Town that sits snugly beneath the rocky outcrop of Akronafplia. Its eventful history is writ in stone, from the massive fortifications of the Palamidi castle on the hill to the multicoloured marble-paved and mansion-lined pedestrianised streets that lead down to the harbour.

It's easy to do nothing in Nafplio, but the town has a handful of attractions worth seeking out. Its one-time military significance is obvious in the presence of not one, not two, but three castles. The picturesquely sited little fortress of Bourtzi sits out in the harbour (no public access); it was built by the Venetians in 1470 and then remodelled by them during their second period of occupation at the end of the 17th century. Akronafplia was the site of the Byzantine town and a series of strongholds, though only remnants of their walls remain. The key destination for castle-lovers, however, is the mighty **Palamidi Fortress**, which can be reached by car, or, for the fit, by an extraordinary 913-step staircase that snakes up the almost-sheer slopes of the hill from the town. The Venetians constructed its extensive fortifications in the early 18th century. Explore the endless crenellated walls, dark passages, wide stairwells and look-out points and enjoy the wondrous views.

Back in the Old Town there are a couple of museums worthy of a look. The award-winning **Peloponnesian Folklore Foundation** contains a beautiful selection of Greek folk costumes, though disappointingly little information about them. On the wonderfully central café-edged square of Platia Syntagmatos stands the **Archaeological Museum**, which has a decent selection of local finds, though, again, with precious little explanation. The collection's prize exhibit is a very rare Mycenaean armour. There are also some frescoes from Tiryns, a once-mighty Mycenaean city, the remains of which lie a couple of kilometres outside Nafplio.

Tiryns itself is well worth a visit, not least because it's mostly ignored by the tour bus convoys that hurtle round the better-known sites in the area, and you are thus quite likely to be able to enjoy its ruins alone. Some parts of Tiryns have been dated to 2600 BC, though the majority of what you can see today dates from a millennium later. The height and strength of its walls were famed in antiquity, and what is left still impresses, particularly when you hear they were originally twice their current height.

When you've had your fill of ancient stones and want nothing more than to laze on a beach, head for **Karathonas**, a five-minute drive east of the town. This long, greyish, likeable strand

Sitting on the dock of...

is popular with Greek families and holds a scattering of beach bars and restaurants. For something more lively, a 15-minute drive will take you to the resort of **Tolo**.

Archaeological Museum

Platia Syntagmatos (27520 27502).
Open 8.30am-3pm Tue-Sun. **Admission** free.

Palamidi Fortress

27520 28036. **Open** 8.30am-6.30pm daily.
Admission €4; concessions free-€2.
No credit cards

Peloponnesian Folklore Foundation

Ypsilantou 1 (27520 28379/28947/25267/ www.pli.gr). **Open** 9am-3pm Mon, Wed-Sun.
Closed Feb. **Admission** €4; concessions €2-€3.
Credit DC, MC, V (gift shop).

Tiryns Archaeological Site

27520 22657. **Open** 7am-8pm daily. **Admission** €3; concessions €2. **No credit cards.**

Where to eat & drink

Nafplio teems with tavernas. The main food thoroughfare is pedestrianised Staikopolou, which is filled with outdoor tables and waiters exhorting you to choose their joint over their neighbours'. Don't let this put you off, though. **To Fanaria**

... **Nafplio** bay.

(No.13, 27520 27141, main courses from €7)
is excellent; try their lamb cooked with tiny
pasta in tomato sauce if it's available.

If you want to eat where the locals eat,
and don't mind sitting by a road opposite a
car park near the cargo port, then you can enjoy
some bargain-priced classic Greek cooking at
Nafplios (corner of Bouboulinas and Syngrou,
27520 97999, main courses €5-€10), which since
1966 has been knocking out the likes of superb
spit-roasted pork with crackling and the most
generous Greek salads you'll ever encounter.

For a more romantic setting, and some
seriously good fish, head round the end of
the peninsula, where a couple of restaurant-
bars enjoy an impossibly lovely setting right on
the water. The pick is **Agnanti** (Akti Miaouli,
27520 29332, main courses €8-€30). It's hard to
beat this spot for a sundowner, but if you want
a livelier drinking scene, the boisterous back-to-
back bars along Bouboulinas will deliver. For
dancing, head to one of the purpose-built clubs
around the bay, or hop in a cab to the youthful
resort of Tolo, 15 minutes' drive away.

Where to stay

As a well-established resort, there's no shortage
of places to stay in all categories in Nafplio. In
summer 2003 it even got its own design hotel,
the chic, sleek **Amphitryon Hotel** (Spiliadou

21, 27520 70700, www.nafplionhotels.gr,
doubles €200-€320); each room has a terrace
with wonderful sea views. Another luxury
option, the **Nafplia Palace** (Acronafplia,
27520 28981-5, www.nafplionhotels.gr,
doubles €200-€270), is perched just above it.
You don't get the views at **Ilion** (Elthimiopolou
4 & Kapodistriou 6, 27520 25114/22010,
www.ilionhotel.gr, doubles €74-€132), back
in the Old Town, but you do get a lot more
idiosyncratic character, with individually
themed rooms flamboyantly decorated
and decked out with antiques.

More affordable options include the
six properties that make up the **Pension
Acronafplia** (Papanikolaou 34, Vas
Konstantinou 20 & Agios Spiridou 6, 27520
24481/24076, www.pension-acronafplia.com,
doubles €45-€70). A good mid-range choice is
Kapodistrias Traditional House (Kokinou
20, 27520 29366, www.hotelkapodistrias.gr,
doubles €50-€100), while a popular budget
spot is the **Dafni Pension** (Fotomara 10 &
Iatrou 5, 27520 29856, mobile 6972 708133,
www.pensiondafni.gr, doubles €45-€70).

Tourist information

The information office is on 25 Martiou
(27520 24444, www.nafplio.gr, open 9am-1pm,
4-8pm daily).

Patra, Athens' raffish little brother. *See p254.*

Getting there

By bus

There are buses to Athens and to the nearby resort of Tolo every hour, and to Argos every half hour. Three buses a day go to Mycenae and four a day to the Theatre of Epidaurus. The bus station is on Syngrou (27520 27323/27423). On weekends during July and August there are extra buses to Epidaurus from Nafplio at 7pm and from Athens at 5pm laid on for the drama performances at the Ancient Theatre. They return right after the performance.

By car

Nafplio is 146km (98 miles) from Athens.

By train

Two trains a day run between Nafplio and Athens and Piraeus via Argos and Corinth. An additional train goes only as far as Argos. The rail station is by the port (for more information, call 27520 29380).

Olympia

Ancient Olympia, the ancient Sanctuary of Zeus and home of the first Olympics, is deservedly the main tourist attraction of the western Peloponnese. Though packed during the summer months, it's well worth braving the crowds to explore the impressive site.

Olympia is about five hours from Athens, so we advise an overnight stay somewhere nearby or, better still, that you make it part of a longer trip exploring central or south-western parts of the Peloponnese. If you try to do it in one day you'll likely end up exhausted and too overwhelmed by the experience to fully appreciate everything that Olympia has to offer.

Named after Mount Olympus much further north in Central Greece, Olympia was the most important sanctuary of the ancient world. The cult of Zeus started to develop around 1200 BC and, according to myth, Zeus's son Heracles appointed him patron of the Olympic Games. The Games took place every four years and were reorganised in 776 BC by Iphitus, King of Elis, who introduced the Sacred Truce (*ekecheiria*). Before and during the celebrations a ceasefire was declared among all Greek city-states for a month. Only free-born male Greeks were allowed to participate or spectate: neither slaves nor women could pass the gate of Altis, the sacred precinct – with just one single exception recorded throughout history. Kallipateira, a woman from Rhodes, disguised herself as a man and managed to enter the stadium, but her identity was revealed while celebrating her son's victory. Claiming her blood relationship with more than one Olympic champion, she was spared the death penalty, but thereafter it was decided that all participants and trainers should appear naked (*see also pp44-5*).

The most important monuments of the archaeological site include the Temple of Zeus (as large and impressive as its contemporary, the Athenian Parthenon), which once featured the now-lost gold-and-ivory statue of Zeus, one of the Seven Wonders of the Ancient World, by Phidias; the Temple of Hera, where the famous statue of Hermes by Praxiteles was discovered in 1877; the Pelopeion, dedicated to the cult of the ancient hero Pelops; the Treasuries, small edifices that operated as storage chambers of valuable offerings; and the Stadium, capable of accommodating up to 45,000 spectators.

The **Archaeological Museum of Olympia** (26240 22517) holds some of the most magnificent examples of ancient Greek sculpture, including Praxiteles's Hermes and Paionios's Nike. It closed for pre-Olympic refurbishments and was scheduled to reopen some time in 2004; call to check before visiting.

Olympia is sited at the fertile confluence of the Alfeios and Kladeos rivers, and the surrounding rural areas have a lot of natural and historical interest, though Pyrgos, the regional capital, is somewhat less than scenic. The locals are looked down on as hicks by their compatriots, and though they do try to be helpful with foreigners they tend to come across as rather brusque and stand-offish. The modern town of Olympia, tediously overrun with souvenir shops, gives the impression that it was built just to serve the archaeological site. The **Museum of the Olympic Games** is its one and only drawing point.

After so many hours under the hot Olympian sun, you undoubtedly deserve a relaxing dip and you will get it if you head south to **Kaiafas** and its idyllic stretch of sands. To the west the beaches around **Katakolo** are a fairly good option as well. Also try **Skafidia**, just three kilometres (two miles) north, and the so-called **Aldemar** beach, named after the nearby five-star hotel (*see below*). It will take you around 30 minutes to reach any of these beaches by car.

From mid July to mid August the **Floka Festival** at the recently built Olympia Theatre features drama, music, dance and other cultural happenings. For more information, contact the Municipality of Olympia (26240 22549).

Archaeological Site of Olympia
26240 22517. **Open** 8am-7pm daily. **Admission** €6; concessions free-€3. **No credit cards**.

Museum of the Olympic Games
Spiliopouliu (26240 22544). **Open** 8am-3.30pm Mon-Sat; 9am-4.30pm Sun. **Admission** €2; free under-18s. **No credit cards**.

Where to eat & drink

Good value for money and a friendly atmosphere is what you will get at the traditional taverna of **Kladeos** (26240 23322, main courses €7-€11), right behind the railway station in Olympia. Try **En Plo** (26210 41300, main courses €8-€12) in Katakolo for home-made specialities by the sea. Popular with the locals, **Aigli** (4km off the Pyrgos-Patras road, 26210 22502, main courses €8-€10) serves delicious cooked dishes speedily.

Where to stay

The **Aldemar Olympian Village** (Skafidia, Pyrgos, 26210 54640, www.aldemarhotels.com, closed Oct-Apr, doubles €145-€200) is about a half-hour drive from Olympia, but the facilities and service will definitely recompense you. The **Amalia Hotel Olympia** (210 607 2000, www.amalia.gr, doubles €125-€145), two kilometres before Ancient Olympia, offers clean and comfortable rooms and well-kept patios. For an exceptional view of Olympia, try the recently refurbished **Antonios Hotel** (Krestena, 26240 22348, www.olympiahotels.gr, doubles €56-€114). A good budget option is **Camping Diana** (26240 22314, €5.50 per person, €3.50 tent, €3.50 car), a 15-minute walk from the archaeological site; facilities include a swimming pool and a mini-market for basic supplies. There is also a **Youth Hostel** (Praxiteli Kondyli 18, 26240 22580, €8 per person plus €1 for extra sheets).

Getting there

By bus

KTEL buses to Olympia leave Kifissos station (Kifissou 100, 210 513 4110) twice daily (5.5hrs; €19). Call ahead to check the timetable.

By car

Olympia is 334km (208 miles) from Athens via Patras (coastal drive, national highway) or 323km (200 miles) via Tripolis (inland drive, many curves). Both routes are well signposted.

By train

Trains to Olympia leave Athens' Larissis station (Karolou 1-3, 210 529 7777) twice daily (5hrs; €14). Call ahead to check the timetable.

Getting around

There is no direct bus service from Olympia to Katakolo, Kaiafas and the nearby villages. You'll need to get to Pyrgos first and then continue your trip. Buses leave from Olympia for Pyrgos and from Pyrgos for the coastal and mainland villages every hour. For more information, contact the offices of KTEL Ileias in Athens (210 513 4110).

Patra

Patra doesn't get the best of press. For most visitors, the only reason to journey to this port 225 kilometres (141 miles) west of Athens, on the north-west edge of the Peloponnese, is to catch a ferry to Italy or the Ionian islands. Yet this irrepressibly lively little city (Greece's third largest, and its second port) is not without its charms, particularly when the sun goes down and the pavement cafés start to fill. In fact, it's Patra's zesty, youthful nightlife that is its primary draw – and it's at its fullest during the mayhem of the biggest and best Carnival in Greece, which runs for seven weeks up to Lent. And the city is only likely to improve. It will be European Cultural Capital for 2006, setting in train a slew of much needed renovations and improvements to its infrastructure.

Patra is laid out on a grid plan, stretching uphill from the busy port, and becomes steadily more attractive the higher you climb. Its modern lower reaches are dominated by constant traffic and nondescript blocks, but the shopping here is good, particularly in the streets between and around Platia Olgas and Platia Georgiou.

A half day is plenty to take in the few sights. Overlooking the town is the ruined **Kastro** (Castle) (2610 623 390, closed Mon, Sun afternoon, admission free), built on the site of the ancient acropolis in the sixth century AD, and continually in use until World War II. There's not a lot to see, but the archaeologically inclined might enjoy untangling the architectural legacies of successive Frankish, Byzantine, Venetian and Turkish rulers.

Nearby stands the **Roman Odeon** (2610 220 829, open mornings Tue-Sun, admission free), described by Pausanias around 170 AD as the second-finest odeon in Greece (after that in Athens). It was built some time before 160 BC and went out of use by the third century AD. Today, it's the venue for theatre and music events during Patra's enjoyable **Summer Arts Festival** (early June-late Sept, 2610 620 236).

Some of the local finds from classical times are laid out around the Odeon. Others are on display in the two-room **Archaeological Museum of Patra** (Mezonos 42, 2610 275 070, closed Mon, admission free). The highlight is a superb Roman mosaic pavement from a villa uncovered in the town.

You might also want to visit the vast bulk of the Byzantine-style church of **Agiou Andreou** (St Andrew), which was completed in 1974 and dominates the south-western corner of the city.

If you need a break from metropolitan life, a popular (though touristy) trip is to the **Achaïa Clauss** winery (Petroto Patron, 2610 368 100), just outside Patra, where the famed Mavrodaphne dessert wine is made.

If lying on a beach is more your thing, then the nearest is Plaz, a ten-minute, two-euro cab ride north of the city. Bikes are available free of charge from the extremely helpful Info Center on the waterfront, which also has an excellent English-language guide to the city.

Where to eat & drink

Though Patra is abuzz with traffic noise from dawn until well after dusk, there are sanctuaries to be found on a number of pedestrianised, café-lined streets. The hippest alleyway in town is Radinou, one block south of Platia Olgas, which throbs with the chatter of Patra's sizeable student population and the clubby sounds pulsing out of a strip of bars named Time, Lobby, Blue Monday and the like.

For a little more space and a little less volume, head a further block south to the cafés on Agiou Nikolaou, or those not far from the church of Agiou Andreou on tree-lined, traffic-free Trion Navarhon. The best eating in Patra is to be had at taverna-style places, and there's a great one here, on the corner with Riga

Convivial street-corner dining at **Mythos**.

Fereou, called **Mythos** (2610 329 984) –
it's cosy, candlelit, much loved by locals and
serves up great meaty dishes, meze and salads.

The other main pedestrianised nightlife area
is at the top end of Gerokostopoulou and along
the cross street Ifestou, just below the Odeon.

For somewhere more chilled, keep heading
upwards until you reach Papadiamandopoulou,
immediately below the castle. Try meze and a
carafe of the dark local wine at **Mourias** (No.34,
2610 276 797, closed Oct-Mar and lunch Apr-
Sept, main courses from €4.50) or **Kastro**
(Panagouli 22, 2610 622 584).

Bars stay open into the early hours, but
Patra isn't great for clubs. The city's dance kids
decamp during summer to the Rio resort, eight
kilometres (five miles) north-east (a ten-minute
No.6 bus ride away), where the waterfront is
a continuous strip of bars and discos.

Where to stay

Until recently, accommodation options in Patra
weren't exactly appetising. The big, blocky 120-
room **Astir** (Agiou Andreou 16, 2610 277 502,
www.greekhotel.com, doubles €103-€124)
dominated both the waterfront and the classier
end of the market. Its rooftop bar and pool still
appeal, but two smaller hotels now easily trump
it for style. The 25-room **Byzantino Hotel**
(Riga Fereou 106 & Asklipiou 26, 2610 243 000,
www.byzantino-hotel.gr, doubles €140-€170) is
cleanly designed in an updated trad style, while
the **Primarolia Art Hotel** (Othonos Amalias

33, 2610 624 900, www.arthotel.gr, doubles
€118-€177) is an incongruously gorgeous
piece of contemporary design on Patra's
grimy waterfront, with 14 rooms decked
out with Jacobsen and Starck gems and
hung with modern Greek artworks.

Further down the price scale, don't expect
much character. The dull-but-reliable **Galaxy**
(Agiou Nikolaou 9, 2610 278 815, doubles from
€62) is well located, while those on a tight
budget shouldn't have any complaints about
Pension Nicos (Patreos 3 & Agiou Andreou
121, 2610 623 757, doubles €30-€35).

Tourist information

Othonos Amalias 6 (2610 461 740/461 741).
Open 8am-10pm daily.

Getting there

By bus

Buses to and from Athens leave every half hour
(ten of these are express services). Journey time:
3hrs 30mins/2hrs 30mins express. The bus station
is located on Othonos Amalias, the road that
runs along the waterfront.

By car

It takes around 2hrs 30mins to reach Patra
from Athens on the main E94 and E65 roads.

By train

There are eight daily trains to and from Athens.
Journey time: 3hrs 30mins. All call at Corinth. The
station is on the waterfront, close to the bus station.

Island Escapes

If the buzz of the city gets too much for you, hop aboard a ferry.

It's well known that Piraeus is the jumping-off point for ferries to the Greek islands. But what comes as a surprise to many visitors is that some of the loveliest islands – if not the best endowed with beaches – are within a couple of hours of the mainland. It is entirely possible to pop over to **Aegina** (40 minutes by fast boat) for lunch.

The four islands listed below – pine-clad **Spetses** (two hours by fast boat), cosmopolitan **Hydra** (90 minutes), scenic, lively **Poros** (one hour) and engagingly undeveloped Aegina – are all rewarding day-trip or weekend destinations. If you do them as a quick side-trip from Athens it makes sense to take the fast boat rather than the regular ferry: journey times are halved. Two companies, Flying Dolphins (210 419 9200/ www.dolphins.gr) and Saronic Dolphins (210 422 4777), run services to all four, leaving from the dockside at Piraeus about 200 metres south of the metro station, beside (Akti) Miaouli. Ticket booths (credit cards accepted at Flying Dolphins) are open for perhaps an hour before each departure, but note that if you want to travel on a Friday afternoon or Saturday morning and return Sunday afternoon in high season (mid June to September), it is essential to buy tickets in advance. In high season, at least, there are several departures a day, but they thin out at other times. Make sure you don't get stranded.

If you prefer to use the slower, cheaper, conventional ferries, we recommend you book via a travel agent (*see p263*) as services can be confusing.

Aegina

Aegina, an island of 85 square kilometres (33 square miles) and a population of 10,000, is a mere 40-minute jaunt from Piraeus by hydrofoil, but a world away from the fumes and angst of Athens. Here you can visit one of the finest ancient monuments in the country, relax at a seaside taverna, or rent a bike and breeze through the endearing, pocket-sized port capital Aegina Town, where the boats drop you off, taking in the neo-classical buildings from its days as Greece's first capital after the War of Independence, its horse-drawn carriages and its fishing boats bobbing gently at the waterfront. City life will soon be a distant memory.

Twelve kilometres (about eight miles) east of Aegina Town is the intricate and immaculately preserved fifth-century BC **Temple of Aphaia** (22970 32398, admission €4). Aphaia was a local goddess, later identified with Athena. It's a top-rank site and worth the journey, especially since en route are the **Monastery of St Nektarios** and the island's abandoned, atmospheric medieval capital, **Paleohora**.

Antiquary opportunities within walking distance of Aegina Town are at **Kolona**, home of the ruins of the **Temple of Apollo**, and the **Archaeological Museum** (22970 22248, closed Mon, admission €3) located just north of the port.

The best spots for a swim are **Marathona** or **Aeginitsa** on the west coast, and **Kleidi** and **Keri** near the southern village of **Perdika** – an ideal place for a seaside lunch. The more commercialised eastern resort of **Agia Marina** also has some decent beaches. Shuttle boats leave from the main harbour.

Where to eat & drink

For great seafood in Aegina Town, try **Agora** (22970 27308, closed Aug, main courses €5-€15) at the fish market, south of the port and a block inland, or **Lekkas** (22970 22527, closed mid Dec-Feb, main courses €8-€15) on the seafront. The classic waterfront café **Aiakeion** (22970 22249, closed Nov-Mar) has cakes to die for. In Perdika, **To Proreon** (22970 61827, main courses €8-€15) is a first-rate taverna on the seafront.

For nightlife in Aegina Town, **On the Beach**, **Belle Epoque**, **En Aigini** and **Ellinikon** are all lively hangouts. Clubs are clustered on the waterfront.

Where to stay

Most hotels quote a 'door price', but this can often be lowered with bargaining. In Aegina Town, the **Aegenitiko Archontiko** (Agiou Nikolaou & Thomaidou 1, 22970 24968, doubles €50-€70) is traditional and friendly, while **Hotel Areti** (Kazantzakis 4, 22970 23593, doubles €40-€50) offers sea views. In Perdika, **Hotel Hippocampus** (28 Oktovriou, 22970 61363, doubles €35-€40) is traditional and cosy.

Seafood rules supreme in **Aegina**'s tavernas.

The pine-fringed Agia Paraskevi on **Spetses**.
See p258.

Tourist information

Aegina doesn't have an independent tourist information centre. **Aegina Island Holidays** (Dimokratias 47, 22970 26430, closed Sun) is a helpful private travel bureau on the seafront.

Getting around

The bus station on Platia Ethneyersias runs an excellent service to most villages on the island. Regular services run to the Temple of Aphaia, and eight to ten per day run from Aegina Town along the west coast of the island, stopping at Marathona and Perdika. You could also rent a bike or scooter from one of several rental centres near the port, where you can also pick up horse-drawn carriages.

Spetses

The pine-clad island of Spetses is scenic, vibrant and cosmopolitan, steeped in history, and just two hours from Piraeus by hydrofoil. It covers 23 square kilometres (nine square miles) and has a population of about 4,000.

The best way to enjoy the charming courtyards and grand neo-classical mansions of the port capital Spetses Town is by bike or on foot (cars are completely banned on the island). Horse-drawn carriages offer a romantic, if expensive, alternative.

The majestic Mexis Mansion in the town centre once belonged to the island's first governor, Hadziyiannis Mexis, and now houses the **Museum of Spetses** (22980 72994, closed afternoons & Mon, admission €3). It displays relics from the 1821 Greek War of Independence and houses the bones of Spetsiot heroine Laskarina Bouboulina, a leading figure in the fight against the Turks. The **House of Laskarina Bouboulina** (22980 72416, closed Nov-Mar, tours every 45mins 9.45am-8.15pm, admission €4) can also be visited at the cannon-dotted modern port of **Dapia** (a rallying point during the revolution, now the island's commercial centre, and where your boat will drop you off). The island's medieval district of **Kastelli**, the **Old Harbour** and the **Church of St Nicholas** (22980 72423), with its giant pebble mosaics, are all nearby and worth a visit.

The **Anargyreios and Korgialenios School** (22980 72206, call 8am-2pm to arrange a tour), about 15 minutes' walk west of Dapia, was an English public school where British writer John Fowles used to teach.

You can walk to some reasonable coves from Spetses Town, but the best beaches on the island are at **Agia Anarghiri** – a long, sheltered sandy bay in the south of Spetses – and **Agia Paraskevi**, a few kilometres further west (on the hill above it is the **Villa Yasemia** – used

by Fowles as the setting for *The Magus*). Water taxis are an exhilarating way to get to secluded beaches, but they don't come cheap.

The little **Church of Panaghia Daskalaki**, on top of Spetses' mountain, merits a visit – the hike from town is not too strenuous and is a good way to build up an appetite.

Where to eat & drink

For fish and lobster spaghetti, try **Exedra** (22980 73497, closed Nov-Feb, main courses €8-€10), on a jetty at the Old Harbour. **Lazaros** in Kastelli (22980 72600, closed mid Oct-March, main courses €8-€12) serves good cooked dishes and own-make retsina, and the famed **Patralis** fish taverna (22980 72134, closed Oct-7 Jan, main courses €8-€12) in the area of Kounoupitsa, west of the port, is also worth a visit. **Bracciera** and **Figaro**, near the port, are popular clubs.

Where to stay

A short walk from Spetses Town, in Kounoupitsa, the traditional **Economou Mansion** (22980 73400, doubles €100-€205) is much loved for its huge balconies. Also in Kounoupitsa is the luxurious **Nissia** (22980 75000/210 342 1279, doubles €135-€200). For more affordable comfort, a good bet is the **Yachting Club Inn** (22980 73400, doubles €42-€70), near the beach half a mile from town.

Tourist information

The island's tourist police in the town centre (22980 73100, closed after 3pm and Oct-mid May) can provide you with information on accommodation, places to visit and eating and drinking out.

Getting around

You can reach most parts of the island by bicycle or motorbike – visit one of the various rental outlets in Spetses Town. Small boats ferry locals and visitors from Dapia to various beaches during the summer. Sea taxis are an expensive alternative but can take up to ten people for a set price. Horse-drawn carriages are also available.

Hydra

Arriving on this picturesque 50-square-kilometre (19-square-mile) island (population 3,000) after a 90-minute hydrofoil trip from Piraeus is like stepping into a painting. The distinctive neo-classical stone mansions of Hydra Town ascend amphitheatrically around the port, fishing boats bob along the waterfront where tasselled donkeys await their next

Room with a view: the picturesque, car-free island of **Hydra**.

expedition along cobbled lanes (cars are banned on the island) and cafés teem with a cosmopolitan crowd.

For spectacular sea views, follow Boundouri, a pebbly path fringed with poppies that winds upwards from the port and towards the fishing village of Kamini; the route is magical at night. Or climb the mountain from town to the **Monastery of Profitis Ilias** (22980 52540, closed noon-4pm daily), the adjacent **Convent of St Efpraxia** (22980 52484) and the nearby uninhabited **Monastery of St Triada** – the views justify the one-hour trek.

For beaches, try **Mandraki** and **Vlichos**, near the port. For more solitude, head to **Bisti** and **Agios Nikolaos** in the west and **Limioniza** in the south. Sea taxis take up to eight passengers at a time, to the above and other destinations, for a set price.

Drag yourself away from the island's natural beauty to visit the **Panaghia Mitropoleos** cathedral (22980 52829, closed afternoons Sept-Apr), whose distinctive clock tower dominates the waterfront and which houses the ecclesiastical **Byzantine Museum** (22980 54071, closed Mon, admission €1.50). Relics from the 1821 revolution are on display at the island's **Historical Archives & Museum** (22980 52355, admission €3) at the port. Also worthy of a quick tour is the **Mansion of Lazaros Koundouriotis**, 22980 52421, admission €4) – once the home of the island's wealthy 18th-century merchant family – where the **Historical & Folk Museum** and **Public Art Gallery** are housed.

Many contemporary art collectors keep houses on Hydra, which each summer attracts a who's who of the international art scene. A must is the annual exhibition of works from the Ophiuchus Collection housed at **Hydra Workshops**, a gallery space located in the harbour area.

Where to eat & drink

Ydrargyros (22980 54030, closed winter, main courses €8-€15) serves European cuisine in a sophisticated candlelit setting behind the port, while **Xeri Elia** (22980 52886, closed 3wks Nov, main courses €8-€10) offers simple but quality fare in a square near the port. **Kondylenia** (22980 53520, closed Nov-Feb) is situated in a charming location at Kamini. **Spilia Beach Club Café-Bar** (22980 54166, closed Nov-Mar), built into the side of a cliff just before the cannons at Hydroneta, is a good stop for a coffee or a beer during the day. At night, visit the **Pirate Bar** (22980 52711) for rock and 1980s nostalgia, **Nautilus** (22980 53563) for Greek music and **Heaven** (22980 52716) for clubbing.

Where to stay

Bouayia (22980 52869, doubles €70-€120) has a homely atmosphere; more stylish is **Bratsera** (22980 53971, closed Oct-Mar, doubles €130-€150), in a restored 19th-century sponge-processing factory. At the **Orloff** (22980 52564, closed Nov-Apr, doubles €115-€130) guests can enjoy breakfast in a flower-filled courtyard. All are within walking distance of the port.

Tourist information

The tourist police (22980 52205), in the town centre, can provide details on accommodation, eating and drinking out and places to visit.

Getting around

No motor vehicles are allowed on Hydra, so rent a bicycle or prepare yourself for a lot of walking (note that Hydra also has many steps!). Donkey rides from the port are a quainter way of seeing some of the town. Sea taxis (22980 53690) connect the port to all the island's beaches. Set prices: Kamini €7, Mandraki €10, Vlichos €10.

Poros

Covered in pine forests, Poros is a lively, scenic island an hour from Piraeus and close to some of the most striking archaeological sites in the Peloponnese (*see chapter* **The Northern Peloponnese**). It has an area of 31 square kilometres (12 square miles) and a population of around 4,000. Poros (meaning 'ford' or 'crossing') is actually two islands – Sferia (the tiny volcanic peninsula that harbours Poros Town) and the more extensive Kalabria. They are separated from each other by a shallow artificial canal.

As your boat glides in towards the animated café-lined waterfront of Poros Town, the **Clock Tower** rises distinctly from the mass of traditional and neo-classical houses. (One of the most characteristic of the island's historic homes, the **Villa Galini**, in the island's west, has accommodated several writers, including George Seferis and Henry Miller.)

Make sure you see Constantinos Parthenis's magnificent wall paintings at Poros Town's **Cathedral of St George** (22980 23241, open Sat & Sun afternoons only), near the port. Also take a quick tour around the small **Archaeological Museum** (22980 23276, closed Mon, admission free), which features finds from ancient **Troezen** (now Trizini), the legendary birthplace of Theseus and site of the ancient **Temple of Aesculapius**. Trizini is an eight-kilometre (five-mile) bus trip from Galatas, on the mainland. If you make the journey, the Gefira tou Diavolou, or **Devil's Bridge** – a natural rock formation spanning a gorge – en route makes for a pleasant walk, as do the nearby orange and lemon groves.

The sixth-century BC **Temple of Poseidon** (closed Mon, admission free), near the centre of Kalabria, has been reduced to a scant few pillars but remains an arresting sight. Legend has it that the exiled orator Demosthenes drank poison there after having been cornered by his enemies. For a serene excursion, visit the 18th-century **Monastery of Zoodochou Pigis** (22980 22926), in an idyllic setting in southern Kalabria.

Though Poros isn't renowned for its beaches, **Neorion Bay** and **Kanali** are fine for a swim (north and south of Poros Town respectively); the sheltered cove of **Agapi** is also quite nice. More secluded beaches can be found near the ruins of the 19th-century Russian naval dockyard.

Where to eat & drink

For tasty home-cooked food, try **Mourtzoukos** (Neorion, 22980 22438, closed Nov-Mar, main courses €5-€7) or **Panorama** (Askeli Bay, 22980 24563, closed 2wks Nov, main courses €7-€9); for fresh fish, head to **Nikolas** taverna (Monastiri, 22980 23426, closed Nov-Mar, main courses €7-€9), about four kilometres (two and a half miles) from the port.

You're spoiled for choice for waterfront bars. **Scirocco** (22980 25790), south of the port, has a café-bistro upstairs and a club playing mainstream and Greek music downstairs.

Where to stay

The **Sto Roloi** guesthouse (22980 25808, www. storoloi-poros.gr, doubles €40-€180), housed in a restored neo-classical mansion just behind the port, is owned by the same people as **Anemoni** (22980 25808, doubles €60-€200). The latter consists of two renovated farmhouses next to the Church of St Constantine; both are recommended. The newly refurbished **Poros Hotel** (22980 22216, doubles €82-€132) has a prime location on the waterfront at Neorion Bay, while a cheaper option is the **Hotel Saga** (22980 25400, www.sagahotel.gr, doubles €50-€70), with its large balconies overlooking Kanali Bay.

Tourist information

If you have any queries regarding where to stay or eat and places to visit, call the tourist police (22980 22256, closed end Sept-mid May). **Family Tours** (22980 23743) is a helpful travel agent just behind the waterfront.

Getting around

To see the island, rent a scooter or bicycle from one of the rental outlets on the waterfront. Buses regularly leave Poros Town for the Monastery of Zoodochou Pigis. Frequent boats connect Poros Town with Galatas on the mainland from where there are regular buses to Trizini and the nearby Devil's Bridge. Travel agents on Poros can also organise day trips to Nafplio (*see p249*) and to the Ancient Theatre of Epidaurus (*see p249*).

Directory

Features

Directory

Getting Around

Arriving & leaving

By air

Athens International Airport – Eleftherios Venizelos

210 353 0000/www.aia.gr
The Greek capital is served by Eleftherios Venizelos Airport, situated about 27 kilometres (17 miles) north-east of Athens, linked by the six-lane Attiki Odos expressway.

Several public bus routes serve the airport exclusively, linking it with central Athens, Piraeus and the suburbs. All airport buses, known as Athens Airport Express, depart from outside the Arrivals Hall. Routes E92, E93, E95, E96 and E97 run 24 hours a day. E95 goes right to the city centre (Syntagma) in roughly an hour; buses leave every 8-30 minutes depending on the time of day. Route E96 will take you from the airport to the port of Piraeus. The journey time is a little over an hour and buses leave every 20 minutes to one hour, again, depending on the time of day. E92, E93 and E97 go to Kifisia, Kifisou bus station and Dafni metro station respectively. The average journey time is 45 minutes.

Route E94 takes you to Ethniki Amyna, where you'll be able to connect to the city's metro network. E94s run from 5am to 11.30pm and leave every 15-30 minutes, depending on the time of day. The journey time is around 30 minutes. For more details on these routes, contact the Athens Urban Transport Organisation (OASA) on 185. The phones are manned by bilingual staff from 7am to 9pm.

Tickets for the Athens Airport Express cost €2.90 (€3 on the E92) and can be purchased from all metro stations, the blue-coloured public-transport ticket booths or the bus driver – in this last case, make sure you have the right change. Your ticket is valid for one journey to or from the airport and you can use it within the city for 24 hours after the time you validate it (in the machine on board the bus) for an unlimited number of trips on all modes of public transport.

Taxis will drop you off right outside the Departures entrance. There is a queue for taxis at the airport extending from doors 4-1 of the Arrivals entrance. An average taxi ride from Syntagma to the airport costs around €15 during the day or €18 from midnigh to 5am and takes 40 minutes (more in rush hour).

Be aware that frequent strikes and demonstrations can bring the city centre to a standstill so allow plenty of time to get to the airport.

Airlines

Aegean Airlines/Cyprus Airways *210 998 8339/ www.aegeanair.com*
British Airways *210 353 1170/ www.british-airways.com*
Easyjet *210 353 0300/ www.easyjet.com*
Hellas Jet *210 353 1219/ www.hellas-jet.com*
Olympic Airways *210 966 6666/ www.olympic-airways.gr*
Virgin Express *210 690 5375/ www.virgin-express.com*

By rail

The national rail authority is called OSE (210 529 7777/www.ose.gr) and Athens' main stations are Larissa (for trains from northern Greece and abroad) and Peloponnisou (for trains from the Peloponnese). The terminals are near each other in one of Athens' less savoury neighbourhoods. Keep an eye on your belongings and avoid accepting assistance from dodgy types outside the stations. Between 5am and 11.30pm the stations are linked to the city's transport system by buses, trams, metro and cabs, located right outside.

Larissa Station *Deliyianni 31 (210 529 7777). Metro Larissa Station.* **Open** 6.30am-midnight. **Map** p295 D1.
Peloponnisou Station *Sidirodromon (210 513 1601). Metro Larissa Station.* **Open** 6.30am-midnight. **Map** p295 C1.

By boat

From central Athens you can get to the port of Piraeus by metro (Line 1) or the 24-hour 040 bus from Syntagma (Filellinon). For more information, contact the Piraeus Port Authority (210 459 3000). An average taxi ride from Syntagma to the port costs €7-€11 during the day or €15 at night (midnight-5am).

If you're planning to travel by boat in August, make sure you've reserved your tickets well in advance – it's the month when practically the whole of Athens escapes to the islands.

For information on routes and timetables, visit www.greekferries.gr, a useful and fairly comprehensive database detailing many of Greece's main ferry services. Piraeusferry.co.uk also has timetables, information and booking facilities.

Ferry companies

ANEK Lines *Akti Posidonos 32 & Leocharous, Piraeus (210 419 7420/ www.anek.gr). Metro Piraeus.* **Open** 7.30am-8.30pm daily. **Credit** DC, V.
Hellas Flying Dolphins *Akti Kondyli & Aitolikou 2, Piraeus (Cyclades & Sporades 210 419 9000/ Saronic Gulf 210 419 9200/ www.dolphins.gr). Metro Piraeus.* **Open** *Summer* 8.30am-8pm Mon-Sat. *Winter* 8.30am-4pm Mon-Fri; 8.30am-2.30pm Sat. **Credit** AmEx, MC, V.
Minoan Lines *Syngrou 98-100, Syngrou (210 920 0020/www. minoan.gr). Metro Syngrou-Fix.* **Open** 8.30am-8pm Mon-Fri; 8.30am-4.30pm Sat; 3.30-4.30pm Sun. **Credit** AmEx, DC, MC, V. **Map** p299 D8. *Thermopylon 6-10, Piraeus (210 414 5700). Metro Piraeus.* **Open** 7.30am-9pm daily. **Credit** AmEx, DC, MC, V.

Yacht rental

Bear in mind that if you rent a motor sailer without a crew, at least two people on board need to be in possession of a valid yacht licence.
Amphitrion Yachting *Defteras Merarchias 3, Piraeus (210 411 2045/www.amphitrion.gr). Metro Piraeus.* **Open** 9am-7pm Mon-Fri; 9.30am-1pm Sat. **Credit** AmEx, DC, MC, V.
The average price for a ten- to 12-person sailing boat, with crew, is €20,000 a week in high season (June-mid Sept). You can sail from one of four different marinas: Alimos, Flisvos, Kalamaki or Zea.
Nava Yachts Sakkiotis Commercial Centre *Athinon 8, Lavrion (22920 69018/ www. navayachts.gr).* **Open** 10am-5.30pm Mon-Fri. **No credit cards.**

Yachts for periods of seven days and upwards (weekend rentals subject to availability). The average price for a ten-person sailing yacht is €4,500 a week (skipper, cook and cabin crew available on request). You can sail from Lavrion every Saturday or from other bases on the islands of Corfu, Lefkas, Skiathos, Kos and Rhodes.
Triton Yachting *Eleftherias 5A, Alimos (210 981 1044/www.triton-yachting.gr).* **Open** 10am-8pm Mon-Fri; 10am-3pm Sat. **Credit** MC, V. Offers motor sailers, with crew, for periods of two to 20 days. Prices for a four-person boat start from €1,300 during high season. You can sail from Alimos, Lavrion, Kalamaki and various other harbours in Attica.
Vernicos Yachts *Leof Posidonos 11, Alimos (210 989 6000/www.vernicos.gr).* **Open** 10am-7pm Mon-Fri; 10am-2pm Sat. **Credit** MC, V. Offers a wide selection of vessels, from ultra-fast motor yachts complete with swimming pools, to traditional Greek motor sailers. Bareboat cruising and crewed yachts both available. Charters begin and end on a Saturday for multiples of seven days, but in the low season, flexible arrangements can be made. Prices for an eight-person boat start at €7,500.

Marinas

To book a berth:
Alimos Marina *210 982 1850.*
Flisvos Marina *210 982 9218.*

Glyfada Marina *210 8912281.*
Vouliagmeni Marina *210 896 0012.*
Zea Marina *210 451 3944.*

By coach

The intercity coach service in Greece is known as KTEL and offers destinations all over the country. There are two coach stations in Athens: Terminal A (Kifisou 100), with buses to the Peloponnese and western Greece, and Terminal B (Liosion 260), with services connecting to central and northern Greece. For information on tickets and timetables, call 210 512 4910.

Travel agencies

Amphitrion Holidays
Syngrou 7, Makrygianni (210 900 6000/www.amphitrion.gr). Metro Akropoli. **Open** *Sept-May* 9am-5pm Mon-Fri. *June-Aug* 9am-6pm Mon-Fri; 9am-1pm Sat. **Credit** AmEx, DC, MC, V.
Argo *Xenofontos 10, Plaka (210 324 6000). Metro Syntagma.* **Open** 8.30am-4.30pm Mon-Fri; 8am-4pm Sat. **Credit** AmEx, DC, MC, V.
Aspida Travel *Filonos 46, Piraeus (210 413 2258). Metro Piraeus.* **Open** 8.30am-7pm Mon-Fri; 9am-1pm Sat. **Credit** AmEx, MC, V.

Public transport

For information on public transport, visit www.government.gr/citizen and www.ametro.gr, or phone the Athens Urban Transport Organisation (OASA) on 185.

FARES AND TICKETS

Metro tickets can be bought at ticket machines or ticket offices situated at all stations. Ticket machines do not give change for notes or take credit cards. The regular fare is ct60 for Line 1 and ct70 for lines 2 and 3 (ct70 for a combination). A reduced fare of ct40 is available for pensioners and students. Children up to six years old travel for free.

Do not forget to validate your ticket at the special machines before you board the train. Tickets are valid for 90 minutes from the time of validation and for interchanges on all three lines. However, they are not valid for return via the route already covered.

Fares for both buses and trolleybuses cost ct45. Drivers do not issue tickets, which must be bought prior to boarding from OASA ticket booths and kiosks. Tickets must be validated using the special machines on the bus itself.

Yellow peril

You can gaze at fallen pillars and traipse through Plaka till your feet hurt, but for the full Athens experience you have to take a cab ride. Taxis in this city are like drawing lots – you never know what you're going to get. The grimy Lada will get you there as fast as the air-conditioned Mercedes, give or take a couple of 'brief' detours and a lecture in world affairs and football. Athens cabbies don't like being stuck in traffic, and will resort to every trick in the book – short of driving on the pavement – to get the most out of their shift. Their untamed spirit obeys no speed limits, road regulations or personal hygiene rules.

Though nominally obliged to ask for permission before lighting up or taking on additional fares, cabbies are usually happier enforcing their own house rules. 'Creative' charging for newcomers is one of them. Friendly interrogation is another, with topics ranging from a passenger's profession and place of origin to marital status and political beliefs.

While some visitors may find all this entertaining, it has ceased to amuse officials preparing for the 2004 Olympics. The Games will require about 1,500 professionals to chauffeur Olympic VIPs around town. And cabbies that want in on the act will have to improve their manners, because assertive honking and a flair for imaginative shortcuts won't cut it in 2004. Olympic organisers are now providing crash courses in safe driving, protocol and languages. But since this process will take time and is of far from certain outcome, it's best to take a deep, calming breath, brace yourself (literally) and remember that this is the best way to experience Athens' traffic from within. Relax. You're in expert, if twitchy, hands.

Athens is the only European city we know where having one passenger on board is no bar to picking up another. Good for the environment, good for your waiting time and – since he gets two fares out of it – good for the driver's pocket. Now *there's* a surprise.

Directory

A day pass (€2.90) is valid for an unlimited number of trips on the metro, buses and trolleybuses (no need to validate this).

Metro

The new underground train network is called the metro and the older line, which runs both under and over ground, is the ISAP. The stations are clearly marked with 'M' signs.

The network operates from 5.30am to midnight and has three different lines: Line 1 (ISAP) runs from the port of Piraeus to the northern suburb of Kifisia; Line 2 runs from Dafni to Sepolia; and Line 3 from Monastiraki to Ethniki Amyna. Trains run around every five minutes at peak times (ten minutes off peak).

Buses & trolleybuses

Athens is well served by buses and trolleybuses but the routes are generally not of much use for visitors other than for getting out to the suburbs or completing an onward journey from a metro stop. And traffic causes problems for both.

Blue buses and yellow trolleybuses run from around 5am until 11pm/midnight, depending on the route. For more information, contact OASA (185). You can pick up a bus map at metro stations.

Taxis

Taxis can get snarled up in traffic, especially during rush hour, but fares are reasonable and they're virtually a tourist attraction all of their own (*see p263* **Yellow peril**). And after midnight, when public transport stops, they're the only option.

Athenian taxis are yellow, with a 'TAXI' sign on the roof. They can be hailed in the street or booked by phoning a local cab company (€1 surcharge). One useful rank is on Syntagma between Ermou and Karagiorgi Servias.

Though it's pretty hard to find taxis during rush hour, most Athenian cabbies have no qualms about stopping to pick up extra fares. If a taxi slows

You're breaking up

Nobody knows how many potholes there are on the streets and pavements of Athens. Nobody has ever had the time to count them. But they're out there all right. Ahead of the 2004 Olympics, the municipality of Athens allotted €600,000 for mending road potholes – more than a few of which could swallow a cat – and announced that some 65 per cent of the city's pavements would be repaired.

The public works ministry went as far as setting up a hotline in February 2003 for motorists wishing to complain about faulty roads. In the first few days, a staggering 90 per cent of calls concerned potholes on roads. Cyclists, already used to having to pedal for their lives to escape from stray dogs in hot pursuit, will also testify to the number of holes. Nearly every Athenian knows of someone who has fallen over, bruised their foot or even broken an ankle because of a pothole or uneven/slippery pavement, even before the capital turned into a building site for the Olympics.

There are three main reasons for all the potholes and one of them is rather cynical: no important politician has ever broken his or her ankle getting out of a chauffeur-driven limousine. So it's not a major issue.

The second, down-to-earth reason is that, before the onset of the Olympic Games, there had been very few repairs over previous years. This in turn encouraged a widespread and fatalistic acceptance by the public of the state of the roads and pavements.

And, third, YOU SHOULD HAVE LOOKED, STUPID. It's taken as given that the streets of Athens are potentially dangerous, and it's not just the speed of the cars. Out there in the wild, individuals are expected to look after themselves, rather than the state or municipality doing the job for them.

The capital lives by this 'It's up to you' attitude. Lean back on a wall and it might be too late to notice the five-metre drop behind you. In the realm of public safety, Athens is more Mediterranean than European, lacking the 'nanny state' attitude. Unlike in England, for example, there are very few safety signs and warnings. This might well be due to the almost total lack of successful lawsuits. Break your ankle on the street – as some have – and there's no point claiming compensation, even if you're in the right. You just won't get it.

Many Athenians walk on the roads – and not only because of the damaged state of the sidewalks. Cars are routinely parked on pavements – there's little clamping – without the motorist giving a second thought about blocking people's way. On top of this, motorbikes often drive along pavements, either taking a short cut or bypassing snarled traffic. It's not unheard of for a motorcyclist to honk a pedestrian.

With potholes and parked cars, the perverse situation can be reached whereby people walk on the roads and motorbikes ride on the pavements. The anti-pothole crusade, if it lasts beyond the Olympics, might work, but for now visitors should carry on looking down.

down (or flashes his headlights) as he approaches you but has his light switched off, mouth your destination to him and he will stop for you if he is going in the same direction.

Ask your driver for an estimate of how much your journey is going to cost before you set off. If you feel you're being ripped off, suggest that you find a police officer to get a second opinion; if your cabbie really is trying to take you for a ride, this kind of threat is usually enough to bring him back to his senses.

All taxis are obliged by law to use a running meter – if the driver doesn't switch it on when you get in, ask him to. There are two basic tariffs: No.1 and No.2. Depending on the time of day and the journey, the driver needs to select the correct rate. Tariff No.1 is the day rate, used from 5am to midnight, while tariff No.2 is the night rate, valid from midnight to 5am. Also, tariff No.1 is used within city limits and No2 is used outside that zone. The number 1 or 2 should be clearly visible on the meter. The meter starts at ct73 and there is a minimum charge of €1.47. There's also a surcharge of €1.17 for taxi rides to and from the airport, and of ct50 for each item of luggage over ten kilos.

Radio taxis
Athina1 *1203.*
Europe *210 502 9764.*
Express *210 994 3000.*
Ikaros *210 515 2800/ www.athens-taxi.gr.*
Kosmos *18300/www.1300.gr.*

Driving

Extensive roadworks and poor signposting make driving around Athens extremely hard. The city's traffic jams (and its fender-benders) are legendary. In the evening the police are on the lookout for drunk drivers, setting up checkpoints around the club districts. The summer

months are especially messy, with accidents soaring around the coastal club strips. According to the Attica Traffic Police, an average of 500 people are killed and twice that many injured every year.

You really don't need a car in Athens, but if you do have one, map your route before setting off and don't take any of the hussle personally. Drivers should stick to the standard EU speed limits: 30km/h (18mph) in residential areas and around hospitals and schools, 60km/h (37mph) on central roads and 100km/h (62mph) on motorways.

Breakdown services

Check with the company you are registered with at home to find out about affiliated companies in Greece or register with a Greek breakdown service when you arrive.
ELPA Emergency Service *10400.*
Express Service *1154.*
Hellas Service *1057.*
Interamerican *168.*

Fuel stations

Avin Oil *Solonos 56, Kolonaki (210 361 7767/210 362 8202).* **Open** *May-Sept* 6am-9pm Mon-Sat. *Oct-Apr* 6am-8pm Mon-Sat. Open 24hrs every 1, 7, 17, 27 of each month. **Credit** DC, MC, V. **Map** p297 G4.
Revoil *Mesogeion 17, Ampelokipi. (210 770 5876).* **Open** *May-Sept* 6am-9pm Mon-Sat. *Oct-Apr* 6am-8pm Mon-Sat. **No credit cards.**

Parking

Finding a parking place in Athens is notoriously hard. Most Greeks tend to park in the first available space, with no regard for pavements or the blocking in other cars. There are no parking meters in Athens, but there are a few private car parks around the city centre.

Car parks
Lykavitou 3C, Kolonaki (210 361 5823). **Open** 24hrs daily. **Rates** €8 1st hr; ct80 every extra hr. *Zalokosta 8 & Kriezotou, Historic Centre (210 362 8863).* **Open** *Aug-Sept* 7am-midnight Mon-Sat. *Oct-July* 7am-2am Mon-Sat; 6pm-1am Sun. **Rates** €8 1st hr; €1 every extra hr. *Paparigopoulou 9 & Parnassou, Historic Centre (210 323 6606).*

Open *June-Aug* 7am-9pm Mon-Sat. *Sept-May* 7am-10.30pm Mon-Sat. **Rates** €6.50 1st hr; ct50 per extra hr. *Platia Klafthmonos, Historic Centre (210 323 6698).* **Open** 6.30am-11pm Mon-Fri; noon-1pm Sat. **Rates** €5.50 1st hr; ct90 every extra hr.

Vehicle hire

The minimum age for car rental in Greece is 21 and you must have held a licence for at least one year. EU citizens must hold a EU licence, while non-EU citizens must possess a valid national driving licence as well as an International Driving Permit. Seatbelts are compulsory in Greece.
Avis *Amalias 48, Historic Centre (210 322 4951). Metro Akropoli.* **Open** 7.30am-8.30pm daily. **Rates** from €50/day for a Fiat Seicento. **Credit** AmEx, DC, MC, V.
Europcar *Syngrou 43, Makrygianni (210 924 8810). Metro Syngrou-Fix.* **Open** 8am-8.30pm daily. **Rates** from €40/day for a Fiat Seicento. **Credit** AmEx, DC, MC, V.
Hertz *Syngrou 12, Makrygianni (210 922 0102). Metro Akropoli.* **Open** 7.30am-9.30pm Mon-Sat; 8am-9pm Sun. **Rates** from €50/day for a Citroën Saxo. **Credit** AmEx, DC, MC, V.
Reliable International Rent-a-Car *Syngrou 3, Makrygianni (210 924 9000). Metro Akropoli.* **Open** 8am-9pm Mon-Fri. **Rates** from €25/day for a small car. **Credit** AmEx, DC, MC, V.
Sixt *Syngrou 23, Makrygianni (210 922 0171). Metro Akropoli.* **Open** 7.30am-9pm daily. **Rates** from €30/day for a Daewoo Matiz. **Credit** AmEx, DC, MC, V.

Cycling

Although there are plans to introduce cycle lanes in the capital, there are no such facilities as yet and we wouldn't recommend risking it on two wheels.

Walking

The 2004 Games have jolted the Athenian authorities out of their apathy towards the plight of the pedestrian. As a result, they are now widening and improving existing pavements and creating pedestrianised walkways to link the various archaeological sites.

Even so, pedestrians must be permanently alert, as red lights, stop signs, zebra crossings and one-way streets are often ignored by drivers. Even a green man doesn't give the pedestrian right of way. Always look both ways before crossing a street, even in pedestrianised zones, which motorcyclists use as shortcuts.

Directory

Resources A-Z

Addresses

Most street signs in Athens are written in both Greek and Roman characters, so you shouldn't have any problems getting around as long as you follow a good map. Do be warned, however, that spellings can often be quite imaginative due to the fact that there doesn't seem to be a standardised system of transliteration. For example, you could see Lykavitou, Licavittou (phonetic spelling) or even Lycabettus, all referring to the same street. In our listings we have used transliterations that will sound recognisable, in case you need to ask for directions.

Age restrictions

The age limit for drinking, smoking and driving in Greece is 18. However, bars rarely ask for ID and most, especially small bars, will allow children in as long as they are accompanied by an adult. Driving below the age of 18 is strictly prohibited. The age of consent is 15.

Attitude & etiquette

For its laid-back attitude to most things, Greece is really a conservative society. Recent events involving skirmishes between tourists and locals in Athens and the islands have highlighted the need for mutual respect. While you may be on a carefree holiday, bear in mind that you are visiting a country with its own set of social rules and values. Drunk and disorderly conduct, overt displays of affection in public places and rude behaviour, especially towards the elderly, are not acceptable.

While Greeks are not famed for their gushing politeness, they will be helpful and friendly towards visitors. One real point of friction between visitors and locals, however, comes when paying a bill or taxi fare. Presenting a cab driver with a €20 note for a €2.50 fare or paying for a pack of cigarettes with a €50 will trigger a long, heated argument. It is advisable to carry lots of loose change and, when changing money, to break €100 and €50 notes into smaller denominations.

Greeks are notoriously fond of arguing and shouting at each other in the street. Don't dwell on this too much – they never really act on these exaggerated displays. It's just their way of letting off steam.

Many locals still take a siesta at lunchtime in summer. Between 2pm and 5.30pm it's considered unacceptable to be noisy in residential areas or to disturb people at home.

If you plan to visit churches or monasteries during your stay, dress in a respectable manner (long trousers for men; sleeved dresses and no miniskirts for women).

Business

Meetings and conferences in Greece are generally held at the 'host' office or often in the lobbies of the better hotels, like the Divani Caravel, the Grande Bretagne, the Inter-Continental and the Hilton (*see p52* **Where to Stay**), where international delegates can reside. Lunch meetings are popular too.

Greeks may be somewhat lax in keeping time in their leisure hours, but not when it comes to business – be prompt. Dress smartly if it is your first meeting.

Conventions & conferences

Conferences are generally held at the larger hotels. There are also a few official conference centres for fairs and exhibitions.

Helexpo *Leof Kifisias 22, Marousi (210 616 8888/www.helexpro). Bus A7, B7 from Kanigos.*
Piraeus Port Authority Centre (OLP) *Akti Miaouli 10, Piraeus (210 452 0910/www.olp.gr). Metro Piraeus.*
Zita Congress & Travel *1km Paianias-Markopoulou, Paiania (210 664 1160/www.zita-congress.gr). KTEL Koropi from Pedion Areos.*

Travel advice

For up-to-date information on travel to a specific country – including the latest news on safety and security, health issues, local laws and customs – contact your home country government's department of foreign affairs. Most have websites packed with useful advice for would-be travellers.

Australia
www.dfat.gov.au/travel

Canada
www.voyage.gc.ca

New Zealand
www.mft.govt.nz/travel

Republic of Ireland
www.irlgov.ie/iveagh

UK
www.fco.gov.uk/travel

USA
http://www.state.gov/travel

Couriers & shippers

All companies collect from hotels and offices for a fee. Unless otherwise stated, the companies listed offer both courier and shipping services.

DHL *Alimou 44 & Roma, Alimos (210 989 0000/www.dhl.gr).* **Open** 8am-7pm Mon-Fri; 8am-3pm Sat. **Credit** AmEx, DC, MC, V.
SpeedEx (courier only) *Spirou Patsi & Sidirokastrou 1-3, Votanikos, Western Athens (210 340 7000/www.speedex.gr).* **Open** 8am-8pm Mon-Fri.
TNT *Zita 7, Elliniko, Southern Suburbs (210 898 3500/210 898 3509/www.tnt.com).* **Open** 8am-7pm Mon-Fri. **No credit cards.**
UPS *Leof Kifisias 166, Marousi (210 614 6510/www.ups.com).* **Open** 8am-6.30pm Mon-Fri. **Credit** AmEx, DC, MC, V. *Leof Eleftheriou Venizelou 43-45, Glyfada (210 998 4000).*

Office services

Fast Digital Copy Centre *Kolokotroni 11, Historic Centre (210 323 9865). Metro Syntagma.* **Open** 8am-5pm Mon-Fri. **No credit cards.** Map p295 E4.
Fototipies Strilinga *Aristidou 9, Historic Centre (210 321 2623). Metro Panepistimio.* **Open** 8am-7pm Mon-Fri. **No credit cards.** Map p295 E4.

Secretarial services

IBS International Business Services *Michalakopoulou 29, Ilisia, Southern Suburbs (210 724 5541). Metro Evangelismos or Megaro Mousikis.* **Open** 9am-5pm Mon-Fri. **No credit cards.** Also offers translation services and conference organising.
Planitas *Spyridonos Trikoupi 20, Exarchia (210 330 6945-7/ 210 380 5663/www.planitas.gr). Metro Omonia.* **Open** 9.30am-5.30pm Mon-Fri. **No credit cards.**

Translation services

Athens Tower 2 *Mesogeion 2-4, Ambelokipi (210 778 3698). Metro Ambelokipi.* **Open** 9am-5pm Mon-Fri. **No credit cards.** For legal and technical translations.
Com Translation & Interpretation *Xenagora 8-10, Platia Amerikis, Northern Suburbs (210 862 3411/www.pra-zis.gr). Metro Victoria.* **Open** 9am-5pm Mon-Fri. **No credit cards.**

Useful organisations

Athens Stock Exchange *Sofokleous 10 (210 321 1301).*
British-Hellenic Chamber of Commerce *Leof Vas Sofias 25 (210 721 0361/www.bhcc.gr).* **Open** *Telephone enquiries* 9am-5pm Mon-Fri.
US-Hellenic Chamber of Commerce *Mesogeion 109-111 (210 699 3559/www.amcham.gr).* **Open** *Telephone enquiries* 9am-4.30pm Mon-Fri.

Consumer

There is one main consumer protection service in Greece, INKA (Akadimias 7, 210 363 3976, for emergencies 1721). However, although INKA can provide advice, it doesn't have any legal power.

In the case of an argument with a shop owner, hotelier, etc, it is a better idea to seek advice from the tourist police (*see p268*).

Customs

When coming to Greece, you're allowed to bring in duty-free up to 200 cigarettes (or 100 cigarillos or 50 cigars or 250g of tobacco), 1 litre of spirits (or 2 litres of wine or liqueur), 50ml of perfume and 250ml of eau de cologne. EU nationals arriving from within Europe don't pass through customs. For further information about customs, contact Athens International Airport (210 353 0000).

Greece is naturally sensitive about its antiquities, which range from fragments of sculpture and architecture to a pebble picked up while touring the Acropolis, to coins and other relics. Taking antiquities out of the country without a permit is considered a serious offence, and the punishment ranges from a hefty fine to a jail term. To apply for a permit, contact the Central Archaeological Council (KAS) (210 820 1262) or consult the dealer you bought from.

Disabled

Compared to other European cities, Athens is not very accommodating towards the mobility-impaired. Hardly any of the capital's sights make provisions for wheelchair users, and transport is a big headache for those who have problems getting around.

However, the city is getting its act together ahead of the 2004 Olympic Games, when all public transport (buses, trams, urban railway), archaeological sites and cultural sites are to be made fully accessible. All metro stations already have lifts for the disabled. Also, a fleet of 400 buses and thousands of new taxis will be available to carry the disabled during and after the Olympics.

By mid 2004 many hotels will also have been equipped to better accommodate disabled guests.

National Committee for the Disabled
Milerou 1, 6th floor (210 523 8961/www.asaea.gr). Offers advice to disabled visitors.

Drugs

Do not get involved with any kind of drug in Greece, whether it be 'soft' drugs like marijuana or 'hard' drugs like cocaine, ecstasy or heroin. Penalties for possession of even small amounts are harsh and getting harsher. Depending on the amount you are caught with (and whether the crime is judged as a misdemeanour or a felony), you will get a suspended sentence, which you can pay off, or face a jail sentence (between five and 20 years).

Electricity

Greece uses 220-volt electric power (AC 50Hz). Appliances from North America require a transformer and British

Directory

ones an adaptor. Bring one with you to save wasting valuable time searching for adaptors and transformers.

Embassies & consulates

American Embassy
Leof Vas Sofias 91, Ambelokipi (210 721 2951/fax 210 645 6282/ www.usembassy.gr). Metro Megaro Mousikis. **Open** 8.30am-5pm Mon-Fri.
Australian Embassy
Soutsou 37 & Tsocha 24, Ambelokipi (210 645 0404/fax 210 646 6595/www.ausemb.gr). Metro Ambelokipi. **Open** 8.30am-12.30pm Mon-Fri.
British Embassy
Ploutarchou 1, Kolonaki (210 727 2600/fax 210 727 2876/www.british-embassy.gr). Metro Evangelismos. **Open** 8.30am-1pm Mon-Fri. **Map** p297 H5.
Canadian Embassy
Ioannou Gennadiou 4, Kolonaki (210 727 3352/fax 210 727 3480/ www.athens.gc.ca). Metro Evangelismos. **Open** 8am-4pm Mon-Fri. **Map** p297 J4.
Irish Embassy
Leof Vas Konstantinou 5-7, Historic Centre (210 723 2771/fax 210 729 3383). Metro Syntagma. **Open** 9am-3pm Mon-Fri. **Map** p297 E6.
Consulate of New Zealand
Leof Kifisias 268, Halandri (210 687 4700/fax 210 687 4444). **Open** 10am-3.30pm Mon-Fri (by appointment only).
South African Embassy
Leof Kifisias 60, Marousi (210 610 6645/fax 210 610 6640/ www.southafrica.gr). Metro Marousi. **Open** 8am-1pm Mon-Fri.

Emergencies

If you need immediate assistance, dial 100, free of charge, from any phone, or 112 from your GSM mobile.

If you've been robbed, attacked or involved in an infringement of the law, but don't require immediate attention, you can file a formal complaint at the Athens police headquarters (Leof Alexandras 173, Ambelokipi, 210 951 5111/210 647 6000) or at the Piraeus police headquarters (Iroon Polytechneiou 37, Piraeus, 210 411 1710).

For any problem, complaint or enquiry you may have, you can also contact the tourist police, a specially trained section of the Greek police force who speak foreign languages. They can be contacted by calling 171 any time of the day or night, seven days a week from all over Greece.

For hospital listings, *see below* **Health**.

Useful numbers

Coastguard *108.*
Duty pharmacies *1434.*
Fire department *199.*
Poison Control Centre *210 779 3777.*
Road assistance *10400.*
Tourist Police *171.*
Tourist Police Athens *Veikou 43, Koukaki (210 920 0724-727). Metro Syngrou-Fix.* **Map** p299 E7.
Tourist Police Piraeus
New Passenger Terminal, Xaveriou seafront (210 429 0664). Metro Piraeus.

Gay & lesbian

Greeks are fairly tolerant of alternative lifestyles and, in Athens especially, there is a growing gay scene, mainly centred in the districts of Gazi and Psyrri, which have several lively gay clubs and bars.

However, Greeks are also a bit conservative and gay/ lesbian couples should exercise common sense when making public displays of affection.

Help & information

Act Up Greece *Nikitara 8, Historic Centre (210 330 5500). Metro Omonia.* **Open** 6-10pm Wed, Fri. **Map** 295 F3.

Travel/hotels

Magna Graecia Hotel *Mitropoleos 4, Plaka (210 331 8781-4/www. magnagraeciasuites.com). Metro Monastiraki or Syntagma.* **Rates** €80-€110 single; €110-€140 junior suite. **No credit cards. Map** p295 F5. Athens' only exclusively gay hotel. The spacious rooms are tastefully decorated with stunning artwork from local Greek artists. Its café/bar, Sto 54 (*see p200*), serves breakfasts, snacks and drinks.

Gay Travel Greece *210 948 4182/www.gaytravelgreece.com.* Travel agency specialising in gay-friendly hotels and packages for Athens and the rest of Greece, including the Greek islands.

Health

Visitors do not need to be vaccinated against any diseases prior to travelling to Greece. In summer travellers are advised to wear sunscreen, a hat and light clothing to guard against the sun and heat. Mosquitoes can be a nuisance: visitors should wear insect repellent when going out in the evening and invest in a plug-in zapper (available from supermarkets) for the bedroom.

Though in the capital and on the rest of the Greek mainland tap-water quality is generally of a high standard, remember that some of the islands do not have natural water resources and rely on desalination plants for their supply; the tap water in such places is briny and consequently both locals and visitors drink bottled water.

Accident & emergency

All visitors to Athens are entitled to free medical care in the event of an emergency. This may include helicopter transfer if necessary. Call 166 (free from any phone) to request an ambulance. All the hospitals listed below have 24-hour accident and emergency departments.

Agia Sophia General Children's Hospital *Thivon 3 & Mikrasias, Goudi (210 777 1811). Bus A5 or B5.*
Alexandra General Hospital *Leof Vas Sofias 80, Kolonaki (210 338 1100). Metro Megaro Mousikis.*
Errikos Dinan Hospital *Mesogeion 107, Ambelokipi (210 697 2000). Metro Katehaki or Panormou.*
Evangelismos General Hospital *Ypsilantou 45-47, Kolonaki (210 720 1000). Metro Evangelismos.* **Map** p297 J4.
Ippokratio General Hospital *Leof Vas Sofias 114, Ambelokipi (210 748 3770). Metro Megaro Mousikis.*

Contraception & abortion

Condoms are widely available at kiosks (some of which are open 24 hours a day in central Athens), newsagents, supermarkets and pharmacies. If you are on the Pill, however, we advise you to stock up for your holiday – Greek pharmacies require a doctor's prescription.

Though abortion is legal in Greece, there are no family planning clinics as such. Instead, contact one of the general hospitals or clinics or one of the gynaecological clinics below. Call to book an appointment or visit between 9am and noon daily.

Iaso *Leof Kifisias 37-39, Marousi (210 618 4000). Metro Marousi, then 010 bus.*
Mitera *Leof Kifisias & E Stadou 6, Marousi (210 682 0110). Metro Marousi then 010 bus.*

Dentists

Some free dental treatments are available for EU citizens at two centres: Evangelismos Hospital (Ypsilantou 45-47, Kolonaki, 210 720 1000) and at Athens Dentistry University (Thivon 2 & Fidipidou, Goudi, 210 779 5875). Non-EU travellers are advised to contact their embassy (*see p268*).

In case of emergency, check the back page of *Kathimerini*'s English edition for duty hospitals, where you will be able to find a pathologist to advise you, or call the SOS-Doctors on freephone 1016 (*see below*).

Doctors

You can also gain access to medical services by calling the SOS-Doctors on 1016 (call free of charge). This is an international organisation of 'house-call' doctors operating on a 24-hour basis. All you have to do is call the number and the closest doctor will be paged to come to wherever you are staying to assist with any medical need or emergency you might have.

For patients staying in hotel accommodation, SOS-Doctors fees are fixed at €80 (€100 between 11pm and 7am and public holidays).

If you wish to discuss your symptoms, but do not require immediate attention, the best option is to ask a pharmacist.

Opticians

See p182 for optician and optometrist contact information.

Private clinics

For those who feel uneasy about placing their health in the hands of a government-run hospital (though they really needn't – Greek medical services rank among the best in Europe, even if the hospitals themselves might appear in need of a facelift), the following private clinics all have accident and emergency departments and provide a range of thoroughly modern facilities.

If you have private health insurance in your own country, check if this brings any affiliations to private clinics in Greece.

Athens Euroclinic *Athanasiadou 9, Ambelokipi (210 641 6600/emergency 1011/www.euroclinic.gr). Metro Ambelokipi.*
Athens General Clinic *M. Geroulannou 15, Ambelokipi (210 692 1484/www.agclinic.gr). Metro Panormou.*
Central Clinic of Athens *Asklipiou 33 & Navarinou 2-4, Kolonaki (210 367 4000/emergency 1169/www.centralclinic.gr). Metro Syntagma.* **Map** p297 E3.
Metropolitan Hospital Ethnarchou *Makariou 9 & Leof Eleftheriou Venizelou 1, Neo Faliro (210 480 9000/www.metropolitan-hospital.gr). Metro Faliro.*
Hygeia Clinic *Erythrou Stavrou 4 & Leof Kifisias, Marousi (210 686 7000/www.hygeia.gr). Metro Marousi.*

Pharmacies & prescriptions

Generally speaking, the opening hours for pharmacies in Athens are 8am-2.30pm on Mondays and Wednesdays and 8am-2pm and 5.30-8.30pm on Tuesdays, Thursdays and Fridays. Most are closed at weekends, except for emergency pharmacies (of which there is always one in every neighbourhood). To find the one nearest to you, consult a newspaper, look at a chart on the door of your nearest pharmacy, or call 107.

If you have exchanged your E111 form for a health book (*vivliario ygeias*) at the Social Security Foundation (IKA), you can get subsidised prescriptions; otherwise you pay the full whack (as do non-EU citizens).

The following pharmacies are centrally located:

Agamemnon Zisiadis *Pireos 1, Omonia (210 524 8668). Metro Omonia.* **Map** p295 E3.
Litos *Stadiou 17, Historic Centre (210 322 8458). Metro Panepistimiou or Syntagma.* **Map** p295 F4.

Nikolaos Zouberis *Patision 27, Historic Centre (210 522 3205). Metro Omonia.* **Map** 295 E2.
Yiorgos Papaioannou *Asklipiou 144, Kolonaki (210 643 5586). Metro Panepistimio.* **Map** p297 G3.

STDs, HIV & AIDS

Visit the outpatient department of any of the main state hospitals (*see p268*) to arrange for free tests (a prescription issued by a state hospital doctor will speed the process up considerably).

AIDS hotline *210 722 2222.*
Kentro Zois *Antimachou 7, Ilisia, Southern Suburbs (210 725 7617).*

Helplines & support groups

For information call the State Citizens' Information (KEP) centres on 197. They will help you in cutting through red tape and getting paperwork done; call 1464 to access the multilingual 24-hour service to make an appointment at your nearest centre. All the centres listed can deal with English-speaking visitors.

Foundation for Child & Family *12A Herodou Attikou, Marousi (210 809 4419/www.childfamily.gr). Metro Marousi.* **Open** 9.30am-7.30pm Mon-Fri.
HAPSA (sexual abuse/rape support group) *Erifilis 12, Pangrati (210 729 0496/www.hapsa.netfirms.com). Metro Evangelismos.* **Open** hours vary; call ahead. **Map** p297 J6.
Hellenic Red Cross *Likavittou 1, Kolonaki (210 361 3563/www.redcross.gr). Metro Panepistimio.* **Open** 7.30am-2.30pm Mon-Fri. **Map** p297 E4.
OKANA (drug helpline) *Averoff 21, Omonia (210 889 8200-85/www.okana.gr). Metro Omonia.* **Open** 9am-8pm Mon, Wed; 9am-4pm Tue, Thur, Fri. **Map** p295 E2.
The Parthenon Group of Alcoholics Anonymous *Ippokratous 156, Kolonaki (210 645 2972). Metro Panepistimio.* **Open** 8.30pm-10pm daily. **Map** p297 G3.
State Counselling Centre for Violence Against Women *Nikis 11, Plaka (210 331 7305/6). Metro Syntagma.* **Open** 8am-6pm Mon-Fri. **Map** p295 F5.

ID

By law all Greeks must carry their identity cards at all times. Visitors are advised to carry a photocopy of their passports and visa (if travelling with one), especially in the capital, where it is not uncommon for police to carry out random spot checks in their efforts to clamp down on illegal immigrants. An EU driving licence with photo should also be acceptable.

Though you have to be at least 18 years old to legally buy or consume alcohol in Greece, proof of ID is rarely requested.

Insurance

EU nationals should obtain an E111 form (available at post offices), which facilitates their free medical care under the Greek national health service (IKA). Visitors of other nationalities are strongly advised to arrange for private insurance prior to their trips, as private medical facilities in Greece are expensive.

Internet

Internet cafés are widespread in Athens. Most hotels offer net access, though at high rates. And the in-room Web TV gimmick is tedious to use.

Tellas is the only firm to offer free internet connection. Using the username 'tellas' and the password 'free', dial up an internet connection using the telephone number 211 180 5000. CosmOTE and HOL are two other good and cheap providers. For useful Athens websites, *see p278* **Further Reference**.

Arcade *Stadiou 5, Historic Centre (210 321 0701). Metro Syntagma.* **Open** 9am-10pm Mon-Sat. **Rates** €3/hr. **No credit cards. Map** p295 F5.
Bits & Bytes *Akadimias 78, Omonia (210 330 6590/ www.bnb.gr). Metro Omonia.* **Open** 24hrs daily. **Rates** €2.50/hr 9am-midnight, €1.50/hr midnight-9am. **No credit cards. Map** p295 F3.
Quick Net Café *Gladstonos 4, Omonia (210 380 3771). Metro Omonia.* **Open** 24hrs daily. **Rates** €2.50/hr. **No credit cards. Map** p295 E3.

Language

The vast majority of Athenians have a basic grounding in English and many speak it well so you are unlikely to have problems in communicating. However, you will be treated with more respect, especially in business liaisons, if you learn the basics (*see p276*). Most Athenians will be flattered that you are trying and keen to help.

Left luggage

The left luggage facilities at Athens International Airport are situated on the ground floor of the International Arrivals terminal. Do not count on them during the security-aware Olympics.

Travellers can also leave bags at either of the Greek capital's railway stations, Larissa and Peloponnisou, situated next door to each other between Deliyianni and Konstantinoupoleos (*see p262*). Both of central Athens' bus stations have facilities for left luggage.

Legal help

Should you require legal help during your stay in Greece, contact your embassy or consulate (*see p268*) and/or (where appropriate) your insurance company.

Libraries

Visit the following libraries to browse through English-language books (note that the books can only be removed by members).

British Council Library *Platia Kolonaki 17, Kolonaki (210 369 2333). Metro Syntagma.* **Open** 8.30am-7pm Mon-Fri; 11.30am-2.30pm Sat. **Map** p297 G5.
European Union *Leof Vas Sofias 2, Historic Centre (210 727 2100). Metro Evangelismos.* **Open** 10am-2pm, 3.30pm-5pm Mon-Fri. **Map** p297 E5.

Hellenic-American Union *Massalias 22, Historic Centre (210 368 0044). Metro Panepistimio.* **Open** 10am-5pm Mon, Thur; 10am-8pm Tue; 10am-6pm Wed; 10am-4pm Fri. **Map** p297 G4.

Lost property

The Greek transport police have a lost property office on the seventh floor at Leof Alexandras 173 (210 647 6000/ 210 642 1616). Bring your passport when making a claim.

Another lost property office is at Athens International Airport in Arrivals in the main terminal (210 353 0000).

Media

Newspapers & magazines

International magazines and newspapers are widely available at kiosks around the central Syntagma and Omonia squares, and on the main thoroughfares in Kolonaki.

The *Athens News* is a local weekly English-language newspaper that comes out on Fridays, while *Kathimerini* is an English-language daily that comes out with the *International Herald Tribune*. Both newspapers feature news items as well as listings of things going on around the city, TV pages, emergency telephone numbers, duty pharmacies and other useful information.

There is a weekly *Time Out* magazine for Athens. Its listings are in Greek and hard to figure out unless you speak the language – in which case it's by far the best source of news, reviews, listings and opinion. Its summer *Visitors' Guide*, in English and widely available at newsstands, is an invaluable tourist and events guide.

Radio

Though there are no English-language radio stations in Greece, many play a wide range of British and American music, not to mention just about every other type, Greek and other – just zap through the stations until you find one you like.

For news bulletins in English, tune in to the following: Antenna 97.2FM at 8.25am daily; Flash 96FM 8.55am, 3pm, 8pm daily; ERA 91.6FM 5am, 9am, 9.30pm daily. No radio station offers English-language traffic reports.

Who let the dogs out?

During your stay in Athens you will undoubtedly encounter homeless dogs and cats. Many of them are plump, well cared for and sporting collars and tags. Some have even been sterilised – usually by local animal welfare groups but in some areas by animal-friendly municipalities – evidence of which can be seen on cats by the nicked-off ear tip. However, often these stray animals are thin, ill, injured, mistreated or even lying dead at the roadside.

There are several reasons why Greece has such a large population of stray dogs and cats: the first is that sterilisation was – and still is in rural areas – taboo. Trying to convince a Greek man to have his dog neutered is like asking him to remove his own manhood, and many female cats and dogs are left unspayed by owners who consider the operation inhumane and unnatural. And although Greek law forbids the abandoning of animals, those who do so are rarely, if ever, found and punished.

In the cities, strays are, for the most part, fairly well cared for. Kind-hearted citizens often look after 'community' dogs or cats, providing them with food and water, and even taking them to the vet when necessary. Some shopkeepers 'adopt' a street dog or cat, and it's not uncommon to enter a chic boutique by stepping over a large, panting canine that

has commandeered the doormat. Countryside strays tend to be worse off. Island tavernas may put out fish for families of stray cats or at least turn a blind eye when the tourists are there, but before the season starts the animals often fall prey to poisoners. Hunting dogs are abandoned in the fields if they perform poorly, and unwanted puppies of farm or guard dogs are also turned out to fend for themselves.

Greece's stray population has diminished in the last few years, mainly due to humane population control measures of catch-neuter-and-release and by the collection of dogs to take to sub-standard municipal shelters. Some welfare activists pin the falling number of strays on to what they say was government-ordered poisoning of dogs and cats to 'clean the streets' before the 2004 Olympic Games.

There is generally no need to be frightened by Greek strays. There is no rabies, and the city dogs especially tend to be friendly and harmless. Beware, however, of roaming packs of dogs, which have been known to nip the heels – or more – of passing joggers, cyclists or walkers. The car-chasers, which leap out joyfully attempting to bite the wheels of your car or moped, though somewhat distracting, are usually only interested in rubber tyres, not human flesh.

Television

There are three state-run TV channels in Greece (ET1, NET and ET3) as well as several private channels. While the former offer high-quality news and sports coverage and documentaries, private TV stations tend to go for a tabloid style of news reporting. Their programming also includes soaps, quiz shows and late night soft-porn. Both state-run and private television channels in Greece feature many familiar foreign programmes and films, and they're usually subtitled rather than dubbed. You'll find listings in *Athens News*.

Money

Prices have increased significantly since the introduction of the euro in January 2002. Also keep in mind that there has been a

subsequent increase in the circulation of forged euros; check for the silver line through the note and the silver strip down the side, otherwise you may find yourself having to explain yourself to a suspicious bank official or even police officer. Notes in circulation are €5, €10, €20, €50, €100, €200 and €500 while coins come in denominations of €1, €2, 1 cent, 2 cents, 5 cents, 10 cents and 20 cents.

ATMs

ATMs are easily available in Athens. Most accept Visa and MasterCard (you'll pay interest on cash withdrawas) as well as debit cards of internationally recognised networks such as Cirrus and

Maestro. Syntagma and Omonia are focal points for ATMs – the National Bank of Greece and Alpha Bank are two good ones.

Banks

Most banks are open 8am-2pm Mon-Thur and 8am-1.30pm Fri.
National Bank of Greece (NBG)
Karagiorgi Servias 6, Historic Centre (210 334 0500). Metro Syntagma. **Map** p295 F1.
As well as the usual banking services, this location offers a foreign-exchange service on Saturdays and Sundays (9am-1pm).
Other locations: *Eolou 86 (210 334 1000/lost credit cards 210 483 4100).*
Eurobank's 'Open 24'
(8001 111 1144)
Leof Kifisias 41-45, Ambelokipi (210 610 5883). Metro Ambelokipi. **Open** 10am-6pm Mon, Wed; 9am-8pm Tue, Thur, Fri; 9am-5pm Sat.

Directory

Not, as you'll notice, actually open 24 hours as the name might suggest, but still good for an evening visit.
Other locations: *Sofokleous 7-9, Omonia (210 321 4811).*
Central Alpha Bank *(210 326 0000/lost credit cards 210 339 7250) Panepistimiou 3, Historic Centre (210 324 1023/210 236 7366). Metro Syntagma.* **Open** 8am-2.30pm Mon-Thur; 8am-2pm Fri. **Map** p297 E5. *Filellinon 6, Plaka (210 322 9482/ 210 324 8417). Metro Syntagma.* **Open** 8am-2.30pm Mon-Thur; 8am-2pm Fri. **Map** p295 F5/p299 F5.

Bureaux de change

Eurocambio
Apollon 5, Plaka (210 322 1527). Metro Syntagma. **Open** 8.30am-7pm Mon-Fri; 9am-2pm Sat. **Map** 295/299 F5.
Stadiou 58, Omonia (210 331 4241-46). Metro Omonia. **Open** 8.30am-7pm Mon-Fri; 9am-2pm Sat, Sun. **Map** p295 E3.

Credit cards

Most major cards (AmEx, Diners Club, MasterCard, Visa) are accepted at hotels, department stores and some restaurants. Ask first if you're unsure.

If you lose your credit card or it is stolen, call:
American Express *210 324 4975-9 (8.30am-4pm Mon-Fri).*
Diners Club *210 924 5890/ 210 929 0200 (24hrs daily).*
MasterCard *(City Bank) 210 929 0100.*
Visa *210 326 3410/210 326 3395 (24hrs daily).*

Tax

Non-EU citizens travelling in Greece are entitled to a refund of the 18 per cent VAT (value-added tax) paid on certain goods that they have bought during their stay here. Though this doesn't apply to hotel and food bills, it does cover items such as valuable electronic goods, jewellery and furs, which could save you a fair amount of money. The store will provide you with a form to fill in, which you should hand to a customs officer prior to your departure.

If you want to collect your refund before you leave, allow yourself plenty of time at the airport (or port, or border). Normally you receive your refund by mail after you return home; don't be surprised if it takes four to six weeks, this is normal (should you feel that you've been forgotten about, though, call the store where you made the purchase).

If your purchase is cumbersome or fragile we recommend you have the store ship it home for you, in which case you only need to pay the shipping and import duties upon collection or receipt back home, if applicable.

Natural hazards

Greece lies in a seismic zone, so there are occasional earthquakes, but most are mild and result in no damage or injuries. If an earthquake occurs and you are indoors, get under a table or doorway away from windows. Do not use lifts. If you are outside, try to move to an open area to avoid falling objects.

In extremely hot weather, avoid overexposure to the sun and drink plenty of water.

Over-the-counter remedies are available to treat jellyfish stings and mosquito bites.

Opening hours

Opening hours vary according to the business and to the season. Generally speaking, however, business hours are 9am-6pm Mon-Fri (8am-2pm for public services offices). Most banks are open 8am-2.30pm Mon-Thur and 8am-2pm Fri, while post offices open 8am-3pm Mon-Fri.

Shops generally open 9am-3pm Mon, Wed, Sat, and 8am-3pm and 5pm-8pm Tue, Thur, Fri. Large department stores generally open 8am-6pm Mon-Sat (or until 8pm in winter). When it comes to bars and clubs, even those that have set times tend to be flexible – usually closing when most customers have left.

Pets

If you're planning to bring a pet with you, keep in mind that Greeks aren't exactly animal lovers. You'd be hard pushed to find a hotel that accepts pets and you can forget about taking them on public transport. The large number of stray

dogs wandering the streets in the centre (*see p271* **Who let the dogs out?**) is eloquently indicative of the city's policy regarding animals.

Pets coming to Greece need to have an export health certificate, without which they will be refused entry; talk to your vet about this. If you acquire a pet during your stay and want to take it home with you, contact your embassy in Athens (*see p268*) to find out the correct procedure.

Postal services

You can buy stamps from all post offices and many kiosks. Post boxes around town are yellow and post offices are easily spotted by their blue and yellow signs.

Opening hours are 7.30am to 2pm Mon-Fri. There are also four central post office (ELTA) branches (Syntagma, Tritis Septemvriou 28, Eolou 100, Koumoundourou 29) that stay open till 8pm. Local postage charges are approximately ct50 for a regular letter and up to €4.50 for a letter weighing up to two kilos. Within the EU, prices range from €1 for a simple letter to €11.50 for a bulky letter. Prices are almost double for letters going outside the EU. The price for parcels going abroad ranges from €22 (in the EU) to €25 (outside EU) for small parcels, and from €95 (in the EU) to €120 (outside EU) for parcels of 20 kilos.

Tip: Parcels sent abroad are inspected, so don't wrap and seal them beforehand. You can buy brown paper, soft padded envelopes and cardboard boxes at most post offices.

See also p267 **Couriers & shippers**.

Poste restante/ general delivery

If you want to receive mail while you are staying in Greece but will have no fixed address, have it sent 'poste restante' to the main post office just off Omonia (Eolou 100) or the American Express location at 2 Ermou Street, 1st floor. GR-102 25, near Syntagma. You must present your passport upon receipt.

Religion

Greece is a predominantly Greek Orthodox society with only a smattering of other religious groups. It has a large Catholic community that is mostly centred in Athens and on the island of Syros and just a handful of Presbyterians. There are very few Jews and even fewer Muslims, and their communities are mostly found in the north.

For a long time, mosques were not licensed to operate in parts of the country and only recently has the government agreed to the construction of a large mosque outside Athens, in Spata, although this project is facing some local opposition. In the meantime, community centres run worship services in makeshift mosques (often set up in stores or basements) located mostly downtown around the Omonia area.

Anglican
St Paul's Anglican Church, Filellinon 29, Plaka (210 721 4906). Metro Syntagma. **Map** p295/p299 F5.
Armenian Apostolic
Agios Grigorios Kriezi 12, Keramikos (210 325 2149). Metro Thisio. **Map** p295 D4.
Catholic
St Denis Omirou 9, Historic Centre (210 362 3603). Metro Syntagma. **Map** p295 F4.
German Evangelical
Christuskirche Sina 66, Kolonaki (210 361 2713). Metro Syntagma. **Map** p297 G3.
Jewish
Beth Shalom Synagogue, Melidoni 5, Keramikos (210 325 2823/210 325 2773) Metro Thisio. **Map** p294 C4.
Protestant
St Andrews Protestant Church, Paraschou 117, Pedion Areos (210 645 2583). Metro Victoria.
Roman Catholic Chapel
Apostolou Pavlou, Kokinaki 4, Thisio (210 801 2526). Metro Thisio. **Map** p294/p298 C5.

Safety & security

Though the crime rate has risen in recent years, Athens is still considered to be one of the safest cities in Europe. What crime there is tends to be of the organised variety between rival gangs. Also, the threat of terror attacks directed against foreign individuals has decreased since the arrests of suspected members of the notorious November 17 organisation in 2002.

Just to be on the safe side, however, here are a few tips:
● Keep your money and other valuable items hidden away in a safe place while walking around the city, and especially on public transport.
● Avoid poorly lit or dark deserted places at night.
● Beware of bar hustlers. These characters target men out alone at night inviting them for a drink. The unsuspecting male is then taken to a bar where he is introduced to one or more girls whom he will be encouraged to buy drinks for before being presented with an enormous bill. If he should try to dispute the price, the bar owner will probably bring in the heavies to help you recalculate. Don't get into this position.

Smoking

Despite the fact that Greeks are among the biggest tobacco consumers in the world, the recent European wave of campaigns against smoking seems to be making its presence felt here. Smoking is banned on all public transport and in public buildings (shops, banks, post offices, public offices, schools, hospitals, etc.) and most indoor restaurants have no-smoking sections.

Cigarettes are cheap in Greece and the airport duty-free shops helpfully stock a wide range of brands.

Study

Language classes

There are several institutions that hold Greek language classes for foreigners in Athens. The centrally located Athens Centre (Archimidous 48, Pangrati, 210 701 2268) is one of the most popular.

Many teachers of Greek also advertise in the classified ads of the *Athens News*.

Useful organisations

For information on studying in Greece, from summer courses to language lessons, visit the Study Abroad website (www.studyabroad.com/content/portals/Greece_port.html).

If you are interested in longer courses, the Greek Embassy in your own country will also be able to provide information on institutions, courses, prices and procedure.

Telephones

Dialling & codes

Several recent changes to telephone numbers in Greece mean that the numbers displayed in advertisements are not always valid. The area code must be included even if you are calling from the same area: for example, the area code for Athens is 210 and must be dialled whether you are calling from Athens or Thessaloniki. If you are unsure, check with directory enquiries (*see p274*).

The country code for Greece is 30.

Making a call

If you want to make an international call while in Greece, first dial 00, then punch in the area code, before dialling the rest of the number, dropping any initial zeros as necessary (as it is for all British numbers). The country code for the UK is 44; for Australia it's 61; Canada 1; the Republic of Ireland 352; New Zealand 64; South Africa 27 and the USA 1.

Public phones

The cheapest way to make local or international calls is via the Hellenic Telecommunications Organisation (OTE) offices. Just walk in to your nearest office – they're ubiquitous – and grab a booth. At the end of the call, the desk operator will present you with a bill.

Directory

Get in line

Cat Stevens, so the joke goes, was inspired to write *Morning Has Broken* after joining a huge afternoon queue in Athens' main post office. Queues are a fact of life in the capital. Traditional even. At tax declaration time, they stretch out on to the streets. Why so many? Generally because not enough staff serve too many customers for too few hours – 8am to 2pm or 3pm for much of the public sector.

The three golden rules for queueing in Athens are:

a) avoid Monday mornings;

b) if you're second in the queue at a fast-food restaurant and get the chance to lean on the counter, do so, even if it means stepping out of line;

c) take a book.

Service is gradually getting better across the capital. More and more can be done on the internet. Paying bills through standing order and withdrawing cash from ATMs saves buckets of time. The oft-criticised Syntagma Post Office, in the centre of the city, now boasts a deli-counter style ticket machine (for which, encouragingly, there are no queues).

Service has clearly got quicker and if queues can still be a joke at least they don't end in the classic punchline whereby the counter is slammed closed in front of you at your moment of triumph.

As for queue-jumpers, they are rarely punished by staff – they will be served and they know it. Public shame does not exist, and there's not much you can do about it. In the open air, generally speaking, no rules apply. For taxis, just shout along with everyone else and let the cabbie decide. When the bus comes, be a seat-seeking missile. Granny can stand.

Queues are not all bad. They foster community spirit, are an excellent source of gossip and reinforce notions of equality – or at least helplessness. Romance is not out of the question: 'Where did you meet?' 'In a queue' is a not uncommon phrase.

If you've time, try to catch a customer revolt. These typically occur in a smoke-filled bank where two or three staff are on duty with up to 50 people waiting. A couple of customers, hot and tired from standing for an hour, will start shouting, quickly joined by the rest. For those who want to learn Greek, it's an excellent opportunity to hear an impressive variety of swear words.

Local and international calls can also be made from public cardphone booths and kiosks. Public payphones only take prepaid phonecards (*tilecartes*), which cost €3, €10 or €15 and are available from post offices and kiosks. You can also make calls from kiosk shops where the cost of your call is tallied up on a meter and you pay at the end of your telephone conversation.

A cheaper way to make calls, though, is to buy pre-paid cards that work like mobile-phone top-up cards. They cost the same as payphone cards, but give you more call time for your money (approximately ten minutes for a €3 card). Smile and Talk Talk are two that give good value for money; look out for them at kiosks.

As is the case everywhere else in the world, hotels are notorious for charging ridiculously high rates for telephone bills. Avoid making phone calls from your hotel room, or use a pre-paid phone card.

Operator services

Directory enquiries *131.*
International operator *139.*

International inquiries *139.*
International assistance *139.*

Mobile phones

Mobile phone connections in Greece operate on the GSM network, so you probably won't be able to use your phone here if you're visiting from the USA or Canada, unless it's a tri-band. In this case, your best option is to buy a 'pay-as-you-go' SIM card package to use while you're in Greece. B-Free Telestet, Cosmocarta, A la Carte and CU (€15 each, from Germanos) are four good ones; top-up cards cost from €9 upwards.

Visitors from the UK will be able to use their phones here if they have agreed roaming facilities with their service provider, or the terms of their pay-as-you-go deal allow it.

Germanos is a recommended mobile-phone service shop.

Germanos

Stadiou 10, Historic Centre (210 323 6000). Metro Syntagma. **Open** 9am-4pm Mon, Wed; 9am-8.30pm Tue, Thur, Fri; 9am-3pm Sat. **Credit** AmEx, DC, MC, V. **Map** p295/p299 F5.

Kanari 26, Kolonaki (210 361 5798). Metro Syntagma. **Open** 9am-4pm Mon, Wed; 9am-8.30pm Tue, Thur, Fri; 9am-3pm Sat. **Credit** AmEx, DC, MC, V. **Map** p297 G5.

Faxes & telegrams

There are many central print/copy shops from where you can send faxes, and every neighbourhood has at least one grocer or newsagent with access to a fax machine. Hotels also offer a (more expensive) fax service (and sometimes charge to receive, too).

To send telegrams, call 136 or visit the nearest branch of OTE.

Time

Remember to adjust your watch to East European Time when you arrive in Athens. This is two hours ahead of Greenwich Mean Time, one hour ahead of Central European Time and seven hours ahead of Eastern Standard Time.

Daylight-Saving Time starts at the end of March and ends in late September.

Tipping

You should tip in taxis, cafés, restaurants and some theatres. Ten per cent is normal, with some restaurants adding up to 15 per cent to your bill. Always check to see if service has been included in your bill.

Toilets

Public toilets in Athens are few and far between and generally little used. Your best bet is to pop into a fast-food outlet or department store. In bars and restaurants, it is best to ask.

Tourist information

The **Greek National Tourist Organisation** (GNTO) can provide details on places of interest, hotels, events, etcetera, though not for many hours of the day or in a very convenient location (though there's also a desk at the airport arrivals terminal; 210 354 5101). The GNTO office in your country can also supply information.

GNTO
Tsoschas 7, Ambelokipi (210 870 7000/www.gnto.gr). Open 8am-1.30pm Mon-Fri.
GNTO UK
4 Conduit Street, London W1S 2DJ (020 7495 9300/www.gnto.co.uk).
GNTO US
Olympic Tower, 645 Fifth Ave, New York, NY 10022 (212 421 5777/www.greektourism.com).

Visas & immigration

EU nationals can travel without a visa and may remain indefinitely. Non-EU visitors can stay for up to three months without a visa. For longer periods, they should check with the Greek embassy or consulate in their home country.

If you wish to extend your visa during your stay, go to the Aliens Bureau (Leof Alexandras 173, 210 770 5711). Be prepared to wade through a fair amount of red tape.

Weights/measures

Greece uses the metric system (kilometres, kilogrammes, litres, etc) rather than the imperial system (miles, pounds, pints, etc).

1 metre (m) = 3.28 feet (ft)
1 sq metre (sq m) = 1.196 sq yards
1 kilometre (km) = 0.62 miles
1 kilogramme (kg) = 2.2 pounds (lb)
1 litre (l) = 1.76 UK pints,
2.113 US pints

When to go

Climate

Summers in Athens are generally dry with next to no rainfall and plenty of sunshine. Between July and September the temperature hovers at around 35°C (95°F), and visitors should take precautions against the sun and heat (drink lots of water, wear a hat, etc).

Winter is wetter and cooler, with temperatures occasionally dropping to zero. However, mini-heatwaves with temperatures rising to the mid-20s are not unheard of in winter.

Public holidays

Fixed
New Year's Day (1 Jan); Epiphany (6 Jan); Independence Day & Feast of the Annunciation (25 Mar); Labour Day (1 May); Dormition of the Virgin (15 Aug); 'Ochi' (No) Day (28 Oct); Christmas (25-26 Dec).

Changeable
Ash Monday (41 days before Easter); Easter weekend (Good Friday to Easter Monday); Whit Monday (50 days after Easter).
The Greek Orthodox calendar and its Western counterpart often diverge where Easter celebrations are concerned. Check ahead to avoid any unpleasant surprises.

Women

Athens is fairly safe, but it's best to avoid walking alone late at night in some of its dingier central districts (Omonia, Platia Vathis, Victoria, Pedion Areos).
See also **Helplines** and **Contraception & abortion** (*p269* for both).

Working in Athens

EU nationals can work in Greece as long as they have a full passport. If you plan to be in Greece for over 90 days, apply in advance for a residence permit at the Aliens Bureau (*see above*). At the end of the financial year you will have to submit a tax form (available at a local tax office). You will also need to sign up with IKA, the Greek social security foundation, to which your employer has to make monthly contributions.

Non-EU citizens should check requirements with their local embassy/consulate.

Average climate

Month	Temp (°C/°F)		Hours of sun	Humidity (%)
Jan	10.3	50.5	4.12	68.9
Feb	10.7	51.2	4.48	68.3
Mar	12.4	54.3	5.54	66.3
Apr	16.0	60.0	7.42	62.8
May	20.7	69.2	9.24	59.5
June	25.1	77.1	11.12	53.4
July	27.9	82.2	11.42	47.6
Aug	27.7	81.8	11.00	47.3
Sept	24.2	75.5	9.12	53.7
Oct	19.4	66.9	6.42	61.9
Nov	15.5	59.9	5.06	68.9
Dec	12.2	53.9	3.54	70.1

Directory

Vocabulary

Pronunciation

a – 'a' as in cat
e – 'e' as in net
ee – 'ee' as in Greek
i – 'i' as in hit
o – 'o' as in hot

Useful words & phrases

hello – yassoo; (plural/formal)
herete or yassas
goodbye – yasso, ya;
(plural/formal) adeeo or
yassas
good morning – kalee mera
good evening – kalee spera
good night – kalee nihta
How are you? – Tee kanees?;
(plural/formal) Tee kanete?
yes – ne
no – ohi
please – parakalo
thank you – efharisto
excuse me/sorry – seegnomi
open – anihto
closed – klisto

Do you speak English? – Milate
Anglika?
I don't speak Greek (very well)
– Then milao Ellinika (poli kala)
I don't understand – Then
katalaveno
Speak more slowly, please –
Boreete na milate pio seega,
parakalo?

Emergencies

Help! – Voeethia!
I'm sick – Eeme arosti
I want a doctor/policeman –
Thelo ena yiatros/astinomeekos
Hospital – nosokomeeo
There's a fire! – Ehi fotia!

Accommodation

hotel – xenothoheeo
I have a reservation – Eho
kleesimo
double room – thiplo thomateeo
single room – mono thomateeo
double bed – thiplo krevatee
twin beds – theeo mona krevateea
with a bath – me banyo

with a shower – me doosh
breakfast included – me prohino
air-conditioned – kleematismos

Getting around

car – aftokeeneeto
bus – leoforeeo
bus stop – stathmos leoforeeo
coach – pullman
taxi – taxi
train – treno
trolley bus – trollay
aeroplane – airoplano
airport – airothromeeo
station – stathmos
platform – apovathra
entrance – eesothos
exit – exothos
tickets – isiteeria
return – isiteerio met epeestrofis
(I'd like) a ticket to –
(Thelo) ena isiteerio ya
Where can I buy tickets? –
Pou boro n'agorazo isiteereea?
(Turn) left/right – (Strivete)
aristera/thexeea
It's on the left/right –
Eene ekee aristera/thexeea

Greek letters and sounds

The alphabet

Αα alpha	'a' as in cat	
Ββ vita	'v' as in vice	
Γγ gama	'g' as in game	
	'y' as in yes	
Δδ thelta	'th' as in this	
Εε epsilon	'e' as in net	
Ζζ zeta	'z' as in zebra	
Ηη ita	'ee' as in Greek	
Θθ thita	'th' as in thing	
Ιι yiota	'ee' as in Greek	
Κκ kappa	'k' as in key	
Λλ lamtha	'l' as in late	
Μμ mi	'm' as in my	
Νν ni	'n' as in night	
Ξξ ksi	'ks' as in rocks	
Οο omikron	'o' as in open	
Ππ pi	'p' as in pet	
Ρρ ro	'r' as in rope	
Σσ (ς at the end of word) sigma	's' as in snake	
Ττ taf	't' as in tea	
Υυ ipsilon	'ee' as in Greek	
Φφ fi	'f' as in food	
Χχ hee	'h' as in heat	

Ψψ psi — 'ps' as in lapse
Ωω omega — 'o' as in hot

Double-letter combinations

ει epsilon-yiota-	'ee' as in Greek	
οι omikron-yiota-	'ee' as in Greek	
αι alpha-yiota	'e' as in net	
ου omikron-ipsilon-	'oo' as in food	
μπ mi-pi	'b' as in bee	
ντ ni-taf	'd' as in date	
γκ gama-kappa	'g' as in get	
γγ gama-gama	'ng' as in England	
γχ gama-hee	'a' as in inherent	
το taf-sigma	'ts' as in sets	
τζ taf-zeta	'ds' as in friends	

αυ alpha-ipsilon	'av' as in avenue	
	'af' as in after	
ευ epsilon-ipsilon	'ev' as in never	
	'ef' as in left	

Useful words

exit	εξοδος·
entrance	εισοδος
toilet	τουαλετα

Greek for cheats

Every Greek deeply appreciates any foreigner making the effort to butcher their beautiful and ancient language, so give it a go. And if you find Greek too hard, cheat.

For starters, speak slowly. Someone will finish the sentence for you. Speak quietly and your mistakes won't sound so bad. Speak quickly and blunders will be forgotten. This 'speak quickly' rule might appear to contradict the 'speak slowly' rule but Greek's like that.

Use your body (within limits). When you agree don't nod because, in Greece, a nod can mean 'no'. Instead, smile or just say 'Ne', the Greek for 'yes' (pronounced like the 'ne' in 'never'). To say 'no', remember 'hockey' and take off the 'h'. Strictly speaking, the 'ck' sound in 'ockey' should be more like the 'ch' in 'loch' but it's a quibble and cheats ignore quibbles. Hockey stays.

Let out a 'YA-sas' when saying hello to someone you don't know, or greeting more than one person. Why say hello to someone you don't know? It's a very friendly country. Speaking to a friend is YA-sue.

'How are you?' is 'tea-CAR-knees'. The polite and plural version can't be whittled down to a drink, an automobile or a part of the body, so forget it.

Asking the price of something depends on – dear-oh-dear – whether it's singular or plural. You know what? Always say 'PO-sa', which rhymes with 'tosser'. Think pancakes and you'll be fine.

To introduce yourself: 'me-LE-ne Brian' (My name is Brian), the 'me' as in 'met', 'le-' in 'leg', 'ne' in 'net' and 'Brian' in 'Brian'. In this particular example, two Greek letters are needed to make the equivalent sound of the English letter 'B'. This happens quite a lot in Greek and you should either learn all the combinations or change your name to Petros.

What about 'thank you'? Many Greeks speak French, so 'merci' (if you know how to pronounce that) is one option. If you say this in a taverna, be prepared to have all the dishes explained in French.

The Greek for 'thank you' is pronounced 'ef-hari-STO'. Many books mention Mr F Harry Stowe as a way to remember this, cutting out the 'Mr' of course. A clipped version, 'sto', is like saying 'cue' at the end of a fast-spoken 'thank you' and probably works.

One radical but fail-safe solution is never to say thank you.

● *Athens News* columnist Brian Church is the author of *Learn Greek in 25 Years*.

---

straight on – pee-enete eeseea
Could you show me the way to the Acropolis? – Boreete na moo theexete to thromoo ya to Acropoli?

Eating & drinking

I'd like to book a table for four at nine – Thelo na kliso trapezi ya tessera stin enya.
A table for two, please – Ena trapezee ya theeo, parakalo
Can I have the menu – Boro na eho to katalogho
Some water – leegho nero
Waiter/waitress! – servitoros/servitora
Is there a non-smoking section? – Ehete horo pou apaghorevete to kapneesma?
I am a vegetarian – Eeme hortofaghos
Where's the toilet? – Pou eene ee twaleta?
That was (very) tasty – Eetane (polee) nosteemo.
That was not (very) good – Then eetane (polee) oreo.

bill – logariasmo
I think there's been a mistake on the bill – Nomizo ehete kani lathos sto logariasmo.

Shopping

How much does this cost? – Posso kanee afto?

Days of the week

Monday – Theftera
Tuesday – Treetee
Wednesday – Tetartee
Thursday – Pemptee
Friday – Paraskevee
Saturday – Savato
Sunday – Kireeakee
today – seemera
tomorrow – avreeo
morning – proee
afternoon – apogevma
evening – vrathi
night – nihta

Communications

phone – tilefono
stamp – gramatoseemo

letter – gramma
postcard – kartpostal, karta
A stamp for England/the US – Ena gramatoseemo ya tin Angleea/Ameriki
Can I make a phone call? – Boro na kano ena tilefonima?

Numbers

1 – ena; **2** – theeo; **3** – treea; **4** – tessera; **5** – pende; **6** – exhi; **7** – efta; **8** – octo; **9** – eneia; **10** – thecca; **11** – enthecca; **12** – tho-thecca; **13** – theccatreea; **14** – theccatessera; **15** – heccapende; **16** – theccexhi; **17** – theccaefta; **18** – theccaocto; **19** – theccaeneia; **20** – eekosi; **100** – ekato; **500** – penda-koseea; **1,000** – hileea

Times

Could you tell me the time? – Ehete tin ora?
It's – o'clock – **eene** (number) Ee ora.
quarter past – ke tetarto
quarter to – para tetarto
half past – ke meessi

Further Reference

Websites

www.athensguide.com
A wide-ranging and knowledgeable home-made site from an American who clearly loves Athens with a passion.

www.athensnews.gr
The site for Athens' weekly English-language magazine. Good for features and news.

www.ekathimerini.com
The internet version of Athens' daily English-language newspaper. With good general information too.

www.culture.gr
Created by the Culture Ministry, this portal highlights the artistic riches of Greece. It has a thorough list of museums, monuments and archaeological sites as well as a regularly updated diary of cultural events.

www.gnto.gr
The site of the Greek National Tourist Organization offers a wealth of information on where to stay, what to visit and how to get the most out of your stay.

www.gogreece.com
Loads of well-catalogued links provide information on myriad subjects, from arts to travel.

www.hri.org/
Excellent information, media and links database for Greeks and Greek-Americans.

Films

The Attack of the Giant Moussaka
(*Panos Koutras, 2000*)
As silly as its name suggests.

The Dawn (To Harama)
(*Alexis Bistiskas, 1994*)
A Star Is Born set in Athens, complete with Greek ballads.

Edge of Night (Afti i Nighita Meni)
(*Nikos Panagiotopoulos, 2000*)
This film follows the ambitions of Stella, a young Athenian girl who dreams of becoming a famous singer.

End of an Era (Telos Epochis)
(*Antonis Kokkinos, 1994*)
An old man reminisces on his coming of age in Athens in the late 1960s, with the military dictatorship in the background.

From the Edge of the City (Apo tin Akri tis Polis)
(*Konstantinos Giannaris, 1998*)
A tale of sex and drugs set in the immigrant ghettos on the outskirts of Athens.

Hard Goodbyes: My Father (Dhiskoli Apoheretismi: O Babas Mou) (*Penny Panayotopoulou, 2002*)
In the late 1960s a young Athenian boy struggles to come to terms with the death of his father.

Never on Sunday (Pote tin Kyriaki)
(*Jules Dassin, 1960*)
A US intellectual tries to reform a prostitute of Piraeus, believing her to be emblematic of the fall of the great Greek civilisation.

One Day in August (Dekapendavgoustus)
(*Konstantinos Giannaris, 2001*)
Follows a day in the life of three families in Athens at the height of the summer, when the rest of the city has left for the beaches.

Rembetiko
(*Costas Ferris, 1984*)
This film follows the fortunes of a female *rembetika* singer in Athens, from her childhood in the days of the Asia Minor population exchange (1922) to her rise to fame and eventual decline. Featuring original *rembetika* by Stavros Xarhakos.

When Mother Comes Home for Christmas (Otan Erhtli Mama Gia ta Christougenna)
(*Nilita Vachani, 1995*)
This documentary on the life of a Sri Lankan woman hired as a nanny in Athens reveals a dark truth behind some Athenian ladies who lunch.

Books

Classics

Aeschylus
Agamemnon; *Persians*, *Prometheus Bound*; *The Suppliants*

Aesop
Aesop's Fables

Aristophanes
The Acharnians; *The Birds*, *The Clouds*; *The Frogs*; *Lysistrata*

Euripides
Andromache; *Bacchantes*; *The Cyclops*; *Electra*, *Hecuba*

Homer
The Iliad, *The Odyssey*

Ovid
The Metamorphoses

Pausanias
The Guide to Greece

Plutarch
The Rise and Fall of Athens

Sophocles
Antigone; *Electra*; *Oedipus the King*

Thucidides
History of the Peloponnesian War

Fiction

Douka, Maro
Fool's Gold
The story of a young woman who becomes involved with the resistance movement, and her reaction to the events of 17 November 1973.

Fakinou, Eugenia
The Seventh Garment
The lives of three generations of Greek women reflect the history of the country, from the Asia Minor catastrophe, to the years of the Junta and on to modern Athens.

Finlay, David
The Nelson Touch
Nelson's Column is dismantled and robbed from Trafalgar Square and held hostage for the return of the Elgin Marbles to Athens. Comedy and international intrigue.

Haris, Petros
Longest Night: Chronicle of a Dead City
A series of narratives detailing the brutal reality of the Nazi occupation of Athens during World War II.

Kazantzakis, Nikos
At the Palaces of Knossos
The author of *Zorba the Greek* mixes fact and fiction in this tale about the fall of Minoan Crete at the hands of the emerging city of Athens.

Kotzias, Alexandros
Jaguar
In 1964 the wife and the sister of a hero in the resistance who was killed 20 years earlier meet in Athens. Their lives have taken a different path, but they share recollections of the main events in their lives, from the German occupation to the civil war.

Manning, Olivia
The Balkan Trilogy (volume 3: Friends and Heroes)
A young married couple flees from war-torn Romania to Athens, where they have to contend with more historical turmoil. Made into a TV series (*Fortunes of War*) featuring Kenneth Branagh and Emma Thompson.

Mourselas, Kostas
Red Dyed Hair
This best-selling novel spawned a popular TV series in Greece. It focuses on the lives of a group of marginalised Piraeus dwellers.

Somoza, José Carlos
The Athenian Murders
When a student of Plato's Academy is found dead, foul play is supected and Heracles sets about investigating the case. To make things murkier, a literary mystery unfolds within the murder mystery.

Non-fiction

Beard, Mary
The Parthenon
Beard demystifies the sacred temple on the hill in a very readable fashion.

Burn, AR
The Penguin History of Greece
A useful introduction to ancient Greece.

Church, Brian
Always on a Sunday
This irreverent, affectionate look at life in Greece predicts that the 2004 Olympics will take place in 2005.
Learn Greek in 25 Years
A tongue-in-cheek crash course for the linguistically challenged.

Davidson, James
Courtesans and Fishcakes: The Consuming Passions of Classical Athens
Sex, gluttony and booze.

Grant, Michael & Hazel, John
Who's Who in Classical Mythology
A thorough compendium of mythological personalities.

Henderson, John, & Beard, Mary
Classics: A Very Short Introduction
How the classics have influenced our lives.

Holst, Gail
Road to Rembétika: Songs of Love, Sorrow and Hashish
For those who want to find out more about the Blues of the Balkans and its singers.

Mackenzie, Molly
Turkish Athens
The history of Athens during its four centuries of Ottoman occupation.

Sacks, David, et al
A Dictionary of the Ancient Greek World
One-stop volume detailing the people, places and events that shaped the ancient Greek civilisation.

St Clair, William
Lord Elgin and the Marbles
The ultimate volume to learn more about the marbles that were taken from the Parthenon in 1801.

Storace, Patricia
Dinner with Persephone
A New Yorker living in Athens deconstructs the Greek sense of self, culture and attitudes with the clarity that only an outsider can have.

Theodorakis, Mikis
Journals of Resistance
The Greek composer's journal during the years of the Junta.

Vlachos, Helen
House Arrest
Vlachos, editor of newspaper *Kathimerini* during the Junta years, was placed under house arrest when she refused to publish a censored paper.

Wasson, R Gordon, Hoffmann, Albert, & Ruck, Carl
The Road to Eleusis: Unveiling the Secret of the Mysteries
As the title says.

Index

Note Page numbers in **bold** indicate section(s) giving key information on a topic; *italics* indicate photographs.

Advertisers' Index

Please refer to the relevant sections for contact details

Place of interest and/or entertainment	
Railway & bus stations	
Parks	
Hospitals/universities	
Olympic venues	
Neighbourhood . . . . PLAKA	
Metro station . . . . Ⓜ	

Maps

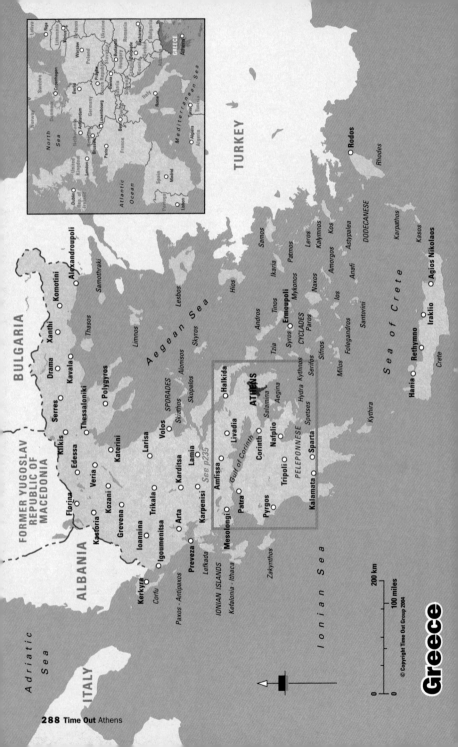

Greece

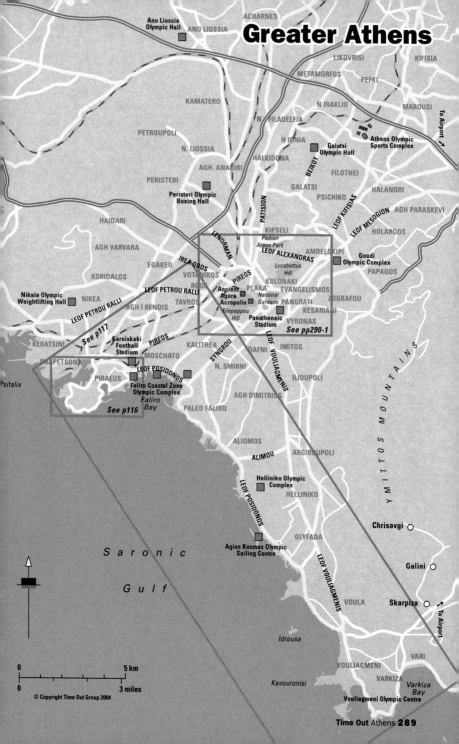

Greater Athens

Ano Liossia Olympic Hall
Ano Liossia
Acharnes

Likovrisi
Kifisia
Metamorfos

Kamatero
N Iraklio
Marousi

N. Liossia
N Filadelfia
Athens Olympic Sports Complex

Petroupoli
N Ionia
Galatsi Olympic Hall

Agh. Anagiri
Halkidona
Filothei

Peristeri
Galatsi

Peristeri Olympic Boxing Hall
Psichiko
Halandri

Haidari
Patision
Kipseli
Agh Paraskevi

Agh Varvara
Pedion Areos Park
Leof Alexandras
Ambelokipi
Holargos

Egaleo
Irea Odos
Votanikos
Pireos
Lycabettus Hill
Goudi Olympic Complex
Papagos

Koridalos
Leof Petrou Ralli
Roui
Plaka
Kolonaki
Evangelismos
Zografou

Nikaia Olympic Weightlifting Hall
Nikea
Agh I Rendis
Tavros
Ancient Agora
Acropolis
National Gardens
Pangrati
Kesariani

Keratsini
See p117
Pireos
Filopappou Hill
Panathenaic Stadium
Vyronas
See pp290-1

Drapetsona
Karaiskaki Football Stadium
Moschato
Kalithea
Syngrou
Dafni
Imitos

Piraeus
Leof Posidonos
N. Smirni
Leof Vouliagmenis
Ilioupoli

*sitalia
Faliro Coastal Zone Olympic Complex
See p116
Faliro Bay
Paleo Faliro
Agh Dimitrios

Aliomos

Alimou
Argiroupoli

Helliniko Olympic Complex
Helliniko

Agios Kosmas Olympic Sailing Centre

Chrisavgi

Galini

Glyfada

Skarpiza

To Airport

Saronic

Gulf

Y M I T T O S   M O U N T A I N S

Voula

Idrousa

Vari

Vouliagmeni
Varkiza

Kavouronisi
Varkiza Bay

0   5 km

0   3 miles

© Copyright Time Out Group 2004

Vouliagmeni Olympic Centre

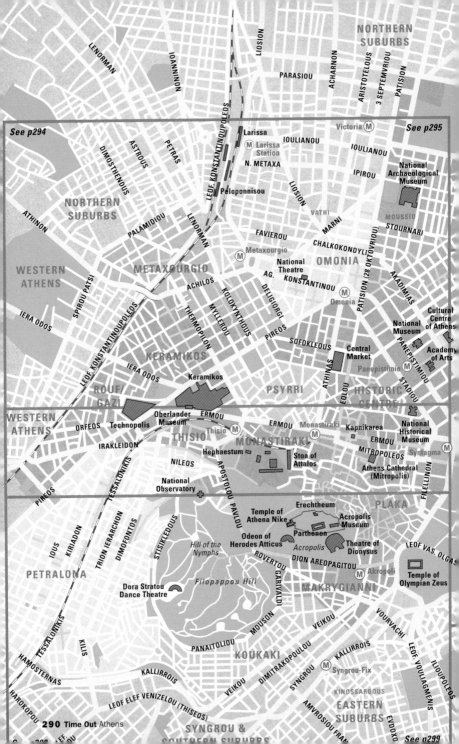

LENORMAN

IOANNINON

LIOSION

NORTHERN
SUBURBS

PARASIOU

ACHARNON

ARISTOTELOUS

3 SEPTEMVRIOU

PATISION

See p294

Larissa

Ⓜ Larissa
Station

N. METAXA

IOULIANOU

Victoria Ⓜ

See p295

IOULIANOU

IPIROU

National
Archaeological
Museum

MOUSSIO

STOURNARI

LEOF. KONSTANTINOUPOLEOS

Peloponnisou

LIOSION

VATHI

MARNI

CHALKOKONDYLI

DIMOSTHENOUS

ASTROUS

PETRAS

PALAMIDIOU

FAVIEROU

Metaxourgio Ⓜ

OMONIA

PATISION /28 OKTOVRIOU

AKADIMIAS

ATHINON

NORTHERN
SUBURBS

LENORMAN

National
Theatre

AG.
KONSTANTINOU

Omonia Ⓜ

National
Museum

Cultural
Centre
of Athens

WESTERN
ATHENS

METAXOURGIO

ACHILOS

KOLOKYNTHOUS

DELIGIORGI

PANEPISTIMIOU

Academy
of Arts

SPIROU PATSI

THERMOPILON

MYLLEROU

PIREOS

SOFOKLEOUS

Central
Market

Panepistimio Ⓜ

IERA ODOS

LEOF. KONSTANTINOUPOLEOS

KERAMIKOS

ATHINAS

EOLOU

STADIOU

HISTORIC
CENTRE

IERA ODOS

Keramikos

PSYRRI

IERA ODOS

ROUF/
GAZI

Technopolis

Oberlander
Museum

ERMOU

Thisio Ⓜ

ERMOU

Monastiraki Ⓜ

Kapnikarea

National
Historical
Museum

WESTERN
ATHENS

ORFEOS

THISIO

MONASTIRAKI

ERMOU

MITROPOLEOS

Syntagma Ⓜ

IRAKLEIDON

Hephaestum

Stoa of
Attalos

Athens Cathedral
(Mitropolis)

FILELLINON

PIREOS

NILEOS

APOSTOLOU PAVLOU

National
Observatory

PLAKA

TESSALONIKIS

Temple of
Athena Nike

Erechtheum

Acropolis
Museum

STISIKLEOUS

Hill of the
Nymphs

Odeon of
Herodes Atticus

Parthenon

Acropolis

Theatre of
Dionysus

LEOF VAS. OLGAS

IOUS

KIRIADON

TRION IERARCHON

DIMOFONTOS

Acropoli Ⓜ

DION AREOPAGITOU

ROVERTOU
GARIVALDI

Temple of
Olympian Zeus

PETRALONA

Dora Stratou
Dance Theatre

Filopappou Hill

MAKRYGIANNI

VOURVACHI

TESSALONIKIS

KILIS

PANAITOLIOU

MOUSON

VEIKOU

KALLIRROIS

LEOF. VOULIAGMENIS

ILIOUPOLEOS

HAMOSTERNAS

KOUKAKI

DIMITRAKOPOULOU

SYNGROU

Syngrou-Fix Ⓜ

HAROKOPOU

KALLIRROIS

VEIKOU

KINOSSARGOUS

EASTERN
SUBURBS

LEOF ELEF VENIZELOU (THISEOS)

AMVROSIOU FRAN

EVDOXO

See p299

SYNGROU &
SOUTHERN SUBURBS

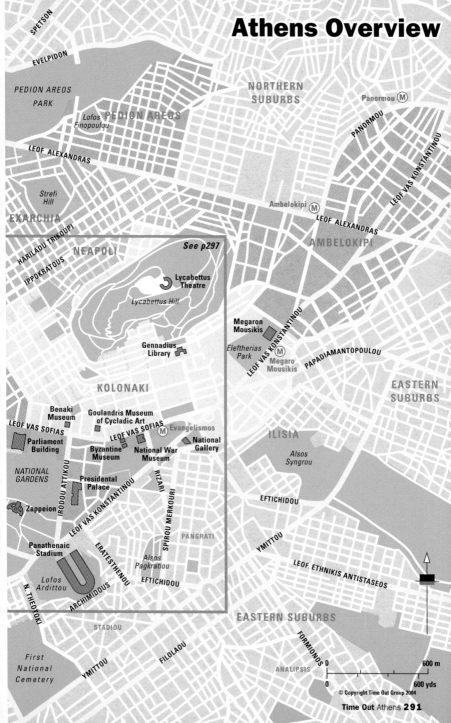

Athens Overview

SPETSON

EVELPIDON

PEDION AREOS PARK

Lofos Finopoulou

PEDION AREOS

NORTHERN SUBURBS

Panormou Ⓜ

PANORMOU

LEOF ALEXANDRAS

Strefi Hill

LEOF VAS KONSTANTINOU

EXARCHIA

Ambelokipi Ⓜ

LEOF ALEXANDRAS

AMBELOKIPI

HARILAOU TRIKOUPI

IPPOKRATOUS

NEAPOLI

See p297

Lycabettus Theatre

Lycabettus Hill

Megaron Mousikis

Eleftherias Park

Megaro Mousikis Ⓜ

LEOF VAS KONSTANTINOU

PAPADIAMANTOPOULOU

Gennadius Library

EASTERN SUBURBS

KOLONAKI

ILISIA

Benaki Museum

Goulandris Museum of Cycladic Art

Alsos Syngrou

LEOF VAS SOFIAS

LEOF VAS SOFIAS

Evangelismos Ⓜ

Parliament Building

Byzantine Museum

National War Museum

National Gallery

NATIONAL GARDENS

IRODOU ATTIKOU

Presidental Palace

RIZARI

EFTICHIDOU

Zappeion

LEOF VAS KONSTANTINOU

SPIROU MERKOURI

YMITTOU

PANGRATI

Panathenaic Stadium

ERATESTHENOU

Alsos Pagkratiou

LEOF ETHNIKIS ANTISTASEOS

Lofos Ardittou

EFTICHIDOU

N. THEOTOKI

ARCHIMIDOUS

EASTERN SUBURBS

STADIOU

FORMIONOS

First National Cemetery

YMITTOU

FILOLAOU

ANALIPSIS

0   600 m

0   600 yds

© Copyright Time Out Group 2004

Street Index

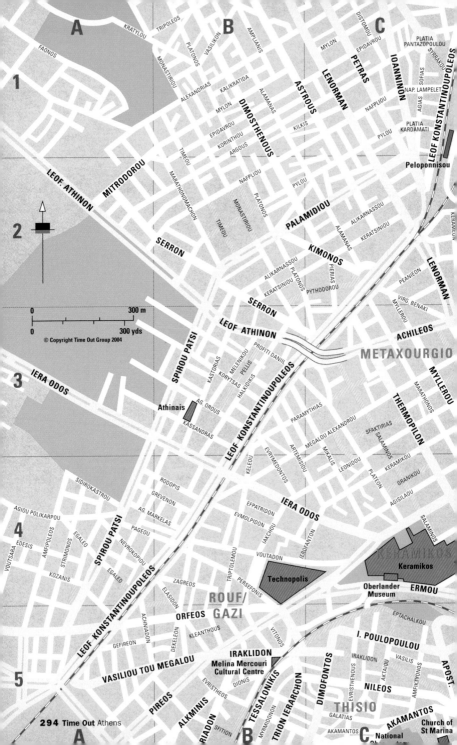

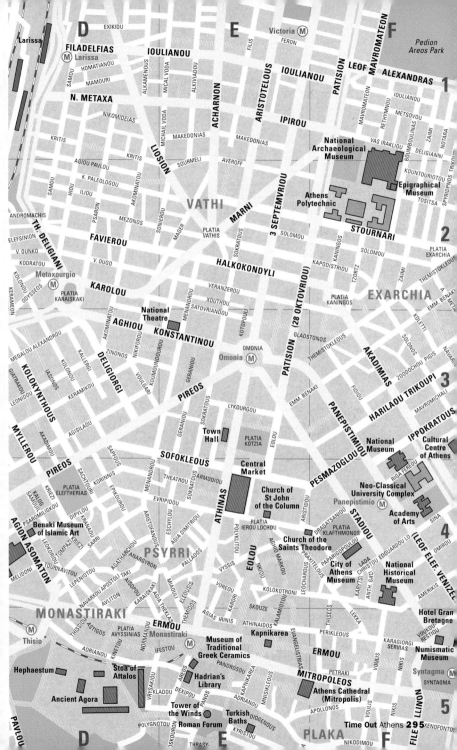

What Londoners take when they go out.

Time Out
London

EVERY WEEK

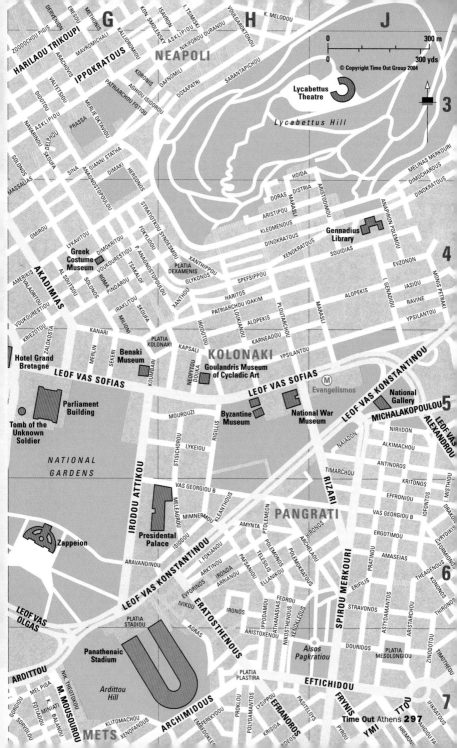

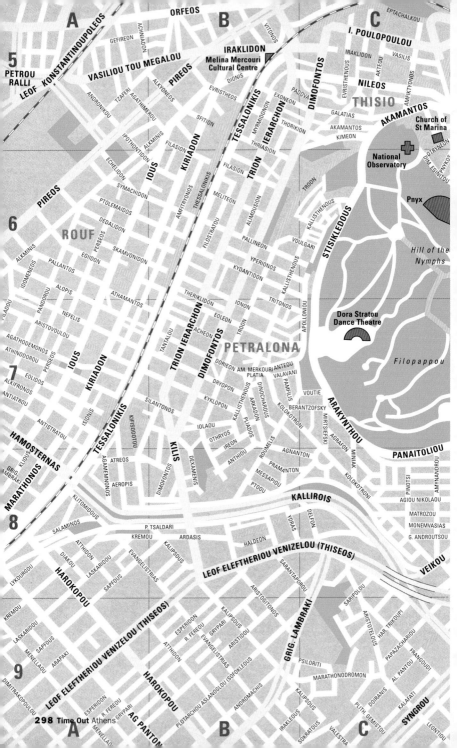

ORFEOS

A

B

EPTACHALKOU

VITONOS

I. POULOPOULOU

C

ACHIADON

GEFIREON

IRAKLIDON

VASILIS

5

PETROU
RALLI

LEOF KONSTANTINOUPOLEOS

VASILIOU TOU MEGALOU

PIREOS

IRAKLIDON
Melina Mercouri
Cultural Centre

DIONIS

EVRISTHEOS

TESSALONIKIS

IERARCHON

DIMOFONTOS

PADOVA

EVRISTHENOUS

NILEOS

AKTEOU

AMFIKTYONOS

THISIO

AKAMANTOS

Church of
St Marina

TZAFERI

AGATHIMEROU

ALKYONEOS

SFITION

EXONEON

GALATIAS

AKAMANTOS

ANDRONIKOU

IFOTHONTIDON

ALKMINIS

FILASION

MYRMIDONON

THORIKION

KIMEON

National
Observatory

DOTRIKEON
DIM.EPIKTOU

SYMACHIDON

ECHELIDON

KIRIADON

IOUS

FILASION

THRIASION

TRION

Pnyx

PIREOS

PTOLEMAIDOS

AMFITRYONOS

TESSALONIKIS

MELITEON

ALIMOUSION

TROON

KALLISTHENOUS

Hill of the
Nymphs

6

ROUF

DEDALIDON

SKAMVONIDON

FILOSTRATOU

PALLINEON

YPERIONOS

VOULGARI

STISIKLEOUS

ALKMINIS

IDOMENEOS

PALLANTOS

PERSEOS

EGIIDON

ATHAMANTOS

THERIKLIDON

KYDANTIDON

KALLISTHENOUS

APOLLONIOU

Dora Stratou
Dance Theatre

Filopappou

LLADOU

PANDROU

ALOPIS

NEFELIS

ARISTOVOULOU

IONON

TRITONOS

TRIDON

AGATHODEMONOS

ATHINODOROU

IOUS

PERSEOS

TANTALOU

ACHEON

TRION IERARCHON

EOLEON

DIMOFONTOS

DORIEON AM. MERKOURI

PETRALONA

VOUTIE

BERANTZOFSKY

ARAKYNTHOU

7

EOLIDOS

KIRIADON

KYKLOPON

DRYOPON

ANTEOU

PLATIA

DINOCHAROUS

VALAVANI

PAMFLIS

KOLOKOTRONI

MIRTSIEFSKI

MINIAK

PANAITOLIOU

ALKIFRONOS

ANTIATROU

SILANTONOS

IOLAOU

OTHRYOS

IREON

KALLISTHENOUS

PLIADOS

ARKADON

AGNANTON

AGRAFON

KOLOKOTRONI

PINOTSI

AMYNANDROU

HAMOSTERNAS

ISIONOS

TESSALONIKIS

KIFISODOTOU

DEKAMENIS

ANTHIOU

ROUMELIS

PRAMANTON

AGIOU NIKOLAOU

MARATHONOS

GRIG.
AMBRAKI

KLIDIOUS

ATREOS

AGAMEMNONOS

DIMOFONTOS

KILIS

MESSAPIOU

PTOU

MATROZOU

MONEMVASIAS

8

AEROPIS

KLITOMIDOUS

KALLIROIS

YDRAS

DELFON

G. ANDROUTSOU

SALAMINOS

P. TSALDARI

KREMOU

ARDASIS

HALDEON

VEIKOU

ATHIDON

DIAKOU

LASKARIDOU

SAPFOUS

EVANGELISTRIAS

KALIPSOUS

LEOF ELEFTHERIOU VENIZELOU (THISEOS)

SARANTAPOROU

LYKOURGOU

HAROKOPOU

ARISTOGITONOS

SARIPOLOU

ARISTOTELOUS

HAR. TRIKOUPI

PAPAZACHARIOU

FRANGOUDI

9

KREMOU

LASKARIDOU

SAPFOUS

MENELAOU

ARAPAKI

ESPERIDON

R. FEREOU

GRYPARI

ATHIDON

LEOF ELEFTHERIOU VENIZELOU (THISEOS)

KALIPSOUS

ARISTIDOU

EVANGELISTRIAS

ISOFOKLEOUS

GRIG. LAMBRAKI

PSILORITI

AL. PANTOU

ARISTOTELOUS

DOIRANIS

KALAFATI

DIMITRAKOPOULOU

HAROKOPOU

AG PANTON

ESPERIDON

R. FEREOU

GRYPARI

MENELAOU

PLOTARCHOU ASLANOGLOU

ANDROMACHIS

MARATHONODROMON

IRAKLIDON

KALIPSOUS

PLITH. GEMISTOU

SOKRATOUS

VALESTRA

SYNGROU

LEONTIOU

A

B

C

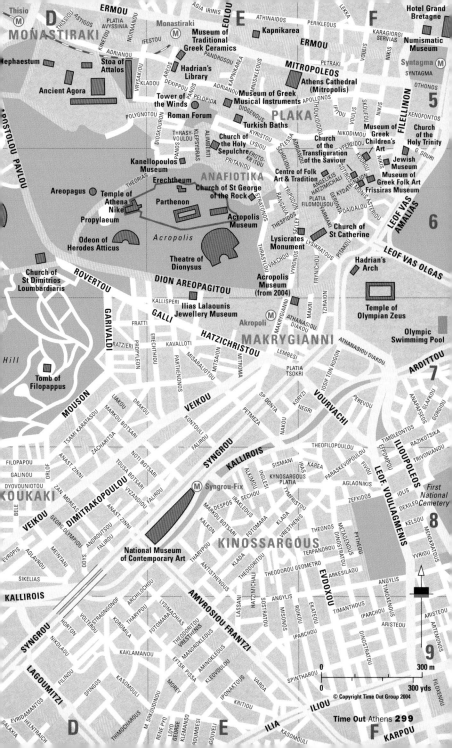

Athens Metro

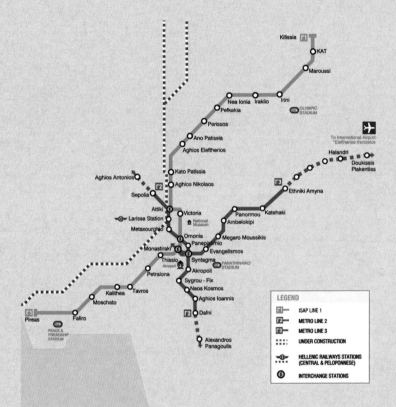